The Demography of Corporations and Industries

The Demography of Corporations and Industries

Glenn R. Carroll

Michael T. Hannan

Princeton University Press
Princeton, New Jersey

Library of Congress Cataloging-in-Publication Data

Carroll, Glenn.
    The demography of corporations and industries / Glenn R. Carroll,
Michael T. Hannan.
        p.   cm.
    Includes bibliographical references and index.   ISBN 0-691-01030-7 (alk. paper)
    1. Industrial statistics—Methodology.   2. Industrial surveys—Methodology.
    3. Demographic surveys—Methodology.   4. Industrial
    sociology—Statistical methods.   I. Hannan, Michael T.   II. Title.
    HD4826.5.C37   1999
    338′.007′27—dc21   99-23937

This book has been composed in ITC New Baskerville with LaTeX by Technical Typesetting
Inc., 1510 Caton Center Drive, Suite E, Baltimore, MD 21227

The paper used in this publication meets
the minimum requirements of
ANSI/NISO Z39.48–1992 (R1997)
(*Permanence of Paper*)

http://pup.princeton.edu

Printed in the United States of America

10 9 8 7 6 5 4 3 2 1

To our students,
whose efforts are making this field

Contents

List of Figures

List of Tables

Preface

Structure and change in contemporary societies follow from the actions of two kinds of actors: natural persons and organizations. The centrality of organizations in the economy, polity, and social structure nearly defines modern society. Yet, knowledge about the two kinds of actors is extremely unbalanced.

Consider the case of demography, the subject of this book. Human demography (the demography of natural persons) has a distinguished 350–year history, beginning with the investigations of mortality rates in London by merchant John Graunt in the mid-seventeenth century. It has become organized as a distinct academic discipline and institutionalized within the structure of all modern states. Because of the success of human demography, social scientists, policymakers, and the general public have easy access to a vast amount of information about the dynamics of human populations.

The situation for organizations could hardly be more different. Although, as we describe below, several attempts were made in the 1950s and 1960s to develop a demography of organizations, none was successful. Organizational demography does not exist, either as an academic field or as an institutionalized component of policy-making. Unsurprisingly, detailed knowledge about the demography of the corporation in the modern world has been slow to develop; corporations and other kinds of organizations remain poorly understood.

This book focuses on corporations and industries. By corporation, we mean not only business firms, but also other types of corporate entities embodied in formal organizations and associations. Our usage accords with the expansive legal definition of the term. Thus the category corporation is sufficiently broad to encompass the firms studied by economists, the political parties, interest groups, and government bureaus analyzed by political scientists, and the myriad types of organizations and associations that interest sociologists.

We use the term industry to refer to the domains in which corporations operate. Much of the research that we discuss examines industries such as auditing, automobile manufacturing, banking, and beer brewing. As the demographic perspective on corporations has developed, it has become clear that it is not very productive to regard these industries as the basic demographic units. Most industries contain a mix of populations of corporations. Consider the higher-education industry, composed of populations of research universities, colleges, junior colleges and community colleges, and free-standing professional schools. One might also argue that these populations should be divided into subgroupings based upon legal standing (public [...] gradations (elite liberal arts colleges vers[...] es the view that the potential of the dem[...] hen the analyst models the demography [...] nat comprise an industry and derives impli[...] f the industry.

By a demogr[...] insights about the ways industries develo[...] processes of organizational founding, [...] and mortality. Much of the work that we cite and on [...] omes from the perspective called "organizational ecology." The foundational statements of this perspective (Hannan and Freeman 1977; Hannan and Freeman 1989) distinguished sharply among demography, population ecology, and community ecology of organizations, based on the levels of analysis used. By this reckoning, organizational demography refers to processes that apply at the levels of populations of organizations, population ecology refers to interactions between localized sets of populations, and community ecology refers to the processes that follow from the full set of population interactions in some system. Although most of the published research in this field is identified as "ecological," it has a strong demographic flavor. That is, theories and research directed at the ecological issues actually used by analysts working from this perspective almost always involve a strong mix of both demography and ecology. In this book, we seek to emphasize the continuities between the theory, models, and methods of general demography and those of comparable investigations of the organizational world. The title we have chosen reflects this emphasis.

A demographic perspective on industry and society shifts attention from *the* corporation to the range and diversity of corporations in the system. Rather than concentrate on an image of a prototype organization, a demographic analysis focuses on whole *populations and communities of corporations*.

Why does this shift in perspective matter? Consider the corporate community in Silicon Valley, a leader in California's recovery from the massive cutbacks in defense industries during the 1980s. Close examination

Close demographic analysis of many diverse industries throughout history reveals that Silicon Valley and Hollywood, though possibly extreme in their recent organizational vitality, are not all that unusual in their demographic heterogeneity. As we describe in this book, study after study reveals that organizational populations contain many more firms (and even more would-be firms) than conventional wisdoms (and even detailed historical accounts) admit. Even old, highly concentrated industries, such as automobile manufacturing and beer brewing, consist of hundreds of firms. Indeed, the number and diversity of firms in these old industries have grown in recent years. Systematic measurement of such heterogeneity in populations of corporations comprises a central task for corporate demography. Analyzing the causes and consequences of organizational heterogeneity is a second key task.

Unfortunately, basic corporate-demographic facts, such as the number of organizations in society or the prevalence of organizations in various sectors of the economy, have received little attention. Even students of particular industries are unlikely to know much about the typical life spans of its organizations or the degree of stability and change over time of organizational phenomena. This situation should not be that surprising. The United States lacks institutionalized sources for most kinds of data on individual organizations, but especially for demographic data on organizations, which need to be collected systematically over time for large sets of organizations. Available data might be quite valuable for particular purposes, but they do not provide the basis for a demographic understanding of the organizational world, as the Population Census does for persons and households.

Demographic knowledge and data on corporations are lacking largely because corporate demography does not yet exist as an institutionalized scientific field. Yet we believe that much of the hard groundwork for building such a field has already been done by organizational researchers. In this book, we seek to organize this material and to present it as a viable and coherent approach. Our main goal is to explain and develop corporate demography, and by doing so to move further toward its establishment as a field of social science inquiry. We examine concepts and theories that we think have promise in corporate demography as well as the appropriate methods and materials (cf. Shryock and Siegel 1971).

The lack of an institutionalized organizational demography means that social and economic policy usually gets formulated without appreciation of implications for the full diversity of corporations and other kinds of organizations. An essential part of our efforts here involves foreshadowing the use of demography for addressing questions about corporate and public policy, showing how this might yield different insights and new ideas.

reveals an astonishing variety of organizations in the Valley (Saxenian 1994; Baron, Burton, and Hannan 1996). One finds giant firms, such as Hewlett-Packard and Intel, which have occupied stable industrial roles for decades, alongside upstarts such as Cisco Systems, Sun Microsystems, and Oracle, each of which became world leaders in its industry within its first decade of existence. For every Cisco, Sun, and Oracle, dozens of other large firms fell behind and got acquired, hundreds (perhaps thousands) of other ventures never got off the ground and faded unnoticed from the scene, hundreds of still other firms persist as small, niche players, and yet others are undergoing rapid growth (the so-called gazelles). One finds classic bureaucracies, firms organized like families or clans, and virtual companies (with a minimal "center" and employees scattered over several continents). Some of the firms ___ ___ ___ fundamental technical break-throughs; these are firms run b___ ___ technical frontier, driven by the intellect___ ___ Others are racing to refine existing techno___ ___ e to users. Still others are trying to make ___ ___ ts for par-ticular customers and building ___

Is there a meaningful pro___ ___ f so, which of the many possible choices ___ ___ entative? A demographic perspective sugg___ ___ e mark for both social science research and public p___, ___ triking features of Silicon Valley are (broadly) demographic: *high diversity of organizational forms and high rates of demographic turnover* (entry and exit of firms).

The vitality of this community of firms stems partly from these demographic characteristics, in our view. At the level of the organizational community, the high rates of turnover of constituent organizations continually reshuffles the human work force. The great diversity of organizational forms and technological strategies means that job-changers find themselves in new and different social contexts. Ideas flow with the people, get recombined, and new technical and organizational innovations result. Analysis of a putatively representative firm would not only miss the point, it would also obscure community-level dynamics.

Surface appearances point to a strong similarity between Silicon Valley and Hollywood, another industrial sector behind California's economic renaissance. Hollywood encompasses large, free-standing production companies, such as the stable Disney Corporation and the upstart Dreamworks, once-independent firms now operating as subsidiaries of giant multinationals, such as Columbia Pictures (now owned by Sony), and a very large number of smaller independent production companies and associated suppliers. Hollywood firms form and disband nearly continuously, causing a continual reshuffling of the human actors. The vitality of the organizational community appears to reflect its demography.

Some of this benefit comes simply from application of demographic methods to different substantive issues. For example, in current policy debates concerning the competitiveness of a nation's firms in the international marketplace, this issue often gets analyzed on the basis of only a few anecdotes or highly publicized cases. As we demonstrate here, corporate demography provides a framework for systematic assessment of firms' experiences as they attempt to penetrate and develop foreign markets. It also offers conceptual frameworks and statistical tools that would facilitate meaningful measurement of the competitive intensity of various markets. A deeper understanding of these issues would undoubtedly have value for policymakers.

For many other policy issues, a corporate-demographic approach suggests new questions or revisions to commonly asked questions. For example, current public and political anguish about the retirement costs of the (relatively) large generation of persons born in Western nations and Japan between 1945 and 1955 (so-called baby boomers) focuses on national social security systems and the ability of large old corporations to fund their pension obligations. These are paramount issues, to be sure. However, corporate demography shows the greatest needs are generated by small new firms—these organizations have the lowest rates of private pension coverage of any kind. These firms also typically have high mortality rates, which exacerbates the problem. Policies that give incentives to these firms to establish pensions would go some way toward addressing the nation's needs. Policy that provides collective solutions to vibrant industries or communities with high firm mortality would go even further.

More generally, much policy discussion builds on normative notions that the interests of various corporate stakeholders ought to be balanced. This discussion builds on the presumption that corporations would function more smoothly and be more beneficial to society if a set of stakeholder rights and responsibilities could be established and applied meaningfully. The backdrop for most of these discussions again consists of an imagined representative corporation. But, the organizational diversity and high rates of change characterizing the corporate world suggest strongly that any single constitutional blueprint of stakeholder rights is likely to be deficient in some contexts. Indeed, we would suggest that these demographic issues might explain why advocates of the stakeholder framework have had such difficulty in agreeing on the appropriate model.

An intriguing alternative approach, based on a demographic understanding of the world of corporations, would assess stakeholder issues at a higher level of analysis, perhaps the industry or organizational community. By this view, some of the organizational diversity found in an industry might play itself out in varying degrees of alignment with particular stakeholders. What would matter, then, from a normative or public-policy stance would be whether every relevant group of stakeholder interests is addressed somewhere in the community, but not necessarily in every company. In fact, it is entirely possible that matching stakeholders' interests with corporations is easier and more efficient when done at this collective level. (Of course, this conjecture overlooks new issues of governance and the like that might arise.)

In introducing policy issues, we hope merely to whet appetites. We understand and appreciate that any serious policy question deserves great study of its own, even if approached from a demographic viewpoint. The book presents illustrative applications of a corporate-demographic approach to issues of regulation/deregulation, employment issues, and to some extent cultural diversity. We believe that these applications do not come close to exhausting the potential value of corporate demography for understanding the changing roles of corporations and populations and communities of corporations.

A Reader's Guide

Demography is a technical field, and this book reflects that orientation. We have tried, nonetheless, to make the book accessible to audiences with a range of technical backgrounds. Most of the book is written for social scientists and other analysts without a strong training in demography or its underlying tools of mathematics, statistics, and logic. Other parts should appeal directly to a more technically advanced audience. We do not think that the book needs to be read from cover to cover to be appreciated. Indeed, we suggest that readers might initially skip over sections that they find too technical, coming back to them after they have had a chance to brush up their knowledge. For those without mathematical training at the calculus level, some parts of Chapters 10 and 11 might be difficult. For those without an exposure to probability theory and statistics, Chapters 6 and 7 might be difficult, as well as parts of Chapters 10, 11, 13, and 14. Finally, for those who do not have a basic understanding of first-order logic, some (clearly identifiable) parts of Chapters 13, 14, 16, and 17 might be hard going.

We also recognize that readers with varying interests might pick up the book, and so we have made many of the chapters relatively self-contained. This is especially true for the chapters in Parts III–V. We recommend that those with such specific interests first familiarize themselves with the general demographic approach by reading Chapters 2, 3, 6, and 7. We think that many of the later chapters might be read in order of interest rather than sequence without much loss. The chapters in Parts III and IV are organized by *theoretical mechanism*; they each address the variety of relevant outcome variables. The chapters in Part V each deal with the implications of corporate demography for a specific topic.

A Note on Style

In order to preserve the readability of the book, we have striven to lower the amount of technical detail to only the most important elements. In particular, we adopted two conventions in reporting empirical findings. First, we do *not* report standard errors of estimates or *t*-statistics in tables of findings, except in Chapters 6 and 7 where estimation is a primary topic. Instead of standard errors or *t*-statistics, we use an asterisk to indicate that an estimated effect is statistically significant at the (usual social-science standard) of 0.05. Second, we do not usually report estimates of complete specifications but only the part that is relevant to the discussion. Most of the tables are adapted from published papers that report the full set of estimates and also give standard errors or *t*-statistics. Readers who would like the full details are urged to check the original papers.

Acknowledgments

We would like to thank the large number of collaborators, colleagues, and students who have helped to make this book a reality. The collaborators whose work is reported or reflected in the book include: William P. Barnett, James N. Baron, David N. Barron, Lyda Bigelow, Christophe Boone, Vera Bröcheler, M. Diane Burton, Stanislav D. Dobrev, Elizabeth A. Dundon, Joon Han, J. Richard Harrison, Heather A. Haveman, Michael Kinstlick, David G. McKendrick, Gábor Péli, László Pólos, Marc-David Seidel, Anand Swaminathan, John C. Torres, Albert C.Y. Teo, Lucia Tsai, Arjen van Witteloostuijn, and Elizabeth West. Dave Barron also helped us with programs for typesetting in LaTeX. We are especially grateful to László Pólos for collaborating with us on Chapter 4.

Colleagues who have read chapters or other material and gave us comments include: William P. Barnett, James N. Baron, David N. Barron, Ronald S. Burt, John Freeman, Roberto Fernandez, J. Richard Harrison, Michael Hout, Jaap Kamps, Tai-Young Kim, Michael Kinstlick, Ronald D. Lee, Peter V. Marsden, David G. McKendrick, Susan Olzak, Joel M. Podolny, László Pólos, Luca Solari, Jesper B. Sørensen, Olav Sorenson, Kenneth W. Wachter, and Ezra W. Zuckerman. We also appreciate the help of Tae-Young Kim in bringing the book to publication.

Finally, we thank the many students who have worked with us—inspired us, helped us, corrected us—across the years. The book is dedicated to them mainly because it is their efforts that have made this field what it is and will determine what becomes of it. While all these students made contributions for which we are grateful, those who did their dissertation work in this area deserve special mention.

From Berkeley, they include: William P. Barnett, Lyda Bigelow, Heather A. Haveman, Will Mitchell, Marc-David Seidel, Anand Swaminathan, Albert C. Y. Teo, Lucia Tsai, and James B. Wade.

From Cornell, they include: Jane Banaszak-Holl, David N. Barron, Alessandro Lomi, James Ranger-Moore, and Elizabeth West.

From Stanford, they include: Terry L. Amburgey, M. Diane Burton, Charles Denk, Joon Han, Stanislav D. Dobrev, Tai-Young Kim, Nancy Langton, Douglas Y. Park, Jesper B. Sørensen, Olav Sorenson, Toby E. Stuart, and John C. Torres.

From Amsterdam, Jeroen Bruggeman and Jaap Kamps.

We also greatly appreciate the financial support of several institutions, whose grants made possible the research behind this book as well as the time required for its writing. The Alfred P. Sloan Foundation should receive greatest credit for the book; it was the Foundation's staff (Hirsh Cohen and Jesse Ausubel, in particular) who sought us out and funded the project on the Demography of the Corporation. Other essential support came, at various times, from the John Simon Guggenheim Memorial Foundation, the National Science Foundation, the Max Planck Institute for Human Development, the Cortese Chair of Management (Haas School of Business at Berkeley), the Institute of Industrial Relations at Berkeley, and the Faculty Trust of the Graduate School of Business at Stanford.

We thank the following publishers for permission to adapt portions of the following copyrighted articles.

William P. Barnett and Glenn R. Carroll. 1993. "How institutional constraints affected the organization of early U.S. telephony." *Journal of Law, Economics, and Organization* 9:98–126; James N. Baron, M. Diane Burton, and Michael T. Hannan. 1996. "The road taken: Origins and early evolution of employment systems in emerging companies." *Industrial and Corporate Change* 5:239–76; James N. Baron, M. Diane Burton, and Michael T. Hannan. 1999. "Engineering bureaucracy: The genesis of formal policies, positions, and structures in high-technology firms." *Journal of Law, Economics, and Organization,* in press; David N. Barron, Elizabeth West, and Michael T. Hannan. 1998. "Deregulation and competition in populations of credit unions." *Industrial and Corporate Change* 7:1–32; Glenn R. Carroll 1997. "Long-term evolutionary change in organizational populations: Theory, models, and findings in industrial demography." *Industrial and Corporate Change* 6:119–43; Glenn R. Carroll and Albert C. Y. Teo. 1996. "Creative self-destruction among organizations: An empirical study of technical innovation and organizational failure in the American automobile industry, 1885–1982." *Industrial and Corporate Change* 5:619–44; Michael T. Hannan, M. Diane Burton, James N. Baron. 1996. "Inertia and change in the early years: Employment relations in young, high-technology firms." *Industrial and Corporate Change* 5:503–36; Michael T. Hannan, Glenn R. Carroll, Stanislav D. Dobrev, and Joon Han. 1998. "Organizational mortality in European and American automobile industries, Part I: Revisiting the effects of age and size." *European Sociological Review* 14:279–302; Michael T. Hannan, Glenn R. Carroll, Stanislav D. Dobrev, Joon Han, and John C. Torres.

1998. "Organizational mortality in European and American automobile industries, Part II: Coupled clocks." *European Sociological Review* 14:302–13, all copyright © by Oxford University Press. All rights reserved.

David N. Barron, Elizabeth West, and Michael T. Hannan. 1994. "A time to grow and a time to die: Growth and mortality of credit unions in New York, 1914–1990." *American Journal of Sociology* 100:381–421; Glenn R. Carroll and J. Richard Harrison. 1994. "On the historical efficiency of competition between organizational populations." *American Journal of Sociology* 100:720–49; Michael T. Hannan. 1998. "Rethinking age dependence in organizational mortality: Logical formalizations." *American Journal of Sociology* 104:85–123, all copyright © by the University of Chicago. All rights reserved.

Michael T. Hannan, Glenn R. Carroll, Elizabeth A. Dundon, and John C. Torres. 1995. "Organizational evolution in multinational context: Entries of automobile manufacturers in Belgium, Britain, France, Germany, and Italy." *American Sociological Review* 60:509–28; James N. Baron, Michael T. Hannan, and M. Diane Burton. 2000. "Building the iron cage: Determinants of managerial intensity in the early years of organizations." *American Sociological Review*, forthcoming, both copyright © by the American Sociological Association. All rights reserved.

Glenn R. Carroll and J. Richard Harrison. 1998. "Organizational demography and culture: Insights from a formal model and simulation." *Administrative Science Quarterly* 43:637–67, copyright © 1998 by Cornell University. All rights reserved.

Michael T. Hannan. 1997. "Inertia, density, and the structure of organizational populations: Entries in European automobile industries, 1886–1981." *Organization Studies* 18:193–228, copyright © 1997 by Walter de Gruyter GmbH & Company. All rights reserved.

Glenn R. Carroll, Lyda Bigelow, Marc-David Seidel, and Lucia Tsai. 1996. "The fates of de novo and de alio producers in the American automobile industry, 1885–1982." *Strategic Management Journal* 17:117–37, copyright © 1996 by John Wiley & Sons Ltd. All rights reserved.

William P. Barnett and Glenn R. Carroll. 1995. "Modeling internal organizational change." *Annual Review of Sociology* 21:217–36, copyright © 1995 by Annual Reviews. All rights reserved.

We also thank Krause Publications of Iola, Wisconsin for permission to reproduce materials from *The Standard Catalogue of American Cars*, Third Edition. Copyright © 1996 by Krause Publications. All rights reserved.

Part I
THE CASE FOR CORPORATE DEMOGRAPHY

THE CHAPTERS in this part of the book address the questions: Why corporate demography? What is the promise of corporate demography? What shape might a demography of corporations and industries take? They do so in steps, drawing from both the basic discipline of demography as well as the multidisciplinary field of organizational studies.

Chapter 1 attempts to whet appetites. It sets conventional views of various organizational phenomena, such as competition and structural transformation, side by side with demographic views. It illustrates that explanations based on considerations of corporate demography sometimes contrast sharply with commonly held beliefs and explanations.

Chapter 2 initiates discussion of demography per se. It begins by presenting some basic demographic facts about firms and other organizations. The presentation includes some general information about the American economy as well as about a variety of specific industries in the United States and elsewhere. It points out that some of these facts represent recurrent empirical patterns that have been the subject of much organizational research. The chapter next moves to a more conceptual level and discusses how demographic theory and research are organized and developed. The structure of what social scientists call a "demographic explanation" is reviewed in some depth. The chapter also distinguishes several disparate areas of organizational study that are sometimes called demographic.

Chapter 3 addresses head-on the theoretical and conceptual challenges of a demography of corporations and industries. It reviews prior attempts to establish such a demography and suggests ways to make a more fruitful corporate demography. The chapter then delves into the most important conceptual issues and explores current thinking and research practice. The issues considered here include: demarcation of vital

1

events, requirements for models of internal organizational transformation and for corporate vital events, specification of units of analysis, and treatment of organizational environments. The chapter concludes with a discussion of the design of theory-driven cumulative research programs.

Chapter 4 tackles a thorny issue for all organization research: how to bound the analysis to meaningful and comparable sets of units. In the case of corporate demography, this question concerns the specification of organizational forms and organizational populations. The chapter reviews previous practice and advances a more precise definition of forms as cultural codes. It develops the notion in depth using formal tools and tracing through their implications for identifying organizational populations. Examples are drawn from several industries.

1

About Organizations

CORPORATE DEMOGRAPHY looks at organizations in a special way: through the scientific examination of their vital rates of founding, growth/decline, and mortality. In this book, we seek to advance, explain, and develop the demographic view of organizations. Understanding of corporate demography among social scientists and policy analysts is incomplete at best. So before we undertake our mission in earnest, we offer in this opening chapter some glimpses of how a demographic perspective potentially enhances our understanding of the world of corporations.

As demographic matters have not been given broad attention, analysis of corporations and industries too often rests on stylized misconceptions. When social science and policy debates miss basic demographic facts and processes about corporations, the ramifications are frequently important. Consider the following series of issues.

1.1 Organizational Aging and Learning

Are young firms more fragile than old ones? According to a well-known fact about organizations, this is indeed so: young organizations have much greater risk of failure than old ones. Most empirical research, ranging from studies of single industries to representative samples of firms in many industries, shows this fact to be true. At a basic level, the best studies demonstrate that the probability of corporate failure is higher in the earlier years than in later years. Theoretical ideas about the fact refer to it as the "liability of newness" and explain the high mortality hazard of young organizations as the consequence of such varied factors as the difficulty of coordinating strangers, lack of experience and tacit knowledge, insufficient assets, and difficulties in establishing networks of suppliers and customers (Stinchcombe 1965).

3

Research in corporate demography suggests that the "fact" of negative age dependence in the hazard of firm mortality might be wrong. A long-recognized alternative explanation for apparent negative age dependence in organizational mortality rates involves the effect of unobserved heterogeneity. Suppose that an industry has only two types of firms, call them type A and type B. Suppose that all of the firms of each type have a constant hazard of death, meaning that the probability of death does not depend upon age. Suppose further that firms of type A are more fragile than those of type B; that is, the mortality rate of type-A firms exceeds that of type-B firms (by the same ratio at every age). A researcher who followed this set of firms over time and calculated mortality rates of all firms without knowing their type (in other words, using a combined but unlabeled sample of types A and B) would observe that the mortality rate declines with age. This pattern would appear because the hazard in the combined sample is a weighted average of the two rates (with the weights depending upon the mix of types). At the beginning of the observation period, both types of firms are present and contribute to the observed hazard. As time passes (and firms age), more of the high-hazard type-A firms will fail and thus leave the sample than will the lower-hazard type-B firms. So, the weighted average trends toward the hazard of type B over time. In other words, the rate declines from some initial weighted average of the two rates toward the lower rate. In our example, the trend corresponds with organizational aging; so the observed hazard declines with age. This example is a special simple case (called the "mover-stayer" model). This form of explanation has great generality. It applies to many types of possible factors and represents a continuing challenge to stories about negative age dependence.

Recent research reveals that the most important unobserved variable in many studies of firm mortality is organizational size. Small size elevates the hazard of mortality, because small firms can be destroyed by small environmental shocks. Moreover, age and size are almost always positively correlated for organizational populations. So the apparent effect of age might really be an effect of size. Size varies over firms' lifetimes, and adequate control for this factor requires information on growth and decline over time for each firm over its entire existence. Recent research shows that, when complete size data of this kind have been collected and statistically controlled in analyses of mortality, the liability of newness often disappears. Indeed, a liability of senescence/obsolescence (whereby failure rates increase with age) replaces it in many studies. That is, rigorous demographic analysis suggests that corporate mortality rates might be characterized by *positive*, rather than negative, age dependence (Chapter 13).

Now consider a similar question about the industry or organizational population: Are old industries or populations "wiser" than young ones?

According to a common belief, as industries age and mature, their individual and organizational members accumulate a great deal of beneficial collective learning. This view is buttressed by data on performance and productivity, which usually show large improvements over the life of an industry. Some of this improvement comes as the result of technical innovations; but some also stems from organizational changes, involving improvements in the processes for getting work done.

It is tempting to generalize from these few specific facts of industry evolution to other aspects of possible learning. Many analysts do so; they see mistakes as less common in old industries. This thinking is often applied to entrepreneurs, as well as to established organizations. It suggests that organizations founded in mature industries will have lower failure rates than those founded in new industries. It also implies that old firms in established industries should have lower failure rates than firms of equal age in new industries.

Corporate demography suggests that collective learning stops or reverses itself in many industries, at least insofar as organizational structures are concerned (Chapter 16). Failure rates of new organizations often are not lower later in an industry's history. If late entrepreneurs know more, then they apparently cannot implement the knowledge effectively. Likewise, existing organizations often display higher death rates in old industries. This is probably because organizational structures sometimes become obsolete and senescent with age, rendering them incapable of incorporating improvements found in competitors. In other cases, dominant firms become stagnant and fail to learn at the same rate as firms in highly competitive contexts. These findings suggest that collective learning might be rare and fragile; it likely occurs only under certain conditions that are not yet understood.

1.2 Organizational Inertia and Change

An important parallel question arises at the level of the individual organization: How flexibly do organizations respond to changes in their environments? Corporations and other kinds of organizations can be regarded as social tools for achieving work and other kinds of collective action. The organizational tool might be viewed as an awkward or cumbersome one, but it is still usually thought to be subject to the control of its managers, who direct it to accomplish the tasks at hand. As the nature of task requirements changes, managers attempt to redesign the organization, making it a flexible tool. The management literature regularly extols such flexible organization as the ideal. The obstacle to good organizational design, by this view, lies in figuring out the right changes, what new configuration would best suit the current technologies and markets, not in getting the organization to change.

Research in corporate demography suggests that an organization's history strongly constrains its subsequent possibilities. In particular, research shows that the social and economic conditions at the time of an organization's founding have a lasting effect upon its structure and operation—sometimes spanning decades of existence (Chapter 9). Overcoming this inertia is much more difficult than the literature on management implies, especially for core features of an organization such as its mission and its form of authority. Perhaps for this reason, established organizations often find it beneficial to buy existing start-ups as a way to learn new technologies or business practices or to create semiautonomous units when attempting to do new or radically different things.

Of course, some organizations do manage to transform core elements of structure. Do their life chances typically improve as a result? Many observers think that they do. However, a program of empirical research in corporate demography supports the opposite conclusion. This research examines sets of similar organizations systematically over time and keeps track of attempts at major change. This research, though somewhat mixed in its conclusions, tends to find that organizations undertaking major structural changes experience increased risk of failure. Why? It could be that only those organizations already experiencing serious problems enact such profound change. However, ample theory and evidence suggest that the *process of change* itself might be so disruptive that attempting radical change elevates the risk of mortality (Chapter 16). This seems to be especially the case for organizations attempting to make radical shifts in their cores (those structures whose modification requires the reworking of many apparently unrelated secondary and tertiary routines in the organization). The precariousness of this process endangers organizations in the short run, even if the intended new structure would actually benefit the firm and enhance its viability in the longer run.

The common, but distorted, view of organizational change as easy and beneficial likely arises from the unsound way many observers collect data on corporations. Frequently, analysts and popular management authors collect information on a set of organizations currently performing very well and then look at the evolution of their strategies and structures. This selective, retrospective view of firms often shows that successful firms went through one or several previous transformations that led to later good performance. It is tempting—and many analysts succumb—to infer from this information that, had other organizations attempted the same changes, they too would have experienced success. Unfortunately, this inference comes from considering data that are heavily biased toward the successful firms. The information available does not justify an inference of cause-

and-effect with respect to the changes. Nor does it provide the basis for generalization to other firms. Such a sample cannot support dependable analyses of the consequences of change.

1.3 Competitive Intensity

How does variation in the number of firms in an industry affect the intensity of competition? Assessment of the levels of competitive intensity in industries holds great interest to practitioners, policymakers, and academic analysts. A common rule of thumb relates the number of competitor organizations within an industry to its overall level of competition. Most commonly, analysts assume that the level of competition in an industry rises with the number of organizations it contains. Subtler developments of the idea often incorporate market share concepts. These hold that new organizations increase competition only if they are roughly the same size as existing organizations. For instance, Porter (1980) cites "numerous and equally balanced competitors" as a major structural factor in intensifying rivalry among firms within an industry. High competition or rivalry within an industry manifests itself in lower founding rates and elevated mortality rates.

Empirical research in corporate demography shows evidence supporting this general conjecture. A well-developed model of longterm organizational evolution assumes that the level of competition in a population rises with the number of constituent organizations, that is, *density*. According to this theory, as the number of competitors increases linearly, the number of potential competitive ties between organizations increases geometrically. Organizations are assumed to be of equal size in the theory (and time-varying controls for size differences are introduced in empirical work). However, this research also shows the situation to be more complicated and more interesting.

Demographic research on founding and mortality supports the simple association between competition and density only in the high ranges of density. In the low ranges of density, a very different relationship dominates: founding rates increase with density and lower mortality rates decrease with increases in density. These population-enhancing effects are widely thought to be the result of *legitimation*, a social process by which organizational forms become institutionalized or socially "taken for granted." According to the density model, legitimation increases as a decreasing function of the number of "competitor" organizations in an industry (Chapters 10 and 11)

Taken together, legitimation and competition processes predict curvilinear (specifically, nonmonotonic) relationships between the number of organizations in an industry and their vital rates. In the low ranges of density (especially during a population's early years), legitimation dominates industry evolution: founding rates rise with density and mortality rates fall. At high ranges, competition dominates, leading founding rates to decline and mortality rates to rise. So in models of both founding rates and mortality rates, the effect of the number of organizations on vital rates is often specified as a function of density and density-squared, with the effects of these two terms differing in sign. Many empirical studies have found support for these predictions.

Do large size and positional advantage insulate firms from competitive pressure? A tradition of thinking in sociology and economics sees great power in the hands of large corporations and their executives. For instance, sociologist Perrow (1986, 175) writes:

> The dominant organizations or institutions of our society have *not* experienced goal displacement and have been able to institutionalize on their own terms—to create the environments they desire, shape the existing ones, and define which sections of it they will deal with. (emphasis in original)

Economists, while usually more tempered in their views, still often see large dominant firms as capable of exercising their market power to limit competition and exclude new competitors. Industrial economist Porter (1980) advocates designing a firm's business strategy around its bargaining power relative to suppliers and buyers, which get determined in large part by relative size comparisons.

Economic history shows that most large dominant firms cannot maintain their dominance over extremely long periods. Hannah (1999) reports that, of the world's hundred largest firms, by market capitalization, in 1912, only 19% remained in the top 100 in 1995. More surprisingly, 29% had experienced "liquidation, bankruptcy protection, extensive corporate breakup, or nationalization." Leading firms in 1912 who have left little if any trace of their organizations include J & P Coats (3rd in 1912), Pullman (4th), Anaconda (6th), Armour (16th), and Westinghouse Airbrake (21st).

Corporate demography shows that large firms frequently cannot even control entry into their own industry during their periods of dominance. In fact, empirical research on a variety of industries (including beer brewing, wine making, music recording, airline passenger service, and others) documents that the rate of entry is high in many contexts precisely when large firms are most dominant (in the sense of controlling great market share). Moreover, the new firms entering under these conditions typically fare better than had they entered in times where the large firms exerted less dominance. The ability of giant firms to control their fates is thus sometimes illusory.

The demographic theory of resource partitioning explains why entry rates sometimes surge when large firms dominate a market (Chapter 12). According to this theory, large firms compete by achieving economies of scale in markets of consumers with diverse tastes. These firms increase their scale by becoming generalists, tailoring their product(s) to consumers in the "center" of the market. They become dominant by ramping up scale faster than their competitors, which allows them to offer higher quality to consumers for the same price. Left unfettered for a long period, this competition process eventually produces a market monopolized by a single large firm. However, this result rarely occurs. As the largest firms attempt to make their products appeal to a larger, more diverse consumer base, they lose their appeal to those with unusual tastes. This untapped part of the market becomes attractive to entrepreneurs, and they start specialist firms targeted to it. In contrast, when many generalists occupy the market, competition forces them to differentiate (even though each strives for a large market share). A market with many or even several differentiated generalist firms leaves less untapped space at the periphery of the resource space than a market covered by a single large generalist firm. So dominance by one firm creates conditions more favorable to entry than the presence of several large less-dominant firms.

1.4 Global Competition

Does globalization intensify competition? The answer to this question would surely seem to be affirmative. As the business world becomes increasingly global, many firms and industries design strategies for coping with increased competition. Executives often worry that their firms will not be able to thrive in the competitive global world (or at least that they might need to rethink their firm's strategy in order to be competitive). Labor leaders and employees fear that jobs might be lost if firms fail in the face of fierce new global competition. Politicians and governmental officials respond to these concerns by seeking to erect trade barriers to thwart international competitors or by refusing to tear down existing barriers. A common presumption lies behind these and many other beliefs and actions: globalization of industry concerns primarily—if not solely—competition, particularly competitive relations between organizations from different countries.

Comparative historical research on corporate demography traces the developments in national industries as they become international. Such research reveals that an exclusive focus on competition misses some important processes. Relations other than competition often develop between

various organization populations in different countries. Some of these relationships benefit organizations in multiple national industries. For instance, demographic study of the European automobile industry shows
that early automobile producers in a country experienced lower rates of
failure when other countries had many producers than when they had few
(Chapter 11). Why?

The density model of organizational evolution suggests that the process of legitimation (whereby organizational forms get institutionalized)
operates at a relatively high level of analysis, one that transcends political
and geographical barriers. Cultural images about organization often flow
freely across national boundaries, meaning that those starting firms of a
new kind in a "late" country benefit from the ideas and cultural understandings developed elsewhere in "early" countries. This occurs because
the cultural images have diffused prior to establishment of the national industry, making institutionalization processes proceed more rapidly. In this
process, globalization actually assists the development of national organizations.

International relations in the post–cold-war period have become increasingly concentrated on matters of trade and national competitiveness.
Analysts and policymakers understand that a country's international competitiveness depends less on its natural resources or its price of labor than
on the productivity and innovation of its firms and industries. Put simply,
countries with internationally competitive firms have internationally competitive economies. Much industrial policy seeks to enhance and sustain
the competitiveness of a nation's large companies, which are regarded as
having strategic and other advantages in the world marketplace. The ways
this goal might be achieved, ranging from governmental orchestration and
protection to fostering national competition to investing in infrastructure
and education to changing management practice, are actively debated.

This debate operates on what we regard as a misconception about the
organizational world: the (frequently implicit) premise that the longterm
competitiveness of a nation depends on its best firms retaining and sustaining their competitive advantage. For instance, Porter (1990, 20) claims
that a fundamental issue in industrial policy is understanding "how a nation provides an environment in which its firms can improve and innovate
faster than foreign rivals in a particular industry." In our view, this fram-
ing of the issue implicitly invokes one or, perhaps, several implausible
premises, including organizational flexibility and environmental stability.
We think it is unreasonable to assume that any particular organizational
form will prevail for long periods of time in the uncertain world of international trade. Likewise, we doubt that organizational structures are mal-
leable enough to keep pace with rapid and unpredictable environmental
change (Chapters 16 and 17). Should industrial policy be based on such

assumptions? In our view, it would be much wiser to accept these organizational realities and to base policy on them rather than on more fanciful ones. Doing so would shift focus from sustaining the advantages of existing dominant firms to considering how best to facilitate the construction and development of new firms with innovative organizational forms. In other words, the focus would be on building—and constantly refreshing—the *diversity* of organizational solutions for a national economy rather than on continuing to prop up a few current successes.

1.5 Historical Efficiency

A related question asks: Do the fittest firms survive? The field of strategic management traditionally concerns itself with questions of organizational competitiveness. Among the firms in an industry, which will succeed? What factors produce competitive success? Strategy theory offers many answers to these questions. The answers point to the importance of factors such as market positioning, innovative capability, organizational flexibility, and human-resource practices. Debate is spirited. Research in the area attempts to demonstrate the impact of specific strategic factors on firm growth, profitability, and survival. Much of this work gets turned into prescriptive advice for executives, transmitted through popular trade books, executive education seminars, management consulting, and so forth.

Both academic and practitioner discussions of effective strategies often rely on the presumption that once a firm adopts a "key success factor" (something enhancing firm competitiveness), it will have an advantage that consistently and quickly generates a dominant position, unless competitors can also make similar moves. In other words, competitive strength of a firm translates efficiently into industrial dominance.

Although historically efficient adjustment does characterize some industries, theory and research in corporate demography suggest that industries adjust slowly, much more slowly than is typically assumed (Chapter 17). That is, even when a set of firms has demonstrably more competitive form (due, say, to better technology), it still takes a very long time for the superior form to reach a position of dominance when populations built on other forms have gotten a head start—and there is even some chance that the superior form might never win. Why? The evolution of organizations and industries often displays *path dependence*, a condition where the present possibilities depend on the previous trajectory of events. Path dependence often produces surprising outcomes; early trajectories get driven one way or another by a few random events. Firms in path-dependent markets then can develop strong positional advantages that are difficult for new firms to overcome, even if they possess inherently superior structures and capabilities.

1.6 Employment and Entrepreneurship

Has the rate of involuntary termination of employment diminished in recent years? Many analysts claim that it has. They argue that American employment relationships have been changing. They note that the once-mighty labor movement has declined substantially, and unions have lost their appeal for many employees. Although the reasons for this decline are many and varied, changes in both employment practice and labor law have played a part. Many companies now appear to treat their employees as assets to be protected and nurtured rather than resources to be exploited. This means that many employees face more benevolent employers as well as a greater and more attractive range of benefits and privileges. The rights of employees have been strengthened and expanded steadily. Employees not only have legal guarantees of equal protection but also potential remedies for use against arbitrary and capricious actions by employers. The law has developed especially in areas concerning due process and employee termination.

These developments have led many observers to conclude that an increasing share of job mobility comes from voluntary employee decisions. It does appear to be the case that employer control over termination has eroded. However, this does not mean that the rate of involuntary termination has declined, as is commonly claimed. Not all (or most) involuntary terminations result from decisions by employers to terminate the jobs of particular individuals. Empirical research shows that many (perhaps most) involuntary employee terminations result from corporate demographics, the closing of plants and firms and the merger and reorganization of viable firms (Chapter 19). Demographic activity among corporations varies strongly across industries, and it bears no simple relationship with historical time. In particular, there is no convincing evidence of a general shift in corporate demography of the kind that would be necessary to make the overall rate of involuntary employee termination diminish. So, although the sources of involuntary employee termination might have shifted, it is unclear that the rate has also changed. Understanding the forces shaping the employment relationship clearly requires attention to the dynamics of the corporate world.

Over the last 10 to 15 years, American corporations have undergone substantial restructuring and transformation. Perhaps the best known is the downsizing trend whereby large corporations lumped off many units, layers, and employees. Indeed, we discuss evidence in Chapter 2 that the

average size of corporations and other business entities has declined dramatically in recent decades. Much, if not virtually all, of this decline in
size has been attributed to adjustments made by companies in response to
changes in technology (in particular, the advent of information technology) and in the environment (in particular, competition from foreign competitors). This view assumes that organizational structures adjust downward
in size to internal and external contingencies much as they adjust upward
in periods of growth.

Corporate demography suggests that this view of the downsizing trend
likely involves two misconceptions. The first is that much of the decline in
size results from transformations of existing organizations. In fact, evidence
suggests that most of the decline comes from the selective replacement of
old (large) firms with new (smaller) ones. This replacement process has
occurred hand in hand with the shift in the economy from the manufacturing sector to the service sector (Carroll 1984b). The economic shift to
the service sector has, of course, received much media attention, but it has
not usually been related to the larger downsizing trend of which it is a
major cause.

The second misconception concerns the speed of downsizing by large
firms in response to changing technologies and market conditions. Even
though they do not account for a great amount of the overall decline in
size, large firms such as Citigroup, Chase Manhattan Bank, Kodak, Phillip
Morris, Woolworth, Xerox, and many other firms reduced their employee
bases by thousands in the 1990s. Have these firms adjusted quickly to their
changing circumstances, much as they did to previous growth conditions?
Carefully controlled corporate demography studies of the organizations experiencing growth and decline show that adjustment is much more rapid
to growth than to decline and has a much stronger relationship to environmental conditions (Freeman and Hannan 1975). The reason for the slower
adjustment likely has to do with internal politics: managers find it much
more difficult to make negative decisions about each other and their loyal
employees than they do to make positive decisions about future employees.

The entrepreneurs who start firms are celebrated as strong-willed, aggressive persons. According to this image, their toughness gives them the
ability to withstand the trials and tribulation of starting risky new ventures.
Despite this characterization, most observers still attribute rationality to entrepreneurial motives and actions. By this view, entrepreneurs might have
a higher threshold for risk, but they still behave rationally in that they respond to perceived market opportunities. When considered collectively, this
view implies that entrepreneurial start-ups should increase when markets
and industries abound with opportunities and dwindle when they do not.

Research on corporate demography suggests that this view is incomplete at best. Organizational founding rates typically do not show straight-

forward consistent relationships with variables that measure environmental marketlike resources and opportunities. Instead, entrepreneurial actions are often associated with changes in individual life situations such as unemployment or early retirement. Some evidence suggests an association of entrepreneurship with supply-side variables that make it easier to acquire resources necessary to build a new organization. Both findings suggest that observed rates of organizational founding might be the result of a two-stage process whereby the first stage involves attempting to start an organization and the second involves acquiring the resources necessary. While we would not call those who make it through these stages irrational, it does seem a stretch to use "rational" in the conventional way as a description of a process in which adverse life events push people into the first stage and the existence of unclaimed resources propel them through the second.

1.7 A Look Ahead

In this chapter, we tried to show that certain common beliefs about corporations and industries might not be accurate when approached from a demographic perspective. Of course, we realize that many analysts already understand this. But many others will likely need to be convinced, given our sketchy presentations and informal arguments above. We hope that both groups of readers will bear with us and continue to the more formal presentation below. We want to present the demographic approach to organizational studies in its entirety. This involves motivating, explaining, and developing corporate demography. We will examine theory, models, and methods. We will also briefly explore some implications of corporate demography for public policy on several issues. We strive to present the collective achievements of the active group of organizational researchers who work in this area. We also want to explain the approach in enough detail to allow those others whose imaginations we might seduce to attempt to undertake this work themselves. In any event, we feel confident that those who read and embrace this book will develop a demographic intuition of their own, one that will allow them to see and develop new insights about corporations and industries.

The book proceeds as follows. In the remaining chapters of this section, we explain what a demographic approach to the study of corporate organizations entails. Chapter 2 describes the demographic perspective and discusses it in the context of organizational analysis. This chapter also discusses the differences between our view of corporate demography and other popular types of demographic analyses of organizations. Chapter 3 initiates the formal analysis of corporate demography. It discusses the modifications in classical human demography that are needed for the corporate context. This chapter motivates and develops much of the conceptual structure that is used throughout the book. Chapter 4 deals in depth with a core conceptual issue for corporate demography—how to define organizational forms and populations.

Part II explains and develops the methods of corporate demography. Chapter 5 presents a brief overview of the observation plans commonly used to study organizations. It pays special attention to the choice between designs that seek broad representativeness and those that seek detailed coverage of a narrow part of the organizational world. Chapter 6 introduces the formal modeling machinery used in corporate demography: stochastic process models of vital rates. It discusses various types of processes and the statistical methods used in their estimation. Chapter 7 continues the review of relevant stochastic models. It explains the ways corporate demographers incorporate the effects of covariates and time dependence into the models. It discusses special problems that arise when relevant differences among organizations cannot be measured directly, the unobserved heterogeneity problem. This chapter also presents results of simulation studies that compare the value of common alternative research designs for estimating models of corporate demography. This part ends in Chapter 8 with a nuts-and-bolts discussion of demographic data on corporations, including the commonly used types of sources and their advantages and disadvantages. This chapter reviews and comments on a variety of specific source materials used by organizational demographers.

Part III contains four chapters treating processes that apply to organizational populations. Chapter 9 discusses processes that reflect the impact of the organization's environment, broadly conceived. By way of illustration, it includes analyses of two populations and their environments: early telephone companies and high-technology companies. Chapters 10 and 11 also deal with constraining effects of environments but for population processes that have an endogenous character. These chapters feature the model of density-dependent legitimation and competition, including its many various extensions. Chapter 12 turns to models of population segregation, a special class of endogenous processes. It reviews the model of resource partitioning as well as models of size-localized competition.

Part IV of the book examines demographic processes operating at the organizational level. Chapters 13 and 14 review theory and research on the effects of age and size on the vital rates in organizational populations. These chapters show the importance of proper model specification for sound inference about these complicated matters. They also develop theory about age dependence by formalizing the arguments typically advanced to account for various empirical patterns. Chapter 15 considers how organizations get started. It explores the organizing process prior to the actual opening of the firm for business. The empirical analysis described

in this chapter examines preproduction organizing in the American automobile manufacturing industry. Chapter 16 addresses questions of organizational transformation. It reviews models and studies of the mortality
consequences of major structural change in individual organizations.

Part V explores selected implications of corporate demography. Chapter 17 turns to basic questions of organization theory. It explains why demography is relevant to all organizational theories and suggests some ways
that it might be used to develop theory about organizational change. Chapters 18 and 19 concern policy-oriented topics. Chapter 18 addresses regulation and deregulation from a demographic viewpoint. It contains illustrative analyses drawn from the telephone and banking industries. Chapter 19
considers the implications of corporate demography for employment and
related issues. The final chapter of the book (Chapter 20) returns to the
issue of organizational diversity. It speculates about how diversity might affect careers as well as important outcomes in two particular industries. It
also suggests some ways researchers might go about examining diversity
effects.

2

The Demographic Perspective

THIS BOOK looks at corporations and other kinds of organizations from a demographic perspective. It presents theories, methods, and empirical findings that exemplify a demographic approach. Although the demographic perspective figures prominently in much recent theory and research on organizations, the connections with the broader discipline of demography have not received much attention. We think that there is much to be gained by emphasizing these linkages.

For organizational studies, exploiting the models and methods of demography promises to generate new ways of studying corporations. It should increase rigor in organizational theory and research as well. For demography, a new subfield can be developed, one that brings demographic theory and methods to bear on issues of growing importance: the dynamics of organizational change and their socioeconomic consequences. The new substantive problems encountered in studying corporations will also likely spur innovation in demographic theory and methods.

Unfortunately, the demographic perspective of social science often gets misunderstood and underestimated. Too many social scientists and other analysts subscribe to the view that demography amounts to little more than an accounting system for populations. Demography is commonly considered as just a methodology, and an established boring methodology at that. While we admit that demography (like all domains of social sciences) has its share of uninspiring efforts, we believe that this general characterization is grossly inaccurate. Demography has, to be sure, an institutionalized set of methodological procedures, usually involving aspects of counting. Yet, these methods are not ends in and of themselves. Instead, they serve as tools for producing reliable empirical facts that inform a particular way of looking at research questions and developing theory. When used properly, demography yields unique and deep insights into social phenomena.

This chapter begins our introduction to the demographic perspective by presenting some basic demographic data on corporations. The exposi-

17

tion continues the theme of the preceding chapter in that it aims to provide some glimpses of how corporate demography differs from usual views of industry, to show that the facts produced by this perspective do not always square with conventional wisdom. The next part of the chapter describes generally how demographic theory gets constructed and empirical research is conducted. This discussion tries to give a concise, but sharp, overview of the conceptual and logical elements of the demographic perspective. The remainder of the chapter explains how our particular vision of corporate demography differs from several other styles of analysis of demographic factors in organizational contexts.

2.1 Basic Demography of Business Organizations

Although demographic intuition about the human population might be fairly elementary, it appears to be reasonably accurate. For example, we would venture that many Americans know that the population of the United States consists of approximately 250 million persons. Many also probably know that the United States ranks as one of the larger countries in the world population-wise but that it falls well behind China and India in terms of sheer size. Most Americans also know of the demographic bulge in the population known as the "baby boomers" (the disproportionately large group of persons born between 1945 and 1955). There is even a sense among the general public that the baby boomer bulge in the population exerts disproportionate effects on the country's cultural, political, and social life.

Demographic intuition about the corporate population appears to be much more limited and more often wrong. What, for instance, is the size of the American corporate population? Its ranking relative to other countries? Its age structure? Or any possible effects of its demographic structure on American society and economy? Although the use of publicly available data imposes severe limitations, we can nonetheless construct estimates of some of these basic demographic facts. For instance, Table 2.1 shows the

Table 2.1.   *Counts (in thousands) of U.S. business organizations, 1970–1990.*

	1970	1980	1990
Corporations	1,665	2,711	3,717
Partnerships	936	1,380	1,554
Proprietorships	6,494	9,730	14,783
All business entities	9,095	13,821	20,054

Source: *Statistical Abstract of the United States.*

Table 2.2. *Size distribution of U.S. corporations, 1990.*

Size-class (by receipts)	Number (thousands)	Percent
Under $25,000	879	23.6
$25,000 to $49,999	252	6.8
$50,000 to $99,999	359	9.7
$100,000 to $499,999	1,162	31.3
$500,000 to $999,999	416	11.2
$1,000,000 or more	649	17.5

Source: *Statistical Abstract of the United States.*

federal government's estimate of the number of American business entities from 1970 to 1990. It includes a breakdown by three generic organizational forms, corporations (which typically have limited liability) and partnerships and proprietorships (which typically have other levels of liability). Obviously, this population has grown rapidly in recent decades. The number of corporations more than doubled between 1970 and 1990. Partnerships and proprietorships also soared, making the total number of business entities rise rapidly as well. In 1990, the number of business entities stood at roughly 20 million, with roughly one independent business for every 12 or 13 persons.

Table 2.2 gives some basic information on the size distribution of American corporations in 1990. It shows size classes as measured by annual business receipts. As might be expected, a large proportion of these companies were small, with annual receipts below $25,000. Nonetheless, the largest size class by this grouping is for medium-size corporations, those with receipts between $100,000 and $500,000. The substantial size of the largest group also deserves note.

How has organizational size changed over time in the United States? Table 2.3 presents some estimates of average size of business organizations from 1960 to 1990, based on aggregate data on business and the labor force.[1] It indicates clearly that the major trend in firm size over this period runs toward smaller organizations. No matter which of the four

[1] These figures are calculated as the number of relevant persons (counts of the economically active population and major occupational classes taken from the *Labor Yearbook*) over the number of relevant organizations (counts of business entities by major class taken from the *Statistical Abstract of the United States*). That is, they are ratios of independent aggregate counts of persons and organizations. The estimates of size are imprecise in several ways. Most notably, the employee counts include those who work in the public and nonprofit sectors but the firm counts exclude public and nonprofit employers; the numbers also exclude overseas employees of American businesses. Other methods of estimating organizational size sometimes yield radically different estimates.

Table 2.3.   *Estimates of average business size in the United States, 1960–1990.*

	1960	1970	1980	1990
Economically active persons per corporation	61.2	51.6	39.4	34.0
Economically active persons per business entity	na	10.3	8.2	6.3
Employees per corporation	50.6	46.4	35.7	30.9
Employees per business entity	na	9.2	7.4	5.7
Administrative and managerial employees per corporation	4.8	5.0	4.1	4.0
Employees per administrative and managerial employee	10.5	9.9	8.6	7.8

Note: na means not available.

Sources: Calculations using data from the *International Labor Organization Yearbook* and the *Statistical Yearbook of the United States.*

"average" size calculations (shown at the top of the table) one prefers, the same pattern appears from 1960 to 1990. Such a decline represents a profound change in the organizational structure of the American economy, one with potentially far-reaching implications, given the close association of size with many other features of organizational life, including especially employment. It must be meaningful, for instance, that many Americans now work in smaller firms. For comparable jobs, small firms typically pay less, offer fewer opportunities for advancement, provide less generous benefits, and experience less stability than large firms. Table 2.3 also reveals that the management structure of American corporations might have changed over this period in that the number of administrative-managerial employees per corporation has declined (but note too that employees per administrator–manager has also dropped).[2]

What about specific industries? Although many commentators on the economy apparently regard their intuition about industrial demographic matters as good, we sense that it usually is not. Complete demographic counts of the number of firms within an industry commonly surprise most people. Consider, for example, the automobile manufacturing industry. Many social scientists are startled to learn that as many as 2,197 producers have operated within the United States sometime during 1885–1981.[3] Figure 2.1 shows their distribution across history. At its peak, in the second

[2] Caution should be used in interpreting these patterns as we are making inferences about micro patterns based on aggregate data—the trend shown is suggestive at best.

[3] We discuss the sources for these data in Chapter 8.

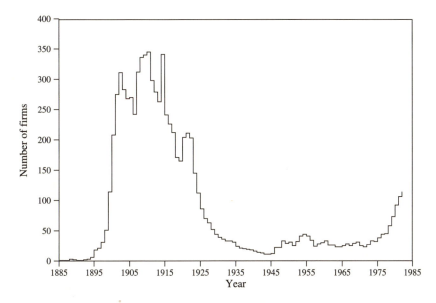

Figure 2.1. *Number of automobile manufacturers in the United States, 1885–1981. Copyright © 1995 by Glenn R. Carroll and Michael T. Hannan. Used by permission.*

decade of the century, this industry was home to 345 automobile manufacturers. Even in the recent era, with a highly concentrated market for the largest automakers, there are many more producers than most people know (mainly because they do not know about small specialist producers making alternative fuel cars, kit cars, vintage cars, and the like).

American society generated more automobile producers than other countries, but it is not unique in spawning what many social scientists find to be a startling abundance of car manufacturers. Figure 2.2 shows historical demographic counts for France and Germany. By our count, during 1885–1980 the French population of automakers included 828 firms and the German population numbered 373.[4] Interestingly, the populations show roughly the same general pattern of growth and decline as well as peaks around the same period, 1920 to 1925. This type of regularity across

[4]Three complications arose in these data from border changes. When Alsace was returned to France in 1918, two firms changed nationality. We coded these firms as censored on the right (Chapter 5) in 1914, and we coded them as entering the French industry in 1918 by a special event: change of national boundary. Another firm experienced a similar event when the Polish–German border changed in 1945. These events are not included in the counts of entries reported here. We also did not include East German firms in the count of the German industry.

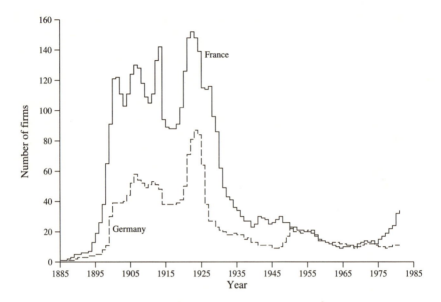

Figure 2.2. *Number of automobile manufacturers in France and Germany, 1885–1981. Source: Hannan et al. (1995). Copyright © 1995 by American Sociological Association. Used by permission.*

different countries constitutes an important empirical fact to be explained. Was there something inherent in automobile technology or production systems that produced it? Or might automobile producers have been— somewhat unexpectedly in these early days of trade—linked socially or economically across countries?

Consider a different example: banking. Figure 2.3 compares two populations of organizations but in this case the two are subsets of a single industry.[5] The figure shows the growth in numbers of two types of commercial banks in Singapore from the time of founding of its first bank in 1840 until 1990. The first type is the *full-license bank,* which can operate in all aspects of commercial banking in Singapore. The second type is the *off-shore bank,* which cannot operate freely in the local commercial market but which specializes in money-center banking for the region. The explosion of off-shore banks in the 1970s and 1980s reflects the effect of regulation: this organizational form was first authorized in 1970 with the establishment of the Monetary Authority of Singapore.

---

[5] These data were kindly provided by Albert C.Y Teo. Description of sources and coding can be found in Carroll and Teo (1998).

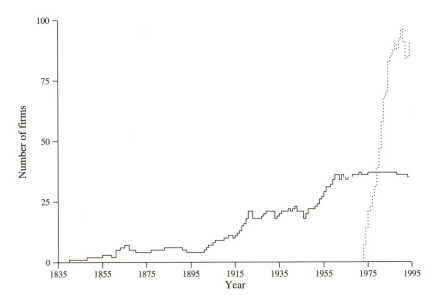

Figure 2.3. *Number of full-license (solid line) and off-shore (dashed line) commercial banks in Singapore, 1840–1990. Copyright © 1998 by Albert C. Y. Teo. Used by permission.*

For further comparison, Figure 2.4 presents historical counts of beer brewers in the United States. Notice again a general longterm pattern of population growth to a peak and then decline. The decline here is dramatic. However, it is followed in the most recent period by an even more dramatic upsurge in the number of brewers. Against the backdrop of the automobile producers, these observations raise two research questions. First, can some process account for the longterm evolution of organizational populations generally? Second, is there some way to explain the apparent late-stage reversals in the process?

What about "modern" industries? Figure 2.5 shows counts of firms in the worldwide hard-disk drive industry.[6] Despite its short history, this industry shows a pattern of early growth and decline similar to that seen above, except that it occurs over a shorter time frame. Perhaps industrial evolution moves with greater speed in modern high-technology industries. However, no reversal is yet evident.

---

[6] These data were kindly provided by David G. McKendrick. Description of sources and coding can be found in Barnett and McKendrick (1998).

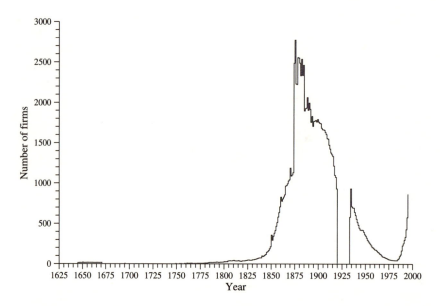

Figure 2.4. *Number of brewing firms in the United States, 1633–1995. Source: Carroll and Swaminathan (1998). Copyright © 1998 by Glenn R. Carroll and Anand Swaminathan. Used by permission.*

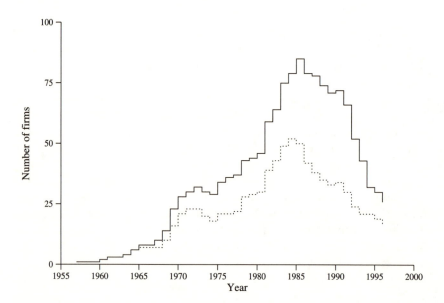

Figure 2.5. *Number of disk drive manufacturers in the world (solid line) and in North America (dashed line), 1957–1996. Copyright © 1998 by David G. McKendrick. Used by permission.*

2.2 Organizing Principles of Demography

Demographic facts about corporations and industries might be interesting; but what should we make of such phenomena? How should the empirical facts of corporate demography be analyzed? Before addressing these questions directly, it is instructive to review more generally the way demography looks at the world, its conceptual organizing principles. We identify five principles that arguably constitute demography's core.

Demography adopts a *population perspective*. This means that demographic analysis does not concern itself much with any given individual or even sets of individuals. Instead, demography seeks to explain properties of populations such as their composition (e.g., age distribution) or their dynamics (e.g., growth rates). Except in the case of an extremely homogenous population, it makes little sense to speak of a representative individual from a population. Adequate description of a population almost always entails distributional measures.

Demographic analysis examines the occurrence of events. The central objects of study in demographic analysis are the so-called *vital events* of birth and death. Other kinds of events draw attention insofar as they affect the flow of vital events. So, for instance, events of marriage and divorce frequently get brought into the picture in human demography because they affect rates of natality. For populations with permeable boundaries, rates of emigration and immigration also constitute significant events since they generate population changes.

Formal analysis in demography concentrates on the flows of events in time and the implications of events for population structure. *Age is the master clock* in standard demographic analyses of biological populations. That is, demographers assume that age differences summarize the dominant sources of variation in the outcomes of interest, leading Keyfitz (1977, 1) to proclaim that "age is the characteristic variable of population analysis." Analysis of the vital rates (of natality and mortality) in animal or human populations invariably begins with the calculation of age-specific hazards (or rates). It then proceeds to make comparisons of these rates across time and among various groups.

Events occurring to individuals are related back to the population level by the use of *counting* procedures. The demographic researcher calculates and recalculates population-level measures based on counts of events among individuals in the population. In the simplest case, population size gets incremented or decremented as a result of the simple aggregation of birth and death events. Distributional measures of the population such as the mean and variance in age require more elaborate counting systems. In other analyses, events might be assigned differential weights (special counting rules) based on specific characteristics of the event or those individuals experiencing the events.

Models of demographic systems possess a *coherent and consistent internal logic*. This logic allows demographers to move freely across parts and levels of the system, confident that the consistency of their theories can be checked and that theory fragments can potentially be unified. In a common exercise of this logic, information on vital rates and population characteristics get used in analytical procedures to derive implications for population change and stability.

2.3 Formal Demography and Population Studies

Demographers often make a distinction between formal demography and population studies. We think that this distinction provides a useful orientation for understanding how demographic research on corporations might relate to established traditions in demography and organizational studies. In their overview of the discipline, Shryock and Siegel (1971, 2) define formal demography as "concerned with size, distribution, structure and change of populations." This means that formal demographic analysis addresses the flows of vital events in time and develops population-level implications of the flows. Births and deaths (and sometimes migrations) comprise the vital events in biological and human demography. These events occur to individuals in the population, and certain regularities in their timing make it possible to develop mathematical models for their occurrence. From these models, demographers often deduce important information about the population. For example, assuming that birth and death rates do not change, it is straightforward to predict how long it will take a given population to stabilize, meaning that its overall growth or decline rate ceases to vary. It is also possible to derive the age structure of the population at any given time.

What of population studies? According to demographers Hauser and Duncan (1959, 2–3),

> Population studies examine not only classic population variables but also the relationships between population changes and other variables: social, economic, political, biological, genetic, geographical, and the like.

This means, of course, that population studies encompass a far broader range of issues and types of research than does formal demography. Population studies is such a broad category that Hauser and Duncan equate the field with the study of the "determinants and consequences of population trends." This definition would include such diverse topics as the impact of war on the population age structure and fertility, the relationship between the automobile and sexual behavior of teenagers, the drinking patterns of middle-aged men during economic depression, the relationship between the strength of familial bonds and the economic incentives to migrate from underdeveloped countries, and the effects of large young cohorts on national consumption, savings, and economic development.

Formal demography and population studies play complementary roles in enhancing our understanding of population processes (Keyfitz 1971). In its classical forms, demography rests on strong assumptions of homogeneity: the only source of variation in vital rates is age (and sometimes sex). This assumption still characterizes much formal demography. It facilitates greatly the development and analysis of mathematical models, which are both elegant and extremely useful. As Kreps (1990, 6–7) has noted, a formal model possesses the advantages of: (1) clarity ("It gives a clear and precise language for communicating insights and contributions."); (2) ease of comparability ("It provides us with general categories of assumptions so that insights and intuitions can be transferred from one context to another and can be cross-checked between different contexts."); (3) logical power ("It allows us to subject particular insights and intuitions to the test of logical consistency."); and (4) analytical precision ("It helps us to trace back from 'observational' to underlying assumptions to see what assumptions are really at the heart of particular conclusions.").

Population studies typically relax the assumption of homogeneity. They might build on the formalisms of demography, but they get much closer to reality by incorporating explicitly information about differences among members of the population. In actual demographic analyses, this heterogeneity is typically linked to individuals, but the source of the heterogeneity might lie at any level, including the environment, the individual's location in the population structure, or intrinsic properties of individuals. Population studies identify the important dimensions of heterogeneity by empirical means, by adding and testing the effects of covariates in models, and by weighting and reweighting various explanatory factors. A population study usually has a more specific concern with the idiosyncratic features of a situation than does a typical formal modeling effort; population studies frequently attempt to explain all the variance in the outcomes of a particular historical context (e.g., fertility rates of Chinese emigrants to California) while formal demography seeks generality. Consequently, population studies might be more informative about any given research problem, but they also tend to be less elegant and less general than formal analyses.

The differences between the orientations of formal analysis and population studies generate some intellectual tension. This can be healthy: formal demography and population studies ideally build on each other in ways that prove productive to each. Population-studies researchers usually find it helpful to have a general model as a point of departure on which to build complexity and heterogeneity, as the specific research context requires. Conversely, formal theorists often look to empirical population studies for facts worth incorporating into their models. In some fields, the interplay between the two orientations spawns a fertile middle ground where beneficial features of both can be found. For example, in the field of evolutionary ecology (which we discuss again later in Chapters 3 and 5 because it has strong parallels with corporate demography), theoretical analysis typically results in the development of formal models of the populations of species and their habitats. Much of the information about species behavior (and interrelationships with the environment) used in the model-building enterprise comes from natural-history studies in which researchers have spent years observing and documenting species activity in particular habitats.

Successful research programs in demography typically reflect the orientations of both formal modeling and population studies. Consider again evolutionary ecology. For many research questions, the field contains one or two basic general models of the relevant process along with a series of increasingly detailed models where analysts have built in layers of complexity for certain specified contexts (MacArthur 1972). Such nested series of models develop in research programs whose field investigators uncovered empirical regularities of ever-increasing detail while its theorists devised ways to incorporate these systematic patterns into models of the underlying basic process. This type of theoretically driven, cumulative research program characterizes much demography (Keyfitz 1977).

2.4 Demographic Explanation

Demographers and other social scientists often refer to certain explanations as "demographic." What exactly does this mean? For many, it means that outcomes of interest are related to certain types of variables and processes: those related to population characteristics, especially growth and decline. For instance, the argument that China experienced fast economic growth after the reforms of the 1980s because of the vast size of its potential market (approximately 1.2 billion persons) fits this type. For others, a demographic explanation implies mainly a counting of observable indicators. So, in this sense, to explain demographically a firm means to enumerate its employees by age, sex, ethnicity, location in the organizational structure, and the like.

Although neither of these meanings is necessarily misleading, each fails to convey the full analytical potential of demography. In our view, an explanation should be regarded as demographic when it is based on a *decomposition* of the population. An important class of such explanations relates change in the composition of a population to change in social structures and outcomes (Coleman 1964; Stinchcombe 1968). For instance, a simple explanation of this type might be used to explain the trends in firm size discussed above: the longterm decline in size coincides with the dramatic shift of the American economy into the service sector, which is populated by smaller firms (Carroll 1984b).

To give another simple example, consider variations in pension coverage of workers in the United States, which some analysts fear might be declining (thus placing greater pressure on the government's Social Security system). A way to explain this change would be to collect information on a sample of firms and then count those that do and do not provide pensions as part of the employment relation. (We ignore important differences in the types and levels of the pension plan.) Say that 50% of the employees in the whole set of firms have such coverage. Decomposition of the set by various characteristics of firms would typically reveal some large differences in the rate. A demographically inclined decomposition would look first at firm age and size: it would likely show strong associations with rates of pension coverage. For example, firms with more than 1000 employees have coverage rates near 85% while those with fewer than 25 have almost half that level (Reich and Ghilarducci 1997). A finer decomposition would look at such factors as whether the firm's employees are unionized, which would also show a strong association with pension provision (unionized firms have higher rates of coverage across all size classes; the disparity seems greatest for small firms).

Turning back to the original question, why has pension coverage been declining, this type of analysis attempts to explain the decline by examining the growth and decline in groups of firms with differing rates of coverage. In other words, a demographic explanation posits that changes in vital rates alter the compositions of populations and thereby change features of the social structures based on these populations.

The simplicity of our examples comes in large part from our regarding the vital rates of the various groups of firms composing the population as exogenous. More realistic portrayals relax this assumption and recognize that subgroup vital rates depend upon demographic characteristics of the group or the subpopulation defined by the form. The most interesting of these have to do with population dynamics within and among the compositional elements; these processes tend to be complex and nonlinear.

For example, the figures reviewed above on the historical automobile manufacturers across different countries all show a similar longterm trend of population growth and decline. This regularity reflects in part the operation of endogenous demographic processes of *density dependence* whereby the vital rates depend on the population's size: as population density rises, founding rates climb to a peak and then fall while mortality rates drop and then go up (Chapters 10 and 11). Similarly, the figures above on the historical number of American beer brewers display a dramatic late upsurge in the population. The increase results wholly from the high founding rates (and low mortality rates) of particular specialist organizational forms (microbrewers, brewpubs, and contract brewers). These form-specific founding rates and mortality rates in turn depend strongly on the extent to which a few organizations in the other population (mass production breweries) dominate the market for beer (in a process called resource partitioning—Chapter 12).

Demographic explanations frequently invoke the effects of environmental conditions as well. In organizational demography, researchers analyze the effects of resource abundance, technology, industry structure, sociopolitical institutions, and the presence and scale of other organizational populations in the corporate community (Chapter 9). Consideration of these kinds of effects also adds complexity to the analysis. In fact, modern analyses treat these factors as covariates in specifications of (unit-specific) functions of vital rates (Chapter 7). For example, estimated mortality models for beer breweries (Carroll and Swaminathan 1992) typically specify effects of variables measuring the size of the potential market (human population), the state of the economy (gross national product), and periods of relevant legislation (the Volstead Act and its later repeal). Other variables (often associated with organizational characteristics) are used as controls (in the case of breweries, organizational size).

From a research-design viewpoint, these specifications represent a middle ground between the approaches of formal demography and population studies. They seek to retain the elegance and generality of a formal model while still incorporating the complexity and specificity of a multivariate analysis.

Figure 2.6 summarizes the general structure of demographic explanations of social structure, using corporate organizations as the focal point. It shows the four general components of argument used in a demographic analysis: the social structure to be explained; the decomposition of the entire set of organizations in the system into constituent organizational populations; the estimation of population-specific vital rates; and the specification of environmental conditions affecting the rates. The solid arrows depict the dominant flows in the causal structure. Sometimes researchers analyze one or several of these in isolation and treat the causes as exogenous. At other times, analysts consider one or more of the feedback mechanisms in the system, shown by dotted lines in the figure, and build models with endogenous causes.

Finally, there are other, perhaps longer-term feedback mechanisms in the system, shown by the dashed line. Although many theorists agree that

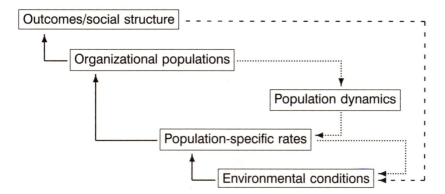

Figure 2.6. *General structure of demographic explanations.*

these forces operate at some level and over some time frame, they often do not get modeled explicitly, in part because available theory is not up to the task (Chapter 9).

2.5 The Demography of the Work Force

Corporate demography is not the only kind of application of demography in organizational settings. A second type involves the demography of the work force of organizations, especially its turnover and mobility. Research in this tradition usually adopts an organization-level analysis and posits theory from the perspective of a focal organization. Theoretical arguments often focus on the factors associated with mobility within the organization; however, they obviously have implications for external mobility as well.[7]

Research on mobility within an organization typically focuses on the characteristics and effects of established internal labor markets, which Doeringer and Piore (1971, 1–2) define as:

> an administrative unit, such as a manufacturing plant, within which the pricing and allocation of labor is governed by a set of administrative rules and procedures. The internal labor market ... is to be distinguished from the external labor market of conventional economic theory where pricing, allocating, and training decisions are controlled by economic variables.

The boundaries between such an enclosed market and the larger labor market mean that the usual effects of sex, ethnicity, social class, industrial

---

[7]This section is adapted from Carroll, Haveman, and Swaminathan (1990).

sector, and the like will often be muted for internal mobility. That is to say, mobility within an organization with an internal labor market tends to be rationalized according to some personnel plan, be it implicit or explicit (Weber 1968). A person's mobility chances, however, also depend upon his or her location within the structure of the organization itself.

Organizational research on mobility has gone in two directions, one focusing on the work force of the organization and its demographic characteristics, the other based on dimensions of organizational structure. Research on internal work force demography usually involves temporal analysis of career-mobility patterns within a single organization. Studies have demonstrated that rates of mobility within and across organizations are affected by rates of growth and decline of organizations (Keyfitz 1973; Stewman and Konda 1983), the distribution of employee cohorts (Ryder 1965; Brüderl, Preisendörfer, and Ziegler 1989), early career history (Turner 1960; Rosenbaum 1984), vacancy chains (White 1970), and career lines (Spilerman 1977; DiPrete 1987).

Early research on organizational structure and mobility drew pictures of relationships between organizational characteristics, such as the presence of departmental boundary-spanning units, and average levels of wages and status; Baron (1984) provides a review. Recent work in this tradition addresses issues such as the determinants of internal labor markets, sex segregation in jobs, fragmentation of work, and the opportunity structure within organizations; Carroll et al. (1990) give an overview.

Research on the work force demography of organizations reveals that a wide variety of factors are associated with mobility within and across organizations. Yet very little of this work takes seriously the basic notion that organizational populations change over time and experience demographic pressures of their own. There is, for instance, little consideration given in this literature to the mobility consequences of organizational founding and mortality (for an exception see Haveman and Cohen 1994). Since even a single event might generate massive job turnover and mobility, the demography of corporations and industries deserves consideration in this research context. So, despite the very different orientations of these two demographic approaches to organizations, we explore briefly some of their possible interrelations in Chapter 19.

2.6 Internal Organizational Demography

A third line of demographic research on organizations also goes by the name of organizational demography, but it could more appropriately be labeled as *internal* organizational demography. Most contemporary research on internal organizational demography stems from Pfeffer's (1983) theoretical essay on the topic. In that essay, Pfeffer (1983, 303) defines demography as "the composition, in terms of basic attributes such as age, sex, educational level, length of service or residence, race and so forth of the social unit under study." He adds that "the demography of any social entity is the composite aggregation of the characteristics of the individual members of that entity." Pfeffer makes the straightforward observation that organizations can be readily described this way and he presents a persuasive case for the study of internal organizational demography.[8]

In an approach akin to that of the population-studies tradition, Pfeffer also advances a number of specific theoretical propositions about the causes and consequences of demographic phenomena in organizations. Most of these specific arguments concentrate on the properties of demographic distributions of persons in the focal organization, especially the tenure or length of service (LOS) distribution of members of the organization or its top-management team. The arguments that have attracted the greatest research attention concern the consequences of the LOS distribution on a wide variety of organizational outcomes, including employee turnover, organizational innovation, internal control structures, the power distribution, interorganizational relations, and firm performance (Carroll and Harrison 1998). Although the details of the theorized process depend on the particular outcome, the common general theoretical formulation used in each argument focuses on the unevenness or heterogeneity in the LOS distribution as the demographic variable of primary interest.

In fact, the idea that unevenness (heterogeneity) in the LOS distribution should affect organizational outcomes, such as turnover, constitutes the standard operational framework for virtually all empirical research on internal organizational demography. The framework might seem theoretically stark in that it relies on the statistical association between only two variables: the homogeneity/heterogeneity of the LOS distribution and an organizational outcome. Studies investigating LOS effects, however, usually invoke some kind of social process to motivate the framework theoretically. For example, Wagner, Pfeffer, and O'Reilly (1984, 76) justify investigating the relationship between variation in LOS and turnover with the following explanation:

> Similarity in time of entry into the organization will positively affect the likelihood of persons communicating with others who entered at the same time ... the more frequent the communication, the more likely it is that those interacting will become similar in terms of their beliefs and perceptions of the organization and how it operates.

---

[8]This section draws from Carroll and Harrison (1998).

Other processes used for explaining LOS-outcome associations include psychological processes of similarity and attraction, social psychological processes of homophily and group dynamics (including especially communication patterns), and sociological processes about norms (Boone and Van Olffen 1997).

Carroll and Harrison (1998) reviewed the 21 major empirical studies conducted within this framework. By most standards, the set of studies is impressive. It includes studies of organizations in the public and private sectors, in a variety of different industries, and in two major national economies (the United States and Japan). Turnover is the most frequently studied outcome; however, various other outcomes have also received attention. Over time, the focus of this research has shifted from entire organizations to work groups within organizations, especially top-management teams. The coefficient of variation in tenure (the standard deviation of tenure divided by the mean of tenure) has also become the most common measure of LOS heterogeneity. Most of the evidence presented in these studies supports theory about the effects of the LOS distribution. By Carroll and Harrison's (1998) count, eleven studies present solid supporting evidence, another four provide weak support, and six offer no support.

So, the main difference among approaches is that we treat the demography *of* corporations and the other two styles of research treat demography *within* corporations. With these distinctions in place, we turn now to a more formal statement of our vision of corporate demography.

3

Toward a Corporate Demography

IF DEMOGRAPHY CONSISTED primarily of a set of methods and statistical techniques, then development of a corporate and industrial demography would be very straightforward. Researchers could simply apply the received procedures mechanically to data on corporations and other organizations. Given the failure of several such efforts in the past, however, either corporate demography has little to offer organizational studies or the purely methodological approach misses something.

We believe that successful development of the demography of the corporation requires significant effort beyond the narrowly methodological. This chapter initiates our discussion of the requirements. Here we identify and discuss the major conceptual and theoretical developments necessary to build a foundation for corporate demography. We start by reviewing briefly several earlier attempts at corporate demography, and we speculate about why they failed to spark widespread interest. We then discuss the potential application of demography's general conceptual framework to corporations and industries. We identify some of the important ways in which corporate entities differ from biological organisms, and we explore the implications of these differences for demographic analysis.

Some of these differences are obvious but far-reaching, such as the ways organizations begin and end their lives. Despite the parallels to biological birth and death, corporate vital events also involve a broader range of types of events. Other conceptual issues are subtler, such as the potential immortality of corporate organizations and the complexity of the mechanisms of information transmission across units. Complexity also arises from the great diversity of relevant characteristics of organizations. So, we also discuss how to deal with the range of possible units of analysis that might be employed in studying the world of organizations. The chapter concludes with a discussion of general research strategy for corporate demography, taking account of the special features of organizational processes.

3.1 Earlier Efforts

The idea of applying demographic techniques to corporations and other types of businesses is not new. Our search of the literature uncovered three different spurts of activity of this kind that predate the recent work. The first, beginning between the two world wars and continuing for several decades, typically examined business failure within particular industries or locales for fairly short periods, usually 5 to 10 years. Early studies investigated failure among American automobile producers (Epstein 1927), retail stores (Converse 1932; Cover 1933; Starr and Steiner 1939), shoe manufacturers (Davis 1939), grocery stores (Vaile 1932; McGarry 1947), and others (Heilman 1935; Hutchinson, Hutchinson, and Newcomer 1938). Some of these studies reported impressive data collection efforts and provided useful—if piecemeal—empirical facts about failure rates. They rarely offered much by way of analysis, however, often adopting a somewhat Baconian posture. The intended audience for these studies appears to have been governmental officials and other policymakers who might have found a use for the facts.

A second set of efforts was more ambitious. Three studies, which appeared after World War II, adopted more comprehensive research designs and used demographic techniques more analytically. The first (Frasure 1952) examined the longevity of all types of manufacturing concerns in Allegheny County, Pennsylvania (the Pittsburgh area) from 1873 to 1947. It included extremely detailed analysis of the longest-lived firms in an attempt to ascertain the causes of longevity. The findings attribute longevity to the general managerial abilities of specific individuals and to the reputations of the firms and their products. The second study (Crum 1953) addressed similar issues but took a more macroscopic view. Relying on U.S. Treasury data from 1945 and 1946, this investigation analyzed data for the 477,949 corporations present in the U.S. economy at the time. The findings of this study highlighted the strong negative relationship between firm age and mortality. The third study (Mayer and Goldstein 1961) resembles the project on Allegheny County. It examined in detail a set of diverse businesses in Rhode Island from 1957 to 1960, concentrating on firms that failed in their early years. The study found that smaller firms had higher mortality chances and that the rate of failure was associated with the owner's age and level of education.

Both Frasure (1952) and Crum (1953) were professors of accounting who envisioned major roles for demography in studying and understanding corporations. Frasure (1952, xi) claimed that research on the longevity of corporations in a community would constitute "a contribution to the understanding of a community's life." Crum (1953, 1) made a bolder claim:

A comprehensive and continuous system of vital statistics of corporations would supply information on births and deaths, length and perhaps expectation of life, age structure at any particular time, and morbidity and mortality from various causes for the entire corporate population and various important sections thereof. Such vital statistics would be immensely helpful guides for attempts to understand the functioning of a major, and in some respects dominant, section of the private enterprise system. Such statistics would also assist in formulating policies, public and private, designed to improve that functioning.

The third set of efforts appeared within the discipline of economics, where demographic data and techniques were used to make inferences about economic processes. The most comprehensive single work of this kind that we know is by Wedervang (1965), a statistician who analyzed data on a set of Norwegian industrial firms. Although Wedervang examined rates of firm founding, failure, and growth, his study apparently had little influence. Much more influential was the theory and research on firm growth and size distributions associated with Simon and colleagues (Chapter 13). This work typically used comprehensive data on firms either to estimate growth models directly or, if the data were cross-sectional, to infer growth patterns from the size distribution, which was usually assumed to be in equilibrium.[1]

Another influential application of demography to corporations within economics was due to Stigler (1958), who pioneered what is known as the "survivor technique" for identifying economies of scale. Stigler argued that the sizes of surviving firms would reflect the minimum efficient scale. He argued that, under certain specified market conditions, comparisons of size distributions over time would detect changes in scale economies. Stigler (1958, 56) advocated determining optimum firm size as follows:

> Classify the firms in an industry by size, and calculate the share of industry output coming from each class over time. If the share of a given class falls, it is relatively inefficient, and in general is more inefficient the more rapidly share falls.

The technique is still described in many economics textbooks, although it rarely (if ever) gets used in articles appearing in the major journals.

Despite these many admirable efforts, the demography of the corporation did not really begin to take shape until the 1980s. Why? What caused these earlier efforts to stall? We think that the first two sets failed to take hold due to a lack of sufficient anchoring to either demography or the

---

[1] This approach has been revived recently after a dormant period; Sutton (1997) gives a review.

social sciences. The lack of a demographic foundation meant that major technical errors were common.[2] The lack of connection to mainstream social science meant that these efforts were not well informed about corporations, that they often treated organizations in the same way as human and biological demographers would analyze humans and animals. Consequently, these occasional demographic studies of corporations constituted novelties that had no great appeal to social scientists working on other issues.

The third set of efforts did not suffer from these deficiencies; and, as a result, it was much more successful and has a continuing legacy today. Yet for the most part, it failed to develop much beyond its original narrow technical role as a tool for economic analysis. Many demographic processes and problems never received attention at all. The techniques themselves (for example, survivor studies) were not explored generally but were, instead, used in ways tightly wedded to the neoclassical economic assumptions of the day, including market equilibrium and firm homogeneity. Other disciplines, such as organizational sociology, did not see the value of these approaches because sociologists disdained the neoclassical assumptions. As economics, itself, moved away from unvarnished neoclassicism, the techniques lost favor.

What does this history imply for the prospects of a new corporate demography? What lessons can we draw from it? We conclude that for corporate demography to be successful—for it to become an established and productive line of inquiry—three general conditions must be satisfied. The first is that demographic tools need to be modified to accommodate the special features of organizations. Received demography is based on analyses of biological populations; certain aspects of demography require significant reconceptualization for the applications to organizations to be worthwhile. Much of this chapter considers these issues, which include the special (and often complex) ways in which organizations start, grow, and die. Second, we believe that the demography of the corporation must generate new research problems and new models and theories about organizations. Demographic analysis of the corporation must be compelling in its own right, not just a set of technical tools for other disciplines. Third, corporate demography must connect to the mainstream of organizational studies. Although many organizational problems might not intersect with corporate demography, at least some important ones must, if demography is to have a significant impact.

---

[2] Key examples include Frasure's (1952) analysis of a sample selected on the outcome variable and Crum's (1953) reliance on backward recurrence times to make inferences about time variation in hazards of mortality—Chapters 6 and 7.

The success of contemporary research on corporate demography reflects in broad part the ability of researchers to begin to meet these general conditions. Continued development of the area, however, requires sustained attention on the relevant issues. In our view, this is hardly the time for organizational demographers to feel satisfied and become complacent. Many of the interesting facts and relationships between facts that have been uncovered by demographic research in the last few decades cry out for sharper conceptualization, more rigorous model-building, tighter theoretical integration, and greater relevance. At least some of these issues require rethinking basic concepts and approaches.

3.2 Retaining the Classical Structure

What should be the form of the demography of the corporation? In our view, the resemblance to other forms of demography should be strong, if the errors of the past are to be avoided and if corporate demography is to keep abreast of technical developments. This means that, at its core, corporate demography should be primarily concerned with the flows of corporate vital events over time and their interrelationships. That is, the formal structure of corporate demography should model mathematically the occurrence of vital events in time for corporations and other kinds of organizations, just as formal human demography does for natural persons. Part II of this book describes a fairly well-developed framework for the formal representation of organizational vital events that already finds widespread use. This framework relies heavily on the estimation and theoretical interpretation of relationships between observable variables and the rates of occurrence of vital events.

Among other things, use of a formal framework potentially allows analysts to develop implications of variations in vital events for the overall structure of corporate and industrial populations. For instance, based on a model of competitive intensity among individual organizations in a population, Barnett (1997) makes inferences about the extent of concentration in an industry. Likewise, models of age dependence in mortality rates imply an age distribution of firms, which likely has a relationship to the flexibility or adaptability of firms in an industry (Hannan, Carroll, Dobrev, and Han 1998a; Hannan 1998). So, development of the formal side of corporate demography potentially provides many connections to other theories about organizations.

Not every linkage between corporate demography and organization theory needs to come through the formal structure of models. Indeed, we imagine that the bulk of research in corporate demography might consist of substantively motivated organizational population studies, just as population studies comprise the bulk of human demography. In general, these studies would be of two kinds. The first relates changes in environments (from both endogenous and exogenous sources) to changes in the composition in populations of corporations (Figure 2.6 in Chapter 2). Much of the current research on corporate demography has this form. We examine a great deal of it in this monograph; other general reviews can be found in Carroll (1984b), Singh and Lumsden (1990), Barnett and Carroll (1995), and Baum (1996). The second investigates how organizational population structure and composition affect changes in social structural processes and outcomes. The last section of the book, containing Chapters 18 through 20, describes some preliminary ideas about connections between organizational population structure and issues related to employment patterns, public policies, and industrial outcomes. Many of these notions are not yet highly developed and almost all of them need stronger empirical validation. There are also multitudes of other potentially interesting research possibilities. The field of organizational population studies thus represents a potentially rich vein for those analysts hoping to mine new research gems.

3.3 Making Demography Organizational

Corporate organizations are constructed social entities, not biological organisms. This fundamental feature of organizations has major implications for certain aspects of corporate demography. While many of the tools of human and biological demography can be borrowed without collateral, others require new intellectual investment to accommodate the social nature of organizations. In our assessment, constructing the demography of the corporation requires awareness of eight differences between social organizations and biological organisms: (1) the greater variety of types of events that define organizational births and deaths; (2) the potential immortality of formal organizations; (3) the lack of clear parentage for organizations; (4) the absence of genetic transmission of information in the organizational world; (5) the multilayered, partly decomposable structure of formal organizations; (6) the great heterogeneity found within organizational populations; (7) the ability of organizations to transform themselves and change populations; and (8) the potentially high levels of endogeneity in the environments of organizations. We discuss each difference, noting some of the challenges it presents. For many differences, we also describe how the framework for corporate demography deals with the issues involved. We also note that not all of the pertinent matters are resolved at this point.

Demarcation of Births and Deaths

In standard human demography, lifetimes are marked naturally by one kind of starting event—birth—and one kind of ending event—death. An interesting and challenging feature of corporate demography is the natural occurrence of multiple types of fundamentally different "vital" events identified in research in corporate demography.

Organizational Founding and Entry Events

Organizations start in one of several common modes. Sometimes organizations are begun *de novo* as members of a certain population or industry. So, for instance, Henry Ford was involved in the creation of three automobile manufacturing firms. The first, the Detroit Automobile Co., was begun in July 1899 and disbanded in January 1901. The second, the Henry Ford Co., began in November 1901; Ford left in February 1902; it eventually became the Cadillac Automobile Co. The third, Ford & Malcomson Co., began in October 1902 and reorganized with additional capital in 1903 as the Ford Motor Company. We refer to initiation events, such as these three entrepreneurial actions, as *organizational foundings*.

What distinguishes foundings from other kinds of entry events in our terminology is that the entity has no prior organizational existence. This is not to say that the individuals who start the organization have no prior organizational experience, as Henry Ford surely did in his second attempt to found an automobile manufacturing firm.

A second type of starting event is the result of *merger*: two or more autonomous firms merge to create a new firm. In this case, "new" means that the resulting firm combines elements of the merger partners in such a way that the new entity is distinct from each of the "parents." For instance, the Nuffield Organization (itself begun by a merger of MG, Morris Motors, Riley, and Wolsley in 1936) merged with Austin Motors in 1952 to create the British Motor Corporation.

The third starting event is a *spin-off* from an existing firm. In many cases, such spin-offs are planned. With the recent wave of deconglomeration, many conglomerate firms are selling off some of their unrelated businesses, providing current examples. For instance, AT&T took its Bell Laboratories and some of its other research and development shops and created Lucent Technologies, an independent public corporation.

In some other cases, conflict within an organization (often concerning choice among a series of business developments to pursue) causes a dissident faction to in effect secede from the parent corporation and begin a new one. For instance, most of the key figures in the development of Silicon Valley's semiconductor industry were originally employees of Shockley

Semiconductor Corporation, founded by William Shockley, one of the inventors of the semiconductor. A key group left en masse, after a dispute with Shockley, and founded the Fairchild Semiconductor Company. Such an event can be regarded either as a spin-off or as a founding (by a group that previously worked together), depending on the research question.

In the fourth type of starting event, an organization enters, *de alio*, from another population or industry. De alio entries are the organizational analog to migration in the context of human demography. For corporations, however, physical migration usually does not matter as much as movement across population and/or industry boundaries. Corporations often appear as members of some population or industry as a result of "migration" from another population. For instance, several of the early important automobile manufacturing firms came from the bicycle industry (e.g., Peugeot), the carriage industry (e.g., Studebaker), and the engine-making industry (e.g., Rover). Other huge firms, such as Germany's AEG, entered this industry and left after a few years. Although these firms were not new organizations in any sense when they initiated automobile manufacturing, they were certainly new to the industry.

By moving to some other industry or population, organizations also frequently end a duration of participation in their previous industry or organizational population. For example, Westinghouse Corp. (not long ago, a major manufacturer of household appliances) has left manufacturing and become a radio and television broadcasting company; and Monsanto Corp. has sold its entire chemical business (once the core of the firm) to concentrate on biotechnology. Such cases represent the obvious complement of de alio entry.

How prevalent are the different types of starting events? For illustration, Table 3.1 shows the distribution of starting events for four populations of automobile producers: the three largest European automobile industries—those in Britain, France, and Germany—and the world's largest automobile industry, that of the United States. It uses data on nearly the full history of these industries from 1885, the start of the industry, through 1980 (the last year of full coverage from our most comprehensive source of data). Although the American data provide reasonably complete coverage of type of entry, this information is unavailable for most cases in the European populations. For the obscure European firms, we know only that they began automobile production but not whether they migrated from other industries. This set presumably includes both newly founded firms and entrants from other industries. The more complete American data indicate that both types of entry were very common.

The life chances of de alio entrants and firms that arise by merger or fission of automakers were better than those of firms that began de novo or whose type of entry is unknown in these populations (Hannan

Table 3.1. *Starting events among automobile makers in four countries.*

	Britain	France	Germany	U.S.
De novo founding	135	84	39	985
De alio entry	206	122	94	723
Merger of automakers	15	7	5	20
Acquisition	33	26	13	19
Restart bankrupt firm	30	14	11	33
Reentry	0	12	0	0
Split from an automaker	13	4	1	15
Unknown	563	559	210	402
Total	995	828	373	2,197

Source: Hannan et al. (1998a). Copyright © 1998 by Oxford University Press. Used by permission.

et al. 1998a; Hannan, Carroll, Dobrev, Han, and Torres 1998b). However, research shows that using the distinction between de alio entry and start by merger or fission does not improve mortality model fits significantly. Among those U.S. firms that did enter in de alio mode, there are nonetheless important distinctions by industry origin. Specifically, firms coming from the carriage and bicycle manufacturing industries had longevity advantages over those from other industries, including engine manufacturing. Carroll, Bigelow, Seidel, and Tsai (1996) attribute this advantage to economies arising from experience in assembly operations.

Organizational Mortality and Ending Events

Previous demographic research also identifies several kinds of common ending events. Sometimes organizations simply *disband*. If the firms operate in societies with modern commercial law, disbanding usually involves a bankruptcy filing and a court judgment dispersing the remaining assets. Henry Ford's first automobile manufacturing firm experienced this fate in 1901. This was also the fate of the vast majority of firms in the industries that have received systematic study.

Except during times of war, revolution, or other major disruption of the society and economy, disbanding typically befalls small and middle-sized organizations. Large organizations, no matter how battered, normally possess some valuable assets. Instead of disbanding, large firms often have their lifetimes ended by *acquisition or merger*. Sometimes acquisitions take place to firms that are about to go bankrupt or whose fortunes are otherwise declining. High-performing firms can also experience acquisition, when some of their organizational capabilities are valued more highly by another firm than by its owners. Many firms, especially in high-technology industries, are established with the goal of ending with a favorable acquisition. Many large, established firms find it cheaper—or at least faster—to enter new technical markets by acquiring small firms that pioneered such technologies rather than by trying to develop the technical capacities themselves.

Given the difference between "fire-sale" acquisitions and those in which firms pay a large premium to acquire a firm as a way to gain some capability, it is natural to wonder whether the two kinds of events ought to be regarded as one. Research on corporate demography would be well served by efforts to gain detailed information that would allow these events to be treated differently.

Finally, as noted above, mergers also end the independent existence of the merger partners, as when Citicorp and the Travelers Group combined to form Citigroup. The notion of treating such events as endings has caused some confusion. Many social scientists unthinkingly translate "ending" to "failure" and assume that failures are never intended. They sometimes criticize corporate-demographic analysis by claiming that, because mergers (and, sometimes, acquisitions) are clearly intended outcomes, it is a mistake to regard them as failures. The confusion here comes from the conflation of ending and failure. A true merger ends two or more corporations as independent social actors and creates a new actor. This is surely true with respect to the legal standing of the actors and their governance. Consider, for example, the film studio Metro–Goldwyn–Mayer (MGM). It was created in 1924 by the merger of Metro Pictures, Goldwyn Pictures, and Louis B. Mayer Productions. By the time this firm went through a series of acquisitions and resales, beginning in 1986, one would be hard pressed to find any trace of the three original firms. Who now would doubt that Metro Pictures, Goldwyn Pictures, and Louis B. Mayer Productions ended not only as legally autonomous firms but also as corporate actors?

The multiplicity of naturally occurring corporate starting and ending events means that the lifetimes of members of a corporate (or other organizational) population can take as many forms as there are combinations of the various types of possible events. In technical terms, the analysis of events needs to be conditioned on the state space. In Part II, we discuss how this is done, provide examples, and demonstrate how important such conditioning is.

Table 3.2 shows the distribution of ending events for the populations of automobile producers. The most important distinctions concern (1) disbanding, (2) exit to another industry, (3) merger, and (4) acquisition. Disbanding has an unambiguous meaning: the firm failed as a collective actor. Exit to another industry also suggests a lack of success in automobile

Table 3.2. *Ending events among automobile makers in four countries.*

	Britain	France	Germany	U.S.
Disbanding	122	62	34	918
Exit to another industry	129	82	56	669
Merger	22	13	7	33
Acquisition by another firm	66	46	34	80
Takeover by creditors	11	5	3	0
Nationalization	0	2	0	0
Ended by war—no reentry	4	11	8	2
Unknown	584	574	219	389
Right censored in 1981	57	33	12	106
Total	995	828	373	2,197

Source: Hannan et al. (1998a). Copyright © 1998 by Oxford University Press. Used by permission.

manufacturing. The other ending events are harder to interpret. Although merger and acquisition both result in the loss of one or more independent collective actors, firms merge and acquire for diverse reasons, as we noted above. Sometimes a firm flounders and its owners seek to recover some fraction of their investment by selling the firm. In other cases, a thriving firm's competencies command great value from potential acquirers or merger partners. Given the ambiguous meaning of mergers and acquisitions, our analysis of these data (much of which is described throughout this book) has concentrated on disbanding and exit to another industry.[3]

Organizational Longevity

Obviously, a corporation can persist as an operating social entity long after its initial members have departed. Indeed, many organizations continue to function without disruption after several generations of members have been replaced. Indeed, a corporation can outlive any known animal (but the oldest plants are apparently older than the oldest organizations). It is not unreasonable to think that organizations are potentially immortal.

[3]We often do not know exactly what happened to most firms when they dropped from the set of producers, especially in the European populations; this is invariably the case when spells of automobile production were short. Apparently, automobile historians rarely could reconstruct the details about an exit unless a firm had become reasonably well established. Knowledge that a certain firm disbanded, was acquired, or left the industry usually means that it persisted in the industry long enough that its exit event received notice in the press. Our reading of the historical materials suggests to us that most exits of unknown type were disbandings or exits to other industries. This is clearly the case in the American population.

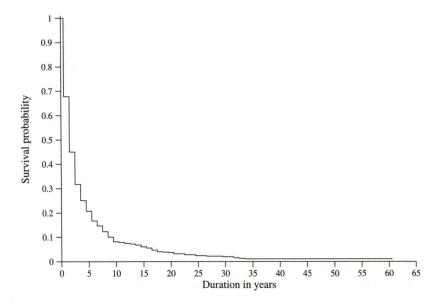

Figure 3.1. *Distribution of durations in automobile production in the U.S. industry.*

Potential corporate immortality must be accommodated even though most corporations die very quickly. For example, Figure 3.1 shows the distribution of lifetimes for American automobile producers.[4] It plots the "survival probability" (the probability that an organization's lifetime exceeded a given age) against age. Obviously, the mortality chances of new organizations are quite high, thus resembling the elevated levels of mortality often found for infants in biological populations. Among the complications that very long-lived organizations introduce into the analysis is the technical problem known as right censoring, which occurs when not all events of interest can be observed; commonly the study ends before all units die. With potentially immortal population members, censoring is likely to be a problem for corporate demography even with very long observation plans spanning, say, centuries. Chapters 6 and 7 describe in detail the appropriate estimation methods for dealing with right censoring.

Of great interest for longevity is the form of *age dependence* in the hazard of mortality. As we explained in Chapter 1, casual observation suggests that older organizations are less likely to die than younger ones. Simple inspection of mortality data such as that of Figure 3.1 apparently supports such a view; moreover, most early demographic studies confirmed these im-

---

[4] The mortality event here is disbanding of the firm or exit from the industry.

pressions with more sophisticated models. However, many of these studies failed to collect and analyze age variations in the sizes of organizations in the population. As age and size are highly correlated, any observed negative age dependence might be spurious. As we discuss in Chapters 13 and 14, recent empirical studies suggest that this might be the case: introducing complete controls for size and other factors often makes age dependence positive rather than negative. It appears that age dependence will continue to be an extremely complicated issue in corporate demography.

Longevity and Performance

How well does organizational mortality map onto corporate performance? Many think it does not map well; it is common to hear descriptions of firms or corporations ceasing to exist only because they was acquired or dismantled as a result of prior success. As we discussed above, this issue can be readily dealt with in contexts where it might be problematic by treating various types of mortality as competing risks in a multiple-state mortality model. That is, the methodology we advocate allows for isolation of those mortality events that are likely associated with failure.

A more serious challenge to using mortality as performance comes from those who contend that the performance-related component of mortality lacks sufficiently fine grain, that it fails to capture important subtle variations in performance. While organizational mortality might not be a perfect measure of performance, neither is any available alternative. Researchers in applied business fields often use as outcomes some financial ratio, such as return on assets or return on investments. As Schmalansee (1989) notes, there are serious technical problems in using accounting-based measures of this kind. Typical accounting-based constructions of efficiency, profit, and other firm-level outcomes contain noise, usually of an unknown but systematic nature. Across industries and across time, these problems likely compound on each other.

More substantively, Meyer and Gupta (1994) have noted a tendency for any performance-based measure to "run down" as it gets used. That is, with sustained usage a wide variety of performance variables might lose variability and hence no longer discriminate well between good and bad performance. According to Meyer and Gupta (1994, 330), this running down occurs for a number of reasons, including:

> . . . positive learning where genuine improvement takes place, perverse learning where there is the appearance of improvement but not actual improvement, selection where poor performers . . . are displaced by better performers, and suppression where persistent differences in performance outcomes are ignored.

Given these deficiencies, it should not be surprising that most accounting-based performance measures fail to meet theoretical expectations. For instance, extant theories of market power in economics predict far more variation in rates of return among firms than ordinarily gets reflected in these measures (Schmalansee 1989). Clearly, social scientists should not be content to use only these measures. Other measures need to be developed; alternatives might tap different aspects of performance and perhaps even prove superior overall.

We believe that, when properly formulated, organizational mortality is potentially valuable as a performance indicator. As we explain below, proper formulation means thinking in terms of firm-specific instantaneous rates of failure. Such rates have a number of attractive features as performance measures. First, mortality can be measured with a minimum of ambiguity and noise. Second, hazard function models—the usual modeling framework for investigating organizational mortality—provide for precise comparability across firms, industries, and sectors (Chapters 6 and 7). Third, variations in firm-specific mortality are likely greater than variations in financial accounting measures, meaning that this outcome might prove more helpful in reconciling theories with the real world. Fourth, organizational mortality is one performance standard that it is difficult to envision becoming run-down over time.

On the other side, there is the issue of weak or absent historical efficiency, as pointed out in Chapter 1. When processes are path dependent, relative mortality rates do not map neatly onto orderings of quality of performance. So the idea of using mortality rates as measures of performance must be qualified when we make comparisons between populations with different forms that have entered a competitive arena at different times.

Nonparental Organizational Heritage

Organizations do not spring naturally from one or more parents. Although many corporations have an individual person as a founder, not all do. Sometimes corporations are started by groups of persons or by other corporations and organizations. In general, the clarity of corporate parenthood is variable and ambiguous. Given the lack of any definable group of potential parents for organizations, corporate demography usually must work without clear parallels to fertility and generations in human demography, concepts that play central roles in modeling vital events.[5] Yet, to model birth-type events as a stochastic process, some meaningful entity must be designated as the unit at risk. What to do?

---

[5] In fact, migration might be the closer parallel in human demography; it too suffers from the lack of a natural and tractable set of units at risk to experience the event.

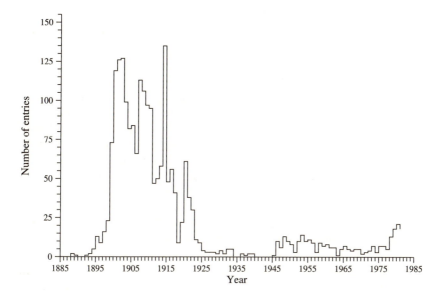

Figure 3.2. *Annual entries into the U.S. automobile industry, 1885–1980.*

The general analytical framework that has developed within corporate demography involves treating the population as the unit at risk of experiencing founding and other entry events.[6] As we explain in Chapters 6 and 7, researchers typically condition on the start of the population (the initial founding event) and then attempt to explain variations in the rate of events from that time. Although this conceptualization does not involve the exact causal imagery of biological parents and births, it does dovetail well with social science theory about entrepreneurship and organizational innovation, which often posits industry-level forces.

Aggregating data mutes variability, but this does not seem to be a problem for organizational foundings. Populations show large variations in founding events across time location. Figure 3.2 plots a typical time series of organizational foundings. It shows the annual number of entries into the population of U.S. automobile producers from 1885 to 1980. The greatest number of foundings occurs in the early periods; the rate drops substantially in later periods. Models of the founding process must be able to account for both shortterm and longterm variations.

---

[6]In Chapter 15, we exploit a rare type of data set containing information on the initial mobilizing activities of many automobile producing firms before they enter production. These data allow us to examine mobilizing activities and foundings in a unique way, to ask some novel questions, and to check the validity of widely used theories. For a variety of reasons, we do not think it is feasible as a general approach for studying organizational foundings.

Information Transmission

In organizational populations, information about organizational structure and routines gets transmitted from generation to generation by many and varied processes. Unless many of its members live a very long time, populations retain their special character over time by intergenerational information transmission. In biological populations, genetic inheritance constitutes the main way information gets transmitted from organism to organism. As Hannan and Freeman (1984, 21) note, "social and cultural information passes in many different directions among generations, and it is not nearly as invariant across transmissions as genetic information." The ability to construct organizations of a given type gets passed among individuals and groups at least by movement of people among organizations, media, specialized schools, and third-party experts. It can also be borrowed from other distant populations (Hannan, Carroll, Dundon, and Torres 1995) and be retained in collective societal institutions (Dobrev 1997).

Complexities of information transmission have not received much attention from organizational demographers. Perhaps this is because sound demographic research on corporations and other organizations can be conducted without specifying exactly how information gets transmitted. Instead, researchers simply assume that information does get transmitted (an assumption supported by the high levels of structural inertia observable in organizations and industries). Such an assumption might not be problematic, but it does leave interesting questions unexplored. We would like to know how different transmission mechanisms operate and what implications they have for population structure and evolution. In an attempt to stimulate thinking about this matter, we introduce and develop a way to define organizational forms in terms of cultural codes—systems of cultural rules (in Chapter 4). We hope that a focus on this particular form of organizational information might improve our understanding of transmission processes.

Multilayered Organizational Structures

In the demography of human populations, there is usually little debate over how to identify an individual member—this is regarded as self-evident. A corporation, on the other hand, often exists as a set of multilayered structures, each of which might operate relatively autonomously. The near-decomposability of subunits might pose conceptual problems. How do we decide the unit for specifying the demographic processes? Practice differs greatly in this matter. Various studies of organizations treat corporations, strategic business units, departments, and establishments as appropriate units of analysis. Defining the appropriate unit of analysis for organizational studies is complicated. There are no easy answers, the casual way in which this matter often gets treated in empirical research notwithstanding. In the long run, corporate demography must resolve the unit issue in a theoretically meaningful way (Freeman 1978). In the short run, it is imperative for comparative purposes that researchers be clear about how and why they chose units of analysis in their studies.

Units of Analysis

As just noted, a wide range of possible units of analysis might be employed in corporate demography. It is worth reviewing them to understand how to make principled decisions in setting the unit for research purposes.

At the lowest possible level of analysis are *establishments*, the physical sites where corporations operate. These might be factories, sales offices, and service centers in a manufacturing firm, for instance. Some corporations, mostly small in size, operate a single establishment and there is no meaningful distinction between the firm and the establishment. Think of locally owned service firms such as restaurants, law firms, and hospitals. Many other corporations, including virtually all very large ones, consist of hundreds or even thousands of establishments. While there is a positive relationship between the size of a firm and its number of establishments, it is far from exact. Establishment structure reflects interindustry differences in products and markets; it also reflects firm-level strategic choices within an industry.

At the highest possible level of analysis one finds sets of complexly intertwined, but legally distinct, firms. Thermo Electron Corp., headquartered in Massachusetts, has spun out 24 "daughter" and "granddaughter" firms. Most of the progeny are themselves publicly traded corporations. Thermo Electron owns a dominant share in all cases, and members of Thermo's top management serve on their boards. Other conglomerates, e.g., GE Corp. and Hanson plc., hold their constituent strategic business units as subsidiaries. In Asian countries, the business enterprise groups such as Japanese *keiretsu* and Korean *chaebol* define such organizational structures. Obviously, the number and diversity of constituent firms within such structures varies a great deal. There is also great variability in the types of relations that hold the constituent firms together (Lincoln and Gerlach 1996).

Between these two extremes, we find a welter of other possibilities, including franchises, subsidiaries, strategic business units, corporate divisions, and the legal entities known as firms. Examples include most of the social entities commonly referred to by formal names, including Columbia Pictures (a wholly owned subsidiary of Sony Corp.), Daimler-Chrysler Aerospace (a strategic business unit of DaimlerChrysler), GE Capital (a division of General Electric Corp.), and British Air (a publicly owned firm). Much (but not all) extant theory and research about organizations invokes assumptions about certain levels of organizational autonomy and environmental coherency of the basic units. These accounts usually square best with one of these intermediate-level units.

It is, of course, possible to conduct demographic analysis at any of the levels. A number of highly visible studies use the establishment or plant level of analysis, fueled perhaps by the Census Bureau's data collection schemes. Many recent demographic studies of corporations delineate the research problem by industry boundaries and attempt to collect information on all independent entities operating within them. This procedure usually leads to a mix of units at one of the intermediate levels. For instance, the organizations currently operating in the investment banking industry include partnerships such as Goldman Sachs & Co., public firms such as Merrill Lynch and Morgan Stanley Dean Witter & Co., wholly owned subsidiaries such as BT Alex Brown (owned by Bankers Trust, which is about to be acquired by Deutsche Bank as we write) and BankBoston Robertson Stephens, and strategic business units such as Warburg Dillon Read (part of the Swiss banking group UBS AG). At the highest levels, demographic analysis would record the rise and fall of conglomerates, business enterprise groups, and the like. We do not know of any studies of this kind.

Choice of unit has major implications: it determines what events count as *corporate-demographic* events. For instance, bank branches open and close regularly in response to residential shifts in the human population. A study of the demography of banks cast at the establishment level might record considerable demographic activity for this organizational form even though the larger banking firm remains basically stable as a corporation. Conversely, when two large banking firms merge and only one firm results, their underlying establishment structures might not change at all. In such a case, the combination (at the parent level) would be virtually invisible at the establishment level. Another likely possibility is that, following the merger, branches get consolidated—some closed and some merged—but at staggered dates. Then, an establishment-level study would record many corporate events, but none of them would coincide with the merger. What goes on in the bank holding companies that overarch the firms might involve a completely different story. Finally, when a banking company closes, all of its establishments close; counts of events at the establishment level grossly overstate the demographic reality.

Some Guiding Principles

How to choose among the possible units? Which level should be the basis for corporate demography? Based on current knowledge, we do not think it makes sense to try to fix all corporate demography at any particular level. Nonetheless, we believe that the choice of analytical unit should always be principled.[7] The principles that we think will best serve the current development of corporate demography are twofold. First, the choice of unit should lead to meaningful counts of demographic events. Meaningful in this case means that recorded events (and their timing) correspond highly with either (1) real-world conceptions of events (and their timing) or (2) theoretically defensible conceptions. It also means that their occurrences are not defined by dependence on other events. Corporate demography that focuses on artificial or obscure events and processes runs the risk of theoretical and practical irrelevance.[8]

Second, the choice of unit should facilitate analysis of systematic processes that generate demographic events, especially in relation to the environment. This principle means that the unit choice must lead to tractable research problems and that the underlying processes are stable enough to allow their parameters to be identified and to allow knowledge to cumulate. The emphasis on the environment is pivotal to maintaining a connection to mainstream organizational theory.

Despite the head-nodding agreement likely induced by mention of these principles, it is worth pointing out that application of these suggestions would almost always eliminate corporate demography at the highest and lowest levels of analysis. The highest level would be ruled out by sparseness in the numbers of units implied and the tremendous (theoretically unreconciled) heterogeneity among them would make demographic research intractable. At a minimum, corporate demography at this level awaits better description of the relevant social structures and deeper insight into the processes that drive them.

At the lowest level, the establishment level, accuracy for counting and dating events for corporations and industries that result from systematic environmental processes would be problematic. Events at the establishment level usually emanate from the decision-making processes of individuals and higher-order authority structures; these events are also often definitionally interdependent in that a single decision leads to many events (e.g., a downsizing decision to close all small outlets in the firm).

The two principles still leave a wide range of possible units as choices for conducting sound demographic analysis. We envision that choice among them will vary by the historical time and the context of the study

---

[7]To be clear, the opposite of a principled decision in this context is pure opportunism. An opportunistic strategy lets the availability of data determine the unit.

[8]It is worth remembering that human demography originally became a scientific field by studying the most basic of social facts: death.

but that the choice will still be reasoned. To us, the paramount consideration involves the definition of the organizational population. Once a population has been defined clearly, a choice of unit(s) consistent with the above principles needs to be made. In Chapter 4, we discuss at length the issues involved in defining organizational populations and propose the use of social codes to do so. As we conceptualize them, social codes about organizational forms reflect the market, technological, and institutional imperatives that bound sets of potentially interrelated organizations.

Organizational Heterogeneity

Demographic analysis proceeds by estimating models of vital rates and making inferences about them. In a homogenous population, the rates themselves tell the story: researchers need only to estimate and compare them across contexts. In a population with limited heterogeneity, say two or three basic types of members, researchers can usually break down the comparisons by type as well.

For most studies of biological populations, however, this process quickly reaches a point where the comparisons are meaningless because there are too few observations per category. For studies of corporations, the problems of heterogeneity seem to be even more severe. In our view, most industries and organizational populations are characterized by even greater levels of heterogeneity. The research literature on organizations documents vast within-industry differences in scale, resources, organizational form, prior experience, and the like.

This ubiquitous heterogeneity is not benign; many of these variable characteristics have strong effects on the vital rates of organizations. These powerful effects simply cannot be ignored or downplayed. The challenge for corporate demography, therefore, consists of finding ways to acknowledge and incorporate this heterogeneity, while still retaining the ability to derive general implications for population-level and social structural processes. The modeling framework we describe in Part II does just that. In a nutshell, we specify models that treat vital events as stochastic processes controlled by instantaneous rates. We introduce heterogeneity into the rates by making them explicit functions of covariates and estimating the strength and direction of their effects (Chapter 7). We prefer to analyze the effects of observable covariates, because this choice facilitates comparative analysis.

An observable organizational characteristic of special interest is size. Size differences occur in every organizational population; and these effects are almost always very consequential. Empirical studies of organizations invariably find that size is one of the strongest predictors of structure and behavior. For demographic issues, proper treatment of the effects of size is crucial because size is invariably highly correlated with age, the fundamental modeling variable. Despite this central role, some contemporary lines of corporate demography routinely use research designs that exclude significant portions of population size distributions. In Chapter 7, we investigate the consequences of these and other observation schemes with simulation methods.

Transformational Properties

Social scientists have long marveled at the durability of the structures and cultures of organizations. Not only do organizations persist beyond the presence of particular individuals but they usually do so with great structural inertia. If this observation is correct, then it suggests that models of the development and transformation of individual population members need not assume a high priority in the formal demography of the corporation. This would be the case whenever most of the variability in a population arises from entry and exit processes rather than from organizational change.

Of course, the extent to which structural inertia prevails is itself an empirical matter. As we explain in Chapter 16, an active line of contemporary organizational demography investigates the process of organizational transformation and its consequences for longevity. Although these results are not uniform, a number of the studies conducted within this framework suggest that major structural transformation rarely succeeds in enhancing organizational life chances, once all relevant factors are taken into account. Should evidence begin tipping in the other direction, this would urge a rethinking of the emphasis on entry and exit.

Endogeneity of "Environmental" Factors

Organizational analysts generally agree that corporate organizations can shape as well as experience their environments. Although gene–environment interactions sometimes occur in biotic evolution, most social scientists would contend that the potential for environmental interaction is stronger for organizations. In some cases, the interaction can be simple but profound, such as when large corporations (such as Chrysler Corp. in the 1960s or Crédit Lyonnaise in the 1990s) are bailed out from imminent bankruptcy by authorities who regard them as too big to be allowed to fail. In other cases, such as a technology race between competing companies, the interactions might be complex: each time one firm makes a move the competitive environment changes for all of the others, who then make corresponding adjustments, and so forth. How much environments change in response to organizational actions determines whether the elements within them should be treated as exogenous.

Two different kinds of endogeneity of environmental forces might be considered, with differing implications for modeling. The first concerns feedbacks in the demographic system: do changes in the population at one point in time affect the behavior of its members at a later point? Often this is the case for organizational populations, the nonmonotonic effects of organizational density on vital rates being perhaps the best documented example (Chapters 10 and 11). Feedback effects of this kind might be complex and difficult to understand, but we can often develop meaningful models by incorporating lagged or historical specifications of the relevant variables.

The second kind of endogeneity involves interdependence among units and environmental elements at every point in time. Taking this kind of endogeneity seriously means modeling demographic processes as simultaneous systems of equations whereby events in the population affect environmental conditions and vice versa. Such models are extremely difficult to identify and estimate meaningfully. When one or more of the equations predicts a stochastic rate of event occurrences, then the technical demands are even higher and possibly insurmountable (Tuma and Hannan 1984). For many possible applications (notably, institutions), there is also a lack of explicit theory that might be used to specify the effects of organizational populations on particular environmental conditions (Chapter 9). The importance and complexity of these challenges have only recently become recognized and research practice often assumes exogeneity as a matter of modeling convenience. Although not ideal, this practice at least seems reasonable provided that environments change slowly relative to organizational changes and that major causal inferences are not made with respect to the endogenous elements of the environment.

3.4 A Research Strategy

How should organizational demographers proceed? How should the search for relevant processes and covariates unfold? The approach of bioecology again proves instructive. As mentioned in Chapter 2, theoretical bioecologists develop theory by building models of species growth and interaction with their habitats, including other species. These models are general, but not universal; they contain features that apply to more than one species or habitat (and often to many) but not to all. Although much bioecological work relies at its start on one of several basic models of population dynamics, these are usually modified for the specific context. For any given process, there is thus a series of models graded by level of detail (Roughgarden 1979).

In bioecology, one does not expect that the detailed models apply broadly, even if the underlying basic model does. However, models developed within a related series often have great comparative value. This is because they are based on common observable variables (such as counts of the numbers of members of a species) and because their coefficients are estimated in ways that do not depend on specific data structures.

A similar strategy underlies many of the research programs in contemporary organizational demography. Model building and empirical research proceed incrementally down different avenues based on various fundamental processes thought to link observables. For that reason, this book devotes considerable attention to demographic phenomena that are arguably found in *all* organizational populations: age dependence in mortality rates, density dependence in vital rates, and interorganizational population dynamics including segregating processes. We examine the core theoretical representations of these phenomena. We also review and discuss many of the context-specific complexities that researchers have discovered and represented in their models as research programs have developed. Sometimes these complexities take the form of specifying particular additional covariates as research uncovers the substantive factors summarized in effects of variables such as organizational age. At other times, these complexities involve extensions of the model to fit particular situations, such as geographically contiguous markets.

There are, of course, many more interesting complications than can be developed, or even mentioned, here. We believe that future efforts often will not need to reinvent the wheel. Rather, researchers can build on to the existing frameworks presented here, using as much of the general apparatus as seems relevant and dropping the more specific elements when warranted. In this way, the demography of the corporation will construct a cumulative research record at the same time that it portrays the complexities of the world of organizations.

A difficult question arises with this research strategy: How cumulative should model specifications be? Should analysts follow exactly the specifications of previous studies of a phenomenon unless there is a strong reason to the contrary? The goal of cumulative knowledge might seem to dictate an affirmative response, perhaps even a hard-line position. However, such requirements might stifle creativity and limit discovery, especially if the received specification is deficient in some (perhaps unknown) manner. Then, too, there is always the issue of whether an analysis is intentionally headed down a new branch of contextual complexity and thus should be freed from at least some prior requirements. Obviously, no absolute rule applies. Nonetheless, we believe that the lack of any public discussion about this issue is unhealthy. Among other things, it allows some researchers to change specifications radically from one article to the next, even though they address the same dependent variable with the same data. It would seem reasonable to expect at least some rationale to be offered when specifications appear to be departing from cumulativity.

4

Forms and Populations

with László Pólos

THIS CHAPTER EXAMINES how researchers define the basic units of study in corporate demography: organizational populations. Demographic and ecological analyses usually define an organizational population as an instantiation of an organizational form. Forms are abstract specifications of types of organization. Populations are concrete manifestations of the types, bounded in time and place. In a well-known example, the founding father of organizational sociology, Max Weber, provided a detailed specification of the rational-legal form of bureaucratic organization (Weber 1968). He defined the form in terms of the nature of organizational authority (professional expertise in evaluating abstract rationalized rules), procedures (impersonal exercise of authority, reliance on written rules and files), and the employment relation of the official (bureaucratic employment as a career of full-time work, office separated from the private sphere, and compensation by salary). Weber contrasted this particular form of rational-legal bureaucracy with other bureaucratic forms such as "prebendal bureaucracy."

Weber introduced his specification of rational-legal bureaucracy as an "ideal type," meaning (among other things) that he had abstracted from the historical details in identifying the core features that define the form. Nonetheless, it was crucial to Weber's analysis—and is also crucial in our approach to defining organizational forms—that the rational-legal form was instantiated in real organizations. That is, the idealized form does not constitute a thought experiment; it provides an abstract characterization of some organizational reality. For instance, Weber sought to capture the essential features of the bureaucratic organizations of the later nineteenth-century Prussian state. Yet, he noted that the form was not limited to its Prussian instance; for instance, he noted that the civil-service bureaus created by the Progressive reform movements in the United States in the first decades of the twentieth century also fit the form. In the language of contemporary theory, the Prussian and American instances are two different

59

organizational populations that share a common form: rational-legal bureaucracy.

What exactly is a form? What roles do forms play in the explanatory structures of theories in organizational analysis and, especially, corporate demography? Although the literature uses the form notion indis-
criminately, little attention has been paid to clarifying and developing the
theoretical concept. Accordingly, this chapter explores the organizational
concept of form from several angles. We begin by discussing why the organizational form concept is important. We next look at the various definitions
of form used by organizational theorists and researchers, including what
are sometimes referred to as trait-based and boundary-based approaches.
The chapter then considers the various uses of forms in current research;
it explains how the main use of form in population studies differs from
that of market-based approaches. This section also suggests that prevailing
practices are not always consistent and could be improved.

In the bulk of the chapter, we sketch informally a formal theory of
organizational forms that we have been developing with László Pólos of
Eotvos University, Budapest and the University of Amsterdam.[1] This formal
theory strives to create a representation general enough to incorporate the
insights of both the trait-based and the boundary-based approaches to form
currently in use. We also want the definition to allow the possibility that
forms change over time, that forms are not timeless Platonic elements but
rather social definitions subject to elaboration and simplification. Finally,
we want the definition to be capable of representing the organizational-
science analog of an "evolutionary tree."

4.1 Population versus Form

Why go to the trouble of specifying abstract forms when research in corporate demography focuses on organizational populations? In our view,
clarifying the meaning of organizational form and developing systematic
principles for specifying sets of forms would generate several important
advantages for corporate demography.

First, a well-developed system of organizational forms would provide
a map for negotiating the confusing terrain of the organizational world.
Clearly, there is great diversity in the world of organizations, including
such disparate kinds as voluntary social and political movement organizations, public bureaus, churches, banks, mining companies, and electronic
commerce ventures. No single type fits all. Yet, it does not seem helpful

---

[1] Full details are provided in Pólos, Hannan, and Carroll (1998, 1999), from which this
chapter draws heavily.

to assume that each organization is unique. Churches are usually much more similar to each other than any of them is to a mining company, to take one example. Knowing that an organization is a bank tells us a great deal about what to expect from the organization. More generally, knowledge about the distinctions among forms provides the basis for describing the topography of the organizational world.

Another substantial benefit of relying on the form concept involves issues of continuity in time and space. Start with time. Unlike the case of biotic evolution, organizational evolution allows "extinct" populations to be reestablished. Consider the examples of governmental prohibitions on the sale of alcoholic beverages and bans on publication of "free press." When the U.S. Federal government initiated the national Prohibition, brewing firms, wineries, and distilleries were forced either to close or to shift to some other lines of business. Likewise, the victories of various forms of authoritarian regimes has meant the suspension of the existing newspaper industry, often for long periods of time. When prohibitions end, breweries spring up (Swaminathan and Carroll 1995); when authoritarian regimes are replaced by more open ones, independent newspapers reemerge (Delacroix and Carroll 1983; Dobrev 2000). In a less dramatic example, the history of American national labor unions includes periods in which the number of organizations fell to zero. For instance, the initial members of the population were founded in 1836 and failed in 1837, and no new national unions were founded until 1843 (Hannan and Freeman 1989). In each case, one could conclude, with some justification, that the earlier population went extinct and that a new one formed at a later date. Such a conclusion seems to run counter to our conception of historical continuity; yet, this conclusion seems hard to avoid if one regards the organizational population as the fundamental unit.

The notion of form provides a natural way of defining the continuity of organizational populations over gaps in existence. If a form persists (as we suggest below) as a cultural object even when some local population goes extinct, then organization builders do not have to invent the form to restart the population. Instead, they can apply the known specification of form to newly mobilized resources to build organizations that reinstate the form in the locality.

As to the spatial dimension, it would be desirable to have a systematic means of accounting for the spread of forms over weakly connected (or unconnected) systems. If organizational populations with similar identities emerge in many nations, as has so often been the case, then what exactly is the entity that diffuses? The concept of form provides an easy answer to this question. A form as cultural object has the capacity of spreading over system boundaries. A form diffuses with the proliferation of localized populations of organizations that implement it.

A final advantage of beginning with forms is that this analytic strategy clarifies important issues in the study of structural change. Most accounts of organizations agree that some features can be changed easily with little risk to the organization making the change but that change in other features is hard and dangerous to the organization (Chapter 16). Often this distinction gets phrased in a core/periphery image: peripheral features are easy to change and core features are not (Hannan and Freeman 1984).

What makes some features core and others peripheral? Answering this question turns out to be hard without reference to organizational forms. The proposal sketched below holds that some organizational features matter for determining membership in an organizational form and other features do not. Changing those features that determine form membership exposes the organization to risk. It blurs the organization's identity and lessens the legitimation that flows from membership in a form. In contrast, changing the features that do not decide form membership does not have such consequences. If researchers have a clear delineation of forms and the elements that determine form membership, then they have a way to discriminate fundamental structural changes from peripheral changes. Existence of a systematic accounting of forms would even provide leverage for scaling fundamental changes, as we explain below.

Definitions of Organizational Forms

Now consider the ways that organizational theorists and researchers currently define forms. The most popular social scientific approach to organizational forms regards them as *clusters of features*. The par-excellence example is Weber's (1968) specification of the form of rational-legal bureaucracy, discussed above. Subsequent development of the feature-based conceptions of forms recognized that some features are more important than others in distinguishing forms. In this vein, analysts have utilized the distinction between core and peripheral features and have identified forms with a set of core features. That is, organizations having the same core features belong to the same form. Various analysts' notions of form differ mainly in that they envision different sets of features as core.

The feature-based approaches to defining forms make forms a function only of structural elements, with the implication that forms can be assessed in purely technical terms. Such a possibility can now be realized in the study of biotic evolution. Organizational sociology seems unlikely to reach such a position, because distinctions among forms appear to reflect social processes of boundary creation.

This possibility has been explored in another, less developed, line of work that defines forms in terms of the clarity and strength of *social boundaries*. Hannan and Freeman (1986) argued that forms are bounded sets of features and that the existence of a sharp boundary results in a clear form. The existence and location of the boundary matters more than the details about what features are contained within it. That is, the processes that create and reproduce the boundaries—social network ties, closed flows of personnel among a set of organizations, technological discontinuities, social movements articulating the interests of a set of organizations—are the key to understanding forms. When these processes operate strongly (and dominate the processes that blur forms), then the world of organizations is organized by forms.

DiMaggio (1986) proposed a similar approach, based on identifying discontinuities in patterns of *network ties* related to resource flows—see also Burt (1993). He suggested defining form membership in terms of structural equivalence in such flow networks. Two organizations are structurally equivalent if they have exactly the same relations with other actors. Because structural equivalence is a transitive and symmetric relation, it is in fact an equivalence relation. Equivalence relations introduce partitioning, and this kind of partitioning of a set of organizations gives the equivalence classes that represent forms.

This proposal would actually define an organizational population, in our framework (explained below), because it pertains to a localized set of interacting organizations among particular actors.[2] Forms, as we construe them, are more abstract entities—they potentially apply over space and time. Nonetheless, bringing network ideas into the picture is a very valuable step. So, we follow this lead. That is, our proposed definition of forms can be built partly or wholly in terms of network ties or other kinds of relational properties, such a position in a status distribution or size distribution.

Our proposal combines elements of the feature-based, network-based, and boundary-based approaches. Like the first, it begins by specifying potential identities in terms of constraints over features. And like the third, it allows identities be to defined relationally. Like the second, it emphasizes the importance of the judgments made by outsiders in transforming potential identities into real identities and, under certain conditions, into forms.

---

[2] Hannan (1996) argued that there is a problem involved in trying to use structural equivalence to define forms as stable entities over time. This is because structural equivalence defines relationships among particular (named) actors. That is, the identities of the actors matter. Suppose that there are three classes of organizations with two instances of each. Call them a_1, a_2, b_1, b_2, and c_1, c_2 and suppose that c_1 has ties to one member of each class, say a_1 and b_1 and that c_2 has ties to a_2 and b_2. Then c_1 and c_2 occupy the same kind of position (they are automorphically equivalent); but they are not structurally equivalent (Borgatti and Everett 1992).

Roles of Organizational Forms

In corporate demography, researchers typically use notions about organizational form to define populations for study. In the usual framework, localized sets of organizations belonging to the same form constitute a population. A great deal of recent research conducts analysis on populations defined in this manner. The set includes research on such populations as audit firms (Boone, Bröcheler, and Carroll 2000), automobile manufacturers (Hannan et al. 1998a), banks (Barnett and Hansen 1996), baseball teams (Land, Davis, and Blau 1994), brewers (Carroll and Swaminathan 1992), cooperative banks (Lomi 1995a), credit unions (Barron, West, and Hannan 1994), day-care centers (Baum and Singh 1994), ethnic newspapers (Olzak and West 1991; West 1995), ethnic and women's social-movement organizations (Minkoff 1993), investment banks (Park and Podolny 1998), savings-and-loan associations (Haveman 1992), semiconductor manufacturers (Podolny, Stuart, and Hannan 1996), telephone companies (Barnett 1997), and wineries (Swaminathan 1995). Empirical research proceeds by collecting information on all the organizations in the specified population and then estimating models of organizational and population processes. To a great extent, the value of such research depends upon the degree to which the population studied represents an instance of a clearly bounded form.

Corporate demographic usage of the form concept differs from two widely used other meanings. In a second common role, form refers to a *selection-favored* conglomerate of features. So, for instance, when Williamson (1975) refers to the divisionalized corporation as the M-form, he implies that it is a successful form of organization. Most discussions about new forms of organization imply a certain degree of environmental fitness. For instance, such claims have been made recently for the "network form" of organization (Podolny and Page 1998).

The examples of the M-form and the network form illustrate yet another facet of the meaning of form. These examples refer to *organizational architectures*. Architectures and forms in our sense are quite different. Forms, as we see it (and explain below), are related to identity. Architectures rarely matter decisively for identity in two senses. First, architectures vary considerably within forms. For instance, M-form organizations can be found in many populations of differing forms. Second, organizations routinely change their architectures without changing their identities. So, without denigrating the importance of architecture, it seems imperative to distinguish architecture and form.

A third usage of form differentiates between possible local adaptation steps and deep structural changes. According to inertia theory (Chapter 16), changing a core feature exposes an organization to great risk of mortality, but change in peripheral features does not increase mortality chances and might indeed reduce them. According to this theory, the core features are those that regulate membership in a form. Testing this (and related arguments) demands clear and detailed specifications of forms. The form concept should also play a role in explaining why changing form is more difficult and precarious than other kinds of organizational changes.

Organizational Populations and Markets

It is worth noting that the form-based population framework used in corporate demography differs in some basic ways from other approaches to industry. For instance, many approaches to the economics of organizations begin with a conception of the market rather than form; they commence analysis by examining organizations competing directly within the specified market. Corporate demography, by contrast, views the market boundaries as potentially the consequence of organizational actions, as possibly endogenous. Demographers begin analysis with a conception of the organizational population, defined broadly as the set of organizations characterized by a particular organizational form and dependent on a common set of material and social resources. Demographic analysis starts by identifying all organizations that might plausibly compete and then proceeds by modeling the vital rates as well as the interdependencies—including but not limited to competition—that emerge among them.[3] The resulting analysis might cover several interdependent organizational forms and populations.

An example clarifies these differences. Carroll and Swaminathan's (1992) analysis of contemporary American brewers focused on the period from 1975 to 1990 and featured an analysis of two emerging organizational forms, microbreweries (producers of ale and beer by traditional "handcrafted" methods) and brewpubs (producers of ale and beer who sell for consumption at the site of production, typically a brewery-restaurant), as well as traditional mass production breweries. The data collection effort identified 200 breweries as operating in late 1989. These included 25 mass producers, 71 microbreweries, and 104 brewpubs. The analysis examined the founding rates and mortality rates of each of the three types of breweries, including the ways that numbers (densities) of the other forms affected them. Carroll and Swaminathan (1992) paid special attention to the different market contexts and consumer bases of the various organizational forms of breweries, including the fact that brewpubs operated in local markets and competed against other dining and drinking establishments.

---

[3] This section is drawn from Carroll (1997).

An industrial economist who has published a number of articles on the brewing industry objected to this analysis (Tremblay 1993). He complained that microbreweries and brewpubs do not compete with the mass production breweries. In his words,

> It is inappropriate to include microbreweries and brewpubs in the same market with the mass producers ... [because following the logic of substitutability in] ... the 1982 Merger Guidelines. ... it is hard to believe that a 5% increase in [the price of] Budweiser beer (the best-selling mass producer beer in America) will cause consumers to switch to the stouts and ales (which sell for about twice the price of Budweiser) produced by the microbreweries. ... microbrewery beer competes more directly with imported than with the average domestic beer. Imported beers and microbrewery products have similar characteristics, being more full-bodied and having higher alcohol contents, and sell for about twice the price of the average mass-produced domestic beer. (Tremblay 1993, 94)

Tremblay's position was supported by an anonymous reviewer who called microbrewers and brewpub operators the "almost-hobbyist counterparts" of the larger brewers. He recommended publication of Tremblay's comment as a "useful corrective" to the Carroll and Swaminathan (1992) article.

Why did Carroll and Swaminathan (1992) include the two organizational populations defined by these new forms even though their combined market share was small? They did so because both were involved in production of the same generic product as the mass producers. All three types of producers used the exact same ingredients; all three used roughly the same production techniques (albeit with great differences in scale); and all three made beverages purchased by the consumer for the same purposes.

So, despite different organizational forms and despite dependence to some extent on separate consumer markets, the two new forms were potentially competitive with mass producers. Including them in the analysis allowed Carroll and Swaminathan (1992) to investigate the extent and exact nature of their relationship with mass producers. The fact that the forms were incipient and not strongly competitive at the time of analysis was no reason to exclude them from a study designed to shed light on organizational evolution.

Indeed, excluding these forms until they become competitively important entails selection bias and blinds one to many of the underlying processes of evolution, whatever the eventual outcome. Consider the possible extreme outcomes of the competition. Should mass producers remain dominant as these new forms emerge, then it would be important to know the details about the potential competitors that were warded off. Conversely, should the new forms rise to prominence, then records of their early histories would likely be central to their analysis.

It winds up that the outcome has not yet been determined in American brewing. However, the numbers and market shares of the new forms have continued to rise. In September 1998, the so-called craft brewing segment of the industry included: 37 regional specialty breweries (making microbrewery products), 423 microbreweries, and 910 brewpubs. Most mass producers now make at least one beverage aimed directly at this segment and many "microbreweries" have reached substantial scale (annual production of 100,000 barrels or more) and distribute their products nationwide. Even taking Tremblay's (1993) argument on its own terms (direct competition as evidenced by substitutability), exclusion of the two new organizational forms is no longer warranted. Analysis proceeding according to his reasoning would be forced to choose some arbitrary starting point in the early 1990s (when direct competition became discernible at some arbitrary level) as the "beginning" of the microbrewery movement. We believe that it would be preferable to choose the *actual* origins.

4.2 Identity and Form

Our review of the organizational form concept does not mention identity for a simple reason. Currently used definitions of organizational form do not reflect on corporate identities. Yet, many analysts expect that, under specific circumstances, a strong identity might enhance an organization's life chances. If form is unrelated to identity, then we cannot speak about identity-related selection without risking inconsistency. In our view, a better construction would define identity and form in closely related terms.

We propose a new definition of form as a recognizable pattern that takes on rule-like standing. Our choice of language for expressing this idea deserves some discussion. We want to use a term whose denotation and connotation include both *cognitive recognition* and *imperative standing*. In early drafts, we phrased the theory in terms of social and cultural "rules." We reasoned that rules both specify the objects to which they apply and offer prescriptions about the objects and their behavior. However, the connotation of articulated regulation appears to be so strong that the cognitive dimension gets slighted. So we have chosen to speak of codes. "Code" refers both to (1) a *set of signals*, as in the "genetic code" and (2) a *set of rules of conduct*, as in the "penal code." We intend that our use of the term code reflect both meanings.

In Pólos et al. (1998, 1999), we proposed a new formal definition of form as a kind of externally-enforced identity.[4] We sketch this definition below in informal terms. Our discussion begins with the notion of identity. We define identity in terms of social codes (comprised of sets of social rules and signals) that specify the features that an organization can legitimately possess. These codes can be enforced by members of the organization (insiders) or by external actors on which the organization depends for resources and support (outsiders). We claim that one knows that a social code of this kind exists when one observes that departures from the rules (after periods of conformity) cause a devaluation of the organization by relevant outsiders.

We concentrate on the subclass of identities that possesses two properties: the codes apply to classes of organizations (social rules might apply to unique organizations) and they are enforced by outsiders. We define forms as identities that are externally enforced and that apply to some (form-specific) number of actors. We conclude that knowing a form implies knowing the constraints on features that are enforced for the organizations belonging to the form. Crossings of the form boundaries appear as violations of identities, and they are sanctioned accordingly. An organization that crosses such a boundary loses the benefits that result from conformity with the rules.

4.3 Codes

What provides the basis of identity? A natural answer says that identity inheres in the constancy of some set of features. Yet, in the case of organizations, at least some changes do not disrupt identity. So, defining identities in terms of permanent features does not work. We conclude that neither the actual values of the features nor the features themselves can be the carriers of identity.

So what do organizations preserve when they maintain their identities? We claim that an identity constrains what an organization would/could do and what is expected and not expected of it. On the formal side, this idea can be expressed as follows: organizations are described in terms of features and constraints over features.

Restricted Alternatives and Indispensable Properties

The sets of feasible feature values can be considered as given in analyzing identity, because they are set by considerations that do not depend upon

---

[4]This effort developed a formal language for organizational forms using set theory, algebra, and logic. Here we describe the conceptual machinery informally.

the organizations under consideration or on the rules defining their identities. For instance, some features are constrained by technological possibilities. Widespread availability of inexpensive information technology has increased the range of production possibilities in some industries (e.g., the option of marketing and selling products over the Internet was not in the feasible set until recently). Other features are constrained by laws and general cultural rules (e.g., slave labor is now excluded in most societies from the set of options for the form of the membership relationship).

Some identities impose restrictions on features that go beyond the technological and legal constraints. We refer to these restrictions as identity-restricted alternatives. If an identity allows only one value for a particular feature, then an organization cannot change the value of this feature without giving up its identity. These features might be called indispensable properties. Some restrictions that support identity have a conditional nature. Think, for instance, of an identity that allows a wide range of values for both of two properties but assumes that, if the value of one of them falls in a given subset of the possible values, then the other value gets restricted to a certain subset. For instance, the property of brokerage requires that an actor have ties to two or more other actors who are not directly tied. Such a restriction on a pattern of ties can be expressed as a sentence that states restrictions on properties. We refer to these restrictions as *constraints*.

Potential Identities

An organization can, of course, claim several identities simultaneously. It should not matter at all that an organization claims two identities, if these two identities are equivalent in the sense that they necessarily apply to the same objects. This situation can be characterized by the notion of extensional equivalence. Two potential identities are extensionally equivalent in a period if (1) both are defaults for the very same organizations in that period and (2) both are satisfied by the same actors at the start of that period. Because extensional equivalence is (obviously) an equivalence relation, it partitions the set of potential identities. The equivalence classes of such a partition might be regarded as the "real" potential identities.

Organizations generally have many identities. For instance, a proper microbrewing firm rightfully claims such identities as microbrewer, brewer, manufacturer, and firm. It is easy to see that an organization might continue to satisfy one or another of its potential identities while changing some of its feature values.

Grading Potential Identities

Social identities, including organizational identities, are often nested. Of course, it is ultimately a matter for empirical research to document exactly how this nesting gets organized. Our experience in studying organizational populations suggests that organizational identities are usually partially ordered. For instance, if we know that an organization has the identity of "craft labor union," then it usually also has the identity "labor union." Thus, we would conclude that craft labor union is a refinement of the labor-union identity or that "craft labor union" is a sharper identity than "labor union."

We conjecture that sets of organizational identities sometimes are graded (in terms of the sharper-than relation): If an organization cannot or will not satisfy the constraints that maintain its sharpest potential identity, it still might be able to keep a fraction of its identity, i.e., maintain a less-sharp identity. This in practice would appear as a redefinition of identity in more general terms.

Not all pairs of identities are nested in the sense of one being sharper than the other. This is the case for the identities "labor union" and "brewing firm." How do we know in general that two identities are distinguishable? Clearly, when one of a pair of identities is strictly sharper than the other,[5] then they are distinguishable.[6]

Valuation Functions

Organizations and other corporate actors face evaluation by members, particular external constituencies, and the society at large. The various kinds of evaluators might have different perspectives and impose different, perhaps conflicting, demands. At this stage of the development of the theory, we elide these differences, and we assume that evaluations can be aggregated meaningfully. The more positive the (aggregate) evaluations of an identity, the more resources will be available for the organizations with that identity. Such judgments are made both by insiders and outsiders. Members decide how much loyalty to give to an organization, constituencies decide whether to engage in transactions with the organization and whether to support it in disputes, and so forth. To represent this abstract content, we specify two evaluation functions, one pertaining to the judgments of "insiders" (members of the organization) and one pertaining to "outsiders." Although it would be important in empirical research to measure these functions directly, we simplify here by concentrating on the changes in valuations over a period. We want to consider situations in which deviation gets punished. So we single out the case in which valuations decrease substantially over a very brief (instantaneous) period.

---

[5] This means that the former is sharper than the latter but the converse is not true.

[6] Pólos et al. (1998) also show that two identities are distinguishable even when neither is strictly sharper than the other, provided that: (1) each is weakly sharper than a different other identity, and (2) different other identities are weakly sharper than one but not the other.

Valuation involves all sorts of social reactions to organizations based upon their identities. For instance, valuation can involve judgments by members about whether an organization has remained faithful to its traditions and culture. Valuation can also mean general social approval by controllers of resources, the belief that organizations possessing a certain identity are valid organizations deserving of support. Valuation can also mean the literal calculation of pecuniary value in the sense that investors in stock markets explicitly or implicitly make calculations of the expected value of firms. When these expectations take form of organization into account, then the process bears on the definition of identities. Zuckerman (1999) provides a vivid account and empirical analysis of such a process in the world of securities analysts, employees of stock brokerages who "follow" industries and firms and make forward-looking assessments of the (stock) market prospects of firms. The research shows that firms that enter sets of markets and industries that do not conform with the category schemes used by the analysts suffer in valuation. Such deviant firms are less likely to be followed by analysts (which reduces their attractiveness to investors) and their stock market returns fall accordingly.

Valuations of features can change over time, as new practices emerge, technologies evolve, and cultural and political views shift. In this context, we must address the volatility of the evaluations of identities. If big changes in the evaluation of an identity can take place instantaneously, then evaluations of identities do not serve as a basis for potentially stable social identities. So, we make the seemingly reasonable assumption that valuation functions change smoothly over brief intervals, that the views that underlie evaluations do not change sharply and discontinuously.

A Definition of Social Identity

As we have defined them, the set of potential identities is unbounded. For instance, adding irrelevant features to the set or making irrelevant restrictions over the ranges of pairs of features (or triplets, quadruplets, and so forth) creates new identities. So, we need some principle for distinguishing *actual* (socially meaningful) identities from potential identities. Our proposal builds on the idea that real identities come to have a code-like status in the sense that they consist of sets of rules whose violations have observable consequences (Meyer and Rowan 1977; Jepperson 1991). The rules contained in these codes are often implicit—sometimes even tacit— yet they might be fully articulated and explicit.

Discontinuities in Valuation Functions

Pólos et al. (1998) propose a way of identifying codes by examining possible violations. Violation of a code (after a period of conformity with the code) lowers an actor's valuation precipitously. However, a violation has negative consequences only when the actors controlling consequences believe that the code in question applies to the organization.[7]

The issue of applicability complicates the job of assessing codes. We do not want to assume that all relevant codes are already known to an observer-evaluator inspecting some social world. Suppose that an evaluator comes across an organization that does not conform to some expected code-like pattern. Should she conclude that this unusual organization violates a code? We think that the answer to this question is No, because the organization might satisfy some other not-yet-known code. To accommodate this complication, we propose a more limited test. This test focuses on a set of organizations that conform with what might be a code and examines the consequences of an organization's violating the possible code after an observed period of conformity to it. If violation of the code (after a period of conformity) causes evaluations to drop sharply, then we decide that we have identified a code.

This reasoning holds even when an organization changes such that it violates one social code but satisfies another code that it did not satisfy previously (e.g., an organization departs from its long-standing tradition and switches to some currently fashionable set of features). In this case, the organization does not satisfy some social code for only a vanishingly small interval of time. Even in this case, the violation of the former code should be costly. The matter turns on evaluators' judgments concerning what codes apply to the organization. If the organization has an observed history of conforming with a given code, then the relevant evaluators will ordinarily form the belief that this code applies.[8] If this is so, then the shift to conformity with some other code does, in the example, constitute a violation.

---

[7] A very fundamental and difficult problem in the social sciences concerns understanding how normative judgments by individuals combine to create, sustain, and apply cultural rules and codes. We do not pretend to offer a general solution to this problem. From the perspective of our proposal, all that is required is that such rules come into existence and that controllers of valued resources use these rules in granting and withholding access to resources. We imagine that the details vary enormously from form to form and system to system. In the case of organizations, the relevant evaluators often include individuals: potential investors, employees, or customers, all of whom make judgments of organizations seeking their favor. In other circumstances, the relevant evaluators are authorities, state regulators, judges, officials of professional associations, and so forth. The processes that translates individual judgments into consequences of organizations' conforming to codes and rules and violating them presumably differ in these two kinds of cases. Nonetheless, the theory proposed by Pólos et al. (1998) has not developed to the point that it can attend to these differences. In the present state of development of their theory, we simply assert that certain codes exist and get enforced, without specifying who does the enforcing and how.

[8] If codes are known, then violation can be defined irrespective of prior conformity. We introduce the special restriction here only because we are considering situations in which codes might not be known to the researcher.

Accordingly, we define code violation as follows. An organization violates a code during a time interval if the code applies to the organization and it satisfies the code at one time during the period but does not satisfy it a (very) short time later. Furthermore, a social code is a constraint (code) with the property that an organization's violation of an applicable rule causes a discontinuous drop in its valuation (by insiders and/or outsiders). We define social codes in this way so as to narrow down the class of identities that matter. A potential identity is an actual identity if and only if the identity applies to the organization as code and the code has rule-like status (the force of a social code) in the period of interest.

The obvious final step in developing the notion of code-based identity considers the consequence of violating such an identity. A violation of an actual identity ⬚ the valuation of an organization by insid⬚ (a theorem in the formal model) provi⬚d to provide a definition of identity that⬚ implicitly defines a potential identity as ⬚al identity as a potential identity that h⬚ the code harms the organization's valuati⬚

4.4 Organizational Forms

We define an organizational form as a special kind of identity. Whereas identities meaningfully apply to single organizations, forms applies to classes of organizations. Moreover, whereas identities might be established primarily or even exclusively by evaluations of insiders (think of a secret society whose structure has avoided notice by outsiders), forms are cultural objects.

So, in our view, an identity is a form in a period if and only if the following conditions are met:

1. the identity applied to and was satisfied by a form-specific constant number of organizations at the beginning of the interval; and
2. violation of applicable identity causes the outsider evaluation functions to drop sharply.

This definition allows forms to become empty for a time without the relevant identities changing or ceasing to exist. Under such circumstances, internal enforcement is vacuously true, and the external enforcement is obviously counterfactual in nature. We have in mind situations such as a state action that bans a form of organization (e.g., prohibitions against the manufacture and sale of alcoholic beverages, bans on newspaper publishing, elimination of the productions of classes of consumer products such as automobiles during times of war). When such bans get lifted, organizations that satisfy the persisting cultural rules can reappear and a form can be repopulated with no new legitimation needed (Dobrev 1998). In other words, this definition allows for the possibility that a form persists (for a time) even when no organization currently satisfies the identity, provided that the enforcement of the identity has persisted since at least two organizations conformed with it previously.

According to this definition, a form is an abstract, code-like specification of organizational identities. The next step ties forms to organizations. An organization is classified by default as having an organizational form if the codes specifying the form apply to the organization by default (i.e., as a code). Our definition of form implies that if an organization violates the set of identities that specify a form of which it is a "member," then the valuation of the organization by outsiders drops sharply.

Subforms

If, as we conjectured above, identities are nested, then form distinctions are ordinarily (partially) nested, because forms are special kinds of identities.[9] This means that organizational worlds tend to contain sets of forms that have subforms that in turn have subforms, and so forth. Such a hierarchical arrangement allows the set of forms to take an especially simple form: hierarchy. Hierarchical systems are easy to comprehend. Code violations in such a world are especially visible and therefore are easy to punish.

The key property for conceptualizing hierarchical relations among forms is the *subform relation*. Pólos et al. (1998) define the subform relation as the weakly sharper relation among identities applied to organizational forms. Membership in forms propagates "upward": membership in a subform of a form means membership in that form.

4.5 Organizational Populations

As in previous treatments, we define populations as bounded sets of organizations with a common form. Populations are bounded by some kind of social-system boundary (chosen to reflect the barriers to the operations of relevant social processes such as the flow of information, competition, and regulation). A crucial part of defining a population is getting this part of

---

[9] Of course, in the actual social world, these nestings might not be so neatly organized or even logically consistent. Indeed, the structure is currently unknown. The structure we assume here has very desirable formal properties and serves as a baseline default.

the specification right. In this respect, nothing has changed in the definition of population. However, the new definition of form does imply some other changes in the definition of organizational populations.

The conventional definition of organizational population contains a fundamental ambiguity, not noted previously. The ambiguity arises because the codes that specify forms are (partially) nested: an organization that conforms with the cultural code specifying a particular form also (by implication) conforms with the codes defining all forms higher up all of the branches of the tree that reach it. So, which of the many possible entities is a meaningful population?

We think that population definitions are most productive for theory and research when they pertain to the most specific (sub)form whose cultural specification a given set of organizations fits. So, we introduce the concept of the minimal externally enforced identity that an organization satisfies, the cultural code whose constraints are the most specific. We define a population as the set consisting of the organizations defined by a given minimal external identity in a bounded system in some period.

With this definition of population and the definition of the subform relation, we might visualize an accounting system for populations defined over a set of external identities. Start at the top of the hierarchy. The population of "plain vanilla" organizations (those with no more specific identity than "organization") is the count of all organizations in the local system minus the numbers in all proper subforms of the "unit organization" identity. At each branching point, the rule is the same. For instance, suppose we work our way down to the node for brewing firms. The local population of brewers is the number of brewing firms minus the numbers of all of the proper subforms of brewing (industrial brewers, microbrewers, brewpubs, and contract brewers). In other words, the population of "brewers" is the local count of firms that satisfy the cultural rule for a brewing firm but do not satisfy any of the more specific identities that control membership in any of the proper subforms.[10]

The population defined by a given form in a particular system is the set of organizations in that system that are members of the form minus the set of organizations in that system that are classified by default into any of the proper subidentities of the identity. It is helpful to display this representation graphically. Figure 4.1 uses a Venn diagram to represent the situation for three external identities, ϕ_1, ϕ_2, and ϕ_3, where ϕ_2 is a proper subset of ϕ_1 and ϕ_3 is a proper subset of ϕ_2. The rectangle represents the set of organizations that are members of the population defined by identity ϕ_1 in some local system. The subregion with light shading represents the

---

[10] So the population of "brewers" might contain firms that employ a mixed strategy, e.g., combining industrial production and microbrewing.

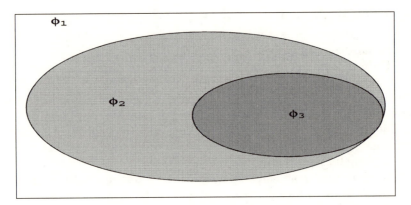

Figure 4.1. *Decomposition of a localized set of organizations into populations.*

set of organizations that are classified by default as ϕ_2 and the heavily shaded region represents the set of organizations that are classified by default as ϕ_3. The population associated with ϕ_1 is the "white space" inside the rectangle. The population associated with ϕ_2 is the region with only light shading, and the population associated with ϕ_3 is heavily shaded region.

4.6 Systems of Forms

At the outset, we suggested that a useful definition of form would be capable of supporting a metric for measuring the "distances" among forms (in a cultural space). Such a metric would permit researchers to distinguish between structural reorganizations that entail movement between closely related forms and those between more distant ones. Our conceptual framework does not yet contain all the requirements for establishing such metric. In this section, we sketch what else we think is needed and show that our framework can usefully express the required structures.

With definitions of forms and subforms in hand, we now consider the implied structure of the system of forms. It would be analytically convenient if the structure possessed the property of hierarchy. Distances between forms could then be calculated in a straightforward manner. Such distances would provide a metric for distinguishing radical (that is, long-distance) change from local change and provide some needed discipline in testing the theory of structural inertia (Chapter 16).

The subform relation is reflexive and transitive; this means that the set of forms has a partial ordering. If the system of forms is to have a tree-like structure, then two other properties must be satisfied. First, there must be a maximal form, a form that sits above all of the others. Does it make sociological sense to envision such a form? We think that it does. Sociological treatments of organization theory routinely posit that all (formal) organizations possess a common set of properties. Commonly, the properties asserted are

1. The object is a corporate actor, more than the aggregation of the individual members;
2. The object mobilizes resources and legitimation based on a claim to achieve specific and limited purposes; and
3. The object is intended to last beyond a single collective action.

We argue that these properties do define an actual form in the sense that organizations are distinguished and favored kinds of actors in modern societies (Stinchcombe 1968; Coleman 1990; Hannan 1986b). A corporate actor gains legitimacy by adopting the form of organization. If this assertion is correct, then corporate actors that have acquired legitimacy (a form of positive valuation) by adopting the form "organization" will experience devaluation if they depart from the form. It should be noted that the cultural distinction between "organization" and other kinds of social actors gets reflected in the legal systems (with some provisions applying only to corporations and other kinds of organizations) and in industry practices (e.g., organizations and persons are often charged different prices[11]). So we contend that the general form "organization" actually exists.

The second condition that must be satisfied involves a complicated idea we call coherence of forms. The coherence criterion states that if two forms are subforms of two other forms, then the common core of the two subforms should be codified culturally as a form in its own right.

We are thinking of situations such as the following. Two forms appear to have emerged in the United States in recent years that are subforms of both the brewer form and the restaurant form. One subform combines a microbrewery (that produces beer, sometimes is considerable quantities, for consumption on premises as well as for sales through other channels) with a restaurant. For lack of a better label, we might call this the microbrewery restaurant. The second form has completely local operations. It produces beer only for sale on premises and also serves meals. We might call this the local brewpub form. Now, each subform is subject to the constraints imposed by default from both lines of "ancestry." That is, they are subject to evaluation as brewers and as restaurants.

It fits our notion of coherence that a form that is a subform of both the brewing and restaurant forms and a superform of the microbrewery restaurant form and local brewpub form is coded as a form in its own

---

[11] Sometimes the organizations pay more, as in the case of subscriptions to scholarly journals, but normally organizations pay less as in the so-called corporate rates charged by hotels.

right: the brewpub form. Whenever an organizational changes form from microbrewery restaurant to brewpub, or the other way around, it suffers a drop in its evaluation function. However, this drop is less than would be the case if it eliminated the brewer identity or the restaurant identity. This difference in the two drops of the evaluation function suggests that this system of codified identities and forms is coherent in the sense that the common constraints that apply at the lowest level are organized and coded in a single intermediate form. To understand the constraints operating at the level of the most specific forms in our example, one needs to go only one level "up" in the system.

When these assumptions are satisfied, systems of forms are semilattices. Furthermore, if one can trace upward (to the unit element) by only one path from any point in the structure, then the system is a tree. Within branches (including the whole tree), more "primitive" or more basic properties are implied by the less primitive ones. We can arrange the properties in descending order of primitiveness, with the first properties in the list being those that define the general organization. With this arrangement, the order of a property in the listing tells the level at which the form distinguished by that property branches in the tree.

4.7 Implications for Corporate Demography

The new definition of organizational form advanced here leads to a definition of organizational population that differs from earlier ones that rely on identifying forms in terms of "core features." The new definitions have several important implications for research practice.

First, meaningful specification of an organizational population depends upon (a) precise understanding of the relevant codes and (b) proper delineation of the system boundaries. These are challenging requirements. Getting the externally enforced identities and system boundaries right requires intensive study of the institutional context that encompasses a set of organizations.[12] We think that these requirements have strong implications for designs of empirical studies.

Current research pursues two main design philosophies: one tries to get broad representativeness of the world of organizations over relatively short time periods (e.g., the National Organizations Survey (Kalleberg, Knoke, Marsden, and Spaeth 1996)) and the other, the population design,

---

[12] In our experience, it usually takes several years of such close study to make meaningful form distinctions for even a very small group of related forms such as the various forms of brewing firms and labor unions.

focuses narrowly on a segment of this world but uses a long temporal perspective (Chapter 5). The representativeness design maximizes variability in forms while the population design minimizes such variability. From the perspective of learning about forms, the representativeness design would seem preferable as it provides information on so many forms. However, it seems implausible, in the present state of knowledge, to identify the forms meaningfully. If there are hundreds or thousands of forms potentially represented, then the analyst needs to be able to specify correctly an enormous number of cultural rules.

Our experience, based on application of the simpler population design in a relatively small number of arenas (audit companies, automobile manufacturers, banks, credit unions, life insurance companies, manufacturing firms, brewers, labor unions, newspapers, and semiconductor manufacturers), indicates that several years of close study are required to grasp the important institutional details that provide the key information about forms.

We devote considerable attention to the two design alternatives in Part II. Whatever one decides about the merits of the two designs, an appreciation of the centrality of social codes in defining forms leads to a deep reexamination of the issues involved.

Second, because social codes and relevant system boundaries vary over time, forms are historically specific and change over time. Therefore, it is usually a mistake to impose an invariant population specification over long historical periods. American brewing provides a handy illustration of the challenges (Carroll and Swaminathan 1998). Over several centuries, all brewers were what today are called microbrewers, because they used hand-crafted methods and traditional ingredients. They also operated in local markets, with the city or town defining the boundaries of competition. Over this period then, the "industry" consisted of a great many localized populations, with each population exemplifying the same form. During this century, the industry bifurcated in form, as some firms began to produce beer using industrial methods and new recipes (which included many additives not culturally sanctioned previously) and others retained traditional methods. By the end of World War II, the industrial brewers had attained dominance in the industry, which became exceedingly concentrated. At the same time, the boundaries shifted to the national (and even international) level. At this time, there was a national population of mass (industrial) brewers and a lingering population of traditional brewers.

Within the past two decades, population boundaries have shifted once again. Movements of local associations of hobby brewers succeeded in gaining legislation in various states that permitted traditional brewers to operate in a new mode. Specifically, the new form integrates production, sale, and consumption at a single site (which had been—and still is—

forbidden to the major brewers). It has come to be known as the brewpub form. The brewpub's emergence occurred hand in hand with development of another form: the microbrewery, which is a small-scale brewery producing for distribution. The numbers of both types of breweries have grown into the hundreds in little over a decade. A crucial part of the story of the rise of these two types is that they became forms in our sense of the term. The activists in the movement succeeded in creating two distinctive identities that differ sharply from the identity of mass brewer. The key was posing the issues in terms of *authenticity* (involving slavish conformity to a set of specific traditional methods) and invoking nostalgic images of craft production.

The rise of the two forms (which, of course, amounts to a recreation of the historic forms in the industry) has complicated brewing's topography of forms in two ways. First, the diversity of forms has increased. Second, the boundaries of the populations defined by these forms differ. The industrial, mass-brewer population is still national. So there is a single population of mass brewers. The brewpub population is, by virtue of its dependence on consumption at the site of sale, exceedingly local (with respect to market competition, but not flows of information and legitimacy). And the microbrewer population stands in an intermediate position, with some brewers emphasizing their local roots and others striving to operate on a national level. According to this account, the brewing "industry" has persisted for hundreds of years, but the populations of brewers have changed markedly over time.

A third implication of the definition bears on the enumeration of populations when form distinctions are nested. Consider the example of national labor unions. Hannan and Freeman (1989) analyzed the ecological dynamics of the entire population of American labor unions and conducted analyses of the two important subforms: craft unions (which organize workers according to craft or occupational distinctions) and industrial unions (which organize workers by site of employment irrespective of craft or occupation). According to their understanding of the situation, the craft and industrial forms were the minimal forms. The proposed definition would suggest that the Hannan–Freeman study amassed data on three populations: craft unions, industrial unions, and unions that did not fit either minimal form but still fit the labor-union form. In this view, the set of all unions does not comprise a meaningful population and should not be the main focus of analysis. Instead, the analyses of the subforms should be given priority. Similarly, our sketch of the brewing industry shows that the same kind of implication holds for analysis of the contemporary period: the set of brewers does not constitute a single population.

Finally, we also believe that the reconstructed form concept paves the way for possible greater theoretical unification. It makes clear that the strongly defended boundary between institutional and ecological views of organization does not demark an intellectually sensible divide. Our form concept employs knowledge about processes shaping identities and rules in building specifications of forms. Consider, for instance, issues of robust identity (Padgett and Ansell 1992) as applied to forms. Stark (1996) provides a vivid account of the ambiguity surrounding rules about property and organizational forms in post-Socialist Hungary. He argues that, because it is unclear which codes will prevail, savvy strategists adopt robust identities, which potentially conform with many different cultural codes. Viewed through the lens of our model, the argument has an interesting general implication. The codes defining forms become clouded and ambiguous during times of transition and/or revolution, when some old codes are challenged and new, potentially conflicting codes contend for support. Refined form distinctions presumably lose their meaning in such a context, in effect pushing many organizations and populations to the highest-level category of "organization." More generally, form distinctions lose force when social codes clash.

Part II
METHODS OF CORPORATE
DEMOGRAPHY

THIS PART of the book reviews and explains the methods of corporate demography. It uses a broad definition of methodology that includes the design of observation plans, the choice of modeling frameworks, the specification of models, the identification of sources, and the collection of data. Taken together, the chapters are intended to give a conceptual and practical overview of the conduct of research in corporate demography.

Chapter 5 begins the methodological discussion by considering observation plans used by organizations researchers. It starts by reviewing the basic design features of empirical studies appearing in a leading specialty journal. The review shows that researchers increasingly rely on observation plans that either cover a large number of diverse organizations for a short period of time or cover a homogenous set of organizations for a much longer period. The chapter then considers the trade-offs inherent in particular (but common) instances of these two plans (specifically, representative sampling and the single-population census) as well as those of a third plan (the multipopulation census). The discussion of trade-offs identifies some potentially severe problems with the broader observation plans that have not been widely recognized. An illustration from internal organizational demography shows the possible impact of observation plans on inferences.

Chapter 6 explains how to analyze vital rates. It starts by examining the ideal form of data for demographic research: event histories. The chapter then discusses models for stochastic processes and the interrelationships between various fundamental constructs. This section uses several corporate populations of automobile producers as illustrations. The chapter next reviews various estimation techniques (including life-table estimation) using data from a banking population. It concludes with a discussion of constant-rate models, the baselines for all demographic models of vital rates.

Chapter 7 extends the modeling framework for vital rates to cover complications that arise routinely in corporate demography. The extensions incorporate duration dependence in the vital rates as well as variation corresponding to observable characteristics of corporations and their environments. It discusses specification and estimation for each complication, and it illustrates their use with data on banks. The last part of the chapter returns to questions about observation plans. It uses computer-simulation methods to examine the performance of the modeling framework under various observation plans. The simulations investigate the quality of estimates of vital rates as well as those of more conventional models of organizational structure and functioning. The findings demonstrate the value of the single-population observation plan.

Chapter 8 considers data sources for corporate demography. It first proposes a set of criteria for evaluating demographic data. The chapter then explores the various types of sources that researchers commonly use, at times examining specific source documents for illustration. The sources described include industry directories, encyclopedic compilations, governmental registries, censuses, and surveys. The use of multiple sources is also discussed.

5

Observation Plans

As DISCUSSED in foregoing chapters, many social scientists agree about the importance of formal organizations in modern society for understanding collective action (Coleman 1990). This consensus implies that organizational studies could be central to the development and progress of social science. Yet, little consensus exists about the best ways to study organizations and, unless this situation gets resolved, organizational analysis will likely not fulfill its potential.

Much of the methodological debate over how to study organizations revolves around issues of measurement and appropriate levels of analysis. On measurement, the discussion typically centers on problems of objectivity, reactiveness, and interpretation. At one extreme, some analysts claim that the complexity of meaning in organizations requires a subjective approach by the researcher. At the other extreme, positivists insist that social settings are amenable to objective measurement, even when they are complex and multilayered.

Views on levels of analysis diverge so strongly as to produce a bifurcation of the field into micro organizational studies, which use the individual (or group) as the level of analysis, and macro studies, which commonly use the organizational level. Both sides claim priority, with some justification, given research findings to date.

Almost all current discussions of methods for studying organizations presuppose a sampling scheme and an associated observation plan.[1] To our minds, these are two of the most unsettled aspects of organizational research. While many organizational analysts apparently embrace as ideal a design involving a broadly representative sample covering all kinds of organizations, we do not. In our view, this design possesses many potentially

---

[1] As Kalleberg, Marsden, Aldrich, and Cassell (1990, 658) note: "despite the importance of sampling issues, they are rarely considered in organizational research reports."

severe drawbacks. Yet, these deficiencies do not seem to be recognized or fully appreciated in the field of organization studies.

Just because a design potentially generates bias does not mean that it should never be used. Rather, it means that the design must be evaluated in light of the questions that it is expected to answer. It should also be compared to feasible alternatives. In other words, decisions about research design involve trade-offs, and these need to be evaluated thoroughly. Although such thinking motivates much social science research, it does not always seem to permeate decisions about sampling organizations.

In this chapter, we consider various organizational sampling schema and observational plans. We first review the organizations literature and identify the types of designs in wide use. The review leads us to focus on three basic types of designs: (1) a broad multipopulation design that attempts to be representative by sampling diverse organizations drawn from all populations; (2) a limited multipopulation design that collects data on all but the smallest organizations in several populations for a particular time period; and (3) a comprehensive single-population design that collects data on all the organizations in a population over its full history. The chapter then lays out the basic dimensions of each design and describes several key trade-offs that do not appear to be widely recognized. We conclude with an illustration of the impact of observation plan drawn from internal organizational demography.

We postpone a second step in evaluating observation plans until we have reviewed the relevant demographic models and statistical estimation methods. In Chapter 7, we report the results of computer simulations designed to allow us to assess the bias in estimation of demographic models for the various designs. The simulation experiments potentially offer a much stronger foundation for understanding the consequences of observation plans for research on organizations. They show that, under typical circumstances, the drawbacks of some widely used designs manifest themselves as bias in estimates of many important organizational processes—demographic as well as conventional structural ones. While our efforts here and in Chapter 7 will clearly not resolve research-design questions for organization studies, we do hope to stimulate discussion and analysis of issues often taken for granted.

5.1 Designs in Organizational Research

How do researchers study organizations? Even a cursory review of the journals shows that organizations researchers use a wide variety of different sampling designs. In an attempt to make sense of this methodological diversity, we systematically examined the articles of *Administrative Science*

Table 5.1. *Design features of research published in the* Administrative Science Quarterly, *1960–1995.*

Publication period	Empirical studies	Sampling scheme			Time span	
		Diverse sample	Sector types	Single type	≤ 5 years	> 5 years
1960–1966	6	3	1	2	5	1
1970–1975	28	8	4	16	23	5
1980–1985	32	14	2	16	18	14
1990–1995	39	17	4	18	14	25

Quarterly or *ASQ*, a leading journal in organization studies. Our efforts focused on systematic empirical research that used the organization as the unit of analysis. We identified each such empirical article and recorded the type of organization(s) studied, the sampling method used, the time period examined, and the geographical area covered. We examined the journal from its inception in 1956 through early 1997.[2]

Table 5.1 shows a summary of the designs that were used in papers reporting systematic empirical research published in *ASQ* from 1960 through 1995. It describes the patterns in some basic design features for the articles published in the first six years of each decade. It gives the number of qualifying empirical studies for each period and groups them by sampling scheme and by time frame. For sampling scheme, we classify the studies according to whether the data come from a sample of diverse types of organizations, a sample of different types of organizations within a common general sector (for example, manufacturing firms), or a sample of organizations of a single functional type. For time frame, we divide the studies by those that analyze data spanning more or less than five years.

Comparisons across the periods reveal some general trends in designs. First, the number of systematic empirical studies has increased steadily. The early years reported few studies, and recent years show many more. Second, the proportion of research using designs with diverse types of organizations (diverse samples and sector samples) versus that using single types of organizations has not changed dramatically. Although the numbers vary somewhat by period, each scheme shows high popularity recently as well as in the past. It would be reasonable to assess the schemes as equally popular. Third, the time span of organizational studies has lengthened in

[2] We thank Tai-Young Kim for assistance in this effort.

recent years. Far more studies now examine periods greater than five years, often much greater.

The table does not reveal clearly the emergence and increased usage of two general design types in *ASQ* and other journals. One of these is the comprehensive single-population design, whereby data are collected on all the organizations of a particular type for (almost) the entire period of the organizational form's existence. For example, in examining organizational mortality of newspaper publishers, Carroll and Delacroix (1982) used data covering the entire nineteenth-century for Argentina and the nineteenth and twentieth centuries for Ireland. Similarly, in studying major structural changes in organizations, Amburgey, Lehtisalo, and Kelly (1988) collected and analyzed data on all newspapers published in Finland from 1771 to 1963. Much of the trend in length of time spans in Table 5.1 reflects the use of this kind of design.

The other increasingly popular general design type relies on representative data from the largest organizations in the economy or a sector. This design culls data from many types of organizations and industries, usually for a relatively short period; these samples of diverse organizations are often weighted by importance to the economy (or employment base). For example, in investigating selection of company directors, Westphal and Zajac (1994) compiled and analyzed information on the largest U.S. industrial and service firms given in the 1987 *Forbes* and *Fortune* listings. Likewise, in their study of the diffusion of governance innovations, Davis and Greve (1997) collected data on the 500 largest U.S. publicly traded industrial firms (from *Fortune*) in 1980 and 1986; they supplemented the file in 1986 with data from the 50 largest publicly traded commercial banks, the 25 largest publicly traded diversified financial service firms, the 25 largest publicly traded retailers, and the 25 largest publicly traded transportation companies.

Diverse sampling schemes remained popular from 1960 to 1995. Researchers shifted from other types of diverse samples to this type, which has a compelling rationale to many (in that it includes so many powerful firms) and for which data are readily accessible. For example, in discussing her use of Compustat data on publicly traded (large) manufacturing firms, Hall (1987, 585) states:

> These data cover approximately 90 percent of the employment in the manufacturing sector in 1976 although they account for only about one percent of the firms in this sector... We would argue that these are the firms of interest, since their relative sizes are the main determinants of concentration in most markets.

5.2 Trade-offs in Observation Plans

Obviously, many studies of firms and other organizations rely on observations across very diverse sets of organizations and industries. In contemplating the role of diversity in observation plans, it is useful to focus initially on representative-sampling schemes, which potentially generate the greatest observed diversity. By definition, sampling that seeks representation of the full range of the organizational world involves taking a probability sample of organizations drawn from the multipopulation universe of organizations.[3] Probability sampling means that every element in the universe has a known nonzero probability of being sampled.[4] The probabilities need not be equal, of course. In fact, organizational sampling commonly weights the probabilities by size, legal form, or industry. A popular design that mitigates the need for an organizational sampling frame uses random sampling of employed individuals to obtain an (employment) size-weighted sample of organizations (Kalleberg et al. 1990). As long as the probabilities of sampling particular units are known, a probability sample can be used to construct a representation of the universe by reweighting the sampled units.[5] This representation can be used, among other things, to calculate estimates (of known quality) of the means and proportions of various characteristics of the universe. Estimates of such descriptive facts are, of course, often invaluable to the scientific enterprise.[6]

Organizational theorists who advocate the use of representative sampling of organizations stress the importance of building general theories and testing them on data spanning the universe of all organizations. From this point of view, evaluation of representative sampling involves more than quality of the sample (which can be judged relative to any theoretically defined universe, such as, all telecommunications firms); it also involves generalizability of the sample to a highly diverse universe (Freeman 1986; Kalleberg et al. 1990). Typically, these analysts strive to have "a large, representative sample of organizations ... drawn from the population of *all* organizations in the United States" (Freeman 1986, 299) (emphasis added). Indeed, assessments of the representativeness of organizational samples

---

[3] To avoid confusion, we use the term universe here to mean what is usually referred to as a population in the sampling literature. We reserve the term population for its organizational meaning.

[4] Many of the samples found in the organizations literature do not use probability sampling. Convenience samples of diverse organizations have many widely acknowledged drawbacks (Freeman 1986). For that reason, our discussion here focuses on the stronger version of the diverse sample, that using probability sampling.

[5] Reweighting might or might not produce high-quality representative estimates, depending on the sampling variance.

[6] For instance, in Chapter 14 we use such figures to estimate the share of individual job mobility attributable to corporate demography.

usually invoke an implicit criterion of generalizability to a very broadly
defined universe of diverse organizations, much as public opinion polls
usually attempt to represent all the individuals in a society. This posture
makes even more ominous the claims of analysts such as Kalleberg et al.
(1990, 658):

> If representative sampling procedures are not followed [in studies of
> organizations], there is little more than an intuitive basis for general-
> izing cases beyond the specific cases studied.

The ability to generalize to a broad universe of organizations often
comes to be regarded as a virtual necessity to the development of cumulative knowledge. Kalleberg et al. (1990, 658) claim "the adequacy of sampling
procedures is central to [the] goal of . . . cumulating research findings by
building on what other investigators have accomplished." Freeman (1986,
299) conjectures that, if a broad representative sample were publicly available, "such a data base could be the basis on which other studies build."

Although for many analysts representative sampling seems to go hand
in hand with the development of a cumulative science of organizations,
this need not be so. In bioecology, a discipline that most observers would
characterize as scientific and cumulative, empirical research usually examines particular species (e.g., purple finches) and sometimes specific habitats populated by several interacting species (e.g., a food chain). That is,
despite the great diversity of the biological world, bioecologists do not use
the representative multipopulation design[7]—and the single-population design yields cumulative general knowledge.

Science proceeds in bioecology by the development of theoretical models of the species and habitats studied empirically. The models developed
are general, but not universal: they embody features that apply to more
than one species or habitat (and often many) but usually not to all. As
Roughgarden (1979, 279) explains, "ecological processes never share a *universal* mechanism and the mechanisms are never *simple*" (emphasis in original). He goes on to say that although much work relies at its start on basic
population dynamics, these almost always undergo challenge and modification for the specific context. He also notes that for any given process
"there is usually a graded series of models with increasing detail." In other
words, no one expects these detailed models to apply widely even if the
underlying basic model might.

---

[7] It is instructive to recognize that a random sample of biological organisms from the
universe of all such creatures would be intractable and not useful. For instance, such a sample
might mix elephants with algae, storks, and newts. Even if these differences were known and
identified, mixing the species-groups (and controlling for group membership) to estimate
models would be uninformative at best and misleading at worst

Organizational analysts differ in their views about how truly universal the mechanisms might be. However, few question the notion that some general principles of operation and functioning apply to all organizations. The main divide concerns the question of how general the theories should be, how much detail they should contain. As with those who advocate representative sampling, we believe that organizational theory should be highly general. In our view, the world of organizations likely contains less variability in forms than the biotic world. At the same time, we doubt that organizations and their environments are any less complex than comparable biological systems. Contemporary research on organizations shows the powerful influences of a variety of elements including strategic competitors, resource providers, governmental agents, and social institutions. The complexity of each of these elements sometimes requires nonlinear network formulations. Moreover, increasing evidence suggests that organizational dynamics are not historically efficient but are instead path dependent (Chapter 17).

The complexity of mechanisms driving organizational-environmental relationships bears on observation plans in at least three important ways. First, samples of diverse organizations likely reflect the results of many different processes, probably mixed in ways that depend on the context. Even if only a handful of highly general mechanisms exist, we would not expect them to mix similarly in different environments. Likewise, if organization-environment processes do not equilibrate quickly or deterministically, then we would not expect different realizations of the same process to look the same. These observations imply that for a representative sample of diverse organizations to have a chance at detecting and estimating these processes it must be big—very big. In other words, the sampling variance will be high and this requires a large sample; otherwise the number of observations per relevant "cell" is too small to be useful.

Second, causal complexity in organization-environmental mechanisms places extraordinarily great demands on observation and data collection. Researchers must collect detailed information on competitors, suppliers and buyers, institutions, and the like for each organization sampled. The menu should include not only the featured independent variables of a theory but also the control variables likely to affect the outcomes. These data demands are difficult, time-consuming, and ultimately limiting, even for researchers who study single populations. Often the best way to overcome these problems is by constructing variables from the population elements themselves: relative size, density (number of organizations), competitive history, niche overlap, ordering of competitive moves, etc. (For many theoretically interesting processes, it would be virtually impossible to do otherwise.) Unfortunately, this option usually does not present itself in broadly representative samples, because there will be only one or several units from any given population.

Third, dynamical complexity in the ways organizations respond to environments means that observation plans should cover the relevant time frames. If organizations respond slowly to environments or if industrial processes are age dependent or path dependent, then these time frames need to be long. Unfortunately, efforts at representative sampling commonly gather only cross-sectional snapshots (as with the National Organizations Study) because prohibitive investments would usually be required to update the sampling frame on a regular basis. This means, among other things, that representative-sampling schemes find it very difficult to adequately sample vital events such as founding and mortality.[8]

Of course, many empirical studies of organizations stop short of full representation and opt for incorporating organizational diversity by investigating fewer industries but in greater depth. For instance, Hall's (1987) analysis of firm growth rates confines itself to industries in the manufacturing sector. Perhaps the most ambitious of these types of data collection efforts is the Longitudinal Research Database (LRD) of the U.S. Census of Economic Studies. Among others, the highly visible studies of Dunne, Roberts, and Samuelson (1989) and Davis, Haltiwanger, and Schuh (1996) rely on these data, which cover plants in the U.S. manufacturing industries from 1963 to the near present.

These kinds of limited multipopulation observation plans overcome many of the most problematical aspects of representative-sampling schemes. The intensity of the data collection within industries means that researchers can construct relevant measures of environments as a by-product of data collection. Moreover, the narrowed industrial scope usually makes it feasible to lengthen the observation period to several years or even decades, thus allowing examination of dynamic processes. For instance, many researchers who study top management teams use designs like that of Finkelstein and Hambrick (1990), which examined firms in three industries (computer, chemical, and natural gas) over a five-year period.

---

[8] When surveys are used, another serious practical problem of representative sampling involves nonresponse or incomplete sampling. The quality of a sample usually depends heavily on acquiring data on a very high proportion of the units sampled; inability to collect information on a case (nonresponse) is usually not random but systematic. In organizational sampling, the response rate rarely exceeds 50%, and it is very unlikely that units are not excluded in some systematic way. For example, the National Organizations Study could only obtain data on 50.9% of the establishments it drew in its initial sample. Kalleberg et al. (1996) did, however, conduct comparisons of the marginal distribution of their sample with those of the Current Population Survey of the Bureau of Labor Statistics and the General Social Survey. These comparisons suggest that, at least on certain dimensions, the NOS sample is reasonably representative.

Even though they are sometimes referred to as censuses, multipopulation designs usually fall quite far short of full coverage. A very common (but often neglected) limitation concerns *size truncation*. Only organizations above a certain size are included. On this score, even the Census Bureau's LRD file is problematic. It is, first of all, a sample of manufacturing *plants*, not firms. It also is heavily weighted toward only firms with the largest plants: firms with plants of 250 or more employees are followed in their entirety, those with less than 250 but more than 5 employees are sampled but likely excluded over time unless they grow to over 250 and remain there, and those with fewer than five employees are excluded entirely. By the Census Bureau's own assessment these procedures exclude a very large proportion of manufacturing firms, especially small ones. For example, Davis, Haltiwanger, and Schuh (1994, 11) note that

> ...since 1963, Census has excused certain small single-unit plants (i.e., the company contains only one plant) from completing the Census of Manufacturers to reduce respondent burden. These plants ...represent about *one-third* of the manufacturing universe of 350,000 plants and about 4 to 7 percent of manufacturing employment. (emphasis added)

Exclusions such as these mean that industrial variables constructed from the firms in the observation plan will contain measurement error, the extent of the error depending on the exclusion criteria. The vital events of the excluded firms will be missed as well.[9]

By contrast, a single-population study that covers the full history of an organizational population does not suffer from many of these problems. This design has the attractive feature of (potentially) including *every* organization in the population, large or small, long-lived or ephemeral. When data on all organizations can be found, researchers can construct measures of aspects of population structure by aggregating and performing other operations on the file. For instance, many measures of a firm's competitive environment (e.g., number of competitors and proximity on a variety of dimensions) can be constructed in this way, as we show in later chapters. Researchers using the single-population design also usually gain great historical industry-specific knowledge, allowing them to identify and access specialized sources of data as well as to develop coding schemes reflecting the industry's institutional environment.

The comprehensive single-population design possesses other drawbacks. The most obvious, of course, is its inability to allow estimation of the

---

[9] Freeman (1986) claims that most organization theorists blame these limitations on small research budgets, the implicit idea being that with sufficient funding the dream of diverse representative sampling would be realized. The experiences of the Census' LRD project suggest that ample funding alone will not solve these problems.

means and proportions of characteristics of the multipopulation universe. The greatest potential analytical drawback concerns the possibility that the specific population examined behaves peculiarly with respect to the issues of interest. Then, too, there is the danger that a researcher will misinterpret or incorrectly attribute developments in a single industry's history that would readily be seen as otherwise in a multipopulation study. We do not, however, suggest that only one or several industry studies should be conducted. Ideally, comparison of findings across many different population studies makes aberrations obvious and also provides grist for the theory mill. Indeed, such metanalyses often feature critically in the development of cumulative general knowledge. Finally, in the practical realm, single-population studies that reach back over long historical periods often must rely on archival sources that contain little or no systematic information on certain variables potentially of interest.

Tables 5.2 summarizes the main points of our discussion of organizational observation plans. They show the typical properties of the three generic schemes we have examined: (1) the representative sample of diverse organizations drawn from all populations; (2) the multipopulation census design that collects limited temporal data for all but the smallest organizations in several industries; and (3) the comprehensive single-population census that collects complete temporal data on all organizations in the population. Although many other schemes get used in research, we believe that these three generic designs display many of the relevant features that need to be compared to assess trade-offs.

For designing sound research, the central questions that arise from the comparison of designs concern the costs of the trade-offs. Obviously, we believe that, given the current state of knowledge about organizational processes, the gains from increasing organizational diversity in a sample

Table 5.2.   *Typical features of observation plans.*

	Representative sample	Multipop. census	Single-pop. census
Coverage			
Organizational diversity	Great	Limited	Narrow
Temporal coverage	Short	Limited	Complete
Coverage of size distribution	Full	Truncated	Full
Vital events observable	No	With error	Yes
Ability to measure key			
Industrial covariates	Very limited	Limited	High
Institutional covariates	Very limited	Limited	High

beyond that spanning a single population usually do not repay the costs in terms of lost information on critical covariates. Recognizing that this conclusion rests on judgment and intuition, we now turn to an illustration that shows how strongly observation plan might affect theoretical insights from empirical studies. In Chapter 7, after reviewing relevant models and methods, we return to the design trade-off issue. There we use computer simulations to conduct systematic and precise evaluations of the trade-offs in observation plans.

5.3 An Illustration: The Impact of Observation Plans

In Chapter 2, we described an active area of research that we call internal organizational demography. Recall that the bulk of work in this area examines the effects of heterogeneity in the tenure or length of service (LOS) distribution of individuals in organizations. The outcome variables investigated span a variety of phenomena including turnover, innovation, firm growth, and performance. Virtually all of the published studies in this area use a cross-sectional design, often with cross-industry sampling or some other kind of multiple-industry observation plan.[10]

The research program on internal organizational demography posits that LOS heterogeneity affects outcomes by operating through processes such as social integration and cognition. Despite its achievements, the program has conducted only three studies (O'Reilly, Caldwell, and Barnett 1989; Glick, Miller, and Huber 1993; Smith, Smith, Ollian, Sims, O'Bannon, and Scully 1994) that examine directly the explanations used to account for the predicted associations between LOS heterogeneity and outcomes. Collectively, the results of these studies constitute a questionable empirical foundation for the demographic research program. Two of the studies (O'Reilly et al. 1989; Smith et al. 1994) find supporting evidence; but both use small, nonrandom convenience samples with low response rates. Both constitute contributions, but neither would classify as a benchmark empirical study of the kind found in more developed areas of social science. The other study (Glick et al. 1993), perhaps the most ambitious empirical project, finds no supporting evidence.

We regard the questionable empirical support for these theoretical stories as problematic, because a very simple alternative explanation exists for many of the established findings. Although not commonly recognized in research on internal organizational demography, a simple aggregation of individuals with negatively declining turnover rates generates—in the cross section—a positive association between the coefficient of variation

---

[10] This section draws from Carroll and Harrison (1998).

Table 5.3. *Cross-sectional correlations between the coefficient of variation in*
tenure (CV) and turnover in simple aggregates of individuals with simulated
negative tenure-dependent rates of turnover.

Number of persons	Observation window	r(CV, dummy)	r(CV, event count)
		Gompertz model	
5	3 months	0.30	0.29
5	12 months	0.41	0.34
20	3 months	0.27	0.25
20	12 months	0.42	0.38
		Makeham model	
5	3 months	0.22	0.25
5	12 months	0.37	0.29
20	3 months	0.18	0.28
20	12 months	0.08	0.30

Note: Simulations were run for 120 time periods with 1000 trials for each condition. All correlations are statistically significant at the 0.05 level or less. The
dummy variable indicates that a turnover event occurred; the event-count variable records the number of events.
Source: Carroll and Harrison (1998). Copyright © 1998 by Cornell University.
Used by permission.

in tenure (for the set of socially unconnected individuals) and turnover.
Table 5.3 illustrates this built-in cross-sectional relationship by showing
the correlation between LOS heterogeneity (measured by the coefficient
of variation in tenure) and turnover for simulated sets of socially unconnected individuals with tenure-dependent quit rates. It reports findings
from Carroll and Harrison (1998), who simulated the turnover process with
two closely related tenure-dependent functions that are commonly used in
studies of individual turnover and mobility, the Gompertz and Makeham
processes (Chapters 6, 7, and 13). For the Gompertz process, the simulated
model for turnover as a function of tenure (u) is

$$h(u) = 0.20 \exp(-0.15u). \tag{5.1}$$

For the Makeham process, the simulated model is

$$h(u) = 0.025 + 0.20 \exp(-0.15u). \tag{5.2}$$

LOS heterogeneity and turnover are positively correlated in cross sections for all simulations and estimates. (Estimates with other parameter settings support similar conclusions.) Moreover, the similarity of magnitude
of this correlation with those reported in many of the empirical studies

of internal organizational demography raises questions about the substantive explanations offered. The positive correlation arises from the fact that unevenness in a LOS distribution implies that some members have relatively short durations. It is precisely these members who are the most likely to leave in a duration dependent turnover process. Presumably, any duration-dependent process might have a similar built-in spurious relationship with aggregated LOS measures of heterogeneity.[11] In any event, the built-in cross-sectional link between LOS and turnover is especially problematic, because turnover is a frequently studied outcome (see the review by Carroll and Harrison (1998)).

Using a longitudinal observation plan gives a very different view of what processes might lie behind the effects of LOS heterogeneity. For instance, Table 5.4 shows the detailed tenure distribution of a hypothetical (but typical) top-management team over time. The entries represent tenure times of individuals on the team (members). Whenever a demographic event of hiring or exit occurs, the coefficient of variation in LOS changes sharply in the next time period (this simple observation has been confirmed with regressions on simulated data). For example, in Table 5.4, the coefficient of variation in tenure jumps from 0.383 to 0.665 between periods 21 and 22 when one member leaves and is replaced. Of course, the new individual, with a tenure score of 1, replaces an individual with a score of 17.

More generally, Carroll and Harrison's (1998) extensive simulation studies document a strong relationship between demographic events of entry and exit to the team, on the one hand, and measures of LOS heterogeneity, on the other hand. This relationship challenges standard interpretations of the conventional cross-sectional heterogeneity measures (the coefficient of variation in tenure). It implies that effects of diversity get inextricably mixed with dynamic effects of disruption (caused by the comings and goings of team members). To make matters even more complicated, the widely used coefficient of variation of tenure (or any similar diversity measure) is viewed, at various times, as representing the effects of at least three conceptually distinct social processes: socialization, group cohesion, and common historical experiences.

In any given context, all three processes likely operate simultaneously, in different directions (with respect to tenure), and with unknown weights. In other words, the combined effect of all three processes might produce

---

[11] Unobservable heterogeneity has not been dealt with satisfactorily in many studies of internal organizational demography, despite their population-studies orientation (Chapter 2). In fact, this line of research has the odd feature that it possesses the sparseness of formal demography but lacks a clear underlying model. We think that the program would benefit from moving in the direction of formal representation, towards a modeling orientation.

Table 5.4. *Coefficient of variation in tenure (CV) over time for a team with demographic events.*

Period	Tenures at start of period	CV of tenure at start of period	Members departing in period	Tenures of leavers	Members hired in period
11	1,4,5,7,9	0.583	0		0
12	2,5,6,8,10	0.489	1	6	1
13	1,3,6,9,11	0.687	1	1	0
14	4,7,10,12	0.424	0		1
15	1,5,8,11,13	0.628	1	1	1
16	1,6,9,12,14	0.611	0		0
17	2,7,10,13,15	0.546	0		0
18	3,8,11,14,16	0.493	0		0
19	4,9,12,15,17	0.450	0		0
20	5,10,13,16,18	0.414	0		0
21	6,11,14,17,19	0.383	1	17	1
22	1,7,12,15,20	0.665	0		0
23	2,8,13,16,21	0.610	0		0
24	3,9,14,17,22	0.563	0		0
25	4,10,15,18,23	0.522	0		0
26	5,11,16,19,24	0.488	1	5	1
27	1,12,17,20,25	0.609	0		0

Source: Carroll and Harrison (1998). Copyright © 1998 by Cornell University. Used by permission.

nearly any pattern of diversity, and it is impossible to check the possibilities with any confidence.

Carroll and Harrison (1998) do not fully resolve the matter, but they do propose three tenure-based measures that disaggregate these processes. Their suggestions might assist in identifying the social processes that drive the impressive empirical findings of internal organizational demography. Using simulated data, they show that the three proposed measures perform well compared to the conventional, combined measure and that each represents a different source of variation. The measures can be readily implemented with available data. That is, they do not impose additional data requirements.

Use of these measures provides only intermediate solutions on the road to a more complete modeling strategy for internal organizational demography. However, they do serve to push internal organizational demography into examining the dynamic processes underlying LOS diversity. This push will be helpful, we believe, if it moves researchers away from the cross-sectional multipopulation designs common in this field and toward longitudinal designs of one or several populations. (Sørensen (2000a) provides an initial, promising effort in this direction.) As we demonstrate with computer simulations in Chapter 7, targeted longitudinal designs of organizational populations usually provide a stronger empirical base for analyzing organizational dynamics.

6

Analyzing Vital Rates

THIS CHAPTER EXPLAINS recommended ways of analyzing life histories of organizations and testing demographic hypotheses. It discusses how event-history data can be analyzed as realizations of certain stochastic processes and how the vital rates of organizational populations can be estimated. Chapter 7 addresses particular models, especially those that posit that the vital rates vary as functions of time, characteristics of organizations and populations, and environmental variations.

6.1 Event-History Designs

Demographic data on organizations come in many forms. Ideal designs for demographic study of corporations would meet at least two conditions. First, they would record event histories for a meaningful set of organizations. Such data would contain information on the exact times and character of all demographic events experienced over the lifetimes of the organizations in the set. Information on exact timing means that the ordering or sequence of events is known for the life of the individual organization and for the set of organizations under study. By character of events, we mean the qualitative distinctions in the conceptual state space used to define events (e.g., start-up, diversification, dissolution, and acquisition). Second, an ideal design for corporate demography would provide complete and comprehensive coverage of one or more populations of organizations. This means that the event histories are recorded for all organizations in the population from its inception to the time of data collection.

To fix ideas, we begin with a stylized illustrative example of the data that might be produced by such a research design. Table 6.1 summarizes a narrative history of an organizational population with two subgroupings. The narrative is arranged chronologically. Each relevant event has an index (or sequence) number and a date along with information about the

Table 6.1.   *Narrative history of an organizational population with two forms.*

Index	Time	Event
1	15	Org. 1 is founded with ▲ form; this initiates the organizational population.
2	35	Org. 2 enters from another pop. with ♦ form.
3	55	Org. 1 gets absorbed by org. 2.
4	60	Org. 3 is founded with ▲ form.
5	70	Org. 4 enters from another pop. with ▲ form.
6	90	Org. 5 is founded with ▲ form.
7	100	Org. 4 and org. 5 merge to create org. 6.
8	200	Org. 7 is founded with ▲ form.
9	230	Org. 7 changes from ▲ to ♦ form.
10	250	Org. 8 secedes from org. 7.
11	275	Org. 3 disbands.
12	300	Org. 7 disbands.
τ	350	Observation ends.

kind of event that occurred. In this example, the organizations have one of two subforms, denoted by ▲ and ♦. Moreover, organizations begin in one of four ways: founding, entry from another population, start by merger, or secession. They end in three ways: disbanding, merger, or acquisition.

It is helpful to express the narrative information in a graphical form. Figure 6.1 provides such a display, a kind of family tree of the illustrative population. The time lines in this figure represent the lifetimes of identifiable, autonomous organizations. The length of a line indicates the length of the lifetime. So the topmost line in the figure (firm 1) represents a firm that begins at time t_1 and ends at time t_3 (when it gets acquired by firm 2). The fact that firm 2's time line continues but firm 1's does not indicates that the former continues as an independent organization but the latter does not. The time τ tells when the observation plan ends: nothing can be observed beyond τ.

The marks at the start of a lifeline in Figure 6.1 distinguish between two forms of entry: a vertical line denotes a founding and a circle denotes entry from another population. Start by merger appears as a new line running from two organizations. Finally, a start by a split from an existing organization appears as a line diverging from the time line of another organization. The three kinds of ending events in the narrative history are represented as follows. A disbanding of an organization is indicated by the end of a time line without a tie to any other organization. When an organization ends by absorption, its time line ends with a vertical line tying it to the absorbing organization. Finally, an end by merger appears as a vertical line tying the ends of two organizations' lifelines.

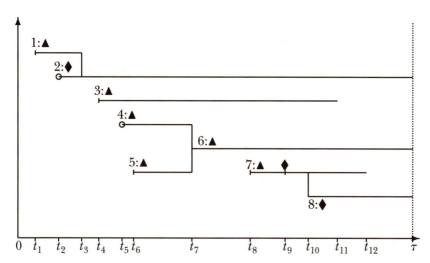

Figure 6.1. *Illustrative life-history data for organizations based on the narrative in Table 6.1.*

The geometric shapes above each line denote each organization's subform as noted above. In the illustrative example, only firm 7 changes its form (from the triangle to the diamond form).

As we noted above, the vertical dotted line at time τ in Figure 6.1 represents an arbitrary times of cessation of observation. Because firms 2, 6, and 8 persist as independent corporations at τ, their histories are right censored by the design.

Starting Events

Different forms of data are needed for analyzing the starting and ending events. Ending events (and their absence) can be associated with identifiable organizations at risk of experiencing the event. In other words, the unit of observation for ending events is the individual organization.

In contrast, the occurrence and nonoccurrence of entries cannot be associated meaningfully with properties of the individual organizations observed to enter. This is because nonevents—the absence of entries during some interval—provide just as much information about the process as do the observed entries during an interval. Meaningful estimation of an arrival process must use information about entries and the absence of entries within periods or geographical units. The two kinds of information must be treated alike. Here we have the reason why properties of entering firms cannot be used to explain the arrival process: one cannot describe the organization involved in the absence of a founding at some time. Thus, entries should be regarded as *population-level or economy-level events*.

Two strategies for analyzing the beginnings of organizations need to be distinguished. One strategy seeks to analyze the *emergence* of a population and subsequent starts of organizations within it. For instance, one might want to analyze the appearance of the first commercial bank within some economy and the subsequent foundings of other commercial banks. In such an analysis, the organizational population itself is not a meaningful unit of analysis for the reasons discussed in the previous paragraph: the absence of emergences needs to be considered on a par with observed emergences. Instead, some sector of the economy or an organizational community stands as the relevant unit for analysis of founding processes. (The sector might be the whole economy or community.) This approach, which we call sectoral analysis, appears to be the natural one for addressing questions about the rise of new kinds of variability.

The second strategy, which we call population-level analysis, takes as given the time of the first founding. That is, it does not attempt to explain the origin of the organizational population. Instead, it addresses the variations in the flow of entries that follow the first appearance of the population (the first entry).

Thus we might follow two approaches in empirical analysis: (1) treat a sector of the economy or a community as the unit and analyze the timing of first and subsequent foundings of each population of organizations; or (2) condition on the appearance of the first organization in a population and analyze the timing of subsequent foundings within the population.

Most empirical work in corporate demography takes the second approach. It seems that this choice reflects the difficulty of assigning a meaningful starting time of the process in the case of sectoral analysis. For example, at what point does France, the pioneer in the automobile industry, become meaningfully at risk of giving rise to the first automobile manufacturing firm? Is it when the steam engine is invented?[1] Is it when the first gasoline engines are invented? Any answer to this question seems at least partly arbitrary.

Luckily, the situation is not always so complicated. For example, in the case of semiconductor manufacturers (or any other kind of firm whose identity gets defined in terms of a particular technical development), one can meaningfully assume that the invention of the technology for producing semiconductors begins the process. The length of time from invention (or perhaps licensing) of the product or process until the first founding of an organization specialized to using it has substantive meaning.

For both of the main forms of analysis, an appropriate state space for the stochastic process is the set of nonnegative integers, by which one can

---

[1] The historical record reveals numerous experiments to drive farm wagons with steam engines at least fifty years before the acknowledged start of the automobile industry.

count the number of foundings. Any organizational entry process might be regarded as an *arrival process*. Such a process counts the number of arrivals to some state, such as events of radioactive decay, arrivals to a waiting line, cell divisions, and births. In the case of foundings and other kinds of entries, we analyze the distribution of *interarrival times*.

Suppose we are interested in the flow of entries in historical time and do not want to distinguish the various forms of entry. Then a figure like Figure 6.2 would provide the relevant information. This figure (built from information in Table 6.1 and Figure 6.1 on the times of entries) displays the cumulative number of entries by historical time. The times noted on the horizontal axis tell when entries were recorded. The slope of this plot over an interval of historical time gives the entry rate during that interval. (Of course, given the ruggedness of the plot, one would have to use some way of smoothing the data to obtain a meaningful estimate of the slope.)

Analysts often think that different causal processes affect the rates of occurrence of the different kinds of entry, and they do not want to aggregate all kinds in one count. So, for instance, one might focus on the founding process (the subclass of entry events given by foundings rather than by lateral entry or other types of entry). Figure 6.3 gives the cumulative count of foundings in historical time for the illustrative population.

As we explain below, researchers ordinarily do not use historical time as the primary clock in analyzing entry processes. Instead, they focus on the distribution of interarrival times (and control for historical time). This

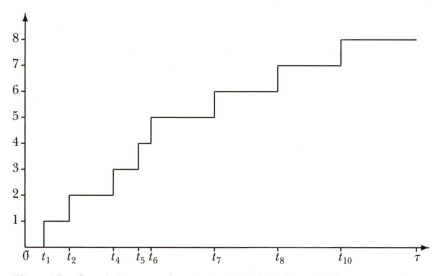

Figure 6.2. *Cumulative count of entries (of all kinds) in historical time corresponding to the population life history in Table 6.1.*

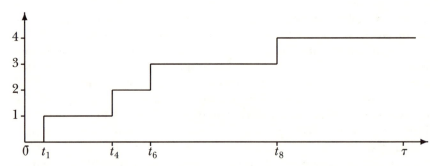

Figure 6.3. *Cumulative count of foundings in historical time corresponding to the population life history in Table 6.1.*

focus allows researchers to examine the possibility that the occurrence of entries depends upon the flow of entries, and especially on the time elapsed since the previous entry in a population.

The interfounding times (times between successive foundings) in Table 6.1 are $u_1 = t_4 - t_1$, $u_2 = t_6 - t_4$, $u_3 = t_8 - t_6$, and (right-censored) $u_4 = \tau - t_8$. Figure 6.4 shows a standard way to display the distribution of interarrival times and other measures of duration. The vertical axis in this figure records the complement of the cumulative distribution function of the interarrival time, usually called the survivor function, as we explain below. The slope of this function provides information about the rate as a function of the time elapsed since the previous event.

Data available to researchers do not always contain such complete information. In many cases, coverage of a population in a data source begins many years after the emergence of the population, as we noted above. Such observation plans are said to be left truncated with respect to the entry process. For instance, if the observation window on the process

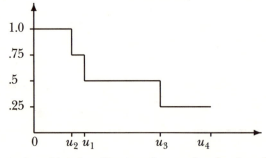

Figure 6.4. *Proportion of interfounding times that exceed u, based on the population life history in Table 6.1.*

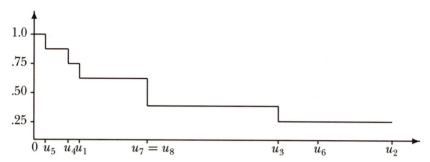

Figure 6.5. *Proportion of organizational lifetimes that exceed u, based on the population life history in Table 6.1.*

in Table 6.1 begins at some time after t_1, then several of the interarrival times are left truncated for each kind of starting event.

Ending Events

The information in Table 6.1 relevant to analyzing ending events also consists of the dates of each vital event and the kinds of events that took place. Although one could analyze ending events in historical time, analysts almost always focus on a different clock, one that tracks a dimension of organizational lifetimes. (We discuss several possible clocks below.) Then relevant information is contained in the collection of lengths of lifetimes or, more generally, distributions of durations, and the information on the types of starting and ending events.

Suppose that an analyst is interested in the clock that simply measures the lengths of lifetimes and does not want to distinguish among the various kinds of ending events. The shortest tenure in Table 6.1, ten time units, is for organization 5 which was founded at $t_6 = 90$ and ended by merger at $t_7 = 100$. We write this as $u_5 = t_7 - t_6$, and we note that an ending event is observed.[2] Organization 1's tenure is observed to end at $u_1 = t_3 - t_1 = 40$. Other cases are still alive when observation ends. So, for instance, organization 2 entered the population at $t_2 = 35$ and has not yet ended by $\tau = 350$. So we record that $u_2 = \tau - t_2 = 315$ and we note that no ending event was observed. Figure 6.5 contains the complement of the cumulative distribution of lengths of lifetimes (as independent corporations)—the survivor function—derived from the illustrative data in Table 6.1.

The basic strategy in mortality analysis involves exploring how and why the distributions of lengths of lifetimes (or other relevant durations)

---

[2]As we explain below in discussing alternative clocks for corporate demography, we denote times that refer to the operation of a demographic process by u. In the last subsection, u referred to interarrival time; here it refers to organizational age.

Table 6.2. *Illustrative data file for population members described in Table 6.1 and Figure 6.1.*

Org.	Start time	End time	Waiting time	Start state	Org. form	End state
1	15	55	40	11	▲	22
2	35	350	315	12	◆	12
3	60	275	215	11	▲	21
4	70	100	30	12	▲	23
5	90	100	10	11	▲	23
6	100	350	250	13	▲	13
7	200	230	30	11	▲	24
7	230	300	70	15	◆	21
8	250	350	100	14	◆	14

State space:

1*x*: in operation
    11: started by founding;
    12: started by lateral entry;
    13: started by merger;
    14: started by secession;
    15: changed form.

2*x*: no longer in operation
    21: exited via disbanding
    22: exited via acquisition
    23: exited via merger
    24: changed form

vary. In corporate demography, researchers typically investigate how these distributions are shaped by the types of starting events, characteristics of organizational form, and environmental conditions (Chapter 9). These analyses commonly involve specification of types of starting and ending events as well as specification of covariates; they might also entail specification of assumptions about unmeasured factors.

It might be helpful to see how life-history data are normally entered into an analysis file (for event-history analysis). Table 6.2 shows such a file.[3] Note that each organization's lifetime produces one record in the file, except for Org. 7, which experiences a form-change event and remains in the population. Note that we have coded "origin" and "destination" states. We have followed the convention (implemented in most relevant software as the default) that right-censored cases are indicated by the fact that the destination is the same as the origin (nothing relevant has yet changed).

---

[3] As we explain in Chapter 7, most analysis files are actually more complicated. When the covariates used in analysis change over time, analysts typically "split spells" and update covariates at the start of each subspell. A split-spell data file would therefore contain many more records than the kind of file we are illustrating here.

Demographic Clocks

Before undertaking demographic analysis of events, it is helpful to recognize the multiplicity of possible "clocks" available to record time and the principles that analysts use to choose among them. In discussing the illustrative population history above, we used two different clocks in representing the processes of entry and founding: historical time and inter-arrival time. In organizational demography, several clocks usually deserve attention. For instance, analysis of mortality processes often considers organizational age and the age of the population (Chapter 13). And, as the illustrative history shows, one can analyze mortality as a function of an organization's age or its tenure in a (form-defined) population.

Specifying a stochastic process for vital events requires the choice of a master clock for recording the flow of events. In contrast to human demography in which age normally serves this role, corporate demography measures the passage of time in a variety of ways. Two classes should be distinguished: external clocks and process clocks.

Historical time is external: the time scale does not depend upon any events in the population. That is, one does not have to know anything about the evolution of the organizational population to calibrate historical time. Population (or industry) age can also be regarded as externally given, even though it is initiated by an organizational event (the first emergence of an organization of a given form in the localized system of interest or the emergence of the first firm in an industry). Population age can be considered external in the sense that, given the knowledge of the initiation of the population or industry, the clock runs independently of events in the population (or industry). Indeed, it is nothing more than a linear transformation of the historical clock (set to zero at the initiation of the population).

Organizational age and tenure in a population are both process clocks. Each measure is defined with reference to the durations between events to organizations. An organization's completed age records the difference between the (historical) time of its ending and the time of its start. Likewise, the clock that records the timing between arrivals, such as foundings or entries, is a process clock.

Both external and process clocks play a role in corporate demography. Most prior research in this field has used some process clock as the basis of analysis. When researchers take a population perspective, process clocks are more informative than external ones. So research that collects life histories of firms within clearly defined populations invariably uses organizational age or tenure in the industry as the master clock in analyses of mortality processes. Research on foundings and entry from a population perspective most often measures the passage of time in terms of the duration between successive entries.

To help clarify the nature of the various time measures in this book, we follow a simple convention. When the difference matters substantively, we denote readings from external clocks by t (and sometimes s) and those from process clocks by u (and sometimes v).

6.2 Stochastic-Process Models

Analyses of the flows of entries and exits in an organizational population build (implicitly or explicitly) on probability models. That is, researchers regard the occurrences of vital events as realizations of a stochastic process. In formulating stochastic-process models for vital events, investigators face a number of choices.

One basic choice concerns the temporal structure of the process, whether to regard time as discrete or continuous (in addition to which clock to use). Research on corporate demography uses both options. The choice often seems driven by the form of the observation plan. When information on exact timing of events can be found, researchers usually adopt the assumption that time is continuous, that events can occur at any time. But, when data are aggregated in time, e.g., the observation plan records only the year of an event, then many researchers adopt the assumption that time is discrete, that events occur only at fixed intervals.

Allowing the form of the data to determine the probabilistic model, though common practice in the social sciences, hinders the cumulation of knowledge over studies. It makes patterns in results hard to identify, by hindering comparisons across studies. This means that patterns will be harder to discern across studies even when the organizational world operates by simple rules. It would be far better for researchers to use a common probabilistic structure (adapted to take account of the exact form of their data). A considerable body of research finds that vital events in organizational populations can and do occur at *any* time. Therefore, we argue that considerations of realism in representing processes favor the use of continuous-time models (Tuma and Hannan 1984).

A second basic choice in model building involves the assumptions made about the role of randomness, whether to use deterministic or stochastic formulations. Research in corporate demography usually assumes that the occurrence and timing of mergers, changes of forms, and dissolutions are affected by a large number of factors other than those emphasized in general theories. Stochastic models, which reflect the operation of the set of excluded factors that affect the rate, are needed to describe these histories.

Combining our preferred choices on the two basic questions about timing and randomness, we argue for assuming that the organizational histories under study are realizations of continuous-time, discrete-state stochastic processes. This class of processes has played a productive role in dynamic analyses of many kinds of social phenomena (Coleman 1964; Tuma and Hannan 1984).

The principal methods for analyzing such processes empirically are called *event-history* and *event-count* methods. As we noted in the first section of this chapter, an event-history (or sample-path) observation plan records information on all changes in state within some observation period. In the case of ending events, let $Y(s)$ denote the random variable indicating an organization's state at time s (measured by any of the relevant clocks) and let $y(s)$ denote a particular realization of this random variable. For instance, $Y(s)$ might denote the distinction between "dead" ($Y(s) = 1$) and "alive" ($Y(s) = 0$), or it might denote which of a set of alternate forms an organization displays.

The set of all the distinct possible values of $Y(s)$ constitutes the state space of the process. For applications in corporate demography, the qualitative variables have a countable number of states. In the case of mortality, the number of possible ending states is usually small, e.g., the four possibilities noted above.

For starting events, the relevant random variable, $X(u)$, counts the cumulative number of entries by time u (assuming that we are considering a process time measure). Again, $x(u)$ denotes a particular realization of this random variable: the observed number of entries by time u. In this case, the set of natural numbers serves as a reasonable choice for the state space.

The period of time between successive events is usually called a *spell* or *episode*. The nth spell refers to the period between the $(n-1)$th and nth events. The length of time from event $n-1$ until event n is called the *waiting time* to the nth event. We usually refer to the waiting time until an event as the *duration* in a state.

In analyses of organizational mortality, the relevant duration measures the length of an organization's existence in the population. When social codes defining forms are very strongly enforced and organizations cannot change forms without paying a big penalty in terms of evaluations (as explained in Chapter 4), then the costs of migration (changing form and thus changing population) are high and migration should be uncommon. If migration is low, then duration is nearly equivalent with age. When migration is common, then tenure in the population can differ from age. In analyses of organizational entries, the waiting time or duration measures the time elapsed since the previous entry. Such a duration is often called an interarrival time.

Event histories can be described using a number of parameters (or functions of the underlying stochastic processes) such as hazards, transition probabilities, waiting times, and so forth. We concentrate on *hazards*. This section explains the advantages of analyzing effects on hazards and describes the models and methods used to analyze event histories. It also shows how event-history data can be used to estimate causal parameters and to test demographic hypotheses when data are censored.

More detailed treatments of most of the matters discussed here and of the advantages of the general approach can be found in Tuma and Hannan (1984) and Blossfeld and Rohwer (1996). Good technical references include Kalbfleisch and Prentice (1980), Lancaster (1990), and Cox and Oakes (1984). A thorough but challenging account of the modern counting process formulation for such analyses can be found in Andersen, Borgan, Gill, and Keiding (1993). A wonderful software package for event-history analysis (and many other kinds of analysis relevant for corporate demography) is Transition Data Analysis (TDA 6.2). The freeware program and an extremely extensive manual are available (Rohwer and Pötter 1998).[4]

Single-Origin, Single-Destination Processes

We start with the simplest case: a process for only one kind of event. The prototypical instance in demography involves "mortality without regard to cause."[5] Standard life tables, calculations of life expectancy, and related statistics are based on analysis of single-destination processes. In corporate demography, the parallel case involves exit from a population "without regard to the type of event."

The case of organizational entries also fits. Each entry might be regarded as an instance of the same kind of event, and the process simply counts repetitions of this type of event. In each case, all of the relevant information about the stochastic process is contained in the distribution of the random variable (U) that tells the length of the spell. As noted above, we assume that this random variable has a continuous distribution.

It is conventional to summarize the distribution of durations (of either type) in terms of the survivor function:

$$G(u) = 1 - F(u) = \Pr\{U \geq u\}. \tag{6.1}$$

Associated with the survivor function is a density function:

$$f(u) = -\frac{dG(u)}{du}.$$

---

[4] The TDA program and associated manual and materials can be accessed from Professor Rohwer's site on the world wide web at http://www.ruhr-uni-bochum.de/sowi.

[5] This means ignoring the difference between accidental death and death from so-called natural causes as well as ignoring the differences within the two types.

The survivor function tells about the global behavior of the process in the sense that it records the cumulative probability of surviving over successively longer intervals. Ordinarily we want to focus on the local behavior of the process. In this context, this means focusing on the hazard, a parameter that tells the rate at which events occur very near (just after) some time point:

$$h(u) = \lim_{\epsilon \downarrow 0} \frac{\Pr\{u \le U < u + \epsilon \mid U \ge u\}}{\epsilon}.$$

The hazard is a fundamental parameter: many other interesting features of a set of event histories can be expressed as functions of the hazard (Cox and Oakes 1984; Tuma and Hannan 1984).

By the definition of conditional probability, the hazard can be expressed as

$$h(u) = \frac{f(u)}{G(u)} = -\frac{1}{G(u)} \frac{dG(u)}{du} = -\frac{d \ln G(u)}{du}. \tag{6.2}$$

Solving the differential equation in (6.2), with initial condition $G_j(0) = 1$, gives the so-called integrated hazard function:

$$H(u) = -\ln G(u) = \int_0^u h(s) \, ds. \tag{6.3}$$

Equation (6.3) shows that the hazard defines the survivor function, and vice versa. This relationship proves important in empirical analysis, because the survivor function can usually be estimated from available data, as we show below.

Multiple-Origin, Single-Destination Processes

Next consider multiple origins. Suppose that the theoretical and substantive motivations for an analysis dictate that the hazard of a certain event depends on how a unit entered the population. For instance, analysis of the life histories of corporations in a population routinely distinguishes between those firms founded as new corporations in that population, those that entered from other populations, and those that began by merger of firms in the population. Research usually reveals that mortality rates are higher for newly founded firms than for those that enter by merger or migration from another population.

How can the effect of origin on the hazard be taken into account? The standard approach generalizes the setup for the single-origin case to allow multiple origins. Instead of the single (overall) survivor function, we define a survivor function for each origin state:

$$G_j(u) = \Pr\{U > u \mid y(0) = j\}, \qquad j = 1, \ldots, J.$$

The corresponding origin-specific hazards and integrated hazards are

$$h_j(u) = -\frac{d \ln G_j(u)}{du},$$

and

$$H_j(u) = -\ln G_j(u) = \int_0^u h_j(s)\,ds.$$

Empirical analysis for this case parallels that of the single origin case but with estimation performed separately for each origin state. In the language of multivariate statistics, the strategy of distinguishing several origin states and allowing the parameters of the stochastic process to differ by origin state amounts to allowing full interaction by origin.

The top and middle panels in Table 6.3 compare estimates of a multiple-origin specification with the single-origin one, which ignores differences among types of origins. The population considered is the set of

Table 6.3. *Estimates of constant-hazard models of mortality in the French automobile industry, 1885–1981, for various state spaces (duration is tenure in the industry measured in years).*

Specification	$\widehat{\alpha}$
Single-origin, single-destination:	
Event: firm ended as an autonomous automobile manufacturing firm	0.181
Multiple-origin, single-destination:	
Event: firm ended as an autonomous automobile manufacturing firm	
Origin:	
New firm (de novo)	0.233
Entrant from another industry (de alio)	0.110
Firm resulting from events to other automobile mfg. firms (de ipso)	0.098
Single-origin, multiple-destination:	
Type of ending event:	
Disbanded	0.014
Exited to another industry	0.019
Merged	0.003
Acquired	0.011
Taken over by creditors	0.001
Other	0.002
Disappeared from the record	0.131

firms that ever manufactured automobiles in France. We have records on 828 firms. All but 33 of these firms had ended their spells as automobile manufacturers by 1981 when the data are right censored by the ending of coverage of the most comprehensive source of data.

Three kinds of origins are both common and substantively interesting. These are what we call de novo entries: firms appear in the record for the first time as automobile manufacturers; de alio entries: firms start in some other industry before migrating to the automobile industry; and de ipso entries: firms with some prior history in the automobile industry begin as autonomous automobile manufacturing firms (by reentering the industry, starting as a merger of automobile manufacturers, secession of part of an automobile manufacturing firm, or a restart using the assets of a bankrupt automobile firm).

The top panel in Table 6.3 shows that the overall hazard of ending (ignoring type of starting event) is 0.181 (per year). The panel breaks out the hazards by origin. It shows that life chances differed substantially by type of origin. Firms that enter de novo have by far the poorest life chances. Their hazard of ending is more than double that of firms that enter by the other two routes. The hazards of mortality for de alio and de ipso entrants differ only slightly, with the latter having a lower rate.

Multiple-Origin, Multiple-Destination Processes

Now consider the general case of research that distinguishes several origins and several destinations. For example, corporate demographers recognize that organizations might leave a population by disbanding, by merging with another, or by changing form; and many of the relevant substantive arguments hold that different processes hold for different outcomes. Unlike the shift from single-origin to multiple-origin models, introducing multiple destinations makes a real difference for the probability model. It no longer suffices to consider a single random variable U that records the length of lifetime (or tenure in a population).

Instead, we must consider the joint distribution of the random variables telling the time of the transition and the specific destination (or type of event). This joint distribution can be specified in terms of the separate instantaneous transition rates:

$$r_{jk}(u) = \lim_{\epsilon \downarrow 0} \frac{\Pr\{u \leq U < u + \epsilon, Y(u + \epsilon) = k \mid U \geq u, Y(u) = j\}}{\epsilon}. \quad (6.4)$$

Much empirical work in corporate demography estimates such rates. Below we show how such rates can be estimated meaningfully by maximum likelihood (ML) from event-history data.

Although specification of the joint distribution in terms of transition rates has most direct value for empirical research in corporate demography, it is not the only meaningful parameterization. Another common way of specifying the joint distribution of (U, Y) relies on the notion of competing risks. If moves to Ψ different destinations (risks) can occur, each organization can be thought of as having Ψ unobserved or latent waiting times, one for each destination. Let these latent random variables be denoted by U_{jk}^*. The conditional survivor function for a particular destination is defined in terms of the corresponding latent waiting time:

$$G_{jk}(u) = \Pr\{U_{jk}^* \geq u\}, \qquad j = 1, \ldots, J.$$

If no event has occurred before some t, this means that $U_{jk}^* \geq u$ for all k. Unless we note otherwise, we assume that the Ψ processes are independent. Notice that:

$$G_j(u) = \prod_{k=1}^{\Psi} G_{jk}(u),$$

when the competing risks are independent. These conditional survivor functions (sometimes called pseudo survivor functions) can be estimated meaningfully only in the case of independence of competing risks (Tsiatis 1978). Thus they do not provide generally useful descriptions of a population process in empirical applications (where the assumption of independence often strains credulity).

The nonidentifiability of the pseudo survivor functions, $G_j(u)$, often causes confusion about the estimation of transition rates. It might seem that one must assume independence of competing risks to estimate transition rates, but this is not so. Estimation of the hazards (or transition rates) as defined in (6.4) does *not* require the assumption of independence of competing risks. That is, the possibility of nonindependence of competing risks does not affect the identifiability of transition rates (Kalbfleisch and Prentice 1980; Cox and Oakes 1984).

The bottom panel in Table 6.3 shows the result of distinguishing several ending events for the population of French automobile manufacturers. In the most common form of ending, a firm ceases to produce automobiles and drops from the record. For the 574 firms with this kind of history, we cannot tell whether the firm ceased to exist as an autonomous firm or continued in some other industry. In the other cases, we can distinguish disbandings (62 events), mergers (13 events), acquisitions by another firm (46 events), exit to another industry (82 events), and several other types (takeover by creditors, nationalization, and destruction by war), which we combine in the category "other" (18 events). The estimated rates of the

Table 6.4. *Estimates of constant-hazard models of mortality in the French automobile industry, 1885–1981, for selected multiple-origin, multiple-destination models (duration is tenure in the industry measured in years).*

	Type of origin		
Ending Event	De novo	De alio	De ipso
Disbanded	0.013	0.011	0.031
Exited to another industry	0.009	0.041	0.010
Disappeared from the record	0.197	0.042	0.018

various kinds of ending, of course, reflect these counts. The rate of disappearance runs many times higher than the rates of the other kinds of ending events.

We have already seen that type of origin affects the life chances of automobile manufacturing firms. So it makes sense to use processes with multiple origins and multiple destinations in analyzing their life histories. Table 6.4 reports estimates of the rates of transition from the three relevant origins to three of the destinations: disbanding, exit to another industry, and disappearance. Note that the firms that enter from another industry (de alio entrants) have a much higher rate of leaving the automobile industry for another industry than do the firms with other kinds of entry. Firms that begin spells of automobile production as either de novo or de ipso entrants have nearly the same (much lower) rate of moving to another industry. In this sense, it appears that the event of disappearance falls closer substantively to disbanding than to exit. That is, it seems likely that the firms that disappeared tended to fail as firms rather than migrate.

6.3 Life-Table Estimation

This section begins our sketch of the standard approach to estimation of vital rates from event-history and event-count data. Although we might begin with the case of complete data, this case has little application in corporate demography. Data on entries and exits are invariably incomplete. In empirical research on entries, an analyst cannot know with certainty that a process has ended and that no subsequent entries are possible. All of the organizational populations whose mortality experience has been analyzed have one or more surviving members in the data set. In both cases, the data sets analyzed are censored on the right.

Right censoring turns out to be a manageable problem given assumptions that are usually plausible. Analysis is especially straightforward when right censoring is *noninformative* about the process. This means that censoring might depend upon the past but not on the future (Andersen et al. 1993). In this case, knowing that a case is censored does not provide any information about the length of its (uncensored) duration. In the most common case in corporate demography, right censoring arises from the ending of the observation scheme. Sometimes, as with our studies on the world automobile industry, observation ends when a key source of data stops its coverage. In others, the source of information continues but the researcher stops collecting data so as to begin analysis. The decision by the investigator or the producer of the basic data to stop collecting the data does not depend on the durations of the spells, and censoring can therefore safely be considered to be noninformative.

Much of human demography constructs and interprets life tables. A life table relates some dimension of duration to the probability of survival. Two forms of estimation of the life table have wide currency: the actuarial and the product-limit estimators (Cox and Oakes 1984).

Actuarial Estimation

The actuarial estimator is the workhorse of human demography. With it, analysis focuses on counts of events within preselected periods. One chooses a temporal dimension for arraying events. In human demography, age normally serves as the basic dimension. (In contrast, the basic dimension in corporate demography might be any of the clocks we have discussed.) The analyst then picks a set of breakpoints on the chosen time axis. These points define the ranges of the intervals for grouping the events:

$$0 \leq \tau_1 < \tau_2 < \cdots < \tau_P.$$

Demographic analysis adopts the convention that $\tau_P = \infty$, which means that there are P intervals (open on the right):

$$I_p = \{t : \tau_p \leq t < \tau_{p+1}\}, \qquad p = 1, \ldots, P.$$

We need counters for the number of spells that experience events and undergo censoring within each interval:

$$N_p = \text{number of spells that enter } I_p;$$

$$E_p = \text{number of spells with events in } I_p;$$

$$C_p = \text{number of spells censored in } I_p.$$

The relations among these three counters are given by $N_1 = N$ (where N denotes the number of spells under study) and $N_p = N_{p-1} - E_{p-1} - C_{p-1}$.

We want to define survivor functions and hazards in terms of these quantities. However, right censoring introduces an ambiguity. How should we treat the experience of censored cases? In particular, should censored cases be regarded as having faced the risk of experiencing the event for the whole interval or only a part of it?

The classic actuarial approach adopts the convention of assuming that the censored cases on average experienced this risk for half of the interval. We can implement this assumption by defining the set of cases at risk of experiencing the event (the risk set) appropriately. That is, the standard actuarial approach defines the risk set for an interval as

$$R_p = N_p - \frac{C_p}{2}.$$

With this assumption in hand, the life-table estimate of the probability that a spell survives an interval is

$$\widehat{p}_p = 1 - \frac{E_p}{R_p},$$

and the survivor function is

$$\widehat{G}_1 = 1 \quad \text{and} \quad \widehat{G}_p = \widehat{p}_p \widehat{G}_{p-1}.$$

For all save the last interval, a discrete-time estimator of the hazard is

$$\widehat{h}_p = \frac{\widehat{f}_p}{\widetilde{G}_p},$$

with the density and survivor functions evaluated at the midpoint of the interval:

$$\widehat{f}_p = \frac{\widehat{G}_{p-1} - \widehat{G}_p}{\tau_{p+1} - \tau_p},$$

and

$$\widetilde{G}_p = \frac{\widehat{G}_p - \widehat{G}_{p+1}}{2}.$$

We introduce data on another corporate population at this point to illustrate life tables and other methods described in this chapter. Joon Han (1998) compiled a population life history with unusually detailed coverage of exact dates of start and finish. The population consists of all banks that have ever operated in Japan over the history of the industry. We use here the subset of banks in the Tokyo prefecture, because banking was localized over its early years. This subset contains information on 310 firms. The growth and decline in the density of this population is shown in Figure 6.6.

In analyzing founding processes, Han (1998) concentrates on the period running from the inception of the population in 1873 until 1926 when

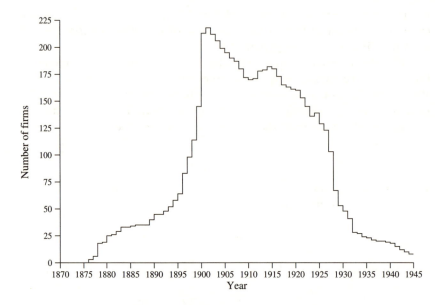

Figure 6.6. *Number of banks in the Tokyo prefecture, 1873–1945. Source: Han (1998). Copyright © 1998 by Joon Han. Used by permission.*

bank panics led to tight government controls on the system, which pushed the founding rate to zero. During 1873–1926, 270 banks were founded. Figure 6.7 shows how this process unfolded in historical time. It plots the cumulative number of foundings by historical time. Increments in the count tell the exact time of foundings. The slope of the curve tells the founding rate. Note that the founding process was incredibly intense in the last years of the nineteenth century, for which the slope runs nearly vertical. The process slowed dramatically near 1900, and it continued at a slow pace thereafter.

The surge of foundings of banks in Tokyo during 1890–1900 appears to reflect a contagious process, meaning that the occurrence of foundings stimulated other foundings. We examine this possibility by shifting the time dimension from historical time to interarrival time. The records of founding times for the 270 banks provide 270 interarrival times: 269 uncensored spells between the observed foundings and a last right-censored spell that runs from the time of the last founding observed in this historical period and the end of 1926.

Does the founding rate vary with the time since the previous event? If the process is contagious, then the rate would be high just after an event and then decline with duration. In other words, the duration dependence would be (monotonic) negative. However, other possibilities need to be

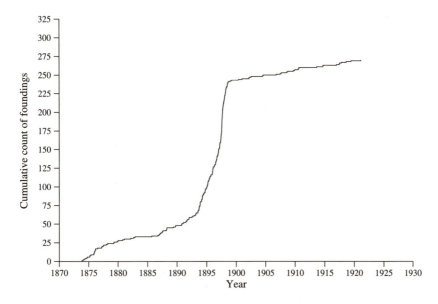

Figure 6.7. *Flow of Tokyo bank foundings over time, 1873–1926.*

considered. Duration dependence in vital rates might be (monotonic) positive or have some complicated nonmonotonic form.

One way to describe the duration dependence in the founding rate is by constructing a life table in interarrival times. To start, we must choose the breakpoints of the time axis for constructing the life table. Human demography has strong conventions about this choice that make it seem unproblematic. In analyzing human mortality, for instance, demographers invariably use life tables defined over five-year age classes. At present, corporate demography lacks such conventions. How should we proceed? Two principles apply here. First, the chosen breakpoints ought to match shifts in the underlying hazard. (If the hazard stays constant over the whole interval, then only the second principle applies.) Second, each interval (defined by the breakpoints) must contain at least one event (for the interval to contribute). This means that intervals generally have to be wider in regions of the time interval in which events are sparse.

With these considerations in mind, we break the interarrival times at 2, 5, 10, 25, 50, and 75 days. Table 6.5 presents the actuarial estimate of the life table for foundings that results from this choice. Note that the median waiting time between foundings (or half-life of a spell), given when $\widehat{G}_p$=.50, falls between the 10-day and 25-day breakpoints; its actual estimate is 12 days. And many durations are very short. For instance, just over 15% of the spells last one or two days (shown by the drop in $\widehat{G}_p$ in the first two

Table 6.5. *Actuarial estimates of the life table for foundings of Tokyo banks, 1873–1926 (duration is the interarrival time measured in days).*

Start	Midpoint	N_p	Censored (C_p)	Events (E_p)	$\widehat{G}_p$	$\widehat{h}_p$
0	1.0	270	0	41	1.000	0.082
2	3.5	229	0	48	0.848	0.078
5	7.5	181	0	40	0.669	0.050
10	17.5	141	0	44	0.520	0.025
25	37.5	97	0	29	0.357	0.014
50	62.5	68	0	18	0.249	0.012
75		50	1	49	0.182	0.012

Median duration (half life) $= 12.0$

periods). The last column of the table shows that the hazard of founding declines sharply with the time since the previous founding. That is, this founding process displays negative duration dependence.

Now consider the mortality process. Recall the founding process stopped in the early 1920s (to resume again after World War II with the banking reorganization imposed by the occupation authorities). The mortality process, however, did not stop. So we follow Han (1998) and examine mortality rates over the period from 1873 to 1945. We analyze a combined mortality event, one that combines several distinguishable events: failure, acquisition, and merger to create a new bank. Although only 270 banks were founded over this period, 60 more banks were created as the result of merger. So 310 banks existed at one time or another in Tokyo between 1873 and 1945.

The pattern and time scale for mortality of Tokyo banks differ considerably from those for founding. The relevant clock is age (not interarrival time), and the relevant time scale is years (not days). Table 6.6 reports the estimated life table for this mortality process. The half-life (median duration) of Tokyo banks falls between 20 and 25 years; its estimate is 24 years. That is, half of the banks last at least as long as 24 years. Unlike the case for the founding process, the survivor function for mortality does not drop steeply near the origin of the process. Instead, the decline in this function appears to be nearly linear. The implications of this pattern are seen more easily when we switch from the survivor function to the hazard.

Product-Limit Estimation

The classic actuarial life-table approach requires temporal aggregation of events into periods. Such aggregation has two disadvantages. First, like any

Table 6.6. *Actuarial estimate of the life table for mortality of Tokyo banks, 1873–1945 (duration is age measured in years).*

Start	Midpoint	N_p	Censored (C_p)	Events (E_p)	$\widehat{G}_p$	$\widehat{h}_p$
0	2.5	310	9	26	1.000	0.018
5	7.5	275	3	37	0.915	0.029
10	12.5	235	2	26	0.791	0.024
15	17.5	207	7	35	0.703	0.038
20	22.5	165	3	29	0.582	0.039
25	27.5	133	0	46	0.479	0.084
30	40.0	87	4	72	0.313	0.073
50		11	1	10	0.048	0.073

Median duration (half life) = 24.0

other kind of aggregation, it provides only a rough description of the underlying data. Second, different analysts might choose different intervals for calculating life tables (in the absence of a strong convention). This would make it hard to compare patterns across studies.

For these reasons, most event-history analyses (including most published research in corporate demography) uses a continuous-time version of the life table, one that does not aggregate the timing of events. This variant uses the product-limit estimator developed by Kaplan and Meier (1959), another nonparametric maximum likelihood estimator (MLE) of the survivor function. In defining this estimator, we need some additional notation. Assume that the data set contains N cases. Let the exact durations of an event occurrence to one or more of the cases be denoted as

$$s_1 < s_2 < \cdots < s_Q,$$

with $s_Q = \infty$.

We redefine the counters to use the information on exact timing:

$$E(s_q) = \text{number of spells with events at } s_q;$$

$$C(s_q) = \text{number of spells censored at } s_q,$$

$$R(s_q) = N(s_q) - E(s_q) - C(s_q).$$

The Kaplan–Meier estimator is defined as

$$\widehat{G}(u) = \prod_{q: s_q < u} \left[1 - \frac{E(s_q)}{R(s_q)} \right].$$

Empirical work typically relies on Greenwood's formula for generating an estimate variance of the product-limit estimator:

$$\text{Var}[\widehat{G}(u)] = \widehat{G}^2(u) \sum_{s\,:\,s_i < u} \frac{E(s_q)}{R(s_q)[R(s_q) - E(s_q)]}.$$

Figures 6.8 and 6.9 display graphically the relationship between the product-limit survival probability and duration for founding and mortality of Tokyo banks. The two patterns of duration dependence differ sharply, as would be expected given the results presented in the previous section. The survival probability drops very sharply with duration for the founding process but not for the mortality process.

The hazard function at duration u equals the slope (time derivative) of $H_j(u)$. So any graphical or analytic technique for evaluating this function's slope gives a possible method for estimating the hazard function. Equation (6.3) shows that the logarithm of the Kaplan–Meier estimator can be used as an estimator of the cumulative hazard function. The large-sample properties of MLE are preserved under monotonic transformations (including the logarithmic transformation). So this estimator of the cumulative-hazard function has good asymptotic properties.

Figure 6.10 plots this estimator of the cumulative hazard of founding of Tokyo banks against duration (the interfounding time). Note that the

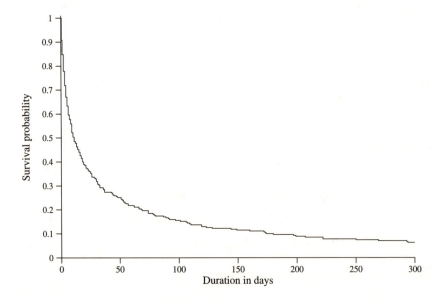

Figure 6.8. *Product-limit survivor function for interfounding times of Tokyo banks, 1873–1926.*

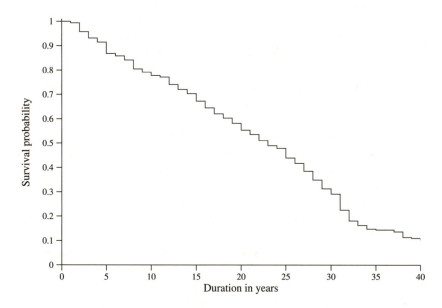

Figure 6.9. *Product-limit survivor function for mortality of Tokyo banks, 1873–1945.*

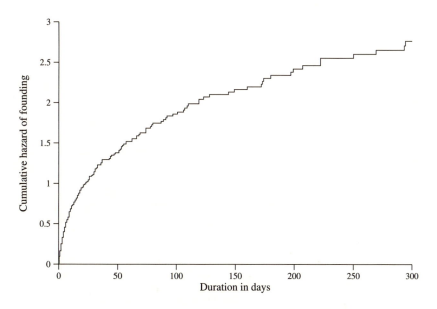

Figure 6.10. *Cumulative hazard of founding by duration for Tokyo banks.*

cumulative hazard rises sharply at small durations and then flattens out. Taking slopes at different segments of this curve to obtain estimates of the founding rate shows that the rate is high near the origin and drops fairly regularly with increasing duration. In other words, the rate of founding of a bank is high just after another bank has been founded; but as the time since the previous founding increases, the founding rate declines. The duration dependence is negative, as we have already seen from the life table.

Figure 6.11 examines mortality; it plots the cumulative hazard of mortality of Tokyo banks against duration (length of lifetime). Contrary to what we saw for the founding process, the cumulative hazard of mortality rises slowly near zero and then rises more and more steeply as length of lifetime increases. In this case, the duration dependence is *positive*.

Above we noted that the negative of the logarithm of the survivor function provides an estimator of the cumulative-hazard function. Although this estimator has good asymptotic properties, it is biased in small samples due to the nonlinearity of the transformation in (6.3). Aalen (1978) used martingale theory to derive the properties of an empirical estimator proposed earlier by Nelson (1972). The Nelson–Aalen nonparametric estimator of

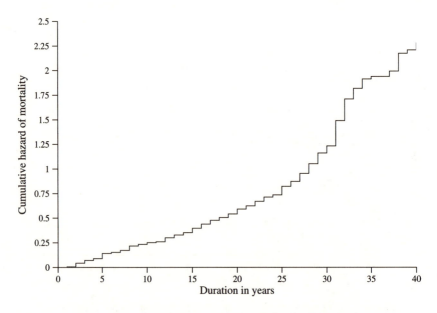

Figure 6.11. *Cumulative hazard of mortality for Tokyo banks.*

the cumulative hazard function is

$$\widehat{H}_j(u) = \sum_{i\,:\,s_i < u} \frac{E(s_i)}{R(s_i)}.$$

This estimator is unbiased, consistent, and asymptotically normal. Its variance can be defined as

$$\mathrm{Var}[\widehat{H}_j(u)] = \sum_{i\,:\,s_i < u} \left[\frac{E(s_i)}{R(s_i)}\right]^2.$$

6.4 Constant-Rate Models

The simplest case, which forms the starting point in all kinds of efforts to build models for vital rates, is the constant-hazard model. It will help fix ideas to discuss estimation of this model for each of the classes of processes that we introduced above (concerning the number of origins and destinations considered). We do so for two common forms of data. The first is a right-censored event history. The second is a temporal aggregation of such a history, that is, counts of events within periods.

Single-Origin, Single-Destination Processes

If only a single transition is possible, then the constant-hazard model takes the form

$$h(u) = \alpha, \qquad u > 0,$$

which implies that

$$G(u) = e^{-\alpha u},$$

assuming that the process begins at $u = 0$. Because the assumption of a constant hazard implies an exponential distribution of durations, this specification is commonly called the *exponential model*.

Event Histories

We begin with the case of ideal data: event histories. An event-history observation plan yields information on the exact timing of all relevant events within some interval. Such data allow the analyst to construct an analysis file on the entry process; here the key information involves the distribution of times between successive entries (the interarrival times). It also allows the analyst to construct analysis files appropriate for studying ending events such as exit from the industry, mortality, and so forth. In this case, the relevant time measure refers to some organization-level duration, e.g., age, tenure in an industry, and so forth. Here we consider ML estimation of a constant hazard from such data.

In the simple case of noninformative censoring, it is easy to construct a MLE of a constant hazard from event-history data. The data contain two kinds of cases: censored and uncensored. For an entry process, only the last spell—the duration between the last observed entry and the end of the observation period—is censored. In mortality analysis, the observations on all organizations that remain in the population at the ending of observation are censored. We construct an indicator function that distinguishes between censored and uncensored spells:

$$D_i = \begin{cases} 1 & \text{if the event is observed for case } i, \\ 0 & \text{if the record for case } i \text{ is right censored.} \end{cases}$$

The likelihood for the data is

$$L = \prod_i f(u_i)^{D_i} \, G(u_i)^{1-D_i}, \tag{6.5}$$

where u_i denotes the length of the spell for the observation on the ith case (the time elapsed from the origin to either the censoring time or the event time). In this version of the likelihood, the censored cases clearly do contribute valuable information about the process, namely that they were at risk of the event for a known duration without experiencing it.

According to (6.2), $f(u) = h(u)G(u)$. Thus the likelihood can be rewritten as

$$L = \prod_i h(u_i)^{D_i} \, G(u_i) = \prod_i \alpha^{D_i} \, e^{-\alpha u_i}. \tag{6.6}$$

To form a MLE, take the log of the likelihood, differentiate with respect to α, set the resulting expression to zero:

$$\frac{d \ln L}{d\alpha} = \frac{1}{\alpha} \sum_i D_i - \sum_i u_i = 0,$$

and solve for α:

$$\widehat{\alpha} = \frac{\sum_i D_i}{\sum_i u_i}. \tag{6.7}$$

The numerator in this expression counts the uncensored observations, and the denominator gives the sum of all observed durations. That is, the MLE for the exponential model is the famous *occurrence/exposure ratio* from classical actuarial mathematics.

Consider the illustrative data given in Table 6.1. We have already noted that five of the eight organizations in this example experienced ending events. The sum of the exposure times for the eight organizations in the table is 1060. Therefore the MLE of the mortality rate in this example is $5/1060 = 0.0047$.

Event Counts

Next we consider the possibility that available data have been aggregated over time. We treat event-count analysis explicitly because information on vital events within populations of organizations can often be found only in such a temporally aggregated form in a reasonably broad class of situations. For instance, most efforts to record entries into organizational populations have succeeded in obtaining yearly (or, sometimes, monthly) counts. Many analyses of organizational mortality also rely on temporally aggregated data. Chapter 8 points out that many common data sources on organizational life histories tell only the *year* of entry and exit.

What does such temporal aggregation mean for modeling and analysis? Some analysts, when confronted with temporally aggregated data, redefine the model so that it has a discrete-time structure. We question the value of allowing the form of the data to determine the form of the model. In the cases we have examined, events can and do occur at all times during the year. In other words, the actual time structure of the process appears to be continuous.

In the case of founding processes, most available data are aggregated to the year. However, some studies do manage to obtain data with refined timing, e.g., the studies of foundings of Japanese banks by Han (1998) and credit unions in New York by Hannan, West, and Barron (1994) obtained the exact date of each event. If we want to identify regularities that hold across populations, then it makes sense to employ models and methods that fit all of the cases, regardless of the degree of temporal aggregation in currently available data. This consideration dictates that we maintain the assumption that the time parameter in these processes is continuous. In the case of temporally aggregated data (count data), this strategy entails building models for counts from specific continuous-time models.

The implications of a constant-hazard process for aggregated counts are well known. The relevant version of the model has as its state space the natural numbers ($\mathcal{N} = 0, 1, 2, \ldots$). Transitions flow only from n to $n + 1$. Such a "pure birth process" is the natural specification for a model of a count of arrivals in historical time. (The possibility of using interarrival times is vitiated by the temporal aggregation.) A pure birth process with a constant hazard is called a *Poisson process*. The constancy of the hazard implies that the rate of arrival does not depend on the history of previous arrivals (including the time of the last arrival) and on the current state of the system. Among other things, this assumption implies that the order of the event and the waiting time since the previous event do not affect the rate.

The relevant hazard concerns the *rate of arrival* of organizations in the population (or environment). In particular, the rate of arriving at state $n + 1$ at *historical time* t is

$$h_n(t) = \lim_{\epsilon \downarrow 0} \frac{\Pr\{X(t + \epsilon) - X(t) = 1 \mid X(t) = n\}}{\epsilon}.$$

It normally turns out to be more informative to analyze the arrival rate in terms of a process time: the clock that records the time since the previous arrival. Let t_x denote the (historical) time of the xth arrival. We might regard this arrival as initiating a new interfounding spell and setting the clock for this spell to zero. Times within the spell can be measured in terms of the interarrival clock as $u = t - t_x$. The definition of the hazard for the arrival process in *interfounding* time can therefore be expressed as

$$h_n(u) = h_n(t - t_x) = \lim_{\epsilon \downarrow 0} \frac{\Pr\{X(t - t_x + \epsilon) - X(t - t_x) = 1 \mid X(t_x) = n\}}{\epsilon}.$$

If the hazard of arrival is a constant,

$$h_n(t) = h_n(u) = \lambda,$$

then the arrival process is Poisson.

The properties of the Poisson process can be exploited to yield an explicit solution to the problem of temporal aggregation. The data structures available for analyzing organizational entries typically provide annual counts. So analysis focuses on year to year variation in the counts. (Any other regular temporal spacing are treated analogously.) Let $A(t + \tau) = X(t + \tau) - X(t)$ denote the number of arrivals during the period of length τ that begins at historical time t. According to the Poisson formula, the expected number of arrivals with a period of length τ is

$$\Pr\{A = a\} = \frac{e^{-\lambda \tau}(\lambda \tau)^a}{a!}. \tag{6.8}$$

When the temporal intervals of the aggregation are the same (e.g., each count pertains to a single year), we set $\tau = 1$, without loss of generality, giving the standard representation of the Poisson probability law:

$$\Pr\{A = a\} = \frac{e^{-\lambda} \lambda^a}{a!}. \tag{6.9}$$

In the standard data structure for analyzing entries, the analyst has a time series of annual (or monthly) counts of entries for equally spaced time points: a_q. (This notation reflects the fact that, unlike t which refers to any historical time, q tells the times at which the available counts are given.)

Consider the MLE of the hazard for this framework. The likelihood for a time series of counts of an event, say organizational foundings, driven by a constant hazard is

$$L = \prod_q \frac{e^{-\lambda} \lambda^{a_q}}{a_q!}, \tag{6.10}$$

and the log-likelihood is

$$\ln L = \sum_q (-\lambda + a_q \ln \lambda - \ln a_q!).$$

Differentiating with respect to λ and setting the resulting expression to zero gives

$$\frac{d \ln L}{d\lambda} = \sum_q -1 + \sum_q \frac{a_q}{\ln \lambda} = 0.$$

We obtain the MLE by solving for λ:

$$\widehat{\lambda}_{\mathrm{MLE}} = \frac{\sum_q a_q}{\sum_q 1} = \frac{A}{Q}.$$

The numerator in this expression counts the total number of events observed. Because the duration of each time interval, τ, in (6.14) has been set to 1, the denominator gives the total period of exposure (that is, observation), Q. So again, the MLE is an occurrence/exposure ratio. Time aggregation has not altered this estimator.

Multiple-Origin, Single-Destination Processes

Earlier in the chapter we noted that interesting issues in corporate demography often involve transitions among multiple states: organizations enter populations by different routes (different kinds of entry events) and leave by different routes (different kinds of ending events). This subsection and the next discuss the generalization of the estimation strategy just sketched to these more interesting and more complex cases. Suppose that the analyst continues to focus on a single outcome (e.g., mortality of all types considered alike) but makes distinctions among several kinds of entry events.

If a process has only a single destination and multiple origins with different hazards, then the constant-hazard model has the form

$$h_j(u) = \alpha_j, \qquad u > 0, \quad j = 1, \ldots, J,$$

and

$$G(u) = \prod_{j=1}^{J} e^{-\alpha_j u} = \exp\left(-\sum_{j=1}^{J} \alpha_j u\right) = e^{-\alpha u}.$$

Now we construct an indicator function for censoring that takes account of the different origins:

$$D_{ij} = \begin{cases} 1 & \text{if the event is observed for case } i \text{ starting in state } j, \\ 0 & \text{if the record for case } i \text{ starting in state } j \text{ is right censored.} \end{cases}$$

The likelihood is

$$L = \prod_j \prod_{i=1}^{I_j} f_j(u_i)^{D_{ij}} G(u_{ij})^{1-D_{ij}},$$

which is equivalent to

$$L = \prod_j \prod_{i=1}^{I_j} h_j(u_i)^{D_{ij}} G(u_i) = \prod_j \prod_{i=1}^{I_j} \alpha_j^{D_{ij}} e^{-\alpha u}.$$

To form a MLE, take the logarithm of the likelihood, differentiate it with respect to α_j, set the result to zero:

$$\frac{d \ln L}{d\alpha_j} = \frac{1}{\alpha_j} \sum_i D_{ij} - \sum_i u_i = 0,$$

and solve for α_j:

$$\widehat{\alpha}_j = \frac{\sum_i D_{ij}}{\sum_i u_i}. \tag{6.11}$$

The numerator in this expression tells the number of uncensored observations that begin in state j, and the denominator gives the sum of the observed durations of the cases that start in that state. In other words, the MLE is a conditional occurrence/exposure ratio, one that is specific to the origin state (calculated only for the spells that share a particular origin).

Similar reasoning applies in the case of analysis of event counts. If data are aggregated to period counts and several origins must be taken into account, then we simply analyze multiple series of event counts, one for each origin.

Single-Origin, Multiple-Destination Processes

Finally, consider the constant-rate version of the general formulation with multiple origins and destinations. The only challenge for estimation involves accommodating the fact that several types of events are possible. It simplifies notation, without loss of generality, to consider the case with only one origin and several kinds of destinations. We use the notation $r_{*k}(u)$ to

denote the rate of moving from the undifferentiated state (which we denote by $*$) to state k (or, equivalently, the rate of occurrence of the event
of type k for cases in the undifferentiated starting state $*$).

$$r_{*k}(u) = \alpha_{*k}, \qquad u > 0, \ k = 1, \ldots, K,$$

with

$$G(u) = \prod_{k=1}^{K} \exp(-\alpha_{*k} u).$$

The trick in estimating the rate of a given event involves regarding
the cases that experience different events as being right censored at the
times of those events. This trick works because such cases are at risk of the
event until they have a different event and cease being at risk at that time.
This means that they provide valuable information about the process, the
information that they have not experienced each of the events over the
period. So we construct an indicator function for censoring that is specific
to the destination state:

$$D_{i*k} = \begin{cases} 1 & \text{if the event of type } k \text{ is observed for case } i, \\ 0 & \text{if case } i \text{ has a different event or is right censored.} \end{cases}$$

As above, u_i is case i's duration at the time of its event (of any kind) or its
time of censoring.

The relevant likelihood is

$$L = \prod_i \prod_k f_{*k}(u_i)^{D_{i*k}} G(u_i)^{1-D_{i*k}},$$

which can be rearranged as:

$$L = \prod_i \prod_k \alpha_{*k}^{D_{i*k}} G(u_i) = \prod_i \prod_k \alpha^{D_{i*k}} \prod_k e^{-\alpha_{*k} u_i}.$$

To form a MLE, again take the logarithm of the likelihood, differentiate
with respect to α_{*k}, set the resulting expression to zero:

$$\frac{d \ln L}{d\alpha_{*k}} = \frac{1}{\alpha_{*k}} \sum_i D_{i*k} - \sum_i u_i = 0,$$

and solve for α_{*k}:

$$\widehat{\alpha}_{*k} = \frac{\sum_i D_{i*k}}{\sum_i u_i}.$$

The numerator in this expression counts the number of observations observed to have event k, and the denominator tells the sum of the observed
durations of those units at risk of having this event. It bears noting that,
once again, the MLE is an occurrence/exposure ratio.

Again, similar reasoning applies in the case of analysis of event counts. If the data are aggregated to period counts and several origins and several destinations must be taken into account, then one should analyze the series of event counts for each origin–destination pair.

Demographic analysis of corporations and other kinds of organizations usually goes beyond estimation of vital rates. Analysts usually want to understand the forces that shape the vital rates. This interest leads them to analyze how vital rates depend on various dimensions of duration and on measured and unmeasured heterogeneity. The next chapter sketches the main approaches used in such analyses.

7

Modeling Corporate Vital Rates

IN THE PREVIOUS CHAPTER, we devoted considerable attention to the constant-rate model, using it as a simple framework for examining core demographic ideas. Instructive as this exercise might be, research in organizational demography has never, to our knowledge, uncovered a case in which a vital rate was plausibly truly constant. How should the model be modified so as to accommodate substantively interesting and empirically important departures from the constant-rate model?

In addressing this question, corporate demographers have developed two main classes of elaboration of models, often in combination. The first builds specifications that allow vital rates to vary systematically with the passage of time. The second common type of elaboration incorporates information on the observed and unobserved heterogeneity that affects vital rates. This means analyzing how measured and unmeasured characteristics of organizations, populations, and environments affect the rates of entry and exit. In this chapter, we describe and explain the main classes of extensions.

This chapter also considers complications arising from research design. With the basic technical tools in hand, we return to the issues involving trade-offs among observation plans, which we discussed in Chapter 5. We pay special attention to the issue of left truncation. We compare alternative designs (with and without left truncation in duration and size truncation) using computer simulation methods.

7.1 Duration Dependence

Duration dependence in vital rates bears on a number of core theoretical issues in organizational demography and ecology (Chapter 13). So a widely used class of models for corporate demography specifies that the hazard depends on time, as measured by one of the relevant clocks, usually a process clock. We assume the latter choice in what follows. Each of the models makes sense if the rates and parameters are defined separately for each of a class of possible transitions. For simplicity, we concentrate on processes with a single origin and a single destination. Generalizing the methods we consider to cases with multiple origins and destinations does not introduce any new ideas or complications.

Piecewise-Exponential Specifications

A flexible and widely used strategy for representing temporal variation in transition rates breaks the relevant temporal dimension into pieces and fits constant rates within segments (Tuma and Hannan 1984; Blossfeld and Rohwer 1996). This procedure produces the so-called piecewise-exponential specification. This kind of specification constrains temporal variation in the rate to be a step function in duration (as in the discrete-time life table, discussed in Chapter 6); the analyst sets the width of the steps and allows the data to determine the height (positive or negative) of each step. We denote the breakpoints as

$$0 \leq \tau_1 \leq \tau_2 \leq \cdots \leq \tau_P.$$

With the assumption that $\tau_{P+1} = \infty$, there are P periods:

$$I_p = \{t \mid \tau_p \leq t < \tau_{p+1}\}, \qquad p = 1, \ldots, P. \tag{7.1}$$

Then the piecewise-exponential model can be written as

$$h(u) = \alpha_p, \ u \in I_p. \tag{7.2}$$

Estimation turns out to be nearly as simple as for the constant-rate model. As it will prove useful in describing how to employ information on time-varying covariates below, we sketch the derivation of the MLE for this case. Consider the first (earliest) period, starting at zero. All units observed are at risk ("in the risk set") at $u = 0$. Some fraction have events during this period; some might be censored during the period, and some (usually most) are censored at τ_1, the end of the period. This is exactly the situation that we considered in developing a MLE for the constant-rate model. Not surprisingly, the MLE of α_1 is the same: the ratio of the number of events during the period to the total time at risk (total exposure) during that period.

Nothing changes for the second period, except that those units that had events during the prior period or were lost to observation by prior censoring cannot be observed to experience the event in the second period—they should be dropped from the risk set. So the MLE $\widehat{\alpha}_2$ is simply the occurrence/exposure ratio during the period for those units in the risk set at the start of the period, τ_1. This principle generalizes to subsequent periods.

Table 7.1. *Estimates of constant and piecewise-exponential models of duration dependence in the founding rates of banks in Tokyo.*

Exponential: $h(u) = \lambda$	
$\widehat{\lambda}$	0.016 (6.81)
$\ln \mathscr{L}$	-1382.5
Piecewise exponential: $h(u) = \lambda_p$, $u \in I_p$	
$\widehat{\lambda}_1$ $(u < 5)$	0.083 (23.4)
$\widehat{\lambda}_2$ $(5 \leq u < 15)$	0.042 (24.4)
$\widehat{\lambda}_3$ $(15 \leq u < 25)$	0.024 (18.7)
$\widehat{\lambda}_4$ $(25 \leq u)$	0.007 (48.4)
$\ln \mathscr{L}$	-1241.5

Note: The figures in parentheses are t-statistics. The time unit is days.

We continue to use the case of banks in the Tokyo prefecture for illustration. Table 7.1 presents estimates of parameters of models of the founding rate in this population over the period 1873–1926.[1] The topmost panel gives the estimates for the constant-hazard (exponential) specification. Next we show estimates of a piecewise-exponential model, with the (interarrival) time axis broken into four segments.

Notice that the exponential model can be considered a constrained version of the piecewise-exponential model in the sense that it results from constraining the four parameters of the latter to be equal. Thus one can construct a likelihood-ratio test of the null hypothesis that the founding rate was constant over durations between foundings against the alternative that the rate varied as a step function with the given breakpoints. The test statistic for the specifications reported in Table 7.1 is $-2[\ln(L_0) - \ln(L_A)]$, where L_0 and L_A denote the null hypothesis and the alternative hypothesis, respectively. Under the null, this statistic is distributed as chi-square with degrees of freedom equal to the difference in parameters between the two models: three in the case at hand. For this example, the test statistic equals $-2(-1382.5 + 1241.5) = 282.0$. Such a large value is incredibly implausible under the null hypothesis with three degrees of freedom.

---

[1] A note of caution in interpreting these results: Han (1998) shows that this rate depends strongly on the values of covariates such as population density and changes in legislation pertaining to banks in Japan; adding effects of such covariates will alter the estimates of the effect of duration on the rate—see Han (1998) for the complete results.

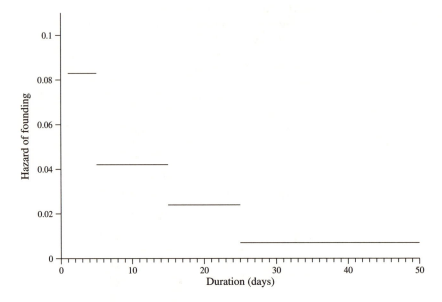

Figure 7.1.   *Estimated piecewise-exponential model for founding rates of Tokyo banks.*

Thus we can reject the null in favor of the alternative, that is, duration dependence.

Figure 7.1 plots the implications of these estimates for the hazards: the step function that relates the duration to the founding rate. Note that the duration dependence implied by the piecewise-exponential model is monotonic negative. According to these estimates, the rate is very high just after a founding and drops sharply as the time of the most recent founding recedes.

Parametric Specifications

Estimation of piecewise-exponential specifications serves as a useful preliminary step in almost all efforts at parameterizing the temporal variation in vital rates. In some cases, the pattern of duration dependence will be so complex that it does not make sense to try to represent it with some simple parametric model. In other cases, such as the one just illustrated, the $\widehat{\alpha}_p$ display some kind of fairly regular pattern, e.g., increasing or decreasing roughly monotonically or rising and then falling. Then it will often prove productive to move to simple parametric models of duration dependence in the interest of parsimony and simplicity. This step involves analysis of models of the form

$$h(u) = \vartheta(u),$$

where $\vartheta(\cdot)$ is some (parametric) continuous function. A number of these parametric models have been used in corporate demography, especially the study of organizational mortality. Chapter 13 discusses these parametric models in the context of mortality processes, along with the theoretical and substantive ideas used to motivate them.

7.2 Dependence on Covariates

Although establishing the existence and forms of time dependence in vital rates forms a natural part of any kind of demographic analysis, modeling efforts do not usually stop there. If anything, more attention has been paid to addressing variations in vital rates associated with environmental conditions and—in the case of exit—organizational properties. In considering the effects of covariates, as in considering duration dependence, substantive questions have paramount importance: How do vital rates depend upon variations in explanatory variables?

Available theories do not provide guidance about the functional forms of organizational processes. Therefore, researchers typically choose simple, tractable functional forms that agree qualitatively with the substantive arguments. They use a variety of models that specify relationships between transition rates and explanatory variables that are log-linear in parameters, because negative rates do not make sense. In the language of generalized linear models (McCullagh and Nelder 1989), this means that the link between outcomes and predictors is log-linear. Restricting models to those that are log-linear in parameters is not very confining.

Suppose that a hazard turns out not to be a constant. One possible source of the nonconstancy is the effect of *heterogeneity* among the sample members. Assume, for the moment, that such heterogeneity can be represented well with a vector of measured variables, $\mathbf{z}$, whose first element is set to 1 (to allow estimation of a constant term). Suppose further that these covariates are fixed over time but vary over cases (that is, among organizations in mortality analysis and among interarrival spells in entry analysis). Then the generalization of the duration-dependent hazard model to incorporate the heterogeneity has the form

$$h(u, \mathbf{z}_i) = \varrho(u, \mathbf{z}_i). \tag{7.3}$$

In this general form, the model allows the possibility that the effects of covariates depend upon duration, that duration and covariates "interact" in determining the hazard.

It might be substantively important to allow such complex effects. For instance, we describe research in Chapter 14 that shows that the effect of organizational size on mortality rates varies with duration. However, nearly all published research in corporate demography imposes the assumption of *proportionality of effects*. This means that (7.3) can be factored into the product of two pieces, one that gives the effect of duration and a second that gives the effect of the covariates:

$$h(u, \mathbf{z}_i) = \vartheta(u) \cdot \beta(\mathbf{z}_i). \tag{7.4}$$

As hazards must be nonnegative, analysts commonly use a log-linear specification of the effects of the covariates on the hazard:

$$\beta(\mathbf{z}_i) = \exp(\mathbf{b}'\mathbf{z}_i).$$

The assumption of log-linearity of effects creates the following formulation for the model of proportional effects:

$$h(u, \mathbf{z}_i) = \vartheta(u) \cdot \exp(\mathbf{b}'\mathbf{z}_i). \tag{7.5}$$

If the assumption of proportionality of effects is warranted, then we have the option of using a semiparametric estimator, called the partial-likelihood (PL) estimator developed by Cox. The strategy behind PL estimation regards the duration dependence expressed in $\vartheta(u)$ in (7.5) as a "nuisance function." Instead of forming a likelihood for the full model in (7.5), the PL estimator ignores the nuisance function and maximizes the partial likelihood involving the effects of the covariates as if it were a genuine likelihood. It does this by conditioning on the fact that an event occurs at each given observed event time, u_i, and forming the likelihood the ith case experienced this event (instead of each of the other cases at risk). Even though the PL estimator is not an MLE, it turns out to have surprisingly good properties for estimator of proportional-hazards models. Nonetheless, because the strategy of PL estimation does not seek to obtain high-quality estimates of duration dependence, it gets used much less frequently in research on the demography of corporations than the alternative discussed next.

The piecewise-exponential specification estimated by ML has the decided advantages that it (1) accommodates nonproportionality of effects, (2) does not require strong assumptions about the exact forms of duration dependence, and (3) provides information about duration dependence. For the piecewise-exponential specification, the nonproportional assumption might be represented as

$$h(u, \mathbf{z}_i) = \exp(\mathbf{b}'_p\mathbf{z}_i), \ u \in I_p.$$

In this form, the effect parameters vary by period (p), meaning that they vary with duration. The proportional version imposes the constraint that only the constant b_{1p} varies by period, that is, $b_{ip} = b_i, i \neq 1$.

Finally, specifications of the form of (7.3)–(7.5) with parametric specifications of duration dependence can be estimated by ML. The various common parametric specifications contain two or more parameters connected to duration dependence; and the analyst must decide which parameters (if any) depend upon the covariates. See Tuma and Hannan (1984) and Blossfeld and Rohwer (1996) for details.

Time-Varying Covariates and Spell Splitting

To this point we have treated the covariates as fixed over time. However, the environmental factors and competitive relations that engender population dynamics rarely remain stable. A simple and useful way to allow the levels of covariates to change over time involves a generalization of the piecewise-exponential model to include effects of preselected periods. For instance, common practice in empirical research sets the periods to coincide with calendar years to reflect the timing of changes in the values of covariates in common source documents. More generally, breakpoints might be defined to coincide with the times of observed changes in covariates. In this case, analysts assume that the covariates are step functions in time, that they remain constant within periods and change values at the start of each period.

Event Histories

We start with spell splitting in analysis of event-history data. In the simplest case, we impose the assumption of proportionality of effects (that is, we constrain the effect parameters to be constant over periods), and we update the values of the covariates at the beginning of each period:

$$r(u|\mathbf{z}) = \vartheta(u) \cdot \exp[\varphi(\mathbf{z}_p)], \qquad u \in I_p, \tag{7.6}$$

where I_p is defined as in (7.1) and $\varphi(\mathbf{z}_p)$ is some log-linear relationship (or link) between the covariates and the rate.

Implementation of this idea usually relies on the tactic of *spell splitting*. This means taking the observation for each unit and splitting it into a set of pieces. Figure 7.2 illustrates the idea for a hypothetical case. The observation in the figure experiences the event at u_1. The contribution of such a case to the likelihood defined in (6.6) is

$$L_1 = h(u_1) G(u_1).$$

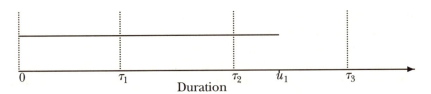

Figure 7.2.   *Illustration of spell splitting.*

In spell splitting, we want to generalize this expression to take account of the subspells. In the case in Figure 7.2, we break the observation into three pieces: $(0, \tau_1]$, $(\tau_1, \tau_2]$, and $(\tau_2, u_1]$, and we observe that the first two (sub)spells are right censored and the third is uncensored. We need to write an expression for $G(u_1)$ that takes account of the spell splitting. First, note that, by the definition of the survivor function,

$$G(u_1) = \Pr\{U \geq \tau_1\}\,\Pr\{U \geq \tau_2 \mid U \geq \tau_1\}\,\Pr\{U \geq u_1 \mid U \geq \tau_2\}.$$

The first of these terms, $\Pr\{U \geq \tau_1\}$, is simply $G(\tau_1)$. The second term, $\Pr\{U \geq \tau_2 \mid U \geq \tau_1\}$, can be expressed (using the definition of conditional probability) as $G(\tau_2)/G(\tau_1)$. Using the definition of the survivor function in (6.1), we put this expression in a more convenient form:

$$\frac{G(\tau_2)}{G(\tau_1)} = \frac{\exp[-\int_0^{\tau_2} h(s)\,ds]}{\exp[-\int_0^{\tau_1} h(s)\,ds]} = \exp\left[-\int_{\tau_1}^{\tau_2} h(s)\,ds\right] = G(\tau_2 - \tau_1).$$

And the third expression can be written analogously as $G(u_1 - \tau_2)$. Therefore, the case's contribution to the likelihood is

$$L_1 = h(u_1)G(\tau_1)G(\tau_2 - \tau_1)\,G(u_1 - \tau_2).$$

We write an explicit likelihood for the whole set of observations by first defining the number of full periods of exposure for each unit as $p_i^{\max} = \{\max p : u_i > \tau_p\}$. With this notation and the usual event indicator D_i, the likelihood is

$$L = \prod_i h(u_i)^{D_i} \prod_{p \leq p_i^{\max}} G(\tau_p - \tau_{p-1})G(u_i - \tau_{p_i^{\max}}). \tag{7.7}$$

This idea typically causes confusion at first encounter, because it appears that we have greatly increased the number of "cases" by splitting spells. It is important to see that we have not changed the likelihood by spell splitting. The number of spells per se does not matter as long as we have not changed either the number of occurrences or the periods of exposure. Consider what would happen if we estimated a constant-rate model in two ways: one uses the version of the likelihood in (6.6) applied to the unsplit spells and the other uses the likelihood in (7.7) and the split spells. The results (point estimates, asymptotic standard errors, likelihoods) will be the same.

This result on spell splitting has widespread application in estimation of specifications with time-varying covariates. The basic idea is that we split spells to take account of the refinement of the time-series information on the covariates. If, as in the example considered above, the values of the covariates get updated yearly, then one splits observations into yearly spells and associates with each subspell the levels of the covariates that obtain for the year associated with the subspell.

Event Counts: Poisson Regression

Now we address these issues in the context of temporally aggregated counts of events. Experience shows that the pure Poisson model, introduced in Section 6.3, is far too simple for organizational founding processes (Barron 1992; Hannan and Carroll 1992). A standard extension adds effects of covariates, forming the so-called *Poisson regression model*. We obtain this model by substituting a log-linear relationship between the arrival rate and a set of covariates:

$$h_a(q, \mathbf{z}) = \exp[\varphi(\mathbf{z}_q)],$$

into the probability model in (6.9), which gives

$$\Pr\{A_q = a_q\} = \frac{\exp(-\exp[\varphi(\mathbf{z}_q)]) \exp[\varphi(\mathbf{z}_q)]^{a_q}}{a_q!}.$$

Although the baseline probability law is Poisson instead of normal, this specification bears a resemblance to standard regression models. However, Poisson regression and standard regression differ in two ways that matter for demographic applications. First, as just noted, the probability laws differ. In particular, Poisson regression uses a probability law that imposes the constraints that counts be nonnegative and that they have integer values. Second, as the derivation above makes clear, the coefficients in the Poisson regression model give the effects of covariates on the underlying hazard, rather than on the event count directly. Thus the regression coefficients have direct interpretation in the general stochastic-process framework.

Unmeasured Heterogeneity

Even if an analyst does a good job of representing the systematic effects of duration and organizational and environmental covariates on corporate vital rates, some sources of variation undoubtedly get overlooked. That is, a realistic appraisal of specifications used in corporate demography must admit that some heterogeneity affecting the rates remains unmeasured. In general, the unmeasured factors might vary over spells and over duration for a given spell. For instance, an organization's mortality rate might depend upon some organization-specific constant (reflecting, say, its distinctive culture or some other enduring feature) and some random factors that reflect the quality of its interaction with other actors (say the strength of its position in some network).

How much attention should be given to the issue of unobserved heterogeneity and how should it be addressed? This enormously complicated subject cannot be addressed fully here.[2] We will nonetheless sketch the main lines of our views on the issues and point to some valuable sources for more detailed treatments.

The importance of the problem of unmeasured heterogeneity depends upon its "strength" (the fraction of variation in the rates that reflects the operation of the unmeasured factors) and its association with duration and the measured covariates. The problematic cases are those in which unmeasured heterogeneity is both strong and highly associated with the measured factors (duration and covariates). Although these guidelines are reasonably clear, applying them in research turns out to be anything but straightforward. By definition, we do not know the identities of the unmeasured factors. Therefore, it is highly unlikely that we can propose credible answers to questions about the strength and pattern of association of unmeasured factors in any one analysis.

How might analysts deal with problems of unmeasured heterogeneity? We think that three possibilities should be explored: (1) using research designs that minimize the problem, (2) conducting replications in contexts that differ considerably, so that the strong unmeasured factors likely differ, and (3) controlling for the effects of unmeasured factors statistically.

Consider first the issue of research design, which we have already discussed in contrasting the representative design and the population design (Chapter 5). One of our main reasons for questioning the value of broad representative designs for corporate demography comes directly from considerations of problems of unobserved heterogeneity. Any broadly representative sample of, say, employers in a modern economy will contain firms in service industries (e.g., restaurants, plumbing contractors, and

---

[2] Useful references include Andersen et al. (1993), Heckman and Singer (1984), and Hougaard (1987).

schools), financial services (e.g., banks, check-cashing services, and insurance companies), manufacturing (e.g., brewers, steel mills, and semiconductor manufacturers), transportation (e.g., airlines, railroads, and taxi companies), business services (e.g., accountancies, bicycle messenger services, and management consultancies), as well as government agencies (e.g., police, forestry, and treasury departments) and voluntary associations (e.g., labor unions, charitable foundations, and churches).

We contend that a sample of such diverse organizations presents nearly insurmountable problems of heterogeneity. The set of relevant environmental factors in such a sample is huge—some of these organizations operate only in one town and others operate globally, some face intense governmental regulation and others do not, and so forth. The diversity of strategies that affect vital rates is also enormous. The diversity of relevant causal factors is so great that it overwhelms efforts to "control" for heterogeneity with measured covariates (including period effects). When such factors cannot be controlled by design or estimation of effects of the relevant covariates, their effects contribute to unobserved heterogeneity.

In contrast, using more focused designs reduces the number of relevant factors to be considered and greatly enhances the ability of researchers to measure many of these relevant factors. In other words, the population observation plan mitigates some of the problems of unobserved heterogeneity by design.

Replication in diverse settings serves as a possible safeguard against mistaken inference due to issues of unobserved heterogeneity. As we describe in the next several parts of the book, some basic corporate-demographic processes have been examined separately in very diverse contexts. Researchers have published estimates of, say, density dependence in vital rates using data on many different kinds of organizations, including accountancies, automobile manufacturers, banks, brewers, labor unions, newspapers, semiconductor manufacturers, and social protest organizations (Chapters 10 and 11). Moreover, studies have replicated patterns for one type of population in different countries, e.g., banks in Denmark, Japan, Singapore, and the United States and newspapers in Argentina, Finland, Ireland, and the United States. The value of such replications comes from the diversity of settings examined. The challenges to sound inference that might plague a study of brewers presumably differ from those that would challenge studies of banks or labor unions. Likewise, the idiosyncratic heterogeneity that might be relevant in a study of Danish banks presumably differs somewhat from that relevant to Japanese banks.

If similar patterns turn up in estimates of the same basic model (tailored to include the relevant local factors), then either: (1) unobserved heterogeneity is not very damaging to sound inference in these cases, or

(2) some systematic unobserved factors operate across many diverse contexts. Unless credible stories can be told about the systematic factors (which has not yet been done), the first alternative appears to be more plausible.[3] In any event, replication in diverse settings provides a valuable supplement to appropriate research design in dealing with the ubiquitous problem of unobserved heterogeneity.

Finally, analysts sometimes attempt to control statistically for the effects of postulated forms of unobserved heterogeneity. Work pursuing this strategy makes the hazard model doubly stochastic by introducing a stochastic disturbance term in the specification of the hazard or rate.[4] The strategy works somewhat differently in event-history and event-count analysis.

In the case of event-history analysis, researchers typically assume a distribution that summarizes the effects of the unobservables. These choices are based primarily on issues of analytic tractability rather than on theoretical or other substantive considerations. See Kalbfleisch and Prentice (1980) and Lancaster (1990) for reviews and Hannan (1989) for an application to organizational mortality.

These procedures do not find much use in current research in corporate demography. Perhaps the main reason for this situation is the great complexity of estimating specifications with both time-varying covariates and stochastic disturbances.[5] Generally available packages for event-history estimation do not implement such procedures. Because researchers understandably want to devote more attention to the factors that they can measure than to those that they cannot and because measured covariates generally change over durations, most researchers opt to forego estimation of doubly stochastic specifications for event-history data.

Event Counts: Negative Binomial Regression and QL Estimation

The situation differs for analysis of event counts, where dealing with unobserved heterogeneity has long been central to the development of models and estimators. This difference in emphasis is due, no doubt, to recognition of the consequences of temporal aggregation. Creating a time series of counts of events almost surely creates unobserved heterogeneity when the underlying (disaggregated) process has duration dependence but not

---

[3] If patterns diverge across contexts, then the result is inconclusive from the perspective of judgments about unobserved heterogeneity. Lack of similarity might mean that the process under study lacks generality or that a general process has gotten confounded with unobserved heterogeneity.

[4] This modification can be seen as involving a "doubling" of the stochastic nature of the process because the process driven by a rate without the disturbance term is already stochastic.

[5] To the best of our knowledge, MLE has not been found to be feasible for such cases. Some alternative, usually the EM algorithm, must be used.

unobserved heterogeneity. Indeed, as we explain below, the standard extensions of the Poisson regression framework are usually considered as "fixes" for either duration dependence or unobserved heterogeneity.

Empirical research on organizational vital events seldom finds that the mean of a time series of arrivals equals the variance, even approximately, as the Poisson process implies. Instead, it has been common to find the variance of event counts exceeds the mean, often by a considerable margin. This condition, commonly called *overdispersion*, arises for a number of different reasons, including unobserved heterogeneity and time dependence.

It has often proven insightful in prior research to regard the Poisson model as a special case of a *negative binomial model*. The most common representation assumes that a Poisson process operates but is disturbed by a (continuous) multiplicative error process,

$$h_a(q) = \lambda \, \eta_q, \tag{7.8}$$

where η_q is uncorrelated over units at risk (time periods, regions, and so forth, depending on the application). The probability law for the event counts is then a mixture of Poisson processes. That is,

$$\Pr\{A_q = a_q\} = \int \frac{e^{-\lambda} \lambda^{a_q}}{a_q!} \, f(\theta) \, d\eta,$$

where $f(\eta)$ is the density of the disturbance (the mixing distribution).

The negative binomial model follows from the assumption that η has a gamma distribution. Analysts often specify the mean of the process to be a log-linear function of the covariates to maintain the parallel with the Poisson regression model:

$$E(A_q) = \exp[\varphi(\mathbf{z}_q)].$$

Unlike the case of the Poisson process, the variance does not necessarily equal the mean; this model accommodates overdispersion.

Two special cases of this formulation have been used in empirical research on founding processes. One assumes a constant coefficient of variation (ratio of the variance to the mean). The second assumes that the coefficient of variation increases linearly with the mean. In either case, setting $\eta = 0$ reduces the model to a Poisson process. Thus one can form likelihood-ratio tests of the Poisson process versus the negative binomial. An alternative derivation assumes "contagion" in the process over time within the intervals chosen (within years in the case of much research). This means that the occurrence of an event affects the rate of subsequent occurrences, meaning that the occurrences are not statistically independent within time intervals. Positive contagion leads to overdispersion.[6]

Either interpretation fits common applications in corporate demography. Analysts usually have reason to think that founding rates fluctuate randomly over time, net of the effects of the covariates, due to unmeasured changes in environments. Contagion likely operates *within* years as well, with the result that the occurrence of one or more foundings early in a year increases the rate for the rest of the year. This would be an instance of unobserved contagion in the process. Research on the demography of organizations has not yet been able to choose convincingly between these alternative sources of overdispersion. Analysts simply control for overdispersion to try to ensure that estimated standard errors are reasonably accurate.

Model testing here relies on a statistic due to Haberman (1977) that parallels the likelihood-ratio test of a restricted model (L_2) against a less restricted alternative (L_1):

$$\mathrm{X}^2(L_2|L_1) = \sum_q \left[\widehat{\lambda}_{1q} - \widehat{\lambda}_{2q}\right]^2 / \widehat{\lambda}_{2q},$$

where $\widehat{\lambda}_{1q}$ and $\widehat{\lambda}_{2q}$ denote the fitted values under models L_1 and L_2.[7]

Another approach for dealing with the implications of unobserved heterogeneity makes weak assumptions about the form of such heterogeneity.[8] One promising alternative uses the method of quasi-likelihood (QL) estimation.

Yearly counts of entries might not be independent from year to year, as is assumed implicitly in conventional MLE of either Poisson regression or negative-binomial regression.[9] Some previous research has addressed this potential problem by specifying that the unobservable in (7.8) is autocorrelated. This change in the model has major implications for estimation, even when one assumes a very simple structure of autocorrelation. In particular, the task of deriving the likelihood functions for such structures has not yet been accomplished.

---

[6] More precisely, the negative binomial arises as a limiting distribution of an Eggenberger–Pólya urn scheme in which the probability of an event depends on the previous number of events.

[7] This statistic converges asymptotically to the analogous likelihood-ratio test statistic; and it has an asymptotic chi-square distribution with degrees of freedom equal to the number of restrictions on L_2, even when expected counts are small (Haberman 1977).

[8] Lomi (1995b) provides a convincing application of a flexible parameterization of unobserved heterogeneity in use of pooled cross-section and time-series data on organizational foundings.

[9] This issue is not, however, restricted to time-series analysis. Data from cross-sectional observation plans are also subject to spatial autocorrelation or network autocorrelation, in which case similar issues would arise.

The most feasible approach for dealing with autocorrelation in time series of event counts at this point relies on QL estimation. This technique differs from ML estimation in that it relies only on assumptions about the mean and variance of the outcome; no assumptions need be made about the underlying probability distribution. McCullagh (1983) demonstrated that this estimator is consistent, asymptotically Gaussian, and robust in the sense that consistent estimates of effects can be obtained given only that the mean is specified correctly. Moreover, the QL and ML functions are equivalent in the case of Poisson regression. Indeed, the two estimators are equivalent for all members of the linear exponential family (McCullagh and Nelder 1989). Barron (1992), Barron and Hannan (1991), and Hannan and Carroll (1992) discuss and illustrate applications to corporate demography.

7.3 Note on Left Truncation

Chapter 5 noted that a good deal of published research on the demography of organizations analyzes reasonably small slices of a population's late history, e.g., the last ten or fifteen years in history of a hundred years or more. In such cases, data on the states $Y(u)$ and the relevant covariates are lacking for the beginning of the history of the population; the observation plan is said to be left truncated.[10] Left truncation presents far more difficult analytic problems than right censoring. Much research shows that the past shapes the present, but we do not expect the future to shape the past.[11]

This is a problem that ought to be eliminated by design rather than by analytic technique. That is, researchers would be well advised to invest heavily in designing research so as to avoid left truncation rather than in technical fixes to easily available but left-truncated data. However, left truncation can surely sometimes not be avoided even in well-designed research. What then should a researcher do (other than give ample warnings to the readers)?

The best answer we can offer does little more than state the obvious (which, nonetheless, often goes unrecognized in the research process): do not ask the data to answer questions for which they are ill suited. Consider the example of duration dependence, say age dependence, in mortality processes. A typical left-truncated design includes observations on some

---

[10] See Andersen et al. (1993, 152–160) and Guo (1993) for examples of various forms of left truncation and discussions of the estimation problems that result.

[11] Expectations about the future might often affect present decisions. But this is not the issue, because expectations must be formed based on the past and present conditions and not on the true future conditions.

long-lived organizations. These are the survivors from cohorts founded many years before. The fact that they survived and were already old when the observation window started means that these observations do not provide any useful information about the effect of early aging on mortality rates. They do, however, provide useful information about the effect of age on mortality rates for the ages over which they are observed, if they are handled properly.

However, it is important to recognize that the left-truncated design confounds cohort and age. In the kind of examples we are considering, the only observations on youthful organizations are for those that are founded within the observation window, and the only observations on aged organizations are for those that were founded well before the observation window. So there is no hope of disentangling age- and cohort-related effects with this design. Moreover, if the effect of age varies with other conditions (as we show in Chapter 13 that it does, at least for some populations), then left truncation makes it very problematic to obtain high-quality estimates of the effect of aging. More generally, left truncation greatly complicates inference concerning corporate-demographic processes and should be avoided whenever possible. At a minimum, left-truncated designs and findings from them should be treated with caution.

7.4 Comparing Designs by Simulation

In contrasting the common research designs for studying organizations, we noted in Chapter 5 that some designs involve heavy left truncation and/or size truncation. Now we examine the consequences of these and other design features under controlled conditions. Our research strategy for making such comparisons involves the extensive use of computer simulations. We state the main results in this section.

Basically, the analysis proceeds as follows. We first simulate the emergence and growth of one or more organizational populations with known and empirically plausible models of the vital processes. The simulated data record the life experiences of every organization to appear in each population. Next, we impose an observation scheme on the simulated data; the scheme chooses a specified subset of the data for analysis. For instance, a left-truncated observation scheme ignores all of the data prior to the point of left truncation. Then we use the scheme-selected data to obtain estimates of a chosen organizational process. We record the estimates and repeat the entire procedure numerous times. Finally, we calculate descriptive statistics for the parameters and compare them to the known true values used to simulate the data initially. Comparing the statistics of the estimated parameters for different observation schemes reveals their relative quality under these conditions.

Our simulation model uses a set of functions for organizational founding, size, internal structure, and mortality.[12] The model incorporates empirically supported specifications of age-, size-, and density dependence (Chapters 10, 11, 13, and 14) as well as a common specification relating size and age to internal organizational structure. Each simulated population follows its own self-governed trajectory. That is, there is no interpopulation competition or other type of cross-population relationship in these simulated data.

Founding Rate Function. Organizational foundings follow a duration-independent, population-level process with the following well-documented (nonmonotonic) density dependence:

$$\lambda(t) = \exp(\alpha_0 + \alpha_1 N_t + \alpha_2 N_t^2), \tag{7.9}$$

where t is the time since the first founding in the population and N_t is density (the number of organizations) at time t. Following empirical studies explained in Chapters 10 and 11 in Part III, we set $\alpha_1 > 0$, $\alpha_2 < 0$; but this part of the model is not particularly important since we do not use the data generated from the simulation to estimate the founding rate function.

Distribution of Size at Founding. We simulate initial size as a realization from negative exponential distribution. With the parameter settings we use, the expected mode is 1.0 and the expected median is 4.47. Given that we use an employee-size imagery, we round size values to integers. Under this regime, an illustrative simulated distribution generates a mode of 1, a median of 4, a mean of 5.6, and a maximum value of 38.

Mortality Rate Function. The hazard of mortality for organization i depends upon its age (u), its size (S), contemporaneous population density $(N_t$—a count of the number of organizations at $t)$, and population density at the time of the organization's founding (N_0):

$$\mu_i(u, t) = \beta_0 \exp(\beta_1 N_t + \beta_2 N_t^2 + \beta_3 N_0 + \beta_4 S_{iu} + \beta_5 u). \tag{7.10}$$

As explained in the chapters in Part III, researchers commonly find that the values of these parameters obey the following inequalities: $\beta_1 < 0$,

---

[12] The simulation program, known as *CorpSim*, was written and developed by Michael Kinstlick in the C language. J. Richard Harrison also made important contributions to the design and implementation of this simulation. Indeed, both contributed in major ways to the simulation analysis reported here.

$\beta_2 > 0$, $\beta_3 > 0$, $\beta_4 < 0$, and $\beta_5 < 0$. Therefore, we used values within these ranges in the simulation.

Growth/Decline in Size. The size of an organization changes each period in integer increments via a linear stochastic arrival–departure model, resembling the arrival and departure of individual employees. We set the "arrival" component (positive increments in size) to be Poisson distributed with a rate that depends upon current size, recent growth in size (from last period), and age. The predicted changes in size are likely serially correlated. The "departure" component (decrements in size) has a parallel structure.

The function we use is

$$S(t+1) = S(t) + A(t) - D(t) \tag{7.11}$$

where $S(t)$ indicates the organization's size at time t, $A(t)$ indicates arrivals between t and $t+1$, and $D(t)$ indicates departures. We generate the flow of arrivals $A(t)$ as a realization of a Poisson process with rate ϕ:

$$\Pr\{A = a\} = \frac{\phi^a e^{-\phi}}{a!}. \tag{7.12}$$

The rate for the period t to $t+1$ is given by

$$\phi_t = \exp\left(a_0 + a_1 \ln S_t + a_2 \frac{\Delta S_t}{S_{t-1}} + a_3 u\right), \tag{7.13}$$

where $\Delta S_t = S_t - S_{t-1}$. Likewise, we generate the flow of departures $D(t)$ as a realization of a Poisson process with rate ψ:

$$\Pr\{D = d\} = \frac{\psi^d e^{-\psi}}{d!}. \tag{7.14}$$

The rate for the period t to $t+1$ is given by

$$\psi_t = \exp\left(b_0 + b_1 \ln S_t + b_2 \frac{\Delta S_t}{S_{t-1}} + b_3 u\right). \tag{7.15}$$

A special problem arises with this specification: the projected size changes sometimes generate a zero or negative value of size, which is meaningless given our reliance on employee-size imageries. Although this situation might be regarded as a sort of "shrink-death," letting organizations die in this manner greatly complicates the true mortality model.[13] To preserve a simple model for evaluating observation schemes, we fix a floor on size of unity and set any organization's value to unity when it

---

[13] The mortality process becomes a combination of the result of the hazard of mortality and a "first-passage time" of a diffusion process.

would be predicted to go lower. With the parameter settings we use (specified below), the resulting distributions of size have the general shape and character of real organizational population size distributions: they are unimodal skew distributions with long right tails. For example, after 300 months an arbitrarily chosen simulated population shows a modal size of 1, a median of 7, a mean of 27, and a maximum size of 535; after 400 months the same population shows a mode of 1, a median of 9, a mean of 39, and a maximum of 851.

Organizational Structure Function. Now we consider the implications of alternative designs for estimation of common specifications of interorganizational variation in some feature of internal structure, such as degree of hierarchy or formalization. Explaining variation in such features constitutes one of the main programs of organization theory. In the simulation, internal organizational structure is given by a single variable calculated as a function of size and age for each organization at each point in time:

$$V_i(u) = f(S_{iu}, u). \tag{7.16}$$

Based upon the results reported by Kalleberg et al. (1996, 84) from the National Organizations Study (NOS), we use a log-quadratic formulation for the size–structure relationship and a linear formulation for the age–structure relationship:

$$V(u) = \gamma_0 + \gamma_1 \ln S_u + \gamma_2 [\ln S_u]^2 + \gamma_3 u + \epsilon, \tag{7.17}$$

where ϵ is normally distributed error term with mean 0.[14] Note that the specification for internal organizational structure is completely *static*. In other words, there is no time lag or other temporal dimension in the underlying simulation model for this process. Representative sampling is often thought to be the ideal observation plan for this type of outcome and process.

Assessing Design Trade-offs

Our main criterion in evaluating observation plans involves assessing the quality of estimates of structural parameters across the major features of the observation plans. Accomplishing this task requires first simulating full population data (following the model specified above) and then comparing coefficient estimates for various subsets of the data defined by observation plan.

---

[14]We set the variance of the disturbance so as to yield in our regression estimates of structure model explained variance values of around 0.50, figures roughly comparable to those reported in the NOS.

The orienting question for this analysis concerns the trade-offs between multipopulation and single-population designs under various observation schemes, including those with common flaws (e.g., size-truncated observation). Does the comprehensiveness of the multipopulation design make it superior? When, if ever, will the single-population design be preferable in that it produces less bias?

Simulation Framework. To set up the analysis in an evenhanded way, we assume that outcomes for organizations in every population are governed by a set of universal processes. That is, we assume that, for any given process, a single parameter value (θ) governs all organizations in a multipopulation system. We further assume that the process for any single population of organizations will be governed by a value near but not exactly equal to θ due to heterogeneity. Let this single-population parameter be $\theta_k = \theta + \delta_k$ for population k, where $E(\delta_k) = 0$ for all k. Thus, for any given single population even an unbiased sample estimate of θ will likely not yield the "true" universal value (it would yield that population's specific θ_k). A combined sample of many populations might very well do so if the values of θ_k are random and symmetrically distributed.

Once we have simulated the population data, we apply ML techniques to estimate the values of all parameters, but we focus on estimates of θ. We estimate θ with data drawn from observation plans created to resemble the major features of the three generic designs: the single-population census, the multipopulation census, and the multipopulation representative sample (Chapter 5). For the single-population census, we use the complete historical population data generated by the industry-specific parameter θ_k.

For the multipopulation designs, we use a temporal "slice" of each population's history and combine a set of slices, thus giving less historical information on any given population but giving observations across data generated with a range of θ_k values centered on the "true" universal value. Given that the dates of the slices are chosen randomly, the multipopulation designs yield data with observations from populations of varying ages, as does a random sample of organizations drawn at any particular date. To capture differences in the measurement capabilities of the representative sample and the multipopulation census, we vary model specification in estimation. Representative sampling in the cross section usually does not allow measurement of covariates that refer to conditions in the organization's past (e.g., its density at founding). We reflect this fact in the model specifications, as we explain below.

We contend that these schemes represent fairly the main trade-off contained in actual designs: full temporal coverage for a unrepresentative single population versus shorter temporal observation of a broadly representative set of populations, sometimes with measurement and specification problems.[15] So that the data sets have roughly equal statistical power, we fix the length of the slices so that a combined set (intended to represent a multipopulation scheme) contains roughly the same number of observations (data points) as a full-population sample.

7.5 Simulation Findings

Mortality Rates

We structure a first set of simulations with ten different populations indexed by k. Each population has exactly the same parameters except for the constant parameter associated with the baseline mortality rate β_0 in the model specification above. That is, we choose β_0 to be the population heterogeneity parameter θ discussed above. For this parameter, we randomly assign to each population k a value by drawing δ_k and adding this value to β_0 to set the value of β_{0k}. This randomly assigned value of β_{0k} is fixed for each population k for the entire simulation. The random component δ_{0k}, drawn from a normal distribution with mean 0 and variance 1, is used to set the standard deviation of the parameter β_0 to 0.04 across populations. We set the value of the "universal" parameter β_0 to 0.10 so that the random component essentially creates 40% heterogeneity in the baseline mortality rate across populations. This setting might be construed to represent the effects of industry-specific factors and institutions.

We chose a set of parameters that resemble those estimated from population data collected empirically and that behave well in the simulation program. In terms of the function specified above, these are: $\beta_0 = 0.100$, $\beta_1 = -0.015$, $\beta_2 = 0.000018$, $\beta_3 = 0.006$, $\beta_4 = 0$, and $\beta_5 = -0.021$. We simulated each population on a monthly basis for 50 years of time. We ran 50 different independent populations, each time using a different "seed" for random number generation. For multipopulation data, we combined the populations into unique nonoverlapping sets of ten populations, thus yielding five multipopulation data sets.[16] Figure 7.3 shows a realization of a set of five populations using these parameters.

We first compare parameters estimated from the simulation data using two different observation plans: (1) a *full-population* observation plan

---

[15] We also examined multipopulation data where the slices are all taken at the same point late in each population's history (last six years). Estimates from these data perform much more poorly than any others reported here.

[16] In order to have equal numbers of point estimates for the various plans, we have also recombined the populations into 50 possibly overlapping sets of ten populations by randomly resampling the data. These estimates are not independent, so we do not report them in detail. It is reassuring to know, however, that they do not yield different conclusions from the estimates reported here.

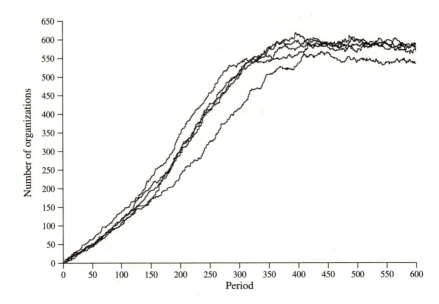

Figure 7.3.   *Time paths of simulated populations.*

whereby a single population's data for the entire 50 years is used (we obtain 50 sets of estimates of this kind); and (2) a *window-truncated, multipopulation* observation plan with a randomly chosen six-year window of data for each of ten populations (we obtain five sets of estimates of this kind). The window-truncated observation plan resembles the multipopulation designs where the industries would be of various ages. At least some research that uses this observation plan (e.g., that based on representative sampling) cannot collect data on firm histories prior to the start of the window. Among other things, this means that density at founding (N_0) cannot be measured due to the inability to record the histories of all of the relevant firms.[17] So, for the window-truncated sample, we estimate a model with the effect of N_0 omitted as well as (for analytical comparison) one with it included.

Table 7.2 shows how the estimates obtained from using these three observation plans performed with the simulated data. It reports the mean bias across a set of estimates (calculated as the estimated value minus the true value) as well as the mean squared error (MSE), calculated as the absolute value of mean bias plus the standard deviation of estimates.

---

[17] Of course, representative-sampling also might not allow for measurement of contemporaneous density and multipopulation censuses might not allow for measurement of density at founding. Our goal is not to reproduce exactly these designs in their entirety, but to isolate and allow assessment of certain features.

Table 7.2. *Quality of estimates of the mortality function in (7.10) with* $\beta_4 = 0$ *for various designs.*

	Parameter				
	β_0	β_1	$\beta_2/100$	β_3	β_5
True value	0.1000	−0.0150	0.0180	0.0060	−0.0210
Full window, single-pop. design					
Bias	0.0022	−0.0002	0.0005	0.0000	0.0019
MSE	0.0584	0.0027	0.0044	0.0006	0.0098
Misspecified, window-truncated, multipop. design					
Bias	−0.0664	0.0239	−0.0225		−0.0756
MSE	0.1014	0.0436	0.0435		0.0825
Window-truncated, multipop. design					
Bias	−0.0742	0.0178	−0.0257	0.0008	0.0156
MSE	0.0972	0.0315	0.0401	0.0017	0.0331

Note: The true values of β_0 have a standard deviation of 0.04 across populations. For exact comparability, the same underlying data are used with each set of estimates; only the observation windows differ.

The estimates for the full single-population data look quite good, especially considering that there is 40% heterogeneity in the β_0 parameter across the populations. Estimates of β_0 are biased upward very slightly, with a mean of 0.102 instead of the true value of 0.10. However, estimates of the other parameters in the mortality model are also all of very high quality with this observation plan.

The window-truncated data yield estimates of much poorer quality. The β_0 parameter gets underestimated by a large fraction of its value. Moreover, estimates of the other parameters vary wildly from their true values, often showing even the wrong sign (the mean bias is larger in absolute value and opposite in sign from the true value). This pattern holds for both the realistic misspecified model as well as for the one using the data on density at founding.

What happens if we include an effect of size in the mortality function? We addressed this question by generating data with size effects from the size-change function above with parameters $a_0 = b_0 = -0.10$, $a_1 = b_1 = 1.0$, $a_2 = b_2 = 0.30$, and $a_3 = b_3 = -0.03$. We fix a floor of size at 1.0 and set any organization at this level if its size-change functions try to drive it lower. The resulting distribution of size in 50 simulated populations has, for example, at year 10 a median of 5.4 and a mean of 17.0 (maximum size of 495) and, at year 50, a median of 10.8 and a mean of 62.9 (maximum of 2936). In the mortality function, we set $\beta_4 = -0.25$ and keep the other parameters in the model the same.

Because many multipopulation censuses exclude organizations below a certain size, we examine size-truncated observation plans here as well as full single-population and window-truncated designs. The size-truncated designs exclude all spells with a size of less than 10. We examine size-truncated observation plans in isolation and in conjunction with window truncation. As before, we look at both misspecified (omitting density at founding) and correctly specified models, both with window truncation.

Table 7.3 reports the bias and MSE of estimates with size effects included in the mortality model. The full single-population data again yield high-quality estimates: the mean estimates all fall within 10% of their true values, and the standard deviations are relatively small. Only the constant, β_0, and the size effect, β_4, seem to be even slightly affected by the 40% heterogeneity in the base rates.

Table 7.3. *Quality of estimates of the mortality function in equation (7.10) under left truncation and size truncation.*

	Parameter					
	β_0	β_1	$\beta_2/100$	β_3	β_4	β_5
True values	0.1000	−0.0150	0.0180	0.0060	−0.2500	−0.0210
Full window, single-pop. design						
Bias	−0.0085	−0.0002	0.0000	−0.0002	0.0222	0.0003
MSE	0.0640	0.0020	0.0003	0.0008	0.0482	0.0077
Size-truncated, single-pop. design						
Bias	−0.0588	−0.0001	−0.0135	−0.0004	0.0460	−0.0055
MSE	0.1076	0.0231	0.0177	0.0018	0.1329	0.0244
Misspecified size- and window-truncated, multipop. design						
Bias	−0.0840	0.0299	−0.0186		0.0496	−0.0839
MSE	0.1008	0.0534	0.0243		0.7300	0.0933
Size- and window-truncated, multipop. design						
Bias	−0.0789	0.0137	−0.0175	−0.0009	0.0196	−0.0073
MSE	0.0980	0.0331	0.0222	0.0028	0.0422	0.0299

Note: The true values of β_0 have a standard deviation of 0.040 across populations. For exact comparability, the same underlying data are used with each set of estimates; only the observation windows differ.

The estimates for the multipopulation data with only size truncation have inferior quality in all but one instance (for β_1), despite being generally in the neighborhood of the true values. However, when size truncation and window truncation are combined, the bias increases substantially for most parameters whether the model is correctly specified or not (the single exception is β_4). Obviously, window truncation leads to poor-quality estimates of parameters of mortality rate functions.

Internal Organizational Structure

We now turn to the relationship between internal organizational structure and organizational size and age. This analysis is substantively important, because those who advocate multipopulation sampling schemes often focus on cross-sectional relationships among such variables rather than on corporate vital rates or other dynamic processes. For instance, Kalleberg et al. (1996, 13) state that

> The NOS is well-suited to testing implications of some of the organizational theories we have mentioned...for example...on organizational structures and elements of the employment relation. As a cross-sectional survey, however, the NOS is not an effective vehicle for examining the dynamic propositions included in organizational ecology, for example.

Our investigation of these issues uses the same basic simulation setup, with a modification for heterogeneity in internal organizational structure across populations. We generate a set of simulations with ten different populations indexed by k. Each population has exactly the same parameters with two exceptions: (1) the constant (β_0) associated with the baseline mortality rate; and (2) the constant (γ_0) in the internal structure function specified above. That is, we choose both β_0 and γ_0 to be *population-specific* heterogeneity parameters. We treat β_0 and γ_0 as before. To wit, each population k is randomly assigned a value by drawing η_k and adding this value to γ_0 to set the value of γ_{0k}. This randomly assigned value of γ_{0k} is thus held constant for each population k for the entire simulation. The random component η_{0k} is drawn from a normal distribution with mean 0 and variance 1; it is used to set the standard deviation of γ_0 to 0.05 across populations. Given that we set the value of the "universal" parameter γ_0 to 0.10, the random component essentially creates 50% heterogeneity in the baseline level of internal structure across populations. Again, this setup might be interpreted as representing the effects of industry-specific factors and institutions.

To specify the structural relationships, we chose a set of parameters that fairly closely resemble those estimated by Kalleberg et al. (1996,

84) from the cross-sectional, multipopulation NOS. In terms of the cross-sectional internal-organizational structure function specified above, these are: $\gamma_1 = 0.5$, $\gamma_2 = -0.033$, and $\gamma_3 = 0.05$.

We conducted the simulations as described above: we simulated each population on a monthly basis for 50 years of time. We calculated the structure function for each organization at each month of its existence. We ran 50 different independent populations, each time using a different "seed" for generating random numbers. For multipopulation data, we again combined the populations into unique sets of ten populations. We estimated the coefficients from the simulated data by regressing the values of the structure variable $V(u)$ on the values of the covariates based on size and age.

For size-truncated schemes, we based estimation on only those observations with size exceeding 10. For window truncation, we used observations from only a single point in time in order to mimic the fully cross-sectional data commonly used to estimate relationships between structural variables.[18]

Table 7.4 shows the quality of the estimated internal-organizational structure function under the different observation schemes. The full-window, single-population design performs quite well, despite the lack of information on population heterogeneity. The estimates of all three coefficients show minimal bias across the runs; variability is also low except for the constants (γ_0), which reflects the differences across populations.

Size-truncated observation produces estimates of lower quality. The biases for all coefficients (except age) are roughly an order of magnitude larger than those of the full single-population design. The MSE values of the estimates are also larger. Although the quality of the estimates of the size effects might be expected to deteriorate under this plan, it is interesting that the estimates of γ_0 do as well.

The impact of observation plan on the quality of estimates of the effect of age differs because of our simple linear specification of the age effect. Indeed, other simulations that we have run show clearly that making the size specification linear also reduces the severe bias shown here. It is important to recognize, however, that most theories and empirical studies of internal structure posit nonlinear specifications for *both* size and age (Kalleberg et al. 1996).

The estimates from the multipopulation observation plans also have very poor quality. With only window truncation (in fact, a single period of time), the quality of the estimates runs roughly similar to that for only size truncation: the bias and MSE are lower for the constant γ_0 but higher for

---

[18]We also estimated models using wider windows for truncation and reached similar conclusions.

Table 7.4. *Quality of estimates of the organizational-structure function in equation (7.17).*

	Parameter			
	γ_0	γ_1	γ_2	γ_3
True value	0.1000	0.5000	−0.0330	0.0500
Full window, single-pop. design				
Bias	0.0039	−0.0026	0.0005	0.0000
MSE	0.0544	0.0219	0.0042	0.0001
Size-truncated, single-pop. design				
Bias	−0.0518	0.0247	−0.0029	0.0000
MSE	0.3567	0.1776	0.0217	0.0001
Window-truncated (cross-sectional) multipop. design				
Bias	−0.0417	0.0462	0.0145	−0.0005
MSE	0.2967	0.2397	0.0747	0.0016
Size- and window-truncated (cross-sectional), multipop. design				
Bias	-10.171	0.6482	−0.0732	−0.0011
MSE	20.575	10.365	0.1683	0.0020

Note: The true values of γ_0 have a standard deviation of 0.050 across populations. For exact comparability, the same underlying data are used with each set of estimates; only the observation windows differ.

the other coefficients. So, in moving to short multipopulation observation plans, the gains in quality of γ_0 are offset by losses in quality elsewhere. When size truncation is also incorporated, the quality of all estimates (except the effect of age) becomes downright embarrassing. As the last line of the table shows, the biases and MSEs under these common conditions are very large.

Sensitivity of results to specific parameter settings and other procedural choices is an important issue in evaluating any simulation. Although we cannot examine all of the myriad combinations of simulation choices in exhaustive detail, it does behoove the investigator to explore a range of settings and procedures for the major features. We have done so for many of these simulations by altering: (1) model parameters; (2) length of simulation period (up to 200 years); (3) level of heterogeneity in β_0; (4) location of heterogeneity in mortality model parameters; (5) timing of window truncation period; (6) minimum size used in size truncation schemes; (7) specification of the size-change function; and (8) inclusion rules for firms that drop below the size truncation level after surpassing it. We do not find anything in the results of these numerous simulations that suggests to us that the findings reported above are misleading.

In general, the simulation findings presented here illustrate vividly some of the problems associated with multipopulation research designs and observation plans. These problems emerge in typical implementations of both broad representative samples and multipopulation censuses. By contrast, the single-population study covering a long period performs much better than the other designs, despite lacking representativeness. In our view, this design does much better than many analysts would expect. So, we imagine that these findings will stimulate discussion and inquiry into this important methodological issue. Nonetheless, we believe that it is clear now that the single-population design usually provides a sounder basis for empirical research on corporate demography and organizational change.

8

Demographic Data Sources

MODELING IN CORPORATE DEMOGRAPHY involves specifying theoretical processes in mathematical form and then estimating the parameters of the specified models. Chapters 6 and 7 showed how the class of models that we recommend—continuous-time models of stochastic events—can be estimated with a variety of different types of data, provided certain assumptions can be sustained. Indeed, a major attraction of these models is that parameter estimates can be compared meaningfully across different data structures. So, for instance, a researcher whose data cover a period of twenty years can estimate the same model as researchers whose data cover periods of five, forty, and three hundred years. Likewise, researchers with data in the form of event counts, event histories, and longitudinal panels can all estimate comparable parametric specifications (Tuma and Hannan 1984). This feature greatly facilitates comparative analysis and therefore assists theory construction as well.

Of course, the generality of continuous-time demographic models does not mean that concerns about data quality are irrelevant. Meaningful estimation of parameters still depends, first, on the use of appropriate observation plans, second, on high-quality measurement of the observable aspects of underlying processes, and third, on the use of plausible assumptions about the processes (given the observation plan). So, in this chapter, we discuss data sources and data quality for corporate demography.

We first discuss some general standards for evaluating research designs for corporate demography. These standards concern both the structure of data and the measurement properties. The bulk of the chapter then examines a variety of types of data sources commonly used by researchers studying corporate demography. These include annual directories, governmental registries, archives, censuses, surveys, and others. When appropriate, we show illustrative documents. We also discuss the typical scope of the data available and the quality of measurement of key variables for each type of source. Overall, we hope that this chapter will provide a sense of the issues involved in evaluating and using available demographic data on corporations and other organizations.

8.1 Criteria for Evaluating Sources

What criteria should be used in evaluating source data? Given the complicated possibilities, we think it is practical to evaluate sources against a set of specific dimensions. Human demographers evaluate census data in terms of *coverage* and *content*. According to Shryock and Siegel (1971, 56), coverage errors "result from persons being missed or counted more than once" while content errors correspond to "errors in the characteristics of the persons counted." For organizational-population data, it makes sense to refine this general scheme to include errors of four possible types. These involve: (1) organizational coverage; (2) temporal coverage; (3) the precision in the timing information; and (4) accuracy of organization-specific information. The first two might be considered coverage issues and the last two, content issues.

By quality of organizational coverage, we mean the extent to which the source includes information about *all* organizations that fit the definition of the population or industry. The most common deficiency is *underinclusion*, especially of small and marginal organizations, as we discuss below. Often sources include only organizations above some certain size or within some conventional product definition of the industry. At a theoretical level, industry boundaries might be regarded as somewhat arbitrary and ambiguous. However, in empirical research, the coding rules must be clear-cut, which means that the boundaries must be clear-cut. One issue with organizational coverage consists of whether all operating organizations that satisfy the rules for inclusion appear in the source. A related issue concerns whether these organizations can be readily identified.

Oddly enough, a lack of identifying information in an abundant source might indicate another deficiency: *overinclusion*. This problem exists when the source contains unwanted "extra" organizations, perhaps those from a related but different population. A particularly problematic type of overinclusion occurs when the source lists "phantom" or "paper corporations" that have no social basis. For instance, in our research on the American automobile manufacturing industry, the major source (the *Standard Catalog* discussed below) included listings for many companies and individuals that were likely not to have actually engaged in production or even a serious attempt to enter production. For instance, some are described as "stock swindles." Researchers will, of course, want to exclude these types of entries from a source and need sufficient identifying information to be able to do so.

Quality of temporal coverage refers to the extent to which the observation period covers the critical times in the population's history. Obviously, this criterion would imply that a good source should cover the times of initiation, major transformations, and renewals for a corporate population. However, for comparative purposes it also implies that other periods should be observed—otherwise, there is no sound way to assess a period's uniqueness. In other words, the periods of stability convey information as do the periods of turmoil. Good designs collect information on both.

In general, long observation periods are better than short ones. Two other considerations are important for getting good estimates of many important population processes. First, the start of the observation window should be set as close as possible to the population's inception, ideally to the time of first founding or entry. This is because, as we show in later chapters, many of the relevant population processes are strongly path dependent or time dependent. Failure to observe the early phases of such processes exacerbates problems of left truncation in estimation, as the simulations in Chapter 7 show. Second, the width of the observation window should be made wide enough that many ending events are observed. Narrow windows with few observed events create inference problems; they also usually make it very difficult to detect time dependence in vital rates.

Precision concerns the dating of events. Assuming high reliability in a source, the more precision in dating the better; exact dates of events are best. Among other things, exact dates allow the recovery of full information on the ordering of events within the population. However, reliability might be low, meaning that dates are not always recorded in the same manner for each organization. In many of the data sources that we have studied closely, exact dates (day and month) of certain events are reported for some organizations and only years are reported for others. We advise that all of the detail available be coded and that the analyst try different ways of treating the dates to learn about the robustness of the empirical patterns to the varying accuracy of the information on timing.[1]

Organizational detail matters because it allows individual organizations to be distinguished from one another. Good source data provide, at a minimum, information about ownership, organizational form, and the size of each organization. Each type of information should be recorded regularly across the lifetimes of every individual organization. Initial ownership arrangements and organizational form should be recorded along with the sequence and timing of all subsequent changes in ownership and form. Likewise, size at founding should be recorded along with periodic updates

---

[1]A special class of industries (e.g., newspaper and book publishers) produce material products that occasionally survive across the years and can possibly be examined themselves for dating information.

for the life of each organization. Updates should be spaced so that most temporal variation in the information is captured in the record. Considerations of efficient use of resources might require some compromise, such as when corporate size gets updated annually even though changes occur on an almost daily basis for large corporations.

Obviously, real sources rarely match the ideal of providing a complete and fully accurate representation of the population history. Although the ideal will be unknown in most real research settings, external information can often be used to uncover clues about the quality of a source. For instance, historical references sometime tell when the first organization began operating in a population. Hannan and Freeman (1984) noted that Mittleman (1927) reports that the first American national labor unions appeared in 1836. This piece of information can be used to evaluate the coverage in a source. If the source contains records about labor unions as far back as 1836, then it passes this first test. If it begins coverage at a later date, then it is obviously incomplete.

Sometimes external information about a set of well-known cases can be used in the validation exercise. This kind of test is a weaker one, because information on well-known cases is much easier to come by than information on short-lived and unimportant ones. Perhaps a more helpful use of external information would involve taking a random sample of information from an incomplete but authoritative source to validate a more complete source whose quality is unknown. This evaluation procedure involves comparing the sample from the source against a set of independent facts known or believed to be accurate. These uses of external information provide convenient and efficient ways to evaluate a source prior to engaging in the expensive and time-consuming process of coding and cleaning all of the data in a source.

Another efficient method for evaluating a data source often proves productive: comparing aggregate numbers or marginal distributions tabulated from a data source with those reported elsewhere. Sometimes aggregate counts on, say, the number of firms in an industry in a particular year (and perhaps by size class) appear in the summary data provided by governments and industry associations. For instance, Barnett and Carroll (1993) found that *Telephony's Directory* reported annually a table that indicated the number of operating telephone companies by state and by organization form.

A source listing of individual firms might contain a similar count; or one can be calculated with modest effort. Comparing the two sets of aggregate numbers gives some indication as to how a source stacks up (for example, whether it is more or less inclusive than the standard). This procedure can also sometimes be undertaken prior to full data collection.

A third way to evaluate a source prior to data collection involves soliciting the opinions of industry experts. Generally speaking, an expert is someone who knows the industry and its firms; this might include industry historians, industry analysts in the investment banking and stock brokerage industries, employees of firms, and customers or suppliers of the industry. Experts usually can provide valuable information about the design of a source and also assess its accuracy. These assessments should not be taken at face value; however, they clearly suggest good leads for the researcher to pursue.

A fourth method of assessing the quality of data sources can be used only after all of the data have been collected. Thus, it suffers by comparison to the other options in efficiency. However, this method has proved to be handy for demonstrating the quality of data with some known flaws. The method consists of estimating known baseline models of organizational and population processes with the data (e.g., the model of density dependence discussed in Chapters 10 and 11) and comparing these estimates to the range of previously reported findings. No method is foolproof. This one might be more questionable than others in evaluating a data source in that it depends so heavily on theoretical assumptions about demographic processes. Still we dare say that data generating estimates on baselines within the range expected should often be regarded as acceptable (certainly, the exercise supports this assessment). Of course, estimates that fall outside the range might be the result of either flawed data or a unique population of organizations. Only additional study could lead to a firm conclusion.

8.2 Commonly Used Data Sources

What do demographic data look like in raw form? This section identifies and evaluates the types of sources most commonly used to build analysis files on organizational populations. Before getting to the specifics, we would like to comment generally on the availability of various types of sources for particular populations. In the course of about twenty years of demographic research, we have found that each population that we have studied differs in terms of the kinds of data sources that are available and that prove to be valuable. One never knows in advance what kinds of unique sources might be found. The reference librarian or the computerized search will likely identify only the most obvious sources; finding unusual ones often requires a detective's nose, hard work, and luck. There seems to be no substitute for rummaging through the stacks of good research libraries and poring through mounds of old documents. A good

source makes all the difference for a researcher interested in reconstructing the past.

Merton (1987) refers to a source with valuable unique information as
a "strategic research material." It is strategic because it gives us leverage in
making inferences about social and organizational processes. Sometimes
such a source covers only a limited period but allows us to conduct analyses
that add to our confidence about data collected from other sources. For instance, Carroll and Swaminathan (1991) collected data on the life histories
of American breweries from 1633 to 1985 from the primary source of Bull,
Friedrich, and Gottschalk (1984). The source reports the dates of founding
and failure of each brewery, but it does not provide production levels or
capacity. Many small breweries have operated in the United States, and it is
important to know whether estimates of population processes are damaged
by the inability to observe any good measure of size. A partial answer was
provided by an ancillary source, a complete list of breweries by size in 1878
and 1879 found in Salem (1880). By using this snapshot measure and invoking certain assumptions about growth, Carroll and Swaminathan (1991)
could introduce controls for organizational size for this period. Estimates
of the effects of theoretically important variables did not differ substantively in analyses with and without these controls, thus justifying greater
confidence in the original estimates and data.

Industry Directories

Perhaps the most commonly used type of source is the industry directory.
Typically, an industry association or a third-party publishes an annual that
provides information to suppliers and buyers to the industry. Annual directories can be found for many industries; multiple directories exist for some
industries. Directories often spring up early in an industry's development;
so for established industries, long series of directories sometimes exist. By
obtaining a complete series of (accurate) directories and comparing entries
across years, researchers can usually go a long way toward reconstructing
the demographic history of an industry.

Figures 8.1, 8.2, and 8.3 show the listings in N.W. Ayer and Son's *American Newspaper Annual and Directory* for Evansville, Indiana for 1910, 1911,
and 1912, respectively. N.W. Ayer and Son is an advertising agency, which
publishes the directory as a service to its clients and the public. The Ayer's
Directory dates from 1880. (Another directory, published by G.P. Rowell,
started in 1869 and was subsequently acquired and merged with Ayer's.) It
aims to report a complete list of all newspapers published in the United
States and its possessions and Canada. It covers daily newspapers, monthly
and weekly publications, and so-called class publications. The *Directory* ex-

EVANSVILLE†, pop. 63,957 (B 9) ; VANDERBURG CO. (S.W.), pop. 71,769. On Ohio R., 195 m. bel. Louisville. Railroad center, having the S'thrn and five other railroads. Tel. Exp. Banks. Extensive manufactures, including 12 flour mills, and several foundries and machine shops, breweries, planing and saw mills, woolen mills, a cotton factory, employing 400 hands, and many others. Surrounded by extensive beds of coal (10 mines). Center of a great tobacco producing section, one of the largest hardwood lumber markets in the United States, and has an extensive shipping business in corn, wheat, pork and tobacco. Willard Library and Art Gallery, a United States Marine Hospital and Southern Indiana Hospital for the Insane.

Advocate ....Saturday............Labor	1906	4	17×22	.50	
JAUS & DRAIN, Editors and Publishers.					
Architect, Builder and Con-⎫ tractor ....⎬ Monthly ....Trade	1907	22	9×12	2.00	
SPEED PRINTING AND PUBLISHING COMPANY.					
Courier ....⎰ Every Morn......Democratic....	1865	10–20 17×22	2.50	⋆**17,322**	
⎱ *Sunday edition*..................	30–40 17×22	2.00	⋆**13,750**			
EVANSVILLE COURIER PUBLISHING COMPANY (Inc.), 125 Main St.					
Demokrat (German)..................⎰ *Morn. ex. Mon*...Ind. Dem........	1864	8–16 18×23	4.00	‡4,972	
⎱ *Sunday edition*..................	16–36 18×23	2.00	‡5,320			
Demokrat (Ger.)—*in two parts* ⎰ Weekly ....Ind. Dem........	1864	16 18×23	2.00	‡8,320	
Tues. & Fri...............................⎱					ᶳᴱᴱ ᴬᴰᵛᵀ
HANS SCHELLER and Associates Editors ; FREDERICK W. LAUENSTEIN, Pub., 403 Main St.					
Economist ....Saturday............Republican. ...	1896	4	18×24	1.00	1,500
G. W. DANNETTELL, Editor and Publisher.					
Furniture Industry ....Monthly ....Trade	1901	56	9×12	1.00	‡3,961
J. S. REILLY, Publisher.					
Indiana Post und Freie Presse ⎱ Saturday.............Independent ..	1879	8	17×24	2.00	
(German) ....⎰					
CARL LANGNER, Editor and Publisher, 110 Upper Fourth St.					
Journal-News ....Evg. *ex. Sun*......Republican.....	1851	10–12 17×24	5.00		
Journal-News ....Sunday ....Republican.....	1871	24–36 17×24	2.00		
EVANSVILLE JOURNAL-NEWS COMPANY, Editors and Publishers.					
Journal—Public Health...............Monthly ....Hygienic.......	1903	36	6×9	.50	1,250
COLUMBIA PAXTON-WOOD, Editor and Publisher, 108 Powell Ave.					
Press..Evg. *ex. Sun*......Independent ..	1906	8	18×22	3.00	⋆**7,143**
WARD C. MAYBORN, Publisher, 212 Vine St.					
Pythian Knight (Eng. & Ger.)......Monthly ....I. O. K. of P.....	1894	8	11×16	.50	‡6,500
HENRY ROSENTHAL, Editor and Publisher.					
Star-Bulletin ....Saturday ....Ind. & Liquor..	1905	8	18×24	2.00	‡4,000
WILLIAM L. AYRES, Editor and Publisher, 308½ Upper Third St.					
Sternenbanner (German)..............Friday ....Cath. & Dem...	1882	8	18×24	2.00	1,500
PETER WALLRATH, Editor and Publisher, 118 Locust St.					
Visitor ....Saturday............Republican.....	1900	8	12×17	1.00	
MRS. NELLIE FRITZ, Editor and Publisher.					

Figure 8.1. *Entries for Evansville, Ind. in N.W. Ayer and Son's American Newspaper Annual and Directory, 1910.*

cludes those publications "having no value for the general advertiser or the general public" (1912: 5). This rule excludes papers published by

> ... private and high schools, the smaller colleges, local church papers, papers issued by business houses primarily for the exploitation of their own goods, and generally known as 'house organs' and publications issued in the interest of institutions, unless otherwise having an influence outside of the particular one by or for which they are published.

The *Directory* also tells us that

> ... care has been exercised in the selection of periodicals which rightly come within the scope of this work. Experience teaches us that it is not wise to insert every paper when it is first issued, for while the exclusion might be unfortunate in a few instances, much dead matter is thereby kept out of the book; as many of these ventures have very short lives. (1912: 5)

Even with these exclusions, the *Directory* lists a very large number of papers. In 1912, for instance, it listed 23,345 publications, including 1,635 new ones.

EVANSVILLE†, pop.‖69,647 (B 9); VANDERBURG Co. (S. W.), pop. 71,769. On Ohio R., 195 m. bel. Louisville. Railroad center, having the S'thrn and five other railroads. Tel. Exp. Banks. Extensive manufactures, including 12 flour mills, and several foundries and machine shops, breweries, planing and saw mills, woolen mills, a cotton factory, employing 400 hands, and many others. Surrounded by extensive beds of coal (10 mines). Center of a great tobacco producing section, one of the largest hardwood lumber markets in the United States, and has an extensive shipping business in corn, wheat, pork and tobacco. Willard Library and Art Gallery, a United States Marine Hospital and Southern Indiana Hospital for the Insane.

Advocate ....Saturday............Labor .... 1906 4–8 17×22 .50							
P. D. DRAIN & W. F. JAUS, Editors and Publishers.							
Architect, Builder and Con- } Monthly ....Trade .... 1907 22 9×12 2.00							
tractor .... }							
SPEED PRINTING AND PUBLISHING COMPANY.							
Courier .... } Every Morn......Democratic..... 1865 10–20 17×22 5.00∗**17,144**							
} *Sunday edition*..... .... 30–40 17×22 2.50∗**13,015**							
EVANSVILLE COURIER PUBLISHING COMPANY (Inc.), 125 Main St.							
Demokrat (German)................. { Morn. *ex. Mon.*..Ind. Dem........ 1864 8–16 18×23 4.00 ∗5,072							
{ *Sunday edition*................. 16–36 18×23 2.00 ∗5,380							
Demokrat (Ger.)—*in two parts,* } Weekly ....Ind. Dem........ 1864 16 18×23 2.00 ∗8,151							
Tues. & Fri. .... }							
HANS SCHELLER and Associates Editors; FREDERICK W. LAUENSTEIN, Pub., 403 Main St.							
Economist ....Saturday............Republican. ... 1896 4 18×24 1.00 1,250							
G. W. DANNETTELL, Editor and Publisher.							
Furniture Industry ....Monthly ....Trade .... 1901 56 9×12 1.00 †2,500							
J. S. REILLY, Publisher.							
Indiana Post und Freie Presse } Saturday..... ....Independent .. 1879 8 17×24 2.00							
(German) .... }							
CARL LANGNER, Editor and Publisher, 110 Upper Fourth St.							
Journal-News ....Evg. *ex. Sun*......Republican..... 1851 10–12 17×24 5.00 10,000							
Journal-News ....Sunday ....Republican..... 1871 24–36 17×24 2.00 12,000							
EVANSVILLE JOURNAL-NEWS COMPANY, Editors and Publishers.							
Journal—Public Health.................Quarterly...........Hygienic .... 1903 36 6×9 .50							
COLUMBIA PAXTON-WOOD, Editor and Publisher, 108 Powell Ave.							
Press..Evg. *ex. Sun*......Independent .. 1906 8 18×22 3.00∗**10,560**							
F. R. PETERS & MARK L. FELBER, Editors; EVENING PRESS Co., Pubs., 212 Vine St.							
Pythian Knight (Eng. & Ger.)......Monthly ....I. O. K. of P.... 1894 8 11×16 .50 †6,000							
HENRY ROSENTHAL, Editor and Publisher.							
Star-Bulletin ... .Saturday ....Ind. & Liquor.. 1905 8 18×24 2.00 4,000							
WILLIAM L. AYRES, Editor and Publisher, 308¾ Upper Third St.							
Sternenbanner (German)..............Friday ....Cath. & Dem .. 1882 8 18×24 2.00 1,750							
PETER WALLRATH, Editor and Publisher, 118 Locust St.							
Visitor ....Saturday............Republican..... 1900 8 13×20 1.00 **1,200**							
MRS. NELLIE FRITZ, Editor and Publisher.							

Figure 8.2. *Entries for Evansville, Ind. in N.W. Ayer and Son's American Newspaper Annual and Directory, 1911.*

Ayer's *Directory* for 1912 reported that 11,413 towns had local newspapers. One of these is Evansville, Indiana, a modest-sized place (population at the time about 70,000) located in the southwestern end of the state near Illinois and Kentucky. As the entry in Figure 8.1 shows, Evansville was home to 16 publications in 1910. The *Directory* organizes its entries by publication rather than by publishing firm. Therefore, several entries must be combined (e.g., the multiple entries for the German-language *Demokrat* and for the *Journal–News*) to obtain firm-level information. Doing so identifies 14 newspaper publishing companies in Evansville in 1910; four of them printed daily newspapers: the *Courier*, the *Demokrat*, the *Journal–News*, and the *Press*. Comparing these entries with those for 1911 (Figure 8.2) indicates that no demographic events occurred in the intervening year: we again see the same 16 newspapers and 14 firms.

A second comparison, this time of entries for 1911 and 1912 (Figures 8.2 and 8.3), shows that several events occurred. First, three publishers listed in the 1911 edition do not appear in the 1912 edition: the *Indiana Post und Freie Presse* (founded in 1879), *Journal–Public Health* (established 1903),

EVANSVILLE†, pop. 69,647. B 9); VANDERBURG CO. (S. W.), pop. 77,438. On Ohio R., 195 m.
bel. Louisville. Railroad center, having the S'thrn and five other railroads. Tel. Exp.
Banks. Extensive manufactures, including 12 flour mills, and several foundries and machine shops, breweries, planing and saw mills, woolen mills, a cotton factory. employing 400
hands, and many others. Surrounded by extensive beds of coal (10 mines). Center of a
great tobacco producing section, one of the largest hardwood lumber markets in the United
States, and has an extensive shipping business in corn, wheat, pork and tobacco. Willard
Library and Art Gallery, a United States Marine Hospital and Southern Indiana Hospital
for the Insane.

Advocate ....Saturday...........Labor .... 1906 4-8 17×22 .50
    P. D. DRAIN & W. F. JAUS, Editors and Publishers.

Architect, Builder and Con- } Monthly...........Trade .... 1907 22 9×12 2.00
  tractor .... }
    SPEED PRINTING AND PUBLISHING COMPANY.

Courier......................................{ Every Morn......Democratic..... 1845 10-20 17×22 5.00∗**18,244**
                          { *Sunday edition*.................... 30-40 17×22 2.50∗**12,339**
    EVANSVILLE COURIER PUBLISHING COMPANY (Inc.), 125 Main St.   SEE ADVT

Demokrat (German)..................{ Morn. *ex. Mon*...Ind. Dem........ 1864 8-16 18×22 4.00 †5,001
                          { *Sunday edition*................... 16-36 18×22 2.00 †5,361

Demokrat (Ger.)—*in two parts*, } Weekly ....Ind. Dem........ 1864 16 18×22 2.00 †8,230
  Tues. & Fri.............................. }
    HANS SCHELLER and Associates Editors; FREDERICK W. LAUENSTEIN, Pub., 403 Main St.

Economist ....Saturday...........Republican. ... 1896 4 18×24 1.00 1,100
    G. W. DANNETTELL, Editor and Publisher.

Furniture Industry.......................Monthly ....Trade .... 1901 56 9×12 1.00 2,400
    J. S. REILLY, Publisher.

Journal-News...............................Evg. *ex. Sun*......Republican..... 1851 10-12 17×24 5.00 10,000
Journal-News ....Sunday ....Republican..... 1871 24-36 17×24 2.00 12,000
    EVANSVILLE JOURNAL-NEWS COMPANY, Editors and Publishers.

Press..Evg. *ex. Sun*......Independent .. 1906 8 18×22 3.00∗**11,059**
    EVANSVILLE PRESS COMPANY, Publishers, 212 Vine St.

Pythian Knight (Eng. & Ger.)......Monthly ....I. O. K. of P... 1894 8 11×16 .50 †3,000
    HENRY ROSENTHAL, Editor and Publisher.

Star-Bulletin ....Saturday ....Ind. & Liquor.. 1905 8 18×24 2.00 †3,000
    WILLIAM L. AYRES, Editor and Publisher, 308½ Upper Third St.

Visitor ....Saturday...........Republican..... 1900 8 13×20 1.00 1,200
    MRS. NELLIE FRITZ, Editor and Publisher.

West Side Herald........................Thursday ....Local............... 1911 4 17×24 1.00
    ISRAEL BRENNER, Editor and Publisher.

Figure 8.3. *Entries for Evansville, Ind. in N.W. Ayer and Son's American Newspaper Annual and Directory, 1912.*

and *Sternenbanner* (from 1882). Second, one new firm appears: the publisher of the *West Side Herald*. A check against subsequent years and other
sources would be necessary to verify that these events were indeed beginnings and endings of firms. Nonetheless, the comparisons above show how
industry directories are used to reconstruct the demographic history of a
population or industry.

Industry directories have value for corporate demography because they
enumerate the membership of the organizational population at regular intervals, often once a year. The precision of the dates given in these sources
is always an issue—it is not unusual to find some slippage between actual
dates and when a firm is entered into and removed from a directory. At
best, precision is bounded by the length of the interval between successive
publications of a directory (unless the source reports the dates of firm incorporation and dissolution directly). So, for instance, annual directories
yield dates with precision at best only to the year.

Directories might also miss organizations with lives so short that they
appear and die between publications. However, the comprehensiveness of
coverage of many directory listings usually more than outweighs these de-

ficiencies. Moreover, the periodic nature of directories usually eases the task of collecting time-varying values of important organizational characteristics.

Annual directories have been used as the primary sources for corporate demography studies of newspapers (Carroll 1987; Dobrev 2000; Boone, Carroll, and van Witteloostuijn 1999), semiconductor manufacturers (Hannan and Freeman 1989), banks (Barnett 1997), hotels (Baum and Mezias 1992; Ingram 1996), art museums (Blau 1995), trade associations (Aldrich, Zimmer, Staber, and Beggs 1994), telephone companies (Barnett 1990), wineries (Swaminathan 1995), paper mills (Ohanian 1994), auditors (Buijink, Majoor, van Witteloostuijn, and Zinken 1993; Boone et al. 2000), microprocessors (Wade 1996), and health maintenance organizations (Wholey, Christianson, and Sanchez 1992).

Encyclopedic Compilations

Another source of demographic data comes in the form of encyclopedic compilations. These source books compile information across a variety of organizations and over time. Encyclopedic compilations differ from industry directories in covering many years (whereas directories usually cover only one point in time) and often aggregating information by organization or by their products or services.

A good example of an encyclopedic compilation is the three-volume set on American automobile manufacturers published by Krause Publications of Iola, Wisconsin entitled, *The Standard Catalog of American Cars* (Kimes and Clark 1989; Kimes and Clark 1996; Gunnell, Schrimpf, and Buttolph 1987; Gunnell, Schrimpf, and Buttolph 1992; Flammang 1989). The editors organized their compilation by car marque (or make, the more common American idiom) rather than by firm. So we find entries for such marques as Oldsmobile and Buick but not for corporations such as General Motors. Figures 8.4 and 8.5 reproduce illustrative entries from the first volume (p. 918, volume 1, covering 1805–1942).

Figures 8.4 and 8.5 reproduce four entries. Each contains a different amount of detail, based on what is available in the historical sources underlying *The Standard Catalog*. As its Introduction makes clear, the compilation builds on decades of previous efforts to record the history of the American automobile industry. It also reports the findings of original research by its many expert contributors.

The Standard Catalog is unusual in that it systematically categorizes entries by type. The catalog distinguishes entries for major marques and minor marques (referring to the marque's market presence). As might be expected, this encyclopedia reports much information for the major marques. Major marque entries sometimes consist of many pages; they contain

MALCOLM — Detroit, Michigan — (1914-1915) — In late November of 1913 the Malcolm-Jones Cyclecar Company was launched into business as the 30th new venture in the United States organized to produce a cyclecar. Stockholders included E. Malcolm Jones, C.H. Lawrence and Charles H. Bennett. Their product was to be a two-cylinder tandem two-seater with provision for a third passenger if desired and a single headlight mounted atop the radiator. The price was projected as $395. Only prototypes were built. During the summer of 1914 there was an interim attempt to reorganize as the Malcolm Cyclecar Company and move to another factory in Plymouth, Michigan. Ultimately, however, the decision was made to remain in Detroit and reorganize as the Malcolm Motor Company, since the very word "cyclecar" by now had a negative connotation. For 1915 the Messrs. Jones, Lawrence and Bennett provided their earlier car with two headlights, two more cylinders, a longer wheelbase, and shaft drive instead of the former belt. This Malcolm was called a light roadster, and its price was $425. Memories in Detroit, unfortunately, were not quite as short as the Malcolm people might have wished them to be.

1914 MALCOLM
Cyclecar — 2-cyl., 10/15 hp, 100" wb

	FP	5	4	3	2	1
Roadster	395	2000	3000	4200	6500	14,000

1915 MALCOLM
Four — 18 hp, 106" wb

	FP	5	4	3	2	1
Roadster	425	2200	3200	4400	7000	15,000

MALDEN STEAM — Malden, Massachusetts — (1898/1902) — Although the Malden Automobile Company of Middlesex Court in Malden built its first experimental steam car in 1898, it does not appear the car was marketed until 1902. Among the features claimed for the Malden were a pilot light guaranteed not to burn out and a gasoline tank that could be filled "while the fire is burning." The automatic boiler was fitted with a "fusible plug" also guaranteed not to burn out. Speeds of up to 40 mph were promised. Whether the Malden delivered on all this is very much open to question. What cannot be disputed is that the firm was taken over by the Lynn Automobile Company of Lynn, Massachusetts, in early 1903.

Figure 8.4. *Illustrative entries in The Standard Catalog of American Cars, type 1 and type 3 entries. Source: Kimes et al. (1996). Copyright © 1996 by Krause Publications of Iola, Wisconsin. Used by permission.*

considerable detail on technical matters and prices. (The main purpose of *The Standard Catalog* is to provide information to collectors of old cars and other automobile hobbyists.) The examples in Figures 8.4 and 8.5 pertain to minor marques. They illustrate three basic types of entries. The types of minor marque entries differ mainly in how much data about prices and technical details of the cars are available. The listing for Malcolm exemplifies the *Catalog*'s type 1 entry, which identifies marques known to have gone into "series production." The entries for Malley illustrate type 2; the

MALLEY — The Malley Motor Company was organized in New York City during the spring of 1910 with a capital stock of $500 to manufacture and repair motor vehicles. Thomas Malley of Brooklyn, and W.H. Pumphrey and M.G. Crawford of Manhattan, were the incorporators. Manufacture of a car is doubted.

The Malley Motor Vehicle Company was organized in Boston, Massachusetts, during the summer of 1911 with a capital stock of $50,000 to manufacture and deal in automobiles. Manufacture is doubted, but the firm subsequently became dealers for the Warren and the Flanders Electric.

MALLEY — **Boston, Massachusetts** — **(c. 1905)** — On Huntington Avenue in Boston G.H. Malley built himself a 3-1/2 hp automobile, according to the New England Motor Vehicle Registration Roster published in 1905.

Figure 8.5.   *Illustrative entries in The Standard Catalog of American Cars, type 2 entries. Source: Kimes et al. (1996). Copyright © 1996 by Krause Publications of Iola, Wisconsin. Used by permission.*

Malden Steamer entry is type 3. Both type 2 and type 3 entries describe relatively obscure marques.

For corporate demography, a critical feature of *The Standard Catalog* concerns its reporting of dates of vital events. It would be best if the source reported both the events that begin and end the firms and the onset and end of production. *The Standard Catalog* contains only partial information on events to the firms (such as dates of incorporation, bankruptcy, acquisition, or merger) and much more consistent information on the dates of the start and end of production. The years of these production dates appear in boldface at the top of each entry (in parentheses); greater detail about the timing of events, including month and day, is often found in the text of the entry. Sometimes the dates given are approximate (as with the year of 1905 for Malley) or seasonal (see the text for Malcolm). The researcher might wish to code these quality differences and treat them later in analysis. According to our experience, encyclopedic compilations take particular care in reporting dates, probably because they represent syntheses of other sources reporting dates.

Despite the wealth of information found in encyclopedic compilations, such as *The Standard Catalog*, coverage might be far from complete. Researchers usually need to check and supplement this information with data from other, perhaps incomplete sources. In creating a data set on American automobile manufacturing, we relied on sources such as Kutner (1974) and a special issue of the *Automotive News* (1993) to improve the coverage and detail of the population data (Carroll and Hannan 1995a). Among other things, supplemental sources are usually needed to collect values of time-varying organizational covariates, which are not commonly found in encyclopedic compilations.

Encyclopedic compilations have been used to collect demographic data on automobile manufacturers (Carroll and Hannan 1995a; Hannan et al.

1995; Torres 1995; Bigelow 1999; Tsai 1999), unions (Hannan 1995), newspapers (Amburgey et al. 1988), breweries (Carroll, Preisendorfer, Swaminathan, and Wiedenmayer 1993), political newspapers (Blau and Elman 1998), bicycle manufacturers (Dowell and Swaminathan 2000), and social movement organizations (Minkoff 1997).

Governmental Registries

In many countries, businesses and other corporate entities must register with the government and report regularly on their financial and other status. Of course, such requirements are ubiquitous for public corporations that trade equity on government-sponsored exchanges. In places such as Hong Kong, all businesses—public and private, large and small—face such requirements. In some other places, only businesses engaged in certain types of activities or industries (e.g., banking or life insurance) are required to register. Given that the public agencies involved often represent the central government, the reporting might be standardized for the nation. Gaining access to complete registration files for particular industries or populations can thus be a great boon for the demographic researcher.

For example, the Companies Ordinance (Chapter 32 of the Laws of Hong Kong) requires that the following register with the Companies Registry: (1) all local companies incorporated under the prevailing Companies Ordinance; (2) all overseas companies registered under Part XI of the Companies Ordinance; and (3) all companies incorporated outside Hong Kong and which have established a place of business in Hong Kong.

In addition, companies must file annual reports as well as notifications of name changes, director changes, and other major legal changes. Failure to do so in timely fashion meets with severe sanctions: "if a company fails to file an annual return for two consecutive years, it might be struck off the register under Section 290A of the Companies Ordinance whereupon the company will be dissolved" (brochure, Hong Kong Companies Registry, 1996). It is because of such requirements that the Hong Kong government can say with some confidence that on September 30, 1995 there were 467,794 companies operating in the Territory including 6,312 public and 461,482 private companies.

The Hong Kong Company Registry data are publicly available. One can go to the Registry offices at 66 Queensway and use free public access terminals to locate and research any particular company or set of companies that exist now or previously (at least since registration was instituted) in Hong Kong. The file on a company tells what documents it has filed across the history of its operation; one can purchase any and all of these documents for set fees. In fact, a CD–ROM is available for purchase; it contains all the basic listing data (showing name, dates of incorporation and dissolution, as well as documents filed with the Registry) on companies currently or previously registered.

However, the data on the CD–ROM can only be accessed with companion proprietary software that prevents reading the data in raw form and analyzing it statistically. (If the raw data were readily accessible, then the CD–ROM would have little market value as users could just copy the files from each other.) Without accessing the raw data, only individual companies can be examined. Although one could in theory unpack the data set by going through each and every company individually, this would be incredibly tedious (and would likely violate the user agreement entered into when purchasing the CD-ROM). Furthermore, the data cannot be sampled in tractable subsets such as all companies in the newspaper industry due to a lack of reliable identifying information. (In Hong Kong, company names seem especially opaque. For instance, it would be hard to guess that Forever Smooth Investments Ltd. is the name of a brewery.) It would apparently take official permission to gain access to the underlying data in a form readily amenable to demographic analysis.

The Hong Kong data illustrate an irony of some governmental registry data: the comprehensiveness of coverage often makes these data difficult to access and analyze. Complete historical registration data for an entire economy are almost sure to constitute an enormous database. Without some way to reduce the data to meaningful subsets composed of industries, or geographic regions, the analyst's task is likely to be overwhelming. This level of organizational detail might not be present; or it might be available but not coded reliably. Or, as with the example of Hong Kong, the government might realize the potential monetary value of the information in the complete date set and structure its availability to preclude full access.

Governmental registration data tend to be used for current policy formulation and analysis. So it is sometimes more difficult to gain access to historical data, especially information about failed firms. To overcome this limitation, it might be necessary to gain access to older files and to check across years in a concatenated file as to whether a particular firm is registered. From a sequence of old previously contemporaneous data sets, one could reconstruct complete event histories in this way. It is our understanding that Brüderl and Schüssler (1990) used such procedures in studying business failure in Bavaria.

Despite the potential problems with governmental registration data, they represent some of the highest-quality information on corporate demography available to researchers. So these data are usually worth pursuing, even if it means running around the bureaucracy for a while. Demographic studies of businesses relying on governmental registration data include analyses of new business in diverse industries in Bavaria (Brüderl and Schüssler 1990; Brüderl, Preisendörfer, and Ziegler 1996), airline passenger service carriers (Seidel 1997), child care service organizations (Baum and Oliver 1991), and many studies of banks (Han 1998; Greve 1998; Lomi 2000; Carroll and Teo 1998) and other financial service organizations (Hannan, Ranger-Moore, and Banaszak-Holl 1990; Haveman 1993b; Barron, West, and Hannan 1995; Lomi 1995a).

Censuses: Governmental and Other

Human demographers call an attempt to enumerate all the persons inhabiting an area a census (Shryock and Siegel 1971). A parallel definition for the organizational world would involve efforts to count (and likely list) all the firms and companies operating in a particular place, regardless of industry or economic activity. In many countries (including the United States), the central government conducts censuses of business and industrial populations much as they do for human populations. Other private and state entities also sometimes conduct and publish censuses. Some of these are of a general nature, such as the annual *Thomas' Registry of American Manufacturers*. Others, such as the state Unemployment Insurance files and Dun and Bradstreet's credit-rating data, are compiled for special purposes but still attempt to include virtually all operating businesses.

Censuses might seem to be the ideal data for corporate demography. If censuses are adequately executed and the detailed data are available, they can indeed prove invaluable. Governmental census data typically get used for policy planning and evaluation as official figures; firms face legal mandates requiring participation. Because these data are confidential and privacy rights have the force of law, government census agencies typically make them available only in aggregate form. This means that researchers cannot use them to trace the life experiences of individual firms.[2] Special census data vary in quality and level of detail (see Kalleberg et al. (1990) for a comparison of various data sources in one locale); each source should be evaluated thoroughly. Private census data might be prohibitively expensive to obtain, especially for recent periods when the data might still have commercial value.

Recent efforts by the U.S. Census Bureau have made it possible for bona fide scientific researchers to access and analyze disaggregated census data from 1972 to the present (and a few selected earlier years). These data have generated significant interest among social scientists and have led to a number of empirical articles on a variety of topics. The U.S. Census Bureau's main data set available for scientific analysis is the Longitudinal

---

[2] In some countries, gaining access to the individual records does not present an insurmountable barrier.

Research Database (LRD). The LRD contains establishment-level information on firms in the manufacturing sector over time, i.e., data on plants. The data come from two sources: the Census of Manufacturers (for 1963, 1967, 1972, 1977, 1982, 1987, 1992) and the Annual Survey of Manufacturers (annually from 1972 to 1993). The Census of Manufacturers (CM) is a comprehensive data collection effort that attempts to include all operating plants. The Annual Survey of Manufacturers (ASM) is a probability-based sample of manufacturing plants containing between one-seventh and one-fifth of all plants and about three-fourths of manufacturing employment.

The LRD has been organized so that a plant's records can be linked over a specified temporal window. Information collected and available for analysis includes location, ownership, and information about costs. Recent efforts have linked the LRD with other topical micro data sets on such issues as research and development and pollution abatement. Finally, plans are underway to extend the project beyond the manufacturing sector, eventually to cover the entire economy. According to the Center for Economic Studies (1995), the starting point for this effort would be the 1987–1992 period and would focus initially on the service sector.

The LRD has considerable value for many research purposes. However, its design does present certain serious limitations on its use in corporate demography. One of these derives from the CM; others derive from the sampling scheme used for the ASM. The CM does not require certain very small, single-establishment firms to respond. The cutoff varies depending on payroll levels, but, in most industries for recent years, it amounts to a total employment of five employees (Davis et al. 1994). This rule excludes "about one-third of the manufacturing establishments and about 4 to 7 percent of manufacturing employment" (Davis et al. 1994, 11). Data for these firms must be imputed; for population level research problems, a third of the data is a large amount to impute.

The ASM samples all plants with 250 or more employees; smaller plants are sampled with a probability inversely related to size (relative to all other plants in the same primary product market). In any given year, plant closings and exits are offset by the addition of data on new plants taken from the Census' Company Organization Survey (for new plants of existing firms) and the Social Security Administration's Employer identification files (for new firms). These additions make it possible to generate estimates representative of the manufacturing sample for any given year, although there are minor timing problems with the new plant data (Davis et al. 1994).

The LRD has a major deficiency for applications to corporate demography: the available longitudinally linked data cover large plants almost exclusively. Small plants, those with fewer than 250 employees, are not followed from year to year; and plants with fewer than five employees are not included at all. As a result, the LRD contains a high-quality subset of large plants from multiestablishment firms followed over time and a lower-quality subset of small plants from single-establishment firms covered intermittently (Center for Economic Studies 1995). This disjuncture makes the longitudinal data a highly selective sample that would generate biased estimates of many demographic processes. Moreover, the establishment-level data would need to be aggregated to the firm level and the exclusion problems would then get compounded.

Examples of research using governmental censuses for demographic research on corporations include Wedervang (1965) for Norway, Dunne et al. (1989) and Davis et al. (1996) for the United States, and Mata and Portugal (1997) for Portugal. Studies relying primarily on private census-like enumerations include Gort and Klepper (1982) and Klepper and Simons (1997), who used the *Thomas' Register of American Manufacturers*, and Fier and Woywode (1997) and Evans (1987), who used credit-reporting-agency data.

Restricted-Inclusion Databases

What we call restricted-inclusion databases contain information on corporations that qualify for inclusion only by virtue of engaging in some particular activity or experiencing a specific type of event. (Some of these are also proprietary data sets.) Examples include data recording joint ventures and other strategic alliances by firms (Stuart 1998), patents by firms (Podolny and Stuart 1995), and business ventures involving the venture-capital investment community (Freeman 1996; Podolny 1998). When available over time, these data sets often prove useful in supplementing basic corporate life-history information or in constructing unique demographic data defined by the inclusion criteria.

For example, Podolny et al. (1996) used data on U.S. patents in the semiconductor industry to supplement data on growth rates of firms over time. They formulated relational data on patents having to do with, among other things, which firms possess patents receiving citations from other firms with newer patents. The firms with disproportionate citations were shown to have higher growth rates, especially in the less-crowded areas of the technical space. Podolny et al. (1996) interpret this finding as an effect of technological prestige or social status.

Restricted-inclusion data can often complement basic life-history data. Although certain firms in the population are not included in such data, their values on the relevant values might be known to be zero or negligible. In other words, exclusion from the restricted data set implies a known value—in this example, no patents—rather than a missing value.

So, in essence, the restricted data set allows for complete coding of the population. Furthermore, a great deal of confidence in the patent measure is justified because it is public information available from the government; it is not possible to obtain a patent without being recorded in this data set.

Consider an example of restricted-inclusion data used for constructing demographic life histories based on the inclusion criterion itself: Freeman's (1996) analysis of business ventures collected since 1987 by the San Francisco company, VentureOne. Freeman uses these data to construct life-history data on the business ventures themselves. He then estimates models of the rate of venture liquidation (through outcomes of acquisition, failure of initial public offering). The analysis uses as covariates venture characteristics such as age, size, and location as well as covariates on the investors in the ventures including their position in the social networks of the venture community.

The VentureOne data give social scientists a rare and valuable opportunity to look at the important phenomenon of venture capital (VC). However, this design potentially suffers from a number of inherent limitations. First, although coverage of VC-led ventures might indeed be very high, there is no way to know how high it is. Participation in the survey is voluntary and there is no obvious outside referent point for comparison. The fact that Freeman (1996) identifies 4,073 ventures suggests that coverage is significant. Second, the observation starting date of 1987 suggests that many earlier joint ventures are likely omitted. There is also a selection issue with the set of joint ventures operating but first observed in 1987; these cases are left truncated. Third, many ventures are apparently identified and included only after operating for several years. This implies that smaller and more trivial ones are possibly missed. It also means that the covariates are sometimes not measured—at least contemporaneously— in the earliest years. All these limitations suggest caution in the use and interpretation of such data.

Each restricted-inclusion database appears to have some idiosyncrasies, and these require careful evaluation. A good place to start is with the inclusion criteria. How meaningful is the sample defined by the criteria? How accurately and systematically are the criteria applied? A second set of issues concern how the data are to be used, as supplementary information or as a self-delineating sample or population. Finally, one should assess the data along the usual dimensions of coverage and accuracy.

Demographic studies that use data sets from restricted-inclusion sources include studies based upon patent citations in the semiconductor industry and in biotechnology (Podolny and Stuart 1995; Sørensen and Stuart 1998) and listings of venture capital investments (Freeman 1996; Podolny 1998). Many other nondemographic studies of joint ventures, strategic alliances, and diversification moves also use data sets based on restricted-inclusion rules.

Proprietary Databases

Proprietary databases on industries and corporations owned by private companies and services often appear to be gold mines of information. For instance, the Dun and Bradstreet credit-rating data ostensibly cover every operating business in the United States, from the largest to the smallest. Furthermore, these data get updated regularly and include information on both new businesses and failed ventures. In principle, it should be possible to use these files to construct event-history data on all corporations of a certain kind for a specified period. Other proprietary sources specialize to particular fields or industries at the outset. For example, the accounting firm of Ernst and Young (1996) produces a list of biotechnology firms. The file contains information on 666 independent biotechnology firms founded in the United States during 1973–1994.

The major hitch with proprietary data is that they are not readily available for inspection and scrutiny by the scientific community. Usually, one must purchase the data and agree to not sell or redistribute it to others. Even when access is granted, certain limitations on openness must usually be adhered to. Thus, critics and others have to rely on the judgments of others; replication essentially gets ruled out. This situation might be acceptable if all proprietary data came from similar observation plans and exhibited similar high levels of quality. But these conditions do not hold.

Our impressions and experiences lead us to conclude that virtually every proprietary source abounds with unique features, both positive and negative. Some producers of proprietary data take pains to ensure quality in collection and verification of information. Other producers employ shoddy practices that do not meet minimal standards. Unfortunately, outsiders have great difficulty distinguishing the two: both types of producers claim high quality, and there is no way to make independent assessments. Until such issues get resolved, questions will be raised about basing research on such data, about whether the mines contain gold or fool's gold.

Survey Data

Organizational data can also be collected from individual-based surveys. Indeed, much of the data used in the early development of organizational theory came from individual responses to survey questionnaires. This tradition continues today in many studies conducted by individual investigators, notably, McPherson (1983), as well as in large projects such as the General Social Survey-based National Organizations Study (Kalleberg et al. 1996).

Survey sampling of individuals has considerable potential for corporate demography.[3] Random sampling of individuals can be used to generate samples of organizations with known desirable properties, even though it is often difficult to obtain access to high-quality organizational sampling frames. McPherson (1982) made this clear in the fundamental hypernetwork sampling theorem. Suppose one takes a probability sample of individuals (generated from, say, random-digit-dialing telephone sampling systems) in some system and asks the respondents to identify the organizations to which they belong. The set of organizations identified by the full set of respondents is a size-weighted probability sample of the organizations in the system.

The most productive application of this approach has examined so-called voluntary associations (clubs, churches, sports teams, labor unions, etc.) in cities and towns (McPherson 1983; McPherson, Popielarz, and Drobnič 1992). These researchers surveyed random samples of household heads in 10 cities and towns in the state of Nebraska in 1983 and again in 1989. Consider the second study, which uses the more interesting design. Each respondent was asked to list all of the voluntary associations (VAs) to which he/she belonged at the beginning of 1974 and to tell all subsequent affiliation changes over the intervening period (month and dates of each joining and leaving of a VA). The resulting responses give an unbiased size-weighted sample of VAs at the time of the interview and valuable information on rates of joining and leaving. (They do not give useful probability samples for prior times, because the current respondents might not be representative for earlier periods, due to death and migration.) McPherson's research team visited meetings of each VA identified as current and collected information about other members and the organization itself. Thus this design yields information about individuals and organizations that is unusually rich.

In principle, this method can scale up to provide data on individuals and organizations in larger systems. One ambitious study used the method to analyze employment relations in organizations from a national sample of employed persons (Kalleberg et al. 1996). In this case, the membership relation is the employment relation: a national representative sample of employed persons yields a national, employment-weighted, random sample of employers. The design had two steps of data gathering. First, questions were added to the ongoing General Social Survey (GSS) that asked individuals to identify the *establishment* in which they were employed along

---

[3] A special demographic use of individual surveys is to predict who becomes self-employed and how long they stay in this labor market position (Carroll and Mosakowski 1987; Evans 1989). Although self-employment sometimes involves the start of a new firm or other organization, it does not always. For reasons discussed in Chapters 3, 4, and 6, we prefer to use the population as the unit at risk to experience foundings.

with its address and the name of the head of its human-resources (HR) department. Second, a research team attempted to contact the head of the HR department and collect information about the establishment (e.g., its size) and its employment policies. Then the researchers related the establishment-level information to information given by respondents (e.g., earnings).

The potential value of this approach arises from gaining *representativeness* of the employment base in the sample. Yet, there were difficulties in scaling this approach to the national population of employers. In particular, it was not feasible for the research team to visit every "nominated" organization. The researchers were able to gain information from only 64% of the establishments that were noted by respondents. Since some 14% of the respondents were unable or unwilling to identify the establishment at which they were employed, only slightly more than half (55%) of the respondents could be matched with an organization with available data. Moreover, the research team apparently did not even attempt the trickiest step: connecting establishments to firms.

For many analyses, a highly diverse representative sample might actually prove to be a deficiency. Why? First, organizational diversity implies a diversity in source documents and information. The time saved initially might actually get lost in trying to uncover this information. Worse yet, the data will likely not be collected in the same way from organization to organization, thus introducing unknown measurement error.

A second reason, related to the first, has to do with the enormity of the task of introducing adequate controls for the idiosyncratic elements of the diverse sample. Some of this difficulty might be due to unavailability of key data; data sets on diverse samples ordinarily contain only very general information on firms such as age, size, and industry. Another source of difficulty in constructing adequate controls for organizational heterogeneity is that the researcher's institutional knowledge is unlikely to span across such diverse arenas. Without the ability to introduce adequate controls, it might be difficult to identify and compare systematic patterns on the general feature of organizations (Chapter 5).[4]

The sampling-related limitation (for corporate demography) of hyper-network samples of organizations concerns the sampling weights. Having an employment-weighted sample means that large organizations are more likely to be included and small ones less likely. In fact, a great many small organizations will be excluded; the excluded firms would constitute a large proportion of the sample of firms. Note also that it would be extraordi-

---

[4]Note that diversity could be limited by restricting the sample initially by asking certain qualifier questions of respondents [e.g., Do you work in the telecommunications industry?] but this would reduce the advantage of the technique.

narily difficult to continue the data collection over time in a way not biased towards survivors. Of course, all existing firms could be followed and
those that die could be recorded as such. However, using the method for
re-sampling to include new firms each year would miss many new small
firms, exactly those firms most likely to disappear quickly.

The primary value in the hypernetwork-sampling approach consists
of providing a representative cross section. Such a cross section of firms
would potentially have great value for summarizing aspects of demographic
distributions (e.g., age, size, and other characteristics). However, as Kalleberg et al. (1996) make clear, it cannot adequately support an analysis of
demographic change or vital rates.

Lists of Prominent Firms

Several popular magazines and journals publish lists of prominent firms
on a regular basis. These frequently serve as the basis for defining sets
of organizations for analysis. For example, to study how company directors are chosen, Westphal and Zajac (1994) collected data on the largest
U.S. industrial and service firms given in the 1987 *Forbes* and *Fortune* listings. Similarly, to examine how governance innovations diffuse, Davis and
Greve (1997) compiled data on the 500 largest U.S. publicly traded industrial firms (from *Fortune*) in 1980 and 1986; they supplemented the file in
1986 with data from the 50 largest publicly traded commercial banks, the 25
largest publicly traded diversified financial service firms, the 25 largest publicly traded retailers, and the 25 largest publicly traded transportation companies. A long series of this kind was constructed by Fligstein (1990), who
constructed a data set based on the 100 largest public firms in the United
States every ten years from 1919 to 1979. Fligstein dealt with changes in
the list over time by including information on firms ten years before they
were added to the list and ten years after they were dropped. He used this
data set to investigate a variety of corporate activities including firm growth
rates (Fligstein and Brantley 1992).

Lists of prominent firms often appear in widely available form; and
this accessibility is one of their chief virtues. Because the lists often include
only public corporations, it is also possible to find and integrate other information on firm characteristics from annual reports and governmental
filings. Many researchers trumpet the restriction of these lists to large and
public firms as an asset, because these firms control a highly disproportionate amount of the economy's capital and employment base. While this
claim is true, the exclusion of smaller firms creates analytical problems, especially problems of sound causal inference. Size is often related to prior
success; so the sample might suffer from selection bias. Such bias is particularly worrisome for questions of corporate demography: small firms are

much more likely to die than large firms (Chapter 14). More generally, size is strongly related to many organizational characteristics, so a sample of size-truncated firms will be truncated on many dimensions.

8.3 Using Multiple Sources

Single authoritative sources such as annual directories and encyclopedic compilations cannot always be found for particular industries or populations. On close inspection, sources that appear to be authoritative are often found to be lacking on completeness of coverage or accuracy of reports on dates of events or on organizational characteristics. Thus corporate demographers usually find themselves in the situation of having to use multiple sources. Two of the more commonly used techniques for searching for such sources are archival search and Internet-based search. After discussing each, we consider the general scientific issues raised by these and related practices.

Archival Searches

Sometimes researchers are forced to identify and combine a set of disparate sources discovered by a more open-ended archival search. The data set on American national labor unions compiled by Hannan and Freeman (1987) resulted from this kind of effort. These researchers attempted to collect life histories on every national labor union that ever existed in the United States, however briefly. A national labor union organizes in two or more states; that is, national labor unions cross state boundaries. No known single source or set of sources reports lists of such unions for the early periods; from 1932 to the mid-1980s, annual reports issued by the Department of Labor do provide such information.

Hannan and Freeman (1987) compiled lists of names of unions (with starting dates) contained in ten one-of-a-kind reports, each claiming exhaustive coverage at some particular point in time. These lists, supplemented in later years by the Labor Department annual reports, yielded an initial historical master list of unions. The researchers extended the master list by consulting standard histories of the labor movement and an encyclopedia (Fink 1977), especially for 1830–1870. Pertinent life-history information was recorded for each union from whatever source was discovered. As the search for information progressed, records were uncovered of marginal and short-lived unions that had been omitted previously. Each newly identified union was then added to the master list and detailed information was sought for it.

These procedures eventually identified 633 national labor unions with usable data operating at one time or another from 1836 to 1988. (Another fifty cases showed some evidence of existence but it was too fragmentary or unreliable to be used in analysis.) In collecting the detailed data on individual unions, this research group relied heavily on published histories of unions, of the union movement, and of industries. When feasible, they also used union periodicals and proceedings. They did not try to code data from general newspapers because the relevant events occurred in many cities over a very long period of time. In other words, had they pursued this strategy they might still be coding!

Use of open-ended archival searches to collect demographic data on corporations include studies of labor unions (discussed above), early telephone companies (Barnett and Carroll 1987), worker cooperatives (Staber 1989), voluntary social service organizations (Singh, House, and Tucker 1986), state bar associations (Halliday, Powell, and Granfors 1993), investment banks (Park and Podolny 1998), anti-drunk driving associations (McCarthy, Wolfson, and Baker 1988), medical products (Mitchell 1994), microcomputers (Anderson and Tushman 1990), and biotechnology firms (Barley, Freeman, and Hybels 1992).

Internet-based Searches

The search capabilities of the Internet provide new ways of identifying and collecting demographic data on corporations. That is, researchers might use available software search engines on the Internet to find companies doing business in particular areas and industries. The search would discover many individual companies with home pages containing information about them. The variations here are endless, with some companies providing a wealth of information and others a small amount. An especially handy feature of some companies' home pages is that they contain downloadable Annual Reports and other legal documents. Thus, use of the Internet might save considerable time in accessing these documents.

For some industries, one can find listings of all companies operating in an industry on the Internet. For example, the *Airlines of the Web* homepage (developed by Marc-David Seidel and now operated by the Internet Travel Network at http://www.itn.net/airlines) lists all the airlines around the world currently offering passenger service. It also contains Internet links to the pages of all these airlines (if they have them). Obviously, a page such as this one can be extremely useful in identifying companies and collecting demographic data. As with industry directories, these pages often represent the work of industry associations (e.g., the Institute for Brewing Studies in Colorado maintains such a site at http://beertown.org)

or suppliers or their agents. Some lists have been produced by groups of hobbyists and amateur industry historians.

The Internet is a technology-in-progress; and it is difficult to make general statements about its possible value for future research. Based on current development, however, we regard the Internet as a potentially useful supplemental tool for generating an initial list of companies or for finding information about a particular known company. We think it would be rare today for one to be able to rely exclusively on Internet data and to generate a high-quality demographic data set. Our main reason for thinking this is that the Internet appears to be focused on current information (pages are regular updated and maintained) and historical data are often replaced or removed. It would, for instance, be unusual to find home pages of long deceased companies or lists of industries from several years back.

The availability of information on the Internet for companies varies widely. We would venture that two types of companies will be more prevalent and provide more information: (1) those that sell directly to the consumer and thus view the Internet as a marketing device (e.g., beer, airlines, autos, etc.); and (2) those that rely on informal social networks for sharing of information and collective action and thus view the Internet as a means of communication and organization (e.g., the electric car manufacturing industry). However, we are quick to note that this is only speculation. Indeed, how to ascertain the likelihood that given types of organizations will be included is one of the major uncertainties of Internet-generated demographic data.

Combining and Integrating Sources

Open-ended research based on multiple sources does not have the closure or systematic discipline that results from reliance on a single authoritative source or series. Due to this lack of structure, such research efforts remain open-ended in the sense that additional useful sources might always be found and might change the course of the work dramatically. The lack of a natural stopping point also means that enormous time and effort might be spent on such searches. Indeed, one can easily imagine all sorts of extensive archival searches that simply are not practical for social scientists to undertake (Hannan and Carroll 1995). So caution should be exercised before embarking on such an enterprise.

A problem that arises in studies that use multiple sources is that using different sources for different periods sometimes artificially creates "events" that reflect only differences in the inclusion and exclusion rules used by the various sources. Of course, even the same periodic sources can change their rules and conventions over time, but these are usually announced and explained, perhaps allowing corrections. By contrast, the differences among disparate sources are likely to be much more difficult to discern.

A potential general problem arising from reliance on multiple sources concerns the difficulty of exact replication. The lack of structure in the search and the use of multiple sources makes it more difficult for another researcher to replicate the resulting data exactly. Careful documentation would help to overcome this deficiency; making data publicly available along with any notes made in collection is also potentially helpful. In reality, these are unreasonable expectations given most social scientists' research budgets. In any case, it is clear that as the number and complexity of sources grows, the ease of replication declines.

It would be wrong to conclude from this observation that researchers should prefer single-source data sets. Researchers usually combine information from various sources in pursuit of greater accuracy, much as historians do. This is common practice in corporate demography even when the researcher relies primarily on one of the major source types discussed above, such as annual directories. Presumably, a researcher gains a great deal of institutional knowledge during the course of studying an industry or population over a long period. If so, this knowledge can be used to judge and weigh the value of various sources and information.

8.4 Data Realities

Raw data on corporate demography come in many different forms, some of which are unique. This chapter reviews the most common sources that organizational researchers have discovered and used in empirical analyses. Our comments on the various types of sources reflect our experiences and observations in using (and watching colleagues and students use) these data. Obviously, any particular source might or might not contain the deficiencies of the class we describe here. Indeed, we advise evaluating each data source critically on its own, using the criteria outlined above: organizational coverage, temporal coverage, precision, and organizational detail. Often, insightful evaluations can be conducted via sampling or some other procedure prior to extensive data collection and coding.

We suspect that most sources will show some deficiencies on one dimension or another. This should not be discouraging, at least initially. Rather, the extent of the deficiency should be the major issue. How many cases does it involve? What proportion of firms? How great is the error variability relative to true variation? Obviously, if these numbers are large, then the data might not be worthwhile. Many times, they will be small. A second issue concerns the nature of the errors. What kinds of bias do the errors introduce? Are the errors random or systematic? Again, experiments based on samples of the data might prove beneficial. Random error does not usually damage sound inference fatally, provided it is not extensive. Systematic error can often be corrected if it can be identified precisely. So even data sets that appear flawed initially might wind up proving to be very useful. After all, perfect data do not exist.

Part III
POPULATION PROCESSES

THIS PART OF THE BOOK examines theoretical mechanisms that operate at the level of the organizational population. The chapters consider both exogenous and endogenous processes. The exogenous processes involve environmental factors such as resource abundance, technology, and politics. The endogenous processes concern transformations of the organizational population with respect to itself; some of these operate on all member organizations similarly, others result from differentiated response.

Chapter 9 discusses organizational environments and their conceptualization in corporate demography. It opens by illustrating the power of environmental forces in shaping corporate populations with data on early American telephone companies. The chapter then discusses the ways corporate demographers model the major exogenous forces of organizational populations: resources, political forces, technology, and ethnic identity. It also explores issues of measurement and estimation. The second part of the chapter looks closely at a particular environmental process that has proven important to demographic concerns: imprinting. After examining theory about imprinting at founding, the findings of a major empirical study of the process are described.

Chapter 10 examines processes of density dependence for organizational populations. The singular characteristic of this important class of processes is that organizational density governs population vital rates. In the basic theoretical formulation, density affects vital rates through its relationships with the social legitimation of the population's organizational form and with the diffuse competition among population members. Empirically, density shows nonmonotonic relationships with both vital rates. The chapter reviews stochastic models appropriate for representing these relationships and gives a comparative empirical illustration. The chapter next discusses many extensions of the framework involving schemes for weighting density. Models of weighted density have proven to be productive in studies of competition among organizations.

Chapter 11 continues the examination of density-dependent processes. It returns to the basic theoretical formulation and addresses several of its primary limitations. These have to do with its inability to explain certain features of longterm trends in organizational density, especially late-stage declines and renewals. Several models designed to deal with these issues are advanced and illustrated with empirical estimates. Another major complicating issue treated in this chapter concerns geographical levels of analysis. A promising extension of the model to multilevel processes is reviewed and illustrated.

Chapter 12 also examines late-stage declines and renewals in density, but this time from the point of view of population segregating processes. This class of processes posits mechanisms that bifurcate or segment the population into subgroups. The major theoretical mechanism examined here is resource partitioning; it is illustrated with the American beer brewing industry, which has experienced both a late-stage decline and a subsequent renewal. Another segregating mechanism, size-localized competition, is also discussed.

9

Organizational Environments

MUCH OF THE THEORY and research in this book concentrates on processes that operate at the level of the organization or the population of organizations. This work seeks to find regularities in demographic regimes that hold for broad classes of corporations and other kinds of organizations. It is important to recognize that such processes operate in a broader environmental context and that environments play a crucial role in shaping the life histories of organizations and organizational populations.

At its most general level, the notion of environment summarizes the relevant parts of the social and physical world that lie outside the organization. In social science applications, the environment includes other organizations, natural actors, political structures, technologies, and physical environments. Analyses of organizations often define environments with reference to identifiable social units such as nation-states, economies, industries, and markets. Environmental variations are typically assessed by measuring and assessing the relationships of measures of these dimensions with vital rates.

We distinguish two broad classes of environmental processes. The first class, discussed in this chapter, we call exogenous processes. These environmental processes shape and change organizations and organizational populations, but they are not directly affected by organizations themselves (at least in known, systematic ways). The second class, reviewed in the next several chapters, we call endogenous processes. In these types of environmental processes, the organizational population comprises the primary environment for organizational activity and demography. In endogenous processes, as organizations and populations change, so too do their environments. In terms of the general explanatory structure laid out in Figure 2.7 of Chapter 2, exogenous environmental processes would usually fall within the box for "environmental conditions" while endogenous processes fit under "population dynamics."

Organization theory abounds with abstract and sophisticated characterizations of environments. Most of these theories seek to explain how specific organizational designs arise and persist in environments with particular types of characteristics. To many organizational theorists, it might seem that these theories of internal structure and functioning have little to do with corporate demography. In a sense, this characterization hits the mark: organization theory contains few arguments that directly predict corporate-demographic activity such as foundings and mortality. In another sense, however, this depiction is dead wrong. Virtually all well-known theories of organization presuppose some process of organizational change over time (usually dealing with adaptation to changing environments and markets). The type of processes that are usually assumed implies a more or less central role for corporate demography. Given this conceptual embeddedness, the issues involved in relating organizational theory to corporate demography are complex. So, we delay serious discussion of organization theory until later in the book (Chapter 17).

This chapter takes a very basic, but essential, approach to considering the ways environments affect corporate activity. It starts with an illustration, one that shows some of the unexpected ways that environments shape organizational populations. It then discusses how demographic researchers typically analyze and model the effects of environmental factors. It touches on the dimensions associated with large variations in demographic activity among organizations across the social units commonly used to define environments. These are resource availability, ethnic identity, technology, and political forces. General theoretical understanding of the effects of these factors is somewhat limited. However, we believe that, as corporate demography develops and stronger empirical patterns emerge, deeper theoretical insights will be forthcoming. The final parts of the chapter deal with a specific type of environmental effect that plays a large role in determining organizational life chances: environmental imprinting, especially at the time of organizational founding.

9.1 Environments and Telephone Companies

The early American telephone industry provides an interesting point of departure for discussion of environmental effects in corporate demography. The early industry saw dramatic differences in the number of telephone companies operating in various states. Some states—for example, Alaska, Delaware, Nevada, and Rhode Island—had fewer than 10 telephone companies in 1908. Others—including Illinois, Indiana, Iowa, New York, Wisconsin, and Ohio—were each home to more than 500 companies. Did environmental factors produce these variations in organizational populations across states? If so, how?[1]

Barnett and Carroll (1993) analyzed these issues by focusing on potential market resources as well as political variations across the states. They analyzed counts of the numbers of telephone companies by type (commercial and mutual organizational forms) and by size class (large and small independents) for each state in a given year (not all data were available for all years). For independent variables, a number of state-level resource variables were used, including urban human population, rural human population, land area, indexed average wage, and indexed average value of farmland and buildings. For political environments, the internal political differentiation of a state was measured by three indicators: number of counties, number of urban incorporated places, and number of rural incorporated places.

Table 9.1 presents estimates of the effects of the various environmental dimensions on the number of telephone organizations in a state.[2] Among those variables measuring resource dimensions, average wage, rural population, and land area show no significant effects on the number of telephone companies. Urban population has a positive effect on large independents and commercial companies. The effects of the average value of farmland and buildings are more robust across type, showing positive effects on both large and small independents (but these are not significant for commercial and mutual forms). So, resource variables show some effects of munificence, but these are not consistent across all measures.

The most interesting results in Table 9.1 concern the effect of internal political differentiation in states. The number of rural incorporated places has a strong positive effect in every equation. Moreover, this effect is larger for the small companies than for the large ones. The number of counties also usually has a positive effect, although it is not significant. The effect of the number of urban incorporated places is negative and significant in three of the four equations. Overall, the pattern of findings suggests that large and small telephone companies operated in different "niches," with the large companies being organized around city boundaries and the small companies around towns and villages. To the extent that there were many cities in a state, the niche of the large organizational form apparently encroached on that of the small form.[3]

---

[1] This section is abstracted from Barnett and Carroll (1993).

[2] These are weighted least squares estimates of pooled cross-sectional regression equations.

[3] The variance in the number of telephone companies also increases with the number of political units, a relationship that suggests that the degree of autonomy granted to political units might differ across states.

Table 9.1. *Effects of environmental conditions on the number of telephone companies by type across states.*

	Large indep. companies 1907–1942	Small indep. companies 1907–1942	Commercial systems 1902	Mutual systems 1902
Constant	−24.1	−243	−74.1	−41.6
Average wage	−0.039	−0.968	1.70	0.463
Average value of farm bldgs	0.084*	0.499*	0.033	0.086
ln(Urban pop.)	6.95*	8.26	20.0*	8.95
ln(Rural pop.)	-0.885	21.9	−3.81	−2.04
ln(Land area)	−2.26	−15.6	−2.52	−0.348
Incorporated urban places	−0.038	−0.689*	−0.489*	−0.317*
Incorporated rural places	0.116*	0.550*	0.275*	0.173*
No. of counties	0.026	0.561	0.347	−0.098
R^2	.684	.389	.760	.701
$N \times T$	384	384	48	48

* $p < .05$.
Source: Barnett and Carroll (1993). Copyright © 1993 by Oxford University Press. Used by permission.

Social scientists (Stinchcombe 1965; Hannan and Freeman 1977) typically expect resource factors to increase the market's capacity to support a given form of organization. So, the positive relationship between telephone-market variables and numbers of organizations seems natural. Why do the numbers of political units (incorporated places and counties) within a state also show a positive relationship to the number of telephone companies? Barnett and Carroll (1993) argue that the political boundaries of towns, cities, and counties constrained the expansion of individual telephone companies—and so greater political differentiation led to greater numbers of companies—for at least two institutional reasons.

First, local political units must have affected and reflected, at least in part, the taken-for-granted normative conceptions of the market; entrepreneurs would have readily adopted these boundaries when thinking of organizing telephone companies (Meyer and Rowan 1977). This was especially likely for the mutual telephone companies, which often sprang up in populist fashion in places where Bell and the commercial independents refused to locate (Fischer 1994).

A second reason has to do with the fact that local governments were the first regulators of the telephone industry (Brooks 1976). This came about because the initial proliferation of companies resulted in direct price competition in some places (Gabel 1969). In fact, nearly one-half of the nation's 1051 incorporated places with telephone service had more than one company by 1902 (Phillips 1985). To attract customers in these places, companies reduced prices—sometimes offering service at no charge—which often resulted in poor-quality service (Gabel 1969). In other cases, opportunistic entrepreneurs would enter local markets intending simply to prompt existing competitors to buy them out. Consequently, local governments began requiring telephone companies to obtain charters—often for a fee—that controlled rates, acquisitions and mergers, and rights-of-way for cable (Stehman 1925).

The combined effects of many such local constraints creates at the state level what Meyer and Scott (1992) call *institutional fragmentation*. Empirical research in a variety of contexts has demonstrated that such a fragmentation makes it difficult to design, monitor, and enforce a unified and coherent public policy (Meyer, Scott, and Strang 1987; Carroll, Delacroix, and Goodstein 1988). Therefore, states with greater numbers of political units would have been less capable of rationalizing the telephone industry.

Political boundaries also prevented market factors from operating freely. For example, the Pittsburgh and Allegheny Telephone Company served most of the market in Pittsburgh by 1910. Unconstrained, one would expect that this company would also have served the entire metropolitan area surrounding Pittsburgh in Allegheny County. However, the area was very fragmented politically; it included 120 distinct political units in 1910. As a result, this area was not completely dominated by the Pittsburgh and Allegheny Telephone Company, but instead was served by 11 different telephone companies at that time.

9.2 Modeling Environmental Conditions

The usual corporate demography study examines organizational life histories and the rates at which vital events occur, not the type of cross-sectional distribution investigated above for telephone companies. Often these analyses begin with simple comparisons of the vital rates of various observable organizational forms. For instance, Harhoff, Stahl, and Woywode (1995) investigate the effects of legal form on the growth and exit of firms in West Germany. Likewise, Mata and Portugal (1997) compare many types of foreign and domestic firms, showing that foreign firms exhibit significantly lower exit rates.

Most corporate demographers also attempt to incorporate environmental variations into the analysis. Environmental conditions often change substantially over the periods for which corporations and organizational populations are at risk of experiencing the relevant events. When environmental characteristics can be measured directly, these changes can be modeled as time-varying covariates.[4] To the extent that relevant theory gets developed, it might provide guidance about the functional form relating environmental covariates to vital rates. We illustrate such arguments with brief discussions of each of the four major classes of exogenous environmental factors: (1) resources, (2) political forces, (3) technology, and (4) ethnic identity.

Resources

Building and sustaining organizations depends on the availability of resources, both human and material (Weber 1968; Stinchcombe 1965). Resource availability for new organization means that levels of potentially mobilizable resources are ample and claims on these resources by other social units can be contested. Under norms of rationality, the founding rate of new organizations increases when the levels of resources rise and other groups and organizations do not control them. Population growth and economic development are classic examples of environmental conditions in which resources rise: however, these conditions obviously do not always result in new organization because existing firms often hold entrenched and advantaged competitive positions that allow them to absorb the resources before new firms can.

Consider, for example, the resources available to the early American automobile industry. Technological knowledge, labor, and consumer wealth all increased rapidly and steadily throughout much of the twentieth century—and so too did the number of cars built and sold. Nonetheless, the number of automobile producers did not grow with resources; instead it declined through much of this period (see Figure 2.1 in Chapter 2). A major research question for corporate demography thus involves identifying the conditions under which growth in resources generates growth among existing firms or population expansion in the form of new organizations.

Durkheim's theory about the causes of the division of labor in society provides one version of an argument relating the size of the resource base to organizational diversity. According to Durkheim (1947, 266), "if work becomes divided more as societies become more voluminous and denser, it is not because external circumstances are more varied, but because the struggle for existence is more acute." Durkheim developed the imagery of a set of isolated communities whose economic enterprises have expanded

---

[4]As Chapter 7 discusses, the conventional approach to estimating the effects of these covariates involves splitting the spells of risk exposure, updating the covariate values, and treating the spells as censored unless an event is observed.

to the limits of the local markets and local competitive interactions. When these isolated communities are brought into close contact by declines in the costs of communication and transportation, a competitive struggle ensues. Consider the following:

> There is always a considerable number of enterprises which have not reached their limits and which have, consequently, power to go further. Since there is a free field for them, they seek necessarily to spread and fill it. If they meet similar enterprises which offer resistance, the second hold back the first ... But if some of them present some inferiority, they will necessarily have to yield ground heretofore occupied by them, but in which they cannot be maintained under the new conditions of conflict. They no longer have any alternative but to disappear or transform, and this transformation must necessarily end in a new specialization.... Although the preceding examples are drawn particularly from economic life, this explanation applies to all social functions indiscriminately. (Durkheim 1947, 268–270)

To the extent that new specializations come about by the creation of new enterprises, increased "moral density" increases rates of both organizational founding and failure (Hawley 1950).

Political Forces

Another broad type of environmental change that potentially creates pervasive organizational change reflects political processes, especially those associated with political discontinuities in national government. The major political forces that affect organizational diversity are tied to social revolutions, that is, processes by which some class structures and political structures are destroyed and others built. Social revolutions and political crisis almost invariably change the mix of organizations in society. Breaking the hegemony of ruling groups means destroying the organizations with which they ruled and extracted economic value. Social revolutions normally involve both the large-scale destruction of existing organizations and the creation of new ones. National revolutions, in particular, often espouse ideologies, for example, egalitarianism, communism, democracy, that prescribe new or different organizational forms.

The establishment of state socialist governments has historically produced some of the most dramatic changes in the organizational panorama, lowering overall levels of organizational diversity. The East German case provides a nice illustration. Between 1971 and 1987, the state of the German Democratic Republic directed its nationalization efforts towards the abundant *Mittlestand* (medium-size companies). The result was a decrease in the numbers of smaller companies. In 1971, over 8,000 firms with fewer than 199 employees operated, but there were fewer than 1,000 in 1987. Average firm size increased dramatically.[5] Upon the collapse of the socialist system, the situation reversed itself almost immediately. Between November 1989 and December 1994, over 450,000 new companies were established in the territory that had been East Germany (Fier and Woywode 1997).[6] Many of these were small organizations with good life chances, in many instances better than their counterparts in West Germany (Hinz and Ziegler 1998).

In contrast to revolution, political change by ordinary institutional means (in response to political and social crises) usually involves the addition of new organizations and new organizational forms without the destruction of much existing organization. That is, solving political crises usually means constructing new organizations either to repress dissent or to incorporate contending groups into the polity. For example, the incorporation of organized labor into the polity in the United States during the 1930s involved the creation of numerous state and local agencies designed to enforce the newly won rights of unions. Subsequent attempts by conservative governments to roll back New Deal concessions to labor unions often involved attempts to eliminate agencies. Similar reactions followed the War on Poverty program development.

Less profound organizational change often occurs with routine regime change. Once in power, new governments frequently provide the authority and funds to proliferate their preferred organizational forms. For instance, the dramatic increase in offshore commercial banks in Singapore after 1971 (shown in Figure 2.3 in Chapter 2) is directly attributable to the government's establishment of the Monetary Authority of Singapore. Likewise, taxes and other incentive mechanisms might be changed with this end in mind, (e.g., tax credits for college tuition to support the educational system). Much of this kind of activity can appropriately be considered as a facet of regulation, which we discuss in greater length in Chapter 18.

Technology

A third broad class of important environmental changes involves technological developments occurring through innovations and other discontinuities. Often arising from the periphery of an industry, these major breakthroughs in technology typically substitute for and eventually supplant an

---

[5] This is typically the case under state socialism, even when the guiding ideology favors small producers, as was the case in Nicaragua between 1979 and 1983 (Colburn 1986).

[6] It is interesting to note that the founding rates of these new firms followed well-known patterns of density dependence (Chapters 10 and 11) typical of new populations (Fier and Woywode 1997). See also Dobrev's (1997) study of newspapers in Bulgaria before and after the collapse of state socialism.

existing technology. The initial discovery is often called paradigmatic because it renders obsolete previous ways of doing things (Dosi 1982). Further technological progress proceeds incrementally down a few uncertain
but directed trajectories to an accepted regime. The organizational structures associated with the new technology differ from those associated with
the old technology (Tushman and Anderson 1986; Utterback and Suarez
1993; Klepper and Simons 1997).

A well-known example of technological change severely affecting organizational change involves the modern evolution of the world watch
industry. From the industry's earliest days until about 1950, mechanical
watches using pin-lever and jewel-lever technologies dominated the market. Swiss firms overwhelmingly produced these watches; they tended to
be fairly small operations consisting of highly trained craftsmen who were
not involved in the distribution of their products. Between 1950 and 1970,
alternative types of watches appeared, using new electric and tuning-fork
technologies. These watches were produced primarily by large American
firms, which usually had their own distribution and retail networks. The
biggest technological change occurred in the 1970s, however, with the successful development of quartz-watch technology, resulting in numerous
electronic watches, many inexpensive. The popularity of this new technology virtually eliminated the old Swiss watchmaking companies whose
products suddenly seemed less reliable and much more expensive. The
quartz-technology regime in the world watch industry was initially dominated by large, vertically integrated Japanese firms such as Hattori–Seiko.
Hong Kong companies also participated in this reorganized industry.

Technical innovation plays a key role in the creation of new organizations and especially new forms of organization (Sutton 1999). Each wave
of technical innovation produces new sets of opportunities. Sometimes
these new opportunities get exploited by members of existing organizational forms. Quite often, however, only new organizational strategies and
structures can meet the demands of efficiently producing, servicing, and
marketing the new products and services that arise from application of
the new techniques. Recent examples of technology-driven organization
building come from biotechnology, which depends on new knowledge of
recombinant DNA biochemistry, and from the overnight delivery business,
which depends critically on extensive computer networks and scheduling
algorithms.

Ethnic Identity

Changes in the distributions of socially constructed identities in human
populations also often constitute important environmental changes for organizations. Consider, for instance, the effects of the changing demog-

raphy of ethnic groups for the demography of corporations. Often these changes occur as a result of large-scale immigration of minority groups into advanced economies, but they can also involve the increased salience of identities or the activation of new or latent identities (e.g., the black power movement). In any case, blocked-upward mobility channels (because of discrimination directed against the minority group), labor market competition, and ethnic solidarity by ethnic consumers (reinforced by concentrated geographic settlement patterns, caused in part by discrimination) create new ethnic-based forms of organization often situated in ethnic enclaves and providing numerous sources of opportunity (Olzak 1989).

An example of organizational change following from ethnic change can be found in the history of the U.S. newspaper industry. Waves of ethnic (often foreign-language) papers were generated by waves of immigration. The peak of the American ethnic press occurred during World War I, when many German-language newspapers went out of business; however, new immigrants from Asia are sparking a new wave of newspapers in places such as California and New York. Russell (1995) documents a similar link in Israel, where waves of immigration have fostered the building and maintenance of cooperative organizations. His study finds a strong positive association between immigration and the rate of cooperative founding. As Russell (1995, 73) explains,

> ...the formation of worker cooperatives has long been viewed in Israel as a particularly appropriate technique for the absorption of new immigrants—by many of the immigrants themselves, by the Histadrut and international Zionist philanthropic organizations and by the Israeli government.

Measurement Issues

Organizational populations—and even individual organizations—sometimes span centuries of time. In these cases, environments commonly develop and change in many dramatic ways. However, it is often difficult to find systematic data that record environmental variables in reliable and consistent fashion across the entire period. Demographers face two options when confronted with this situation. The first limits the analysis to periods with adequate measurements of detailed environmental conditions. The second option periodizes the history and seeks to estimate period-specific effects. Such periodization uses historical and institutional knowledge to identify periods where environmental conditions (of any kind) are thought to differ significantly from each other. The former strategy allows for precise estimation of environmental effects, but it limits the scope and potential generality of the study. The latter strategy allows for full use of the corporate-demographic data, but it summarizes environmental effects in imprecise fashion.

Corporate demographers often use a combination of the two strategies, relying on those covariates that can be measured consistently for the entire observation window but also introducing period effects to pick up other unmeasured environmental changes. For example, our studies of the automobile industries (Carroll et al. 1996; Hannan et al. 1998a) relied on measured variables such as gross national product and human population size as well as period dummies representing the industry regimes identified by Altshuler, Anderson, Jones, Roos, and Womack (1984). Both types of variables show strong and significant effects, as is typically the case.

Estimation Issues

Some theoretical analyses of organizational environments postulate that the competitive structure of an industry has much to do with the types of resources, technologies, institutions, and regulatory structures that develop and evolve within that industry. Those very same factors might influence and change later competition. For instance, institutional theorists seek to explain how specific organizations and organizational forms get institutionalized and become sociopolitically legitimated. In its usual form, this type of analysis relies on historical understanding of the authority structures prevailing over an organizational population, be they governmental, professional, or normative. Analysts seek to identify those specific endorsement actions by the authority leading to institutionalization of the organization or organizational form (for example, certification of a hospital by Medicare or recognition of acupuncture as an acceptable treatment mode by insurance companies). Theory presumes that institutionalization accords favorable treatment by social actors or other important advantages, often generating more resources. Hypotheses typically link organizational fates to the specific endorsement actions, predicting that particular organizations will show lower mortality rates as a result.

Sociopolitical legitimation of an organizational form is usually represented by dummy variables associated with the endorsements received by particular organizations or the timing of governmental actions implying endorsement of particular organizational forms (for example, a legislative act authorizing the right of certain organizations to exist and operate or providing them certain advantageous rights (Sutton, Dobbin, Meyer, and Scott 1994)). Effects of this kind have been successfully identified in a wide variety of organizational and industrial contexts, including voluntary social service organizations (Singh et al. 1986), labor unions (Hannan and Freeman 1987; Hannan and Freeman 1988), banks (Hannan et al. 1990; Han 1998; Carroll and Teo 1998), day care centers (Baum and Oliver 1991), newspapers (Miner, Amburgey, and Stearns 1990) and railroad companies (Dobbin and Dowd 1997). Of course, the actions of authorities are not always benign. Particularly dramatic examples of state actions that damaged life chances of populations of organizations include the imposition of censorship of the press (Carroll and Delacroix 1982) and local, state-level, and federal prohibitions against the production and sale of alcoholic beverages (Carroll and Swaminathan 1998; Wade, Swaminathan, and Saxon 1998).

Institutional theorists do not view the endorsement acts of authorities as random or as unrelated to the organizational population. Indeed, a long-standing claim of institutionalists holds that organizations can in varying degrees influence, manage, and even control this part of their environment (Perrow 1986; Fligstein 1990). In other words, institutionalists argue that endorsement acts by authorities are tightly interrelated to the structure of the organizational populations. If this is so, and sociopolitical legitimation is the primary focus of the analysis, then the endorsement acts should be treated as *endogenous* rather than as exogenous. However, the technical challenges of making this shift to simultaneous equations are nontrivial, especially with typical data. The processes potentially represented by the two sets of equations (one for endorsements, the other for organizational events) operate at different levels of analysis and at vastly different rates (typically generating only a few relevant endorsements over a long period and many vital events).

As one imagines solving these technical problems, it becomes apparent that accommodating full endogeneity requires specifying the processes that generate acts of sociopolitical legitimation. Current research practice entails identifying specific relevant acts by assessing their likely beneficial consequences on an organizational population (for example, lower death rates because of greater legal protection or more resources). Theory constructed in this way does not usually contemplate the general causes of the endorsement acts or factors affecting their timing. Indeed, such theory does not often even describe the general characteristics of endorsement acts leading to sociopolitical legitimation, making it difficult for other analysts to develop theory or to connect the research program to other areas of potential application, such as positive political theory. So, even if one could estimate the simultaneous system of equations required to make sociopolitical legitimation endogenous, it would be difficult (based on the current state of development of the field) to specify models of endorsement acts. Accordingly, the research problem is underdeveloped theoretically and needs to pay more attention to modeling sociopolitical legitimation appropriately.

9.3 Environmental Imprinting

Imprinting refers to a process in which events occurring at certain key developmental stages have persisting, possibly lifelong, consequences. Environmental imprinting is a form of imprinting whereby specific environmental characteristics get mapped onto an organization's structure and affect its development and life chances. Research on corporate demography has identified several types of environmental imprinting including imprinting at founding, an exogenous process which we discuss at length here.

Imprinting at Founding

The idea that firms and other kinds of organizations tend to be imprinted by their environmental conditions at founding comes from Stinchcombe (1965). This seminal essay argued that social and economic structures have their maximal impact on new organizations. In attempting to accumulate financial and human capital, entrepreneurs expose their designs to intense scrutiny. Proposals get tested against taken-for-granted assumptions about structural forms and employment relations. Because conventional wisdoms and taken-for-granted assumptions change over historical time (as new forms flourish and others wane), the tests imposed on proto-organizations also change. Consequently, the kinds of organizations that emerge reflect the social structure of the founding period.

Stinchcombe (1965; 1979) examined this process for employment relations at the industry level. He noted that industries formed in different centuries still reflect today some of the character of their formative periods. For instance, those formed after the "organizational revolution" of the closing years of the nineteenth century and the early years of the twentieth century typically employ a higher fraction of administrative workers than those with earlier origins.[7]

If Stinchcombe is right, then certain features of the employment relation get imprinted. Moreover, the character of the employment relation gets set, at least implicitly, very early in the organization's existence, when the first employees join, and later when jobs are formalized. Arrangements made at that time might have long-lasting consequences.

Baron and colleagues' investigation of employment systems in agencies of the California state government found such an imprinting effect. Baron and Newman (1990) found that jobs with mainly female incumbents

---

[7] Carroll and Mayer (1986) used Stinchcombe's historical typology of employment systems in industrial sectors in analyzing patterns of individual careers. They found that time of origin of industry affects mobility regimes centuries and decades after founding.

tended to have lower prescribed pay rates and that this effect increased significantly with the age of the job. Baron and Newman (1990, 172) interpret this effect as indicating that

> ...notions of imprinting and inertia thus might fruitfully be extended to the study of work roles: cohorts of jobs founded during the same period might be expected to evince common features, such as shared selection and promotion criteria and similar degrees of ascription.

Organizational age also affected the rate at which gender composition of jobs changed in response to changing composition of the relevant work force. Baron, Mittman, and Newman (1991) reported that the youngest and oldest state agencies integrated their work forces more quickly than agencies of intermediate age. They interpreted the effect for younger jobs as agreeing with the idea that inertial pressures on youthful structures are weaker than on older ones.[8] This study makes clear that organizational age matters for the employment relationship and that the observed patterns are consistent with the hypothesis of inertia in organizational structures and practices.

Modeling Environmental Imprinting

Environmental imprinting requires two conditions: (1) a mapping of an environmental condition onto the organization, and (2) inertia (or at least a fair degree of hysteresis) in the imprinted characteristics. If the second condition does not hold, then later modifications of the structure will erode the association of founding conditions and those features.

Environmental imprinting can be detected by estimating the effects of covariates measuring environmental characteristics on life chances over temporally defined observation windows. The simplest case is imprinting at *founding*. Here the observation window is defined as the moment of founding. Covariates are measured at founding and then treated as fixed for the life of the organization. A simple case of importance to corporate demography involves density at time of founding (Chapter 11).

A related idea says that *experience* at some later time has enduring effects (Barnett 1997; Barnett and Hansen 1996). When the organization's entire life experience matters, then the window must be wide enough to include all previous experience. The covariates vary over time and get updated in every new period of the organization's existence. That is, the relevant information is summarized across the organization's lifetime. The

---

[8]Baron et al. (1991) suggest that the effect for the oldest agencies reflects the survivor bias in their data (the set of very old jobs is unusual in having survived for a long time and have been, therefore, perhaps more responsive to environmental pressures).

more common case specifies a historical period of specific length over which observations are made (say, the last five years) and updates values as warranted.

9.4 Imprinting in High-Technology Firms

The Stanford Project on Emerging Companies (SPEC) provides an opportunity to examine how organizational design features get imprinted. This panel study of more than 170 young, high-technology firms in California's Silicon Valley (Baron, Burton, and Hannan 1999) seeks to understand how founding conditions and early decisions affect organizational evolution, which necessitates information about the earliest days of the organization. The sample was restricted to firms no more than 10 years old and with at least 10 employees when sampled. The focus on firms in a single region and sector of economic activity controls for many labor market and environmental conditions that might be relevant to organizational design. In 1994/5, semistructured interviews were conducted with a founder, the current chief executive officer (CEO), and a key informant whom the CEO nominated to provide information about human-resource practices.

Models of Organizing in Young Technology Firms

Founders were asked about how they had thought about the organization-building process and about employment relations, including whether or not they had "an organizational model or blueprint in mind when . . . founding the company." A large fraction reported that they had a specific organizational model in mind, often patterned to reflect—or diverge from—a particular firm with which they had prior experience. Analyses of transcripts from these interviews suggested that their organizational models reflect a set of premises about three dimensions of the employment relationship:

- *Attachment.* Is the primary intended basis of employee attachment and retention: (a) monetary rewards (money); (b) opportunities for challenging work and professional development (work); or (c) a strong emotional bond to the organization and its members (love)?
- *Selection.* Was the primary consideration in selecting employees to be: (a) their command of specific skills necessary to perform well defined and immediately needed tasks effectively; (b) the potential to perform effectively on a series of projects (often not yet even envisioned) through which the employee would move over time; or (c) values and organizational fit?

- *Basis of control*. Is control and coordination of work to be achieved principally through: (a) direct oversight; (b) formal rules, systems, and procedures; (c) informal mechanisms (peers or organizational culture); or (d) professionalism?

Premises about the employment relation can thus be classified into three types of attachment, three types of selection, and four types of control, yielding $3 \times 3 \times 4 = 36$ possible combinations. The observations turn out to be highly clustered. Roughly half of the responses fall in five of the 36 cells. These five cells, which Baron et al. (1999) call basic model types, correspond with well-known images:

- *Engineering model*: attachment through challenging work, peer group control, and selection based on specific task abilities. This is generally thought to represent the default blueprint for a high-tech Silicon Valley start-up, and it is the most prevalent model among the SPEC founders (espoused by roughly a third of them).
- *Star model*: attachment based on challenging work, reliance on autonomy and professional control, and selection of elite personnel based on their longterm potential.
- *Commitment model*: emotional or familial attachments to the organization, selection based on values or fit, and peer group control.
- *Bureaucracy model*: attachment based on challenging work and/or opportunities for development, selection based on qualifications for a particular role, and formalized control.
- *Autocracy model*: monetary motivations, control and coordination through direct oversight, and employees who are selected to perform a set of prespecified tasks.

Most of the responses that do not correspond to one of these basic model types differ from a single type on only one of the three dimensions. A variety of analyses reveal that these observations can be combined with the basic-type observations without significant loss of information. The results discussed below followed this procedure (and combined responses that do not fit the types into a sixth type called "non-model type").

Founders' Models and Subsequent Events

Founders' models of employment relations significantly affected the early careers of their firms. Hannan, Burton, and Baron (1996) reported analysis for the 100 firms sampled in 1994 (analysis for the full sample is ongoing). They concentrated on the rate of transition from a founder as CEO to a nonfounder CEO and the rate of initial public offering (IPO) of stock. They examined the effects of the employment models of founders. They also analyzed the employment models of the then-current CEOs (who had been asked similar questions about their organizational blueprint for their companies). For each outcome, they found that the founders' models matter but the CEOs' models do not. In other words, the initial premises matter more than the premises employed by those who are best positioned to control later events.

In the case of the transition to a nonfounder CEO, the commitment, engineering, and star models of employment have higher transition rates than the bureaucratic and autocratic models. If the bureaucratic and autocratic models stand at one extreme, the star model stands at the other. Estimates imply that the transition rate for firms with star-model founders is approximately 8.5 times higher than for firms with bureaucratic and autocratic founders. This difference in rates is highly significant. The difference between the commitment model and the bureaucratic and autocratic models is also large (the ratio of the rates is roughly 3).

Many founders report that their initial business plans called for their firms to become public companies at some point. Succeeding in going public is an important concern in many—if not most—young, high-technology firms. Such firms frequently offer inexpensive "founders' stock" and/or options to purchase the firm's stock on favorable terms at a future date to some—if not all—early hires. Both types of compensation are largely illiquid unless a firm becomes a public company. Not surprisingly, completion of an initial public offering (IPO) is widely regarded as an early sign of success in the Silicon Valley business community. Nearly a third of the firms in the SPEC sample had completed an initial public offering by mid-1994.

The founder's model of employment also has a surprisingly strong impact on the rate at which firms manage to conduct an initial public offering. The rate of IPO for the firms founded with commitment, engineering, or star models is much higher than that for the bureaucratic and autocratic models. The difference is large and statistically significant for the star and commitment models. Holding constant age, size, and industry, firms whose founders had star or commitment models go public at roughly ten times the rate of firms whose founders had either a bureaucratic or autocratic model.

Effects of Founders' Models on Managerial/Administrative Intensity

The founders' models (or blueprints) vary in how strongly they presume that control and coordination will be effected through the standard devices of bureaucratic administration—rules, procedures, reporting relations, specialization of tasks, performance evaluation, and the like—rather than through informal, tacit means of generating commitment or through personal oversight by the founders themselves or their agents. Empirically, these blueprints profoundly shape the extent (and speed) of some aspects of formalization and bureaucratization in firms over their early years, even controlling for other features of organizations and their environments likely to influence organizational design. Indeed, the current level of managerial and administrative intensity in these enterprises is more strongly related to the founders' espoused organizational blueprints than it is to the contemporaneous organizational models of the current CEOs. Founders' early premises about employment relations exert enduring effects on the managerial and administrative intensity of the organizations they build, even when/after the initial founder(s) departs.

Managerial or administrative intensity provides a handy summary measure of the tendency toward bureaucratization. Baron, Hannan, and Burton (1999) examined the relationship of founders' and CEOs' models on bureaucratization by estimating multivariate regressions relating the (ln) number of managerial and administrative full-time equivalent positions (FTEs) in 1994/5 to the founder's organizational model, controlling for the (ln) number of nonmanagerial, nonadministrative FTEs in 1994/5. They also controlled for other factors that might influence bureaucratization, including: occupational composition, industry, strategy, firm age, whether the firm ever went public and/or received venture capital, growth, executive succession, and the level of managerial and nonmanagerial employment observed at the end of the firm's first year of operations.

As hypothesized, the bureaucracy and commitment models were at opposite extremes in terms of managerial intensity. Firms whose founders championed a bureaucratic model had significantly more managerial and administrative specialists by 1994/5 than otherwise-comparable firms. At the other end of the spectrum, commitment firms were significantly less administratively intense than otherwise-comparable firms (with the exception of star firms, where the contrast was not statistically significant).

Baron et al. (1999) also examined the impact of the employment models of the then-current CEOs. As a group, the set of CEO organizational models does not have a statistically significant effect on managerial/administrative intensity in 1994/5; moreover, adding measures depicting the CEO's model does not reduce either the magnitude or the significance of the effects associated with the founder's model. In other words, how the founder conceptualized the organization at its inception, not how the then-CEO conceived of it, predicts bureaucratization in 1994/5. Baron et al. (1999) construe this result as providing quite compelling evidence of imprinting at founding.

It turns out that patterns of bureaucratization and formalization are also influenced by the social composition of the work force (specifically, in this sample, the gender mix) early in a firm's history. Women's proportional representation in the labor force at the end of the firm's first year of operations has a significant negative effect on managerial and administrative intensity, even controlling for founder's model, industry, strategy, organizational age, and whether the firm had gone public. The results imply fairly dramatic differences in administrative intensity for firms of a given size by 1994/5, based on women's proportionate representation in the first year.

As was the case in contrasting the effects of founders' versus CEOs' organizational models, early work-force demography was more decisive than the current state of affairs. That is, the present-day gender mix was less relevant to current managerial intensity than was the gender mix at the firm's inception.

Effects of Founders' Models on the Formalization of Human-Resources Policies

The SPEC researchers also examined how founders' organizational models and the firm's early gender mix affected the rate of formalization of the employment relationship.[9] The researchers constructed scales (ranging from 0 to 11) indicating how many of the relevant employment practices each firm had adopted: (a) by the end of its first year of operations; and (b) by the time it was first interviewed by the SPEC research team in 1994/5. Analysis of the number of formalized HR practices adopted by each firm by 1994/5 reveals that commitment-model firms display less employment formalization than all other types. However, the differences across organizational models are small and far from statistically significant.

In a parallel analysis, the SPEC research team analyzed the hazard of adding practices using a monthly split-spell file built using information on the month and year of adoption (if ever) of each of the 11 human-resource practices comprising the index of employment formalization. This kind of analysis focuses on rates of adoption (rather than on the total count of practices adopted over some period), and it controls for the number of practices adopted at the start of each monthly spell and uses information on changes within the study period for some covariates. Employment size is updated yearly, based on information collected from secondary sources (e.g., commercial publications listing technology companies); however, these data give only rough approximations of the time paths of

---

[9]This analysis was based on a survey, completed during 1994/5 by the person in each organization most knowledgeable about human-resource (HR) matters. It indicated whether (and when) a number of employment practices, policies, forms, and documents were adopted. Eleven of these items seem directed at formalizing, standardizing, and/or documenting employment practices: organization chart; standardized employment application; written job descriptions; personnel manual or handbook; written employment tests; written performance evaluations; standard performance evaluation forms; written affirmative action plans; standard employment contract for exempt employees; employee grievance or complaint forms; and human-resources information system.

changes in firm size. This analysis finds controls for the number of HR practices previously adopted at the start of each monthly spell. It finds that firms founded along commitment-model lines add employment practices at a somewhat lower rate than firms whose founders espoused other models. The estimated model implies that the rate of formalization in commitment firms is 0.47 that of otherwise-identical firms founded along bureaucratic lines.

In sum, early differences in the overall extent of employment formalization, reflecting founders' organizational blueprints, are essentially absent after a period that averages around six years. This suggests a pattern of convergence, rather than path-dependent development, as was found for managerial intensity. Event-history analyses suggest that it is not primarily a matter of how much, but rather how fast, technology companies adopt various standard HR practices designed to formalize and routinize employment relations. In particular, commitment-model firms resemble firms founded along bureaucratic lines in doing somewhat more extensive organization-building early on. However, commitment-model firms are somewhat slower to formalize, presumably reflecting the capacity for self-organizing and self-managing that such firms seek to cultivate. On balance, however, there is less evidence of enduring effects of founders' models on the extent or pace of employment formalization than on the evolution of managerial-administrative intensity.

A question might be raised about whether demonstrating an enduring imprint of founding conditions on technology companies that are almost all still in their first decade provides powerful evidence of path dependence. The issue is an empirical one. As Hannan and Freeman (1984) noted in discussing the tendency toward structural inertia in organizations, one must assess the rate and direction of organizational change relative to trends in the relevant environment(s). Demonstrating strong tendencies toward path-dependent development in the evolution of religious organizations, for instance, would presumably carry little shock value, given the mission and environment of a typical church. In contrast, Baron et al. (1999) contend that the organizations they studied—nascent technology companies in Silicon Valley—are subject in their early years to very turbulent environments, intense product and labor market competition, strong selection pressures, and numerous other influences that should encourage structural isomorphism.

10

Density-Dependent Processes I

ONE OF THE MAJOR discoveries of human demographers concerns an empirical regularity known as "the demographic transition." Put simply, the demographic transition involves the changes associated with the movement of a society from a preindustrial to an industrial stage (Landry 1909; Landry 1934). In terms of vital rates, the demographic transition refers to a specific chronological sequencing of changes in vital rates from a point of roughly stable population size: first mortality rates decline, then fertility rates drop at some later time (Notestein 1945). As societies undergo the transition, the rate of population growth changes from low to high and then to low again. The details depend on the differences in the vital rates and the age distribution of the population (Kirk 1944; Davis 1945). Some societies pass through the transition rapidly. Other societies experience a significant lag between the decline in mortality rates and the decline in fertility rates, with the result that populations grow very large. However, as Chesnais (1992, 513) describes it, "the nature of demographic upheavals has evolved in almost identical manner from country to country." Comparative analysis of the demographic transition consists primarily of describing and explaining variations in the onset of declines in the vital rates and the magnitudes of change.

The demographic transition produces rapid population growth because of a particular pattern of historical *time dependence* in vital rates. In corporate demography, researchers have discovered that similar historic periods of rapid organizational population growth often arise because of a particular pattern of *density dependence* in vital rates. Such density dependence has been documented in scores of organizational populations in many different countries. The empirical regularities have also been the subject of theoretical debate. The major outcome of these efforts has been the establishment of a general model of longterm organizational evolution: the density model of legitimation and competition (Hannan 1989; Hannan and Carroll 1992). This model assumes that change proceeds mainly through the selective replacement of different organizations, rather than through the adaptations of individual organizations. It posits two general forces as the drivers of selection: social legitimation and diffuse competition. Both forces are linked to the organizational density of a population (the number of organizations in the population).

This chapter and the next examine density dependence in organizational populations. In this chapter, we start by examining classical demographic models and the role played by density dependence in them. We then move to empirical evidence and theory, first showing the typical patterns of density dependence observed in organizational populations and then explaining the theory that has been advanced to explain them. Finally, we discuss some extensions of the density-dependent modeling framework that have appeared and proven valuable in organizational analysis, especially in modeling competition.

10.1 Classical Models of Population Growth

As noted above, models of density dependence figure centrally in efforts to explain the dynamics of corporate populations. To place these developments in a general demographic context, we first outline the main features of classical models of population growth. We want to show the centrality of density dependence in standard models for the growth of human and animal populations.[1]

A cornerstone of mathematical demography is the logistic model of population growth in limited environments:

$$\frac{dN}{dt} = aN_t - bN_t^2, \qquad a, b > 0.$$

Solving this differential equation (subject to the initial condition $N(0) = N_0$) yields an S-shaped growth path:

$$N(t) = \frac{a/b}{1 + (\frac{a/b}{N_0} - 1)e^{-at}}.$$

The connection between the logistic model and the models for corporate populations discussed below can be seen clearly when the logistic is derived as the implication of *density dependence* in vital rates. In order to

---

[1] For treatments of density dependence in human demography, see Lee (1987), Tuljapurkar (1987), and Wachter (1988).

highlight this similarity, we sketch a derivation of the logistic model as a special case of compound growth:

$$\frac{1}{N_t}\frac{dN_t}{dt} = r(N_t).$$

Here $r(N_t)$ is the density-dependent function for the (per capita) population growth rate. In applications to biotic populations, it makes sense to specify the growth process in terms of the birth rate (λ) and the death rate (μ). The rate of population growth is the product of population size and the difference of the two vital rates: $r(N_t) = \lambda(N_t) - \mu(N_t)$.

Malthusian arguments about population growth treat the two vital rates as constants. If the Malthusian assumptions are correct, then the overall growth rate is a constant and the population grows exponentially if the birth rate exceeds the death rate or falls exponentially to zero otherwise.

In contrast, the logistic model posits that the vital rates depend upon density. In particular, it assumes that the birth rate falls linearly with density,

$$\lambda(N_t) = \lambda_0 - \lambda_1 N_t, \qquad \lambda_0, \lambda_1 > 0,$$

and that the mortality rate rises linearly with density,

$$\mu(N_t) = \mu_0 + \mu_1 N_t, \qquad \mu_0, \mu_1 > 0.$$

Substituting these expressions into the growth process yields

$$\frac{dN}{dt} = (\lambda_0 - \mu_0)N_t - (\lambda_1 + \mu_1)N_t^2.$$

This process has steady states at 0 and at $K = (\lambda_0 - \mu_0)/(\lambda_1 + \mu_1)$. Which steady state obtains in a given case depends on the sign of $r = \lambda_0 - \mu_0$. If this term is negative, then the population size collapses exponentially to zero; if it is positive, then the logistic growth process generates S-shaped growth to a nonzero steady state, called the carrying capacity of the environment for the population.

In treatments of biotic growth, the model is commonly reexpressed as

$$\frac{dN}{dt} = rN_t\left(1 - \frac{N_t}{K}\right),$$

which serves as the basis for the well-known multipopulation Lotka–Volterra formulation (Wilson and Bossert 1971). In this parameterization, r (which equals $\lambda_0 - \mu_0$) is called the "natural" rate of increase because it tells how fast a population grows when no resource (or other) constraints apply—that is, when density falls very far below the carrying capacity (K).

10.2 Corporate Density Dependence

Demographic models of growth in corporate populations have turned out to be more complicated than the classical demographic models of population growth. In particular, the theoretically motivated models specify *nonlinear* density dependence. We now review these models and provide an empirical illustration; then we discuss the theory that generated the models and continues to guide research.

Founding Rates

The model that initiated research on density dependence in corporate populations (Hannan 1986a) specifies the founding rate as

$$\lambda(t) = l_t \, N_t^\alpha \, \exp(\beta N_t^2), \tag{10.1}$$

where l_t summarizes the effects of conditions other than density that affect the rate. Because (10.1) reduces to a Yule process when $\alpha = 1$ and $\beta = 0$, it has become known as the generalized-Yule (GY) model. The usual empirical findings (whose theoretical interpretation is discussed extensively below) show that the first-order effect of density lies between 0 and 1 and the second-order effect of density is negative:

$$0 < \alpha < 1; \text{ and } \beta < 0. \tag{10.2}$$

Estimates that satisfy these inequalities make the relationship between density and the founding rate *nonmonotonic*. Under these conditions, the relationship has a maximum at

$$N_\lambda^* = \sqrt{\frac{\alpha}{-2\beta}}. \tag{10.3}$$

So, the founding rate rises as density increases until the level of density indicated in (10.3) is reached; then it falls with increasing density.

The most common alternative to the GY specification comes from the first study of density dependence in organizational mortality rates. In analyzing data on the lifespans of American national labor unions, Hannan and Freeman (1989) could not obtain convergent ML estimates of a GY model. So, they used a specification that can have a similar qualitative interpretation: log-quadratic (LQ) density dependence. This specification has been used in some analyses of founding rates as well.

The log-quadratic (LQ) specification of density dependence in founding rates has the form

$$\lambda(t) = l_t \, \exp(\gamma_1 N_t + \gamma_2 N_t^2). \tag{10.4}$$

The log-quadratic model implies nonmonotonic dependence on density when

$$\gamma_1 > 0; \ \gamma_2 < 0; \ |\gamma_2| < |\gamma_1|. \tag{10.5}$$

Then the founding rate given by this model rises with increasing density to the maximum given by

$$N_\lambda^\circ = -\frac{\gamma_1}{2\gamma_2}. \tag{10.6}$$

Above N_λ°, the founding rate decreases with increasing density. The LQ model, therefore, can also imply an inverted-U-shaped relationship between density and the founding rate.

Mortality Rates

Density-dependent specifications of mortality rates parallel those of founding rates in obvious ways. Hannan's (1986a) original model of density dependence in mortality specified the rate as:

$$\mu(t) = m_t \, N_t^\delta \, \exp(\zeta N_t^2), \quad \delta = -\alpha. \tag{10.7}$$

In typical studies, the first-order effect of density is negative and the second-order effect is positive. In terms of (10.7), the estimates follow the pattern

$$\delta < 0; \ \zeta > 0. \tag{10.8}$$

The log-quadratic (LQ) version of density-dependent mortality in corporate populations has the form

$$\mu(t) = m_t \, \exp(\theta_1 N_t + \theta_2 N_t^2), \tag{10.9}$$

where m_t summarizes the effects of conditions other than density and with coefficients typically within the range

$$\theta_1 < 0; \ \theta_2 > 0; \ |\theta_2| < \theta_1. \tag{10.10}$$

This LQ specification of mortality rates yields an inverted-U relationship between density and mortality rates. The mortality rate falls with any initial increase in density; but eventually the process reaches a point at which further growth in density increases the mortality rate. The LQ specification has been used in almost all published research on density dependence in organizational mortality.

Growth Rates

Although the original statements of the theory did not attend to issues of growth, later work has made such a connection. Barron et al. (1994) reason that both foundings and growth require that resources be mobilized from the environment. Any process that makes it easier for entrepreneurs to mobilize resources ought also to make it easier for existing organizations to grow. Likewise, any process that slows the rate of foundings ought, by symmetry, to slow rates of growth. So, they argued that the relationship between growth rates and density will have the same form as the relationship of founding rates and density.

Empirical Findings: Rates of Founding and Mortality

After initial discovery of density dependence in organizational populations, many other analyses were conducted. Some studies examine founding rates, some mortality, and some both. Conducted on a highly diverse set of populations, the overwhelming majority of these tests yield the nonmonotonic patterns described above. These include populations of organizations in the following major economic sectors:

- **Manufacturing:**

    automobile manufacturing (Rao 1994; Hannan et al. 1995),
    beer brewing (Carroll et al. 1993),
    bicycle manufacturing (Dowell and Swaminathan 2000),
    newspaper publishing (Carroll and Hannan 1989b; Olzak and West 1991; Blau and Elman 1998),
    semiconductor manufacturing (Hannan and Freeman 1989),
    biotechnology (Hybels, Ryan, and Barley 1994),
    wine making (Swaminathan 1995);

- **Financial services:**

    banks (Ranger-Moore, Banaszak-Holl, and Hannan 1991; Han 1998; Lomi 1995a; Carroll and Teo 1998; Lomi 2000),
    credit unions (Hannan et al. 1994),
    life insurance companies (Ranger-Moore et al. 1991; Ranger-Moore 1997),
    investment banks (Park and Podolny 1998),
    bank cooperatives (Teo, Chong, Lim, and Ng 1998),
    savings and loans associations (Haveman 1994),
    venture capital partnerships (Manigart 1994);

- **Health care:**

  health maintenance organizations (Wholey et al. 1992);

- **Social services:**

  daycare centers (Baum and Singh 1994),
  voluntary social services agencies (Singh, Tucker, and Meinard 1991);

- **Telecommunications:**

  telephone service providers (Barnett and Carroll 1987),
  fax transmission services (Baum, Korn, and Kotha 1995);

- **Entertainment and leisure:**

  film production companies (Kim 1998),
  professional baseball teams (Land et al. 1994),
  hotels (Baum and Mezias 1992; Ingram and Inman 1996);

- **Nonprofit sector:**

  labor unions (Hannan and Freeman 1989; Hedström 1994),
  trade associations (Aldrich et al. 1994),
  social movement organizations (Minkoff 1997),
  research and development consortia (Barnett, Mischke, and Ocasio 2000).

For many organizational forms, the tests have been conducted with data from more than one country (for reviews, see Aldrich and Marsden (1988), Singh and Lumsden (1990), and Hannan and Carroll (1992)).

The disconfirming tests that have appeared typically come from analyses of data produced by flawed research designs, notably left-truncated observation schemes that exclude the early history of a population (Singh and Lumsden 1990; Hannan and Carroll 1992; Hannan and Carroll 1995; Baum 1996). We have already seen in the simulation studies of Chapter 7 that substantial left truncation wreaks havoc with efforts to estimate effects of density. Furthermore, substantive efforts to delineate classes of nonconforming populations have generally failed to be convincing.

Empirical Findings: Growth Rates

Far fewer studies have examined the effect of density on growth rates. Those that have addressed this issue find the expected pattern: the first-order effect of density is positive and the second-order effect is negative. Studies that report such results include analyses of credit unions (Barron et al. 1994), banks (Han 1998), and research and development consortia (Barnett et al. 2000).

Table 10.1. *Estimates of density dependence in vital rates for Singapore banks, 1840–1990.*

	Founding rate	Failure rate
Density	0.046*	−0.059*
Density squared/100	−0.026*	0.041*

* $p < .05$.
Source: Carroll and Teo (1998).

An Empirical Illustration

As an illustration, Table 10.1 presents estimates of density-dependent effects in the vital rates of the banking population in Singapore.[2] As shown, the estimates all follow the nonmonotonic patterns typically found in corporate populations. Moreover, the relevant estimates are all statistically significant. Figures 10.1 and 10.2 show the predicted relationships between density and the vital rates, as given by these estimates. The figures illustrate clearly the common nonmonotonic relationships between density and organizational vital rates.

The parallel in turning points in Figures 10.1 and 10.2, which is characteristically seen in most populations, shows why nonmonotonic density dependence resembles (in some fashion) the demographic transition of human populations. When founding rates are at their maximum and mortality rates are simultaneously near their minimum, population growth will be exceedingly high. Indeed, the population density trajectories for these and many other organizational populations often show an initial stage of slow growth, followed by one of rapid growth, and then proceeded by a stage of stabilization or decline (see the figures in Chapter 2).[3]

Despite the general similarity of estimated relationships between density and vital rates across many organizational populations, there is great diversity in the strength of the effects of density. Differences in these estimated effects imply high variation in the levels and speed at which the vital rates will turn with increases in density. As Chesnais (1992, 513) has noted for the demographic transition of human populations, the point is that: "similarity of trajectory does not preclude diversity of rates."

---

[2] These models also include the estimated effects of other covariates—see Carroll and Teo (1998) for full specification.

[3] Of course, many simpler models (e.g., those with linear density dependence in vital rates discussed above) imply S-shaped growth trajectories as well. And, some models with time dependence but not density dependence, such as the Gompertz model, also imply such a trajectory in density. So claims that the S-shaped growth of density forces the vital rates to have the form of nonmonotonic density dependence described here are clearly misinformed.

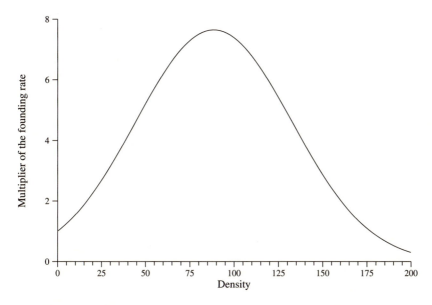

Figure 10.1. *Predicted relationship between density and the founding rate of banks in Singapore.*

Comparative analysis of such variations in density-dependent rates across populations and contexts holds great promise for corporate demography, in our view. Hannan and Carroll (1992) made some initial efforts in this direction. They estimated and compared models of density dependence in five organizational populations in three countries.[4] However, the widespread availability of measures of organizational density in a multitude of contexts means that the scope of comparative analysis could be much greater. A glimpse of the possibilities can be found in the research on the demographic transition in human populations, where many countries are often studied over long periods of time. For instance, Chesnais' (1992) authoritative treatment of the transition examines 67 countries over 1720–1984. The ability to make comparisons of this magnitude allows one to understand in a serious way the empirical patterns (and departures from them). For instance, Chesnais can identify several general types of demographic transitions, based on the rate of natural increase implied and the

---

[4]More recently, Hannan et al. (1998a) conducted a comparative analysis of the major automobile producer populations in the United States and Europe. We discuss this study in the next chapter.

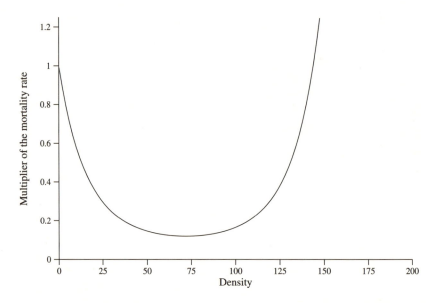

Figure 10.2. *Predicted relationship between density and the mortality rates of banks in Singapore.*

length of time required for the transition to be completed. It also allows him to examine extant theoretical claims rigorously and to advance novel nuanced arguments. Comparative work on corporate density dependence could be even more impressive, because there are many more organizational populations than countries or societies.

10.3 Theory of Density-Dependent Evolution

Good comparative social research uses a theoretical framework to guide investigation and facilitate interpretation. Research on corporate density dependence has from its inception been driven by a specific theory of organizational evolution. The theory of density-dependent organizational evolution holds that the general forces of social legitimation and competition drive changes in vital rates over time. It also contends that social legitimation and competition are themselves molded by organizational density.

The history of legitimation and competition for any organizational population arguably depends on idiosyncratic features of its form, the conditions under which it evolved, and the detailed texture of temporal and spatial variations in its environment. In other words, reconstructing the exact details of changing levels of legitimation and competition over the history of any one population demands attention to all of the unique features of that population's history. A key question in trying to understand organizational evolution concerns the importance of idiosyncrasy. Do special features of populations and their histories dominate, or do population histories work out minor variations on common patterns? The theory used in corporate demography takes a strong stance in favor of generality in terms of the overall forms of relationships.

Next we discuss the two main components of the theory. The first relates density to legitimation and competition, two concepts that researchers find difficult to measure directly over the full histories of organizational populations. The second links the vital rates to competition and legitimation.

Legitimation

What does it mean for an organizational form to be legitimated? One common answer holds that a form receives legitimation to the extent that its structure and routines follow the prevailing institutional rules. In this usage, legitimation means conformity with a set of rules, what DiMaggio and Powell (1983) termed coercive isomorphism. A second answer holds that an organizational form gains legitimation when it attains a socially taken-for-granted character (Meyer and Rowan 1977). A form acquires this second kind of legitimation, which we call *constitutive legitimation*, when relevant actors see it (perhaps implicitly) as the natural way to effect some kind of collective action.

These two conceptions of legitimation differ. What a society's laws endorse and prohibit might not correspond closely with what its members take for granted. It turns out that the conception of constitutive legitimation (taken-for-grantedness) has been more productive for developing theory and research on organizational demography, because it has a clear-cut link with density. So, we restrict our attention to constitutive legitimation here; we discuss this restriction in some detail in the closing section of the chapter.

When a new organizational form appears, say automobile manufacturing in the late nineteenth century, it usually lacks constitutive legitimation.[5] This situation makes organizing difficult: capital sources are wary; suppliers and customers need to be educated; employees might be hard to

---

[5] In some cases, organizational forms might inherit legitimation from closely related existing forms, especially superforms as discussed in Chapter 4. For instance, Boone et al. (2000) argue that the population of auditing firms inherited the legitimacy of the well-established population of accounting firms.

identify and recruit; and in many instances hostile institutional rules must be changed. As the form is promulgated, legitimation increases. Initially, when there are few organizations in the population, the returns to legitimation of adding another organization are great. However, when the population contains many organizations, constitutive legitimation increases very little—perhaps not at all—as the density of the population rises. In other words, the constitutive legitimation of an organizational population increases with density at a decreasing rate and approaches a ceiling at high levels of density.

So, it seems clear that extreme rarity of a form poses serious problems of constitutive legitimation. If almost no instances of a form exist, it can hardly be taken as the natural way to achieve some collective end. On the other hand, once a form becomes common, it seems unlikely that increases in numbers will have a great effect on its institutional standing. In other words, legitimation responds to variations in density in the lower range, but the effect has a ceiling. The ceiling, denoted as $\mathcal{L}$, might be interpreted as the point at which the percentage of relevant actors who take the form for granted reaches a sufficiently high level to make it a normative prescription. At this point further increases in the percentage of persons who take the form for granted do not affect its cultural standing.

The key premise about the relationship between density and constitutive legitimation can be stated as follows.

Assumption 10.3.1. *Constitutive legitimation increases with density, but it cannot exceed a finite ceiling* ($\mathcal{L}$):

$$L_t \propto \min[\vartheta(N_t), \mathcal{L}], \qquad \vartheta' > 0, \ 0 \leq \mathcal{L} < \infty.$$

(In our notation, $\vartheta\prime$ indicates the first derivative of ϑ with respect to its argument; the symbol $\propto$ stands for relationship of proportionality.)

The founding rates of populations surely must be affected by the constitutive legitimation of the organizational forms used. A taken-for-granted social form can be more readily visualized by potential organizers than one with dubious or unknown standing. Institutional rules endorsing particular organizational forms as the appropriate means for attaining collective goals also affect the ease of founding those types of organizations. The capacity to mobilize potential members and resources increases greatly when those who control resources take the organizational form for granted. Reducing the need for such justifications lowers the cost of organizing.

Assumption 10.3.2. *The founding rate in an organizational population is proportional to the level of constitutive legitimation:*

$$\lambda \propto L.$$

Constitutive legitimation also has a straightforward link with organizational mortality. Most institutional theories imply that legitimation enhances the life chances of organizations. Legitimation eases the problem of maintaining flows of resources from the environment; it also enhances the ability of organizations to fend off challenges (Meyer and Rowan 1977).

Assumption 10.3.3. *The mortality hazard in an organizational population is inversely proportional to the level of constitutive legitimation:*

$$\mu \propto \frac{1}{L}.$$

Competition

Competition refers to some kind of negative effect of the presence of one or more actors on the life chances or growth rates of some focal actor. Some important kinds of competition are structured or directed, as when two actors engage in rivalry or so-called head-to-head competition. In other cases, the effects are indirect or diffuse, as when a set of actors are dependent upon a pool of limited resources. In such cases, the entry of additional actors into the arena lowers the life chances of a focal actor by increasing the demand on the resource base. Such diffuse competition does not require that the actors take account of each others' actions or even be aware of their existence. Both structured and diffuse competition are important to understanding the life chances of organizations.

The demographic theory of density dependence focuses on diffuse competition because of its clear relationship with density, viz., the intensity of diffuse competition within an organizational population rises as a function of the number of potential bilateral competitors. In a population of N organizations, as N increases linearly, the number of possible competitive relations increases geometrically (Hannan and Carroll 1992). This implies that diffuse competition rises with a population's density at an increasing rate. In other words, variations in the range of high density (relative to abundance of resources) have more impact on strength of competition than do variations in the lower range. When numbers are few, an increase of population size by a single organization increases the frequency and strength of competitive interactions slightly if at all. However, when density is high relative to the carrying capacity, addition of another organization greatly increases the competition. Viewed from the viewpoint of the actions of a single organization, the difficulty of fashioning a strategy that works against all (or most) competitors becomes extraordinarily difficult when very many pairwise interactions must be considered simultaneously.

Assumption 10.3.4. The intensity of competition increases with density at an increasing rate:

$$C_t = \varphi(N_t), \qquad \varphi' > 0 \quad and \quad \varphi'' > 0.$$

(In this notation, φ' indicates the first derivative of φ with respect to its argument, and φ'' indicates the second derivative.)

Organizational analysts generally believe that intense competitive pressure within an organizational population depresses organizational founding rates. As the level of diffuse competition increases, more of the resources needed to build and sustain organizations have already been claimed by other organizations. Intense competition causes supplies of potential organizers, members, patrons, and resources to become exhausted. When diffuse competition is intense, fewer resources go unclaimed and markets get packed tightly.

Given a finite carrying capacity set by environmental conditions, as the number of potential competitors increases, the potential gains from founding an organization decline. Actors with the knowledge and skills to build organizations would be expected to defer attempts at building organizations in densely populated environments. This sort of process contributes to a negative relationship between competition and the founding rate. Capital markets and other macrostructures often reinforce this tendency. For example, rational investors typically avoid participating in new ventures in highly competitive markets. Likewise, professional associations and government agencies often try to restrict entry under intense competition. These arguments point in the same direction. The founding rate of an organizational population is inversely proportional to the intensity of competition within the population.

Assumption 10.3.5. The founding rate in an organizational population is inversely proportional to the intensity of diffuse competition:

$$\lambda \propto \frac{1}{C}.$$

In the case of mortality, all relevant arguments imply that competition increases the hazard. Every organization must maintain a flow of resources from its environment to keep its structures intact. As competition intensifies, maintaining life-sustaining flows of resources becomes problematic for many, if not all, organizations in a population. Therefore, increasing diffuse competition lowers the life chances of organizations by complicating the task of maintaining a flow of essential resources. In other words, if competition is already intense, then further growth increases mortality rates, after controlling for the environmental conditions that affect carrying capacities.

Assumption 10.3.6. *The mortality rate in an organizational population is proportional to the intensity of diffuse competition:*

$$\mu \propto C.$$

Relationships Between Observables

Although it might not yet be apparent, this theory implies certain empirical facts about density dependence in rates of founding and mortality. These implied facts constitute the primary way that researchers evaluate and extend the theory. As noted above, comparison of these facts across populations might someday prove to be an interesting and insightful form of meta-analysis in corporate demography.

A subtle issue that must be addressed explicitly concerns the behavior of density-dependent legitimation when density is close to zero. Density can actually equal zero in empirical cases after a population's initiation, because the early entrants perish before any additional organizations are founded. For instance, this was the case for the population of American national labor unions (Hannan 1995). We realize that legitimation does not drop to zero with density in such cases, at least not immediately (Chapter 4). It seems reasonable to assume that legitimation is nonnegative at all levels of density (once a population's history has begun). What about competition at low density? When a population contains fewer than two organizations, intrapopulation competition does not exist—there are no potential competitors in the population. For this reason, we assume that legitimation exceeds competition at very low densities.

Assumption 10.3.7. *Legitimation is stronger than competition at very low densities:*

$$\vartheta(N_t) > \varphi(N_t) \quad \text{when} \quad N_t < 2.$$

To see the theory's implied empirical facts, start with founding rates. Assumptions 10.1, 10.2, 10.4, 10.5, and 10.7 jointly imply the following.

Theorem 10.3.1. *A population's founding rate rises with increasing density initially, reaches a peak, and then declines with further increases in density:*

$$\lambda(t) = \kappa_\lambda(t) \frac{\min(\vartheta(N_t), \mathfrak{L})}{\varphi(N_t)},$$

and

$$\lambda(t)' \equiv \frac{d\lambda(t)}{dN_t} \quad \begin{cases} > 0 & \text{if} \quad N_t < N_\lambda^* \\ < 0 & \text{if} \quad N_t > N_\lambda^*, \end{cases}$$

where N_λ^* denotes the turning point in the relationship (the density at which the relationship between density and the founding rate changes sign from positive to negative) and $\kappa_\lambda(t)$ summarizes the effects of other relevant conditions operating at time t.

In other words, the theory yields an empirically testable implication: the relationship between density and the founding rate has the form of an inverted U. At low density, the marginal effect of density is positive: growth in density increases the founding rate. At some level of density, N_λ^*, the relationship changes sign. Above the turning point, an increase in density has a negative marginal effect on the rate. In other words, further growth in density depresses the founding rate. The legitimation process dominates at low density, and the competition process dominates at high density.

A parallel theorem follows for the effect of contemporaneous density on mortality rates. Assumptions 10.1, 10.3, 10.4, 10.6 and 10.7 imply a theorem for mortality rates parallel to Theorem 10.1.

Theorem 10.3.2. *Organizational mortality rates initially fall with increasing density, reach a minimum, and then increase with further increases in density:*

$$\mu(t) = \kappa_\mu(t) \frac{\varphi(N_t)}{\min(\vartheta(N_t), \mathfrak{L})},$$

and

$$\mu(t)' \equiv \frac{d\mu(t)}{dN_t} \quad \begin{cases} < 0 & \text{if} \quad N_t < N_\mu^*, \\ > 0 & \text{if} \quad N_t > N_\mu^*. \end{cases}$$

Again, the theory yields an empirically testable qualitative implication about nonmonotonicity in density dependence. In this case, the relationship has a U-shape. At low density, growth in density lowers the mortality rate by increasing legitimation more than competition. Beyond the turning point, (N_μ^*), further growth in density increases competition more than legitimation and thereby raises the mortality rate. The tests of the theory discussed in Section 10.2 focus on these qualitative implications of the theory.

10.4 Interpreting Density Dependence

As might be expected given its fast popularity, the theory of density-dependent legitimation and competition has not escaped criticism. Virtually all of this commentary has been directed at the theory or at theoretical interpretations of the evidence. Little debate has centered on whether the widely observed empirical associations of nonmonotonic density dependence in vital rates are valid.[6]

---

[6] See, however, Petersen and Koput (1991), Hannan, Barron, and Carroll (1991), and Hannan and Carroll (1992, 132–138).

Some Criticisms

Critiques of the theory and its interpretation convey three general themes. The first deals exclusively with the social legitimation process. Economists usually find this part of the theory intriguing; sociologists sometimes find it lacking. Why? What would cause sociologists to question the operation of a key sociological process? Some of the criticism is pure folly. However, the serious complaints usually call for either more direct measures of legitimation or for a broader conceptualization that includes legal or sociopolitical legitimacy. Nothing is wrong with either suggestion. Nonetheless, waiting for a breakthrough in measurement technology that allows one to assess directly and to compare across contexts the taken-for-granted nature of persons and other actors living decades and even centuries in the past might delay the research project for many years, perhaps forever. In the meantime, using a formal model to infer the operation of legitimation processes seems a sensible strategy.[7]

In the view of most sociologists, legal or sociopolitical legitimacy is distinct from constitutive legitimation (Hannan and Carroll 1995). Little value would result from mixing the two into a single concept or measure, thus muddying up the waters. Taken alone, no one doubts that legal or sociopolitical legitimacy powerfully shapes organizational evolution. Consider, for instance, the organizational consequences of the Volstead Act, which prohibited the production and sale of alcohol products from 1920 to 1933. However, it is hard to build a predictive general theory around idiosyncratic, historically specific acts of legislation and the like. Instead, the better approach would seem to be to incorporate these developments as control variables based on an understanding of a population's history. Without such controls, tests of the density-dependent theory of legitimation and competition would be flawed. But this is clearly not the case, as examination of any major study of the theory shows that analysts have taken pains to control for such events.

The second general theme of critiques focuses on the density variable itself. According to these views, analysis of organizational density is an incomplete way to model evolution (Winter 1990; Haveman 1994). The opinion expressed recently by Nelson (1995, 69) typifies this position: "In assessing the relative importance of a particular routine in the industry mix, or analyzing whether it is expanding or contracting in relative use, it is not sufficient to 'count' the firms employing it. One must consider their size, or whether they are growing or contracting." Again, it is hard to disagree. Any theory or model is an abstraction and must involve simplifications. So, it is also not entirely clear what the critique implies for research on the density model.

---

[7] This subsection and the next follow closely parts of Carroll (1997).

One interpretation holds that tests of density dependence in organizational evolution need to control for organizational size, industry size, and temporal variation in both. No debate here. Although early tests often ignored these factors because of data unavailability, numerous recent tests all include such measures. These tests show unequivocally that density dependence is a unique and general phenomenon. Another interpretation of remarks by Nelson (1995) and others' remarks implies that other, possibly complementary, possibly competing general evolutionary theories of organizations based on characteristics such as size ought to be developed. Sure enough; the world of corporate demography is certainly big enough for multiple theories to coexist.

The third critical theme targets the diffuse-competition component of the model, whereby all organizations in the population potentially compete with each other. It argues that a better formulation for many contexts would be based on *direct* competition, using subsets of organizations that clearly draw from similar or overlapping resources. The operational consequences of this position entail either redrawing the boundaries for counting density so that only direct competitors are included or weighting density counts of population members based on proximity along some competitive dimension such as price or geography (McPherson 1983; Barnett and Carroll 1987; Baum and Mezias 1992; Baum and Singh 1994). As we discuss below, this approach might best be regarded as an extension or refinement of the basic density model (involving weighted density) applicable to particular contexts. Studies to date demonstrate high promise for its use in understanding and modeling interorganizational relationships. Nonetheless, questions remain about whether diffuse competition as modeled in the basic density model captures a distinct process or simply represents a good shorthand approximation to direct competition averaged across an entire population.

Qualitative Evidence

A complementary way of establishing the plausibility of theory involves examining the natural histories of organizational populations and looking for evidence of the large-scale operation of processes of constitutive legitimation and diffuse competition. Does a population's natural history conform to the general predictions of initial growth and development driven by legitimation and later, high-density evolution fueled primarily by competition? This approach is decidedly subjective, but it does lend plausibility to the theory when, for example, diverse histories portray similar longterm struggles for establishing constitutive legitimation or taken-for-grantedness, which has generally been the case in those histories reported. For instance,

Hannan and Freeman (1989) describe how early labor unions faced hostile employers and laws that questioned their right to exist. Carroll (1984a) discusses Mott's (1962) and Schudson's (1978) accounts of battles of the legality of publishing as well as the difficulties of establishing a market for advertising. If constitutive legitimation had existed initially at the low-density points of these populations, then we believe that these histories would read differently.

Natural histories of organizational populations also suggest some intriguing possible embellishments of the theory. An interesting recurring observation of this kind concerns the level of and nature of social organization found early in the history of many industries or organizational populations. Simply put, actions in the origin periods of industries typically look and feel to sociologists like the actions of social movements. This is true for telephony (Barnett and Carroll 1993), newspapers (Olzak and West 1991), automobiles (Carroll and Hannan 1995b), labor unions (Hannan 1995), credit unions (Barron 1998), and health maintenance organizations (Strang 1995). Other industries have for the most part not been examined in this way.

What does this observation mean? A social movement is generally considered to be "the organized, sustained, self-conscious challenge to existing authorities" (Tilly 1984, 304). It is defined as

> a deliberate collective endeavor to promote change, in any direction and by any means possible... a movement's commitment to change and the raison d'être of its organization are founded upon the conscious volition, normative commitment to the movement's aims or beliefs, and active participation on the part of the followers or members. (Wilkinson 1971, 27)

So, to say that the origin periods of industries resemble social movements means that (1) they represent challenges to existing companies and industries and (2) they are populated with individuals and organizations devoted to causes, lifestyles, and visions of a better future for all (rather than with profit-maximizing entrepreneurs engaged in competitive battles based primarily on self-interest).

The theoretical implications of this observation have yet to be explored in any depth. They might be profound. Consider that the usual explanations of industry emergence and initial growth have to do with either market needs (demand-driven explanations) or the great potential of unleashed technologies (supply-driven explanations). Comparable explanations of social movements rely on the severity of particular social problems or the economic and social deprivation of particular social groups. However, these intuitive explanations have proven spectacularly unsuccessful in empirical research on social movements.

Instead, to explain social movements analysts now rely primarily on theories highlighting the organization and solidarity of social groups as well as their ability to mobilize resources (Tilly 1984; Olzak 1992). Among other things, these theories feature the roles of preexisting organizational structures (which provide forums for discovering solidarity as well as focus and resources for articulated interests), social movement entrepreneurs (evangelical individuals who engage in building institutions and mobilizing resources), and social movement organizations (entities designed to foster and protect the interests of the movement). These phenomena are all associated with processes that generate mutualism or positive feedback in the organizational population. Do similar phenomena and processes account for early industry and organizational growth among latent and nascent industries or organizational populations? If so, then conventional views of industry origins would be radically changed.

10.5 Extensions Involving Weighted Density

The basic density framework outlined above assumes that all organizations in a population have equal influence on each other. For instance, it assumes the effect of any single organization on the failure rate of another organization does not depend on the characteristics of either organization or any possible other relationship between them. While recognizing the value of this general formulation, many analysts nonetheless wish to dig deeper into the nature of interorganizational relationships, especially issues of competition. A potentially valuable and flexible way of doing this consists of building models that use specific weightings of density. (Of course, the weights must be based on theoretical and substantive considerations.) Sometimes these weighted-density effects are used in conjunction with full-population density effects; at other times they are viewed as substitutes that get closer to the action.[8] These studies have produced a large number of interesting and important contributions to various areas of organizational analysis, including especially strategic management.

---

[8] Occasionally, analysts claim that the greater statistical power of some weighted-density models demonstrates a weakness of the basic density framework. These analysts often fail to take into account the loss of generality entailed in weighting schemes; they also sometimes do not recognize the additional information employed by these schemes. To us, it does not seem surprising that a model formulated for a specific context and using more information outperforms a general model using less information. Moreover, in our view, the ability of a model to adapt and to be tailored to many specific contexts in ways that improve its explanatory value is a genuine strength, not a weakness. Such model development corresponds with our views about cumulative research programs (Chapters 3 and 5).

Although not restricted to such ties, the models of weighted density that have been developed focus overwhelmingly on competitive relations.[9] A major class of these models relies on notions of direct competition, discussed briefly above. They use an extension of the density framework that incorporates assessments of the probability of various pairs of organizations competing strongly. These models require a priori assessment by the analyst about organizations are likely to compete with a focal organization. The assessment might be based on theory, observation, or prior analysis; its validity is determined by whether or not the relevant weighted-density has significant effects. The weighting scheme used can be categorical (indicating either a firm is a potential competitor or not), as with Barnett and Carroll's (1987) classification of local and nonlocal telephone companies in Iowa (based on county of operation). Weighted densities constructed using categorical schemes simply count the subset of those organizations that are potential competitors (e.g., local telephone companies).

Empirical studies using a categorical weighting scheme have specified that the probability of competition depends upon geography (Swaminathan and Wiedenmayer 1991; Carroll and Wade 1991; Hannan and Carroll 1992; Barron et al. 1994; Hannan et al. 1995; Bigelow, Carroll, Seidel, and Tsai 1997; Barron 1999), technology (Barnett 1990), organizational form (Hannan and Freeman 1989; Greve 1998; Barron 1999), and overlap in resource base (Baum and Singh 1994).

Alternatively, the weighting scheme can be continuous and based on a metric (indicating the likelihood that a firm is a potential competitor or not). For example, the study by Hannan et al. (1990) uses similarity in size as the basis for assessing the probability of competition. In cases such as this, the density variable is constructed by weighting the value of each organization by some measure of similarity (or conversely, distance) on a relevant dimension prior to aggregation. Empirical studies using continuous weighting have based the probability of competition on similarity in price, and physical location (Baum and Mezias 1992; Haveman 1993a) and on location in technology space (Podolny et al. 1996; Stuart 1998).

The theoretical challenge presented by the direct-competition approach concerns the issue of where to draw the boundaries for density counts (or, alternatively, how to weight potentially competing organizations in a complete population). The extremes involve, on the one hand, following the basic density model and counting (equally) every organization in the population and, on the other hand, following the logic of direct competition and circumscribing local competition very narrowly, so

---

[9] Given the relevant theory, it is a straightforward matter to develop corresponding models of weighted density based on mutualistic relations.

narrowly that every focal organization appears as an island and its relevant density count is 1 (Hannan 1997). Obviously, something between these two extremes is what direct-competition theorists have in mind; yet, there is a lot of room between them. Exactly where the boundary should be drawn is a theoretical issue, and at the moment no compelling general theoretical rule has been advanced; instead, researchers circumscribe local competition on an ad hoc basis.

Oddly enough, progress has been made in developing general theory about the appropriate geographical boundaries of social legitimation and diffuse competition relative to each other. As we explain in Chapter 11, we have argued previously that legitimation operates on a broader geographical scale than diffuse competition, mainly because political and physical barriers disrupt the flow of plants, products, and people more severely than they do cultural images. The argument leads to a multilevel specification of density dependence where the measures of density associated with legitimation are counted across political boundaries and those associated with competition are counted only within boundaries.[10] So, for instance, automobile manufacturers in European countries benefited from the legitimation processes of other countries but experienced competition primarily from firms operating in the same country (Hannan et al. 1995). The specification shows promise but has yet to be thoroughly tested in a wide variety of contexts. Among the questions it raises is whether competition gets restricted by geographical constraints or by political constraints (Bigelow et al. 1997). Current evidence is unclear.

An important second class of weighted-density models has been proposed and developed by Barnett (1997). These formulations organize the extension of density dependence around ideas about the competitive strength exerted by various competitors. They also require a priori assessment by the analyst, in this case about which types of competitors are strongest. For example, in an analysis of two distinct organizational populations (telephone companies and breweries), Barnett (1997) argued that older organizations are more powerful competitors than younger ones. Accordingly, he estimated effects on vital rates of density weighted by the ages of the organizations, that is, the sum of the ages of all organizations in the population at each point in time. Age-weighted density had a negative effect on founding rates and positive effect on mortality rates in both populations. Empirical studies of this kind have used the following weighting dimensions as the basis of competitive strength: age (Barnett 1997), size (Barnett 1997), and organizational form (Barnett and Freeman 1997). In general, this approach generates findings about the intensity of

---

[10] A similar argument has been applied to the multiform context by Carroll and Teo (1998) and Teo et al. (1998).

competition in various environments based on observable organizational characteristics of the population.

The Red Queen

The most sophisticated of the weighted density models are based on a theory known as "the Red Queen."[11] According to Barnett and Hansen (1996, 139), this theory holds that a reciprocal process of learning and competition drives organizational evolution:

> ...an organization facing competition is likely to respond, but ...its response is likely to be limited—merely 'satisficing' through a localized search and decision process. ...This response then marginally increases the competition faced by the organization's rivals, triggering in them a similar process of search and decision, which ultimately increases the competitive pressures faced by the first organization. This again triggers the search for improvements in the first organizations and so the cycle continues.

The theory implies that (1) organizations that experience intense direct competition become stronger competitors; and (2) the longer organizations are subject to direct competition and the more recent this experience, the stronger they will be (Barnett and Hansen 1996; Barnett and Sorenson 1998).[12] Model specification for tests of the Red Queen hypothesis involve density weightings based on the experience distributions of direct competitors. For example, in investigating competing banks within local counties in Illinois, Barnett and Hansen (1996) use two weighted densities summing the temporal length of competitive experiences by rival banks. The first weighted-density is the number of rivals weighted by the recentness of their competitive experience; the second is the number of rivals weighted by their distant competitive experience. The analysis shows that banks facing environments filled with competitors possessing high amounts of recent competitive experience are more likely to fail than those facing environments with banks having less recent competitive experience. Barnett and Sorenson (1998) found parallel effects for the founding rates and growth rates of Illinois banks.

Note that these analyses testing the Red Queen theory involve a combination of *both* of the two general classes of weighted-density models. By

---

[11] The label comes from Van Valen (1973), who makes an allusion to Alice in Lewis Carroll's *Alice in Wonderland*. It refers to a scene in which Alice races the Red Queen. Alice notices that she never gains in the race even though she is running. The Red Queen tells her that she is from a slow world because those from fast worlds run simply to stay still.

[12] Conversely, the theory implies that monopolists will slow or cease learning and become less formidable as competitors.

examining only banks within the same locality, these analyses are based on assessments of the probability of competition. By weighting density counts by the length of competitive experience, these analyses are based on assessments of the strength of individual competitors. Such combined weightings show great potential for understanding how organizations compete with each other; we expect that many studies of this kind will appear in the strategy and organizations literature (see, for example, Ingram and Baum (1997)).

10.6 Programmatic Issues

Research on the demographic transition in human populations continues despite its widespread recognition as social fact a half century or more in the past. This is because of the continuing importance of documenting and understanding variations in the timing, levels, and speed of the transition in different societies. There is also considerable effort devoted to refining and extending the theoretical explanations (Chesnais 1992).

The research program on corporate density dependence shows signs of experiencing a similar development. Despite its considerable success in establishing empirical regularities and a general theoretical explanation, significant research activity continues within the density framework. Much of this work does not get highlighted because acceptance of the model has meant that its basic specifications are often used as baselines in studies with other agendas. So new findings on the basic patterns of density dependence often go unremarked. Nonetheless, we believe that enough evidence is piling up to allow soon an authoritative comparative meta-analysis of patterns of density dependence in a wide variety of organizational populations.

A great deal of other work in the framework focuses on developing theories and models that let some weighted function of density play a central role. Following Barnett (1997), these models can be organized according to whether the extension incorporates: (1) the probability of various organizations competing with each other; or (2) the competitive strength exerted by a competitor. We find it interesting that the ideas and specifications developed in this way are often cast by their proponents as challenges to the received wisdom about density dependence. They are not, in our view. The extensions grow from the same tradition and family of models in corporate demography. We believe that extensions of this kind have great promise for advancing our understanding of interorganizational relations, especially competitive ones.

Despite these important developments, some issues pertaining to the original model and evidence remain to be fully resolved. Two major research questions sit at the top of the agenda in the sense that their resolution is required to round out the model. Both concern late-stage evolution, organizational change in mature or well-established industries.

The first major question remaining unresolved in the program on density dependence is how the precipitous decline in density frequently observed in mature organizational populations might be explained. For instance, the number of automobile producers drops from a peak of almost 350 around 1910 to fewer than 50 in 1945 and then stays at relatively low levels (see Figure 2.1 in Chapter 2). Simulations of the basic model of density dependence show that with the usual nonmonotonic relation in vital rates, the projected population follows an S-shaped pattern (Hannan and Carroll 1992; Carroll and Harrison 1994). So the standard model of density dependence can reproduce observed population trajectories up to and including a peak, but it cannot account for the subsequent common decline in density. However, as Chapter 11 explains, certain specific extensions of the density dependence model can explain these interesting features of population trajectories.

The second unresolved research problem is to account for the resurgence in organizational density that sometimes occurs very late in a population's evolution, usually after a major decline. An example of this pattern, not widely known, can also be detected in Figure 2.1, where the number of American automobile producers rises from 1970 to the end of observation in 1981. (Data we are currently collecting for the period to 1995 suggests that the trend has not reversed itself.) An even stronger reversal of this kind has occurred in American beer brewing, where the number of brewers has climbed to over 1,350 producers in late 1998, after experiencing a low of 43 in 1983. Although not ubiquitous, and not as regularly observed as late-stage declines, these renewals are common enough to require attention in any model of longterm evolution.

In principle, the basic density model can explain late-stage resurgences in organizational density—these would be the result of diminished and then reinvigorated legitimation (see the next chapter). However, this interpretation does not seem plausible to many analysts, who note that once established, legitimation as social taken-for-grantedness in organizational forms does not erode rapidly (Chapter 4). That certainly seems to be the case for the two populations we considered as examples for the renewal phenomenon: automobile manufacturing and beer brewing.

A slight reformulation of the density model does, however, make it applicable and potentially powerful in explaining renewals. The reformulation involves identifying new organizational forms and populations associated with the renewal period and arguing that these forms require distinct (but perhaps not total) legitimation (Chapter 4). For instance, Carroll and Swaminathan (1998) argued that the two organizational subforms fueling the renewal process, microbreweries and brewpubs, both initially lacked recognition and social acceptance, despite the fact that each is related to the well-known brewery organizational form. (Some empirical evidence supports this position: microbreweries and brewpubs show positive density dependence.) They also described an institutional arena surrounding these forms displaying the social movement character typically found in populations undergoing the legitimation process. Our hunch, based on preliminary research in the contemporary automobile industry, is that the renewal process there consists largely of producers of alternative fuel cars, who also show great collective commitment and zeal.

The reformulated model shifts the research problem from explaining the renewal to predicting the emergence of new organizational subforms. Unfortunately, we lack the necessary theory. We do not have good models for predicting the appearance of new organizational forms generally (Romanelli 1991). The question of subform emergence adds to this problem the conceptual one of distinguishing subforms from forms. Although these problems might very well be solvable, their current status leaves the door open for other possible explanations of the renewal process often observed in organizational populations.

11
Density-Dependent Processes II

THE THEORY of density-dependent legitimation and competition (discussed in detail in the previous chapter) implies that, ceteris paribus, organizational populations evolve to *steady-state* densities. According to the theory, increased density initially enhances a population's (constitutive) legitimation, thereby raising its founding rate and lowering its mortality rate. These effects initially induce further growth in density. However, persistent increases in density eventually generate intense competition, which depresses founding rates and elevates mortality rates. If the effects of competition and legitimation balance each other, then density stabilizes. Shocks that drive density away from the steady state are countered by resulting changes in rates of founding and mortality that eventually restore the steady state.

In many well-documented cases, however, organizational densities decline sharply after an extended period of early proliferation; and they sometimes rise again. Consider, for instance, the time path of densities of American, French, and German automobile manufacturers over 1885–1981 (see Figures 2.1 and 2.2 in Chapter 2). The number of firms in these populations grew for roughly forty years, then declined steeply and remained far below the peaks for the next fifty years; then they began to rebound toward the end of the histories. Can the model of density dependence be extended to explain these kinds of population declines and resurgences? In this chapter, we suggest that the answer might be Yes. We explain and review several promising modeling efforts aimed in this direction. These extensions of the theory focus on density delay and population aging.

The second half of the chapter takes up another general problem of longterm organizational evolution, namely, the geographical dispersion of populations. Such dispersion makes it hard to know where to draw the boundaries of processes of legitimation and competition. And, because organizational populations often evolve in proximity to other populations, it might be unrealistic to assume that each evolves independently. Promising extensions to the density model reviewed here relax this assumption and specify legitimation and competition as multilevel phenomena.

11.1 Density Delay

How can decline and later resurgence of forms be explained? One obvious way is to retain the existing theory and attribute reversals to environmental changes following the strategy laid out in Chapter 9. For example, large shifts in environmental munificence or government regulations might turn out to coincide with turning points in density. Abundant research shows that events such as economic depression, war, technological innovation, cultural change, and shifts in regulation affect founding rates and mortality rates (Chapter 9). Nonetheless, attributing sustained declines in density to environmental conditions does not appear promising as a general explanation of decline and resurgence.

Numerous studies find that the estimated effects of density on vital rates are stronger and more robust than the effects of environmental conditions. Moreover, the pattern of growth, decline, and mild resurgence holds for very diverse populations operating in very different environments, e.g., automobile manufacturers, beer brewers, credit unions, labor unions, railroad companies, and telephone companies (Hannan and Carroll 1992; Carroll and Hannan 1995b). Intensive study of these and other cases reveals more similarity in population dynamics than in the patterns of environmental change. Thus, organizational demographers have asked whether commonalities in population processes might explain decline and resurgence.

The search for a mechanism to explain decline with reference to population processes began with the model of density delay. In contrast to the theory reviewed in the previous chapter, where density has contemporaneous effects on rates of organizational founding and mortality, this model holds that density also has a *delayed* effect on mortality rates (Carroll and Hannan 1989a). Its central prediction is the following.

Hypothesis 11.1. *Organizations founded during periods of high density have persistently higher age-specific rates of mortality.*

Density delay has important implications for the evolution of the organizational population. If the effect of density at time of founding persists, then organizations founded at high density have elevated rates of mortality for some time. As a consequence, the size of the population falls from the peak, unless the founding rate rises in compensation.[1]

---

[1] We assumed that there is no compensating rise in founding rates.

The density-delay hypothesis was stimulated by work in mathematical population biology. Leslie (1959) proposed a model that relates the hazard of mortality to contemporaneous density and conditions at time of birth. Citing research on human mortality, Leslie (1959, 152) observed that:

> It appears that each generation of young tends to carry throughout life a relative degree of mortality peculiar to itself, and it is supposed that this characteristic mortality ... represents the effect of environmental conditions experienced by each generation during the early years of its life in the population.

Leslie showed that adding delayed density dependence (with an implicit interaction with age structure) produces dampened cycles in trajectories of growth even when the environment does not vary. In other words, this kind of process can generate the kind of trajectory commonly observed for organizational populations.

The appeal of Leslie's model led us to ask whether density at time of founding might affect the mortality hazard of "mature" organizations? We suggested two related affirmative answers (Carroll and Hannan 1989a). The first involves a liability-of-scarcity story. Intense competition at time of founding (due to high density) creates conditions of resource scarcity. When resources are scarce, new organizations that cannot move quickly to full-scale operation face strong selection pressures. Those that survive the period of initial organizing presumably cannot devote much time, attention, and resources to organization building. In cohorts of organizations facing such circumstances, members have little incentive to acquire the organization-specific skills that make it possible for an organization to develop reproducible routines. It might be difficult to recover fully from such deprived initial organizing. Attempts at redesigning poorly fashioned structures might well encounter strong inertial resistance (Chapter 16). For these varied reasons, cohorts of organizations that experience high density at founding will tend to be inferior competitors at every age.

A second story about the deleterious consequences of experiencing high density at time of founding concerns tight niche packing. Few resources go unexploited in high-density environments. Because new organizations seldom compete well in head-to-head contests with established organizations, the new entrants often get pushed to the margins of resource distributions. In other words, tight niche packing causes new organizations to exploit thinly spread and/or ephemeral resources. Even if they succeed in adapting successfully to the inferior regions of the resource space, this commits them to persisting at the margins. The specialized learning, collective experience, and positional advantages that are beneficial for exploiting the inferior regions of the environment are not appropriate for attempts to operate in more abundant regions of the environment. Attempting to shift towards the richer center at some later time entails high risks of mortality during periods of protracted reorganization (Chapter 16). Successful reorganization brings the organization into competition with others specialized in exploiting the center. In either case, these marginal organizations have higher than average mortality rates.

We also discussed a third story involving a "trial by fire." Suppose that each cohort of organizations has a distribution of unobserved frailty, to follow the terminology of Vaupel, Manton, and Stallard (1979). Presumably, the most frail organizations fail at an early age under any circumstance. Those with slightly less frailty might persist if they are founded in favorable environmental circumstances but fail otherwise. Those with moderate frailty will tend to persist unless their founding conditions are highly unfavorable, and so forth. Founding conditions affect population dynamics by altering the "post-trial" distributions of frailty by cohort rather than by elevating the mortality rates of individual organizations. In particular, cohorts founded in periods of high density have a lower mean frailty after the initial year than cohorts founded in favorable circumstances. As a consequence, they have lower mortality rates after the period of initial selection. In this imagery, cohorts of organizations that survived the trial by fire have lower mortality rates than those that did not face the trial.

The most commonly used model of density delay is a variant of Leslie's model. It holds that the density at time of founding matters—not the time of founding per se. The arguments about the liability of scarcity and tight niche packing suggest that density at founding has a monotonic positive effect on mortality rates. Such an effect likely has the same *relative* effect at all ages, which means that the absolute effect is largest at young ages (because the rate is highest at those ages). So the model of mortality has the form:

$$\mu_i(a) \propto \exp(\theta_1 N_a + \theta_2 N_a^2 + \theta_3 N_{f_i}), \tag{11.1}$$

where N_a denotes density at age a, and N_{f_i} denotes density at time of founding of the ith organization. (We assume that contemporaneous density has the nonmonotonic pattern of effects (at all ages) discussed in the previous chapter: $\theta_1 < 0$, $\theta_2 > 0$.) In terms of Hypothesis 11.1, which holds that density at time of founding has a positive effect on the age-specific hazard of mortality and that this effect persists over time, the specific prediction for the specification in (11.1) is

$$\theta_3 > 0. \tag{11.2}$$

The trial-by-fire hypothesis leads to different predictions. Recall that this story can be construed as saying that the intense competition due to high density at founding eliminates predominantly "high-frailty" organizations. Would founding density affect later mortality, net of the effect of contemporaneous density? Thus the trial-by-fire story can be interpreted as claiming that the average unconditional hazard is lower after the founding year for cohorts founded in periods of high density. In terms of the model in (11.1), this means that the persisting effect of founding density on the hazard of mortality is negative: $\theta_3 < 0$.

Swaminathan (1996) argues that this interpretation is too restrictive—he wants to let the shakeout process last longer than just the year of founding. As Swaminathan (1996, 1359) explains, "the length of the trial likely depends on the strength of selection pressures at founding and the speed at which surviving organizations eliminate failure-inducing routines." In developing this idea, Swaminathan (1996) advances a new model that holds that the effect of density at founding is positive but declines with age.

Empirical Findings

Nearly all of the studies of density dependence in mortality processes cited in Chapter 10 estimated the specification of density delay in (11.1). The estimated effect of density at founding is nearly always positive and significant.[2] The estimated effects of density delay usually imply that the mortality rates of organizations founded in times of peak density are five to ten times higher at any age than those of organizations that enter in times of low density.

Simulation studies suggest that the estimated effects of density at founding on mortality rates can explain some of the observed decline in population numbers in mature populations. However, the observed declines are generally steeper than what would be implied by estimated density-delay effects. So, while density delay seems to get us part of the way toward explaining population declines, it does not appear to provide the full story. Recognition of this state of affairs provides the motivation for the next step in the extension of the theory.

11.2 Population-Age Interactions

Sustained declines in density from a peak pose a problem for the main theoretical arguments about density dependence, even with density delay. The intuitions behind the theory fit best a stylized pattern of slow initial growth, subsequent rapid expansion in numbers, and stabilization. If

---

[2] Han (1998) found evidence supporting notions of liabilities of scarcity and tight niche packing by examining the effect of density on the sizes of newly founded organizations. Among Japanese banks, firms founded during times of high density were on average much smaller than those founded during lower density times.

density declines systematically at a later stage, then the plausibility of this story becomes strained because the original theory treats legitimation and competition as *timeless* functions of density. This assumption of timelessness implies that a drop in density reduces legitimation and competition in a mature population, which does not seem credible. In particular, once an organizational form becomes taken for granted, a decline in density is unlikely to diminish this standing in the short run. Similarly, competition might not ebb as numbers fall, at least while industry structure remains unchanged. In other words, density's effects on legitimation and competition plausibly change over a population's life course.[3]

To deal with the dynamics of density of mature populations, Hannan (1997) developed the extension of the density model that we now explore in detail. The extended model builds on the idea that the original theory applies most forcefully to the early phases of population histories and that the nature of density dependence changes as populations grow old.

Temporal Variation in Legitimation and Competition

Suppose that numerical proliferation does establish an organizational form as a feature of the social landscape. Once taken-for-grantedness sets in, what can undo it? Would a decline in density after a long period of growth, as in the example of the American, British, and French automobile industries (Figures 2.1 and 2.2), have such an effect? This seems very unlikely. Falling density presumably does not erase cultural understandings, at least in the short run. According to our understanding, social categories tend to be inert, to react slowly to empirical information. Therefore, relaxing the assumption of timelessness so that dips in density do not reverse the effects of initial proliferation (in the short run) would enhance the credulity of the theory.

The modeling strategy in Hannan (1997) takes a simple tack: it specifies changes in causal structure in terms of the age of the organizational population. One reason for focusing on a population's longevity is that simple persistence can generate constitutive legitimation. The history of the American telephone industry provides a good example. The Bell Company's vigorous exercise of its patent rights depressed the rate of entry into the industry for an extended period at its start (Chapter 18). When the patents lapsed, the number of firms in the industry grew explosively. Barnett (1995) interprets this response as indicating that longevity of the organizational population (through the period of the Bell patents) had legitimated the organizational form. If such a process operates generally, then

---

[3] This section draws from Hannan (1997).

declines in density might not affect legitimation in a long-standing population, at least initially, because longevity alone might sustain its standing as a cultural fact.

There is a second reason for thinking that legitimation becomes less sensitive to variations in density as populations age. If an organizational form comes to be legitimated constitutively, actors in the system take account of the population's existence in structuring their activities. For instance, state agencies take organizational forms into account in establishing rules and regulations (e.g., creating agencies to establish and enforce rules about automobiles and their use). The occupational system and its supporting structures employ the distinctions that define the form in structuring themselves (e.g., creating curricula in automotive engineering and founding unions of automobile workers). Industries and organizational populations develop to supply inputs, absorb outputs, and so forth (e.g., creating specialized populations of automobile parts suppliers, networks of automobile dealers, and automobile insurance companies).

In these and other ways, an organizational form gains institutional standing from the emergence of networks of tangible ties that develop between its members and other kinds of actors. It takes time for such networks to develop and stabilize, which suggests that they are unimportant in shaping nascent populations (DiMaggio and Powell 1983). As a population ages, however, its taken-for-grantedness presumably comes to depend upon its network position. If a population becomes institutionalized in the sense of developing durable ties with diverse actors, then changing density ought not to affect its constitutive legitimation.

These considerations suggest that the relationship between legitimation and density becomes increasingly sticky as an organizational population grows old. During a population's early history, changes in density have powerful consequences for legitimation. With aging, simple persistence and myriad kinds of institutionalization come to substitute for density in preserving a form's taken-for-grantedness. During a population's youth, substantial gains in legitimation result from modest changes in density. However, big changes in density produce little, if any, additional legitimation during a population's maturity. In other words, density strongly affects legitimation during a population's youth, and the relationship between density and legitimation becomes weaker at older ages.

The intensity of competition does not depend on a population's longevity in such obvious ways. Hence, one might begin the modeling process by assuming that only legitimation processes are affected by population aging. Nevertheless, Hannan (1997) speculates that the relationship between density and competition also becomes sticky as an organizational population ages. In this instance, the growing inertia plausibly reflects the development of *industry social structure*. Early in a population's history, the field of action lacks a stable structure. Firms have not had time to develop statuses and reputations; stable distinctions among products have not yet developed; and the boundary marking the population is faint and perhaps contested. Under such conditions, competition has a diffuse ecological character: every organization in the population is a potential competitor. As a result, variations in density strongly affect the intensity of competition in the field.

As time passes, firms can develop identities. For instance, they can acquire reputations and statuses, form alliances, establish classes of products, and so forth. Stable population structures can be built upon such differentiations. Many industries develop some form of center–periphery structure, with a sharp distinction between generalist and specialist organizations (Chapter 12). At the extreme, the population structure takes the form of a status ordering, with each organization's status depending on the statuses of its transaction partners (Podolny 1993).

As diverse forms of structuring develop, the predominant form of competition in the field can shift from diffuse ecological competition to focused rivalry between organizations that occupy similar positions in the industry (e.g., between organizations of similar status or between those with similarly generalist strategies). Diverse patterns of interaction can characterize mature populations, e.g., the self-reflecting role structures of the type treated by White (1981), the tertius-gaudens competitive strategies emphasized by Burt (1993), and the status-graded competitive structures analyzed by Podolny (1993) and Podolny et al. (1996). If the implications of such structures come to dominate diffuse competition in shaping life chances, then the impact of density on competition will decline with population age.

The relevant part of this story can also be cast in terms of growing stickiness in the relationship to density. That is, the relationship between density and competition, strongest during a population's youth, weakens as an organizational population ages.

So far, the argument suggests that institutionalization and the development of population structures diminish the importance of density. Yet, the late resurgence of density in diverse organizational populations hints at another possibility: density might control vital rates even for long-standing populations but by a more complex process than the original theory anticipates. Earlier we speculated that this is so:

> When the number of organizations declines, the market share held by a few firms often increases. This suggests to us that processes of legitimation and competition frequently interact with processes of niche width. More specifically, low density and low concentration (often occurring early in a population's history) seem to create very different conditions than low density and high concentration (often occurring

late in the history). The primary difference pertains to the mix of generalist and specialist organizations. When an industry is highly concentrated, specialist organizations often find small pockets of resources on which they can exist (Carroll 1985). This leads in turn to lower mortality rates and eventually to a larger population. (Hannan and Carroll 1992, 48)

Although this suggestion concerns mortality rates, the original theory's assumption of symmetry for the vital rates (Chapter 10) suggests that this scenario also holds for founding rates.

Investigating whether density affects the dynamics of mature populations can help clarify the source of resurgence. Explanations based on density dependence ought not to be regarded as rivals to those based on effects of population microstructures. The view taken here is that the evolution of density constrains and shapes the possibilities for various forms of industry social structure to emerge. Such a constraining relationship can be seen especially clearly in the models that represent industry structures by decomposing the effect of population density into effects of various sub-densities (or weighted densities), as discussed in Chapter 10. Because big changes in density imply big changes in industry social structure, progress in explaining resurgence would have broad implications for our understanding of population structuring.

Founding Rates

The generalized-Yule (GY) model can be extended to fit these arguments. Instead of the timeless relationships in (10.1), assume that density's effects on legitimation and competition vary with population age (t):

$$L(t) = l_t \, n_t^{\alpha(t)}, \qquad t \geq 0, \tag{11.3}$$

and

$$C(t) = c_t \, \exp\left[\beta(t) n_t^2\right], \qquad t \geq 0. \tag{11.4}$$

With these revisions, the GY model has the form:

$$\lambda(t) = \lambda_t \, n_t^{\alpha(t)} \exp\left[\gamma(t) n_t^2\right], \qquad \gamma(t) = -\beta(t), \qquad t \geq 0. \tag{11.5}$$

(This representation incorporates the potential "direct" effects of population age into the baseline rate, λ_t.)

The substantive considerations discussed above suggest some qualitative implications for the forms of the population-age effects. The next step is to incorporate such qualitative information into the model. At an early

stage of exploration, it seemed prudent to represent population-aging processes with flexible functional forms that can be consistent with the substantive arguments for some ranges of their parameters. This consideration
argued for specifying density's effects as polynomial functions of the age
of the organizational population. The analysis reported by Hannan (1997)
used polynomials of second degree in t (for reasons given below):

$$\alpha(t) = \alpha_0 + \alpha_1 t + \alpha_2 t^2, \tag{11.6}$$

and

$$\gamma(t) = \gamma_0 + \gamma_1 t + \gamma_2 t^2. \tag{11.7}$$

Replacing $\alpha(t)$ and $\gamma(t)$ in (11.5) with these polynomial functions yields the
empirical specification that has been used in empirical research:

$$\lambda(t) = \lambda_t \, n_t^{\alpha_0 + \alpha_1 t + \alpha_2 t^2} \, \exp\big[(\gamma_0 + \gamma_1 t + \gamma_2 t^2) n_t^2\big]. \tag{11.8}$$

Setting $t = 0$ in (11.8) shows that the original GY model (10.1) is a special case. This relation shows concretely that the extended model assumes
that the existing theory applies to the early (and perhaps the middle) histories of organizational populations. Given this interpretation, the hypotheses for the "main effects" of density are those of the original theory.

Hypothesis 11.2. *The Original Density-Dependence Hypotheses*:

$$0 < \alpha_0 < 1 \quad and \quad \gamma_0 < 0.$$

Suppose that density's effect on the founding rate diminishes as populations grow old. In terms of the specification in (11.8), this is the case when
the signs of the interactions of population age with density and density-
squared oppose those predicted for the main effects.

Hypothesis 11.3. *The Population Inertia Hypotheses*:

$$\alpha_1 < 0 \quad and \quad \gamma_1 > 0$$

(*given that Hypothesis 11.2 is true*).

This part of the argument seems to get the "slopes" right in the sense
that a given decrease in density has less impact on legitimation and competition in an old population than in a young one. However, a drop in
density does lower legitimation by at least some small increment in all
cases according to this formulation. In other words, constitutive legitimation is sticky, but it is not stuck.

It would seem preferable, in the context of these substantive arguments, to use a formulation that allows legitimation and competition to
remain constant even if density falls during a population's maturity. Estimation of specifications with this very strong property fit much less well

in analyses of entries in European automobile industries than the formulation discussed here.[4] In any event, graphical representations of the implications of estimates of this model for European automobile manufacturers indicate that the possibility that the proposed specification is not sufficiently sticky is not a practical problem in the empirical research. The surface relating density and population age to founding rates is very flat in the region in which density drops substantially—see below.

The final portion of the argument posits that low density in aged populations favors resurgence. In terms of the model, this means that the interactions of population-age-squared with density and density-squared have the same signs as the predicted main effects of density and density-squared.

Hypothesis 11.4. *The Resurgence Hypotheses*:

$$\alpha_2 > 0 \quad and \quad \gamma_2 < 0$$

(*given that Hypotheses* 11.2 *and* 11.3 *are true*).

Empirical Findings: European Automobile Manufacturers

This model was first applied to analyze entry rates into the populations of automobile manufacturers in Europe (Hannan 1997). The most important result for present purposes concerns the outcomes of tests of the hypotheses concerning population-level inertia and resurgence. Table 11.1 provides the final result. The baseline model [B] contained a constant and the effects of six period effects, lagged entries and its square, GNP, and recession year. The density model, labeled [B,N], added to the baseline the "main effects" of density. The entries in the first row of Table 11.1 test Hypothesis 11.2, the joint null hypothesis that country-level density does not affect entry rates. These test statistics are distributed asymptotically as chi-square with two degrees of freedom. This null hypothesis of "no density effect" can be rejected at the 0.05 level for all five countries.

The most important step tests Hypotheses 11.3 and 11.4, which concern inertia and resurgence. These hypotheses are tested jointly. The relevant test statistics appear in the second row of Table 11.1, which adds the effects of the four interactions of country density and industry age (measured in years and set equal to zero for 1885). This null hypothesis, that the effects summarized by [NT] and [NT^2] are zero, is rejected decisively for each

---

[4] For instance, this is true for analyses that measured density as either (1) a nondecreasing function of industry age: density in any year is coded as the maximum of that year's value and the maximum in the population's previous history, or (2) a cumulative count over the population's prior history. It appears that such alternatives do not work well because they fail to capture the resurgence process.

Table 11.1.   *Hierarchical model contrasts involving the effects of density and industry age on entry rates in European automobile industries, 1886–1981.*

Model contrast	df	Belgium	Britain	France	Germany	Italy
1. [B, N]	2	19.9	136.7	85.3	45.2	38.8
2. [B, N, NT, NT²]	4	23.7	50.0	50.2	46.4	13.5

Note: [B] denotes a vector of covariates and period effects (see text), [N] is log-density and density squared; [NT] is the set of interactions of log-density and density-squared with age of population; and [NT²] is the set of interactions of log-density and density-squared with the square of age of population.

Source: Hannan (1997). Copyright © 1997 by Walter de Gruyter. Used by permission.

country. In other words, this evidence supports the view that the effects of density on entry rates vary with industry age, as hypothesized.[5]

The hypotheses drawn from the revised theory specify the signs of the main effects of country density and its square and the signs of their interactions with industry age and its square. These hypotheses can be checked in detail by examining the estimates reported by Hannan (1997). For present purposes, we summarize and explain the general patterns of findings. First, the main effects of country density have the signs implied by the original theory, as predicted. These hypotheses are supported for all five countries: the first-order effect of density is positive and significant for all five countries and the second-order effect is negative for all countries and statistically significant for all except Italy.

Second, the predictions of the inertia hypotheses (that signs of the interactions of country-level density and industry age oppose those of the main effects) are supported for all countries. That is, each of the ten relevant estimates has the predicted sign, and eight of them are statistically significant. These effects suggest that the force of density weakens as organizational populations age, as hypothesized.

Finally, the pattern expected by the resurgence hypotheses (that the interactions of country-level density and the square of industry age have the same signs as the main effects of density) also holds for all ten interactions; and again eight are statistically significant. So, it appears that density dependence does play a role in population resurgence, as hypothesized, when each national population is considered in isolation from the others.

Figure 11.1 illustrates the implications of the results for France, the pioneer nation in the automobile industry. It shows a two-dimensional

---

[5] It is natural to wonder whether still higher-degree polynomials in industry age are needed to fit these data. This does not appear to be the case. In particular, adding interactions of density with the cube of industry age does not improve the fit significantly for any country.

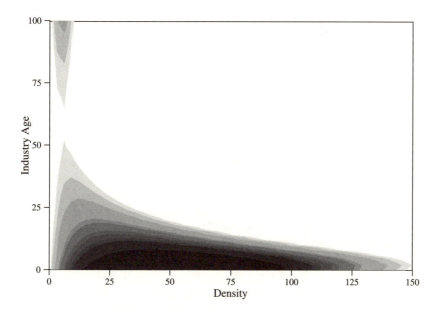

Figure 11.1. *Estimated relationship of the entry rate with density and industry age for the French automobile industry.*

rendering of the three-dimensional response surface implied by the estimates of the industry-age-dependent effect of density. In this figure, the dimension indicated by the intensity of shading is the multiplier of the entry rate (the combined effect of density and industry age). The other two dimensions are industry age (increasing from bottom to top) and density (increasing from left to right). The plotted surface shows how the effect varies over the possible combinations of industry age and density. The response surface is quite steep at the start (the industry's youth). In this period, increasing density causes the entry rate to rise and then eventually fall. As the industry grows old, the surface deforms toward zero (implying that density becomes irrelevant). However, in the late stages of the industry's history (the smaller hill at the top of the figure), the surface again rises and the shape of the relationship resembles the one at the start (at the bottom of the figure). There is something like an echo of the earlier pattern.

11.3 Size Interactions

A recent contribution has explored an alternative way to explain downturns in density in mature populations as a consequence of the interaction of density with some other variable. In this case, the other variable is organizational size. Barron (1999, 429) argues that small organizations with poor life chances (due to the liability of size, which we discuss in Chapter 14) accumulate in populations as they grow towards their peak density:

> As the density model argues, increasing density increases the intensity of competition. Consequently, selection pressure should be stronger: those organizations that are best able to withstand intense competition should have an *increasing* advantage in terms of survival chances. It is important to note that the argument implies an interaction between the intensity of competition experienced by the members of a population and some characteristic that confers a survival advantage. ... The gap between the survival chances of the most robust organizations and the most frail organizations should widen as the population density approaches the carrying capacity.

As noted above, Barron (1999) specifies this argument empirically in terms of organizational size. He finds the predicted relationship in an analysis of failures of credit unions in New York. He finds the usual pattern of effects for contemporaneous density and density at founding; he also finds that size has the expected negative effect on the failure rate. Net of these other effects, the interaction of population density and organizational size is negative and significant.

This analysis also finds that the combination of large size and high population density depresses growth rates significantly. Barron (1999) interprets this result as indicating that the inflexibility of large organizations becomes increasingly disadvantageous as the population nears its carrying capacity.

Finally, Barron (1999) models the founding process in a new way. He points out that density by itself does not govern competitive intensity when organizations in a population differ greatly in size. As populations become concentrated, more of the available resources are locked in at a given density. So he argues that founding rates are depressed by growth in the total mass of the population and by growth in the average size of organizations in the population. Both of these predictions are borne out by analyses of founding rates of credit unions, although neither effect is statistically significant.

Barron (1999) simulated the implications of these new models of founding rates, growth rates, and mortality rates, using the estimates of parameters from the credit union study. He showed that the trio of models can indeed generate patterns of growth to a peak and then decline in density such as we often observe.

11.4 Multilevel Processes

As emphasized in the previous chapter, an organizational form is constitutively legitimated when it takes on a fact-like or taken-for-granted status. In many historical cases, an organizational form develops in one or a few geographical centers. Early development and refinement of a form usually involve social movement processes, with organizations of enthusiasts seeking to define and promulgate a conception of a form. In these cases, the initial accretion of legitimation is highly localized to the birthplace(s): Paris for the automobile industry, medieval Florence for banking, Silicon Valley for the semiconductor and personal computer industries, Seattle and Portland for the modern resurgence of microbrewing, and so forth.[6]

Subsequent proliferation usually involves expansion beyond a form's home ground. Gaining taken-for-granted status elsewhere results from the diffusion of cultural images about organizational populations and their products. Shaped by information about growing densities of organizations at the industry's center, these images can spread with little friction in the modern world.

The infant automobile industry, for instance, developed in this way. The most important sources of diffusion about the growing density of automobile producers were print media: newspapers, journals, and magazines. Conventional understandings hold that these media facilitate the broad spatial spread of information. General-purpose newspapers and journals as well as technical publications within Europe gave considerable attention to the new industry, its technical developments, and the appearances and disappearances of its firms. Within ten years of the start of the industry, specialized publications arose to chronicle the activities of automobile manufacturers: *La Locomotion automobile* in France in 1894; *Autocar* and *Autocar Journal* in Britain in 1895 and 1896, respectively; *Technik* and *Motorwagen* in Germany in 1897 and 1898; and *The Horseless Age* in the United States in 1895 (Laux 1976). These publications produced detailed coverage of technical and organizational developments in the industry in many countries. In particular, "high points of the automobile year for these journals were the automobile shows in Paris, London, and other major cities, which were described in loving detail" (Laux 1976, 33). These exhibitions, which had become annual events during the 1890s, routinely had representation from producers in several countries. However, nothing rivaled the heavily publicized road races, e.g., the Paris–Bordeaux–Paris race in 1895 and the Paris–Amsterdam–Paris race in 1898, in spreading the image of the automobile (Seheer-Thoss 1979; Rae 1984; Flink 1988; Laux 1992).

---

[6] This section is adapted from Hannan et al. (1995).

Technological developments also spread rapidly from country to country during this period. For example, products of the German pioneers Gotlieb Daimler and Carl Benz first gained widespread attention in France. The Daimler engine was the power plant of such important early French firms as Panhard et Levassor and Peugeot and of the British Daimler. Benz's third vehicle was shown at the Paris Exposition of 1889, which Flink (1988, 13–14) regards as a turning point:

> ...after the Paris Exhibition of 1889 virtually no development of importance in automotive technology went unreported in one or another of the engineering journals, bicycle periodicals, automobile trade journals, newspapers, and popular magazines of the day. Consequently, knowledge of such developments was widely disseminated worldwide from the very beginning of the automobile industry.

Parallel developments have reduced the frictions involved in international trade and have broadened the scope of competition, but much more slowly. Competition retains a local character long after cultural images have diffused broadly. This is because organizations have mainly competed for members and employees in local labor markets, and, until fairly recently, for capital and material inputs in local or national markets. Moreover, inflows of labor, capital, and material goods can more successfully be blocked than inflows of ideas and cultural understandings.[7]

The key point is that cultural images ordinarily flow more freely across social system boundaries than the material resources used to build and sustain organizations. This observation led us and our collaborators to speculate that competitive environments tend to be more local than institutional environments (Hannan and Carroll 1992; Hannan et al. 1995)—see also Manigart (1994). Organizational forms in one part of a system can gain legitimation from growth in densities of organizational populations in other parts of the system long before competitive influences from distant parts of the system exert themselves strongly. As a result, legitimation typically operates at broader geographical scales than competition, at least in the early stages of the proliferation of an organizational form.[8]

---

[7] For instance, countries have routinely relied on tariffs to protect national producers from foreign competition. For instance, tariffs on automobiles enacted by the major European countries in the early twentieth century reached as high as 70 percent of value.

[8] Several demographic studies had earlier explored the appropriate scales for such multilevel processes. Carroll and Wade (1991) and Hannan and Carroll (1992) analyzed founding rates and mortality rates of American brewing firms at the national, regional, state, and city levels. Swaminathan and Wiedenmayer (1991) analyzed the rates for Bavarian breweries at the level of the *Land* (state), region, and city. In these studies, analysis at each level related the vital rates to density at the *same* level. That is, these researchers estimated models separately for different levels of analysis and then made inferences by comparing coefficients across equations.

In a world organized politically as a system of sovereign states, nation-state boundaries seem to be especially important in differentiating legitimation from competition. Modern states have succeeded in monopolizing powers of taxation and regulation of trade. Efforts to protect national industries and labor markets from worldwide competition therefore focus on the state. When protectionist sentiments prevail, states attempt to block or reduce inflows of products and labor (and outflows of capital) at their borders. Nation-states have frequently succeeded in creating and enforcing laws and regulations that limit competitive threats from the outside. Yet, even totalitarian states find it difficult to control access to cultural images that set their inhabitants' tastes. Witness the widespread appeal of Western music, literature, clothing, and cigarette brands under the old regime of the Soviet Union. More generally, state boundaries delimit processes of competition more strongly than processes of cultural diffusion. In a system of states, competition processes ought to be more intense within state boundaries than across such boundaries. However, state boundaries tend to be less effective in stemming the flows of information that affect legitimation.

A Multilevel Model

The formalization of these ideas also builds on the theory and research discussed in Chapter 10. We continue to assume that growth in numbers conveys constitutive legitimation and increases diffuse competitive pressures, and we fit differences in the scales of the processes by specifying them at different levels of analysis. Consider a system composed of I bounded subsystems. Recall from Chapter 4 that we define populations with reference to local interactions within bounded systems. So we define populations here at the level of the subsystem. Let n_i denote the density of organizations in the ith subsystem and N denote the density in the whole system ($N = \sum_i^I n_i$). We maintain the premises that the entry rates, $\lambda_i(t)$, are proportional to legitimation, $L_i(t)$, and inversely proportional to competition, $C_i(t)$, with each defined at the subsystem level:

$$\lambda_i(t) \propto \frac{L_i(t)}{C_i(t)}.$$

The premise that the intensity of competition within a subsystem is proportional to density at the same level also remains unchanged.

Assumption 11.4.1. *In a multilevel system, the intensity of diffuse competition in a subsystem is an increasing function of subsystem density.*

We continue to assume that this relationship has the form used in the original theory:

$$C_i(t) \propto \exp(\beta_i n_{it}^2).$$

The change in the model pertains to the assumed scope of the relationship between density and legitimation.

Assumption 11.4.2. *In a multilevel system, the constitutive legitimation in any subsystem depends on density in the entire system.*

As in the original model (Chapter 10), we specify the relationship between numbers and legitimation as a simple power function. Now we use system-level density (N) rather than subsystem density (n_i) as the argument of this function.

$$L_i(t) \propto N_t^{\alpha_i}.$$

This change in the premises leads to a revised GY process for entry rates:

$$\lambda_i(t) = N_t^{\alpha_i} \exp\!\left(\beta_i n_{it}^2\right), \qquad i = 1, \ldots, I. \tag{11.9}$$

We hypothesize that systemwide density positively affects the entry rates in the subsystems ($0 < \alpha_i < 1$) and that subsystem density has a negative effect ($\beta_i < 0$). The implication of this changed assumption for the LQ model can be represented as

$$\lambda_i(t) = \exp\!\left(\gamma_1 N_t + \gamma_2 n_{it}^2\right), \tag{11.10}$$

with hypotheses: $\gamma_1 > 0$, $\gamma_2 < 0$, and $|\gamma_2| < |\gamma_1|$.

This model applies to any hierarchical system where subsystem boundaries can impede flows of material products and labor more effectively than they impede flows of information.

Empirical Findings: Automobile Manufacturers

In specifying the multilevel model for entry into automobile production, we treat national boundaries as the subsystem boundaries and integrated world regions as the system. We start with Europe, where the continent is considered the larger region for each of the major automobile-producing countries.

In the first investigation of the hypothesis that legitimation operates at a broader scale than competition, Hannan et al. (1995) added *density in Europe* as a covariate in the models in models for founding rates that contained the standard GY specification for the first-order and second-order effects of country density. They tried several ways of representing European density. One used the number of automobile manufacturers in the five countries. A second dropped the focal country's count from the first. Choice between these alternatives does not make a substantively important difference in the results. The sharpest results come from the first option: the count in the five countries under consideration. However, if we want to learn whether the densities of populations of other countries really affect vital rates in a given country, a useful first step is to analyze specifications that exclude a country's own density from the count of European density. When this strategy was followed, results for Britain differed sharply from those for the four continental countries. In every variation tried, British entry rates were either unrelated to European density or negatively related to it. In contrast, other-European density did have significant positive effects on founding rates in each continental country.

What happens when the multilevel and population-age specifications are combined? Table 11.2 shows the estimates of the combined model. The density of each focal country i is given by n_i and the (European) density of the entire set of five national populations by N_E. These analyses build on the assumptions that national density affects both legitimation and competition and that European density has only a legitimating effect. This specification constrains the legitimating effect of national density to be the same as that of the density in the rest of Europe's automobile manufacturing core.

The effects of European density in Table 11.2 have the predicted alternating pattern of signs for all five countries: the main effects are positive, the interactions with industry age are negative, and the interactions with industry-age-squared are positive. Fourteen of the fifteen effects are statistically significant. The effects of country-density squared also have the predicted pattern of alternating signs for Britain, France, Germany, and Italy, although it is not significant for Italy.[9]

[9] Replacing the three terms for national density-squared with one main effect does yield significant negative effects for Belgium and Italy. After the fact, it appears that the most interpretable specification for Belgium and Italy is one with the Europe-wide legitimation process varying with age and the national-level competition process invariant with age.

Table 11.2. *Estimates of the combined multilevel and population-age model for entry rates of automobile manufacturers in Belgium, Britain, France, Germany, and Italy, 1886–1981.*

	Belgium	Britain	France	Germany	Italy
$\ln(N_E)$	2.85*	2.60*	1.96*	2.56*	2.05*
$\ln(N_E) \cdot t$	−0.071*	−0.166*	−0.047*	−0.077*	−0.039*
$\ln(N_E) \cdot t^2\, 10^{-3}$	0.481	0.022*	0.393*	0.976*	0.379*
$n_i^2\, 10^{-3}$	−2.49	−0.511*	−0.401*	−4.17*	−3.75
$n_i^2 \cdot t\, 10^{-3}$	−0.245	0.037*	0.022*	0.278*	0.145
$n_i^2 \cdot t^2\, 10^{-5}$	−0.850	−0.061*	−0.031*	−0.436*	−0.132

* $p < .05$.
Source: Hannan (1997). Copyright © 1997 by Walter de Gruyter. Used by permission.

What about the United States, the world's largest automobile producer population? A straightforward application of the multilevel specification used above would cast the legitimation-related density variables at the world, continent, or partial two-continent (Europe and the United States) levels and competition at the national level. After estimating and evaluating numerous alternate specifications of such a model, however, Bigelow et al. (1997) concluded that there was no consistent pattern of effects. This led them to question whether the geographical levels in these models might be misspecified for the U.S. population. More specifically, they suggested that the size and geographical scale of the U.S. industry (as well as its distance from Europe) might have required its own separate legitimation process.

They also noted that anecdotal historical evidence suggests that much competition in the industry was circumscribed by region rather than by the nation-state. In the early period of the automobile industry, the three regions of initial automotive development each spawned and developed its own technology. In particular, the New York metropolitan area cultivated the production of electric cars; the New England region, propulsion by steam technology; and the Midwest, gasoline cars. The association of regions with technologies suggests that local conditions and local resources might have played an important role in subsequent founding patterns. For these reasons, Bigelow et al. (1997) estimated multilevel foundings models with legitimation effects of density cast at the national level and competition effects at the regional level.

Overall, the pattern of estimates reported by Bigelow et al. (1997) suggests that national and regional legitimation work in concert: both regional (n_i^2) and national (N_{US}^2) densities have significant effects on entry rates within regions. More relevant for the multilevel model is the dominant competitive effect of regional density. While the second-order national density effects on founding rates are often negative, none are statistically significant. In contrast, the second-order region-based n_i^2 terms exhibit strong (and statistically significant) negative effects on founding rates. The exception to this pattern is, interestingly, the Midwest, the region with the greatest density and, of course, the eventual geographic center of the auto industry.

The findings reported by Bigelow et al. (1997) suggest an interaction between geography, physical space, and technology. For example, one possible explanation for the exceptionalism of the Midwest depends on the link between geography and technology. The association of three distinct technologies with three regions in the early period of the automobile industry might be accidental or might be due to factors associated with these regions. These factors could include differences in terrain, weather conditions, extant transportation infrastructure, natural resource endowments such as the availability of water for steam or gasoline for gas-powered engines, and/or local technical expertise.

Once the industry's dominant technology emerged, the region first associated with that technology would face increased competition over resources associated with that technology from the other regions, at least until these regions managed to develop their own resource base. However, given their initial experience with the alternative technologies in conjunction with the pressures of local competition, foundings in the regions not associated with the dominant technology are more likely to be sensitive to regional density than foundings in the region associated with the dominant technology. Their late adoption of the ultimate technological winner could adversely impact the founding attempts of organizations in these regions by limiting or hindering access to resources. Local networks of capital, labor, suppliers, and customers, whose limits are defined by physical space, would have to be reconfigured to conform with the new technology, impeding foundings. In other words, local density generates greater competitive pressure than national density, as reflected in the negative second-order regional density coefficient. However, in populations where different standards or competing technologies exist, the region that spawns the eventual dominant technology might be more sensitive to multilevel density dependence, due to its function as a technological source for the entire population. Thus competition effects are difficult to detect at the regional level for this region.

More generally, multilevel models of density dependence show striking similarity to recently developed models of path dependence in economic geography (David 1985; Arthur 1989). The assumptions that founding conditions have enduring and pervasive effects, that density has an initially positive effect on growth, and that chance events can have potentially far-reaching effects on population vital rates are common to both perspectives (Hannan and Carroll 1992; Carroll and Harrison 1994; Krugman 1991; Arthur 1989). The two theoretical perspectives part company, not surprisingly, on the issue of how to incorporate sociological and economic forces in the respective models. Although density-dependent models downplay the role of firm characteristics, they do incorporate firm-specific and industry-specific control variables when possible. In contrast, economic models of path dependence offer little or no consideration of how sociological forces might determine population boundaries or how legitimacy affects population vital rates. The fact that regional populations exhibit both legitimating and competitive forces in this study runs counter to the prevailing notion of competitive processes of spatial dynamics in the work of Arthur (1989) and others.

According to density-dependence theory, changes in density over a population's history induce the waxing and waning of the opposing processes of legitimation and competition. In the early stages of a population's evolution, the observed increase in density reflects the combined effects of strong legitimation processes and weak competitive processes. In the path-dependent economic location models, the initial increase in density in a given region stems from weak or latent competition. Ignoring legitimation, and the underlying social, political, and geographical factors associated with it, makes it difficult to explain the advantages of density. Stories about agglomeration benefits, knowledge spillover, and externalities do not have clear implications about the effects of density across populations. This is precisely the issue that a density-dependent model can explain, once it is respecified at a lower or regional level of analysis.

The three types of models considered in this chapter—involving density delay, population-age interactions, and specifications of legitimation and competition processes at different levels—demonstrate one of the advantages of formal modeling. The starkly simplified model of density-dependent organizational evolution can support a variety of extensions and elaborations that add richness and substantive detail. Its very simplicity proves to be a great advantage in such efforts.

12

Segregating Processes

DIVERSE INDUSTRIES and organizational populations experience a renewal of sorts in the late stages of their evolution. After long periods of decline in organizational density, these industries and populations show a resurgence or upward swing in the number of organizations. A highly visible example involves American beer brewers. After declining in numbers for almost a hundred years, from over 2,800 breweries in 1880 to around 40 in the early 1980s, the trend dramatically reversed itself: the United States was home to over 1,350 breweries in late 1998.

In Chapter 11, we addressed such reversals in mature populations by extending the model of density dependence to include interactions with population age. In this chapter, we examine a different approach and theory, that of resource partitioning (Carroll 1985). Whereas the density model posits that all organizations in the population respond homogeneously to the driving forces of legitimation, competition, and institutional inertia, the resource-partitioning model states that organizational differences in niche width play a pivotal role. Specifically, specialist forms of organization respond differently to competitive forces than do large generalist forms. As we explain below, a central prediction of the theory holds that the late-stage renaissances consist primarily of the proliferation of specialist organizations. So, the theory applies to some, but not all, industry renewals.

Resource-partitioning theory differs from many of the other demographic models discussed in previous chapters in that the operative processes involve a segregation of the population. Segregation might also result from other mechanisms such as size-localized competition within a population. So we review these models in this chapter as well. All segregating models share the implication that organizational populations will eventually display discontinuity along some relevant dimension such as size, niche width, or status.

261

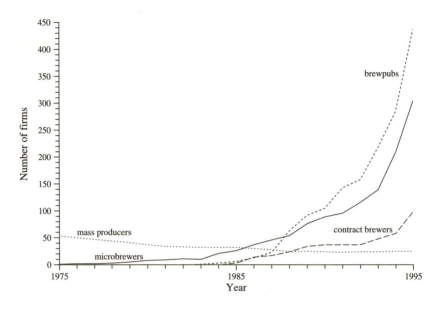

Figure 12.1.   *Number of U.S. brewing companies by organizational form, 1975–1995. Source: Carroll and Swaminathan (1998). Copyright © 1998 by Glenn R. Carroll and Anand Swaminathan. Used by permission.*

12.1 Resource Partitioning

Resource-partitioning theory addresses the interrelationship between two organizational trends not often thought to be related. The first of these is the trend of increasing market concentration found in many industries, especially when the rise occurs gradually and over the longterm, perhaps persisting for decades. For instance, the combined market share held by the four largest firms in the American beer industry rose from under 10% in 1910 to over 80% in the 1990s. The second is the increasingly common appearance of many small specialist organizations in certain mature industries. Figure 12.1 displays this development in brewing, where the specialist organizations consist of those organizational forms associated with the microbrewery movement: microbreweries, brewpubs, and contract brewers.[1] Resource-partitioning theory explains why the two trends sometimes occur simultaneously within the same industry, a development once considered highly implausible.

The theoretical imagery of resource partitioning relies on notions of crowding among organizations in a market characterized as a finite set of

---

[1] See Chapter 4 for an explanation of these definitions of organizational form.

heterogeneous resources. Organizations initially attempt to find viable positions within this market by targeting their products to various resource segments. Some organizations choose narrow, homogeneous targets; others choose broad targets composed of heterogeneous segments.

Location and Crowding in Resource Space

The theory presumes that some aspect of product delivery in the market is subject to a scale advantage; this is typically envisioned as an economy of scale in production, marketing, or distribution. Organizations targeting small resource segments thus have higher costs (per unit of product) than those in larger segments. However, large organizations often do not transform these lower costs into lower prices but rather into expanded products. These expanded products offer more for the same price, thus appealing to other segments of the market without losing their hold on the established ones. Small organizations located in the invaded segments thus face formidable competition, and many will eventually fail. Meanwhile, the large organizations become even bigger, thus enhancing their advantage and allowing them to move into even other segments. As the process repeats itself, these successful organizations become generalists (in that they serve diverse markets and perhaps rely on diverse capabilities) and grow large.

Generalist Competition

Competition among generalist organizations in such markets has the character of an arms race, an ever-escalating contest for resources that can be converted into increased scale (the basis of competitive success in such a market). The assumption of increasing returns to scale implies that the most intense fighting occurs in the densest or most abundant resource areas. The generalist organization that secures a toehold in this dense market "center" possesses a potentially sustainable advantage over all competitors. In typical cases, many generalists seek to establish themselves in this region. But, because each originates from a different location and each seeks to maximize that part of its target without competitors, the set of competing generalists becomes somewhat differentiated. In the long run, this differentiation matters little except as it corresponds to market size: larger generalists will eventually out-compete smaller ones. When the smaller generalists fail, their target markets become free resources. Generalists occupying adjacent regions hold the best positions for securing these newly available areas; and they typically do so. The surviving generalists thus become larger and more general. However, the wide range of each generalist's target area makes it difficult for them to secure the entire free area; doing so might prove more costly than it is worth or entail loss of some of the firm's existing target area. This is especially the case in mature markets where generalists have grown very large and possess extremely broad target areas. So, as the competitive struggle among generalists proceeds to its eventual monopoly equilibrium, two conditions prevail. First, the size and target breadth of the surviving generalists increase. Second, the combined resources held by the surviving generalists decline.

Figures 12.2 and 12.3 depict graphically a simple example of the competitive scenario described above in terms of a market of consumers with taste differences. The respective graphs show the process at two points in time, say t_1 and t_2. In each graph, the horizontal axis indicates the values of some dimension x of the consumer market. The vertical axis represents the proportion or relative frequency, $f(x)$, of consumers who possess any particular value of x. The curved plots of functions show the distribution of consumers on x; the well-behaved normal shape of the distribution ensures that the market has a dense center. The area under any given segment of the curve tells how many resources are potentially available to a firm operating in that part of the market.

Figure 12.2 shows a relatively concentrated market populated by two firms, labeled A and B. The target area of each generalist firm comprises

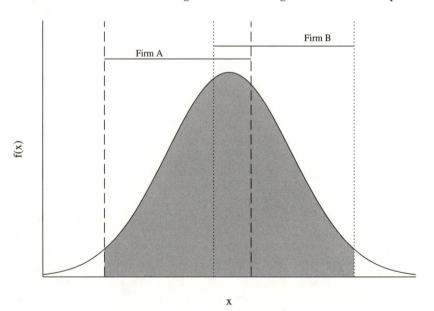

Figure 12.2. *Resource space available under various scenarios about competition with lower concentration. Copyright © 1995 by Glenn R. Carroll and Michael T. Hannan. Used by permission.*

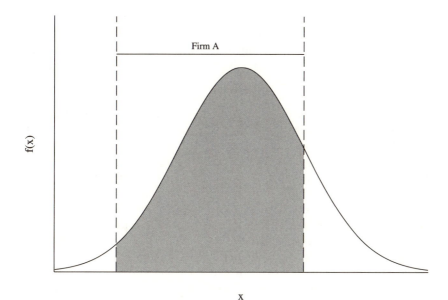

Figure 12.3. *Resource space available under various scenarios about competition with higher concentration. Copyright © 1995 by Glenn R. Carroll and Michael T. Hannan. Used by permission.*

a broad range of x. The target areas overlap to some extent (at the densest part of the distribution), but there is also substantial differentiation. The union of the two target areas covers all but the most extreme and least dense regions of the consumer distribution. Although it is barely discernible, firm A's target area is slightly larger, thus giving it a scale advantage.

Given increasing returns to scale, this advantage eventually proves insurmountable to firm B. By time t_2 (represented by Figure 12.3) this firm has failed and disappeared from the graph. Firm A has, of course, moved to absorb the resources freed up by B's demise and it has for the most part succeeded in this effort. Only the most distant of B's previous target area remains outside its own reconfigured target. Note that firm A has grown considerably in the process.

Specialist Emergence and Proliferation

The illustration in Figures 12.2 and 12.3 depicts in a simple way how scale advantages might generally play themselves out in organizational evolution. The story is consistent with the first general trend noted above, that of steadily increasing concentration within an industry over the longterm.

Of course, there is little novelty in using scale advantages (and economies) to explain this trend; and there are several other plausible organizational scenarios about large firms competing with such forces operating. The resource-partitioning story is attractive in many contexts because it can also account for the second trend noted above: an emergent and blossoming set of small specialist organizations within the industry.

How? The key mechanism involves the resource space that lies outside the generalist target areas. In Figures 12.2 and 12.3 this is the space in the unshaded regions at the tails of the distribution. It is here, away from the intense competitive pressure of the dominant large generalists, that specialist organizations can find viable locations. Because resources tend to be thin in these regions, the specialists located here also tend to be small. Small, highly specialized locations are also less attractive to the ever-encroaching generalists than are broader locations; these locations also tend to be easier to defend.

The basic insight of resource-partitioning theory comes from comparing the amount of resource space available for specialists when overall market concentration rises. Because market concentration derives from generalist consolidation, this comparison can be made by measuring the total area outside generalist targets under different stages of the scale competition scenario. As Figures 12.2 and 12.3 illustrate, this generalist-free area comprises more space when concentration is higher (fewer and larger generalists). By this reasoning, resource-partitioning theory thus yields its novel and central prediction: as overall market concentration rises, the viability of specialist organizations increases as well. This prediction can be interpreted with respect to either founding rates or mortality rates (the specialist segment can expand as a result of changes in either). In either case, however, the empirical implication involves an interaction effect between organizational form (specialist–generalist status) and concentration in affecting a vital rate.

Hypothesis 12.1. (*Under conditions of resource partitioning*) *as market concentration rises, the founding rates of specialist organizations will rise and the mortality rates of specialists will fall.*

The necessary, but not sufficient, conditions for operation of processes of resource partitioning include: (1) a finite and heterogeneous resource environment; (2) the existence of scale advantages for generalist organizations; and (3) limits on the target range and adaptability of both specialist and generalist organizations. Other economic (Porter 1980) and sociological (Perrow 1986) analyses had previously predicted the reverse: dominant large generalists were thought to create barriers to entry that precluded new competitors from entering. Market concentration was considered a primary indicator of the existence of such barriers.

Resource Space Imagery

The initial articulation of the theory of resource partitioning by Carroll (1985) used the two-dimensional space shown in Figure 12.4. Here the generalist firms are represented by circles. In the less concentrated case with multiple generalists, there is again some overlap in target areas but there is also differentiation. Each firm positions itself as near the center as possible while encroaching as little as possible on others' target areas. In the more concentrated case, with only a single generalist left in the market, the size of the circle becomes larger and its location becomes central. The area outside the circles represents the space available to specialists; again the critical observation concerns the greater amount of specialist space in the more concentrated market.

For the central positions in Figure 12.4 to be attractive for scale-oriented firms, resources must cohere near the middle of the resource space. It is the existence of a peak in resources (and the scale advan-

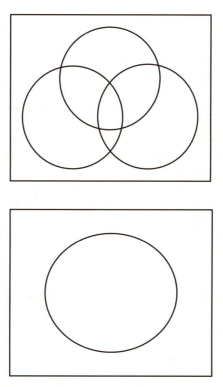

Figure 12.4. *Distribution of niches in a two-dimensional resource space. Source: Carroll (1985). Copyright © 1985 by the University of Chicago. All rights reserved. Used by permission.*

tages associated with exploiting it) that drives organizations to the center
of the resource space, pushing them towards generalism, and also generates a monopoly equilibrium. So, although the figure depicts resources
as evenly distributed, a key assumption needed to generate the expected
dynamics holds that of a well-behaved uneven distribution. Moreover, the
joint distribution needs to be roughly unimodal—there should be a single peak that coincides across the various dimensions of the space. In the
two-dimensional case, this would appear as a sort of hill or mountain in
the middle of the space, as shown by Figure 12.4. (We expect a similar
well-behaved distribution with more dimensions, but higher-dimensional
cases are hard to envision.) This aspect of the theory could be examined with market data on buyer preferences rather than organizational
behavior.

When there is more than one peak, scale advantages might still operate. However, the landscape would likely yield multiple successful generalists, thus allowing less space for specialists than in the unimodal case. It
might seem that the extreme case—an even distribution of resources with
many competing generalists—would eliminate the resource-partitioning effect. But this is not so, as the rigorous theoretical analysis by Péli and
Nooteboom (1999) demonstrates. These analysts envision the generalists
as geometric hyperspheres with radii of fixed length (circles in the two-
dimensional case). In analysis of the central issue, Péli and Nooteboom
(1999) assume that competing generalists' target areas do not overlap. They
examine the proportion of resource space remaining outside the densest
possible packing of hyperspheres, which is assumed to be the area available for specialists. Their mathematical results show that the proportion
of specialist space increases rapidly as the number of dimensions in the
space increases. For instance, with two dimensions, approximately 10% of
the space is uncovered; with three dimensions, the free area rises to 26%;
with four, to 38%; and with five, to 54%. Their analysis holds constant the
target areas of generalists and does not contain a mechanism for consolidation. It generates a complementary set of empirical predictions associating
expansion in resource space with enhanced specialist viability:

Hypothesis 12.2. (*Under conditions of resource partitioning*), *as the number of
dimensions in resource space increases, the founding rates of specialist organizations
will rise and the mortality rates of specialist organizations will decline.*

For industries based on consumer products, such as beer, the resource
space can be reasonably interpreted as consumer demand (Péli and Nooteboom 1999). The dimensions of space can be interpreted as dimensions of
taste preferences; an increase in the dimensions represents an elaboration
of tastes.

Péli and Nooteboom's (1999) finding demonstrates that the general intuition of the graph in Figure 12.4 holds in N dimensions. Moreover, it contributes the additional theoretical insight that specialists are even more viable when many dimensions affect buyer decisions. This aspect of the theory could also be tested with market data.

Note that the target areas of generalists consist of *contiguous* regions of the resource space in all the imagery put forward so far. This constraint on organizational adaptation, which means that organizations cannot operate in widely separated parts of the market without operating in the intermediate regions, plays an important role in the theory. If generalists could combine any set of disparate resources without losing their scale advantage and other advantages, then there would be no opening for specialists: all excess space would be taken over by generalists. In real industries, generalists often do attempt to move into these spaces, especially when they are relatively large or growing in size. However, there are often constraints that prevent them from succeeding and undermining the specialists (Chapter 16 discusses inertial constraints).

12.2 Empirical Research on Partitioning

Specialist Organizations

Empirical studies of resource partitioning have focused on the predictions of Hypothesis 12.1, those relating the vital rates of specialist organizations to concentration levels. Systematic empirical studies reporting an effect of this kind on organizational vital rates span a wide variety of organizational populations. Carroll's (1985) study of the American newspaper industry examined the newspaper populations of seven metropolitan areas and found that specialist paper mortality declined with concentration and generalist paper mortality increased. Subsequent research has considered both vital rates.

Nine studies have focused on rates of founding and/or entry. In a study of the early Iowa telephone industry, Barnett and Carroll (1987) found that the start-up rate of new companies increased when the average size of existing companies grew large. In studying the American beer industry, Carroll and Swaminathan (1992) reported a significant positive effect of concentration in the beer market on microbrewery founding rates. A follow-up study by Carroll and Swaminathan (1998) reported strong positive effects of concentration on founding rates of all specialist breweries. Freeman and Lomi (1994) and Lomi (1995a) found that rates of entry of (specialist) rural cooperative banks in Italy from 1964 to 1988 increased as size and market share of the generalist national banks rose. Swaminathan (1995) reported that the founding rate of American farm wineries (specialists) rose as a function of overall concentration in the wine industry. Torres (1995) reported a positive effect of concentration in the British car industry on the founding rates of specialist automobile manufacturers. Wade (1996) found that high concentration in the microprocessor industry from 1971 to 1989 fostered entry of new firms sponsoring architectural innovations. Seidel (1997) investigated the American airline industry after deregulation and found that concentration among the major airlines (who fly many places and use the hub-and-spoke route structure for scale economies) increased the founding rates and lowered the mortality rates of specialist carriers (who fly a few places from point-to-point). Haveman and Nonnenaker (1998) found that entry by smaller organizations into new markets increased with market concentration in the California savings and loan industry.

In addition to Carroll's original study, six studies have tested the resource-partitioning hypothesis as it applies to mortality rates. Carroll and Swaminathan (1992) reported estimates for contemporary American beer brewing (from 1975 to 1990) showing that the mortality rate of microbreweries declined with market concentration. For mass-production breweries (generalists), they found a nonmonotonic relationship between size and mortality. The follow-up study by Carroll and Swaminathan (1998) reported negative effects of concentration on the death rates of microbreweries and brewpubs. Mitchell (1995) found evidence of resource partitioning in the medical diagnostic-imaging industry. Swaminathan (1998) found theoretically consistent effects of concentration on the mortality rate of farm wineries. Park and Podolny (1998) found evidence of resource partitioning along status dimensions in studying the mortality of investment banks. Finally, Boone et al. (2000) showed that the mortality rates of very small firms in the Dutch auditing industry declined relative to those of large generalist firms as overall market concentration increased.

Dobrev (2000) studied the evolution of the Bulgarian newspaper industry, paying particular attention to the post-Socialist era. He found evidence of a reversal of the resource-partitioning process, namely, that the specialist segment declines with lowered concentration. He interpreted these results as reflecting the presence of two modes in the resource distribution, one pertaining to the remaining structures of the state socialist industrial population and another associated with the independent newspaper population.

Generalist Organizations

Empirical studies of resource partitioning also occasionally examine the parallel (reversed) predictions about generalist vital rates. However, in studies without the complete population history these predictions are difficult to test statistically. This is partly because, at the late stages of many relevant industries, few generalists are present and few events occur (as the theory predicts). Even when tests can be conducted, however, there is a serious problem with the parallel specification for mortality: the theory does not claim that *all* generalists will experience heightened risk as concentration rises, only the smaller generalists. In fact, large generalists' life chances are supposed to be bolstered by the process. Thus, the parallel specification to Hypothesis 12.1 for generalist mortality inappropriately mixes cases with contradictory theoretical predictions. This observation led Carroll and Swaminathan (1998) to develop a new way to model scale advantages and their potential consequences in organizational populations.

Modeling Scale Advantages

The notion that scale advantages in production, distribution, and advertising generate concentration in many industries finds wide acceptance, based in part on examination of cost data and the like. Nonetheless, corporate demography, with its focus on vital rates, needs a stronger link to organizational mortality. How might this be accomplished? In the spirit of Barnett's (1997) models of competitive intensity, Carroll and Swaminathan (1998) proposed using a theoretically motivated specification of the competitive environment faced by each generalist firm. In particular, Carroll and Swaminathan (1998) noted that the theory implies that the competitive pressure faced by a generalist firm depends on the number of larger competitors it faces (who each hold an advantage over the smaller firm) as well as the distance of each from the focal firm on the size dimension (with distance representing the extent of advantage). Carroll and Swaminathan (1998) proposed combining these factors into a single organization-specific environmental measure, yielding the following:

Hypothesis 12.3. (*Under scale competition*), *the greater the aggregate distance of larger competitors, the higher the generalist mortality rate.*

The distances can be calculated according to any number of principles. Because economies of scale drive much competition among generalist brewers, Carroll and Swaminathan (1998) proposed a measure approximating distance on a typical longrun average cost curve. To do this, they first calculated firms' positions on a downward sloping curve represented by the inverse quadratic root of size S after adjusting for minimum size $(S_i - S_{min})^{-1/4}$. That is, they constructed the following transformation of organizational size:

$$S_i^* = (S_i - S_{min})^{-1/4}.$$

Figure 12.5 shows the shape of this transformation. Carroll and Swaminathan (1998) then computed the aggregate distances SD_{it} of each firm i from its larger competitors by summing the differences in scores as

$$SD_{it} = \sum_{S_j > S_i} [S_i^* - S_j^*].$$

Carroll and Swaminathan (1998) reported estimates of the effect of SD_{it} on the generalist mortality rate that agree with expectations from the theory and that support Hypothesis 12.3. This approach might have general value and be used for modeling economies of scale and other scale advantages in a wide variety of contexts. It overcomes many of the deficiencies in Stigler's (1958) widely cited survivor method (Chapter 2), namely, it corrects for censoring, allows for organizational heterogeneity, and does not assume equilibrium.

Product Diversity

Another relevant empirical issue for resource partitioning involves the diversity of products offered by generalists as their numbers decline and concentration rises: the theory predicts a corresponding increase in generalist product homogeneity. Empirical studies of the American music-recording

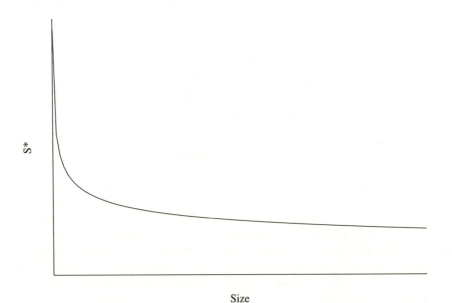

Figure 12.5. *Transformation of organizational size used in modeling scale competition.*

industry show that product diversity and innovation both declined with generalist dominance and consolidation from the mid-1950s to the early 1980s (Peterson and Berger 1996; Lopes 1992; Alexander 1996). For beer, Alison and Uhl (1964) and Jacoby, Olson, and Haddock (1971) conducted blind taste tests of beverages from generalist brewers (before the micro-brewery movement). The findings showed that consumers were incapable of discrimination and identification of these products, including their fa-vorite brands, at this time of high industry concentration.

Beyond Location—Other Interpretations of Resource Partitioning

Resource-partitioning theory places primary emphasis on an organization's location in resource space, especially its location relative to other types of organizations. This emphasis underlies Hypotheses 12.1, 12.2, and 12.3, which state the primary demographic predictions for the phenomenon. It apparently accounts entirely for the partitioning of certain industries such as airline passenger service (Seidel 1997), where physical geography plays a central role. In some other industries, however, other sociological fac-tors might take on greater importance. For example, based on extensive qualitative research, Carroll and Swaminathan (1998) claim that, in Amer-ican beer brewing, the appeal of specialist organizations emanates from their identity as noncorporate, craft-like producers using authentic tradi-tional production methods.

What, if any, systematic empirical implication does the identity appeal have for resource partitioning? Carroll and Swaminathan (1998) suggest that it does not undermine the basic predictions of the theory but rather implies an additional hypothesis, one based on the legitimation of vari-ous organizational forms in specialty production. In brewing, these iden-tity problems confront the mass-production and contract brewers. Com-pared to microbrewers and brewpubs, these other forms do not accord with consumers' normative notions about how specialty beers should be made. Mass-production firms are too large, bureaucratic, and commercial; contract brewers do not even make their own beer.

Comparisons across forms provide research leverage for evaluating and improving the model of density-dependent evolution, which models the effects of legitimation and competition on organizational founding and failure rates (Chapters 10 and 11). This model would lead us to expect that an increase in the density of specialist organizational forms would enhance their legitimation. However, for normative and counternormative specialist organizational forms sanctioned by a tight-knit knowledgeable community, the effects might very well differ. Carroll and Swaminathan (1998) argue that as the density of specialist organizational forms with positive normative sanction rises, the legitimation of all specialist forms is enhanced; and the opposite for counternormative forms: as density rises, the legitimation of all specialist forms should slow. Moreover, among the positively sanctioned forms, we would expect that the strongest effects would come from those with greatest visibility. These arguments can be stated as follows.

Hypothesis 12.4. (*Under resource partitioning based on identity*), *the legitimating effects of specialist organizational density depend on* (12.4a) *the normative status of the specialist form and* (12.4b) *the social visibility of the specialist form.*

Of course, determination of the normative status of an organizational form requires an institutional understanding of the context. In the case of beer brewing, Carroll and Swaminathan (1998) make clear that microbreweries and brewpubs are the positively sanctioned specialist forms. Among these, the brewpub is the more visible form because of its storefront location, its accessibility to the public, and the direct observability of its production capabilities. Unlike with microbreweries, it is not easy to consume a brewpub's beer without some awareness of its origins.

Carroll and Swaminathan (1998) speculate about other industries where identity might play a role in resource partitioning. These include music recording, book publishing, and newspapers. They also suggest that in another set of industries, closely related mechanisms involving the conspicuous status consumption of specialty firms' products appear to be at work. The best example concerns the wine industry (Swaminathan 1995). Finally, in a fourth set of industries, the position of specialist firms seems to be sustained by their flexibility over time. This dynamic capability allows specialist firms to meet the unique and changing needs of certain clients and other customers. Examples here include auditing services (Boone et al. 2000) and banking services.

The conditions for operation of one or the other partitioning mechanisms have yet to be delineated and the implications of each for theory, research, and practice yet to be fully developed. These are important tasks for future scholarly work on resource partitioning. Nonetheless, it is already obvious that each of these latter mechanisms has a stronger sociological character than the original location-based mechanism, which bears a resemblance to some economic models.

12.3 Size-Localized Competition

At equilibrium, resource-partitioning theory predicts a bimodal distribution of organizational sizes: one or several large (generalist) organizations will coexist with many small (specialist) organizations. Compared to many organizational size distributions (e.g., the lognormal), the middle sizes are absent or greatly underrepresented. This same shape of distribution also arises from some other organizational segregating processes, notably from models of size-localized competition.

In developing notions about size-localized competition, Hannan and Freeman (1977) noted that organizations of very different sizes typically employ different strategies and structures, implying they rely on different mixes of resources. If so, then organizations compete most intensely with organizations of similar size. In particular, Hannan and Freeman (1977, 946) maintained that "competition between pairs of organizations in an activity will be a decreasing function of the distance separating them on the size gradient." They also suggested that the competitive balance among organizations of different sizes changes as the size distribution evolves:

> When large-sized organizations emerge, they pose a competitive threat to medium-sized organizations but hardly any threat to small organizations. In fact, the rise of large organizations might increase the survival chances of small ones in a manner not anticipated in the classical model. When the large organizations enter, those in the middle of the size distribution are trapped. Whatever strategy they adopt to fight off the challenge of the larger form makes them more vulnerable in competition with small organizations, and vice versa. That is, at least in a stable environment the two ends of the size distribution can out compete the middle. (Hannan and Freeman 1977, 946)

This conjecture implies a pattern opposite the one produced by adding size-related growth rates to the baseline models (Chapter 14). It holds that the center of the distribution will be sparser than would be expected on the basis of the standard growth theories.

Hannan and Ranger-Moore (1990) contrasted simulation results of two different versions of the above argument. Both assume that the relationship holds strongly in tightly packed regions of the size axis and that the growth rates are relatively insensitive to variations in distance in the upper range. One version assumes that the intensity of competition facing each organization depends on the exact position of every other organization in the population. Hannan and Ranger-Moore (1990) use the Euclidean distance of each organization from all others in terms of size. A second version restricts competition to selected "windows" of the size axis. Organizations are assumed to compete only with organizations within some range of their own size, the window. That is, the measure of distance is

$$D_{it} = \sum_{|S_{it} - S_{jt}| < w} (S_{it} - S_{jt})^2,$$

where w is the width of the window. Using the functional form in this equation with windows localizes the competition process by disregarding the presence of organizations outside the window.

The first version does not produce gaps in the distribution (Hannan and Ranger-Moore 1990). Rather, it generates extreme monopolies. Once an organization moves away from the pack, its growth rate rises sharply, and the process is self-accelerating. The second version does tend to produce the predicted qualitative pattern of a bimodal size distribution with gaps in the center of the distribution.

Size-localized models have proven useful in empirical research as well. The general approach involves using data on the actual sizes of organizations to calculate a D_{it} score for each organization, which is then used as a covariate in mortality models, with the expectation that the coefficient associated with distance will be negative (the further the focal organization lies from its neighbors on the size distribution, the lower will be its death rate).[2] To get estimates of the segregating process, it must be observed well before it reaches the equilibrium state. In other words, the observation plan must cover the period when (at least some of) the middle-size organizations fail. Size-localized models have been estimated in empirical studies of banks (Hannan et al. 1990; Han 1998), credit unions (Amburgey, Dacin, and Kelly 1994), hotels (Baum and Mezias 1992), and insurance companies (Ranger-Moore, Breckenridge, and Jones 1995).

Given the similarity between models of resource partitioning and models of size-localized competition, it is worthwhile comparing the two approaches more systematically. To start with the obvious, the models differ on the number and type of basic dimensions they examine: size-localized competition considers only the single dimension of size, while resource partitioning requires the two dimensions of niche width (generalism/specialism) and market concentration. However, because small size and organizational specialism are generally highly correlated, the two models often highlight exactly the same organizations. Moreover, both models imply that the organizations in the middle of the size distribution have poor life chances (and thus are dramatically underrepresented) because of their precarious competitive position between organizations located at the two ends of the distribution. In both models, too, the gap in the middle might result from either differential entry or failure.

Resource-partitioning theory differs from size-localization in its assumptions about competition. First, small specialist organizations do not compete with each other, according to resource-partitioning theory, unless they target the same resource areas. By contrast, size-localized models assume that all small organizations compete with each other to some extent based on their relative sizes. Second, resource-partitioning theory predicts much more intense competition among large generalists than does size

---

[2] As noted in Chapter 10, size-localized models can be interpreted as weighted-density models.

localization, which posits a competitive process that is virtually symmetric for small and large organizations. The result of these two differences is that resource partitioning predicts far fewer large generalists and far more small specialists than most size-localized specifications.

The two models also differ in theoretical specificity. Resource partitioning posits positional advantages for the largest organizations by way of economies of scale and the like. Size-localized models make no such presumption: large size (like small size) is simply an uncrowded spot on the size dimension. The models and associated theory do not confer any other special characteristics or status on the largest size spot, as resource partitioning theory does. More precise specification of the mechanisms at work would facilitate the use of alternative forms of evidence (e.g., per-unit cost data for economies of scale).

However, the modeling framework used to represent size-localized competition is remarkably general. Basically, any dimension that organizations can be arrayed on continuously can be used to calculate distance measures similar to those shown here for size. The theoretical requirements are that organizations actually compete on the specified dimension and that this competition be intense and sustained enough to generate population segmentation. For instance, Baum and Mezias (1992) show that hotels in Manhattan compete along localized dimensions of price and geographical proximity.

Competition of this kind along multiple dimensions increases the complexity of the equilibrium distribution rapidly. With only a single dimension such as size operating to segregate, we expect a bifurcated distribution. With two dimensions, there are now four viable positions; with three, eight, and so on in geometric fashion. In general, n dimensions of this type generate 2^n viable equilibrium positions. Consequently, the outcome of segregating processes in population distributions with multiple dimensions gets extremely complicated.

Finally, categorical or discrete dimensions of competition are also widely used to model segregation processes in populations. In this case, the literature refers to partitioning models as domain-competition or domain-overlap models.[3] Assume a dimension of k categories. Then construct measures of organizational density by category (or weighted density if organizations can be located simultaneously or partially in several categories). Haveman's (1993b) study of savings and loan associations uses measures of this kind. The categories are various types of investment markets. Similarly, Baum and Singh (1994) specify models of day-care cen-

---

[3]These models are perhaps best regarded as weighted-density models. See the discussion of such models in Chapter 11.

ter competition using target ages of enrolled children as the basis for assessing domain competition.

It is very important to note that the difference between discrete and continuous dimensions involves much more than simply measurement scale. With continuous dimensions, the researcher asserts a basis for competition but lets the data determine the strength and position of the most intense competition along the specified dimension. With categorical dimensions, the researcher essentially asserts the structure of the niche, theorizing the specific locations where competition starts and stops (usually leading to very different judgments about some organizations located nearly proximate in resource space) and asserting that these locations do not change over time. Obviously, this form of analysis requires stronger theory, stronger justification. It also likely requires a deeper a priori understanding of the organizational population and its institutional setting.

Part IV
ORGANIZATIONAL PROCESSES

THE CHAPTERS in this part of the book examine demographic processes operating at the organizational level of analysis. Among the questions addressed are: What happens to organizations as they age? How do changes in size affect organizations? Where do organizations come from? How and when do organizations enact major structural transformations? Research in organizational demography has sharpened many of the relevant issues as well as provided some answers.

Chapter 13 examines age dependence in organizational processes. Numerous theorists and policy analysts have speculated about the liabilities of newness, adolescence, obsolescence, and senescence; each implies a specific pattern of age dependence in organizational mortality and growth rates. The chapter reviews relevant models for studying the various patterns and recounts the relevant empirical evidence. The apparently contradictory state of evidence about age dependence in organizational mortality creates a thorny problem given the centrality of aging processes in demography. The chapter attempts to resolve the dilemma by scrutinizing carefully theories about age dependence with the tools of logical formalization.

Chapter 14 considers size-dependent processes in organizations. It begins by reviewing the role of size in models of organizational growth, focusing on extensions of Gibrat's law based on recent evidence. The chapter next considers the relationship between organizational age and size, especially in the context of mortality processes. It advances a novel specification of the effects of age and size and applies it to populations of automobile producers. The specification shows promise of clarifying issues about age dependence in mortality. The implications of these findings are next incorporated into the logical analysis of theories of age dependence initiated in Chapter 13.

Chapter 15 explores the demographic implications of the mobilizing processes that precede the actual operation of an organization. It exploits an unusual type of data set on preproduction activities in the American automobile industry. The chapter makes arguments about the density-dependent nature of these activities and examines them empirically. The analysis provides a rare glimpse of the demography of actual attempts at mobilizing resources and other preproduction activities.

Chapter 16 considers the structural transformation of organizations. It examines the ideas and theoretical arguments that have been advanced about organizational change and inertia. Special attention is paid to the consequences of transformation for organizational life chances, especially mortality. A theoretically motivated modeling framework that separates content from process effects of transformation is presented. A review of the empirical evidence shows that inertial forces are often—but not always—strong.

13

Age-Dependent Processes

AGE IS THE MASTER CLOCK in human demography; it controls vital rates and plays the central role in models of demographic processes. Should age have a comparable standing in corporate demography? This issue has not been resolved at the moment, in large part because of theoretical tensions over the processes commonly associated with aging in organizations.

Two theoretical images coexist uneasily in standard analyses of organizations. One regards the structural features of organizations as mappings from the environment encountered at founding (Stinchcombe 1965), and it depicts organizations as locked into their initial forms. Structural inertia dominates this image: organizations have very limited capacities to refashion their core structures (their form-defining features, as we termed them in Chapter 4) as quickly as the environment changes (Hannan and Freeman 1977). Efforts at changing core features diminish life chances, at least in the short run (Chapter 16). Therefore, when environments are variable and uncertain, extensive change in the distribution of organizational forms occurs by selection processes operating on organizational populations.

The second view concentrates on the life-history dynamics of organizations. It portrays young organizations as particularly vulnerable to environmental selection—they face a liability of newness (Stinchcombe 1965). Aging conveys advantages, such as improved capabilities and more secure structural positions, that tend to insulate older organizations from damage due to environmental turbulence. Hence, the life chances of organizations improve with aging.

The two images do not necessarily conflict. For instance, large shifts in the environment might increase mortality rates for all organizations in a population and also expose the youngest organizations to the most intense force of mortality. This said, it must be admitted that the two theoretical images do not fit comfortably. Structural inertia in the face of environmental change ought to erode fitness. If new organizations can incorporate current understandings, best practices, and state-of-the-art technology in their core structures and old organizations have the core structures that reflect a bygone era, then why do old organizations have better life chances?

In this chapter, we examine the role of age in organizational demography. We start by reviewing the stochastic models commonly used to represent age dependence in organizational mortality: the Gompertz, Weibull, log-logistic, and piecewise-constant models. We then turn to an empirical illustration, using data on banks in Tokyo. In the following section, we start to discuss the various processes usually associated with aging in organizations. These processes sometimes yield contradictory empirical predictions. To help sort things out, we report an extensive formal theoretical analysis of the various arguments. We believe that the issues deserve such lengthy and careful treatment because of the centrality of aging processes to general demography.

13.1 Models of Age-Dependent Mortality

A simple but powerful type of age dependence lets the hazard of mortality depend on the time since the previous event (duration). Much research makes parametric assumptions about the forms of age dependence. We discuss the most common choices as well as a popular, less restrictive, alternative.

The Gompertz–Makeham Model

The Gompertz model (and its extension, the Makeham model) has been used widely in corporate demography. In particular, this specification served as the basis of most of the early research on age dependence in organizational mortality (Carroll 1983; Freeman, Carroll, and Hannan 1983). This model sets the rate to be an exponential function of duration:

$$h(u) = \beta e^{\gamma u}, \qquad \beta, u > 0. \tag{13.1}$$

Of course, this model imposes monotonic duration dependence. If γ is negative, then the rate declines from β to zero. If γ is positive, then the mortality rate rises exponentially with duration.

Because it is unreasonable to assume that very old organizations escape the risk of mortality completely, organizational researchers have used a variation of the Gompertz model called the Makeham model that allows a nonzero asymptotic rate:

$$h(u) = \alpha + \beta e^{\gamma u}, \qquad \alpha, \beta, u > 0. \tag{13.2}$$

With this specification and $\gamma < 0$, the rate begins at $\alpha + \beta$ and approaches α as $u \to \infty$.

The Weibull Model

Another common parametric specification of time dependence in corporate demography, the Weibull model, sets the rate as a power function of duration:

$$h(u) = \rho\lambda(\lambda u)^{\rho-1}, \qquad \lambda, \rho, u > 0. \tag{13.3}$$

The rate declines monotonically with duration if $\rho < 1$, increases monotonically with duration for $\rho > 1$, and does not vary with duration if $\rho = 1$. The last relationship can be used to construct likelihood-ratio tests of a Weibull model against the null hypothesis of an exponential model.[1]

The Log-Logistic Model

The third common parametric model of duration dependence, the log-logistic model, can imply nonmonotonic duration dependence. This model is typically expressed as

$$h(u) = \frac{\rho\lambda(\lambda u)^{\rho-1}}{1 + (\lambda u)^\rho}, \qquad \lambda, \rho, u > 0. \tag{13.4}$$

The rate decreases monotonically with duration if $\rho \leq 1$. If $\rho > 1$, then the rate rises monotonically to a maximum and then declines monotonically with increasing u.

Piecewise-Exponential Model

As discussed in Chapter 7, a less restrictive way to represent temporal variation in transition rates involves breaking the time dimension (age, here) into pieces and fitting constant rates within segments (Tuma and Hannan 1984; Blossfeld and Rohwer 1996). This procedure constrains temporal variation in the rate to be a step function in duration where the width of the steps is set by the analyst and the height of each step is determined by the data. The piecewise-exponential model can be written as

$$h(u) = \alpha_p, \qquad u \in I_p, \tag{13.5}$$

---

[1] The fit of a Weibull model can also be evaluated by considering plots of empirical log-hazards against age or duration. Whereas the Gompertz model implies that the log-hazard is a linear function of duration or age, the Weibull model implies that the log-hazard is a linear function of the logarithm of age. According to the Weibull model, the integrated hazard of a Weibull process is a power function of the waiting time. So another way to evaluate the fit of the Weibull uses plots of the logarithm of the estimated integrated hazard against the waiting time. Hannan (1989) illustrates the value of these comparisons in a corporate-demographic context.

with preselected breakpoints

$$0 \leq \tau_1 \leq \tau_2 \leq \cdots \leq \tau_P,$$

and the assumption that $\tau_{P+1} = \infty$, giving P periods:

$$I_p = \{t \mid \tau_p \leq t < \tau_{p+1}\}, \qquad p = 1, \ldots, P. \qquad (13.6)$$

Examining the set of $\widehat{\alpha}_p$ tells whether there is a pattern of age dependence, e.g., increasing or decreasing roughly monotonically or rising and then falling.

Industry Tenure Versus Age

What is normally called organizational age in the empirical research literature is often actually a different measure of duration: tenure in a particular organizational population. Of course, basic differences might follow from the ways in which organizations enter a population. As discussed in Chapter 3, some new entrants are formed de novo, meaning that resources have been assembled from scratch for the sole purpose of building an organization of the particular kind. Other organizations enter the focal population from established positions in other geographical locations, or from other industries or sectors. In such cases of de alio (or lateral) entry, the entity is a new member of the population, but it is not a new organization. It is obvious that organizational age is the same as tenure for the former mode but not for the latter.

Although not usually the main focus, previous empirical research often recorded and estimated the effects of de alio status. These studies typically show that de alio entrants have lower mortality rates. For example, studies of automobile producers in the United States (Carroll et al. 1996) and Europe (Hannan et al. 1998a) showed that de alio entrants experienced significantly lower chances of failure. In a study of restaurant longevity, Hannan and Freeman (1989) found that firms with operations in other cities had lower death rates. Likewise, semiconductor manufacturers operating as divisions of larger corporations tended to stay in product markets longer (Hannan and Freeman 1989) and hotels that are affiliated with chains exhibit lower rates of death and failure (Ingram 1996). The greater life chances of these various types of de alio firms might be the consequence of any number of factors including stronger organizational structures, greater experience, or more abundant resources. Future research would do well to sort out these different possibilities.

Tenure-dependent processes themselves might be different for organizations arriving by the two entry modes. Carroll et al. (1996) argue that de alio entrants have an initial advantage (deriving from greater average levels of capital and other resources) but that this initial advantage diminishes as organizations age. They reason that subsidies received by the de alio entrant are likely to decline as time passes (given that the new entrant would normally be expected to become independently viable). They also suggest that de novo entrants likely possess greater flexibility in growth. When opportunities and problems arise, de novo entrants can move more decisively in redeploying personnel, machines, and capital than de alio entrants who are constrained by the justifications, plans, and agreements hammered out in their origin firms at the time of entry.

These arguments suggest that de alio entrants will have initial advantages relative to de novo entrants but these differences will diminish as tenure in the industry increases. If so, tenure-based mortality curves for the two modes will cross, as Carroll et al. (1996) find for automobile producers. Alternatively, the age effect might be consistently stronger for de novo firms, as Mitchell (1994) finds in his study of medical-sector producers.

In general, it is essential to control for a firm's prior experience in empirical research. Otherwise, the quality of estimates of either age-dependent or tenure-dependent organizational processes is potentially affected. In many cases, the only information available tells that the firm is not new; here a dummy variable indicating prior experience must suffice. In other instances, greater detail on the type and length of experience can be codified. For instance, Carroll et al. (1996) could identify the following origin industries for sufficient numbers of early automobile producers: engine manufacturing, bicycle manufacturing, carriage manufacturing, and automobile dealership. Contrary to the expectations of many, the groups with lowest rates of failure in automobile production came from carriage manufacturing and bicycle manufacturing rather than the technical-oriented base of engine manufacturing. Following Hounshell (1984), they suggested that "*assembly* knowledge and expertise propelled both bicycle and carriage manufacturers into automobile production with an advantage"(emphasis added). (Carroll et al. 1996, 134)

An Illustration: Tokyo Banks

We again use Han's (1998) data on Tokyo banks, 1873–1945 (see Chapter 6 for information about these data).[2] Table 13.1 reports estimates of

---

[2] In this case, the time unit is the age of the organization.

Table 13.1. *Estimates of alternative specifications of age dependence in the mortality rates of banks in Tokyo.*

Exponential model: $h(u) = \alpha$	
$\widehat{\alpha}$	0.042*
$\ln \mathcal{L}$	-1170.0

Piecewise-exponential: $h(u) = \alpha_p,\ u \in I_p$	
$\widehat{\alpha}_1$ $(u < 5)$	0.018*
$\widehat{\alpha}_2$ $(5 \leq u < 10)$	0.030*
$\widehat{\alpha}_3$ $(10 \leq u < 15)$	0.024*
$\widehat{\alpha}_4$ $(15 \leq u < 25)$	0.040*
$\widehat{\alpha}_5$ $(25 \leq u)$	0.104*
$\ln \mathcal{L}$	-1109.8

Gompertz model: $h(u) = \beta e^{\gamma u}$	
$\widehat{\beta}$	0.021*
$\widehat{\gamma}$	0.039*
$\ln \mathcal{L}$	-1128.1

Weibull model: $h(u) = \rho \lambda (\lambda u)^{\rho-1}$	
$\widehat{\lambda}$	0.039*
$\widehat{\rho}$	1.62*
$\ln \mathcal{L}$	-1129.0

Log-logistic model: $h(u) = \rho \lambda^{\rho} u^{\rho-1}/(1 + (\lambda u)^{\rho})$	
$\widehat{\lambda}$	0.051*
$\widehat{\rho}$	2.12*
$\ln \mathcal{L}$	-1160.0

* $p < .05$.
Note: the time unit is years.

some specific realizations of the age-dependent mortality models, and Figure 13.1 plots the implications of these estimates. The table shows decisive evidence against the hypothesis that the mortality rate is constant over age. The value of the likelihood-ratio test of the constant-rate model against a piecewise-constant model with five pieces is 120.4 (with four degrees of freedom). Thus, we can reject the null hypothesis of age independence in favor of the alternative, that is, age dependence.

Age has a strongly *positive* effect according to the estimates of the piecewise-exponential model, aside from a slight drop in the rate from the

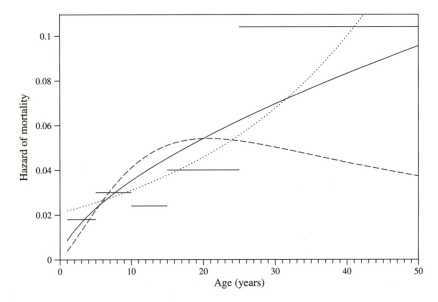

Figure 13.1. *Estimated age dependence in the mortality process for Tokyo banks based on Table 13.1. (The solid horizontal lines give the estimates from the piecewise-exponential model; the solid curve is from the Weibull model; the dotted curve is from the Gompertz model; and the dashed curve is from the log-logistic model.)*

second to the third segment (Figure 13.1). According to these estimates, the rate is very high when a bank's age exceeds 25.[3]

The Weibull and Gompertz models perform reasonably well in terms of model fit as evaluated (informally) by the likelihood ratios adjusting for number of parameters estimated. Yet, neither closely approximates the results of the more flexible piecewise-exponential model. These two parametric specifications fit the piecewise results well for the early years, but neither fits well in the segment in which the rate declines slightly. The Gompertz model is rising very steeply by age 40 and overshoots the piecewise result greatly for older ages. The Weibull model is better in this respect. Finally, the log-logistic specification is a poor one for positive duration dependence as Figure 13.1 shows, because it imposes nonmonotonic age dependence when age dependence is positive.

---

[3] This result holds even when one controls for the effect of the bank panic of 1926 and the subsequent depression in Japan, as well as organizational size, population density, and other relevant factors (Han 1998).

13.2 The Age-Related Liabilities

Theory about aging in organizations has tended to follow empirical evidence, advancing general stories to explain observed patterns. Very early evidence did not introduce many controls and sometimes used inappropriate statistical techniques (Chapter 2). This research generally agreed with popular intuition and found negative age dependence in rates of mortality. The pattern persisted even with the advent of better data and improved statistical methods. However, as even better data and models were brought to bear on the issue, positive age dependence (such as that seen above for Tokyo banks) often appeared. Theoretical accounts of these patterns developed the peculiar tradition of describing the processes involved as "liabilities."

Newness

The sociological literature on organizational age and mortality began with Stinchcombe's (1965) observation that organizations experience a *liability of newness*: new organizations fail at higher rates than old ones. He made this claim based on an assessment of both internal organizational matters and environmental relations. Efficient organization requires trust among members; and trust takes time to build. Setting up and refining roles and routines, learning about the relevant environment, and developing relationships with existing organizations also take time. Once established, these patterns of relationships form a social structure supporting an organization's survival chances.

As discussed in detail in Chapter 16, Hannan and Freeman (1984) derived the liability of newness from an evolutionary argument. They argued that social selection processes favor organizations and organizational forms that have high reliability and accountability that, in turn, depend on high-fidelity reproduction of structure. Only organizations that have established their structures through time and over repeated interactions can faithfully reproduce their structures. So reliability and accountability increase with age, and mortality hazards decrease with age, according to this theory.

A great deal of early demographic research found support for Stinchcombe's argument that mortality rates of young organizations exceed those of old ones. Carroll (1983) showed this pattern holds for 63 samples of diverse kinds of organizations. Freeman et al. (1983) found this pattern for American labor unions, American semiconductor manufacturing firms, and newspaper publishers in San Francisco. Dozens of other studies find this pattern as well—see the reviews by Aldrich and Marsden (1988), Singh and Lumsden (1990), and Hannan et al. (1998a).

Adolescence

Some later research found, however, that mortality rates do not always decline monotonically from founding. Instead, rates sometimes rise during a brief early portion of the life span—while initial stocks of endowments and other resources are exhausted—before declining over most of a typical life span (Carroll and Huo 1988; Brüderl and Schüssler 1990; Fichman and Levinthal 1991; Brüderl et al. 1996). These results have stimulated some to propose that failure rates peak during "adolescence," sometimes referred to as the *liability of adolescence*.[4] Nonetheless, the proponents of this idea continue to assume that mortality hazards decline with age over the great bulk of expected organizational life span.

Obsolescence

The conventional wisdom implies that mature organizations can better withstand environmental shocks than can their newly founded competitors. In other words, negative age dependence suggests that environmental selection operates mainly on new organizations. On the other hand, positive age dependence implies that selection operates more broadly; large environmental shocks can have big effects on old organizations. Dynamics in the two cases differ markedly, as do the relations between organizations and social structure.

Barron et al. (1994) argued that positive age dependence can arise for at least two reasons. The first involves a combination of organizational inertia and environmental change. If inertial forces on organizational structure are strong, then organizations become "locked in" to the strategies and structures adopted during their early years. Initial strategies and structures are molded by prevailing cultural and social understandings and practices (Stinchcombe 1965). As environments change, the appropriate strategies and structures for adapting to them also change. The organizational arrangements that fit the sociocultural environment of, say, a hundred years ago might differ substantially from those that fit today. If inertial forces are strong, then the possibilities of organizational adaptation in response to the changing environment are extremely limited. Attempts at reorganization might, in fact, decrease survival chances.

Carroll (1983, 313) noted the possibility that "organizational age will coincide roughly with the amount of environmental change experienced by an organization." Suppose that this tendency holds on average and that core structures are "imprinted" in youth (Chapter 9). Then older cohorts of organizations have lower fitness in the current environment. If this image

---

[4] The pattern is alternatively described as a "honeymoon" effect.

of organizational development is accurate, then mortality rates increase with age. Notice that this scenario does not attribute causal significance to aging per se. Under these conditions, mortality rates do not vary systematically with age (i.e., they are age-independent) in stable environments. Such a pattern might thus be called a *liability of obsolescence*.

Senescence

The second interpretation of positive age dependence does attribute causal significance to organizational aging (Barron et al. 1994). Suppose, for instance, that organizations accumulate rules, routines, and structures as they age and that these features are durable. Suppose further that accumulating rules, routines, and structures impede an organization's ability to act, especially in a timely fashion, in the face of environmental volatility. Then old organizations are disadvantaged compared with younger ones in changing environments. Alternatively, accumulating rules, routines, and structures might simply impose an overhead cost that reduces the efficiency of organizations even in stable environments. In either case, older organizations have higher mortality hazards, adjusting for size. Here, there is a *liability of senescence*.

13.3 Age and Growth Rates

Despite high attention to the relationship between age and failure hazards, the ways that age might possibly affect organizational growth and decline have not been studied extensively. Sutton (1997) claims that there is a statistical regularity showing a negative relationship between age and growth. As evidence, he cites the empirical studies of Evans (1987) and Dunne et al. (1989). Both studies use very heterogeneous samples; the latter uses plants as the unit and has a large interval between panels of data. Another empirical study, by Harhoff et al. (1995), also uses a diverse sample of approximately 11,000 West-German firms from 1989 to 1994. The findings of this third study call into question the regularity; although negative effects are noted, these are judged by the researchers as only "weakly significant."

Growth, nonetheless, should be subject to many of the same organizational aging processes used in explaining variations in organizational mortality. For instance, if aging signals social and technical obsolescence and/or increasing rigidity of response, then growth rates ought to decline on average as an organization ages. That is, the arguments about obsolescence and senescence imply that *growth rates decline monotonically with age*.

Barron et al. (1994) estimated the following piecewise exponential specification:

$$\ln S_{a+1} = \alpha_p + \beta \ln S_a + \mathbf{z}'_a \boldsymbol{\pi} + \epsilon_{a+1}, \qquad a \in I_p,$$

where a is age, S_a is size at age a, $\mathbf{z}$ is a vector of age-varying covariates, and ϵ_a is a normally distributed disturbance term. The effect of aging in this specification is contained in the constants, α_p.

The estimated constants turn out to display a pattern of monotonic decrease in the growth rate with aging. According to these estimates, growth rates drop sharply after the first few years of the organizations' existence. The finding that growth rates decline with age accords with the view that older organizations are either less attuned to their environments or slow on their feet. However, the fact that the drop in growth rates with age occurs within the young age range suggests another possible explanation. The alternative features the social network character of credit unions.

Barron et al. (1994) argue that credit unions recruit members via the social network ties of their members. In this regard, credit unions resemble other "membership" organizations, which rely heavily on this form of recruitment (McPherson 1983; McPherson et al. 1992). And, as with these organizations, the pool of potential members is limited. In the case of businesses and membership organizations, pools of potential customers or members are often demarcated by social boundaries: people of a particular age group are more likely to buy particular products, while most members of tennis clubs come from the same social class. Membership pools for credit unions have historically been defined explicitly by the requirement that members share a common bond, though in recent years this requirement has become less stringent. Given this limitation of potential membership, the rate of recruitment of new members should decline over time as the proportion of those sharing the common bond who have not already joined declines.

Barnett and Sorenson (1998) conducted parallel analyses for growth rates of banks in Illinois (outside of Chicago). They found that growth rates decline monotonically with age. Likewise, Barnett et al. (2000) found that the growth rates of research and development consortia decline with age.

13.4 Theories of Age Dependence

Obviously, the theoretical accounts entailing liabilities of newness, adolescence, senescence, and obsolescence cannot all be true generally, because they disagree about the form of age dependence in processes of organizational mortality. Can these theories be reconciled and unified?

Can conditions be specified that tell when one theory applies and others do not?

The informal nature of the argumentation makes it hard to discern the premises invoked in each account. We believe that continued theoretical progress might require that the informal arguments be made more precise and formal and that systematic tools be used to evaluate the theoretical claims. So we now try to sort out the relevant theories and use the strategy of logical formalization to clarify some basic differences among them. It seeks to make explicit the tacit premises that inform the various theories about age dependence so that we might better understand the interplay between arguments about age dependence and general sociological theories of organizations.[5]

The first step in formalizing the theories involves a survey of the theoretical terrain. The relevant theoretical arguments can be built from propositions concerning five concepts: endowments, imprinting, inertia, capability, and position.

Endowments

Organizations differ in the quantities and qualities of their initial resources. Some get endowed with extensive financial and social capital, because their founders have great wealth, status, or political influence or because the social conditions of founding are favorable (resources might be abundant and few corporate actors might be competing for them). Others find themselves severely disadvantaged at founding, with these conditions reversed.

Endowments bear on the issues under consideration in two ways. First, developing capabilities is costly, and extensive endowments permit greater investment in capability. In Chapter 11, we discussed the density-delay argument that holds that organizations founded in periods of intense competition for resources face a liability of scarcity. They cannot invest in developing capabilities, and the failure to make such investments at the outset has irreversible negative consequences for life chances. Second, endowments can affect mortality rates directly. A well-endowed organization can maintain its structures and members even if it cannot continually mobilize resources from the environment.

Endowments matter most in the first months and years of operation. Endowments depreciate unless replenished by continuing positive flows of resources from the environment. Until an endowment has been depleted, the organization's risk of mortality is low. Once the endowment gets exhausted, the risk of mortality jumps. The implications for age dependence in mortality rates are clear. At a given level of endowment, the mortality

---

[5]This section draws on Hannan et al. (1998a) and Hannan (1998).

rate remains low during the period of depletion, and it jumps afterward. That is, mortality rates increase with age.[6]

Imprinting and Structural Inertia

Chapter 9 introduced the idea of imprinting, a process in which events occurring at key developmental stages have persisting—possibly lifelong— consequences. The idea that firms and other kinds of organizations tend to be imprinted by their founding conditions comes from Stinchcombe's (1965) insight that social and economic structures have their maximal impact on new organizations. In attempting to accumulate financial and human capital, entrepreneurs expose their designs to intense scrutiny. Proposals get tested against taken-for-granted assumptions about structural forms and employment relations. Because conventional wisdoms and taken-for-granted assumptions change over historical time (as new forms flourish and others wane), the tests imposed on proto-organizations also change. Consequently, the kinds of organizations that emerge reflect the social structure of the founding period.

Imprinting requires an initial mapping of an environmental condition onto the nascent corporate actor. The imprinted characteristics must be inert (or at least possess a fair degree of hysteresis). Otherwise, later modifications of the structure will erode the association of founding conditions and those features.

What does imprinting imply about age dependence in mortality rates? If imprinting occurs, then founders build organizations that fit historically specific environments. If some core features of organizations get set by early decisions and actions and resist change afterwards, then environmental change will erode the fit between organizations and environments. Barron et al. (1994) assumed that the distance of an organization's current environment from its founding-period environment varies directly with its age. Then, the quality of the match declines monotonically with age, and age dependence is positive. In other words, the joint action of imprinting, inertia, and environmental change create a liability of obsolescence.

Capability

An organizational capability is an ability to execute routines and solve problems. An organization's capabilities consist of its stock of solutions to

---

[6] In the usual formulation of this idea (Brüderl et al. 1996), the level of endowment is treated as an unobservable random variable, making the length of the period of exhaustion also an unobservable random variable. If the distribution of endowments is (roughly) continuous, one will observe that the hazard of mortality rises smoothly from zero to a peak (the point of exhaustion for the best-endowed organizations).

the problem of producing collective action in a specified environment. In other words, capabilities are context-specific. Capabilities are often based on routines that codify an organization's dispersed learning (Nelson and Winter 1982; March 1988). An important dimension of capability involves the capacity to reduce friction among the many activities and routines that typically must be undertaken to produce the organization's collective product. The more refined and harmonized an organization's routines, the greater the organization's capability in the specified environment. Therefore, in a stable environment, improvements in capability increase the expected quality of performance and thereby decrease the risk of mortality.

A key part of Stinchcombe's (1965) argument for the liability of newness concerns the relationship of age and capability. In particular, he argues that new organizations suffer from low average quality of performance because they lack experience. As youthful organizations age, they acquire experience and can potentially learn. The stylized image of the learning curve captures this kind of process. As organizations learn from experience, they refine their productive routines and the metaroutines that coordinate them.

Stinchcombe also argues that new organizations face jeopardy because they must rely on the cooperation of strangers. To the extent that trust enhances collective action, lack of familiarity among co-workers is problematic. As time passes, trust tends to develop within work-groups. As a result, the organization's capabilities improve, because an important source of friction has been reduced.

Subsequent theory has followed Stinchcombe's lead in emphasizing that experience improves capabilities. For instance, Hannan and Freeman (1984) argued that norms of rationality demand that organizations achieve low variance in the quality of their outputs and make systematic, rational accounts of their activities. Not all organizations can achieve reliability and accountability; those that do have survival advantages. New organizations lack these capabilities; they must acquire them through learning by doing and the accumulation of organization-specific human capital. Therefore, the development and refinement of these capabilities depend upon age.

Some recent lines of argument about capabilities run opposite this mainstream view. Barron et al. (1994) drew on an analogy to senescence processes observable in animal and human life histories. They suggested that organizations accumulate durable features, such as precedents, political coalitions, and taken-for-granted understandings, that constrain modifications in patterns of collective action. Such encrustation erodes the capability for efficient collective action. According to this view, the liability is one of senescence: mortality rates increase with age.

March's (1991) account of organizational learning tells a cautionary tale about the consequences of the continual refinement of a competence. Organizations that seek to exploit their competencies, by searching for ever-better refinements of their existing capabilities, find themselves in a competency trap if the world changes. Only organizations that have already achieved some competence and follow a so-called exploitation strategy can get trapped by it. Thus this line of argument opposes the mainstream account, at least in the case of the exploitation strategy.[7]

Positional Advantage

A final set of relevant arguments about age dependence in mortality rates concerns the organization's position in the social structure. Stinchcombe (1965) points out that trust matters in building ties with other organizations (e.g., potential suppliers and customers) and important actors in the social environment (e.g., holders of capital, government officials and regulators, and so forth) and that it takes time for trust to develop in external relations. Because maintaining good relations with key external actors enhances organizational performance and also arguably affects survival chances directly, the buildup of favorable external ties over organizational lifetimes lowers mortality rates. This argument, too, implies negative age dependence in mortality hazards.

Positional advantages come in many forms. These include occupancy of positions that bridge structural holes (Burt 1993), favorable reputation (Kreps 1996), high status (Podolny 1993), market power, and political influence. Some positional advantages, such as occupying a bridge over a structural hole, do not seem to depend upon age and experience. Others, such as market power and possibly political influence, appear to be more influenced by size than by age. Still others, such as favorable reputation and high status, presumably depend upon some demonstrated history of performance and thus depend in part upon age. New organizations thus find themselves at a disadvantage when reputation and status matter.

Although not all kinds of positional advantages accrue to experience, we are unaware of any argument claiming that such advantages decline systematically with age. Thus, arguments about positional advantage, if they bear on the issue at all, concur with Stinchcombe's original assertion of negative age dependence.

---

[7]The polar opposite strategy, exploring for solutions that lie far from the organization's current capabilities, has no obvious relationship with aging, as long as the region to be searched is large relative to an organization's radius of search (so that an old organization would not have searched most of the solution space) or the set of possibilities to be searched changes over time.

These arguments about endowments, imprinting, positional advantages, and capabilities have been invoked in varying combinations to explain patterns of positive, negative, and nonmonotonic age dependence. Endowment theories are seen to imply positive age dependence. Theories about imprinting also appear to imply positive age dependence. Arguments about capabilities can suggest either negative or positive age dependence, depending on whether the relevant capabilities are thought to improve or deteriorate with age. However, it is usually claimed that the cumulation of positional advantages as organizations age results in negative age dependence.

Finally, analysts frequently use a mixture of two or more processes to make predictions. For instance, those who emphasize the role of endowments in shaping early mortality experiences have overlaid this process of positive age dependence with standard stories about the age-dependent accumulation of competence and positional advantage. Thus Brüderl and Schüssler (1990), Fichman and Levinthal (1991), and Brüderl et al. (1996) assume that mortality rates rise with age initially due to the exhaustion of endowments and then fall with further aging due to the improvement of capabilities with age. Of course, other combinations are possible.

With the key concepts in hand, we turn now to the formalization. This formalization addresses some of the central ideas about the relationship between age and the rate of organizational mortality. It concentrates on capability and position and treats endowments indirectly as a type of positional advantage. The formalization does not consider either the main effect of size on mortality rates or the interaction of size and age in affecting mortality rates. Doing so would require a substantially more extensive formalization.

13.5 Formalizing Core Assumptions

As noted at the outset, this analysis uses the tools of first-order logic to rationally reconstruct the various theories and to verify the soundness of the derivations.[8] The notation is summarized in Table 13.2. Uppercase strings denote predicates and functions. Lower case letters denote the objects that possess the properties or are mapped by the functions. One-place predicates denote the properties of objects. For instance, the predicate $O(x)$ indicates that an object x is an organization. Predicates with more than

---

[8] Proofs of all lemmas (minor theorems) and the main theorems were verified with OT-TER (Organized Techniques for Theorem-proving and Effective Research) (McCune 1994), a theorem prover for first-order logic with the equality relation.

Table 13.2. *Notation for predicates, functions, and key parameters used in the logical formalizations in Chapters 13 and 14.*

Symbol	Denotation
$O(x)$	x is an organization
$A(x, t)$	organization x's age at time t
$H(x, t)$	organization x's hazard of mortality at t
$EN(x)$	organization x has an endowment at founding
$C(x, t)$	organization x's capability at time t
$P(x, t)$	the quality of organization x's position at t
$IM(x, t)$	organization x has immunity at t
$K(x, t)$	organization x's stock of knowledge at t
$T(x, t)$	the quality of organization x's external ties at t
$F(x, t)$	organization x's level of internal friction at t
$DS(x, t_0, t)$	the environments at t_0 and t are dissimilar
$AL(x, t)$	organization x is aligned with its environment at t
$PA(x, t)$	organization x has positional advantage at t
$FG(x)$	organization x occupies a fragile position
$RB(x)$	organization x occupies a robust position
ϵ	the age at which an endowment ends
σ	the age at which environmental drift destroys alignment and the advantage to fragile position
τ	the age at which advantage accrues to robust position

Source: Hannan (1998). Copyright © 1998 by the University of Chicago. Used by permission.

one argument "slot" and variables denote relations between objects. (Predicates tell that a certain relationship is true; functions define mappings of objects.) For instance, the basic variable in these formalizations is historical time, denoted by t. The function of most theoretical relevance, $A(x, t)$, gives an object's age at time t.[9]

This section presents a set of propositions that—in one form or another—find application in theories of the liability of newness, adolescence, senescence, and obsolescence. These arguments concern the relationship between organizational age and the hazard of mortality. Two properties of the age function deserve note: age is nonnegative and increases monotonically with time in existence:

Meaning Postulate 13.5.1. *Age is nonnegative and monotonic in* t:

$$\forall x, t_0, t \left[O(x) \longrightarrow \{A(x, t) \geq 0\} \wedge \right.$$

$$\left. \{\{A(x, t) > A(x, t_0) \to (t > t_0)\} \wedge \{A(x, t) = A(x, t_0) \to t = t_0\}\} \right].$$

[9] This remainder of this chapter is adapted from Hannan (1998).

[Read: for all values of x, t_0, and t, if an object x is an (existing) organization, then the object's age is greater than or equal to zero, and the statement that the object's age at time t exceeds its age at t_0 implies that time t is greater than time t_0, and the statement that the object's age at t equals its age at t_0 implies that $t = t_0$.]

The dependent variable, $H(x, t)$, is an organization's hazard of mortality at time t. In some earlier formalizations (Péli, Bruggeman, Mausch, and Ó Nualláin 1994; Péli 1997), the mortality rate has been interpreted as a population-level "outflow." In the present context, the rate should be interpreted as an organization-level hazard (Chapter 6).

The substantive core for the first three formalizations involves the relations of endowments capability, position, and the hazard of mortality. The review of the arguments about endowments suggested they provide transitory initial advantages. They buffer new organizations from some of the force of selection processes for a time. However, these advantages get exhausted relatively quickly (in the scale of organizational lifetimes). On this interpretation, endowments can be conceptualized as transitory immunity from the risk of mortality. This idea can be represented in terms of a predicate that tells that an organization possesses immunity at a given time: $IM(x, t)$. Suppose that an endowment lasts until age ϵ. Then, an endowment provides immunity that lasts from founding until age ϵ.

Definition 13.5.1. *An endowment provides an immunity that lasts until an organization's age exceeds ϵ:*

$$\forall x \left[EN(x) \longleftrightarrow \forall t \left[O(x) \wedge \{(A(x, t) \le \epsilon) \to IM(x, t)\} \wedge \{(A(x, t) > \epsilon) \to \neg IM(x, t)\} \right] \right].$$

In the context, it makes sense to make endowments the only source of immunity.

Assumption 13.5.1. *An unendowed organization never possesses immunity:*

$$\forall x, t \left[O(x) \wedge \neg EN(x) \longrightarrow \neg IM(x, t) \right].$$

Finally, we need a specification of the role of immunity in the process of organizational mortality. According to the image used here, the hazard of mortality remains constant at a very low level (possibly zero) during the period of immunity.[10] There are two ideas here. First, the hazard stays constant during the period of immunity.

---

[10] Another, more complicated, possibility is that immunity wears off gradually, so that the hazard of mortality rises gradually during the immunity period. Such a complication does not appear to be needed here.

Assumption 13.5.2. *An organization's hazard of mortality is constant during periods in which it has immunity:*

$$\forall x, t_0, t \, \big[O(x) \wedge IM(x, t_0) \wedge IM(x, t) \longrightarrow H(x, t_0) = H(x, t) \big].$$

Second, immunity has an overwhelming effect on the mortality rate, one that overrides the effects of other potentially relevant conditions such as capability and quality of position.

Assumption 13.5.3. *An organization's hazard of mortality is lower during periods in which it has immunity than in periods in which it does not:*

$$\forall x, t_0, t \, \big[O(x) \wedge IM(x, t_0) \wedge \neg IM(x, t) \longrightarrow H(x, t) > H(x, t_0) \big].$$

Outside of periods of immunity, variations in capability and performance affect the hazard. The function $C(x, t)$ maps an object's capability at time t and $P(x, t)$ tells the quality of its position at time t.

Assumption 13.5.4. *When an organization lacks immunity, superior capability and position imply a lower hazard of mortality:*

$$\forall x, t_0, t \, \big[O(x) \wedge \neg \{IM(x, t_0) \vee IM(x, t)\}$$
$$\longrightarrow \big\{ (C(x, t) > C(x, t_0) \wedge P(x, t) \geq P(x, t_0))$$
$$\vee (C(x, t) \geq C(x, t_0) \wedge P(x, t) > P(x, t_0)) \longrightarrow H(x, t) < H(x, t_0) \big\}$$
$$\wedge \big\{ (C(x, t) = C(x, t_0) \wedge P(x, t) = P(x, t_0)) \longrightarrow H(x, t) = H(x, t_0) \big\} \big].$$

The liability-of-newness theory builds upon assumptions that relate an organization's age to the development of its capabilities and positional advantages. Stinchcombe and others have identified several processes by which aging enhances capability and position in a constant environment. To simplify, this formalization considers the stock of organizational knowledge as an instance of capability and the quality of ties to external actors who control important resources as an instance of the quality of a structural position.[11] The function $K(x, t)$ records an object's collective knowledge at time t, and $T(x, t)$ tells the quality of its external ties at time t.

The main intuition behind the senescence argument holds that organizations develop encrustations of internal frictions, precedents, and political compromises as they age and that these encrustations impede timely collective action. A diminished capacity for timely collective action amounts to a loss of capability. This formalization also considers only one instance

---

[11] It should be obvious that a complete formulation would develop the forms of capabilities and positions more fully.

of the purportedly relevant conditions: the accumulation of internal friction. The function $F(x, t)$ records an object's intensity of internal friction at time t.

According to the standard liability-of-newness story, collective knowledge contributes to capability. Arguments for senescence assume that the accumulation of internal friction diminishes capability. It is helpful to develop a simple framework that applies to both cases so that each theory can be regarded as a special case of the general formulation.

The liability-of-newness proposition will be derived by assuming that internal friction does not vary with age while capability and position increase with age; and the liability-of-senescence proposition will be derived by assuming that internal friction accumulates with age while capability and position remain constant. The core assumptions presented here are tailored to fit these requirements.[12]

Assumption 13.5.5. *Increased knowledge elevates an organization's capability, and increased accumulation of organizational internal frictions diminishes its capability*:

$$\forall x, t_0, t \left[O(x) \longrightarrow \right.$$
$$\left\{ (K(x, t) > K(x, t_0)) \wedge (F(x, t) \leq F(x, t_0)) \longrightarrow C(x, t) > C(x, t_0) \right\}$$
$$\wedge \left\{ (K(x, t) \leq K(x, t_0)) \wedge (F(x, t) > F(x, t_0)) \longrightarrow C(x, t) < C(x, t_0) \right\}$$
$$\left. \wedge \left\{ (K(x, t) = K(x, t_0)) \wedge (F(x, t) = F(x, t_0)) \longrightarrow C(x, t) = C(x, t_0) \right\} \right].$$

Assumption 13.5.6. *Improved ties with external actors enhance an organization's position*:

$$\forall x, t_0, t \left[O(x) \longrightarrow \left\{ \{T(x, t) > T(x, t_0) \longrightarrow P(x, t) > P(x, t_0) \} \right. \right.$$
$$\left. \left. \wedge \{T(x, t) = T(x, t_0) \longrightarrow P(x, t) = P(x, t_0) \} \right\} \right].$$

With these assumptions in place, mortality hazards can be related to knowledge, internal friction, and ties—see Figure 13.2. The following pair of lemmas (minor theorems used to derive the main theorems) establishes the connections. Note that they apply only to periods in which organizations lack immunity (either because an organization lacks endowment or because the period of immunity produced by an endowment has ended). During periods of immunity, the hazard is a constant according to Assumption 13.5.2.

---

[12] It would be valuable to develop a more complete formalization of these issues; but doing so here would detract from the main line of argument and formalization.

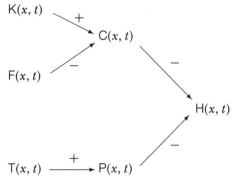

Figure 13.2.   *Schematic representation of the expanded version of the core formalization for organizations lacking immunity. The terms are knowledge* [K(x, t)], *ties* [T(x, t)], *friction* [F(x, t)], *capability* [C(x, t)], *position* [P(x, t)], *and the hazard of mortality* [H(x, t)]. *Source: Hannan (1998). Copyright* © *1998 by the University of Chicago. All rights reserved. Used by permission.*

Lemma 13.5.1.   *When an organization lacks immunity, increased collective knowledge and superior external ties lower its hazard of mortality when internal friction does not increase (from Assumptions 13.5.1–6):*

$$\forall x, t_0, t \left[O(x) \wedge \neg\{IM(x, t_0) \vee IM(x, t)\} \longrightarrow \right.$$
$$\{\{K(x, t) > K(x, t_0) \wedge F(x, t) \leq F(x, t_0) \wedge T(x, t) \geq T(x, t_0)\}$$
$$\vee \{K(x, t) \geq K(x, t_0) \wedge F(x, t) \leq F(x, t_0) \wedge T(x, t) > T(x, t_0)\}$$
$$\left. \longrightarrow H(x, t) < H(x, t_0)\}\right].$$

Lemma 13.5.2.   *When an organization lacks immunity, the growth of internal friction elevates its hazard of mortality when its knowledge and the quality of its ties are constant (from Assumptions 13.5.1–6):*

$$\forall x, t_0, t \left[O(x) \wedge \neg\{IM(x, t_0) \vee IM(x, t)\} \wedge K(x, t) = K(x, t_0) \wedge F(x, t) > F(x, t_0) \right.$$
$$\left. \wedge T(x, t_0) = T(x, t) \longrightarrow H(x, t) > H(x, t_0)\right].$$

13.6 Formalizing the Liabilities of Newness and Adolescence

The liability-of-newness argument, as formalized here, rests on the premise that the processes that improve capability and position—knowledge and the quality of ties—increase monotonically with organizational age.

Assumption 13.6.1. *An organization's stock of knowledge increases monotonically with its age:*

$$\forall x, t_0, t \left[O(x) \wedge A(x, t) > A(x, t_0) \longrightarrow K(x, t) > K(x, t_0) \right].$$

Assumption 13.6.2. *The quality of an organization's external ties increases monotonically with its age:*

$$\forall x, t_0, t \left[O(x) \wedge A(x, t) > A(x, t_0) \longrightarrow T(x, t) > T(x, t_0) \right].$$

The standard argument for the liability of newness does not consider internal friction. For the formalization to remain faithful to the original argument, it should not mix this process with the others. To meet this constraint, this section assumes that an organization's internal friction remains constant over age.

Assumption 13.6.3. *An organization's internal friction does not vary with its age:*

$$\forall x, t_0, t \left[O(x) \longrightarrow F(x, t) = F(x, t_0) \right].$$

These assumptions yield straightforward links between age and capability and quality of position—see Figure 13.3. The following lemmas record the implications of these assumptions for age variations in capability and position.

Lemma 13.6.1. *An organization's capability increases monotonically with its age* (*from Assumptions* 13.5.5 *and* 13.6.1–3):

$$\forall x, t_0, t \left[O(x) \wedge A(x, t) > A(x, t_0) \longrightarrow C(x, t) > C(x, t_0) \right].$$

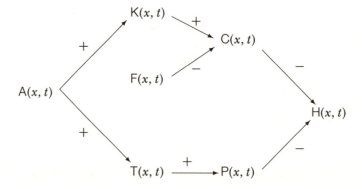

Figure 13.3. *Schematic representation of the liability of newness for organizations lacking immunity. Source: Hannan (1998). Copyright © 1998 by the University of Chicago. All rights reserved. Used by permission.*

Lemma 13.6.2. *An organization's structural position improves monotonically with its age (from Assumptions 13.5.6 and 13.6.2):*

$$\forall x, t_0, t \; \big[O(x) \wedge A(x, t) > A(x, t_0) \longrightarrow P(x, t) > P(x, t_0)\big].$$

The foregoing definitions, assumptions, and lemmas imply Stinchcombe's theorem on the liability of newness as a consequence of age-dependent enhancement of capability and position for the case of organizations lacking endowments.

Theorem 13.6.1 (Stinchcombe 1965). *The liability-of-newness theorem: An unendowed organization's hazard of mortality declines monotonically with its age (from Definition 13.5.1, Assumptions 13.5.1–4, and Lemmas 13.6.1 and 13.6.2):*

$$\forall x, t_0, t \; \big[O(x) \wedge \neg EN(x) \wedge A(x, t) > A(x, t_0) \longrightarrow H(x, t) < H(x, t_0)\big].$$

This formulation also implies a theorem on the liability of adolescence as a consequence of age-dependent enhancement of capability and position for the case of organizations with endowments.

Theorem 13.6.2 (Brüderl and Schüssler 1990; Fichman and Levinthal 1991). *The liability-of-adolescence theorem: An endowed organization's hazard of mortality remains constant during its period of immunity, jumps when its immunity ends, and decreases with further aging but remains above the level during the immunity period (from Definition 13.5.1, Assumptions 13.5.1–4, and Lemmas 13.6.1 and 13.6.2):*

$$\forall x, t_0, t_1, t_2, t_3 \; \big[O(x) \wedge EN(x) \wedge (A(x, t_0) \leq A(x, t_1)) \wedge (A(x, t_1) \leq \epsilon)$$
$$\wedge \, (A(x, t_2) > \epsilon) \wedge (A(x, t_3) > A(x, t_2))$$
$$\longrightarrow H(x, t_2) > H(x, t_3) > H(x, t_1) = H(x, t_0)\big].$$

13.7 Formalizing the Liability of Senescence

Next consider the first of the opposing arguments: the senescence hypothesis. The formalization in this section uses the same general structure as discussed to this point. However, it makes crucial changes in the three assumptions pertaining to the effect of aging on the determinants of organizational performance, Assumptions 13.6.1–3. These three assumptions are replaced with others that reflect the senescence argument as stated in Section 13.2.

The senescence argument emphasizes capability. It identifies processes that diminish capability and argues that these processes increase in strength as organizations age. Here this process is represented by the accumulation of internal frictions. The spirit of the senescence argument suggests that one assume that internal friction increases with age.

Extant statements of the senescence story are silent about the role of knowledge and structural position. Therefore, to represent this argument, assume now that knowledge and the quality of ties to external actors also do not change with age.

Assumption 13.7.1. *An organization's stock of organizational knowledge does not vary with its age (contra Assumption* 13.6.1):

$$\forall x, t_0, t \left[O(x) \longrightarrow K(x, t) = K(x, t_0) \right].$$

Assumption 13.7.2. *The quality of an organization's external ties does not vary with its age (contra Assumption* 13.6.2):

$$\forall x, t_0, t \left[O(x) \longrightarrow T(x, t) = T(x, t_0) \right].$$

Assumption 13.7.3. *An organization's internal friction increases monotonically with its age (revising Assumption* 13.6.3):

$$\forall x, t_0, t \left[O(x) \wedge A(x, t) > A(x, t_0) \longrightarrow F(x, t) > F(x, t_0) \right].$$

With these assumptions about knowledge, position, and friction, only the strength of internal friction depends upon age—see Figure 13.4. These assumptions portray organizations as growing older without growing wiser and accumulating baggage that impedes collective action. The following pair of (trivial) lemmas connects these assumptions to the hazard.

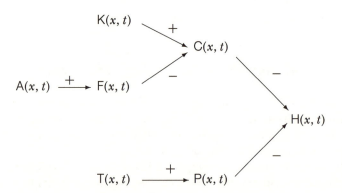

Figure 13.4. *Schematic representation of the liability of senescence argument for organizations lacking immunity. Source: Hannan (1998). Copyright © 1998 by the University of Chicago. All rights reserved. Used by permission.*

Lemma 13.7.1. *An organization's capability decreases monotonically with its age* (*from Assumptions* 13.5.5, 13.7.1, *and* 13.7.3):

$$\forall x, t_0, t \left[O(x) \wedge A(x, t) > A(x, t_0) \longrightarrow C(x, t) < C(x, t_0) \right].$$

Lemma 13.7.2. *An organization's structural position does not vary with its age* (*from Assumptions* 13.5.6 *and* 13.7.2):

$$\forall x, t_0, t \left[O(x) \wedge A(x, t) > A(x, t_0) \longrightarrow P(x, t) = P(x, t_0) \right].$$

The assumptions in this section imply *positive* age dependence in mortality hazard for an unendowed organization (contra Theorem 13.6.1).

Theorem 13.7.1 (Barron, West, and Hannan 1994). *The senescence theorem for unendowed organizations: An unendowed organization's hazard of mortality increases monotonically with its age* (*from Definition* 13.5.1, *Assumptions* 13.5.1-4, *and Lemmas* 13.7.1 *and* 13.7.2):

$$\forall x, t_0, t \left[O(x) \wedge \neg EN(x) \wedge A(x, t) > A(x, t_0) \longrightarrow H(x, t) > H(x, t_0) \right].$$

Previous work did not consider the relevance of endowments in the context of senescence. The formulation in this section carries over to the case of endowed organizations. There is, however, a slight difference: due to initial immunity, the hazard does not rise monotonically at all ages for endowed organizations. Instead, the hazard is constant during the period of immunity and then rises monotonically with age.

Theorem 13.7.2. *The senescence theorem for endowed organizations: An endowed organization's hazard of mortality remains constant during the period of immunity and increases monotonically with its age once immunity ends* (*from Definition* 13.5.1, *Assumptions* 13.5.1-4, *and Lemmas* 13.7.1 *and* 13.7.2):

$$\forall x, t_0, t_1, t_2, t_3 \left[O(x) \wedge EN(x) \wedge (A(x, t_0) \leq A(x, t_1)) \wedge (A(x, t_1) \leq \epsilon) \right.$$
$$\wedge (A(x, t_2) > \epsilon) \wedge (A(x, t_3) > A(x, t_2))$$
$$\left. \longrightarrow H(x, t_3) > H(x, t_2) > H(x, t_1) = H(x, t_0) \right].$$

The reasoning underlying the claims of liabilities of newness and senescence run parallel, but with differing assumptions about the role of age in shaping capability and position. Each story can be regarded as a special case of a more general story of aging both enhancing and diminishing capability, depending on the relative strength of the links of age with the cumulation of knowledge and the intensification of internal friction.

13.8 Formalizing Alignment, Drift, and Obsolescence

This section presents a modification of the formalization to address the implications of imprinting and obsolescence. Making this shift involves some changes in the formalisms. The two theories of age dependence considered in the previous section fit nicely with statements made in terms of functions because the theoretical notions concern processes that increase continuously with age. The obsolescence argument builds on the image of some things (environments) shifting and other things (core features of organizations) getting stuck, and it seems best to represent this argument with predicates that tell whether certain objects have shifted and whether others have not. Because the modeling structure differs from that used in the previous section, this section begins (nearly) anew.

Several features of the core of the foregoing formalization carry over. These are Meaning Postulates 13.5.1 (age is nonnegative) and 13.5.2 (age is monotonic) and the definitions of the functions and predicates. The definition of endowment as providing temporary immunity (Definition 13.5.1) and three assumptions about endowments, Assumption 13.5.1 (unendowed organizations lack immunity), Assumption 13.5.2 (the hazard is constant within periods of immunity), and Assumption 13.5.3 (the hazard is lower during periods of immunity) are also retained.

The theory to be addressed in this section concerns the consequences of the combination of environmental change and inertia rather than genuine aging. The key modeling issue here is how to formalize the relevant part of the imprinting hypothesis. One approach, which is used here, considers external alignment, the fit between an organization's structural features and capabilities and the demands of its external environment (Chapter 17). The obsolescence story posits that *capabilities are specific to environments*.[13] Refining obsolete routines (by, for instance, learning by doing) and better coordinating activities that support obsolete routines do not have mortality-diminishing effects. In other words, external misalignment can be regarded as a mismatch of capabilities and environments. This idea is represented by the predicate, $AL(x, t)$, which tells whether an object, x, is (or is not) aligned with its environment at time t. That is, an organization finds itself either aligned or not aligned with its environment.

Next, consider the issue of environmental change, which drives the obsolescence process. Suppose that the environment can occupy different states at different times, meaning that it imposes different adaptive demands at different times. Does it make sense to think of an organization

---

[13] This idea seems implicit in the theoretical treatments of the liability of newness. However, its implications seem not to have been appreciated.

as being aligned with more than one state of the environment? If the environments impose similar adaptive demands, then it does. However, the notion of alignment also suggests that an organization's capability cannot be aligned with dissimilar states of the environment. In other words, dissimilarity can be defined in terms of alignment.[14] Two states of the environment impose dissimilar adaptive demands if an organization cannot be aligned with both.

This idea can be represented with the three-place predicate, $DS(x, t_0, t)$, which tells whether the environments at times t_0 and t are dissimilar for organization x.[15]

Definition 13.8.1. *Two states of the environment are dissimilar if and only if organizations cannot be aligned with each:*

$$\forall t_0, t \left[DS(x, t_0, t) \longleftrightarrow \left(O(x) \rightarrow \neg \{ AL(x, t_0) \leftrightarrow AL(x, t) \} \right) \right].$$

In the theoretical context, this assumption means that the alternative states of the environment pose very different adaptive demands. Therefore, this formulation applies to situations in which the states of the environment differ greatly when compared with the repertoires of organizational routines available to the members of the population of organizations.

Two properties of the dissimilarity predicate need to be noted. First, there is a piece of "background knowledge" that tells that any environment is similar with itself.

Background Assumption 13.8.1. *The environment at any time is similar with itself:*

$$\forall t \left[\neg DS(x, t, t) \right].$$

Second, Background Assumption 15.8.1 and Definition 15.8.1 imply the following.

Lemma 13.8.1. *The dissimilarity relation is symmetric:*

$$\forall t_1, t_2 \left[DS(x, t_1, t_2) \longleftrightarrow DS(x, t_2, t_1) \right].$$

A strong-form version of the imprinting hypothesis posits that alignment is maximal at (or shortly after) founding, because organization-builders can make use of state-of-the art designs and adapt to prevailing cultural understandings (Hannan et al. 1996). That is, designers have the opportunity to tune structures and routines to the state of the envi-

---

[14] Chapters 16 and 17 present a more thorough analysis of issues of alignment.

[15] Obviously some rule must be used in practice to determine how different two environments must be for them to be considered "dissimilar." One could replace the predicate with a function that tells the degree of dissimilarity of the two environments. However, this choice would make the formalization more complex; and it is not needed to convey the main idea.

ronment at the time of founding. If the environment changes, then the inertial forces on structures, processes, and capabilities restrict the ability of organizations to realign with the new environment.[16]

Assumption 13.8.1. *An organization is aligned with the state of the environment at its time of founding*:

$$\forall x, t \left[O(x) \wedge (A(x, t) = 0) \longrightarrow AL(x, t) \right].$$

According to theories of alignment, organizations have superior capabilities in environments with which they align.

Assumption 13.8.2. *An organization's capability is higher in the state of the environment to which it is aligned*:

$$\forall x, t_0, t \left[O(x) \wedge AL(x, t_0) \wedge DS(x, t_0, t) \longrightarrow C(x, t_0) > C(x, t) \right].$$

Representing the idea of obsolescence requires specification of a time path of change in the relevant environment. According to the general idea of obsolescence, organizations get stuck with core features that fit the environment less well with the passage of time. Although many different scenarios of environmental change are consistent with this image, this chapter considers only one simple case that seems to capture the key insight: *drift*. If an environment drifts, its states at (widely) different times are (strongly) dissimilar. When an environment drifts, the probability that it returns to some previous state is vanishingly small. (In the formalization, this event is assumed to be impossible.) For instance, technological change involves drift: technical standards change over time and do not return to earlier standards.

Environmental drift differs from the broader category of environmental change. Environmental change sometimes involve repeated shifts among alternative states with the possibility of returns to earlier states. For instance, sociological models of niche width (Hannan and Freeman 1989; Péli 1997) consider environments that alternate between two states, e.g., feast or famine. When an organization or population of organizations finds itself misaligned with the current state of such an environment, it should not be regarded as "obsolete." The concept of obsolescence seems most meaningful in the case of drifting environments. The remainder of the formalization specializes to the case of drifting environments.

---

[16] Of course, many organizations begin with poor designs and poor alignment with even the founding environment. Unobserved heterogeneity in initial design and initial alignment is a well-understood source of spurious negative age dependence of the so-called mover-stayer form (Chapter 7). To keep the focus on the role of age, we do not consider such misalignment here.

The notion of drift means that an organization's environment might remain in the close neighborhood of a given position for some time but will eventually move beyond the neighborhood. Suppose the neighborhood boundary encloses the set of similar environmental states (from the perspective of the organization). Then, as long as the environment stays within the neighborhood, the various states of the environment are similar. Suppose that a drifting environment does not return to its initial neighborhood once it leaves and that there is a (common) age, σ, at which the environment drifts beyond a given initial neighborhood. Then, age and dissimilarity are linked:

Assumption 13.8.3. *Environmental drift: The environments at times separated by more than σ are dissimilar:*

$$\forall x, t_0, t \left[O(x) \wedge (A(x, t_0) = 0) \longrightarrow \{(A(x, t) > \sigma) \leftrightarrow DS(x, t_0, t)\} \right].$$

13.9 Formalizing the Liability of Obsolescence

Existing statements of the obsolescence argument consider capability but not positional advantage. To represent these arguments here, we continue to assume that quality of position does not play a role, by weakening Lemma 13.5.1 from the previous formulation to apply only to capability and mortality hazards and implementing the lemma as an assumption in this formulation:

Assumption 13.9.1. *Superiority in capability lowers the hazard of mortality when an organization lacks immunity (specializing Assumption 13.5.1):*

$$\forall x, t_0, t \left[O(x) \wedge \neg\{IM(x, t_0) \vee IM(x, t)\} \wedge C(x, t) > C(x, t_0) \right.$$
$$\left. \longrightarrow H(x, t_0) > H(x, t) \right].$$

Combining the assumptions of environmental drift and constancy of position with the assumptions in Section 13.8 yields two theorems about obsolescence. One concerns unendowed organizations, and the second concerns endowed organizations. Both tell that the mortality rates of old organizations exceed those of young ones. The only difference is the profile of positive age dependence. Age dependence is monotonic positive over the whole age range for unendowed organizations. For endowed organizations, the hazard remains constant during the period of immunity and it rises monotonically with age after immunity ends.

Theorem 13.9.1 (Barron, West, and Hannan 1994). *The obsolescence theorem for unendowed organizations: An unendowed organization's hazard of mortality* *increases with age in a drifting environment (from Definitions 13.5.1 and 13.8.1, Background Assumption 13.8.1, and Assumptions 13.5.1–3, 13.6.1, and 13.8.1–3):*

$$\forall x, t_0, t_1, t_2 \left[O(x) \wedge \neg EN(x) \wedge (A(x, t_0) = 0) \wedge (A(x, t_1) \leq \sigma) \wedge (A(x, t_2) > \sigma) \right.$$
$$\left. \wedge (\sigma > 0) \longrightarrow H(x, t_2) > H(x, t_1) \right].$$

Once again, a parallel theorem holds for endowed organizations. However, this case involves a slight complication because two parameters, ϵ and σ, matter. The following pair of lemmas covers the two relevant cases ($\epsilon < \sigma$ and $\epsilon \geq \sigma$).

Lemma 13.9.1. *When $\epsilon < \sigma$ in a drifting environment, an endowed organization's hazard of mortality remains constant until age reaches ϵ, then jumps to a higher level, then jumps again at age σ (from Definitions 13.5.1 and 13.8.1, Background Assumption 13.8.1, and Assumptions 13.5.1–3, 13.6.1, and 13.8.1–3):*

$$\forall x, t_0, t_1, t_2, t_3 \left[O(x) \wedge EN(x) \wedge (A(x, t_0) = 0) \wedge (A(x, t_1) \leq \epsilon) \wedge (A(x, t_2) > \epsilon) \right.$$
$$\wedge (A(x, t_2) \leq \sigma) \wedge (A(x, t_3) > \sigma) \wedge (\sigma > \epsilon) \wedge (\epsilon > 0)$$
$$\left. \longrightarrow H(x, t_3) > H(x, t_2) > H(x, t_1) = H(x, t_0) \right].$$

Lemma 13.9.2. *When $\epsilon \geq \sigma$, an endowed organization's hazard of mortality remains constant until age ϵ and then jumps to a higher level in a drifting environment (from Definitions 13.5.1 and 13.8.1, Background Assumption 13.8.1, and Assumptions 13.5.1–3, 13.6.1, and 13.8.1–3.1.3):*

$$\forall x, t_0, t_1, t_2 \left[O(x) \wedge EN(x) \wedge (A(x, t_0) = 0) \wedge (A(x, t_1) \leq \epsilon) \wedge (A(x, t_2) > \epsilon) \right.$$
$$\left. \wedge (\epsilon \geq \sigma) \wedge (\sigma > 0) \longrightarrow H(x, t_2) > H(x, t_1) = H(x, t_0) \right].$$

Obviously, the hazard at older ages exceeds the hazard during the youthful (immunized) period.

Theorem 13.9.2. *The obsolescence theorem for endowed organizations: In a drifting environment, an endowed organization's hazard of mortality is constant during the period of immunity; beyond the period of immunity, the hazard rises with age (from Lemmas 13.9.2 and 13.9.3):*

$$\forall x, t_0, t_1, t_2, t_3 \left[O(x) \wedge EN(x) \wedge (A(x, t_0) = 0) \wedge (A(x, t_1) \leq \epsilon) \wedge (A(x, t_2) > \epsilon) \right.$$
$$\left. \wedge (\epsilon > 0) \longrightarrow H(x, t_2) > H(x, t_1) = H(x, t_0) \right].$$

In retrospect, the seemingly straightforward issue of age dependence in organizational mortality turns out on close inspection to be anything but simple. Inconsistency among theories and empirical findings abounds. Such inconsistency reflects the protean nature of the concept of organizational aging.

In one major line of work, aging means learning and solidifying external position. A contrary stream of research regards aging as increasing constraint on collective action, with the buildup of internal friction, precedent, and political deals combining to impede timely and reliable performance. The first set of formalizations presented here shows that these two lines of thinking can be cast as special cases of a general formulation holding that aging shapes the cumulation of knowledge, internal friction, and other constraints, as well as the quality of external ties. The formalization also treats endowments as generating temporary (possibly partial) immunity from mortality. Adding endowments to the picture does not really change the substantive conclusion for the senescence argument. However, it does matter in the liability-of-newness setup, changing the monotonic negative relation between age and the hazard to a nonmonotonic relation, with a liability of adolescence.

The general framework in which these three cases are embedded might serve as a basis for reconciling the conflicting arguments. Allowing the valences of the various effects of aging to vary systematically among different kinds of organizational populations and different contexts would help specify the conditions for each type of liability to operate. Such an effort would also undoubtedly make sense of inconsistencies in empirical findings.[17]

A radically different idea about aging lies at the heart of much of the theory and research on the determinants of organizational mortality. This is the idea that aging per se does not affect the hazard of mortality; instead, age tracks the fit between an organization and its environment. This image builds on ideas of imprinting and structural inertia. According to the imprinting hypothesis, organizations best match their external environments at the time of their founding. According to structural inertia theory, subsequent change to the core of these imprinted features is hard and risky to the organization's survival chances. If environments drift over time, then inert organizations fall further behind as they age—they become obsolete. Under this scenario, the hazard of mortality for old organizations exceeds the hazard for young ones.

The second set of formalizations offered here attempts to represent the logic of this general argument. In this set, age tracks the dissimilarity between an organization's current environment and its founding environment. This argument is specialized to the case of drifting environments, using the idea that there is a (common) age at which the environment becomes sufficiently different from the founding environment that it imposes fundamentally different demands on the organization. Organizations are

---

[17] Pólos, Hannan, and Kamps (1999) have used a more complicated form of logical formalization, using nonmonotonic logic, to begin this kind of effort.

assumed to be aligned well with their founding environments and not to be aligned with environments that are dissimilar to it. In the version presented above, an organization's capability is assumed to be higher when it is aligned with its environment. Thus, alignment unravels because environments drift and inert organizations continue to rely on their old structures and processes. Age tracks environmental drift in this formulation. Hence capability declines as organizations age and the hazard of mortality rises with age. Another, more complex version of this general argument is discussed in the next chapter.

14

Size Dependence

THERE SEEMS TO BE broad agreement that a liability of smallness characterizes the organizational world. Economists routinely build theories based on
economies of scale; these models posit that large firms possess advantages
in terms of cost and other matters. In organizational theory, Hannan and
Freeman (1977) argue that the appropriate time scale for a selection process increases with the size of organizations under consideration (which is
another way of saying that mortality rates fall with size). Large organizations can retrench by reducing their scale of operations over long periods
of poor performance before they are forced to disband. Small organizations have little room to contract; and they fail quickly once fortunes decline.

Insofar as we can determine, most empirical studies about the liability
of smallness measure organizational size in natural units, on an absolute
metric (e.g., dollar value of assets, number of employees, barrels of output).
Such an approach seems best suited to analyzing cross sections or brief histories during which the size distribution in the population remains (nearly)
constant. Over the full histories of an organizational population, however,
the average size of firms typically grows by several orders of magnitude.
The largest automobile manufacturer in the world in 1900, for instance,
would be a tiny firm in today's industry. If large scale conveys advantages
leading to lowered mortality rates, what are we to make of this comparison?
Are these advantages of scale absolute or relative? In other words, does a
firm gain (dis)advantage by virtue of its absolute size or by its position in
the size distribution?

The theory reviewed and developed in the previous chapter indicates
that positional advantages ought to matter. Large size relative to other organizations in a population likely conveys advantage in intrapopulation
competition. This advantage might stem from scale economies in production, which allow larger firms to enjoy lower average costs. Or it might
come from disproportionate influence over suppliers and distributors. In

either case, large size relative to competitors might increase growth rates and lower rates of mortality.

Even if size matters most in this relative sense, very small absolute size might still matter. As Levinthal (1991) recognizes, very small firms exist close to an extinction boundary. Organizations close to such an extinction boundary are very likely to be destroyed by a single random shock, e.g., loss of a key contract or key employee.[1] This risk of very small size does *not* depend on the sizes of the other firms in the population. At the other end of the spectrum, large absolute size gives an organization leverage over its trading partners, regulators, and the like. This effect, too, should persist even if the population contains other large organizations. So, absolute organizational size might affect growth and mortality, even if relative size matters. Obviously, size dependence in organizational processes is potentially more complex than the simple effect suggested by the liability-of-smallness ideas.

Recent organizational research on age-varying size and life chances has also diverged in conceptualizing and measuring organizational size. One strand of research regards size as *capacity*. Examples include: storage capacities of wineries (Delacroix and Swaminathan 1991), production capacity of breweries (Carroll and Swaminathan 1992), license restrictions on enrollment of day-care centers (Baum and Oliver 1991), and room counts of hotels (Baum and Mezias 1992). The other strand regards size as *scale of operations*. Examples include: number of subscribers of telephone companies (Barnett 1990) and assets of banks (Han 1998) and savings and loan associations (Haveman 1992).

The notion of capacity relates to physical limits on the scale of operations. A winery builds storage facilities; a day-care center rents a physical space of certain dimensions; a hotel is constructed with a certain number of rooms. Such capacity constraints are limiting on organizations only as the scale of their operations begins to outgrow the physical plant. Organizations, especially in decline, can operate far below capacity: a day-care center with a permit to enroll a stipulated number of children might operate below capacity, or a large hotel might fail to rent any rooms and remain empty. In such cases, current capacity tells us little about the current

---

[1] Levinthal (1991) formalized this idea as a diffusion process of "organizational capital," which is presumably related to size (at least when measured appropriately). This model assumes that organizations begin with differing stocks of capital and experience random drift in capital over their lifetimes. Organizational mortality occurs when the drift in capital reaches some lower bound. If changes in capital are governed by a diffusion process (meaning that huge jumps cannot take place in a brief period), then the probability of mortality in any period obviously declines with the stock of capital (and thus, perhaps, with size). This formalization captures the essence of the idea that an effect of current size on mortality rates reflects differences in initial endowments and in histories of success and failure in garnering resources from the environment.

scale of operations. Moreover, capacity constraints change discontinuously, even when the scale of operations changes continuously, both in growth and decline.[2] There are lags in adjustment of capacity to growth and decline in scale. For both of these reasons, we think that scale of operations tells more than capacity about an organization's success in acquiring resources from its environment and its capacity to withstand periods of ill fortune. For these varied reasons, we attend in this chapter especially to studies that measure size in terms of scale of actual operations.

This chapter takes up questions about size dependence in organizational processes of growth and mortality. It starts by examining models of growth and then turns to mortality analyses. In both processes, questions about size dependence are closely tied to those about age dependence because new organizations tend to be small and older ones, large. This tight relationship leads us to develop model specifications and theoretical analyses that deal with size and age simultaneously.

14.1 Size and Growth Rates

Models for Growth Rates

Theory and research about the effects of size on organizational growth rates were developed in the context of analyses of firm size distributions. Modern research on the subject began with Gibrat's law, which claims that the sizes of firms, like those of other "naturally occurring" economic units, follow a lognormal distribution (Gibrat 1931). The main idea is the "law of proportionate effect," which holds that growth is proportional to size and the factor of proportionality is random (Kapteyn 1903).[3] Let S_{it} denote the size of an organization in period t. Assume that the size of each organization in each period is a multiple of its size in the previous period:

$$S_{it} = S_{i,t-1}(1 + u_{it}), \tag{14.1}$$

where u_{it} is a random growth rate. According to (14.1), size at any time depends upon initial size, S_{i0}, and the history of random growth rates:

$$S_{it} = S_{i0}(1 + u_{it}) \cdots (1 + u_{i0}). \tag{14.2}$$

---

[2] Barnett et al. (2000) estimate a model for the growth in membership of research and development consortia that takes account of the temporal discontinuities in some kinds of growth processes.

[3] Useful surveys of the genesis of this model can be found in Aitchison and Brown (1957), Steindl (1965), and Sutton (1997).

If the periods are sufficiently short that growth rates are small (or if time is regarded as a continuous parameter), then (14.2) can be well approximated by

$$\ln S_{it} = \ln S_{i0} + u_{it} + \cdots + u_{i0}. \tag{14.3}$$

Gibrat's model for the growth of firms assumes that the random growth rate, u_{it}, (1) is independent from period to period and among firms in each period; (2) is independent of current size ("Gibrat's law"); and (3) reflects the operation of many forces each with small effect, which means that it can be approximated by a normal distribution. That is, Gibrat assumed that the u_{it} are independent, identically distributed, normal random variables with mean μ and variance σ^2. Then it follows that

$$\ln S_{it} = \ln S_0 + \epsilon_{it}, \tag{14.4}$$

where

$$\epsilon_{it} \sim N(\mu t, \sigma^2 t). \tag{14.5}$$

Gibrat's law produces explosive growth in the sense that both the mean and the variance of log-size grow without bound as time passes. A stream of research has explored ways of stabilizing size distributions within the general framework developed by Gibrat, because empirical size distributions are often extremely stable. The key innovation, due to Simon and his collaborators in a series of classic papers (Simon 1955; Simon and Bonini 1958; Ijiri and Simon 1977), introduced an entry process into the smallest size category to stabilize the process.[4]

Simon (1955) initially proposed two models (in the context of explaining distributions of word frequencies in texts). Both models assume that growth is random across a set of ordered size categories with rates following Gibrat's law and entries occurring at a constant rate in (only) the smallest size category. The first model considers an expanding text in which new words enter and existing words remain. The second considers a text of fixed length in which words enter and vanish. The first model is the one that Simon and collaborators applied to distributions of firm sizes.

The first model (of an expanding text) implies that the upper tail of the distribution converges to a Pareto distribution.[5] This distribution implies the famous rank-size rule: a log-linear relationship between rank and

---

[4] Another approach, sketched by Kalecki (1945) and developed at length by Steindl (1965), introduces a negative relationship between the growth rate and size to ensure that the variance of the distribution remains stable.

[5] The second model implies that the upper tail of the distribution converges to Fisher's log-series distribution.

size (in the upper tail). Applications of Simon's first model relied on plots of log-rank against log-size to check the fit of the model to data. Simon and Bonini (1958) showed that the model provides a reasonably good fit to data on diverse giant industrial firms in the United States. In later research, Simon and collaborators noted that plots of log-rank against log-size are convex (from below). Ijiri and Simon (1977) concluded that a combination of autocorrelation in growth rates and mergers accounted for this departure from linearity.[6]

Simon's second model, developed much more fully by Steindl (1965), is closer to the one used in contemporary research. Indeed, the set of empirical studies discussed next implement versions of this model.

Empirical Findings

Gibrat's law served as the focus of much empirical research. In a study of firms quoted on the London Stock Exchange, Hart and Prais (1956) concluded that Gibrat's law was not violated. But, in a study of steel, petroleum, rubber, tire, and automobile industries, Mansfield (1962) found that both growth rates and the variance of growth rates decline with size, violating Gibrat's law. Since those two initial studies, a debate has persisted. Some research has supported Gibrat's law; some has indicated that growth rates are size-independent but the variance diminishes with size (Hart 1962; Hymer and Paskigian 1962); some find that Gibrat's law holds well for large organizations but not for small ones (Engwall 1968; Aaronovitch and Sawyer 1975; Hall 1987); and some find that Gibrat's law fails, with growth rates diminishing with increasing size[7] (Evans 1987; Hall 1987). Sutton (1997) provides a useful summary and analysis of the findings in the economics literature.

Most of the research on these issues in economics uses the multipopulation design, which mixes all kinds of organizations (see Chapter 5). What happens when analysts follow the single-population strategy in analyzing growth processes? Hannan et al. (1994) tested the applicability of Gibrat's law for populations of credit unions in New York by estimating models of the following form:

$$\ln(S_{i,t+1}) = \theta \ln(S_{it}) + r_{it} + \epsilon_{i,t+1}, \qquad r_{it} = \mathbf{x}'_{it}\pi. \qquad (14.6)$$

---

[6] In this and related simulations, these researchers demonstrated that adding various complications does not have much impact on the qualitative implications of Simon's first model. However, each simulation allowed firms to grow but not contract; and most of the simulations excluded the possibility of mortality. So the model, as implemented in organizational research, was a highly restricted one.

[7] Singh and Whittington (1975) find that growth rates *rise* (weakly but significantly) with size.

Notice that this model implies that there is an intrinsic growth rate, r_{it}, that is determined by the values of covariates measuring variations in environmental conditions and properties of individual organizations. The regression (14.6) enables a test of Gibrat's law, as defined in (14.4), as can be seen by subtracting $\ln(S_{it})$ from both sides of (14.6):

$$\ln(S_{i,t+1}) - \ln(S_{it}) = \theta \ln(S_{it}) - \ln(S_{it}) + r_{it} + \epsilon_{i,t+1},$$

$$\ln\left(\frac{S_{i,t+1}}{S_{it}}\right) = (\theta - 1)\ln(S_{it}) + r_{it} + \epsilon_{i,t+1}, \tag{14.7}$$

$$\frac{S_{i,t+1}}{S_{it}} = S_{it}^{\theta-1} + \exp(r_{it} + \epsilon_{i,t+1}).$$

In this regression model, $\theta = 1$ means that Gibrat's law holds (conditional on the values of the covariates). If θ falls below 1, then organizational growth rates decline with size; values of θ that exceed unity indicate that large organizations have relatively high growth rates. Equation (14.6) also shows how to interpret the effects of covariates included in the growth rate, r_{it}. There is a log-linear relationship between proportionate growth, $S_{i,t+1}/S_{it}$, and covariates. Consequently, the magnitude of the effect of change in a covariate depends on organizational size as well as on the effect parameters.

Growth rates of New York credit unions were not simply proportionate to size (Hannan et al. 1994). The estimated effects of lagged log-size fall below unity (the value required for Gibrat's law); in each case, the estimate falls significantly below unity. This finding agrees with much research on organizational growth in the economics literature cited above. To understand the meaning of this finding, recall that this analysis is based on a proportional growth model. So even if large organizations grow more than smaller ones in absolute terms (which they usually do), their percentage growth is smaller on average. The estimated departures from Gibrat's law imply that the differences in average growth rates of large and small credit unions have been considerable. Take, for instance, the estimated effect for New York City: 0.886. In terms of the growth rate, this means that, on average,

$$\frac{S_{t+1}}{S_t} = S_t^{0.886-1} = S_t^{-0.114}.$$

Given the actual distribution of starting sizes, a useful point of comparison is a union with $S = 1{,}000$. A union with $S = 100{,}000$ has an average growth rate slightly less than half (0.45) as high. A union with $S = 100{,}000{,}000$ has an average growth rate about a third as large. Thus, over the range of historically relevant values, differences in growth rates due to size are on the order of two-fold or three-fold differences.

Barnett and Sorenson (1998) conducted a similar study using data on all retail banks in Illinois (except Chicago) from 1900 to 1993. They found that "except for the first few years, age and size dependence appear relatively constant" (Barnett and Sorenson 1998, 32). In particular, this study suggests that violations of Gibrat's law might be restricted to newly founded organizations. Han (1998) reported that growth rates actually increase with age for Japanese banks. So, even the results for even quite sharply defined populations within the financial services sector disagree considerably about the relationship of age and growth. Two other studies find the more usual pattern of growth rates declining with age: Barnett's (1994) study of telephone companies and Barnett, Mischke, and Ocasio's (2000) study of research and development consortia. So, with the exceptions noted, the population-based studies tend to agree with the multipopulation studies that growth rates decline with organizational age.

14.2 Age, Size, and Mortality

The assumption of a liability of smallness in organizational mortality builds on a thin empirical base. Although many studies in corporate demography report mortality models with effects of size included in the specification, few of these use complete size data over the lifetimes of *all* organizations in a population over its history.[8] Moreover, virtually all studies rely on simple specifications of size dependence, consisting of inclusion of size or log-size as a covariate in a proportional-hazard model.

The reported empirical studies do, however, tend to confirm a liability of smallness. This is the case for both studies with limited observation on size as well as those with complete data. Of the latter studies, for instance, Ranger-Moore (1997), Banaszak-Holl (1991), Delacroix and Swaminathan (1991), Baum and Mezias (1992), and Dobrev (1998) all report significant negative effects of size on mortality rates. Two studies (Barnett 1990; Boone et al. 2000) report nonsignificant negative effects. Only Haveman (1992) reports a significant positive effect (in an analysis of data with extreme left truncation).

Three recent studies recast the effect of size on mortality rates in terms of the Hannan–Freeman (1977) hypothesis that life chances of organiza-

---

[8]Failure of most previous studies to account for variations in size over organizational lifetimes does not reflect a lack of attention to this possible specification bias. It reflects the great difficulty of finding data on sizes of all organizations in a population over its history. Nonetheless, research has begun to accumulate (as we discuss) that collects the appropriate data and estimates models that relate mortality rates to age and size, with size measured repeatedly over the life spans of all organizations in a population (over some segment of the population's history).

tions are poor in the center of size distributions (Chapter 12). Wholey et al. (1992) find that this is the case for mortality rates of the subpopulation of group-practice health maintenance organizations in the United States during 1976–1991. For the other subpopulation, independent practice associations, size has a monotonic negative effect on mortality rates. Amburgey et al. (1994) fit a third-order polynomial in size to mortality rates and find that rates are elevated in the middle of the size range. These results suggest interesting possibilities. But they are hard to interpret, because they do not separate the effect of size from the effect of relative position in the distribution. Han (1998) found that relative size of banks in Japan (and separately in Tokyo) had an inverted-U-shaped relationship with the mortality rate, as the size-localized competition theory predicts.

Controlled Comparisons

Note that size variations might account for the observed low mortality rates of old organizations: organizations tend to grow with age and mortality rates decline with size. Consider, for example, the 21 studies with what we consider the best designs and data collection. These studies all report results from analyses relating organizational mortality rates to age and size, with size measured repeatedly over the life spans of all (or nearly all) organizations in a population and size and age having proportionate effects.[9]

Five studies find monotonic negative effects of age, even after controlling for age-varying organizational size. These are studies of savings and loan associations in California, 1977–1987 (Haveman 1992), California wineries, 1946–1984 (Delacroix, Swaminathan, and Solt 1989), New York State life insurance companies and assessment companies, 1881–1931 (Lehrman 1994), producers of certain recently developed medical devices over the histories of the subindustries, 1952–1989 (Mitchell 1994), and American automobile manufacturers, 1885–1981 (Carroll et al. 1996).

Four studies find a variation on the pattern of negative age dependence: an inverted-U pattern of age dependence after controlling for age-varying size. These include studies of American women's and racial/ethnic nationwide activist organizations, 1950–1985 (Minkoff 1993), early Pennsylvania telephone companies (Barnett 1994), newly founded firms in diverse industries in Bavaria (Brüderl et al. 1996), and American peace-movement organizations, 1988–1992 (Edwards and Marullo 1995). The usual explanation for this pattern relies on the initial resource endowments of organizations, which can sustain them through the first few months (or perhaps years) of life regardless of their longrun viability. That is, even very poorly adapted organizations persist until they exhaust their initial endowments.

---

[9]This section and the next are modified and updated from Hannan et al. (1998a).

Twelve studies find positive age dependence once age variations in organizational size have been taken into account. This is the case for New York life insurance companies, 1860–1937 (Ranger-Moore 1997), Manhattan banks, 1840–1980 (Banaszak-Holl 1991), day-care centers and nurseries in Toronto, 1971–1987 (Baum and Oliver 1991), American brewpubs and microbreweries, 1975–1990 (Carroll and Swaminathan 1992), Manhattan hotels, 1898–1990 (Baum and Mezias 1992), American credit unions, 1980–1989 (Amburgey et al. 1994), New York City credit unions, 1914–1990 (Barron et al. 1994), Illinois banks (excluding Chicago), 1900–1995 (Barnett and Hansen 1996), commercial banks in Tokyo, 1867–1985 (Han 1998), Dutch auditing companies, 1896–1992 (Boone et al. 2000), American investment banks, 1920–1950 (Park and Podolny 1998), and American professional sports leagues, 1871–1997 (Dobbs 1999).

Assessing the Pattern

What can we conclude from these studies? A natural way to group them combines studies reporting monotonic negative age dependence with those showing inverted-U-shaped age dependence, because both imply that the mortality rates of old organizations are lower than those of younger ones, and combines those with monotonic positive and U-shaped relationships. Giving equal weight to each study, this grouping yields a slight advantage (12 to 9) for positive age dependence. In our view, however, not all of the studies deserve equal weight in informing issues of age dependence. Moreover, we think that several technical and substantive matters need to be clarified before the joint effect of age and size on mortality rates can be clearly understood. We focus here on the proportional specification of the effects of organizational size.[10]

Almost all of the studies assume that effects of size and age are separable. More precisely, they assume that the effects of age and size are proportional in the sense of Cox (1975). This means that the mortality rate (at any age and size) can be represented as the product of a first component that depends only on age and a second that depends only on size. Such an assumption might not be warranted for at least two reasons. First, large size (absolute or relative) might have a more powerful bearing on the mortality chances of older organizations. This is so because large, old organizations are more likely to have accumulated slack—a set of unused resources, which provide a buffer against adversity, Second, large, old organizations have established networks of suppliers, buyers, and distributors.

---

[10] Other issues dealt with in the analysis include (1) the conceptualization and measurement of organizational size [relative and absolute], (2) variations in organizational form, and (3) the truncation of observation schemes. See Hannan et al. (1998a) for full discussion of these matters.

Actors in this network partly share the fate of the large, old organization; and consequently they are more likely to absorb or share risks, especially in the face of crisis.

14.3 Automobile Manufacturing Populations

Along with Stanislav Dobrev and Joon Han, we studied automobile industries to produce a sharp contrast with the financial service industries (that have been the source of the best data on the issues of age and size dependence in mortality).[11] In particular, unlike banks, life insurance companies, and credit unions, automobile manufacturers did not grow primarily through recruitment in social networks and were not limited strongly by regulatory restrictions. Many firms also entered automobile production as established manufacturers of other products, especially bicycles, carriages, and engines. Comparing these de alio entrants and de novo entrants allows us to examine the implications of alternative entry modes for age variation in mortality processes. For both reasons, analysis of the effects of age and size on mortality rates of automobile manufacturers might reveal the limits of the prior research discussed above.[12]

The analysis covers the mortality experience of firms in the automobile industries of Britain, France, Germany, and the United States. It examines nearly the full history of these industries, from 1885 (the start of the industry) through 1981 (the last year of full coverage from our most comprehensive source of data). As mentioned in earlier chapters, the national populations of automobile manufacturers contained many more firms than people would imagine: 995 firms in Britain, 828 in France, 373 in Germany, and 2,197 in the United States. Not unexpectedly, most of these firms were small, short-lived, and obscure.

The data sources did not always tell exactly what happened to most firms when they dropped from the set of producers, especially in the European populations. This is invariably the case when spells of automobile

---

[11] This section is adapted from Hannan et al. (1998a).

[12] At a more general level, our efforts here represent an attempt to identify and measure the major sources of heterogeneity in organizational mortality rates. This is important, because uncontrolled unobserved heterogeneity has long been known to generate spurious negative age dependence (Tuma and Hannan 1984). As better data and research designs become available, organizational researchers can turn previously unobserved characteristics into observed ones in analyses of mortality processes. In this case, we focus on size (absolute and relative) and entry mode, paying special attention to their joint effects with age in driving mortality processes. Analyses using this more complete information and a more flexible, nonproportional stochastic specification might well lead to different findings about age dependence in organizational mortality.

production were short. Apparently automobile historians rarely could reconstruct the details about an exit unless a firm had become reasonably well established. Knowledge that a certain firm disbanded, was acquired, or left the industry usually means that it persisted in the industry long enough that its exit event received notice in the press. Our reading of the historical materials suggests to us that most exits of unknown type were disbandings or exits to other industries—and this is clearly the case in the American population for which we have reasonably complete information. So we treated these two events alike: the dependent variable in this analysis is disbanding/exit to another industry, defined to include events of unknown type. Firms known to have ended by other events (merger, acquisition, nationalization) are treated as (noninformatively) censored on the right at the times of these events.

Tenures in automobile production can be calculated straightforwardly when dates are exact or nearly exact.[13] The challenging case involves entry and exit in the same year. We reasoned that the tenure (in years) in the industry for such a case is bounded by 0 and 1. We gave such cases a tenure of 0.5 (the expected tenure under the assumption of a uniform distribution of events over the calendar year). We coded exits for such cases as occurring at (just before) the end of the year. When a firm enters in one year and leaves in the next (e.g., a firm is reported to have begun production in one calendar year and ended production during the following year), our coding rules assigned the starting time to the middle of the first year and the ending time to the midpoint of the next year, giving a completed tenure of one year (which is, again, the expected tenure under the assumption of a uniform distribution).[14] These rules generalize to handle all the cases we encountered.

We measured both absolute and relative size. For absolute size, we used a measure of scale of operation: the firm's annual production of automobiles.[15] The models estimated include a time-varying specification

---

[13] The archival sources contain varying degrees of precision in dating events. Sometimes, the sources give the exact date; other times, they give only the month and year or season and year. Most often, they record only the year. To make analysis tractable, we converted all of the information about timing into a common metric. We converted exact dates to decimal years. When dates were given in terms of months or seasons, we converted them to decimal years corresponding to our judgment of the midpoint of the time unit. For example, "early fall" was coded as occurring on October 15 (day 288 in the calendar), giving a decimal-year value of 0.79. Dates given to only the year were coded as occurring at the midpoint of the year.

[14] The general problem concerning data of this kind is known as time aggregation bias. Our procedures are consistent with Petersen's (1991) recommendation for dealing with this problem.

[15] It was occasionally necessary to infer the (presumably very small) size of some short-lived automobile producers. Hannan et al. (1998a) describes and justifies the procedures used in these cases.

of the effect of the natural logarithm of this variable as well as a dummy variable indicating extremely small size (annual production of less than 50 automobiles).

We measured the relative size of a firm in two ways. The first is the ratio of a firm's absolute size to the average of all the firms in its national industry at the time. (In forming such ratios, we used the mean rather than the median as the denominator to allow the scale of giant firms to have full effect.) The second is the ratio of each firm's absolute size to the size of the largest firm in the national population at the time. We obtained better fits and more consistent results across nations when we used the second measure. So we report size relative to the largest firm in the analyses below.

We specified tenure variation as a piecewise-exponential function (presented in Chapter 7). After examining life tables and exploring estimates of a variety of choices of the breakpoints, we decided to break the tenure scale (in years) at: 0.5, 1.0, 3.0, and 7.0. We experimented with other (and more) breakpoints in the upper range. However, the main results are fairly insensitive to these choices, presumably because so few firms experience tenures of greater than seven years.

To summarize, in this analysis, the disbanding/exit rate is specified as a function of tenure in the industry (u), prior organizational existence (e), relative organizational size (r), absolute organizational size (s), a dummy variable indicating very small size (v), and other measured covariates ($\mathbf{z}_t$), including contemporaneous density and density-squared, density at founding, and the macroeconomic covariates (GDP and Depression). The general class of models we estimate has the form

$$\ln[\mu_i(u)] = m_p + \alpha_p \ln r_{iu} + \beta_p \ln s_{iu} + \gamma_p e_{iu} + \theta_p v_{iu} + \mathbf{z}'_{iu} \boldsymbol{\pi}, \qquad u \in I_p.$$

Here m_p denotes a set of tenure effects; the log-linear link imposes the constraint that the baseline rates be nonnegative. The period subscripts on the effects of size and prior experience indicate that we allow these effects to vary by tenure. In this general specification, the hazard of disbanding/exiting is a nonproportional function of tenure and these covariates. We compare this nonproportional specification and one that constrains these effects to be proportional, that is, a specification in which $\alpha_p = \alpha$, $\beta_p = \beta$, $\gamma_p = \gamma$, and $\theta_p = \theta$ for all p. Arguments above about the effects of size suggest nonproportionate effects.

Results from a Proportional Effects Model

The central question is whether effects of age, size, and prior existence on mortality rates are proportional and, if they are not, whether allowing nonproportionality makes an important substantive difference. So we begin with the results of a proportional-hazard specification. The results appear in Table 14.1.

Size affects mortality rates in a complicated way even in a simple specification of proportional effects. Relative size has a large, significant negative effect on mortality rates for all four national populations. The effect of absolute size is negative and significant for Britain and the United States, and the effect of small size (< 50) is positive and significant for all but Germany. So there is a liability of smallness, both absolutely and relatively, as well as a special liability of ultrasmall size. Prior existence lowers rates of disbanding/exiting significantly in each population. This effect is much stronger for the European populations, reducing the rate by one-third to one-half, than for the American one, where the reduction is only one-tenth. We suspect that this difference reflects the different character of the lateral entrants on the two continents.

With controls for size and prior existence (and the other covariates and period effects), the effect of tenure is monotonic beyond the first year for each country—note the steadily decreasing estimates of the tenure con-

Table 14.1. *Estimates of baseline proportional-hazard models of the effects of age and size on the rate of exit of automobile manufacturing firms.*

	Britain	France	Germany	U.S.
Duration ($\widehat{m}_p$):				
$u < 0.5$	−4.90*	−5.69*	−9.77*	−0.690*
$0.5 \leq u < 1$	−4.55*	−5.66*	−9.46*	−0.797*
$1 \leq u < 3$	−5.31*	−6.32*	−10.0*	−1.30*
$3 \leq u < 7$	−5.43*	−6.34*	−10.3*	−1.56*
$u \geq 7$	−5.74*	−6.73*	−10.6*	−1.73*
Prior existence	−0.459*	−0.463*	−0.718*	−0.110*
ln(Relative size)	−1.46*	−1.60*	−3.55*	−0.090*
ln(Size)	−0.054*	−0.028	−0.066	−0.099*
Size < 50	0.580*	0.700*	−0.082	0.338*
Number of spells	5582	5171	2272	8893
Number of events	810	718	309	2051
ln $\mathscr{L}$	−1897.6	−1754.4	−666.1	−3701.2
LR test vs. model with $m_p = m$	203.6	84.4	43.7	291.0
d.f.	4	4	4	4

* $p < .05$.
Note: u denotes tenure in the industry in years.
Source: Hannan et al. (1998a). Copyright © 1998 by Oxford University Press. Used by permission.

stants. So, under the assumption of proportional effects, we see strong support for the notion of a liability of newness.

Results Allowing Nonproportionality

Next we examine possible nonproportionality in the effects of prior existence and size. To retain simplicity and enhance interpretability, we estimated models that allow nonproportional effects but do not entail a great increase in the number of parameters. We began by allowing the effect of prior existence and relative size to shift when tenure reaches three years. This alteration improves the fit substantially for the European populations but not the American. We did not find any evidence from other choices of breakpoints that the effects of prior existence and relative size depended upon tenure in the American population. In contrast, the effects of absolute size and very small size do vary significantly with tenure for the American population but not the European populations. The results reported in Table 14.2 reflect this trans-Atlantic difference in the size effect.

The assumption of proportionality turns out to be a poor one, given the specifications we chose, as Table 14.2 shows. Allowing the effects of prior existence and (some measure of) size to vary by tenure improves the fit significantly (at the .01 level) for all four national populations, as shown by the likelihood-ratio tests reported at the bottom of the table.

The set of baseline tenure effects ($\widehat{m}_p$) in Table 14.2 differs substantially from those in Table 14.1, which decline monotonically after the first year. Now only France and Germany display this monotonic pattern. The British and American baseline rates have U-shapes: the rates fall and then rise as tenure increases. However, given the nonproportional specification, it is not very meaningful to interpret the baseline hazards without taking account of the other relevant effects.

The most interesting results concern the effects of size. The nonmonotonicity of the British and American baseline hazards makes it hard to summarize the overall pattern of size effects over the whole range of tenure. However, clear patterns do emerge if we contrast pairs of tenure segments. It turns out to be most revealing to contrast the segments containing the greatest size variation: 3–7 and 7+.

For the European populations, we consider the following ratio of the multipliers of the baseline rates:

$$\Delta(r) = \frac{\widehat{\mu}_{7+}(r)}{\widehat{\mu}_{3-7}(r)} = \frac{e^{\widehat{m}_{7+}} r^{\widehat{\alpha}_{7+}}}{e^{\widehat{m}_{3-7}} r^{\widehat{\alpha}_{3-7}}},$$

where r denotes relative size. If $\Delta(r)$ exceeds 1 for some value of r, then the rate of disbanding/exiting increases with increasing tenure at this relative size; if the ratio falls below 1, then the rate decreases with increasing

Table 14.2. *Estimates of nonproportional-hazard models of the effects of age and size on the rate of exit of automobile manufacturing firms.*

	Britain	France	Germany	U.S.
Duration ($\widehat{m_p}$):				
$u < 0.5$	−2.73*	−4.30*	−7.68*	−1.00*
$0.5 \leq u < 1$	−2.37*	−4.26*	−7.37*	−1.11*
$1 \leq u < 3$	−9.97*	−4.92*	−7.94*	−1.61*
$3 \leq u < 7$	−6.82*	−7.03*	−11.1*	−1.86*
$u \geq 7$	−6.12*	−8.21*	−18.8*	−0.793*
Prior existence:				
all u				−0.112*
$u < 3$	−0.616*	−0.733	−0.752*	
$3 \leq u < 7$	−0.259	−0.733*[a]	−0.972*	
$u \geq 7$	−0.259[a]	−0.212	−0.323	
ln(Relative size):				
all u				−0.085*
$u < 1$	−0.428	−0.981	−2.53	
$1 \leq u < 3$	−3.43*	−0.981[a]	−2.53[a]	
$3 \leq u < 7$	−1.72*	−1.86*	−3.86*	
$u \geq 7$	−1.49*	−2.21*	−7.10*	
ln(Size):				
all u	−0.052	−0.033	0.087	
$u < 7$				−0.063*
$u \geq 7$				−0.209*
Size < 50:				
all u	0.549*	0.686*	−0.010	
< 7				0.668*
$u \geq 7$				−0.566*
Number of spells	5582	5171	2272	8893
Number of events	810	718	309	2051
ln $\mathcal{L}$	−1891.5	−1750.3	−659.0	−3694.1
LR test vs. model in Table 14.1 (4 d.f.)	12.07	8.31	14.08	14.15

* $p < .05$; [a] estimate constrained to equal the one above it.
Note: u denotes tenure in the industry in years.
Source: Hannan et al. (1998a). Copyright © 1998 by Oxford University Press. Used by permission.

tenure. Figure 14.1 shows the relation between this index of tenure dependence and relative size implied by the estimates.

Consider first the French and German results. Figure 14.1 shows that the implied disbanding/exit rate declines with tenure for relatively large firms and rises with tenure for relatively small firms. For France, $\Delta(r) \approx$

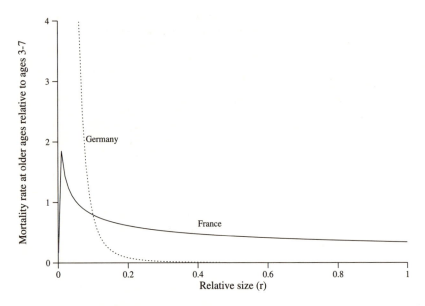

Figure 14.1. *Predicted relationships between relative size, tenure, and mortality for European automobile manufacturers. Source: Hannan et al. (1998a). Copyright © 1998 by Oxford University Press. Used by permission.*

$0.34r^{-0.368}$. So for the largest firm in this population ($r = 1$), the rate after a tenure of seven years is only a third as high as during the years 3–7. At $r \approx 0.05$, $\Delta(r) = 1$, which means that the rate is the same before and after the start of the seventh year. For the many cases in which the firm's size is less than 5% of size of the largest firm, the rate in the seventh year and subsequently exceeds the rate before the seventh year. For instance, the rate rises by 30% after year seven if $r = 0.025$. It is important to point out that many firms in this population were smaller than 2.5% of the largest. Indeed, 63% of all of the firm-year spells meet this criterion, as do 73% of the spells that exceed seven years of tenure.

For Germany, $\Delta(r) \approx 0.00045r^{-3.24}$, which gives a pattern similar to that just discussed for France. The implied rate for the largest firm is nearly zero in the upper tenure category. The rate declines as tenure increases for all firms at least 10% as large as the largest firm. For firms smaller than 10% of the largest, the exit rate increases in the seventh year. This condition holds for a great many firms: 70% of the full set of spells and 48% of all firms whose tenure exceeds seven years were less than 10% as large as the largest firm. These increases are very large for relatively small firms. For instance, if $r = 0.025$, then the disbanding/exit rate is nearly 70-fold higher after the seventh year than before, according to these estimates.

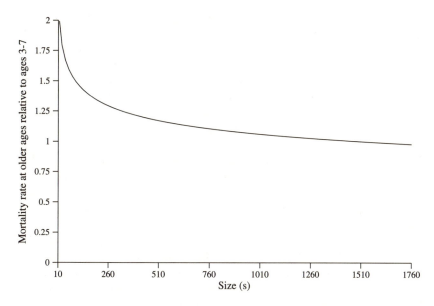

Figure 14.2. *Predicted relationships between absolute size, tenure, and mortality for U.S. automobile manufacturers. Source: Hannan et al. (1998a). Copyright © 1998 by Oxford University Press. Used by permission.*

The American results parallel the French and the British ones over most of the size range (specifically for sizes greater than 50). Replacing relative size (r) with absolute size (s), we have $\Delta(s) \approx 2.91 s^{-0.146}$ for the American population. This expression equals 1 (meaning that the multiplier of the rate is the same in the two tenure segments) when $s \approx 1500$. Figure 14.2 plots the relationship between $\Delta(s)$ and size. For firms larger than 1500, the rate declines with tenure; for firms smaller than 1500 (which comprise 76% of the firm-year spells), the rate is higher in the oldest tenure category. For instance, according to these estimates, a firm producing 100,000 automobiles per year has a disbanding/exit rate that is roughly half (54%) as high in years 7+ as during years 3–7. A firm producing 100 automobiles per annum has a rate 50% higher beyond the seventh year than in years 3–7.

An interesting complication arises in the American results. The direction of the effect of very small size differs for tenures less than seven and greater than or equal to seven. The effect is positive at low tenures ($u < 7$) and negative at high tenures ($u \geq 7$).[16] In other words, there is a reversal

---

[16]This condition holds for a surprisingly large number of cases: 309 firms have one or more year of observation in which their size is below 50 at some time after the seventh year.

for the very smallest firms: their disbanding/exit rate drops considerably after seven years. Taken together, the pair of results for the American population suggests that increasing tenure lowers rates of disbanding/exit for the largest and smallest firms in the industry (Figure 14.2).

The British results paint a different picture. According to the estimates in Table 14.2, $\Delta(r) \approx 1.17\, r^{0.228}$, which implies the mirror image of the French and German pattern.[17] The rate for the largest firm rises 17% after age seven. For firms roughly half as large ($r \approx 0.5$), the rate does not change at $u = 7$. Firms smaller than this have lower rates at higher tenure. For instance, firms whose size is 2.5% the size of the largest would have a drop in the rate by half after the seventh year. In other words, the disbanding/exit rate in the British population increases as tenure increases for the largest firms and decreases as tenure increases for the smallest firms.

Large, old firms face especially high risks of failure in Britain, according to these results. This finding fits some historical accounts of the evolution of the British industry, much of which focuses on the causes of the "collapse" of the industry (meaning mainly the failure of its dominant firms)—see Lewchuk (1987) and Chandler (1990).

Implications

British exceptionalism aside, what do these results tell us about the divergence of the results of prior studies? At the most general level, they imply that the pattern of age dependence one obtains from estimating a model of proportional effects of age and size would depend upon the size distribution over the population's history. If the population has consisted largely of small enterprises, then the pattern of age dependence ought to appear roughly positive. If, on the other hand, large organizations proliferated, then it seems likely that age dependence would appear to be roughly negative.

These implications fit reasonably well the pattern of findings over organizational populations discussed at the outset. Although important details on size distributions are not available in all cases, we think that the following populations contained mainly small organizations: New York City credit unions and hotels, American brewpubs and microbreweries, Toronto daycare centers, early Pennsylvania telephone companies, and Illinois banks (excluding Chicago). Interestingly, the prior research on each, based on proportionate specifications of the effects of age and size, found evidence

---

[17] This difference would be much greater if we compared the segment from years 1–3 and the oldest segment.

of positive age dependence, as our story would imply. And, the population that most clearly contains mainly large firms, that of medical-device manufacturers, shows a negative effect of age.

Not all of the findings fit the story so neatly. For instance, positive age dependence has also been found for populations of commercial banks in New York City and Tokyo, which contain many small banks but also some very large ones. Clearly, more analyses using nonproportional specifications like the one proposed here are needed before we will have a firm grasp of the sources of variation across studies. Nonetheless, this more refined picture of age dependence has promise as a way to understand differences in patterns of age-dependent mortality for diverse organizational populations.

14.4 Extending the Formalization of Aging

Can these new empirical findings be accommodated within the formalization of age dependence developed in the previous chapter? That formalization shows that a reasonably general set of assumptions about capability and position can be altered to represent four theories of age dependence: those implying liabilities of newness, adolescence, senescence, and obsolescence. They differ about the sign of age dependence—it is negative in the first, has an inverted-U shape in the second, and is positive in the other two. We now show that some modifications in the basic formalization can deal with these complexities. We use the set of definitions and assumptions in Section 13.5 but do not use those in Sections 13.6 and 13.7.[18]

Recall that the formalization in Chapter 13 addressed obsolescence as a consequence of organizational inertia in the face of drifting environments. This image forms the core of the extended model. The big change in the model concerns the conceptualization of position. To this point, the model treats position advantages as enduring. However, it seems unreasonable to assume that all positional advantages are preserved when environments drift. And, surely, some positions are more durable than others. This section introduces a distinction between two types of structural position: fragile and robust. *Fragile positions* depend upon some potentially unstable configuration of ties. In this context, instability means that the stability of a position or the advantages accruing to incumbency in a position are very sensitive to the state of the environment—small changes in the environment can destroy the position or its value. For instance, an organization whose positional advantage stems from its ties with a particular

---

[18]This material is adapted from Hannan (1998).

political leader occupies a fragile position. If political conditions change and this leader loses power, then the positional advantage vanishes.

In contrast, *robust positions* depend upon the occupation of highly reproducible positions, those whose value is relatively insensitive to the state of the environment. High status provides a good example of a robust position, because a positive feedback loop runs from high status to capability, e.g., high-status actors can produce signals of high quality at lower cost (Podolny 1993). Because environmental changes likely damage fragile positions more than robust ones, fragile and robust positions can be defined in terms of how well their advantages generalize over environments.

This formalization builds on the assumption that gaining advantage from robust position takes time but that fragile positions provide advantages at founding. This assumption appears to fit the examples of fragile and robust positions used above. Consider examples of each case. If a fragile position builds on a favorable tie to a particular actor, there is no reason why this tie cannot provide advantage from an organization's founding (when, for instance, it depends on the ties between the leaders of the organization and the external actor). If, in contrast, organizations building robust positions invest in high quality, which will eventually generate positional advantages such as favorable reputation and high status that have value in many states of the environment, then such a positional investment is unlikely to pay off immediately. For instance, it takes time for quality to be acknowledged and status to be conferred. For simplicity, assume that an organization does not obtain advantage from robust position until it passes a given age, which we set at τ.

The formulations considered to this point assume a range of positions with varying quality, represented by the function $P(x, t)$. It helps clarify issues here to narrow and consider only two values, using the predicate $PA(x, t)$, which records the presence/absence of positional advantage. Although organizations might be able to change their type of position, this formalization assumes that they cannot.[19]

For fragile position, the key idea holds that big environmental changes destroy the value of the position. It simplifies the analysis to tie loss of advantage from fragile positions to the specification of drift already developed: environmental drift eliminates alignment, and it also wrecks fragile positions. Alignment and fragile position might in general differ in their sensitivity to environmental change. One could incorporate such a difference by introducing another drift parameter that applies to fragile position.

---

[19]This assumption is undoubtedly too strong. The key idea is that positions endure, that they change much more slowly than the environmental variables influencing life chances. We simplify to the assumption that positions remain constant over lifetimes to avoid overly complicating the story at this point.

Not much would seem to be gained by adding such a complication. This formalization employs the simplifying assumption that the same parameter, σ, governs both the loss of alignment and the loss of positional advantage from fragile position.

Definition 14.4.1. *An organization's position is fragile if and only if it provides advantage initially but does not provide advantage after age σ:*

$$\forall x \left[FG(x) \leftrightarrow \{(A(x, t) > \sigma) \to \neg PA(x, t)\} \wedge \{(A(x, t) \leq \sigma) \to PA(x, t)\} \right].$$

According to the image of robust position, drift does not matter. All that needs to be specified is the time that it takes for an organization to begin gaining advantage from occupancy of a robust position. This duration is denoted here as τ.

Definition 14.4.2. *An organization's position is robust if and only if it provides positional advantages even in a drifting environment but only after the organization reaches age τ:*

$$\forall x \left[RB(x) \leftrightarrow \forall t \left[\{(A(x, t) > \tau) \to PA(x, t)\} \wedge \{(A(x, t) \leq \tau) \to \neg PA(x, t)\} \right] \right].$$

If an organization's position can be both fragile and robust, then the foregoing definitions yield contradictions. For instance, for the portion of the age range over which age is less than σ and less than τ, Definition 14.5.1 says that the organization possesses positional advantage and Definition 14.5.2 says that it does not.

Lemma 14.4.1. *An organization's position cannot be both fragile and robust (from Definitions 14.5.1 and 14.5.2):*

$$\forall x \, \neg \left[FG(x) \wedge RB(x) \right].$$

Finally, a rule must be stated for combining the effects of capability and positional advantage on mortality hazards. (This section bypasses the link through performance here to simplify the argument.) In the style of Péli (1997), we introduce ordered levels of the hazard of mortality, using the name constants: *very_low*, *low*, *mod_1*, *mod_2*, and *high*.

Assumption 14.4.1. *An organization's immunity, alignment of capability with the current state of the environment, and positional advantage jointly affect the hazard of mortality with the following ordinal scaling:*

$$\forall x, t \left[O(x) \longrightarrow \{IM(x, t) \longrightarrow H(x, t) = very\_low\} \right.$$
$$\wedge \left\{ \neg IM(x, t) \longrightarrow \{AL(x, t) \wedge PA(x, t) \longrightarrow H(x, t) = low\} \right.$$
$$\wedge \{\neg AL(x, t) \wedge PA(x, t) \longrightarrow H(x, t) = mod_1\}$$
$$\wedge \{AL(x, t) \wedge \neg PA(x, t) \longrightarrow H(x, t) = mod_2\}$$
$$\wedge \left. \left. \{\neg AL(x, t) \wedge \neg PA(x, t) \longrightarrow H(x, t) = high\}\} \right] \right].$$

Derivations require that the inequalities implied by the natural language hold in the formalization for the name constants denoting the levels of the mortality hazards.

Assumption 14.4.2. *The levels of the hazard of mortality are ordered*:

$$\{high > mod_1 > low > very\_low\} \wedge \{high > mod_2 > low > very\_low\}.$$

Note that Assumptions 14.5.2 and 14.5.3 implement the ideas that immunity overrides other potential forces affecting the hazard and that the hazard remains constant during periods of immunity. Thus these assumptions have the same effect as Assumptions 14.5.2 and 14.5.3 in the formalization used in Section 14.5.

Getting determinate results for some cases also requires specification of the relative importance of capability (alignment) and position. This formalization takes the view that positional advantage matters more than the alignment of capability with the environment for the hazard of mortality ($mod_2 > mod_1$). This assumption reflects sociological arguments about the effects of position on the returns to quality performance. For instance, Podolny (1993) shows that a "Matthew effect" applies to organizations: organizations that occupy high-status positions get more credit than those that occupy low-status positions for a performance of a given quality. Likewise Burt's (1993) arguments about "structural holes" also imply that positional advantage dominates. This assumption is implemented by refining this ordinal scaling of the hazards.

Assumption 14.4.3. *Position dominates alignment*:

$$mod_2 > mod_1.$$

It turns out that this assumption does not matter substantively in most of what follows. That is, most of the results also follow if the inequality in this assumption is reversed, because the results usually depend upon a contrast of either of the "*mod*" categories with "*very_low* or "*low*" or with "*high*." Cases in which this assumption plays an important role will be noted in what follows.

What do these assumptions imply about age dependence in mortality hazards? Answering this question requires that one "calculate" alignment and positional advantage by cuts on the age scale for organizations with fragile and robust positions with and without endowments.

Case I: Organizations Lacking Endowments

Consider first the simpler case of organizations lacking endowments. The main result is that the pattern of age dependence in the hazard of mortality diverges by type of position. The top panel of Table 14.3 gives the

Table 14.3.   *Case I: Implications of drift for the hazard of mortality for organizations lacking immunity with robust and fragile positions.*

		Robust position	
	Fragile position	$A \leq \tau$	$A > \tau$
$A \leq \sigma$	$AL \wedge PA \rightarrow$ $H = low$	$AL \wedge \neg PA \rightarrow$ $H = mod\_2$	$AL \wedge PA \rightarrow$ $H = low$
$A > \sigma$	$\neg\{AL \vee PA\} \rightarrow$ $H = high$	$\neg\{AL \vee PA\} \rightarrow$ $H = high$	$\neg AL \wedge PA \rightarrow$ $H = mod\_1$

Source: Hannan (1998). Copyright © 1998 by the University of Chicago. Used by permission.

results, and Figure 14.3 displays the implied pattern of age dependence for unendowed organizations with fragile position. (Note that τ is irrelevant in this case.) The hazard of mortality rises with age for organizations with fragile position without endowment.[20]

In the case of robust position, three cases must be considered: (1) environmental change destroys alignment when advantage can be acquired from a robust position ($\sigma = \tau$), (2) environmental change destroys alignment more quickly than advantage can be acquired from a robust position ($\sigma < \tau$), and (3) advantage can be acquired from a robust position before environmental change destroys alignment ($\tau < \sigma$).

When $\sigma = \tau$, age dependence in the hazard for organizations with robust positions is monotonic negative. Figures 14.4 and 14.5 show the result for the other two cases, one with $\sigma < \tau$ (Figure 14.4) and one with this inequality reversed (Figure 14.5). Note that, when drift produces environmental dissimilarity quickly relative to the speed of payoff to robust position, the hazard of mortality rises with age initially before declining (below the initial level)—there is a "liability of adolescence." In the second case, in Figure 14.5, when advantage can be gained from robust position before drift destroys alignment, then the mortality hazard peaks in youthful periods. The hazard falls with aging initially and then rises; but the hazard at later ages falls below the initial level of the hazard.

Despite the difference in the "middle" period for these scenarios, the comparison between the early and late hazards is the same: the hazard for old organizations falls below the hazard for young ones. So this is one recipe for generating a result that parallels the new empirical findings on

---

[20]The proofs of this and the rest of the results cited in this section can be found in Hannan (1998).

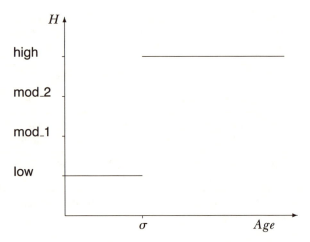

Figure 14.3.   *Implied pattern of age dependence in the hazard of mortality for unendowed organizations with fragile positions in drifting environments. Source: Hannan (1998). Copyright © 1998 by the University of Chicago. All rights reserved. Used by permission.*

mortality rates in automobile industries presented above. Suppose that the form of positional advantage (fragile and robust) corresponds with position in the size distribution and that the organizations lack endowments. That is, assume that small organizations occupy fragile positions and that large ones occupy robust positions. Such an assumption does not appear unreasonable in the context of national automobile industries. Large firms

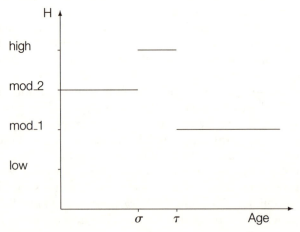

Figure 14.4.   *Implied pattern of age dependence in mortality hazards for unendowed organizations with robust positions for σ < τ. Source: Hannan (1998). Copyright © 1998 by the University of Chicago. All rights reserved. Used by permission.*

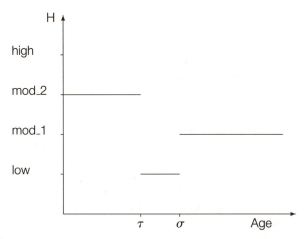

Figure 14.5. *Implied pattern of age dependence in mortality hazards for unendowed organizations with robust positions for τ < σ. Source: Hannan (1998). Copyright © 1998 by the University of Chicago. All rights reserved. Used by permission.*

have positional advantages in distribution (networks of dealers) that appear robust over many important kinds of changes in relevant environments. Such positions are rarely available to very small firms in these industries. Suppose that (1) position matters more than capability, (2) environmental change erodes inert capabilities, (3) fragile-position advantage can be gained at founding, but (4) advantage from robust position takes time to develop. Under these conditions, the theorems fit the result that age dependence in the hazard of mortality is positive for small (unendowed) organizations and negative for large (unendowed) ones.

The assumption that position dominates capability (Assumption 14.5.3) matters in the foregoing argument for the case of organizations with robust positions. If we reversed this assumption, specifying that $mod_1 > mod_2$, then the "shape" of the relationship between age and the hazard would be the same as given in Theorems 14.5.3 and 14.5.4. However, the comparison between the hazard near founding and the hazard at late ages would be different. Instead of the longrun hazard falling below the initial level (as in Theorems 14.5.3 and 14.5.4), the longrun hazard would exceed the hazard in youth. That is, longrun age dependence would be positive for unendowed organizations with robust positions if capability dominates position in shaping life chances.

Case II: Organizations with Endowments

It is intuitively clear that adding endowments to the picture must create a pattern of longrun positive age dependence in the hazard. When organizations are assumed to begin with endowments, then the hazard of mortality for new organizations is *very_low*, whether their positions are fragile or robust. Aging can only increase the hazard, when the immunity ends and when drift eventually erodes alignment. This intuition is correct, that is, it can be derived as a theorem under the assumptions made in this section (Hannan 1998).

In sum, this second version of the general argument about age tracking the fit between an organization and its environment refines the notion of position. It distinguishes two types of structural position: fragile and robust. The difference between these types is that robust positions provide advantage over broader ranges of environmental variations. Fragile positions provide advantage immediately (at founding) but these advantages disappear when the environment becomes dissimilar. Robust positions do not provide advantage immediately; it takes time to build such advantages. Once established, however, robust positional advantages persist in all states of the environment.

If organizations lack endowments, then age dependence is positive for the class of organizations with fragile positions and negative for those with robust positions. This difference in the pattern of age dependence by type of position might clarify the source of divergence in patterns of age dependence in recent empirical research. For instance, suppose that organizational populations in drifting environments vary in the fractions of members with robust and fragile positions. If fragile positions predominate in a population, then simple age dependence will tend to be positive. But, if robust positions are the rule in some other populations, then simple age dependence will tend to be negative.

Allowing endowments to affect the hazard of mortality does not change the result for organizations with fragile positions: age dependence is monotonic positive in drifting environments. However, endowments do complicate the picture for the case of robust positions. Under some of the specified conditions, the presence of an endowment produces the familiar liability of adolescence. Other conditions yield the opposite pattern, a U-shaped relation between age and the hazard, as was found by Boone et al. (2000) and Park and Podolny (1998). The main result is that age dependence in the hazard of mortality is positive over the longrun in drifting environments for endowed organizations with robust positions.

The formalization presented in this and the previous chapter seek to clarify how the various stories about age and size dependence "work" by interpreting them in first-order logic. The resulting formalizations are, of course, interpretations. Although they cannot reflect the full nuance of the natural language originals, they do place the common and divergent features of the contending theories in sharper relief.

15

Initial Mobilizing

ANECDOTAL EVIDENCE SUGGESTS that organizing processes usually begin long before an organization's recognized founding date. We know that entrepreneurs typically must develop plans, assemble resources, and otherwise orchestrate the opening of the firm. Yet, we know very little about the demography of this process, about the rates, durations, and consequences of these preproduction organizing activities. This information might be substantively important. If many organizing efforts fail prior to "official" starting dates, then conventional demographic analyses of organizational mortality (based on time in production) underestimate the actual rates. Indeed, every organization that manages to open its doors and to operate for any length of time might be judged as a success of sorts. Assembling and organizing the resources (capital, labor, technology, and so forth) needed to build an organization can easily get derailed and fail.[1]

Initial organizing activities might also affect other, better understood, demographic processes among corporations. For example, the density model of evolution links the social legitimation of an organizational form to organizational density, the number of organizations in a population (Chapters 10 and 11). As the number of organizations increases in a small population, so too does the social acceptance or taken-for-grantedness of its characteristic organizational form. Density enhances legitimation in part because, when more instances of the form exist, greater numbers of individuals come into contact with it and thereby become aware of its features (Hannan and Carroll 1992, 41–43). By the same reasoning, legitimation should also be affected by the number of entrepreneurs attempting to use the form, the density of would-be organizations. This is because the agents controlling the resources used to found organizations encounter

---

[1] This chapter is adapted from Carroll, Hannan, Bigelow, Seidel, Teo, and Tsai (1994).

these proto-entities as their would-be founders seek support. So, models of density dependence might be enriched by incorporating information about the number of organizing activities.

Relying on an unusually detailed historical source, we describe in this chapter an analysis of preproduction organizing activities in the American automobile manufacturing industry. Many preproduction organizing activities in this industry are identifiable, and the number of preproduction efforts observed historically is substantial.[2] We explore basic questions about preproduction organizing attempts: How frequently do they occur? What is the probability of an organizing attempt succeeding? Do the chances of success change with the length of time spent organizing? To what extent does the rate of organizing attempts depend upon density?

By contributing to an organizational form's legitimation, organizing attempts might also affect an organizational population's evolution. For programmatic reasons, it is important to know if this is so and whether such effects undermine the established relationships between organizational density and vital rates. Moreover, the low or selective visibility of organizing activities suggests some interesting hypotheses about the differences between the effects of density counts based on "preproducers" and those of producers. A major part of our effort here involves developing and testing arguments about rates of organizational foundings based on this distinction.

15.1 Organizing Activities and the Founding Event

As discussed in earlier chapters, organizational founding gets defined in two broad ways in demographic research on organizations. The first is the *formal establishment or legal incorporation* of an organization. For example, studies of foundings of national labor unions defined founding as the ratification of the charter or constitution of the union at an organizing convention (Hannan and Freeman 1989). Studies of banks (Hannan et al. 1990; Han 1998) and credit unions in New York (Hannan et al. 1994) defined establishment of the organization as the granting of a state charter. Studies of biotechnology firms use legal incorporation (Barley et al. 1992). The second, more common, definition of founding is the *commencement of production*. For instance, the many studies of the foundings of newspaper publishers define the founding as publication of a first issue (Carroll 1987; Amburgey et al. 1988). Studies of semiconductor manufacturers and investment banks define founding as the listing of the enterprise in an

---

[2] We focus on preproduction and production here because our analyses of automobile populations use entry and exit from production as the main vital events.

industry directory. It might seem that the first definition should be preferred on the assumption that formal incorporation precedes production or routine operation. In many cases this assumption turns out to be false. For instance, the companies in The Stanford Project on Emerging Companies (discussed in Chapter 9) evidence great diversity in sequences of starting events. Consider, for instance, the simple sequence of key initial organizing activities involving (1) incorporating the business, (2) hiring one or more employees, and (3) producing a product. One might expect that firms would enact these actions in the sequence stated above. But this is not so. Some firms have followed the reverse order, and each of the other possible sequences shows up in these data. Different organizations and different kinds of organizations start in different ways. Exactly which of the many possible starting events ought to be used to mark the beginning of an organization's life history is a substantive decision. We believe it should be based on an understanding of the institutions in the population under study.

Whatever type of activity gets used to mark the beginning of an organization's life history, the defining event will still often not coincide with the initiation of *mobilizing and organizing activities*. For instance, for an organization to begin to function as a national labor union: local unions had to agree to hold a convention to ratify the charter of a national union, the convention had to be held, and the constitution passed. Credit unions had to enroll a stipulated minimum number of members before New York State would grant a charter. Newspaper firms needed to obtain access to printing equipment and so forth. Each case involves a distinction between the initiation of organizing activities and the start of the organizational operation.

Does the difference between initial organizing and the start of business activity matter substantively? That is, does it matter that commonly available data on organizational foundings cover only those organizations that manage to succeed in passing some kind of hurdle? The answer to this question depends upon the dynamics of the initial organizing period. If firms routinely move from initial organizing effort to the state of full-fledged organization, then it presumably does not matter whether demographers have information on only the date of the second event. If, on the other hand, many firms fail to make the transition and the rate of success in making the transition varies with demographic characteristics, then the answer might be different.

At an abstract level, one can conceive of an organizing period—however short—prior to the "official" establishment of every organization. Surely many organizing efforts do not make it very far down the road to full functioning. We would thus be justified in envisioning another stochastic process, one initiated by the decision to found an organization of a particular type and terminated by either the establishment of the organization or abandonment of the effort. This formulation, however, seems to face insurmountable measurement problems (including unobservability, instrument reactivity, ambiguous timing) because the original kernel of a "decision" to start an organization often consists of no more than a passing idea in someone's mind.

Conducting research on organizing activities requires a practical solution to defining and measuring the beginning of the organizing period. The possibilities are numerous and include the establishment of a social compact among the principals involved, the development of a business plan, and the securing of capital or any other essential resource.

We favor linking the choice of the beginning of the organizing period to an event or phenomenon with potential implications for an established theory. With this strategy, research on initial organizing not only informs about the organizing process but also has more general significance. We illustrate this approach here by focusing on American automobile manufacturing. We define preproduction organizing attempts using a set of activities that can be measured in the historical record and can be expected to enhance the legitimation or taken-for-grantedness of the organizational form. These activities include: (1) listing an enterprise in an industry trade directory; (2) formal incorporation as an automobile manufacturer; and (3) building an automobile, usually one thought to be a prototype. We refer to the social entities undertaking these activities as preproducers. Our definition of preproduction organizing allows us to record when particular preproduction efforts begin and end. For each attempt, the duration of preproduction proceeds on its own clock. Spells of preproduction might end successfully, as when the organizing effort enters production, or they might end unsuccessfully in that production never occurs.

With this definition of preproduction, we see the possibility that the density of preproducers plays some role in processes of organizational evolution. This is because the density model (Chapters 10 and 11) posits that the twin forces of legitimation and competition drive evolution. To the extent that preproducer density generates legitimation, it should have predictable effects on organizational vital rates. The rate of initiation of preproducer organizing efforts is also likely to be affected by legitimation and competition.

Obviously, preproducer density needs to reach sizable levels in order for these arguments to be plausible, especially for an industry as vast as the American automobile industry. Figure 15.1, which is based on data we have collected and coded, suggests that it does. It shows density counts over time for both producers (dotted line) and preproducers (solid line) in American automobile manufacturing. Until about World War I, the number of preproducers remained at levels commensurate with those of producers.

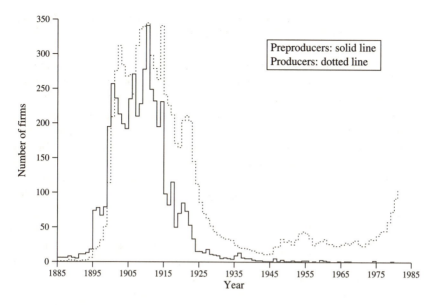

Figure 15.1. *Numbers of producers (dotted line) and preproducers (solid line) in U.S. automobile manufacturing, 1885–1981. Source: Carroll et al. (1994).*

Early in the history of the industry, preproducers actually outnumbered producers, especially around the period 1895 to 1900.

15.2 Theoretical Arguments

We consider initial organizing through the lens of the theory of organizational evolution presented in Chapters 10 and 11. For present purposes, the most important element of this theory is the link between the legitimation of an organizational form and its population density. According to the theory, organizational density enhances a population's taken-for-grantedness because: (1) it facilitates widespread identification and recognition of the form by society at large; (2) it allows for effective collective action by the members of the population; and (3) it aids and accelerates collective learning about the form and its capabilities. Density increases legitimation at a decreasing rate, with the greatest effects coming in the low ranges of density. As density rises, its effects on legitimation diminish until a sort of ceiling is reached. The ceiling might be interpreted as the level where the percentage of persons who take the form for granted is sufficiently high to make it a normative prescription; further increases in the percentage beyond this level do not affect the cultural standing of the organizational form.

As defined here, the density of organizing efforts (preproducers) should exert the same sort of pressures on legitimation as does the density of full-fledged organizations (producers). Building an automobile, listing a concern in an industry directory, or filing incorporation papers expressing an intent to manufacture automobiles would all enhance identification and raise recognition levels of the organizational form. This would be true to some extent for general audiences but especially for specialized and influential ones. For example, formal incorporation more likely gets noticed by legal audiences and by agencies of the state than by the general public.

Individuals and groups engaged in preproduction activities would also likely interact with important societal actors, such as banks and unions, as they attempt to acquire resources. And, through these associations as well as the preproduction activities themselves, individual entrepreneurs in the organizing phase will likely be attracted to and recruited into the social networks of the industry. Their inclusion in these networks should strengthen defensive collective action. The wider network should also provide more information to promulgate collective learning. In these ways, organizing efforts contribute to the development of a social movement around the organizational population (Hannan et al. 1995).

The arguments linking density to competition should also apply, in some degree, to preproducer density. In the standard formulation, density increases competition at an increasing rate. So when density is low, it has minimal impact on competition; when it is high, the addition of another organization to the population generates intensely higher competition. The usual explanation for this relationship has to do with limited resources and the geometrically rising number of possible unit-to-unit competitive links. Because preproducers compete for input resources such as capital, labor (especially highly skilled), automotive designs, machine tools, factory space, and distribution networks, it seems reasonable to expect that their density should affect competition as well.

These arguments imply that the effects of preproducer density on population vital rates parallel those of producer density. At low levels, preproducer density increases legitimation of an organizational form, but the effect diminishes as density climbs. For competition, density has minimal effect at low levels, but this effect rises disproportionately with higher density. Integrating the two relationships in the standard way and applying the usual assumptions about legitimation, competition, and vital rates yields the following hypothesis.

Hypothesis 15.1. *Preproducer density has an inverted-*U*-shaped relationship with the rate of entry into production.*

We think that the effect of the density of preproducers should have the same form as that of the density of producers but be weaker. Why? The producer and preproducer populations differ greatly in *social visibility*. As standing organizations, producers are visible to all; and, even those without a specific reason for interacting with them might come to learn of their existence. Producer advertising, for instance, reaches a much larger audience than simply the customer base of the firm. Preproducers, on the other hand, have much more limited visibility. Only those individuals or groups who have relevant interests or who control sought-after resources are likely to come into regular contact with these emerging entities. This means that a new preproducer is much less likely than a new producer to get noticed generally, for its members to get incorporated into existing social networks, and for it to become an effective lobbying agent for the population.

On average, preproducers also probably consume fewer resources than producers. And, because they experience a precarious stage of operation, preproducers might also get discounted relative to producers in calculations by investors, regulators, and the like. Justification of a new organizational form must be easier when many instances of the form already operate (in the sense of producing a product or service) than when many entrepreneurs simply propose to use it. All of these reasons lead to the following hypothesis.

Hypothesis 15.2. *Producer density has a greater impact on the rate of entry into production than does preproducer density.*

What about the rate of initiation of organizing (preproducer) attempts? Little has been written on this question. Presentations of theoretical motivations for foundings analyses usually conflate conceptually the starting of organizing activities and the start of production. However, as noted earlier, an observed number of founding events likely reflects two underlying parameters: the rate of organizing attempts and the odds of success of organizing attempts (Hannan and Carroll 1992, 198–99). Factors that affect one process might or might not affect the other.[3]

We confront an obvious question: does the success of preproducers depend upon organizational density? Received theory on density dependence in founding processes, concerning entrepreneurs' interpretations of

---

[3]With different data it might be possible to explore the full ramifications of this distinction. What is required is a definition and measurement of the preproduction stage that requires all (or most) entrants to pass through it. The one used here does not, because many producers are not observed as passing through preproduction.

and reactions to the environment, suggests an affirmative answer. Consider, for instance, the following claim:

> ...a taken-for-granted social form can be more readily visualized by potential organizers than one with dubious or unknown standing. ...Rational actors with the knowledge and skills to build organizations might hesitate to make attempts in densely populated environments. (Hannan and Carroll 1992, 36)

Although the basic tests of density-dependent legitimation and competition rely on observed foundings, arguments such as these suggest that they might apply to potential organizers. So we expect the following.

Hypothesis 15.3. *The rate of preproducer initiation has an inverted-U-shaped relationship with the density of producers.*

Now consider the preproduction period itself. Again, we have little guidance from the research literature. The most developed discussion we know about this type of process is a passage in Hannan and Freeman (1989) on "gestation" periods of organizational founding. Most of this discussion presumes that gestation periods are uniform within organizational populations and makes arguments about founding rates based on expected differences across organizational forms. For instance, complex and regulated organizations usually take more time to build, resulting in lower founding rates for such organizations. One of the reasons offered for this prediction concerns the uncertainty of the future and implies a hypothesis for the relationship between duration of organizing and the odds of success at actually entering production. According to Hannan and Freeman (1989, 122):

> The longer the wait from attempted initiation to full functioning, the greater the difficulty in fine-tuning organizational strategy and structure to opportunities and constraints in the environment. Ability to forecast the future declines with the length of the forecast period, probably exponentially.

Recasting this observation as an argument about the rate of movement from preproduction into production yields the following hypothesis.

Hypothesis 15.4. *The rate of successful movement from preproduction into production declines monotonically with the time spent in (preproduction) organizing mode.*

15.3 Automobile Preproducers

The spotlight cast on large automobile manufacturing firms by historians and economists has meant that much of the demographic history of the in-

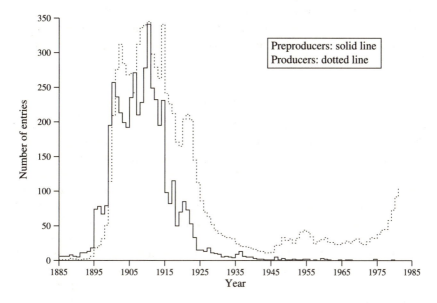

Figure 15.2. *Entries of producers (dotted line) and preproducers (solid line) in U.S. automobile manufacturing, 1885–1981. Source: Carroll et al. (1994).*

dustry has been overlooked. As Figure 15.2 shows, an astonishing number of hopeful producers populated the early industry. By our count, a total of 2,197 producers operated at one time or another in the U.S. market; 1,641 entered the industry between 1900 and 1920. The automobiles they offered varied greatly in technology, design, and cost (Carroll and Hannan 1995a). It is natural to wonder how some of these firms emerged from this free-for-all.

Automobile historian Rae (1984, 17) claims that it was easy to become an automobile manufacturer in the early industry. However, our analysis suggests strongly that much selection occurred prior to actual production. Using the definition of organizing noted above, we identified 3,845 preproduction organizing attempts in the industry. Of these, only 11% succeeded in making the transition to the production stage.[4]

Preproduction organizing efforts varied in longevity. Many lasted less than a year. For example, the Divine Motor Car Company of Chicago was incorporated in the summer of 1913 by three individuals including E.C. Divine with a capital stock of $10,000; but it disappeared from view

---

[4]As these numbers make obvious, many firms enter our data set initially as producers and thus never are observed in preproduction. We discuss the reasons for this below. We also explain analyses we have undertaken to detect any problems that this situation might create.

that year without having manufactured a car. At the other extreme, the
Kirkham Motor Manufacturing Co. of Bath, New York continued as a preproducer for 10 years. The median duration of organizing attempts is less
than one year.[5]

Data and Methods

The data we analyze here come from an attempt to code information on
all producers and preproduction organizers of automobiles in the United
States from 1886 to 1982. We define a producer as an automobile manufacturer that reached a level of production sufficient to generate income,
however small. This definition includes many very small producers; for instance, we have records on little-known companies such as Foster (1908),
Roach and Albanus (1899–1900), Thomas (1900), and Stilson (1907–1909).
Preproducers are "firms" that have begun organizing efforts but have not
yet reached production. Preproducers must also have done at least one of
the following: (1) built an automobile (usually a prototype), (2) incorporated as an automobile manufacturer, or (3) gotten listed in an automobile
industry directory.[6]

Many preproducers disbanded without ever making it into production.
Examples include the marques of Crusader (1914–1915) of Joliet, Illinois,
Fish (1906–1907) of Bloomington, Illinois, Glenwood (1922) of Youngstown,
Ohio, and McHardy (1904) of Detroit. Other preproducers proceeded from
the organizing stage into the production stage, getting coded as each type
of entity in succession. For example, W.B. Robe and Company operated in Portsmouth, Ohio during 1911–1914 as a preproducer building
at least three prototypes of a cyclecar before going into production in
1914. Henry Moyer of Syracuse likewise remained a preproducer for three
years from 1908 before finally entering production with the big, well-built
Moyer cars.

Finally, some producers appeared initially without any record of a preproduction stage. Examples include the producers of the Clark Electric of
Philadelphia (1903–1905), the Durocar of Los Angeles (1907–1912), and
the Economycar of Providence (1914). Firms could enter production without passing through an observed preproduction stage for at least two rea-

---

[5] The actual estimate of the median from our data is 0.5 year. The exact number results,
in part, from our coding conventions about duration, discussed in Chapter 14.

[6] Some apparent preproducers listed in the *Standard Catalog* were not coded because the
entry indicated great uncertainty about whether the preproducer actually existed. For example,
the entry for H.F. reads, "The H.F. Construction Co. of New London CT has been indicated
on various rosters as the manufacturer of an automobile in 1902. This is highly unlikely. Such
a company was not in existence in New London for an entire decade following the turn of
the century" (p. 671). So we did not code this entity (or similar ones) as a preproducer.

sons. First, a firm's preproduction planning and organizing activities might involve activities other than those assessed here. It is possible to enter production without incorporating an enterprise, getting listed in an industry directory, or building a prototype. Second, the source book for the preproduction data might contain measurement error and not record information on some firms that actually engaged in preproduction activities. We believe, in particular, that new enterprises more likely get noticed when they undertake visible preproduction. Established firms in other industries can likely conceal their automobile preproduction efforts.[7]

How accurate are these data? One way to evaluate quality is by comparing counts of firms constructed from these sources with those of previously published analyses. Our coding procedures have identified 3,845 preproducers and 2,197 producers throughout the period of study; the total number of nonredundant "firms" is 5,641. As shown in Figure 15.1, the peak of the combined number of producers and preproducers is 686 in 1910; the number of producers also peaks at 345 in 1910. By contrast, Epstein (1972) finds a peak of 88 manufacturers in 1921, Thomas (1965) finds 250 in 1908, and Klepper and Simons (1997) find nearly 400 concerns listed in the *Thomas* directories in 1910.[8] The Bureau of the Census reported 127 automobile manufacturers in the United States in 1905. Based on these comparisons, we believe that our sources yield more comprehensive coverage.

Although some source entries give exact dates for the beginnings of spells of preproduction and production, many others report only the year of an event. This lack of precise dates means that, consistent with most previous studies of organizational founding, our analysis relies on time-series data of annual event counts (Chapters 6 and 7). For each type of event, entry into preproduction organizing or the movement from preproduction to production, we formulate models of the instantaneous rate of occurrence of events. The rate of entry into preproduction, like any temporally aggregated entry process, is modeled as a function of an external clock (see Chapter 7); in this case the relevant external clock is historical time. Since

---

[7]After checking some specific cases where we can find additional information in other sources, we believe that both reasons apply here. We cannot say what proportion of cases might contain measurement error. But, in many of the cases with additional information, the dates shifted by a year or less. To examine whether such error might have biased our estimates, we re-estimated the models of duration in preproduction (reported in Table 15.3) with simulated supplemental data attaching a preproduction spell to each producer without one. To construct these preproduction spells, we drew randomly from a uniform distribution $U(0, 1)$. We then recalculated all preproducer population variables and reestimated the models. Although point estimates of coefficients shifted with this new data set, the basic pattern of results did not.

[8]Some of the difference in numbers has to do with the definitions used and some has to do with comprehensiveness of coverage.

the data on entries into preproduction are yearly counts, it makes sense to specify a stochastic model for a time series of event counts as follows

$$\ln \lambda(t) = \mathbf{z}'_{t-1} \boldsymbol{\pi} + \eta_t, \quad t = 1, \ldots, T,$$

where $\mathbf{z}$ includes various combinations of preproducer density and producer density (depending on the analysis), control variables and period effects discussed below, and a random disturbance, η_{jt}. We estimate the effects of the covariates on the rates using the method of quasi-likelihood estimation (Chapter 7).

To test Hypothesis 15.4, the hypothesis about duration dependence in the rate of moving from preproduction organizing to production, we use event-history data. In this analysis, the preproduction spell constitutes the unit of analysis: the preproducer is regarded as the entity "at risk" to enter production.[9] Here we consider the random variable U, which measures *time in preproduction* We are interested in the following transition rate:

$$r(u) = \lim_{\delta \downarrow 0} \frac{\Pr\{\text{producer}(u + \delta) \mid \text{preproducer}(u)\}}{\delta}.$$

We use the piecewise-exponential specification (Chapters 7 and 13) with covariates for preproducer and producer densities, period effects, and control variables, as discussed below. After exploring various choices, we found that time variation could be represented well by allowing the rate to shift at the following durations: 0.5, 1.5, 5.5.

As we explain below, the results of the nonparametric analysis of time variation suggest that the log-logistic specification might be appropriate here. So we also report estimates of the specification of the log-logistic model (Chapter 13). In all analyses of transitions from preproduction to production, we split the spells of preproduction every year in order to update values of covariates.

Preproducers and Entries Into Production

Table 15.1 reports estimates of hazard models designed to test hypotheses 15.1 and 15.2, the hypotheses about the effects of density on rates of

---

[9] If all producers passed through the preproduction stage prior to entering production, then this analysis might be the best way to analyze entry into production. Because many producers are not observed in a period of prior preproduction, the event-count analysis of production entry events is nonredundant and necessary for testing hypotheses on founding rates.

Table 15.1. *Estimates of effects on the rate of entry into production in the U.S. automobile industry.*

	(1)	(2)	(3)
ln(Producer density)	0.771*		0.639*
Producer-density squared	−0.112*		−1.02*
ln(Combined density)		0.810*	
Combined-density squared		−0.040*	
ln(Preproducer density)			0.170
Preproducer-density squared			−0.058
Prior entries	0.033*	0.036*	0.034*
Prior-entries squared	−0.175*	−0.181*	−0.173*
Pearson X^2	159.0	178.6	167.0
Number of observations	97	97	97

* $p < .05.$
Source: Carroll et al. (1994).

entry into production. The estimates in the first column represent the usual formulation of the density model; it uses only the two producer-density terms, $\ln N$ and N^2. The estimates of the effects of density are consistent with the theory and with much previous research: the first-order effect of producer density is positive and the second-order effect is negative; both are significant.

Is the model of legitimation and competition improved by the inclusion of effects of preproducer density? The estimates in Table 15.1 provide three different types of tests. Column 2 reports results of replacing the two producer-density effects with effects of the combined density of producers and preproducers. Column 3 contains estimates of a specification that adds the two preproducer-density terms to the specification of column 1; in other words, this model contains four density effects (two for producer density and two for preproducer density).[10]

Estimates of the specifications in columns 2 and 3 suggest that preproducer density affects producer foundings but that specification of the functional form of the effect matters. The additively combined densities used in

[10] We also estimated a model where the densities of producers and preproducers are combined in a different way. In this model, the mathematical operators (taking the natural log of density and squaring density) were applied before the producer and preproducer terms were added. The model represents a constrained version of the model whose estimates appear in column 3, where the coefficients of comparable preproducer- and producer-density terms are equal. Conclusions do not change. See Carroll et al. (1994).

column 2 have strong and statistically significant effects. The four-variable specification of column 3 shows the expected pattern for preproducer density; but neither term is significant.

To what extent does inclusion of effects of preproducer density improve the fit of the models over that of the specification that ignores the density of preproducers? Because the producer-only specification is not nested within the model in column (1), we could not conduct statistical tests comparing the models directly. However, we did compare various specifications against a common baseline model. Such tests yield a set of candidate models, and it appears that preproducer density is important. So, we conclude that the evidence supports Hypothesis 15.1, albeit not in overly strong fashion.

Somewhat paradoxically, weak support for Hypothesis 15.1 implies strong support for Hypothesis 15.2, which concerns the relative effects of producer and preproducer density. The analyses reported above make clear that producer density has strong and significant effects in the directions expected by the basic theory. Effects of preproducer density are more tenuous. When compared with producer density as separate effects in the usual density formulation (column 3), preproducer-density effects are much smaller and not statistically significant. This finding supports Hypothesis 15.2 literally but not in substance, because preproducer density has no effect. However, because the other evidence suggests that inclusion of preproducer density as a combined effect is warranted, we believe the findings as a whole support the argument of Hypothesis 15.2.

Table 15.2.   *Estimates of effects on the rate of entry into preproduction in the U.S. automobile industry.*

	(1)	(2)	(3)
ln(Producer density)	0.890*		0.842*
Producer-density squared	0.066*		0.073*
ln(Combined-density)		0.992*	
Combined-density squared		0.001*	
ln(Preproducer density)			0.063
Preproducer-density squared			−0.024
Prior entries	0.003	0.005	0.003
Prior-entries squared	−0.076	−0.071	−0.075
Pearson X^2	192.5	190.1	195.4
Number of observations	97	97	97

* $p < .05$.
Source: Carroll et al. (1994).

Entries Into Preproduction.

Next we turn to the rate of entering into preproduction, the rate at which organizing attempts are launched. Table 15.2 reports the relevant estimates. Column 1 reports estimates of a specification with only the producer-density effects; column 2 has combined effects of preproducer and producer density (as in column 3 in Table 15.1); and column 3 reports the results of decomposing the density effects of preproducers and producers. Contrary to Hypothesis 15.3, these estimates do not show the typical nonmonotonic patterns of density dependence. Both effects of producer density are significant, but both are positive. The only significant effect of preproducer density is the first-order term, which is positive. Evidently, preproduction organizing efforts are stimulated—and never stifled—by increases in the density of both preproducers and producers. Given the limited resources needed by preproducers, this pattern makes sense.

An intriguing difference between these estimates and the corresponding effects for entries into production in Table 15.1 involves the effect of entries in the previous year. Here this variable does not have significant effects, while it does have significant first-order and second-order effects in Table 15.1. The contrast suggests that entrepreneurs react to actual market developments more strongly in entering production than they do when initiating other organizing efforts.

Transitions from Preproduction to Production

We turn now to tests of the hypothesis about duration dependence in the rate of movement from preproduction to production. Initial nonparametric tests (not shown here—see Carroll et al. (1994)) imply a more complicated pattern of duration dependence than that predicted by Hypothesis 15.4. It appears that the rate is nonmonotonically related to duration: it starts low (first half year), rises rapidly (through year six), and then falls slowly. Table 15.3 shows that the nonmonotonic pattern persists in the face of controls for observable heterogeneity. For the piecewise-constant rate model, the pattern can be seen by noting the sizes of the successive constants. For the log-logistic model, this pattern is indicated by the positive value of the constant ρ. These findings suggest a reformulation of the argument in Hypothesis 15.4.

The estimated effects of the covariates in Table 15.3 tell that the rate of movement from preproduction organizing into production also depends upon density. Statistically significant effects are associated with both preproducer and producer density. However, unlike the estimates of rates of entry into production in Table 15.1, here the strongest and most consistent effects are those for preproducer density. Both the first-order and the second-order effects of preproducer density are significant. The first-order

Table 15.3. *Estimates of effects on moving from preproduction into production in the U.S. automobile industry based on piecewise-exponential and log-logistic specifications.*

	(1)	(2)
ln(Producer density)	0.151	0.156
Producer-density squared	−0.084*	−0.082*
ln(Preproducer density)	0.614*	0.427*
Preproducer density squared	−0.087*	−0.067*
Prior entries	0.005	0.004*
Piecewise age effect (α_p)		
$(0 \leq u < 0.5)$	−15.2*	
$(0.5 \leq u < 1.5)$	−13.5*	
$(1.5 \leq u < 5.5)$	−13.8*	
$(u > 5.5)$	−14.4*	
Log-logistic parameters		
$\widehat{\lambda}$		−10.9*
$\widehat{\rho}$		0.570*
$\ln \mathcal{L}$	−1048.9	−1090.3
Number of events	423	423
Number of spells	5058	5058

* $p < .05$.
Note: u denotes organizational age. Col. (1) uses a piecewise-exponential model, and col. (2) uses a log-logistic model.
     Source: Carroll et al. (1994).

effect is much larger than that of the comparable (and nonsignificant) effect of producer density.[11]

Implications

Organizing attempts are ubiquitous in advanced industrial societies. Yet, we know little about initiation rates and success chances of organizing

---

[11] Might not the larger effect of the preproducers here be a consequence of the shift in level of analysis? Although event-history data are superior for this problem, we examined this possibility by estimating an analogous model using aggregated event-count data. That is, we constructed two new yearly time series of dependent variables, one measuring the number of preproducers entering production in a given year, the other indicating the number of new producers who had not previously been in preproduction. We estimated the basic model of density dependence for each type of count and compared them. Reported by Carroll et al. (1994), the estimates are consistent with the pattern found with the event-history data. The effects of preproducer density relative to producer density are larger for models of preproducer entry into production. In fact, preproducer density shows no significant effects on foundings not previously observed in preproducer mode.

efforts. Part of this disjuncture can be attributed to the ephemeral nature of many organizing activities. Indeed, sound research on organizing activities requires a theoretically meaningful definition of the concept and an observational plan that provides systematic data.

Our approach here has involved tying the organizing process to observable entrepreneurial actions that plausibly contribute to the legitimation or social taken-for-grantedness of an organizational form. This conservative approach to conceptualization clearly overlooks many organizing efforts that do not get very far down the road. The alternative would trace organizing efforts further back in the process to some arbitrarily defined starting point. The further back one goes into the organizing process, the less meaningful the concept is likely to be and the more insurmountable will be measurement problems (not to mention epistemological problems). By contrast, the conservative approach produced ample numbers of identifiable and meaningful preproduction organizing efforts in the American automobile industry. Had these visible and theoretically relevant preproducers not shown any effects in demographic models of organizational evolution, then we would have reason to doubt the merit of further investigation of this phenomenon.

Empirical analyses on preproducers in the American automobile industry suggest otherwise. Using the demographic model of legitimation and competition, we find that rates of organizational founding show some evidence of nonmonotonic effects of the density of preproducers as well as the density of producers. These effects agree with expectations of the general theory. They are also generally consistent with an extension of the argument developed here; it predicts a greater impact of producer density, because preproducers likely enjoy limited visibility.

What do these findings mean for corporate demography? Three possible contributions come to mind. First, the findings extend the theory of density-dependent organizational evolution to preproduction and provide for consistent and meaningful interpretation of this little-studied phenomenon. Second, and perhaps most importantly from a programmatic viewpoint, the results do not undermine established findings and interpretation on density dependence. By our estimates, adding preproducer density improves model fit but it does not appreciably alter estimates or conclusions based only on producer density (which the established literature uses exclusively). Third, the findings suggest that legitimation processes in organizational evolution are even stronger than previously estimated.

As for preproducer organizing efforts, our empirical analyses showed that the rate of initiation depends upon density. Whereas producer density had greater impact on rates of entry into production, preproducer density had a greater effect on rates of movement from preproduction to production. Why should preproducer density have a stronger effect on the rate of initiation of organizing activities? We think the answer lies in recognizing the importance of the social and informational networks available to individuals and groups once they become preproducers. That is, by virtue of their activities and status, preproducers gain access to and become the targets of specialized and timely information. Preproducers can more easily learn about the nature and extent of activities by other preproducers than can those outside the network. Among other things, this means that preproducers will generally have better knowledge about the number of preproducers. It also means that knowing numbers of preproducers are large should increase the competitive pressure one feels to bring his or her own preproduction efforts to production.

Evidence about the relative roles of preproducers and producers in driving organizational evolution suggests the following interpretation. For processes involving the complete organizational population, such as legitimation of the organizational form, preproducers play a smaller role than producers, mainly because of their limited general social visibility. For processes pertaining to preproducers, such as the rate of entering production, preproducers play a larger role than producers, mainly because of their greater salience and visibility to others in preproduction mode. Whether this interpretation has general value remains to be seen; but it does provide a ready framework for extension to other ideas and problems. For instance, we would expect that early automobile producers using different propulsion technologies (steam, electric, and gas) would have greater awareness of others using similar technologies than those using dissimilar technologies.

16

Organizational Transformation

WHY DO ORGANIZATIONS CHANGE? How does change affect their life chances? The answers to these questions seem obvious to many: organizations change when (and how) their managers believe that it will improve performance. Organizational theorists who examine these issues search for regular patterns in the ways that managers decide to change organizations. Going further, these analysts often recognize that attempts at organizational change often take unexpected turns and lead to transformations and outcomes other than those intended. They also realize that change sometimes occurs unintentionally as a by-product of other decisions and actions within the organization. For all these reasons, demographic research on organizational change and transformation tends to focus on what actually happens to organizations over time rather than on the intentions of managers.

Although organizational transformations might not normally be classified as vital events, some such changes do play a central role in corporate and industrial demography. This is partly because the transformation process relates closely to processes of organizational growth and mortality. When organizations grow rapidly or continually, structural adjustments typically follow. (Of course, adjustments also occur for a variety of other reasons including environmental change.) Because the transformation process often cannot be directed smoothly or easily, organizations attempting major structural adjustments sometimes experience mortality in the process. As explained below, how frequently major organizational transformations occur and improve the life chances of those firms attempting them remains a controversial matter in organizational studies (Barnett and Carroll 1995). Different views about this issue get buried in (frequently implicit) assumptions rather than get investigated directly. Demographic research on the effects of transformation on mortality thus promises to inform about basic theoretical questions.

357

From the perspective of corporate demography, instances of successful organizational transformations potentially indicate the stability and permeability of boundaries of populations and industries. When severe transformation occurs, it often signifies a shift in an organization's form (Chapter 4). Much of the discussion in this book assumes that founding and mortality are the dominant corporate-demographic processes. Should successful transformations occur widely, then corporate and industrial demography might need to shift attention accordingly.

16.1 Theory and Research on Transformation

By definition, transformation involves a change in an organization between two points in time. Most analysts want to compare organizations before and after transformations. Making such comparisons entails assessing the *content* of organizational change. Content change refers to what actually differs in the organization at the two points in time. From the perspective of content, major organizational transformations involve many elements of structure or radical shifts in a single, but important, element of structure. At the extreme, content changes so much that an organization changes its form (Chapter 4).[1]

A second fundamental dimension of organizational transformation concerns *process*: the way the change in content occurs—the speed, sequence of activities, decision-making and communication systems deployed, and the resistance encountered. Effects of the process of change on organizational life histories might operate independently of the content that is changed, or the effects might be content-specific. For instance, Gusfield (1957) studied change in the Women's Christian Temperance Union by looking at how the organization's objectives changed over time (analysis of content). Gusfield also analyzed change in content with an eye to how the demography of membership constrained the struggle over different directions that the organization might have taken (analysis of process).

Enough research has been conducted on organizational transformation to make clear that both content and process factors ought to be evaluated. Yet, theories and analyses of organizational change often attend to only one dimension. For instance, the game-theoretic formulations of modern industrial-organization economics (Shapiro 1989) usually involve sophisticated analyses of the costs and benefits of a firm's potential alternative market positions. Yet, these analyses all too frequently assume (often implicitly) that the risks and costs associated with moving to any of these

---

[1] Parts of following sections are adapted from Barnett and Carroll (1995).

positions are nil (see Kreps (1996) for a major exception). In other words, this approach concentrates on content to the exclusion of process. On the other side of the issue, much management theory pays attention only to process. Such work lays out communication systems and political frameworks for implementing organizational transformations (Pfeffer 1992) but ignores the possibility that different types of transformations (in terms of content) might call for different approaches.

Growth-Induced Transformations

Most theories of organizational transformation build on notions of growth. These theories assume that certain structural transformations occur as organizations grow. For example, a well-accepted tenet of organizational theory maintains that successful small entrepreneurial firms must, at some point in their growth, shift from direct and informal control by the owner-manager to a less personal form of control (Lippitt and Schmidt 1967). In their most developed form, these theories posit an organizational life cycle consisting of a fixed sequence of major structural transformations (Greiner 1972). Popular variants of these theories cast the life-cycle metaphor in terms of the age of the organization or its products rather than growth (Boswell 1973; Abernathy and Utterback 1978). Most of these metaphors have been developed by looking retrospectively at the histories of a few large and successful organizations. Such evidence, of course, provides a highly biased picture of the process and cannot support these theories as causal—or even descriptive—models of organizational change.

The same variables that get attention in these theories—organizational size and age—have frequently been used to craft other, less ambitious, theoretical arguments about organizational change. Usually, these arguments build on assumptions about either the bureaucratic nature of large and old organizations or the superior resources controlled by such organizations (Kimberly 1976; Hannan and Freeman 1984; Aldrich and Auster 1993; Barron et al. 1994). The former assumption (large, old organizations are bureaucratic) leads to predictions that large and old organizations will be less likely to change; the latter assumption (old, large organizations command extensive resources) leads to the opposite conclusion. Empirical work directed at adjudicating between these two kinds of stories has generally been inconclusive.

These life-cycle theories share a developmental view of the organization; they concentrate on internal features and ignore environmental ones (Child and Kieser 1981; Cafferata 1982). The continuing strong influence of these ideas is illustrated by the fact that virtually all current studies of organizational change estimate effects of organizational size and many also estimate an effect of age—see, for example, Delacroix and Swaminathan

(1991), Halliday et al. (1993), Miller and Chen (1994), and Barron et al. (1994).[2]

Models of Environmental Effects

Most recent research seeking to explain the systematic source of organizational change looks to the environment. For instance, Miner et al. (1990) find for Finnish newspapers that interorganizational affiliations with external political parties were positively associated with rates of change. Delacroix and Swaminathan (1991) discover a positive relationship between market variability and product changes among California wineries. Many studies show that adoption of certain practices by focal organizations depends upon the pattern of adoption by other organizations. The practices studied include "poison pills" (Davis 1991), acquisition strategies (Haunschild 1993), and diversification (Haveman 1993a). Halliday et al. (1993) document how state actions affect the likelihood of bar associations changing from a market to a governmental orientation. Miller and Chen (1994) find that airline companies are more likely to change when faced with a diverse and growing market.

As interesting as these and similar studies might be, we believe that theoretical specification of the causes and processes of organizational change could be improved substantially. The most commonly used core theoretical ideas in current studies consist essentially of simple models of individual action and decision making extended up to the organizational level. That is, theorists envision environments filled with opportunities and constraints and predict organizational action based on assessment of the choices that a simple unitary actor would make. The logical and conceptual limitations of this approach parallel those of an individual model of rational decision making and action. For instance, it will always be possible to identify opportunities in retrospect; but that does not mean decision makers of the time were aware of them or able to identify them (March 1988). Correctly assessing the ex ante opportunities and constraints retrospectively is also difficult because organizational moves and their associated outcomes are already known.

Viewing these types of studies as a set raises another important question about organizational action. Some studies, such as Haveman's (1993a) analysis of saving and loan associations, implicitly assume that organizations have an action orientation: they seek attractive opportunities and

---

[2] An interesting new twist on these arguments holds that organizational size has a nonmonotonic relationship with the rate of change: small and large organizations are less likely to change than mid-sized ones. Haveman (1993b) finds that this is the case for diversification moves of California savings and loans.

seize upon them. Other studies, such as Halliday et al.'s (1993) analysis of state bar associations, implicitly assume inertia: organizations do not change until almost forced to do so by resource depletion or other crisis. Why should some organizations or some types of changes be pulled by opportunities and others be pushed by impending catastrophe? At present, the available theories do not explain. This might mean that both types of analyses are incomplete, because they ignore the other set of potential factors.

Perhaps the most curious aspect of these recent analyses of organizational change, however, concerns their failure to use basic theories of organization in making predictions about change. Given a set of technological and environmental conditions, most systematic organization theories imply an equilibrium structure (Chapter 17). When coupled with an adaptationist assumption of change (already used by most theories), these implications essentially specify—with proper translation and application—predictions about the content of change. Using such theories to make predictions about organizational transformation would entail analysis of the industrial and organizational context.

So, for instance, a transaction-cost analysis of wineries might suggest that, for reasons of asset specificity, boutique wineries without vineyards would move to integrate such assets. Likewise, a resource-dependence analysis of diversification would predict movement into markets that generate the most uncertainty for the focal firm, a prediction that might contradict expectations from analysis of the focal firm's economies of scope. In fact, when organizational theorists adopt this mode of reasoning, their studies are classified less as pertaining to organizational change than to testing specific theoretical perspectives. Witness the many studies from the institutional tradition in the sociology of organizations that examine organizational change via diffusion of structures (Edelman 1990; Sutton et al. 1994). Although these studies indisputably deal with organizational change, they rarely receive mention in the management literature on the subject.

What does a demographic population-level strategy offer for the analysis of organizational change? Demographic research on corporations highlights two environmental factors in explaining organizational change: technical change and competition. The case for technical change has been made forcefully by Tushman and collaborators, who work from a Schumpeterian perspective (Tushman and Romanelli 1985; Tushman and Anderson 1986; Anderson and Tushman 1990)—see also Barnett (1990), Utterback (1994), and Wade (1996). Because this view emphasizes selection ("creative destruction" in Schumpeter's words), it often gets forgotten in discussions of change. Whether change efforts succeed or not, firms that have knowledge of impending major technical change usually attempt to make adjustments. The contemporary computer industry illustrates this point. With prior industry leaders such as Digital Equipment Corporation (DEC) and Data General falling by the wayside and previous specialty firms such as Dell and Gateway rising in dominance (at least as we draft this book—the situation can change quickly), it is very difficult to know which, if any, of the existing firms will prevail. Virtually all firms in the industry make some kinds of organizational changes as they attempt to position themselves with respect to technological developments.

In a demographic/ecological framework, one organizational population exerts a competitive pressure on another if the presence and activities of the one degrade the vitality of the other (Hannan and Freeman 1989). It is natural in this perspective to assume that the intensity of a competitive effect is proportional to the scale of the competing population. If the competitor is present in the system but has a very small scale, then the life chances of the other organization are not much affected. If the competitor grows in scale, then competition intensifies. In other words, ecological competition is *scale-dependent*.

Demographic researchers use two ways of representing scale, discussed in part in previous chapters. One assumes that the intensity of a competitive threat is proportional to the density of organizations in the competing population (Chapters 10 and 11). The second assumes that competitive intensity is proportional to the mass (aggregate size) of the competing population. Each approach has advantages and disadvantages. Density can often be measured consistently over time for all of the potentially competing populations. It is also unaffected by the rate of inflation and other such variables. On the other hand, mergers and absorptions can decrease density without changing a population's aggregate size (measured, for example, by turnover, total assets, or employment). Measures of mass are often not available consistently for the whole histories of relevant populations.

We turn now to systematic theory and research on the consequences of fundamental organizational change for the life chances of the changing organizations. We begin with the argument that has framed much of the recent research on this issue.

16.2 Structural Inertia

Demographic research on transformation reveals that organizations rarely change their fundamental properties quickly when environmental opportunities and constraints change. Such inertia is often viewed, both by participants and academic analysts, as pathological—if only firms and bureaucracies were better managed or better designed, they would be nimbler. No doubt, many organizations do suffer poor management and poor design.

However, this does not seem to be the crux of the matter. Even organizations that are hailed as paragons of good management and felicitous design often stumble when conditions change suddenly and unpredictably. Consider General Motors in the 1970s and 1980s and IBM in the early 1990s.

Certain lines of social science thinking develop a different imagery, one that suggests that inertia arises as a consequence of sensible, purposeful efforts to adapt.[3] For instance, Arrow (1974, 49) made such an argument in considering specialized investment in information channels:

> The combination of uncertainty, indivisibility, and capital intensity associated with information channels and their use imply (a) that the actual structure and behavior of an organization might depend heavily upon random events, in other words on history, and (b) the very pursuit of efficiency might lead to rigidity and unresponsiveness to further change.

Selection for Reliability and Accountability

Some accounts of inertia resulting from purposive action have been elaborated as theoretical processes in their own right. One prominent theory holds that structural inertia arises as an inadvertent by-product of a particular social selection process imposed on purposeful actors (Hannan and Freeman 1984). The theory holds that inertia derives from the very characteristics that make formal organizations favored kinds of corporate actors in contemporary societies: reliability and accountability. *Reliability* means the capacity to achieve low variance in the quality of performance, including its timeliness. Given uncertainty about the future, potential members, investors, and clients might value reliability more highly than efficiency. That is, rational exchange partners might be willing to pay a premium for the certainty that a product or service of a minimum quality will be available when needed. Therefore, they prefer to transact with corporate actors that demonstrate this capacity. Rational designers will respond to this pressure by building structures that have a capacity for reliable collective action.[4]

---

[3] One of the most persuasive accounts of the sources of inertia is agnostic, at best, on the issue of whether purposeful action plays a central role. Institutional theory points to a powerful symbolic break on radical transformations: the emergence of tacit social agreements about what actions are sensible and proper. Instrumental characteristics, such as routines and structures, tend to become infused with moral value—they become understood as the "proper" ways of doing things. Such institutional process can play an adaptive role, both motivating work and achieving low-cost coordination. But, once such a process takes hold, the costs of radical transformation increase greatly.

[4] This section follows Péli, Pólos, and Hannan (1998)

Accountability means the ability to construct rational accounts for one's actions. Given the pervasiveness of norms of rationality in modern societies, all social actors, natural and corporate, experience pressure to cast decisions in terms of connections between means and ends.

Both accountability and reliability depend on a structure's being reproduced with high fidelity over time. Yet, high reproducibility of structure means that structures resist transformation. As noted above, this means that some aspects of structure can be transformed only slowly and at considerable cost, because many resources must be applied to produce the result. Highly reproducible structures have a deadweight quality: responses to environmental variations trail events at considerable distance. Lags in response often last longer than typical environmental fluctuations and longer than the attention spans of top managers and outside authorities. Thus, inertia often blocks transformation completely.

The Original Statement of the Inertia Theorem

The assumption–theorem structure of the inertia theory (Hannan and Freeman 1984) reads as follows.

Assumption 16.2.1. *Selection in populations of organizations in modern societies favors forms with high reliability of performance and high levels of accountability.*

Assumption 16.2.2. *Reliability and accountability require that organizational structures be highly reproducible.*

Assumption 16.2.3. *High levels of reproducibility of structure generate strong inertial pressures.*

Theorem 16.2.1. *Selection within populations of organizations in modern societies favors organizations whose structures have high inertia.*

Hannan and Freeman (1984) claim that Theorem 16.2.1 follows from Assumptions 16.2.1–3. However, the protean character of natural-language statements makes it problematic to evaluate this claim. The next step in the story is the effort by Péli et al. (1994) to reconstruct the theory so that this claim could be checked.

Péli et al.'s Rational Reconstruction

Péli et al. (1994) sought to use the machinery of first-order logic to evaluate the inertia theory. They took pains to recognize that the verbal statements admit multiple interpretations, as already noted. They offer an interpretation that seeks to stay close to what they saw as the intended meanings of the verbal theory. This subsection notes some important features of the interpretation and states the relevant part of their formalization.

The first consequential decision concerns the *level of analysis*. Assumption 16.2.1 and Theorem 16.2.1 refer to "populations of organizations." However, other assumptions and theorems in the original paper, such as those pertaining to the effects of change in forms on mortality rates, were stated at the organizational level. In seeking to create a unified formalization, these analysts state all formulas as holding for a given organization.

Assume an arbitrary organization. Let Repr, Acc&Rel, and Inert be individual name constants that denote, respectively, that this organization possesses the properties of reproducibility, accountability/reliability, and inertia. In interpreting assumption 16.1, the reconstruction introduces the predicate Favored to indicate that an organization has the property of being favored by selection (in the sense of having favorable life chances).

Assumption 16.2.1a. *If an organization has (high) reliability and accountability, then it is favored by selection*:

$$\text{Acc\&Rel} \rightarrow \text{Favored}.$$

Restating Assumption 16.2.2 in first-order logic requires an interpretation of "require." Péli et al. (1994) interpret the statement that "*A* requires *B*" as expressing a necessary condition ($A \rightarrow B$). So they express the second assumption as follows.

Assumption 16.2.2a. *If an organization has reliability and accountability, then its structures are highly reproducible*:

$$\text{Acc\&Rel} \rightarrow \text{Repr}.$$

Assumption 16.2.3 uses the verb "generates." Péli et al. (1994) interpret the claim that "*A* generates *B*" as a case of causal relation (represented by the relation of material implication: $A \rightarrow B$).

Assumption 16.2.3a. *If an organization has (high) reproducibility of structure, then it is inert*:

$$\text{Repr} \rightarrow \text{Inert}.$$

Finally, the reconstructed inertia theorem is stated as follows.

Theorem 16.2.1a. *If an organization is inert, then it is favored by selection*:

$$\text{Inert} \rightarrow \text{Favored}.$$

With this interpretation, the claim that the inertia theorem follows from the stated assumptions is not correct. That is, Theorem 16.1.1a does not follow from Assumptions 16.2.1a–3a.

Péli et al.'s Reformulation

These formalizers then explored alternative interpretations of the assumptions that would make the theorem go through. They suggested that the direction of the implication arrows be flipped in Assumptions 16.2.2a and 16.2.3a. Because they thought that original arrow directions also make sense in these assumptions, they proposed to use biconditionals (↔), turning Assumptions 16.2.2a and 16.2.3a into "if and only if" statements. These "added arrows" mean adding extra constraints to the premise set. With these modifications in place, Theorem 16.2.1a can be derived from the (revised) premises.

The first assumption (16.2.1a) was kept unchanged. The second and third assumptions were made biconditional, as noted above. The original theorem (16.2.1a) follows as an implication of this revised set of assumptions.

Péli et al. (1998) claim that a high price has been paid to make the theorem go through in this form. Indeed, some of the new theorems that follow from these revised assumptions sound a bit weird; and one can find counterexamples to them. Since the derivations are correct in each case (also checked by theorem prover), it must be the premise set or the formalization of the conclusion that causes the problems. These considerations suggest that alternative ways to formalize the inertial argument be considered, keeping faithful to the larger theoretical program.

An Alternative Organization-Level Formalization

Now we sketch an alternative reconstruction proposed by Péli et al. (1998). The original verbal arguments on inertia clearly do not claim that the presence of inertia, by itself, yields a selection advantage. They claim that inertia arises as an unintended (and unwanted) by-product of a desired property, reproducibility. Roses are favorite flowers. However, they are not popular because of the thorns that come with all (not gene manipulated) roses.

So, inertia accumulates in organizational populations, because the survivor organizations are mainly the inert ones. The presence of high inertia in mature populations is a *consequence* of a selection advantage rather than its precondition. In other words, "A prerequisite for reliable and accountable performance is the capacity to reproduce a structure with high fidelity. The price paid for high fidelity is inertia" (Hannan and Freeman 1977, 162).

Now we consider a formal representation that retains the core of this argument that inertia accumulates as a by-product of selection. This formalization, like the one just sketched, operates at the organizational level.[5] This version keeps Assumptions 16.2.2a and 16.2.3a as above to pre-serve Hannan and Freeman's original interpretation. However, Péli et al. (1998) change the formal representation of Assumption 16.2.1a and Theo-rem 16.2.1a, bringing them closer to the original arguments. The key point is that reliable and accountable performance—not inertia—gives the sur-vivor organizations an advantage. Therefore, the capability for reliable and accountable performance accumulates in groups of organizations that pos-sess selection advantages.

Assumption 16.2.1c. *If an organization is favored by selection, then it has relia-bility and accountability*:

$$\text{Favored} \rightarrow \text{Acc\&Rel.}$$

Consider the argument that inertia accumulates as a consequence of selection processes and consider those organizations that stay alive after a certain period of time, i.e., those that have had selection advantages. The inertia claim says that these survivors have high inertia. So, Péli et al. (1998) propose that the correct reading of Theorem 16.2.1 says that, if an organization is favored by selection, then it has inertia. "If–then" is repre-sented by the material implication ($\rightarrow$), so the inertia theorem is restated as follows.

Theorem 16.2.1c. *If an organization is favored by selection, then it is inert*:

$$\text{Favored} \rightarrow \text{Inert.}$$

The trio of assumptions (16.2.1c, 16.2.2a, and 16.2.3a) implies Theorem 16.2.1c. Under the proposed re-interpretation, the counterintuitive bicon-ditionals ($\leftrightarrow$) in Péli et al.'s (1994) revision of the second and third as-sumptions in the original argument (Assumptions 16.2.2a and 16.2.3a) are unnecessary. In other words, this formal interpretation demonstrates the soundness of the original argument.

To this point, all formal statements have been given as holding for a given organization. However, as noted above, the original argument was stated as holding at the population level. Péli et al. (1998) and Péli, Pólos, and Hannan (1999) show that a property-based formalization meaningfully characterizes the population-based logic. This formalization (sketched in an appendix to this chapter) also supports the logical soundness of the Hannan–Freeman argument.

---

[5] It is enough to employ the simpler propositional logic here (that is, we do not add quantifiers), instead of using first-order predicate logic.

16.3 Transformation and Mortality

Many recent demographic studies have investigated the consequences of major structural change on organizational mortality, in part to explore the arguments formalized above. If selection favors inertia (even as a by-product), then organizations attempting structural transformations should face long odds and be more likely to fail, at least during the transition period. Empirical researchers face challenging problems in conceptualizing and measuring dimensions of structural inertia/change. Most of the demographic studies of organizational populations build on the theoretical and modeling framework of Hannan and Freeman (1984), who argued that "core" structural change is precarious and leads to an elevated probability of organizational failure and mortality. Changes affecting the noncore or periphery structure are not expected to produce the same outcome; they might even lead to a lowered risk of mortality.[6]

What constitutes a core structural change? Hannan and Freeman (1984) gave a hierarchical list of four core features, including an organization's mission, its authority structure, its technology, and its marketing strategy. According to Hannan and Freeman (1984, 156), "although organizations sometimes manage to change positions on these dimensions, such changes are rare and costly and seem to subject an organization to greatly increased risks of death." Presumably, this is because these core changes diminish the organization's reliability of performance and accountability of action, at least in the short run before the new structure gets fully established. In terms of the definitions presented in Chapter 4, we define core changes as those that change organizational-form default classification.

One common way to interpret and generalize this list of core features assesses the *extensiveness* of subsequent other changes in the organization entailed by a given initial change. That is, core changes imply extensive other changes in structures and routines throughout the rest of the organization. In analyzing diversification moves, similar logic leads to assessment of the *relatedness* of new activities to previous core structure. Working hypotheses of this framework hold that (1) the more extensive an organizational change, the more likely is organizational failure, and (2) the more unrelated a diversification move, the more likely is organizational failure.

Table 16.1 provides a summary list of recent empirical studies investigating these arguments. Each of these studies examines a population of like organizations over a period of time, records their actions with respect to a particular type of structural change, and charts their subsequent fates. Effects of change are evaluated with hazard-function models, which spec-

---

[6] Parts of this section are adapted and updated from Barnett and Carroll (1995).

Table 16.1. *Overview of studies of effects of organizational change on mortality.*

Study	Population	Type of change	Effect
Carroll (1984a)	Newspapers	Publisher succession	+
Singh, House, and Tucker (1986)	Social services	CEO succession Location shift Service-area shift	− − +
Zucker (1987)	Hospitals	Technical and administrative	−
Miner, Amburgey, and Stearns (1990)	Newspapers	Various	+
Kelly and Amburgey (1991)	Airlines	Market shift	−
Delacroix and Swaminathan (1991)	Wineries	Add product Land acquisition	− −
Haveman (1992)	Savings and loans	Diversification	−
Amburgey et al. (1993)	Newspapers	Content Frequency	+ +
Barnett (1994)	Telephone cos	Tech. change	+
Teo (1994)	Automobile mfrs.	V-8 engine	−
Carroll and Teo (1996)	Automobile mfrs.	Tech. innovation	+
Barnett and Freeman (1997)	Semiconductor mfrs.	Product change	+
Dowell and Swaminathan (2000)	Bicycle mfrs.	New designs	+
Han (1998)	Japanese banks	Legal form	+
Dobrev (1999)	Communist newspapers	Editor-in-chief change	+

ify an organization-specific instantaneous rate of mortality. As discussed in Chapters 6 and 7, hazard models are very valuable in this context, because they incorporate information on those organizations that do not fail (so-called censored cases). They also allow the researcher to control for differences in organizations and their environments, including organizational age (organizational mortality rates are typically duration-dependent as shown in the foregoing chapters).

By their stated interpretations, the majority of the studies shown in Table 16.1 support the working hypotheses of the core–periphery analytical framework and the broader theory of inertia: mortality rates rise with core changes in structure or unrelated diversification. For instance, Singh et al. (1986) regard CEO succession and location shifts as peripheral changes. Thus they interpret the estimated negative effect as being consistent with the theory. However, the pattern of findings is far from uniform. Several studies report strong effects of core structural change contrary to Hannan and Freeman's predictions. Studies by Kelly and Amburgey (1991), Delacroix and Swaminathan (1991), and Haveman (1992) can be interpreted in this way. So, we have a genuine unsolved puzzle concerning a central issue in the field.

The prospect of solving such an important question will undoubtedly attract many researchers and propel the development of corporate demography. These previous studies might teach us some lessons that will prove beneficial in designing and interpreting future research. One of these concerns the desirability of strictly separating the nature of the change from its outcome. In principle, every researcher would agree that independent and dependent variables must be definitionally and conceptually independent; but in practice the lines sometimes get blurred. Any major organizational change that likely occurs as a result of previous successful performance must be treated with caution in this context because its estimated effects will likely be confounded. An example of this type of problematic "independent" variable comes from Delacroix and Swaminathan's (1991) study of wineries. Land acquisitions and new product offerings are the organizational changes studied; firms need substantial resources to make such changes. Unless an analyst has detailed information on a firm's finances (which would be very rare in the kind of research we are considering), one must worry that the effect of recent success and/or "deep pockets" gets confounded with the effect of the resource-demanding changes.

Another important lesson for future research on the effects of organizational change concerns modeling. As Amburgey, Kelly, and Barnett (1993) point out, Hannan and Freeman's thesis about the deleterious consequences of change relies mainly on notions about the process effects of change: it disrupts routines, undermines relationships, requires learning, and so forth (thereby lowering reliability and accountability). Process effects of change are most pronounced immediately during and immediately following the change and diminish gradually with duration from the change. To estimate such effects meaningfully, one needs to peel away any effects of the content of the change, which might be either positive or negative. So, for instance, in a group of firms diversifying into unrelated areas, some might be moving into markets that are bountiful and uncompetitive while others are moving into markets with scarce resources and strong competitors. If Hannan and Freeman are correct, then all of these firms should experience negative effects from the process of moving into unrelated markets (process effect of change). If, on the other hand, most are going into bountiful markets, then the beneficial returns of participation in such an environment (content effect of change) might overwhelm any simple test of the effects of diversification.

Modeling Framework

Can content and process effects be separated empirically? A general model formulation for all types of organizational change has not been advanced. For organizational changes that have the character of discontinuities or discrete events, however, we have a reasonably well-developed framework. Hannan and Freeman (1984) proposed a model that holds that fundamental change "sets back" the liability-of-newness clock by destroying the value of accumulated experience. They suggested that fundamental change creates a discontinuous increase in the hazard of mortality and that the elevated hazard erodes over time such that organizations that survive the risky period end up with possibly lower hazards of mortality. Amburgey et al. (1993) have elaborated this framework in a way that has generated considerable insight. Their proposal requires estimation of more complex models than we have discussed to this point. The model needs to specify baseline rates, counters for transformations, and clocks associated with each transformation. Without loss of generality, we consider a serviceable specification of the first fundamental transformation in an organization's lifetime:

$$\mu_i(u, v) = \exp[\alpha\Delta_{iu} + \Theta\mathbf{X}_{iu}] \cdot \varphi(u) \cdot \psi(v), \qquad (16.1)$$

where u denotes the master clock for the process, say organizational age, v is a clock that tells the time since the first transformation (and equals zero for an organization until a transformation occurs), $\mu_i(u, v)$ is the instantaneous failure rate of organization i and age u and duration (from transformation) v, and $\mathbf{X}_{iu}$ are variables describing the state-space of organization i at time age u. Δ_{iu}, an indicator variable for change, is set equal to zero from the founding date of each organization i unless and until it engages in a major change. Once an organization has changed, the value of this indicator is fixed at 1. In terms of this specification, process effects of change per se are represented by the terms α and $\psi(v)$. Either type of effect might also interact with other covariates, including organizational age and size. The structural inertia theory of Hannan and Freeman (1984) predicts $\alpha > 0$ and $\psi'(v) < 0$. Amburgey et al. (1993) proposed and estimated a restricted form of this model with $\varphi(u) = \exp(\beta u)$ and $\psi(v) = \exp(\gamma v)$:

$$\mu_i(u, \tau) = \exp[\alpha\Delta_{iu} + \beta u + \gamma v + \Theta\mathbf{X}_{iu}]. \qquad (16.2)$$

Figure 16.1 shows two possible realizations of the model: in the one labeled A the transformation leads to better alignment with the environment, and in the other, labeled B, it actually worsens alignment. Here the vertical axis represents the organization-specific hazard of mortality and the horizontal axis, organizational age. We want to consider the consequences of a transformation at age u_c. The solid line in the figure shows the implications for "no change." In other words, in our example, this is the age-dependent hazard that would apply to the organization if it did not undergo the transformation. As shown in Chapter 13, organizational mortality rates can have complicated relationships with age. We illustrate the change model in terms of negative age dependence. (It is straightforward to translate the results to positive age dependence.) In both realizations, the process of change increases mortality rates (signified by a positive α parameter and shown by the jumps in the lines at age u_c). The trajectory given by the upper dashed line (labeled A) shows an example of a change that worsened alignment. The organization that has chosen this content for its transformation has an elevated hazard at every later age (as compared with the "no change" condition). The lower dashed line (labeled B) shows an example of a case of new content improving alignment. This difference can be seen by comparing the rates before and after the change once the process effects have worn off. Note that the mortality curve for the improved alignment case crosses the "no change" curve. These comparisons can be made fairly easily because we have set the process effects so that they begin at the same level and wear off at roughly the same

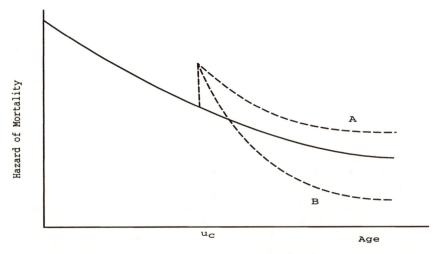

Figure 16.1.   *Two scenarios for the effect of transformation at age u_c on mortality with negative age dependence.*

speed. However, one cannot count on such an extremely unlikely outcome in analysis of real data. The consequence of variations in these effects is hard to understand without a formal model of the process.

Only a few of the studies reported in Table 16.1 estimated the complete form of Amburgey et al.'s (1993) model. In our opinion, most studies of the effects of change mix content and process effects. The full model cannot always be estimated. Among other things, the model requires that changes occur between identifiable states. Otherwise, content effects of the different states cannot be completely controlled. An even stronger requirement of the model is that the organizational changes studied must be either repeatable or of more than one type (yet comparable across repetitions or types). Otherwise, the state space controls are identical to Δ_{iu}. When either of these conditions does not apply, the full model cannot be identified.

Using Amburgey et al.'s (1993) model to examine the consequences of organizational change requires an a priori designation of important differences in the content of change. For some applications, including diversification into new markets, this might be a fairly straightforward exercise of simply distinguishing good practice from bad (movement into bountiful and uncrowded markets versus into scarce and crowded ones). However, we believe that again here, as with models explaining organizational change, researchers have barely tapped the reservoir of relevant knowledge found in basic organizational theory.

Virtually all theories of organization have implications about the organizational configurations that will fare best in a given setting, but these theoretical ideas are rarely applied to conceptualize the content in studies assessing the effects of change. Instead, measures of the content of change are usually taken as given and treated as control variables (for example, the audience, location, and periodicity measures used in Amburgey et al.'s (1993) study of newspaper changes).

The failure to employ theoretically motivated measures of content represents a missed opportunity to study the effects of change for broader purposes. Whether or not Hannan and Freeman's process thesis bears out, it would be informative to learn whether organizations in a particular context changing their structures in the specific ways predicted by, say, transaction-cost theory, institutional theory, or resource-dependence theory, experience enhanced performance and lower mortality rates. Moreover, it might very well be that because of their magnitude, these types of content effects must be considered to get "clean" estimates of process effects.

Finally, many studies of the effects of change fail to control for the competitive intensity of the environments that organizations face. This might seem a minor oversight, characteristic of the treatment of many other possible control variables. However, we believe that addressing the effect of competitive intensity ought to be brought into the picture. When an organization faces strong competition, the consequences of making the "wrong" structural adjustment (content of change) is both more severe and quicker to be realized than when competition is weak. In fact, under weak competition there might be no negative repercussion of retaining (or adopting) inappropriate organizational content. Competition might also determine the threshold at which disruption from change leads to lowered performance (process effects).

16.4 Innovation in Automobile Manufacturing

To illustrate the general issues discussed above, we describe the results of Carroll and Teo's (1996) study of the effects of technical innovations on organizational failure for American automobile manufacturing firms. This study differs from many others in the transformation literature in that it uses an industry-wide conception of innovation: a firm is regarded as having an innovation only when it is the first in the industry to use a particular technical idea. The study uses population data on all American automobile producers operating during 1885–1981. It examines the impact of a firm's own innovations on its life chances as well as those of its competitors in the industry.[7]

Carroll and Teo (1996) used measures of technical innovation from the extensive data-collection effort by Abernathy, Clark, and Kantrow (1983). Using a wide variety of industry sources and relying on their expert knowledge of the industry, these investigators generated a firm-specific chronological list of product and process innovation in American automobile manufacture (Abernathy et al. 1983, 150–151). This effort defines an innovation event as the earliest significant commercial introduction in the United States of a new product or process. The list, which attempts to be comprehensive, enumerates 641 innovations for the period 1893 to 1981 that could be used in this analysis.[8]

Intuition would suggest that innovations improve the life chances of the firms that introduce them. Many socioevolutionary theorists would agree. They usually put technical innovation at the center of their theoretical efforts and envision it as the means by which some firms overcome

---

[7] Parts of this section are adapted from Carroll and Teo (1996).

[8] It includes many innovations by small firms (such as Autocar and Monarch). While the list links most innovations to specific automakers, it also attributes ten innovations to "all producers" or "most producers" (these tend to be regulation-induced innovations such as the safety front shoulder harness). Another 26 innovations are attributed to component suppliers. Because interest lies with the competitive effects of innovation, Carroll and Teo excluded these 36 innovations from the analysis.

or alter their selection environments. The flip side of the coin concerns other firms' innovations. Presumably, a firm in a competitive market stands to lose—at least in the short term—if its competitors introduce technical innovations (especially if those innovations are proprietary or inimitable). The appeal of new products or product features or the lowered costs associated with an innovation represent positive content effects and give the innovating firms a potential competitive advantage.

Suppose that the costs and risks entailed in introducing an innovation depend heavily on the characteristics of the organization. Theory and research on technology frequently investigate the role of organizational size in stimulating or inhibiting innovation (Kamien and Schwartz 1982). A popular theme holds that larger organizations are more likely to generate incremental innovations but small organizations are the likely sources of radical innovations. For instance, Winter (1984) argues that small, entrepreneurial firms face a disadvantage in developing incremental innovations because they lack the necessary complementary assets. Similarly, he contends that large established firms find that existing products and assets constrain their ability to develop radical innovations. Even if generally accurate, this pattern does not preclude the possibility of some nonconforming cases in either direction (Henderson and Cockburn 1995).

Moreover, the organizational context spawning an innovation might not be optimal for its commercial exploitation. Why? First, the resources required to generate an innovation often differ from those needed to implement it successfully; and any given organizational context is more likely to have one or the other set of resources rather than a balanced set of both. Second, the interests and incentives of those persons responsible for potentially spawning innovations and those responsible for implementing innovations frequently diverge in organizational settings. Third, there is the inherent difficulty of accurately predicting the future impact of an anticipated innovation, especially in a complex organizational setting. So, rather than assume that organizational size plays a similar role in both processes, this investigation decoupled questions about effects of innovation from those about sources. More specifically, Carroll and Teo (1996) take the innovation as given and ask whether it is more likely to achieve its potential in small or large organizations.

Large organizations tend to be more complex. Both size and complexity magnify the usual problems of control and coordination within an organization. An innovation introduced into a large firm thus ordinarily entails lots of adjustments—many minor, some perhaps major—by other persons and in other routines. Because so many actors are potentially affected, the chances of encountering opposing interests are high. Even if this is not the case, many actors who need to make adjustments will fail to understand the rationale or will misunderstand what they need to do (in perhaps a process not unlike the one discussed by Kreps (1996)). Indeed, the complementary assets that give large organizations their advantage in many arenas, including perhaps spawning innovation, might create liabilities in innovation: each asset must be integrated, and coordination is costly and risky. For instance, in studying technological changes in the manufacture of mainframe computers, Iansiti and Khanna (1995, 354) conclude that: "the organizational challenge is not simply in the development of specific competences on their own individual merits, but also in the management of the complex web of interrelationships between them and the existing product and production system." For these reasons, Carroll and Teo explored the possibility that the impact of innovation on life chances depends on (interacts with) organizational size.

The empirical analysis centers on a variable, $Innovation_t$, that measures the number of innovations a firm introduces in a year t; this firm-specific variable matches the appropriate firm spell to each recorded innovation. The number of innovations by other firms in a year was measured by constructing annual time-varying measures of the total number of innovations by all other firms in the industry. Because innovations are one-time occurrences and firms are not observed to move from innovation to noninnovation, the full model of Amburgey et al. (1993) cannot be estimated (the baseline rates cannot be identified). As a modeling convenience, Carroll and Teo treated innovations as exogenous and estimated their association with the rate of firm failure as log-linear covariates in a Gompertz model (Chapter 13).[9] The coefficients in this model associated with $Innovation_t$ measure the jump or drop in the mortality rate in the period immediately following development of an innovation in a firm.

Table 16.2 presents the key estimates of two models specified as tests of arguments about the organizational context of technical innovation.[10] In addition to the main effects of innovation and size, the table reports estimates of the interaction of innovation and organizational characteristics. Looking first at the main effects of an innovation by a firm and by its competitors shows the intuitively expected effects. Innovation by the focal firm has a significant negative (beneficial) effect on mortality while innovation by competitors heightens the chances of failure.

Both sets of estimates also suggest strongly that organizational size matters greatly for technical innovations. Although large organizations have lower mortality rates and technical innovation lowers mortality rates, the

---

[9] To test for possible delayed consequences of innovation, Carroll and Teo (1996) also used various lagged versions of this variable. The various lags allowed them to separate shortrun and longrun effects of innovation.

[10] The estimated model contains numerous other covariates, whose effects are not shown here.

Table 16.2. *Effects of innovation on the hazard of mortality for U.S. automobile producers.*

	(1)	(2)
$Size_t$	−0.131*	−0.144*
$Innovation_t$	−1.34*	−2.10*
$Others' innovations_t$	0.035*	0.035*
$Size_t \times innovation_t$	0.011*	0.277*
$Size_t^2 \times innovation_t$		−0.005*

* $p < .05$.
Note: Size is measured in hundreds.
Source: Carroll and Teo (1996). Copyright © 1996 by Oxford University Press. Used by permission.

significant positive effect of the size–innovation interaction in the first column of Table 16.2 shows that innovation in large organizations is initially much less mortality-reducing than it is in small organizations. That is, the larger the organization that makes a technical innovation, the greater are the associated risks.

The second column in Table 16.2 reports interesting estimates of a more complex interaction between organizational size and innovation. This equation specifies an additional interaction between a second-order size variable (size-squared) and innovation. The polynomial interaction allows the detrimental effects of size to decrease for the largest firms, a pattern consistent with the long-lived nature of the industry's largest firms. The estimate of the second-order interaction is negative and significant; its inclusion improves the fit of the model. Thus, it appears that innovation has been precarious for large firms in the industry but not for the very largest.

Appendix: A Property-Based Formalization of Inertia Theory

A crucial aspect of the Hannan–Freeman inertia argument is that certain organizational properties accumulate or disappear over time in organizational populations. The states in which these properties prevail are reached by the proliferation of the carriers of these properties: the organizations. In fact, the focal elements in the inertia theory are the organizational *properties* themselves and not the carrier organizations. Péli et al. (1998) demonstrate this idea by giving an alternative formalization to the just-described model of inertia accumulation, now referring exclusively to organizational properties, using first-order predicate logic.

The only agent in the model is the population in which these properties appear or disappear. Thus, the formulas presented in this section realize a par excellence population-level representation of the inertia argument. As we show, the property-based approach can keep the formalization really quite close to the original verbal arguments.

In Section 16.2, Acc&Rel, Repr, and Inert denoted zero-place predicates (claiming that a certain organization possesses these properties). Now (similar) name strings denote name constants for the properties themselves: a for accountability/reliability, rp for reproducibility, and i for inertia. Péli et al. (1998) define the concept of "favored by selection" as a one-place predicate (it had no argument slots before), denoted as $\Sigma(p)$. The first of Hannan and Freeman's triplet of assumptions can now be restated as holding for the properties of reliability and accountability.

Assumption A16.1. *The property of being accountable and reliable is favored by selection*:

$$\Sigma(a).$$

Péli et al. (1998) restate the second of the original assumptions by using the two-place *requires* predicate, denoted by $\Pi(p_1, p_2)$ with the following interpretation: the incumbent object of the first slot "requires" the presence of the object in the second slot.

Assumption A16.2. *Reliability and accountability require the presence of reproducibility*:

$$\Pi(a, rp).$$

Finally, Péli et al. (1998) restate the third of the original assumptions with the two-place *generates* predicate, denoted by $\Gamma(p_1, p_2)$ in a similar manner; $\Gamma(p_1, p_2)$ means that the object in the first slot "generates" the object in the second slot.

Assumption A16.3. *Reproducibility generates inertia*:

$$\Gamma(rp, i).$$

Two background assumptions and a definition are needed to connect Assumptions A16.1–A16.3.

Assumption A16.4. *If the presence of property p_1 requires the presence of another property p_2 and p_1 proliferates, then p_2 also proliferates*:

$$\forall p_1, p_2 \left[\{P(p_1) \wedge P(p_1, p_2)\} \rightarrow \Pi(p_2) \right].$$

Assumption A16.5. *If property* p_1 *generates the presence of property* p_2, *then the proliferation of* p_1 *also implies the proliferation of* p_2:

$$\forall p_1, p_2 \left[\{\Pi(p_1) \wedge \Gamma(p_1, p_2)\} \rightarrow \Pi(p_2) \right].$$

Note that no explicit time variable appears in these formulas. Yet, the theory concerns temporal processes. In fact, temporality is present in the proposed rendering: it is encapsulated into the meaning of the predicates Γ and Π. Explicit representation of time is not necessary in this rendering.

Finally, selection preference is defined in terms of proliferation of the favored properties.

Definition A16.1. *A property is favored by selection if and only if the property proliferates*:

$$\forall p \left[\Sigma(p) \leftrightarrow \mathsf{P}(p) \right].$$

These assumptions and definitions imply a statement very close to Hannan and Freeman's original claim:

Theorem A16.1. *Selection favors the property of organizational inertia (from Assumptions A16.1–A16.5 and Definition A16.1)*:

$$\Sigma(\mathsf{i}).$$

Part V
SELECTED IMPLICATIONS

THIS PART OF THE BOOK explores some of the implications of a demographic view for selected topics of theory and policy. The chapters aim to suggest how a demographic approach to corporations might make a difference for the social sciences for policy analysis. The topics addressed are those for which the connections to corporate demography seem most salient; however, as will be obvious, the implications of corporate demography for policy have only begun to be developed.

Chapter 17 considers corporate demography in light of basic organization theory. It holds that demographic processes are relevant to *all* theories of organization, not just those with which it is usually associated (i.e., organizational ecology). The claim is demonstrated by examining the mechanisms of organizational change often assumed in theories of organization. Various mechanisms of change are scrutinized and their implications for research considered. Special attention is paid to the speed and efficiency of change processes; these are dimensions that have been undeservedly neglected.

In Chapter 18, we illustrate the implications of a corporate-demographic approach to regulation. The chapter presents the findings of two demographically oriented studies of the consequences of regulation. The first of these concerns state and federal regulation of early telephony in the United States. The second involves an analysis of modern deregulation of banking in the United States. Both studies yield findings whose implications appear to differ from those of typical analyses of regulation.

Chapter 19 investigates relationships between processes of corporate demography and employment. The many ways that vital events of corporations affect careers and jobs are reviewed. The chapter attempts to estimate the impact of corporate-demographic events on job mobility in the United

381

States. The exercise is crude, but it suggests strongly that a sizeable proportion of mobility can be accounted for by corporate demography. The chapter also speculates about the implications of this demographically induced mobility for pensions and other benefits and suggests some research direction. The last part of the chapter identifies some of the reverse processes—those concerning how career dynamics affect organizational demography.

Basic theory and research in corporate demography illuminate how organizational diversity arises and changes over time. Chapter 20 advances some arguments and research ideas about how organizational diversity itself might affect important social outcomes. It first speculates as to how diversity within two particular industries, beer and wine, might affect consumption patterns and related social problems. The case lends itself to empirical research; it also might serve as a model for industry-specific research on the consequences of organizational diversity. The chapter next considers a more general question: how organizational diversity affects careers and associated rewards, leading to variations in inequality. Theory and some initial empirical evidence are discussed. The chapter closes with a brief note about exploring the effects of organizational diversity for society.

17

Organization Theory

IN PRECEDING CHAPTERS, we discussed how corporations experience vital events that parallel birth, death, marriage, and migration. We have also seen that the methods and models of demography can be readily applied to the world of organizations. As the material above shows, using a demographic lens often generates fresh and interesting insights about organizational processes and dynamics. Yet demographic considerations might strike many social scientists as a peculiar, if fascinating, branch of organizational studies, largely disconnected from the mainstream of organizational theory and research. Current textbooks of organizational design, for instance, pay almost no attention to demographic phenomena.

In this chapter, we argue that demographic concerns have important implications for virtually all basic theories of organization. We start by examining the common strategy underlying empirical research on organizations. We explain how the usual approach contains a set of implicit—and often unrecognized—premises about organizational change and corporate demography. We examine and compare the credulity of these premises from a demographic perspective.

Using computer simulation techniques, we also investigate the consequences of using what we claim are generally misguided assumptions. Our analysis suggests that direct investigation of demographic change would be both more appropriate and potentially more interesting than continued reliance on these outdated assumptions. Moreover, we show how greater integration of demographic analysis into basic organizational research promises to sharpen differences between theories and to stimulate exciting new research questions.

17.1 The Equilibrium Orientation

Most theories of organizational structure and performance can be characterized as "equilibrium theories." This means that they make specific predictions only about the organizational designs likely to be found (and operating successfully) in particular situations and contexts. For instance, the influential transaction-cost economics theories of Williamson (1975; 1985) state that, under conditions of high asset specificity, vertically integrated organizations will have lower costs and therefore will be more efficient than other organizational designs. This is because the theory posits that the alignment of a hierarchical governance structure with a highly asset-specific context minimizes transaction costs. Empirical tests of this theory typically compare organizations in conditions of high and low asset specificity and check whether the former show more instances of vertically integrated organizations than the latter. Managerial-action recommendations based on this theory include assessing the asset specificity of an organization's important transaction partners and making appropriate organizational adjustments, i.e., adding or deleting an activity or subunit. Public policy based on this theory would presumably put into place regulations and institutions with incentives favoring organizations with the recommended efficient structures.

Note that corporate demography has little apparent role in this—and other—equilibrium theories, because these theories focus almost exclusively on the organizational forms that will be present in a world where only successful organizations are present. In other words, they consider an equilibrium state of alignment between organizational form and some context.

Such a research strategy ignores the processes by which organizations take on the equilibrium-favored traits. At a general level, two types of processes might operate: a process of *adaptation*, whereby individual organizations acquire and dispose of activities and subunits as they move towards equilibrium, and a process of *selection*, whereby individual organizations come into existence and cease to exist (based on their compatibility with the equilibrium conditions).

Should selective replacement prove to be the major mechanism of organizational change, then corporate demography would inform generally about organizational change, a process of obvious great scientific importance and policy relevance. However, even should organizational change proceed mainly through adaptation, corporate demography would be highly informative: knowing rates of failure or death among adaptive social units tells about the speed and limits of adaptive change.

Equilibrium organizational theories, such as transaction-cost theory and contingency theory, usually assume that the dominant process of organizational change involves adaptation. There is no reason, however, that the theories should be tied to this assumption—transaction-cost minimizing and contingent alignment might very well proceed via selection. In fact, the one systematic study that we know exploring this issue from the perspective of transaction costs finds this to be the case. A study of American paper mills from 1900 to 1940 by Ohanian (1994) finds that the levels of vertical integration match industry conditions as transaction-cost theory implies. However, this alignment obtained overwhelmingly as a result of selective replacement, not the adaptation of individual mills. Selective replacement is, of course, an essentially demographic process.

17.2 External Alignment and Fitness

The equilibrium orientation of much organization theory holds that social structural change reflects a logic of alignment in changing environments. A broadly ecological perspective informs much theory and research on the dependence of organizations on members and environments. According to the central claims of this perspective, the persistence and success of an organization require that it maintain flows of essential resources from its environment.[1]

Organizations possess both identities and structural forms. Identity summarizes both uniqueness and commonality; form summarizes only commonality (Chapter 4). Although both identities and forms might be relevant to the problem of maintaining flows of resources, the garden-variety alignment perspective concentrates on organizational forms. It assumes that organizations differ in form and that the capacity of an organization to maintain flows of environmental resources depends upon its form. Some forms fit better with given environments in the sense that organizations with these forms have a superior collective capacity to mobilize resources in those environments. In the common metaphor of alignment, forms differ in how well they align with a given environment.

Different populations of organizations have different kinds of environmental dependencies. Some, such as populations of automobile manufacturers or integrated pharmaceutical firms, are particularly sensitive to property rights, variations in productive technology, and the availability and cost of financial and human capital. Others, such as drug cartels and guerrilla armies, are especially sensitive to variations in political and legal environments and to the technology of repression.

Despite such differences in details of environmental dependencies, all organizations are subject to a *logic of membership*. Often the members of an organization are natural persons, e.g., the employees of a firm or the activists in a social movement. Sometimes, the members are themselves organizations, e.g., firms and universities participating in research consortia or labor unions joined in a federation. In either case, an organization that

---

[1] This section and the next are drawn from Hannan (1996).

loses all of its members and cannot replace them is not viable.[2] Thus we can formulate ideas about environmental effects and alignment in terms of membership dynamics.

Many social science applications of alignment ideas have been criticized for "circular reasoning." The issue of circularity needs to be addressed in any assessment of selection mechanisms. It is helpful in doing so to shift from the usual informal reasoning about alignment to a more formal statement, representing the alignment story in first-order logic.

The defining characteristics of the populations are structural form in this formulation. That is, this formalization abstracts away from identities and focuses on commonality in structural form. In this sense, the formalization applies to sets of actors with identical forms. The properties considered are the quality of alignment of the form with the environment, the capacity to extract resources from the environment, the capacity to attract and retain (appropriate) members in an environment, and viability in an environment. We employ a one-place predicate $O(x)$ to mean that the object x is an organization and a one-place predicate $E(e)$ that tells that the object e is an environment. And we use the following functions: $A(x, e)$, which tells the level of alignment of object x and environment e, $R(x, e)$, the resource extraction function, $M(x, e)$, the membership function, and $V(x, e)$, the viability function.

The core of the theory depends upon three assumptions about how structural form affects the operation of a population of organizations in a specified environment. As noted above, the general ecological perspective holds that structural forms differ in how well they match a given environment. External alignment has consequences for the capacity to mobilize resources, such as legitimacy, endorsement by state officials, status, financial capital, and human capital, in particular environments.

Assumption 17.2.1. *Superior alignment of form with environment implies a superior capacity to mobilize resources in that environment:*

$$\forall x, y, e \left[O(x) \land O(y) \land E(e) \land A(x, e) > A(y, e) \rightarrow R(x, e) > R(y, e) \right].$$

Resources matter (partly) because they affect the chances of attracting and retaining valued classes of members. Organizations vary enormously in the detailed practices they use to attract members and build attachment. Underlying this great diversity is a common dependence on resources from the environment. That is, to make themselves attractive to members, organizations must acquire generalized resources (such as capital and legitimacy) that can be converted into structures, symbols, routines, activities, and benefits (such as compensation arrangements) that constitute the actor's distinctive appeal.

---

[2] In many, if not most cases, the quality of members also matters.

Assumption 17.2.2. *A superior capacity to mobilize resources from a given environment implies a superior capacity to attract and retain members in that environment:*

$$\forall x, y, e \left[O(x) \wedge O(y) \wedge E(e) \wedge R(x, e) > R(y, e) \rightarrow M(x, e) > M(y, e) \right].$$

The third assumption relates the capacity to attract and retain members to viability. Viability means both the persistence of the organization and its expansion: the more viable an organization is, the greater its probability of survival and the higher its growth rate.

Assumption 17.2.3. *If a form has a superior capacity to attract and retain members in a given environment, then it has superior viability in that environment:*

$$\forall x, y, e \left[O(x) \wedge O(y) \wedge E(e) \wedge M(x, e) > M(y, e) \rightarrow V(x, e) > V(y, e) \right].$$

These assumptions together imply three propositions, including the basic alignment theorem (Theorem 17.2.1).

Lemma 17.2.1. *Superior alignment with the environment implies superior capacity to mobilize members in that environment (from Assumptions 17.2.1 and 17.2.2):*

$$\forall x, y, e \left[O(x) \wedge O(y) \wedge E(e) \wedge A(x, e) > A(y, e) \rightarrow M(x, e) > M(y, e) \right].$$

Lemma 17.2.2. *A superior capacity for mobilizing resources from the environment implies greater viability (from Assumptions 17.2.2 and 17.2.3):*

$$\forall x, y, e \left[O(x) \wedge O(y) \wedge E(e) \wedge R(x, e) > R(y, e) \rightarrow V(x, e) > V(y, e) \right].$$

Theorem 17.2.1. *Superior alignment with the environment implies superior viability in that environment (from Lemmas 17.2.1 and 17.2.2):*

$$\forall x, y, e \left[O(x) \wedge O(y) \wedge E(e) \wedge A(x, e) > A(y, e) \rightarrow V(x, e) > V(y, e) \right].$$

This formulation specifies a simple instance of a selection process. It assumes a stock of initial variability in form, and it postulates a process that links variations in the quality of alignment to the relative abundance of forms. Given a particular environment, well-adapted forms persist longer and expand more than poorly adapted forms.

One can easily add empirical content to the formulation by stipulating the precise meaning of viability. Suppose we limit viability to mean the inverse mortality rate. Then it makes sense to elaborate the statement of initial conditions to include the numbers of members of the two populations (densities) defined by the structural forms. If we let N_{j,t_0} denote the number of organizations with form j at the start of the process and N_{j,t_1}

denote the number at some later time ($t_1 > t_0$), then this formulation implies that, if form 1 is better aligned with the given environment than form 2, then

$$\frac{N_{1,t_1}}{N_{1,t_1} + N_{2,t_1}} > \frac{N_{1,t_0}}{N_{1,t_0} + N_{2,t_0}}.$$

That is, superior alignment implies increased relative abundance.

Alternatively, we can define viability to mean quantitative expansion of individual collective actors. Then the relevant initial conditions include the masses of each form: $M_{j,t_0} = \sum_{i=1}^{N_{j,t_0}} S_{i,t_0}$, where S_{i,t_0} denotes the size of the ith organization at the initiation of the process. Masses at time 2 are calculated only for the surviving actors: $M_{j,t_1} = \sum_{i=1}^{N_{j,t_1}} S_{i,t_1}$. Then this selection process implies that better alignment implies increased relative mass (or market share):

$$\frac{M_{1,t_1}}{M_{1,t_1} + M_{2,t_1}} > \frac{M_{1,t_0}}{M_{1,t_0} + M_{2,t_0}},$$

if form 1 is the better aligned form.

This process differs from the standard *natural* selection process, which lies at the heart of contemporary biology, in two ways. First, in its emphasis on the process of attracting and retaining members, this argument clearly specifies a *social* selection process. Second, this formulation builds a very simple one-period model, thereby avoiding the issue of specifying an intertemporal transmission process.[3] Specifically, this simple selection process operates on a single cohort (the initial stock). The environment is constant. No entry process has been specified. There is also no process of reproduction, and thus no following cohorts (or generations). Any productive analysis of longterm change in social structures would likely extend this structure by considering multiple periods, adding processes of entry and reproduction, and by allowing environments to change between periods. Nonetheless, the bare-bones structure developed here suffices for purposes of contrasting selection processes with other mechanisms of organizational change.

The empirical import of selection arguments has long been a subject of intense debate. Critics have commonly advanced the argument that theories built on selection logic are tautological and untestable. Careful logical analysis does not support this view (Sober 1984; Sober 1993; Brandon 1996).

---

[3]The basic model of natural selection combines a process of selection that parallels the one sketched here with a particular transmission process: Mendelian inheritance and, for the case of sexual reproduction, a mating process.

All theories are tautologies when considered as logical structures. Testability concerns the mappings from the logical structure to the empirical domain in which the theory is postulated to apply. Whether an argument built on a selection model is falsifiable when so applied depends upon defining and measuring alignment independently of viability. It is clearly uninteresting to use observations on life chances of various forms to measure alignment. For such arguments to have empirical import, analysts must be willing to specify what good and poor alignment mean concretely without reference to outcomes. Not all research using alignment images meets this criterion. Nonetheless, there is no logical obstacle to meeting it.

Consider, for instance, The Stanford Project on Emerging Companies, discussed in Chapter 9. This project collects detailed life-history information on several hundred young high-technology firms in Silicon Valley. Based on measurements of aspects of employment relations, business strategies, and external environments during the organization-building phase, variations in degree of alignment of employment relations with internal and external contingencies can be identified. By following firms forward in time, the project seeks to learn whether initial alignment (as measured before having knowledge of the outcomes) affects viability (survival, growth, profitability, and so forth).

17.3 Adaptation and Selection among Corporations

We now compare analytically the dynamics behind alignment. That is, we examine the various processes of change in organizational populations implied by basic organizational theories. According to our reading of the organizations literature, three theoretical images of change dominate contemporary theory and research: atomistic adaptation, network diffusion, and selection. Figure 17.1 depicts stylized examples of the operation of the three mechanisms of alignment following a discontinuous environmental change. In this figure, identities of organizations are denoted by numerals and structural forms are denoted by shapes. The figure illustrates a situation in which the environment of a set of organizations changes between times 1 and 4 such that the best adapted form changes from the △-form to the □-form.

At time 1, three organizations have the same form (△), which, by assumption, is well aligned with the prevailing environment; one actor has the "wrong" form (□). The various scenarios in the figure represent possible consequences of the three processes to the environmental shock that tilts the advantage to the □-form. For simplicity, this discussion brackets the complications that would follow from considering realistic rules for aggregating actions to a social structural pattern. In particular, it considers the simplest possible aggregation relation: counting. The macro pattern is just the *distribution* of structural forms.

Atomistic Adaptation. One common account of alignment treats it as reflecting the intentional adaptations of actors to changing environments. Actors learn from experience and can choose the appropriate responses and implement them. For the case of change in organizational form, this means that the decision makers can learn what form fits best and, if necessary, can switch forms. Panel A in Figure 17.1 sketches an example of one pure form of adaptation, with each actor learning in isolation from the learning of the others. The absence of directed lines between actors in-

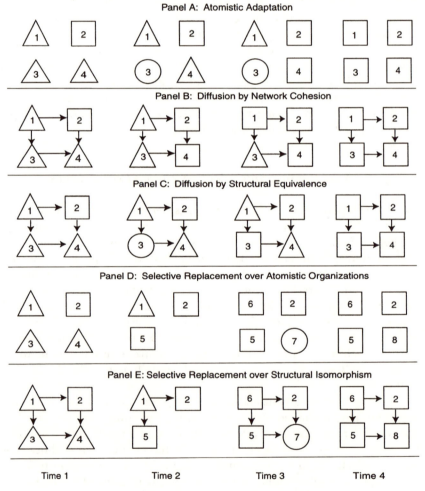

Figure 17.1. *Illustration of three mechanisms for alignment.*

dicates that social ties among them are irrelevant to the mechanism, thus the label "atomistic" adaptation. In this version of the story, each actor learns from its experience. It either experiments with various forms (e.g., actor #3 adopts a ⃝-form by time 2), or it correctly chooses the appropriate □-form and manages to implement it. Eventually, each actor has the □-form, which fits the prevailing environment.

The key feature of this story, for present purposes, is that the change occurs at the level of the *organization*—each organization persists and chooses the best aligned form. None of the actors learns from the experience of the others. Adaptive change at the level of the organization produces aggregate alignment and a replacement of one dominant form with another. In other words, selective replacement occurs in the realm of structural forms but not in the realm of organizations.

This kind of process finds broad use in the social sciences. It is, of course, the one that drives behavior in the standard (textbook) representation of exchange in competitive markets. Actors on both sides have sufficiently small market power that each responds (atomistically) to prices as signals of the relevant environmental conditions (e.g., the balance of buyers and sellers). For instance, a producer facing a large change in the relative price of one of its factors of production will respond by changing its technology of production, which might entail changing its employment relation (one feature of its form). Each producer solves the optimization problem by itself—social learning and influence have no important place in this story.

Sociologists commonly criticize economists for overreliance on atomistic models. However, they would be mistaken to imagine that only economists (writing in introductory textbooks) rely on this kind of mechanism. Even sociological theories that feature the role of institutions commonly rely on images of atomistic adaptation in accounting for alignment. Consider, for instance, John Meyer's influential theory and research on the role of institutional environments in shaping organizational forms (Meyer and Rowan 1977). This theory holds that organizations gain legitimacy by making their observable forms isomorphic to prevailing cultural images (of organization, authority, etc.). Change in a cultural rule "forces existing organizations to incorporate new practices and procedures" (Meyer and Rowan 1977, 340). In other words, organizations respond to changing institutional environments by altering observable aspects of their forms to maintain cultural isomorphism. Thus, individual organizations adapt to preserve alignment. They do so atomistically in the sense that each organization responds alike to changes in an external culture.[4]

---

[4] Current versions of this line of theory place more emphasis on the network-diffusion process.

Network Diffusion. According to the network-diffusion story, an actor's position in a social network influences its choice of form (including decisions to change form). It is conventional to distinguish two versions of this story: cohesion and structural equivalence (Burt 1987; Borgatti and Everett 1992). With cohesion as the mechanism, direct ties govern the flows of information and influence. The probability that an actor changes form increases when its direct ties make such a change. In the structural-equivalence story, actors with identical patterns of ties tend to take similar actions even when they lack direct ties.

Panel B in Figure 17.1 shows a simple pattern of (asymmetric) ties between actors. The sequence of change in panel B reflects a cohesion process. Actor #2 has the well aligned □-form post-change. Actor #4's direct tie from #2 allows it to learn from #2's experience with the □-form in the new environment and follow its lead. Actor #1 with a tie to #2 then learns earlier than the other actors from #2's experience, and so on.

Panel C in this figure shows a sequence consistent with a structural-equivalence story. Again, actor #2's □-form best fits the new state of the environment. Now actor #2's structurally equivalent alter (actor #3) learns from #2's experience with the □-form in the new environment, and it changes its form accordingly. (The subsequent changes have no bearing on this mechanism; one can assume that they occur by atomistic learning.)

In both forms of network diffusion, adaptation at the level of the organization produces a collective alignment; but here (some of) the learning is social. That is, the network structure sets the sequence of adaptations.

Selective Replacement. In the selective-replacement story, alignment of forms occurs at the level of the *population of organizations*. In the pure case, individual organizations cannot change form (e.g., firms get stuck with their initial choices of strategy and structure). Those whose forms align with the environment persist with higher probability; those with poorly aligned forms tend to be replaced by new actors. If some of the new actors have well-aligned forms, they tend to persist, and so on. Panels D and E in the figure depict sequences of change toward improved alignment that reflect pure selection. In panel D the network structure is irrelevant. As in the other examples, one actor (#2) happens by chance to be well aligned (with the □-form) after the environmental shock. Only this actor survives. By time 2, actors #3 and #4 have vanished; a new actor (#5) with the "right" (□) form has entered. By time 3, another of the original cast of actors (actor #1) has disappeared, and two new actors have entered, one with the □-form and one with another, the ○-form. Finally, by time 4, four actors have the well-adapted □-form. One comes from the initial set, and the other three have entered at various times with what turns out to be the "right" form.

The same sequence of changes appears in panel E with the same overlaid network structure as in panels B and C. Here the ties should be regarded as connecting *positions* that can be distinguished from the actors that occupy them. Actors are structurally isomorphic (or automorphically equivalent) if they have the same pattern of unlabeled ties (Borgatti and Everett 1992). In panel E network position shapes selection. Between periods 1 and 2, actors #3 and #4 have disappeared. A new actor (#5) has been formed, and it adopted the same form as its structurally isomorphic alter (#2). Subsequent changes are unaffected by the network structure. Note that the pattern in the fourth period is structurally isomorphic to the original one, even though three of the four actors have been replaced.[5] This example illustrates that selection in the form of selective replacement can operate on the occupants of nodes of the network with the basic structure remaining unchanged (in the sense of structural isomorphism).

The obvious and important difference between selective replacement and adaptation does not concern the final alignment—this does not differ among these examples. Instead, the difference concerns the *locus of adaptation*. In the first three examples (panels A, B, and C), existing actors adapt. In the last two (panels D and E), adaptation in a system occurs through selective replacement among actors with inert forms.

17.4 Speed and Efficiency of Change Processes

Across all kinds of change processes, important differences occur with respect to directionality and the speed of change. These differences might be intrinsic to the process, as when adaptation requires learning that takes time and the acquisition of information. Or, variations in speed and directionality might arise from mixing with some other processes such as competition.

To illustrate such differences, Figure 17.2 shows two scenarios each for adaptation (panels A and B) and selection (panels C and D). In all four scenarios, the same alignment of organizational forms occurs at times 1 and 4; the alignments are also identical to those seen in Figure 17.1. Within each set of paired processes, the speed and directionality of the transformation process differ. Within the two adaptation scenarios, the realization shown in the top panel is faster and more "correctly" targeted than the one in the bottom in the sense that fewer individual transformations are required

---

[5] To highlight the difference between structural equivalence (as conventionally defined in sociological applications) and structural isomorphism, note that actor #3 at time 1 and actor #5 at times 3 and 4 are structurally isomorphic but not structurally equivalent (because the identities of the nodes differ).

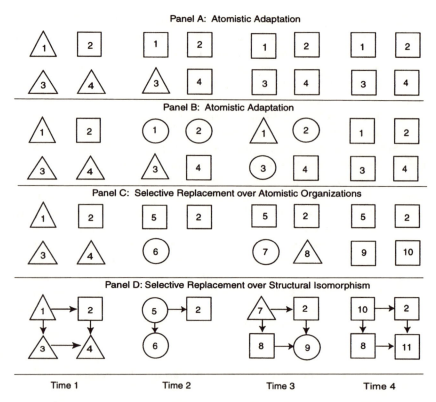

Figure 17.2. *Variations in the speed and directionality of processes generating alignment.*

and these occur faster (it is also better in these respects than the scenario in Figure 17.1). Within the selection scenarios, it is difficult to say which is "better." The scenario in panel C reaches alignment with fewer organizations (specifically, 10 versus 11 organizations in panel D). As compared to those depicted in Figure 17.1, in both of these selection scenarios more organizations appear before alignment at time 4. The major demographic variations in selection as well as adaptation mechanisms become visible once one begins to examine the time paths of organizational change and to enumerate events of organizational founding, structural transformation, and mortality.

To make the alignment process more realistic, consider the founding rates (or arrival rates). Let the founding rates differ for the scenarios painted above, keeping rates of failure and transformation the same. This change in the scenario obviously produces variations in the number of organizations at any point in time, including possibly the last observation at time 4. To make the numbers match, we must introduce competition or some other kind of "winnowing" process (Nelson 1995). Suppose we do so by allowing the first organizations with the better adapted □-form to outcompete later arriving organizations with the same form. Then by this "first-mover" process of advantage, the first four organizations with the better form will persist, regardless of how they acquired the form or how many other organizations appear. In other words, the first movers into the □-form will show a lower rate of mortality once they possess the form than other organizations. Obviously, understanding of this system could only be determined by assessing the relative speeds of both transformational and selectional mechanisms.

Note that, when founding rates vary, the mix of organizations can vary over time. If a particular form has a high founding rate, then organizations of this kind can easily outnumber the environmentally favored form. Organizations researchers and analysts often assume that the existence or relative abundance of particular organizational forms represents the outcome of some process—adaptational or selectional in nature—yielding competitive advantage to those forms. Indeed, the cross-sectional approach to theory testing that we associated with equilibrium theories at the beginning of the chapter implies precisely such an assumption. March and Olsen (1989, 5–6) call this the assumption of "historical efficiency." They explain this idea as follows:

> Institutions and behavior are thought to evolve through some sort of efficient historical process. An efficient historical process, in these terms, moves rapidly to a unique solution, conditional on current environmental conditions, and its destination does not depend upon the historical path. This equilibrium might involve a stochastically subtle distribution or a fixed point, but we require a solution that can be achieved relatively rapidly and does not depend on the details of historical events leading to it.

This assumption, often not made explicit, can be applied regardless of whether the underlying organizational change process is hypothesized to be market-driven efficiency, uncertainty reduction, cost minimization, normative consensus or whatever. In terms of the scenarios we have been discussing, historical efficiency implies that the system moves from time 1 to time 4 quickly in real time. It also implies that the change process has strong directionality in the sense that not many "mistakes" occur along the way in the form of foundings of ill-adapted organizations or transformations to ill-adapted forms.

How realistic is the assumption? In our view, historical efficiency might be plausible in some contexts, but it is far from self-evident that this is the case. The crucial questions concern the strength of the underlying systematic forces yielding competitive advantage to some forms and the extent to which other factors, including random ones, impinge upon organizations. Obviously, in settings where a strong driving force of adaptation or selection operates with little noise, the system will adjust rapidly. Here the assumption of historical efficiency is not only sustainable but practical. However, in settings where the underlying force of adaptation or selection is weaker or where there is a significant amount of noise, assuming historical efficiency becomes potentially problematic. The system might be obscured or even influenced by noise.

For organizations, important substantive considerations bear on the advisability of using the assumption of historical efficiency to infer competitive advantage. Organizational environments might be endogenous or nonstationary, meaning the alignment "target" (favored form) might shift before it is fully realized. Many organizational processes also show signs of positive feedback or self-reinforcement. For example, learning-by-doing and scale economies of production show these features. Such processes create the conditions for path dependence among competing forms of organization. Path dependence deserves attention because it can lead to unexpected outcomes, such as the longterm survival of and dominance by an initially inferior competing form of organization. Analyses by Arthur (1989) and others have shown that systems with positive feedback can generate outcomes strongly affected by random events or noise in the presence of strong systematic forces such as market selection.

To see the power of path dependence, consider the class of stochastic processes known as nonlinear Polya processes (Cohen 1976). Arthur, Ermoliev, and Kaniovski (1987, 294) define nonlinear Polya processes as those characterizing "systems where increments to proportions or concentrations occur with probabilities that are nonlinear functions of present proportions or concentrations." This general definition applies to many organizational population processes including density dependence.

Interesting features of these processes can be seen in even the simplest case, the so-called standard Polya urn-scheme (Eggenberger and Polya 1923; Cohen 1976; Arthur et al. 1987). Imagine that we possess an urn of infinite capacity that holds initially two balls, one blue and one gold. We draw one ball randomly from the urn, examine its color, and return it to the urn. We also place in the urn another ball of the same color as that drawn. We continue this process indefinitely, calculating the proportions of balls of each color in the urn at each step. What happens to the proportions? The counterintuitive answer is that the proportions of blue and gold balls in the urn approach a limit given by a uniformly distributed random variable between 0 and 1 (Eggenberger and Polya 1923; Cohen 1976; Arthur et al. 1987). So, if we conduct the exercise multiple times, each time the proportions will converge to stable values. Across efforts, however, the proportions will differ. Polya processes are path dependent because the probabilities of balls of either color being chosen depend on the sequence of previous draws; and they are self-reinforcing because the more times a color is chosen, the more likely it will be chosen again.

17.5 Historical Efficiency and Competition

The assumption of historical efficiency implies that, when two organizational populations stand in competition with each other, the "stronger" of the two will dominate in a fairly short period of time. For the assumption to be applicable to most real-world contexts, this outcome should not depend on when each population enters the competitive arena or on the size of the other population at time of entry. By contrast, the path-dependent properties of models with positive feedback suggest that, if populations follow trajectories implied by the density model (Chapters 10 and 11), then other outcomes are possible. Because of its wide applicability, the density model provides a good framework for conducting a meaningful detailed examination of the plausibility of historical efficiency.[6]

We summarize simulation findings, produced by Carroll and Harrison (1994), about historical efficiency when the intensity of competition facing organizational populations depends upon density. This research used empirical estimates of the density model to simulate trajectories of competing organizational populations defined by organizational form, a process that theorists often assume to be historically efficient. The simulations were designed so that some populations are "structurally superior" to others, meaning that the chosen parameters lead one to expect that certain populations should outcompete others. Although in common parlance, competitive victory might imply several dimensions of dominance, this analysis uses the simulations to address a specific but central question: How often does the structurally superior population dominate in numbers of organizations?

The simulation study uses the basic model of density-dependent evolution (Chapters 10 and 11). Carroll and Harrison (1994) introduce competition into the model by including simple monotonic effects of the density of each population on the vital rates of each other population. For foundings, a negative interpopulation effect indicates competition: it tells how much the density of another population lowers the founding rate of a focal population. For mortality, competition means that the effect of another population's density on the focal population's mortality rate is positive. With competing populations, the general structure of the relevant part of

---

[6]This section is adapted from Carroll and Harrison (1994).

the model for population i is

$$\lambda_i(t) = \exp\left[\beta_{i0} + \beta_{i1} N_i(t) + \beta_{i2} N_i^2(t) + \sum_{i \neq j} \delta_{ij} N_j(t)\right]$$

for founding rates, where $N_j(t)$ are the densities for the competitor populations, and

$$\mu_i(u) = \exp\left[\alpha_{i0} + \alpha_{i1} N_i(u) + \alpha_{i2} N_i^2(u) + \sum_{i \neq j} \eta_{ij} N_j(u)\right]$$

for mortality rates.

Carroll and Harrison (1994) simulated a world with five potential organizational populations, labeled A through E. The populations always enter the competitive arena in alphabetical order, and the entry times are random. The lexicographical ordering corresponds with competitive strength. Each population is set to be structurally superior to every population that falls below it in this ordering. So the fifth population, E, dominates D in the strength of its competitive effects, D dominates C, and so forth.

More technically, the experiments proceed as follows. Population A begins the simulation with one organization at the start. Populations B through E emerge in order randomly at later points in time set by a constant-rate model. All populations are governed by similar founding and mortality rates with identical baseline rates and identical forms of non-monotonic own density dependence.[7] Each successive population is structurally superior to A and to all other populations emerging previously in that its density exerts negative effects on A's and on prior others' founding rates. Each successive population also exerts positive effects on A's and on prior others' mortality rates. Meanwhile, populations A and prior others exert analogous but much smaller effects on the focal population. Once the density of any population reaches 0, it is considered defunct and cannot reemerge.

The simulation studies were conducted for the equivalent of 500 years (proceeding in monthly increments) for 250 independent trials. Only the seeds used for generation of random numbers were changed between trials. Experimental variation consists of varying the competitive intensity of the relationship between the populations. That is, the absolute values of the competition parameters (δ and η) are changed in different experiments.

Table 17.1 gives a set of competition parameters used in the experiment as well as the outcomes. The top panel of the table shows the exact

---

[7] Exact parameters as well as other technical details can be found in Carroll and Harrison (1994).

Table 17.1. *Experimental settings and outcomes of simulation experiments on historical efficiency.*

Parameter settings: Effects of density on founding rates (δ_{ij})					
Dependent population	Competitor				
	A	B	C	D	E
A	0	−0.008	−0.012	−0.016	−0.020
B	−0.004	0	−0.008	−0.012	−0.016
C	−0.003	−0.004	0	−0.008	−0.012
D	−0.002	−0.003	−0.002	0	−0.008
E	−0.001	−0.002	−0.003	−0.004	0

Number of trials won					
Competition-matrix multiplier	Wins				
	A	B	C	D	E
1	67	25	24	28	106
2	77	18	17	36	102
3	90	26	23	32	79
4	106	36	28	25	55
5	128	25	26	16	55

Note: See text for explanation.
Source: Carroll and Harrison (1994). Copyright © 1994 by the University of Chicago. Used by permission.

structural relationships—it depicts the so-called community matrix of competition coefficients. The table gives values for the community matrix for founding rates (δ_{ij}); the mortality-rate community matrix (η_{ij}) is identical, except that the signs of the coefficients are reversed.

The lower panel of Table 17.1 gives the distribution of dominance outcomes by population at simulation end. Each row shows the number of trials won (meaning numerical dominance at the end of the simulation) by the various populations of a total of 250 trials. Successive rows report separate simulation trials where competitive intensity was increased by multiplying the competition matrix by integer factors. For instance, the last row shows simulation outcomes for experiments with the greatest competitive intensity, where the values of the competition matrix are five times the values shown in the top panel of the table.

In the first group of experiments listed, those with a community-matrix multiplier of unity, the structurally superior competitor, population *E*, wins the most trials: exactly 106. However, *E* wins less than half the time, 106 of 250. Moreover, when E does not win, the most likely winner is A, the "weakest" competitor.

Even more striking is the shift in the distribution of winners as competition intensifies. As the community-matrix multiplier increases, the percentage of trials with E the winner drops by almost half (55 of 250 trials), and the corresponding percentage wins for A almost doubles (to 128 of 250). In the experiment with the most intense competitive relations between populations, those with a matrix multiplier of five, the weakest competitor, A, wins over half the trials. This finding has been replicated for other parameter settings by Carroll and Harrison (1994).

These findings show that the strong assumption of historical efficiency can be very problematic and misleading. Using the well-established general model of density-dependent organizational evolution, we see that outcomes that appear irrational from the point of view of a population's structural superiority or inferiority occur in a variety of experimental conditions. As Carroll and Harrison (1994) demonstrate, these outcomes result from path-dependent consequences of random variations in population growth *before* the emergence of competing populations. More specifically, both previous growth of early populations and entry time of later populations strongly affect outcomes. Early populations that grow fast show remarkable resilience in warding off later but structurally superior competitors. Conversely, competitors that enter the competitive arena quickly can better exert their structural superiority and dominate.

18
Regulation

EVERY INDUSTRY in modern society experiences some sort of governmental regulation. A set of general rules covers many issues such as tax, employment, and competition. Other rules are specific to particular industries, as with sanitation regulations for restaurants, safety regulations for air carriers, and disclosure requirements for financial institutions.

Because of their potentially profound impact on business activity, regulations almost always receive much scrutiny, debate, and study. Among academic scholars, economists have been the leaders in conducting serious analysis of regulatory policy and practice. Economists examining regulation typically undertake theoretical and empirical analysis of the welfare and efficiency effects of particular rules and regulations. Their contributions have literally transformed (and improved) the worlds we live in. There is no question about the value of this kind of work. Still, questions might be legitimately raised as to its possible completeness. Does standard economic analysis of regulation leave some issues and problems unaddressed? More specifically, pursuant to our efforts here, we ask: Might corporate demography play a new or unique role in studying and analyzing the effects of regulations on firms and industries?

There are several reasons for thinking that corporate demography might illuminate new issues about regulation of business and industry. First, a demographic focus on organizational populations implies a comprehensive view of regulation and its effects. Demographic research ostensibly would examine a broad range of relevant corporate actors and their conditions before and after regulatory change. This means that not only might the effects of regulation on specific types of firms be examined but also the interdependencies between various organizational forms found in an industry—a set of second-order effects of regulation. These second-order effects might themselves have important demographic manifestations and likely result in structural change in an industry. Second, corporate-demographic analysis typically uses a long time frame. This means that

regulatory effects that have delayed impact or that take a long time to surface fully might be more likely to be detected. Since organizations often
have trouble adapting to radical environmental change, these delayed effects might be the norm for business regulation.

Both points are illustrated by a study of the American passenger air
carriers after extensive deregulation in 1977. Seidel (1997) collected data on
all firms entering the passenger air carrier market throughout the United
States from deregulation to late-1994. He took pains to gather data on
small carriers, all except the tiny commuter lines (for which the data are
unreliable). He found that airline foundings declined steadily across the
period as a direct function of time since deregulation. He also found that
the interdependence between the two basic organizational forms changed
as deregulation proceeded. Specifically, as the major airlines (e.g., United,
American, Delta, Northwest, TWA, etc.) consolidated and dominated large
volume markets (by establishing so-called fortress hubs), the opportunities
for specialist carriers (flying point-to-point rather than through controlled
hubs) increased.[1] Seidel's study also shows that the effects of deregulation might not yet be fully realized—the system does not appear to have
reached a truly stable equilibrium. Other studies of the impact of air carrier deregulation—and there have been plenty—do not show or highlight
any of these effects.

We illustrate further the potential of corporate demography by describing (collaborative) empirical research on regulatory change in two particular industries, telephony and banking. The telephony study looks at
regulatory institutions in the early history of the American industry. The
banking study focuses on the impact of deregulation in the United States
in the modern era. Although the value of these types of studies for setting
regulatory policy has yet to be determined, we think they suggest that corporate demography has a potential role to play in examining regulatory
issues.

It should be said at the outset that our efforts in this and the next several chapters have a much more speculative character than the treatments
in foregoing chapters, which draw on years of programmatic research that
has yielded not only well-formed ideas but also finely tuned models and a
body of empirical knowledge. Analyses of topics such as the relationship
between corporate demography and regulation and corporate demography
and employment (Chapter 19) cannot draw on nearly as much theory and
research. So the ideas, models, and empirical regularities are not nearly as
well developed. Nonetheless, we believe that promising research possibilities exist in these areas. Our goal here is to try to convince others of this
view so that the promise might be realized.

---

[1] This segmentation exemplifies resource partitioning (Chapter 12).

18.1 Early Telephony

Many social scientists express surprise when they learn the basic demographic facts of the early telephone industry. Literally thousands of telephone companies populated the U.S. landscape in the early period. Data compiled by Barnett and Carroll (1993) show that more than 30,000 independent telephone companies operated at one time or another in the mainland United States, sometimes collectively controlling more than 50 percent of the market in some states. Why did so many companies exist? What kind of competitive relations eventually caused so many to fail and the Bell system to come to dominate? The reasons are, of course, complex and much debated by historians and policy analysts. Barnett and Carroll's (1993) demographic research on these questions focused on the effects of several specific regulatory institutions and constraints: local political boundaries (Chapter 9), state regulations about interconnection, and a major agreement between the federal government and AT&T known as the Kingsbury Commitment (which warded off more hostile regulation, including possible governmental takeover of telephony).[2]

Social science analysis of historical institutions and regulations often focuses on their emergence and their particular form, e.g., the underlying interests that influence the content of a law. Direct investigation of historical institutional effects of the kind we describe here often gets neglected (or finessed away) for theoretical reasons. As Moe (1990, 215) explains, many theorists believe that "a theory capable of explaining institutions...presupposes a theory of institutional effects." They think this is so because, in their view, "institutions arise from the choices of individuals [who] choose among the structures in light of known or presumed effects." If an institution's actual effects coincide with its intended effects, then an explanation of why the institution exists in the form it does might subsume an explanation of its effects. In this case, corporate demography might not have much of a role in the analysis, except perhaps to document what happened in full detail. To the extent that institutions and regulations generate major unintended consequences, however, such a theory will have less to say and corporate demography might allow analysts to reap great new insights.

Do political institutions and regulations affect industry in major unintended ways? If a priori public representations could be accepted as true intentions, then such demonstrations might be a simple matter. But, of course, actors often disguise their intentions, occasionally base their actions on assumed cause-and-effect relations, and sometimes conspire. Once these and other sophisticated action possibilities are admitted, then one

---

[2]This section draws from Barnett and Carroll (1993).

can almost always construct a rational account for an outcome retrospectively. However, the explanation might be very complex, especially when the context involves multiple actors. The plausibility of such accounts sometimes strains credulity, especially if one assumes that actors possess only bounded rationality. Demonstrating that a feature results from unintended consequences of an institution or regulation involves, therefore, not so much denying the possibility of a rational account but assessing such an account as implausible.

18.2 Interconnection Laws

As discussed in Chapter 9, early telephone companies were bounded by local governments. These governments also regulated the telephone companies but they did so idiosyncratically, and the telephone industry became increasingly chaotic (Brooks 1976). Neighboring telephone companies often refused to connect their systems because of feuds over operating areas and methods. In other cases, incompatible technologies sometimes made it difficult to connect, even if the companies were willing (Barnett 1990). The telephone industry thus developed into sets of sometimes overlapping, sometimes fragmented systems (subscribers frequently could not connect to subscribers of other companies).

These and other service delivery problems spurred public discontent with the telephone industry. In response, 40 state governments formed commissions for telephone regulation or expanded existing regulatory commissions to cover the telephone industry. Generally, these commissions were charged with controlling local telephone rates, assuring fair [...] nd resolving consumer grievances.

[...] islation dealing with specific problems in [...]), 34 states passed laws mandating inter- [...] companies. These laws typically required [...] their systems, and ensured that network [...] es were fair. They also often included re- [...] al monopoly franchises. The diffusion of [...] dually and then accelerated rapidly after

How did these laws affect organizational competition in the industry? Barnett and Carroll (1993) assessed the relationships between the Bell system and two size classes of independent telephone companies, large independents (defined as companies with more than 450 subscribers) and small independents (those with less than 450 subscribers). To do so, Barnett and Carroll (1993) estimated state-level difference equations for growth and decline in the numbers (densities) of large and small companies, before and after passage of interconnection laws. These models have the general form

$$\Delta S_{t,t+5} = \alpha_S B_t + \beta_S X_t + \epsilon_S,$$
$$\Delta L_{t,t+5} = \alpha_L B_t + \beta_L X_t + \epsilon_L.$$

where L and S refer to the numbers of large and small companies in a given state, Δ refers to change over a five-year period $(t, t + 5)$, B refers to the Bell-system market share in each state, and the X's are state-level control variables. The error terms ϵ are considered contemporaneously correlated across the equations and estimated in the fashion of seemingly unrelated regressions (Zellner 1962).

Table 18.1 reports the estimates. As indicated by the significant negative effect of its market share, the Bell system exerted a competitive effect on large independent companies before passage of the interconnect laws (the pre-law periods). Meanwhile, Bell's relationship with small independents was apparently mutualistic, although this result is not significant. The competitive effect of Bell on the large independents disappears after interconnect laws are passed, perhaps turning mutualistic (but the market share coefficient is not significant).

The correlation between the residuals of the large and small company models (given by $\widehat{\rho}$ in Table 18.1) indicates whether the small and large organizational forms grew and declined together or in opposing directions (see Barnett and Carroll (1993) for further discussion and justification of this technique). When $\rho > 0$, the relation between the forms is mutualistic; when $\rho < 0$, it is competitive. To see whether this finding is robust, Barnett and Carroll (1993) reestimated the models in Table 18.1 with additional

Table 18.1. *Estimates of organizational interdependence by interconnection law status.*

	Pre-law periods		Law periods	
	ΔL	ΔS	ΔL	ΔS
Constant	8.63*	−95.6*	−5.79	−12.6
Bell market share	−0.119*	1.06	0.036	0.117
$\widehat{\rho}$	.019		.245	
R^2	.022		.003	
$N \times T$	152		184	

* $p < .05$.

Note: ΔL and ΔS refer to changes in the number of large and small companies, respectively. The difference in $\widehat{\rho}$ between periods is significant at the .05 level in a one-tailed test.

Source: Barnett and Carroll (1993). Copyright © 1993 by Oxford University Press. Used by permission.

control variables included. Because of collinearity problems, each control variable alone was included in a separate model along with Bell market share. In every case, interconnect laws generated a statistically significant increase in the positive relationship between these organizational forms.

Comparing the estimate of ρ in the periods before and after the passage of interconnect laws suggests that mutualism among the populations defined by form did increase. The estimate of ρ changes from a weak positive relationship (before the laws) to a strong positive relationship (after passage of the laws); this difference is statistically significant.

In its demands that the telephone system be made more user-oriented and rational, the public provided the impetus for most interconnect laws. Legislatures and regulatory agencies heeded their calls and put into place laws and regulations requiring telephone companies to connect—in effect, to cooperate with each other in providing customer service. The primary intent behind these laws was to rationalize the telephone delivery system, which at the time was characterized simultaneously by numerous service gaps and unnecessary overlaps.

As far as could be determined from the historical record, little thought was given to the organizational consequences of the interconnect laws. This does not necessarily imply, however, that the mutualism such laws generated was an unintended consequence. To the extent that interdependence figured into the design and enactment of interconnect laws, it would have only been natural to think that connecting companies, already loosely organized into functionally based communities, would become more tightly coupled. Such increased interdependence was consistent with the independent movement's belief that companies needed to band together to compete against Bell and would explain why the independent companies supported this legislation. Independents saw interconnect laws as a good thing, deserving of their support, while Bell opposed such requirements.

18.3 The Kingsbury Commitment

After 1896, when its attempts to renew patent protection failed, Bell engaged in price competition and refused to sell its equipment to independent companies (Gabel 1969). The firm also acquired other telephone equipment manufacturers as well as some potential long-distance providers. Nonetheless, price competition did not work to Bell's advantage. Although Bell retained the lucrative urban markets, the presence of direct competitors in many such markets kept profit margins low. Moreover, as the market expanded rapidly nationwide, Bell lost many of the new areas to competition. Bell profit margins, which had been 46 percent during the patent protection period, dropped to 8 percent for the period around 1906 (Brock 1981).

Theodore Vail, who had resigned as president of AT&T in 1887, was restored to office in 1907 by a group of New York bankers holding substantial financial interest in the company. In response to the success of the independent telephone movement, Vail ordered an end to price competition and designed an aggressive set of policies, including denying interconnections for long distance and actively purchasing and merging the telephone systems of competitors. The strategy worked. From 1907 to 1912, national market share of the independents dropped from 49% to 42%. Nevertheless, Bell's tactics created much resentment because many independents lost long-distance capabilities as their previous partners were acquired by Bell. Complaints against the trust ran loud and high; Bell was frequently referred to with disdain as "the monopoly."

In response, the Department of Justice prepared to initiate antitrust proceedings against the Bell system. To prevent this, AT&T vice president N.C. Kingsbury reached an agreement to stop acquiring directly competing independent companies. The Commitment also guaranteed long-distance toll service to any independent company that conformed to fair and reasonable hookup procedures. The leaders of the independent telephone movement, who plauded the Commitment as a major victory over Bell, were described as "jubilant" (MacMeal 1934).

As expected, the Kingsbury Commitment decreased competition between Bell and the independent companies. At the time of the Kingsbury Commitment, Bell and the independent companies competed directly in 1,234 places in the United States. Although acquisitions of direct competitors were technically not allowed under the agreement, interpretation allowed for such actions as long as a property of equal size was sold to an independent company elsewhere. Consequently, mergers continued (although at a much reduced rate) in such a way as to establish geographical monopolies for both Bell and the independents. The decline in geographical rivalry reduced price competition significantly (Brock 1981).

However, the Kingsbury Commitment ultimately proved disappointing to the independent telephone companies. Attempts at coordination by the independents often proved ineffective, despite the formation of a single, national industry association during the period (MacMeal 1934). Atwood (1984) notes that early hopes to form a united system in Southeast Iowa broke down during the period, as conflicts among the various types of companies left the independent systems technically fragmented and organizationally divided. The Federal Communication Commission (1939) reported a similar development nationally, with some companies concluding that a viable independent movement was not possible. Accordingly, many large independents decided to sell to the Bell system.

Meanwhile, service problems during World War I (when all companies were at least formally under national control), topped off by significant postwar rate increases (thought to be due to national control), rendered illegitimate the status quo under Kingsbury, and softened public opposition to the Bell-system expansion (Danielian 1939). These shifts culminated in the Willis–Graham Act of 1921, which effectively ended the pledges of the Kingsbury Commitment by exempting the telephone industry from antitrust review. After the passage of this act, Bell returned to its earlier policy of aggressive acquisition. For the remaining independents, competing against Bell during the post-Kingsbury period proved to be as hazardous as it was pre-Kingsbury. Their plight was summarized by the Federal Communication Commission (1939, 143):

> The vigorous opposition of the independent telephone companies and the United States Independent Telephone Association to the Bell System's acquisition policy...availed them nothing. They insisted that Bell System sales to independents must equal Bell System purchases in order that a strong system of independents might remain. The Bell System refused to accede to such demands.

As a result of these developments and rapid expansion into new areas, Bell attained during the 1920s the position of dominance it would hold for nearly half the century. By 1932, Bell's national market share rose to 79% (in 1970 it was roughly 83%). Bell also emerged from the period with the nation's only significant long-distance network.

How did the Kingsbury Commitment affect the relationships among the various organizational forms in the industry? Descriptive data show that the number of small independents declined dramatically during this period and the number of large independents increased slightly. However, because of strong state-level variations, isolating the effects of Kingsbury requires statistical analysis. The results of such analysis are shown in Table 18.2. Again, the critical estimate is given by $\hat{\rho}$, the correlation of residuals across equations. Notice that this parameter is positive before and after the Kingsbury period, and negative during it. By this evidence, the small and large companies were mutualistically related before and after the Commitment, while they were competitive during the Kingsbury period. That is, the Kingsbury Commitment apparently unleashed competition among the large and small nonBell companies.[3]

The effects of the Kingsbury Commitment can be understood in terms of the sociological distinction between universalistic and particularistic institutional orientations (Parsons 1951). Universalistic orientations apply

----

[3] The result was tested for robustness by sequentially controlling for a variety of additional independent variables. In every specification, ρ changed from positive to negative during the Kingsbury period, and in each case this change was statistically significant.

Table 18.2. *Estimates of organizational interdependence before, during, and after the Kingsbury agreement.*

	Pre-Kingsbury		Kingsbury		Post-Kingsbury	
	ΔL	ΔS	ΔL	ΔS	ΔL	ΔS
Constant	20.4*	58.2	9.70*	−197*	−16.5*	6.18
Bell market share	−0.324*	−1.14	−0.115*	2.43	0.166*	−0.096
$\widehat{\rho}$	.140		−.098		.483	
R^2	.059		.079		.056	
$N \times T$	48		96		192	

* $p < .05$.

Note: ΔL and ΔS refer to changes in the number of large and small companies, respectively. The difference in $\widehat{\rho}$ between periods is significant at the .05 level in a one-tailed test.

Source: Barnett and Carroll (1993). Copyright © 1993 by Oxford University Press. Used by permission.

similarly to all social actors; particularistic orientations apply to only certain sets of actors. The state interconnection laws were universalistic in that they applied to all companies. The Kingsbury Commitment was particularistic: it was designed to constrain the competitive activity of Bell but not of the independents. By constraining only Bell, the Commitment led to an unexpected or unintended *competitive release* (Cody and Diamond 1975; Strong, Simberloff, Abele, and Thistle 1984) among the independents, which prevented them from uniting into a single system. By calming the war between Bell and the large independents, the Kingsbury Commitment had, in fact, started another one between the large and small independents.

This competitive release should have been especially strong for two reasons. First, large independents occupied the middle of the market. As long as Bell battled them aggressively for the lucrative urban markets, the large independents had little choice but to fight back. The power of their aggressor meant, no doubt, that most of their energies were absorbed in the process. During Kingsbury, however, the Bell threat was reduced and managers of large independents could turn their attention to the remaining markets held by the small and mutual independents. Since the companies holding these markets were informally managed and staffed, the relationship between large and small independents became competitive during the period of the Kingsbury Commitment. By contrast, as in the period before the Commitment, the post-Kingsbury period was characterized by symbiosis between the large and small organizational forms. In these periods, the large independents were busy battling Bell, and their fates were again shared by the smaller independents.

There is a second reason for seeing the Kingsbury period as involving a competitive release: large and small independents had distinctly different relationships with Bell during this time. Bell was most concerned with the competition that came from the large independents. These companies were located in the cities, had ample capital and technology, and sought the same customers as Bell. By contrast, the small independents served the more isolated rural markets of only secondary interest to the profit-seeking companies.

Some historical evidence also shows that Bell actually aided the smallest of this organizational form, the farmer lines, by providing technical assistance (Fischer 1994). Apparently, Bell thought that encouraging these sorts of operations would prove an annoying obstacle to their real competitors, the commercial independents, who would be caught in a competitive squeeze. Consequently, there is reason to believe that the potential for strong competition existed among the small and large independent companies—competition that was released by the protections of the Kingsbury Commitment.

The idea of competitive release emphasizes an unanticipated effect unleashed by the Commitment. However, the impact of the Kingsbury Commitment might be interpreted by some as the consequence of purposive action. If Bell executives understood that the effects of the Kingsbury Commitment would fuel competition among large and small independents, then entering into the agreement was a subtle and powerful way to cripple the movement. It was subtle because the independents were weakened considerably by no direct actions of Bell but by their fellow travelers. It was powerful because ultimately it led to the collapse of the independent movement. Furthermore, the Commitment was a clear way to cool out hostile political forces yearning for antitrust action or nationalization.

Barnett and Carroll (1993) argued that such a purposive account strains credulity. In their view, the most important question is whether Bell advocated the Kingsbury Commitment primarily because it would damage the independent movement. Three reasons led them to conclude that the answer is no.

First, given a choice, the most effective policy for Bell's growth was direct acquisition of large and growing independents. Bell had ample capital reserves to continue this policy, and there was no advantage in trying a trickier, more indirect strategy. Second, the independents themselves advocated a restraining agreement of this kind and rejoiced in its enactment. The Kingsbury Commitment was widely regarded as a major victory for the independent movement. Third, the independents who suffered most under Kingsbury were the smaller ones, not the large urban companies that Bell worried about. If Bell's managers understood the cause-and-effect relation inherent in the Commitment, then why would they support it, given that in many instances the strength of the large independents—their primary competitors—was enhanced?

Based on these arguments, it seems unlikely (as an unvarnished rational-action explanation of this institution might) that the reason for the adoption of the Kingsbury Commitment was its eventual major effect on the independent movement. Bell had available many more effective ways of dealing with the independents.

A better explanation for the Kingsbury Commitment might come from considering the political realm. The progressive Wilson administration had just assumed power, and public sentiment at the time ran against large and aggressive corporations. To preempt more aggressive political action, Bell executives searched for a compromise that would remove them from the political limelight with minimal losses. The Kingsbury Commitment did so and provided the progressives an early modest victory against a visible large corporation. That Bell executives understood that the agreement harmed the firm little seems obvious. They might even have understood that it would fuel competition among the independents. However, that understanding or projection was likely not their primary reason for entering into the agreement. Accordingly, the increased competition among the large and small independents, which the Commitment unleashed, must be viewed as, at best, a minor expected consequence (but not one capable of explaining the development and implementation of the agreement). Moreover, given the celebrations among independents and progressives, as well as the enhanced strength of some large independents, the actual outcome for the independent movement as a whole appears to have been an unexpected consequence.

18.4 Regulation and Deregulation in Banking

The American banking industry provides a more contemporary setting for using corporate demography to examine the effects of regulation and deregulation. Until recently, the industry was populated by several organizational forms with clear boundaries among them, boundaries preserved by regulation. Then, over a fairly short recent period many regulatory constraints were lifted or eased considerably. The distinctions among the organizational populations quickly began to erode. What difference did this make for the competitive dynamics in the industry?[4]

The U.S. financial services industry contains a variety of organizational forms. *Commercial banks*, designed to serve agriculture, industry, and commerce, appeared in the late eighteenth century. The Bank of Philadelphia,

---

[4] This section summarizes an analysis by Barron, West, and Hannan (1998).

founded in 1780, is generally considered to be the first U.S. bank. *Mutual savings banks*, modeled on an organizational form first established in Scotland in the early nineteenth century, appeared soon afterwards. They are run by trustees who ensure continuity by electing successors. All profits, after funds are set aside as reserves, must be paid to depositors. *Savings and loan associations* (S&Ls), also a mid-nineteenth century invention, were associations for pooling the funds of members to enable them to purchase their own homes. S&Ls began as mutuals, legally owned by their depositors, among whom all earnings had to be shared.

The market in consumer loans was pioneered by *credit unions*. At the turn of the century, working people had few places to turn when they met a financial crisis. There were a few philanthropic organizations, such as The Provident Loan Society (organized in New York in 1893), which made pawnbroker loans. Otherwise, poor people were at the mercy of loan sharks who charged exorbitant rates of interest. Credit unions were modeled on the cooperative banks and *caisses populaires* of Europe and Québec. These organizations offered savings deposits and small loans to individuals and families who were members of the association. Credit unions have always been organized around a shared characteristic or affiliation, such as membership of an occupational group, a voluntary association, or a community. As not-for-profit associations doing business only with their members, credit unions are tax-exempt, and all of their earnings must be distributed to their members.

Banking in the United States was heavily regulated by both state and federal agencies over the decades following the Great Depression. This regulation sought to preserve some benefits of market competition while decreasing the chance of failure by deposit institutions. Many regulations were imposed during the Great Depression. For example, the Glass–Steagal Act of 1933 strengthened the powers of the Federal Reserve and established the Federal Deposit Insurance Corporation to insure the deposits of small savers and liquidate failed banks. This act excluded banks from the securities market by separating commercial and investment banking activities. It also prevented banks from operating any nonbanking subsidiary, and set limits on their prices. Regulation Q of the Act gave the Federal Reserve the authority to set maximum interest rates on various types of savings and deposit accounts and forbade banks from paying interest on demand deposits. Thus, Depression-era legislation circumscribed banking activities and heightened the distinctiveness of the different organizational populations in the financial marketplace.

After the Depression, the regulatory system was designed to ensure that many small banking organizations served well-defined geographical areas, under the supervision of a tripartite regulatory structure (the Comptroller of Currency, the Federal Reserve, and the Federal Deposit Insurance Corporation). The American banking system remained extremely stable in the post-war era. Between 1945 and 1980, an average of only six FDIC member banks failed per annum. This low failure rate has been attributed to the system of regulation, but it is probably also a result of the prosperous economic climate of the times. As the economy expanded, more households and firms required banking services, ensuring a steady flow of new customers. Interest rates were low, so consumers—whether individuals, small businesses, or large corporations—became loyal customers. Banks found that they could get a steady and secure return from "spread" banking (that is, from the difference between the interest rate charged to borrowers and the cost of funds), so they had little incentive to introduce new products or to penetrate new markets. Indeed, banks were barred from the lucrative markets for life insurance, pensions, and securities.

In the post-war era, then, financial markets were stable and prosperous, especially during 1945–1965. There were few failures and few innovations. The regulatory boundaries demarcating banks and other deposit institutions were clear. Major actors in the financial marketplace offered different products and services to different kinds of consumers.

By the late 1960s, the American financial industry looked less stable. International events, such as the rise in oil prices, led to recession and inflation. Interest rates rose and became more volatile, making consumers more willing to "shop around." This motivated banks to introduce new financial products, such as the negotiable certificate of deposit, designed to evade regulations. "Commercial paper," invented much earlier but little used until the late 1960s, also had a great impact on financial markets by allowing firms and individuals to bypass financial intermediaries altogether by borrowing directly from other firms or individuals. Low-quality corporate bonds (junk bonds) and money-market mutual funds (exempt from Regulation Q interest-rate ceilings) were also opportunistic responses to the unstable market conditions of the time.

Besides the appearance of new financial instruments, many new players entered the financial sector during the 1960s, attracted by high margins. Firms such as General Motors, Ford, and Sears began to offer financial services such as commercial lending, consumer finance, and real estate and mortgage banking. Because such new entrants were "nondepository institutions," they were not forced to comply with many banking regulations, such as geographical restrictions and interest-rate ceilings. These innovations in products, services, and delivery systems strained the regulatory system.

Although deregulation had progressed, unofficially, for some time, a series of legislative acts formalized the trend during 1968–1988. The Depository Institutions Deregulation and Monetary Control Act of 1980 improved the competitive position of commercial banks by allowing them to pay interest on checking accounts. However, the Act also allowed credit unions and mutual savings banks to issue credit cards and offer trust services and business loans. Federally insured credit unions were also allowed to offer share draft accounts similar to interest-bearing checking accounts. These measures enabled thrifts to compete in some of the commercial banks' markets.

The Garn–St. Germain Depository Institutions Act of 1982 encompassed a wide-ranging set of reforms of the financial marketplace. It authorized money-market deposit accounts, ended interest-rate ceilings, removed rate differentials between thrifts and commercial banks, and allowed all depository institutions to offer accounts that were competitive with money-market mutual funds. Mutual savings banks were permitted to participate in consumer and commercial lending, life insurance, brokerage services, and trust management. However, only a few savings banks were big enough to take advantage of all these new powers. Many banks entered the consumer loan market, previously the province of credit unions. Savings and loan associations were also permitted to make commercial loans and accept demand deposits. Federal credit unions were given more leeway in real-estate lending.

Rose (1986, 98) sums up by claiming that deregulation "granted major new asset and deposit powers to commercial banks and their principal competitors—savings banks, S&Ls and credit unions. The net result was to place banks and nonbank thrift institutions on a more equal footing, leveling the competitive playing field for all depository institutions." Most industry analysts think that it is still too early to predict confidently the longrun effects of this revolution in banking. Nonetheless, the methods of corporate demography can be used to assess the impact to date of deregulation on the structure of the depository industry. In particular, they can help answer the question: Did deregulation promote competition among the diverse organizational forms within the financial industry?

18.5 System Dynamics after Deregulation

Barron et al. (1998) investigated the changing pattern of interactions among competing organizational forms in the depository sector of the financial services industry. They considered the four organizational forms of deposit institutions in New York State: commercial banks, savings banks, savings and loan associations, and credit unions. They focused on the organizational masses of these populations, defined as the state-level total assets of all members of a population. Although many other measures could be used, total assets is appropriate for both profit-maximizing and mutual and cooperative organizations. Indeed, it has been argued that total assets is the best measure of performance for organizations (such as credit unions) that have the provision of credit as their primary goal (Pearce 1984; Barron 1998). Figure 18.1 displays the time series of masses of the four populations over 1960–1990. Notice that credit unions have gained in mass compared with other populations while the S&L population has shrunk.

This research modeled the interactions among these four populations using systems of linear differential equations:

$$\frac{d\mathbf{y}(t)}{dt} = \mathbf{C}\mathbf{y}(t) + \mathbf{B}\mathbf{x}(t), \tag{18.1}$$

where $\mathbf{y}(t)$ is a 4×1 vector, each element being the mass of a subject population at time t. In this analysis, mass is the natural log of the aggregate of the assets of all the organizations in the population, measured in millions of (constant) dollars. $\mathbf{C}$ is a 4×4 matrix of interaction coefficients, $\mathbf{x}(t)$ is a $k \times 1$ vector of explanatory variables (including a constant), and $\mathbf{B}$ is a $4 \times k$ vector of effect parameters. Estimation of the parameters $\mathbf{C}$ and $\mathbf{B}$ requires that (18.1) be integrated over time.[5]

To investigate the effect of deregulation, these researchers included interactions between the population masses and a dummy variable identifying the years 1981–1990. They selected 1980 as a significant date because it marks the onset of the most important pieces of deregulatory legislation to affect the banking industry.[6] F-tests comparing the models with

---

[5] Because the time intervals are short (the model is estimated from yearly time series data), it is reasonable to assume that the covariates are constant within each period. Then integrating (18.1) with respect to t gives:

$$\mathbf{y}(t) = \mathbf{\Gamma}\mathbf{y}(t_0) + \mathbf{\Theta}\mathbf{x}(t_0),$$

where

$$\mathbf{\Gamma} = \mathbf{V}e^{\Lambda}\mathbf{V}^{-1},$$
$$\mathbf{\Theta} = \mathbf{C}^{-1}(\mathbf{\Gamma} - \mathbf{I})\mathbf{B}.$$

This implies that e^{Λ} is the matrix of eigenvalues of $\mathbf{\Gamma}$, and that $\mathbf{V}$ is the matrix of right eigenvectors of $\mathbf{\Gamma}$. Therefore, estimates of $\mathbf{\Gamma}$ can easily be used to calculate $\mathbf{V}$ and e^{Λ}. These can then be used, in turn, to obtain estimates of $\mathbf{C}$, as follows:

$$\mathbf{C} = \mathbf{V}\Lambda\mathbf{V}^{-1}.$$

The parameters of this system of equations were estimated by means of seemingly unrelated regression. See Barron et al. (1998) for details.

[6] In particular, the Depository Institutions Deregulation and Monetary Control Act came into force in 1980. This was followed two years later by the Garn–St. Germain Depository Institutions Act. Together, these are generally regarded as the cornerstones of the policy to deregulate the banking industry (Bundt, Cosimano, and Halloran 1992).

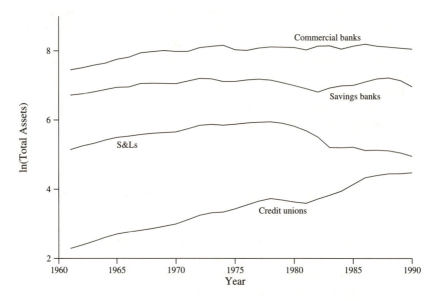

Figure 18.1.   *Mass of banking populations in New York State, 1960–1990. Source: Barron et al. (1998). Copyright © 1998 by Oxford University Press. Used by permission.*

and without the interactions reject the models without interactions as compared with the models with interactions. Thus these tests indicate that the banking-system dynamics changed with deregulation, that the competitive process during the 1980s differed substantially from the one that operated during the 1960s and 1970s.

The easiest way to understand exactly how the periods differ is by examining graphs of the predicted effects based on the estimates. Figures 18.2 and 18.3 show the predicted population masses under the regulatory and deregulatory regimes, respectively. These two figures suggest a dramatic restructuring in the financial services industry. In the earlier period (shown in Figure 18.2), the populations were maintaining their respective positions: all were growing at similar rates. After deregulation, pairs of populations appear to compete. Credit unions and S&Ls come to compete, with credit unions gradually gaining at the expense of S&Ls. We can also see that S&Ls and savings banks compete with each other. As the period progresses, the cycles of the populations appear to dampen and approach a new equilibrium. It is tempting to conclude that we are witnessing the evolution of a new structure of the financial services industry in New York State.

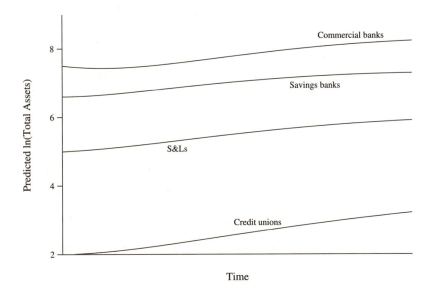

Figure 18.2. *Predicted masses of financial institutions in New York State before deregulation, 1960–1980. Source: Barron et al. (1998). Copyright © 1998 by Oxford University Press. Used by permission.*

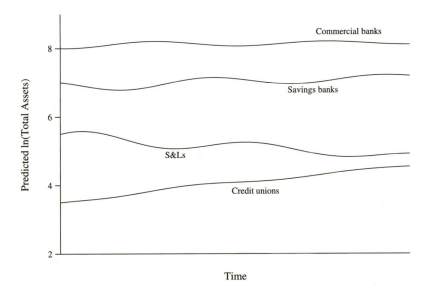

Figure 18.3. *Predicted masses of financial institutions in New York State after deregulation, 1981–1990. Source: Barron et al. (1998). Copyright © 1998 by Oxford University Press. Used by permission.*

18.6 Deregulation and Organizational Growth

Barron et al. (1998) also analyzed the growth and decline of *individual organizations*, looking for evidence that some types of organizations were affected by changes in the interdependencies of the various forms of financial institution. They highlighted the credit-union form for two reasons. First, credit unions are typically much smaller than other kinds of financial institutions, and they could be expected to be affected strongly by changes in competitiveness within the industry. In particular, this population might face the greatest risk of extinction under deregulation. Second, detailed organization-level data were available on a population of credit unions in New York City from the time of the founding of the first such organization in 1914 through 1990, thus allowing this analysis to build on prior research about this organizational population (Barron et al. 1994; Barron et al. 1995).

How did competition from other populations of deposit institutions affect the fortunes of credit unions during 1914–1990? In considering fluctuations in this population's fortune over this long period, Barron et al. (1998) analyzed rates of organizational growth.[7]

A prior study (Barron et al. 1994) found that the following model, an instance of the class discussed in Chapter 14, provides a plausible representation of growth rates of assets of credit unions:

$$\ln(S_{i,t+1}) = \alpha \ln(S_{it}) + \beta \ln(A_{it}) + \gamma_1 N_t + \gamma_2 N_t^2 + \mathbf{x}_{it}'\boldsymbol{\pi} + \epsilon_{i,t+1},$$

where S_{it} denotes the size of an organization in period t, A_{it} denotes the age of organization i at the beginning of year $t + 1$, and N_t is the density at the beginning of year $t + 1$.[8]

This model can be extended by allowing the competitive pressure on the first organizational population to depend upon the (possible) presence

---

[7]Barron et al. (1994) and Barron et al. (1995) found evidence of competition between this population of credit unions and other deposit institutions in analyses of founding and failure rates. However, there were too few foundings and failures in the post-deregulation era to allow them to use these events to test whether competitive interactions have increased in intensity. (In fact, only 35 failures and 9 foundings occurred between 1960 and 1990.) Therefore, the analysis addressed growth rates.

[8]In assessing competition between forms, this research actually considered two ways of representing the scale of the organizational populations. The first assumes that the intensity of a competitive threat is proportional to the density of organizations in the competing population as in the equation in the text. The second assumes that it is proportional to the mass of the competing population. Each approach has advantages and disadvantages. Density can be measured consistently over time for all of the potentially competing populations. It is also unaffected by the rate of inflation. On the other hand, mergers and absorptions can decrease density without changing a population's aggregate size (measured, for example, by turnover, total assets, or employment). Measures of mass are not available consistently for all of the relevant populations.

of the second. The analysis represents this competitive effect in terms of mass (aggregate total assets) of the second population.[9] (The extension to multiple populations is obvious.) Inserting this cross-population competition term into the growth model above yields a model that specifies that the growth rate of the first population depends on its own density and the density (or mass) of the second:

$$\ln(S_{i1,t+1}) = \alpha \ln(S_{i1t}) + \beta \ln(A_{it}) + \gamma_1 N_{1t} + \gamma_2 N_{1t}^2 + \delta_{12} Z_{2t} + \mathbf{x}_{it}' \boldsymbol{\pi} + \epsilon_{i,t+1}.$$

If the second population competes with the first for resources (members, deposits, and so forth), then $\delta_{12} < 0$. Thus this parameter indexes the strength of competition.

Estimates of the proportional-growth model above were obtained using a data set that pooled observations on credit unions over time. (Credit unions that failed during their first year were excluded, because at least two observations on size are required for each organization.) Size was measured in total assets throughout, with the dollar amounts corrected for inflation. These analyses involved regressions of an organization's size at time $t + 1$ (S_{t+1}) on its size at time t (S_t) and other covariates.

The modeling strategy used dummy variables to identify period effects and allows interactions between them and the densities. The models are represented as follows:

$$\ln(S_{i1,t+1}) = \alpha \ln(S_{i1t}) + \beta \ln(A_{it}) + \gamma_1 N_{1t} + \gamma_2 N_{1t}^2 + \delta_{12} N_{2t}$$
$$+ \zeta P_t + \theta_{12}(N_{2t} \times P_t) + \mathbf{x}_{it}' \boldsymbol{\pi} + \epsilon_{i,t+1},$$

with P_t indicating a dummy variable for period. This coding provided a test of whether competitive interactions intensified in either or both deregulatory periods compared with earlier years. Before the period being used, say pre-1960 (versus post-1960), the strength of interpopulation competition is given by δ_{12}. After 1960, competition equals $\delta_{12} + \theta_{12}$. If θ_{12} is negative, then the two populations compete more intensely after 1960 than in earlier years. The period effect is included in the model to ensure that other changes in the environment of financial institutions during the period that might affect growth rates are represented.

Boundaries around different forms of depository institutions were reinforced by several fundamental differences between the organizational forms. These include ownership structures (commercial banks are stock companies, whereas mutual savings banks and credit unions are cooperatives), membership criteria (common bond requirements restrict the category of persons that credit unions could recruit, whereas anyone can open a bank account), size differentials (credit unions were usually much

---

[9] Alternatively, density could be used as the measure of scale to assess competition.

smaller than banks), and the employer sponsorship of credit unions and
their atypical taxation status (Barron 1995; Barron 1998).

Each of these organizational characteristics contributed to the distinctiveness of the various organizational populations in the financial services
sector. In only one area were all of the organizational populations recognized as similar enough to engender competition: deposits. Despite this
area of overlap, credit unions and thrifts have traditionally been regarded
as a source only of indirect competition by the rest of the banking industry.
Therefore, ecological theory would not predict strong direct competition
between these organizational forms for most of their history.

These boundaries have eroded in recent years, and the activities of
different forms have come to overlap more. Has competition among the
populations of organizations in the financial sector intensified in recent
years as many industry analysts claim? Table 18.3 shows estimated effects
of models contrasting two different periodizations of the history of the
population of credit unions over 1914–1990.

The specification in column 1 allows the effects of competition to differ
before and after 1960. The interactions of period with densities of bank
populations tell whether the effect of competition changed. Both period
interaction parameters are negative, which is consistent with the idea that

Table 18.3.   *Estimates of growth models of New York credit unions
by regulatory period, 1914–1990.*

	(1)	(2)
Commercial-bank density	−0.003	−0.003
Savings-bank density	0.002	0.002
Period dummy (1960–1990)	0.514	
Commercial-bank density × (1960–1990) period dummy	−0.001	
Savings-bank density × (1960–1990) period dummy	−0.008	
Period dummy (1980–1990)		0.890*
Commercial-bank density × (1980–1990) period dummy		−0.009*
Savings-bank density × (1980–1990) period dummy		−0.014*
N	4851	4851
R^2	.95	.95

* $p < .05$.

Source: Barron, West, and Hannan (1998). Copyright ©1998 by
Oxford University Press. Used by permission.

the competition from commercial banks and savings banks intensified after 1960. However, neither of these estimates is statistically significant.

The specification in the second column of the table breaks the history into two periods at 1980, that is, the periods are 1914–1979 and 1980–1990. The second-period effect is positive and significant, meaning that deregulation in the 1980s increased average growth rates of credit unions. This estimate implies that the average growth rate doubled during the 1980s. Again, both interactions with the period of deregulation are negative, but they are now much larger than in the previous specification, especially for commercial banks. Furthermore, both these estimates are statistically significant. What do these numbers mean substantively? In the post-1980 period, the mean commercial bank density was 62. At this level, competition from commercial banks slowed credit union growth by one-third more after 1980 than it did in earlier years. The change is very similar for savings banks. The mean density of savings banks from 1980 through 1990 was 26. For a population of this size, these estimates imply competition's effect was 29% stronger in the 1980s than in previous years.

Competition has clearly intensified since the start of deregulation. This was shown in both the population-level and the system-level analyses. There is also evidence that competition continues to intensify. We interpret this intensifying competition as the result of increasing service overlap: different financial institutions now offer a very similar range of financial services. So, to a much greater extent than has ever been the case in the past, different types of financial service institutions are directly substitutable for one another in the retail financial services market.

Although competition by definition has negative consequences, on average, for individual organizations, the evidence suggests that the restructuring of the financial services industry might benefit one section of the industry. Credit-union growth, net of competitive interactions, was higher in the 1980s than in earlier periods. At first sight there might appear to be a paradox in these two results. How can credit unions as an aggregate be advantaged when individual credit unions are disadvantaged?

This paradox can be reconciled by looking at the system-level results. Increased competition plausibly introduced a greater level of instability and uncertainty into the financial services sector. This is shown most clearly in Figure 18.3. System-level instability could increase the opportunities for the population of credit unions to grow by increasing its market share at the expense of other populations of depository institutions. On the other hand, the same systemic changes could be increasing the risks faced by individual credit unions. In other words, financial service industry restructuring might represent an occasion for credit unions to expand their niche in terms of the size of their aggregate asset holdings. However, this benefit might accrue to only a few individual organizations.

We noted earlier that corporate demography might potentially play a larger role in the study of regulation in uncovering any unintended consequences of rules and institutions. The analyses of early U.S. telephony and recent U.S. banking described in this chapter demonstrate a possible approach and suggest its potential value, in our view.

For early telephony, we found that the Kingsbury Commitment, ostensibly a constraint only on Bell and intended to aid the independents, prompted the large independents to compete more intensively with their smaller counterparts. The result was, on the whole, not beneficial to the independent telephone movement. By contrast, our analysis of the effects of state interconnect laws suggested that the anticipated result of increasing mutualism among companies did, in fact, occur. Interconnection laws apparently intensified an existing symbiotic relationship between populations of large and small telephone companies. The difference between this outcome and that of the Kingsbury Commitment is, we speculate, a result of the universalistic nature of the interconnect laws. Rather than aiming at only a segment of the interdependent community, as was the Kingsbury Commitment, the interconnect laws applied to all segments and organizations. Thus, our analysis of telephony suggests that rules and institutions might often have unexpected and unusual consequences as well as more predictable, rational effects. Wade et al. (1998) find similar results for the effects of state-level prohibitions on development of local brewing industries.

For the debate about regulation and deregulation of banking, we reviewed findings that are unexpectedly contradictory. To wit, demographic analysis suggests that the financial industry has become a more unstable system, and so uncertainty has increased. Instability and uncertainty are risky, particularly in the financial industry where stability and confidence are so important. On the other hand, there is evidence that increasing competition is improving performance, at least in the credit-union sector. Credit-union growth has increased despite increased competition, exactly what the proponents of deregulation would expect. So, in a sense we find that the fears of anti-deregulators and the hopes of pro-deregulators are both met.

19

Employment

BESIDES PRODUCING valuable goods and services, firms and other organizations constitute the employment base of the economy. This means, of course, that a single demographic event, such as the failure of a sizable corporation, can greatly affect the lives of many individuals. It also means that knowledge about corporate vital rates and the organizational population processes behind them should serve to increase our understanding of job turnover, career paths, and employment patterns.

These possibilities provoke an obvious question: How important are corporate-demographic events in the overall scheme of things? Although some turnover and job change clearly reflects corporate mergers, failures, and the like, the amount might be negligible relative to total turnover—individuals leave jobs for a wide variety of reasons, voluntary and involuntary. On the other hand, corporate demography might prompt a high proportion of job changes. According to Uchitelle and Kleinfield (1996, 4), "more than 43 million jobs have been erased in the United States since 1979. ... Many of the losses come from the normal churning as stores fail and factories move." Getting a better handle on exactly how many is our first order of business in this chapter. Surprisingly enough, not many analysts have attempted to estimate (even roughly) the proportion of job changes due to corporate demography.

Because so many other social benefits and services come bundled with the employment contract, a next step in our discussion considers what corporate demography means for social welfare. Do individuals and society experience more disruption when corporate-demographic activity rises? If so, why? What might be done about this as a matter of public policy? This topic has obvious social importance; it also raises myriad complexities. Indeed, the issues have rarely been addressed from a demographic perspective. Although we cannot resolve here the many issues involved, we do nonetheless try to sharpen some standard questions and raise some new ones. We also suggest research that might prove productive.

19.1 Effects of Corporate Demography on Careers

The traditional approaches to studying careers in sociology and economics build upon the status-attainment perspective and human-capital
theories, respectively. The two share a common assumption: the opportunity structure for a particular individual can be summarized by a vector
of characteristics that determine the person's productivity (viz., education,
training, intelligence, and experience). Reliance on a single generalized
status (occupation) or capacity (human capital) as a summary measure of
opportunity and constraint came under intense fire in sociology and economics in the 1980s. Critics asserted that industry and firm characteristics
combine with individual characteristics in determining career trajectories.
They argued that the economy divides into sectors with different rules
of the game. Although generalized status and capacity might pay off in
each sector, sectoral location by itself could play an independent role in
determining success. Much of this critical work relies on a Manichaean
image of an economy with two sectors: core (good) and periphery
(bad).

Although the dual economy (or dual labor market) perspective has
given rise to the most extensive attempt to link organizational structures
and careers, it has been largely unsuccessful both theoretically and empirically. Sociologists have shown convincingly that no simple partition of
the world of firms deals well with the enormous diversity of organizational
structures, employment relations, and careers. For example, Baron and
Bielby (1984, 471) conclude their analysis of employment relations in a
large sample of establishments by noting that they found

> ...little evidence of discrete sectors of economic activity, particularly
> along industrial lines ... organizations with a specific structure, tech-
> nology and scale occupy diverse niches, and varied organizational
> types populate the same environment.

In some sense each organization can claim to be unique. If we focus
on uniqueness, then we need a theory of each organization to model careers. This would obviously not be a productive approach. Instead, we need
a middle ground between assuming a unitary organizational world (or its
close relative—a dual organizational world) and assuming that the number of relevant organizational variations is essentially unbounded. How to
do this? We suggest abstracting from the enormous variety by considering
the demographic dimensions of organizational populations and communities. We begin with the connection between the jobs making up a career
and corporate-demographic activity.

19.2 Corporate Demography and Job Shifts

How does the demography of an organizational population affect job mobility? In other words, how much individual job change reflects demographic processes of organizational founding and dissolution, organizational expansion and contraction, merger, reorganization and restructuring, and organizational domain shifting? Some evidence suggests a large share of job changes is due to such dynamics[1]:

> Nearly three-quarters of all households have had a close encounter with layoffs since 1980, according to a poll by *The New York Times*. In one-third of all households, a family member has lost a job, and nearly 40 percent more know a relative, friend or neighbor who was laid off. (Uchitelle and Kleinfield 1996, 5)

Unfortunately, direct microanalytical data on the mobility effects of the corporate-demographic processes are difficult to obtain (but see Haveman and Cohen (1994), discussed below). As a consequence, we must rely on less direct information, on numbers derived from "net" figures of observed changes in firm size over time. These figures thus might be conservative estimates of demographically driven mobility: they ignore job shifts due to changes in the job profiles of organizations whose size does not change. On the other hand, such figures might actually overstate the effects of organizational dynamics on individual mobility, because they record jobs created and eliminated as separate events, whereas an individual might move directly from an eliminated job into a newly created job.

The effects of corporate-demographic events on mobility patterns might be short term in nature. That is, an event of some kind creates or destroys jobs but the aggregate effect wears off quickly. An alternative scenario that must be considered has to do with the possible longterm effects of economic trends. We know of two empirical studies that have addressed this issue.

Jacobson (1984) compared Providence, Rhode Island and Buffalo, New York between 1960 and 1970. He classified industries into comparable growing and declining groups, based on their average employment change during the decade. He equated attrition with the turnover rate in the growing industries (it therefore included both voluntary and some shortterm structural turnover due to growth). He calculated "displacement" as the difference between attrition rates from declining industries and growing industries within a comparable group. Jacobsen's measure of displacement, then, might be interpreted as turnover due to longterm structural change.

---

[1] This section draws on Carroll et al. (1990).

Across all of the industries in the two cities, attrition averaged 13% per year and longterm displacement averaged 2.6%. By these calculations, longterm economic trends account for a much smaller proportion of job mobility than do the ongoing shortterm fluctuations that could possibly be associated with corporate demography.

Investigating similar issues, Leonard (1987) used the Wisconsin Unemployment Compensation Contribution Reports. This source covers all employers in the state except government agencies and nonprofit organizations. His calculations indicate that "frictional" changes in employment (defined as fluctuations in establishment size that are uncorrelated with industry or with geographic region) were much larger than "structural" changes (meaning fluctuations in industry or area employment averages) between 1977 and 1982. Industry and county factors explain little variance in rates of growth and contraction for firms. The within-industry variance in these data is much larger than the between-industry variance. These findings point to the same conclusion as Jacobsen's, namely that fluctuations in ongoing turnover associated with demographic events are of far greater magnitude than longterm turnover trends. If these two studies reflect general tendencies, then corporate demography must be brought into the picture in analyses of trends in job mobility.

The question remains as to how much of the ongoing turnover reflects "pure" demographic processes among organizations. We attempt to answer this question by examining each of the major demographic processes likely associated with job creation and elimination and looking at the research that has assessed the issue. We then shift levels and consider the question from the point of view of the *individual employee* rather than the job. In doing so, we offer rough estimates of the combined consequence of corporate demography on job mobility.

19.3 Job Creation and Dissolution

Foundings and Mortality

We know four empirical studies that assess directly the effects of organizational foundings and failures on rates of job creation and elimination.[2] All use data from the United States, although the times and places studied vary. Birch (1981) looked at the entire U.S. economy, 1974 to 1976. He concluded that 12.4% of the country's jobs were created or eliminated during this period by demographic processes of organizational founding

---

[2] Other studies, such as Kirchhoff and Phillips (1988), report the sources of only the net changes in jobs by demographic process.

and death.[3] Organizational foundings increased the job pool by 6.7%, and failures eliminated 5.7% of all jobs.

A second study, conducted by the Brookings Institution, also covers the entire American economy, but it examined 1978 to 1980 (Small Business Administration 1983). It estimated that 7.0% of all jobs were created or eliminated by organizational foundings or dissolutions. Foundings added 7.7 million jobs to the pool, while failures eliminated 6.4 million positions.

Another study of the whole country, conducted by the Massachusetts Institute of Technology, covered the same time frame but used different assumptions to make estimates (Small Business Administration 1983). It found the total rate of job creation and elimination to be 5.1%. By this reckoning, 6.2 million jobs appeared as the result of organizational foundings, while organizational dissolutions removed 3.7 million jobs. In the Wisconsin study, Leonard (1987) estimated that 3.6% of all jobs are accounted for annually by establishment founding and mortality.[4]

Growth and Decline

The same four studies also assessed the effects of the growth and decline of firms on jobs. Estimates of the effects of firm growth and decline typically run somewhat smaller than the effects of organizational founding and failure. Birch (1981) estimated that 7.8% of all jobs were created or eliminated from 1974 to 1976 as firms grew and shrank. The Brookings study found that 8.7% of all jobs were created or destroyed by firm expansion or contraction during 1978–1980. The MIT study's estimate for the same period is about half of this, 4.2% per annum. Leonard (1987) estimated that 19.4% of all jobs in the state of Wisconsin were created or destroyed each year in expansions and contractions.

Table 19.1 compares the annualized estimates from these different studies of the effects of organizational founding, expansion, contraction, and failure on the number of jobs. Given their different time frames and geographical coverage, it is unreasonable to expect these numbers to be identical or even very similar. All the estimates do show, however, that each of the four demographic processes under consideration has a substantial and regular impact on jobs and the persons who hold them.

---

[3] There is a great deal of controversy about some of Birch's claims; his estimates therefore should be considered in comparison with those of others.

[4] Because Leonard's sample underrepresents one-person establishments, his estimate might be biased downward because small firms tend to have higher founding and failure rates. For example, Dun and Bradstreet (1988) estimates that firms with two or fewer employees account for 57% of all businesses in 1986 and 1987.

Table 19.1. *Estimates of jobs created and eliminated by corporate demography during the 1970s (as a percentage of all jobs).*

Demographic event	Birch 1974–1976 U.S.	Brookings 1978–1980 U.S.	MIT 1978–1980 U.S.	Leonard 1978–1979 Wisconsin
Foundings	3.3	3.8	3.2	2.7
Failures	2.8	3.2	1.9	0.9
Total	6.1	7.0	5.1	3.6
Expansion	2.2	5.8	2.7	12.1
Contraction	1.7	2.9	1.5	7.3
Total	3.9	8.7	4.2	19.4

Source: Carroll et al. (1990).

Mergers

The *Merger Yearbook* (1997) reports that 8,476 American companies were acquired by others in 1997. The value of these companies was estimated at $627.2 billion. These numbers are considerably higher than prior years. In 1995, 7,451 U.S. companies (worth over $429 billion) were completed acquisition targets while in 1994, 6,201 were (worth over $293 billion). These levels of activity raise the obvious question, How do mergers affect job stability?

Birch's (1987) study of the issue traced the history of the 6,046 firms that underwent merger between 1969 and 1976. He compared the merged firms to firms that did not experience merger. He investigated changes in firm employment size. The results show that firms that merged had greater employment shrinkage than did independent firms during this recessionary period. More precisely, by his calculation, merged firms lost 10.5% of their jobs through contraction and 15.9% through dissolution; for independent firms the loss rates were 8.3% and 7.4%, respectively. Although exact data of this kind are not available for divestitures, most likely these events shrink or transfer employment as well. This should be especially the case for leveraged buyouts, which subject firms to greatly increased debt loads.

Reorganization

Corporate reorganization often affects the distribution of jobs within an organization. To the extent that competitive pressures drive reorganization events, the resulting redistribution of employment can be properly classified as demographically induced mobility. The phenomena entailed in this general process are many and varied; they include plant closings, technological changes, domain shifts, strategic realignments, and so forth. It is virtually impossible to find macrolevel data on these processes. However, activity of this kind obviously goes on regularly and with substantial impact on mobility.

19.4 Impact of Corporate Demography on Individual Mobility

Figure 19.1 gives a broad conceptual summary of the demographic processes of organizations that affect the creation and elimination of jobs. How much do these processes matter? How much individual mobility reflects corporate demography? These questions are difficult to answer precisely; however, we can make plausible estimates for the United States based on the studies reviewed above and other data.

To assess the importance of corporate demography in inducing individual job mobility, we need to know the overall amount of individual mobility and the relative magnitudes of its different types. Job shifts by individuals can be categorized along many dimensions: movement within versus across firms, movement within versus across occupations, upward versus downward versus lateral movement, geographic migration, movement into and out of employment, and movement into and out of the labor market (meaning into and out of school, illness, child care, retirement, etc.). The forces driving the job-shift process will vary across categories of change. For present purposes, we choose to take two primary dimensions—movement within versus across firms and movement within versus across occupations—and assess the impact of corporate demography on them.

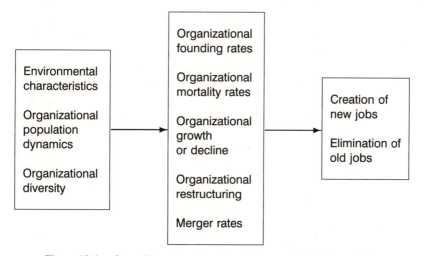

Figure 19.1. *General structure of corporate-demographic effects on jobs.*

Estimates of individual rates of job shifts across firms and occupations are readily available. Perhaps the most exhaustive longitudinal studies have been conducted by the Center for Human Resource Research at Ohio State University. These studies offer estimates for the probability of changing employers, ranging from 7% per year for men over 45 years of age to 23% per year for young men (Kim, Roderick, and Shea 1973; Kohen and Andrisani 1974; Parnes, Fleisher, Miljus, Spitz, and Associates 1970; Parnes, Egge, and Andrisani 1973; Roderick and Kohen 1976). Stated differently, depending on age and gender, between 7% and 23% of all persons shift employers in any given year.

Hall (1982) estimates that over 28% of employees in the American economy have held their current jobs one year or less. Allowing for new entrants to the labor market, this estimate implies an overall annual job turnover rate—encompassing both within-firm and across-firm movement—of about 25%.

Sehgal (1984) estimates that movement across occupational categories averages 9.5% per year. Eck (1984) reports somewhat higher rates, on average 20% per year; movement from an occupation ranges from 1.2% per year for dentists to 58.5% per year for child-care workers. Rosenfeld (1979) estimates that 90% of workers who change occupations also change firms, suggesting that interoccupational movement makes up a large proportion of interfirm movement. Coupled with Hall's estimate of overall mobility, these studies suggest that 20% per year is a reasonable estimate of individual mobility across organizations.

Research on the creation and elimination of jobs offers estimates of the effects of corporate demography on the population of jobs that range from approximately 10% to 23% per year (Table 19.1). Comparing individual mobility rates across organizations to these positional mobility rates requires some guesswork. When a new job gets created or an old job gets eliminated, the action generates at least one individual job change. However, an individual changing jobs might move directly from an eliminated job to a newly created job. This means that, in the extreme case, two structural events in the population of jobs correspond to only one individual mobility event. So, in comparison to an individual mobility rate, the equivalent structural rate changes from the observed figure to half its value.

Even using the conservative estimate, that two structural events involving jobs correspond to one individual job shift, the amount of mobility due to corporate demography is staggering. Taking the structural estimates given above and dividing by two implies that between 5% and 11% of job-holders change employers every year because of demographic processes. (Remember also that these figures are based on net changes in the total number of jobs offered by a firm. To the extent that the distribution of jobs shift independently of changes in firm size, these estimates understate the impact of corporate demography.)

With these estimates in hand, we can now do a rough calculation of the importance of demographic processes for individual mobility. We know that about 20% of all job-holders usually change firms in a given year. We also know that every year between 5% and 11% of all job-holders move to a different firm because of a corporate-demographic event. This means that the job shifts caused by demographic processes constitute between 25% (5/20) and 55% (11/20) of all individual mobility.

Moreover, demographically induced mobility likely accounts for virtually all downward movement and a large proportion of all movement into managerial positions. Because downward mobility within firms is rare, the 20% of movements across firms must capture most of it. Since individuals are unlikely to change firms for a worse job (except in rare circumstances), most movement of this kind must be forced, either by an involuntary discharge or by a demographic event. As involuntary terminations become infrequent (Kalleberg and Sørensen 1979), corporate-demographic factors probably dominate.

Similar reasoning applies to managerial positions, where rates of voluntary quitting are low. One journalist (Magnet 1984) guesses that up to one-half of the employees in merged firms will either leave or shifts jobs within the new firm. Another observer (Kay 1987) estimates that 10% of the entire U.S. work force works in companies involved in an acquisition, merger, or spin-off. When combined, these numbers imply that 5% of all individuals change jobs in a given year because of mergers and related activity.

Adding the estimated effects of mergers to our previous calculations increases the estimated impact of corporate-demographic processes to a level that strains credulity. Suppose that mergers and related activity do indeed prompt 5% of all workers to change jobs in a given year. Suppose also that 60% of those changing jobs also change firms. Then adding this 3% (5% · 60%) to our previous estimates brings the estimated effects of corporate demography up to a range of 8% to 15% of all job-holders per year. Since only 20% of all workers move in a given year, the upper estimate stretches the imagination.

These general estimates accord well with the actual numbers for the California savings and loan industry provided by Haveman and Cohen (1994), in the most sophisticated study of demographically induced mobility that we know.[5] They followed the executive employees of all the savings and loan banks in California from 1969 to 1988. This sample covered the

---

[5] Other informative studies include: Storey and Johnson (1987), Storey (1994), and Brüderl and Preisendörfer (1998).

period of deregulation in 1974–1975 and included information on 5,816 executives. Haveman and Cohen (1994) broke down their analysis by type of job move: into new firms; between firms; and out of the industry. They found that 10% of the moves between firms involved executives moving into newly founded firms. They also found that 25% of the job changes into managerial positions entailed movement into a new firm. For mortality, the numbers run even larger: "Almost half of all moves between firms in the industry occurred when managers left a failing firm. About one-quarter of the exits from the industry came from failing firms" (Haveman and Cohen 1994, 130). The findings show that the effects of corporate-demographic factors are "directly responsible for a large proportion of managerial job shifts in the industry and affect directly a large fraction of the industry's managerial employees" Haveman and Cohen (1994, 146).

These analyses, of course, say nothing about the types of jobs that individuals move to and from in such processes. Some evidence suggests that in recent years demographically induced mobility chiefly propels individuals downward:

> Whereas twenty-five years ago the vast majority of the people who were laid off found jobs that paid as well as their old ones, Labor Department numbers show that now only about 35 percent of laid-off, full-time workers end up in equally remunerative or better-paid jobs. (Uchitelle and Kleinfield 1996, 6)

An important next step in research on corporate demography and mobility would incorporate qualitative and other distinctions in the jobs that individuals move to and from.

19.5 Employment Benefits and Social Welfare

When someone leaves a job, it matters a great deal if he or she moves immediately (or shortly thereafter) to a new job. Those who do not do so usually lose income and status. They also suffer the uncertainty and anxiety produced by unemployment. The direct costs of unemployment to society are obvious; they can be calculated by the level of unemployment subsidy given to individuals out of work in addition to any other benefits provided. The indirect costs to the individual include the loss of experience and associated human capital as well as any stigma possibly attached to the unemployment state. To society, indirect costs involve the loss of productive output and the possible deterioration of the bank of human capital.

Individuals who move directly from one job to another escape many of these problems. Because so many other benefits are tied to employment, however, the losses (or gains) associated with changing jobs might still be very significant. For instance, most employed Americans obtain some form of health insurance and retirement benefit from their employing corporation. Many other corporations provide dental, optometric, and life insurance. In certain areas and industries, the employing corporation also provides housing (or a housing subsidy) and educational benefits (for the employee and perhaps the family). Some progressive corporations maintain child-care centers for their employees and allow long maternity leaves for either parent. And, a variety of modern corporations provide their employees with recreational options including fitness centers, picnic and vacation grounds, organized activities, and clubs.

When a person voluntarily terminates employment, it is reasonable to assume that he or she has made a calculated decision based on a weighted assessment of the various factors associated with a job. The decision is likely rational, based on the person's preferences, and it results in an overall gain. However, when a termination is involuntary, there are no grounds for making such an assumption; indeed the opposite is likely true: the average individual will experience a net loss.

Corporate-demographic processes generate both types of effects. The creation of jobs through the founding of new organizations and the growth of extant firms expands the opportunity set for job-holders and therefore likely induces higher voluntary mobility. Conversely, the elimination of jobs through firm dissolution and acquisition and organizational downsizing undoubtedly prompts great amounts of involuntary termination. So, we expect that industries and periods associated with high mortality and with declines in firm size would experience the highest levels of involuntary job mobility.

From a public-policy viewpoint, the demographic processes associated with these involuntary moves would seem to deserve the most attention because they potentially generate the greatest social costs. The key question is how to mitigate or minimize these costs and losses. Stated another way, the question concerns what benefits might best be tied to the employment contract and what might be provided in other ways, such as through the state. Although we cannot really answer this important and complex question here, we can offer some observations. We hope that these ideas might stimulate research on the issues underlying the question.

Corporate Demography and Benefits

If corporate-demographic activity has negligible effects on stability of employment, then the problem really differs. In this case, the main employment-benefits question concerns the differences in the packages among corporations rather than the periods of interrupted employment without benefits. Of course, in this idealized world, involuntary termination would still occur. But, in modern economies, it would typically take the form of "termination for cause," meaning that an employee has not performed up to some standard. Few would likely think that much policy should be developed to address their problems. At most, the problems of this group would require a very different set of policies.

Conversely, suppose that corporate-demographic activity was so rampant that almost everyone lost his or her job in a year or two as a result. In this case, the problems associated with readjustment would be so prevalent and great that it would likely be a compelling societal problem that would be addressed by the state political apparatus in a global way.

What we actually find lies between these poles. Corporate-demographic activity varies greatly, occurring intensely in some places and times while barely discernible in others. This variability makes it difficult to identify specific problems, especially since the level and type of benefits vary as well. In industries with few or minimal benefits, high firm mortality does not apparently generate much additional cost. Such variability also likely makes it difficult to design remedial policies that do not create unnecessary burdens in unproblematic locations and periods.

In terms of demographic factors, we suspect that the nature and level of employment-related benefits show a strong relationship with an organization's period of founding. In early days of corporations, firms such as shipping companies and railroads often provided virtually all the social functions (security, housing, food, schools, banks) in the company town or its equivalent. The obligation was typically tied exclusively to the employment contract: if you left your job, you lost the benefits.

More contemporary firms—meaning those firms founded after the first part of the twentieth century—operate in a world where the state provides many of the basic functions such as education, security, and transportation. Many of the major functions still retained in these modern benefits packages—retirement, health insurance, and life insurance—are often offered with tightly limited liability to the corporation and are provided through third parties such as investment companies and insurance companies. The corporation in these cases commits only to pay the cost of the service provided by the third party. Sometimes, as with health insurance (because of federal regulations), departing employees have the option of maintaining the service if they continue to pay the relevant fee to the third-party provider. This practice obviously has the potential to mitigate any potential losses arising from employee termination resulting from corporate demography.

We suspect that, as with many organizational features, great inertia holds in the types of benefits a company offers and the manner of their provision. Take retirement benefits for example. In the United States, we see two major types of corporate-sponsored retirement plans, the so-called defined-benefit and the defined-contribution plans. Defined-benefit plans specify exactly what an employee will receive by way of retirement, usually as a function of ending wages, years of experience, and age at retirement. The liability to the company can be estimated (because age-specific death rates of persons are known); but it is still somewhat uncertain. The company funds the program at levels estimated to be adequate given the labor force and expected rate of return on investment, but it maintains its obligation for the promised layouts even if the estimates prove hugely inaccurate.

By contrast, a defined-contribution plan specifies only that the employing organization will contribute a certain amount to an employee's retirement account. The contributed amount might be invested and managed by the employer; but more likely it will remain under the employee's control, at least in a limited way. Under a defined-contribution plan, the employer's financial obligation to fund retirement largely ends with the contribution.

We have not seen systematic data on this issue. Yet, it appears that older organizations are more likely to offer defined-benefit plans and younger ones, defined-contribution plans. This pattern would reflect both the period of founding of the organization and the difficulties of changing such a plan once it is in place (organizational inertia).

Defined-benefit plans are often designed to ensure high levels of employee retention. Thus, a typical such plan has a lengthy initial vesting period that the employee must work until he or she qualifies for the benefits. These plans also often have their benefits heavily tilted toward the latter years, meaning that the gains accruing from a year of employment are greatest for older and more experienced employees. Thus, involuntary termination from such a scheme results in major losses, especially compared to the equivalent event in a portable defined-contribution plan. Moreover, the collapse of such a system because of the failure of the firm could lead to wholesale losses of retirement benefits.

Such considerations suggest that the provision of benefits via portable third-party providers have value as a way to mitigate the potential social costs of corporate-demographic turbulence, especially if the state or other corporate actors will pay for such services during the dislocation. However, it is important to note that, while this approach separates the pieces of the benefits package from the employing corporation, it does not safeguard them entirely from corporate-demographic activity. After all, the third-party providers are themselves organizations subject to demographic processes including failure. So this approach simply shifts the benefits dangers to other domains. Perhaps the new domain is less volatile than that of the employing organization, perhaps not. Research on the demography of the organizations in these domains could be helpful: it could lead to an assessment of the relative risks and rational placement of the benefit.

Of course, many employing organizations do not want to outsource their benefits to third-party organizations because they use them as tools for employee recruitment and retention. That is, selective access to company benefits not available elsewhere assists many companies in attracting and keeping their employees. The issue involves more than the actual cost of supplying the benefit; some benefits greatly facilitate identification with the company and foster commitment and social integration (for example, parties, clubs, and fitness centers). This would appear to be especially likely for those benefits that do not involve high uncertainty in terms of the financial liability.

Corporations operating in environments with intense competition for labor seem most likely to design enhanced packages of employee benefits (broadly construed). This means that they will try to use selective access of their benefits as a competitive weapon, developing local exclusive non-portable benefits except where it is financially infeasible (e.g., retirement, health insurance). Does this mean that competitive environments are ideal places to work? Intense competition also likely makes the mortality rates of firms high and the fluctuations in size substantial. Ironically, the most attractive jobs in the sense of benefits might also be the most unattractive in terms of stability. From the point of view of social costs, the effects of competition are double-edged: they provide more private benefits to employees but at the same time they raise both the levels and the costs of corporate-demographic activity.

We expect that the benefits a firm offers will generally be tied to its human-resource strategy and its overall market orientation. As discussed in Chapter 9, The Stanford Project on Emerging Companies has identified five basic-model-type employment models: (1) a Star model that involves challenging work, autonomy and professional control, and selection of elite personnel based on longterm potential; (2) an Engineering model that combines a focus on challenging work, peer group control, and selection based on specific task abilities; (3) a Commitment model that relies on emotional/familial attachments of employees to the organization, selection based on cultural fit, and peer group control; (4) a Bureaucratic model that is based purely on monetary or task motivations, control and coordination through formal organization, and selection of employees to perform prespecified tasks, and (5) an Autocratic model based on pecuniary attachment, selection based on current competence, and direct oversight and control by managers.

Research on a sample of high-technology companies shows that all five employment models are used in new companies. Moreover, there is a moderate association between the initial business strategy of a company and its initial employment model. Firms pursuing a cost-minimization business strategy are most likely to adopt the Autocratic employment model. Those firms following a strategy of technological leadership are most likely to use the Star model, although the Engineering model is also very common among these firms. Firms adopting a business strategy attempting to refine or enhance an existing technology were likely to use either the Star or the Commitment model as well as the Engineering model. Firms that based their strategy primarily on superior marketing or customer service relied most frequently on the Commitment model, while firms pursing hybrid technology–marketing strategies relied on both the Commitment and Engineering models. As they age, these firms are moving largely toward the Bureaucratic model.

Obviously, almost any industry will be populated by firms pursuing a variety of different strategies. Hence, we would expect a variety of employment models, human-resource strategies, and benefits packages as well. The actual mix will vary across industries. Our discussion suggests that social costs associated with job dislocations caused by corporate demography will be higher in those industries with older firms (higher average age), with intense competition among firms (especially for labor), and where third-party contractors are unstable. These are only speculations, however. Research is needed that examines directly the issues involved.

19.6 Effects of Careers on Corporate Demography

We have assumed so far in this chapter that corporate demography affects jobs. We now consider the reverse causal possibility—that jobs and the characteristics of the individuals who hold them might affect the demography of a population of organizations. Clearly this sometimes occurs. For instance, the probability of self-employment for men increases as they near retirement age, especially if they are managers. Unemployment in general often drives individuals to consider self-employment. Mayer and Goldstein (1961) report that 21 of the 81 owners of the small businesses they studied had opened their firms because they had either lost their jobs or feared job loss. More organizationally, Brittain and Freeman (1986) analyzed the rate at which existing semiconductor firms spawned founders of new firms. They found spin-offs were more likely for firms that followed a generalist strategy, were first movers in a product group, had recently experienced an executive succession, or were recently taken over by a firm from outside the industry. Broadly speaking, institutional and organizational demographics define the set of opportunities and constraints for individuals, while individual choices (taken in aggregate) also shape the dynamics of organizations and institutions.

The fact that causal influences run both ways complicates the study of social change greatly. Analysts always find it tempting to resolve the complication by eliding one side of the causal structure. So, for instance, sociologists influenced by theories of rational choice have begun to insist that we view social movements, organizations, and institutions as relatively simple transformations of individual decisions. Yet a great deal of theory and research on organizations demonstrates the great difficulty of accounting for even particular organizational actions—much less a series of actions—in terms of the preferences of individual actors (March 1988). Difficult as it might be, there seems to be no alternative to modeling the dynamics of social systems with causal influences running both ways.

Because social scientists understandably prefer to consider only two levels of analysis at a time, it is tempting to treat organizations as simple conduits in relating individual careers and social structure. Depending on the starting point, organizations can be thought of as implementing mechanically the dictates of the state and the larger economy or as passively reflecting the interests of their members. In such cases, organizations serve to transmit influences from one level to another.

The simplifying assumption that organizations merely implement goals set by members (micro-level interests) or institutional rules and constraints (macro-level constraints) but do not otherwise affect social dynamics does not fit well with our understanding of the organizational world. For one thing, constructing a permanent organization is a very expensive solution to problems of collective action or institutional control. Constructing an organization requires mobilization and investment of considerable time and resources. Organizations have a high metabolic overhead—they use up considerable amounts of resources in merely maintaining their structures. Typically, only a small fraction of the resources invested in an organization goes into a final product or collective action.

Concerning individual careers and social structure, the key consequence might be that organizations tend to develop their own idiosyncratic dynamics. Their response to the changing interests of relevant populations of individuals and institutional controllers is often halting at best. When the operative time span approximates the career of a typical individual, change in the world of organizations seems glacial by contrast. Even when changing interests among populations of individuals dictate change in organizations, the rate of change in the latter might be so slow that the constraints imposed by organizations can be treated as exogenous or even a constant for the purposes of analyzing a set of individual careers (see Chapter 20 for some initial development in this direction).

A more developed knowledge of relative rates would be very helpful. Under what conditions do individuals change much faster than organizations? When do organizations change more quickly? When are the rates likely to be similar enough that the dynamic processes operate at the same pace strongly linked?

20

Organizational Diversity

IN THIS BOOK, we have tried to lay out the basic elements of a corporate demography and to provide evidence of its promise. The exercise has taken us through a wide range of topics including theory, data sources, observation plans, methods of analysis, and policy. The overarching goal is to develop a set of ideas and tools that will allow analysis of how organizational diversity arises and disappears in industries and entire economies.

We have left somewhat unexplored a question that provides much of the motivation for demographic analysis of corporations and industries: How does organizational diversity actually affect outcomes in the broader economy and social structure? In explaining the relevance of this book in the Preface, we pointed to Silicon Valley and Hollywood. We suggested that the high levels of organizational diversity found in these two industrial communities might explain their sustained economic vibrancy. One general logic behind this supposition holds that a specialized division of labor possesses efficiencies that surpass any increased transaction costs (Smith 1976; Durkheim 1947; Hawley 1950).

Another general logic behind this suggestion follows an old evolutionary principle recognizing that in an uncertain world, diverse systems are more likely to possess appropriate responses than homogeneous systems (Hannan 1986a). As environmental uncertainty rises, so too presumably do the advantages of diversity. Along these lines, Gray and Lowery (1996) examined the relationship between the organizational diversity of political interest representation in American states and the functioning of state economy, policy, and politics.

This general argument that diversity controls the speed of evolution also provides an interesting explanation of the deficiencies of state socialist systems, which lacked (or contained very low levels of) organizational diversity. The transformations of the former state socialist systems provide ample opportunities to examine the implications of growing diversity for economic and social processes. Grabher and Stark (1997), building on organizational demography, argue that great diversity of organizational forms is required for such transformations to move forward.

Yet, it would be fallacious to assume that organizational diversity provides only benefits. Diverse systems carry high overhead costs: many resources are usually underexploited. Moreover, in many contexts, organizational diversity likely influences outcomes that are possibly very important but peculiar to the context. In these cases, institutionally informed research needs to be conducted to assess the consequences of organizational diversity and demographic turnover. Very little of this type of work has been attempted. Yet it clearly represents a major next step for corporate demography, a step that would represent the development of a "population studies" research program about corporations. As noted in Chapter 2, demographic knowledge relies on this component as well as on the more formal modeling component stressed throughout the book.

In this final chapter, we sketch some preliminary ideas about these issues. In particular, we consider how the diversity of organizational forms in a social system determines two kinds of broader societal outcomes. First, we examine the idea that diversity of producers and associated products in a market might affect consumption patterns and their associated social benefits and problems. Given the extensive prior demographic research on populations of beer and wine producers and the great social costs of alcohol abuse, we focus on the beer and wine industries. Second, we consider how the diversity of employing organizations might affect levels of inequality in the quality of individual employment careers and their associated rewards.

In both cases, we shift the level of analysis from the conventional concern with relationships between individual and firm characteristics to relationships between *distributions* of characteristics of populations or communities and distributions of individual outcomes. For consumption, the approach suggests links to a social problem in certain industries; in the case of careers, it generates predictions about social and economic inequality. Our discussion of these ideas culminates in the form of suggested research proposals.

20.1 Consequences of Diversity in Beer and Wine Industries

To illustrate how the effects of context-specific organizational diversity might be examined systematically, we turn to the beer and wine industries. As we discussed in Chapter 12, in both industries in the United States dominance by large firms and associated economic concentration has occurred simultaneously with a proliferation of small specialist producers:

microbreweries and brewpubs in beer and boutique wineries in wine. Both industries have experienced an increase in organizational diversity and product diversity, especially in some areas. Our previous research efforts in these industries leads us to believe that these organizational changes have likely altered consumption patterns. Alcohol abuse and its consequences have possibly changed as well. A number of theoretical arguments and anecdotal observations suggest that some of these changes might be deleterious and others beneficial. We review and discuss these arguments here, suggesting ways that they might be investigated more systematically.

Demographic research shows that the U.S. beer and wine industries have experienced two kinds of interrelated organizational changes in recent decades. The first involves the increased size, scale, and dominance of large firms such as Anheuser-Busch and Gallo. The second change involves the rise and proliferation of small, specialized producers such as those commonly referred to as microbreweries, brewpubs, and boutique wineries. For instance, Anheuser-Busch's share of the beer market grew from 28.2% in 1980 to 44% in 1995, while the number of microbreweries and brewpubs operating in the United States grew from eight in 1980 to 841 in 1995 (and to over 1,350 in late 1998).

As explained in Chapter 12, the theory of resource partitioning holds that (under specified conditions), as the number of large generalist organizations tends toward oligopoly, the opportunities for small specialist producers improve. This is because generalists typically differentiate themselves from each other in terms of their appeals in less concentrated markets; thus, their combined market base is broader than in a concentrated market where the generalist organization(s) aim for the center of the market. Resource-partitioning theory predicts that, as leading generalist organizations become larger and the overall market becomes concentrated, total organizational diversity actually increases. In other words, a market with several large generalist firms differentiating themselves in covering the market has less diversity than one with a single large firm or two that cover most of the market and numerous specialist producers that serve the remainder.

A critical next step in the research program on corporate demography involves learning whether these organizational changes affect important industrial and societal outcomes. Obviously, outcomes such as innovation and industrial performance deserve scrutiny. However, for the alcoholic-beverage industries, other important and relevant outcomes deserving attention are alcohol-consumption patterns, abuse levels, and other social consequences. The importance of these outcomes transcends the industry. We believe that study of these outcomes would assist understanding of the impact of federal and state public policy related to the production and distribution of alcoholic beverages.

Why would organizational diversity in beer brewing and wine making affect consumption and abuse? First, organizational diversity is typically associated with product diversity (Peterson and Berger 1996; Lopes 1992; Gray and Lowery 1996). Certainly, microbrewery and boutique-winery products have increased the range of alcoholic beverages available and might have shaped tastes. These products also reach different consumer groups than those of generalist mass producers; and many of these groups were cultivated freshly for this market. For example, many women who never drank beer regularly now drink beers and ciders from the specialist segment. Second, the quality, high-status image associated with specialty beer and wine products might provide an attractive (and socially approved) inducement to alcohol consumption, especially for particular groups of consumers. Third, the specialty firms in these markets often sponsor highly visible social events such as festivals and tastings. These events provide attractive new public forums for drinking and the celebration of specialty alcohol products.

Based on years of direct and indirect observation of these industries, we believe that consumption patterns have changed with the rise in organizational diversity. We suspect that abuse levels have also changed, along with other social consequences. What is unclear is the exact nature of these changes, including whether the overall impact to society in terms of responsible alcohol consumption has been beneficial or detrimental. On the one hand, the broadened range of products and appeals to potential consumers suggests that consumption and related problems have likely spread into different consumer subpopulations, with perhaps differing consumption patterns. On the other hand, specialty alcohol products are expensive and are designed to be savored in small quantities. They might teach responsible consumption. The social networks developing around these products and associated events might also help control problems, at least for certain consumer subpopulations. There is also the old claim that drinks of moderation might steer at least some consumers away from hard liquor (consumption levels of which are down.)

An interesting research project would examine rigorously the relationships between, on the one hand, organizational diversity in the beer and wine industries and, on the other hand, consumption patterns and abuse and other social consequences. Such a project could analyze data sets that combine detailed historical and demographic organizational data with data sets on consumption, abuse, and their consequences, which have been collected by the federal government and other agencies and firms.[1] The

---

[1] Specifically, one could use two publicly available data sets: the cross-sectional surveys from the National Household Survey on Drug Abuse (Substance Abuse and Mental Health Services Administration, various years), and the series of cross-sectional surveys from the National Alcohol Survey (Alcohol Research Group, various years). Both sets of surveys are

extent and timing of organizational changes in these two industries vary greatly across states and metropolitan areas.

We believe these research questions might be timely in understanding and interpreting certain current trends in alcohol consumption in the United States. According to Midanik and Room (1992, 184), "beer has increased its dominance in the U.S." in the modern era. There is also a baffling apparent change in consumption and in some of its consequences from 1984 to 1990 among persons aged 18–29 years old, a group highly likely to frequent brewpubs and drink specialty products. According to Midanik and Clark (1995), the 18–29 age group showed lower levels of drinking in 1990 than in 1984 but higher rates of social consequences. They describe this finding as "perplexing." Perhaps an examination of new types of beer-drinking outlets and products popular among this age group would prove valuable in understanding these developments.

Addressing these (and related) issues would build an important empirical foundation for policy analysis and formulation. Much of the organizational diversity in the beer and wine industries has either originated from or been propelled by laws and regulations promulgated by the states and the federal government. For beer brewing, the emergence of the smallest-scale producer types, known as brewpubs, required individual states to enact laws authorizing vertical integration of production and sale (usually allowed only for breweries below a certain size threshold). Small brewers also get a break in federal excise taxes. These changes were contemplated against a complex backdrop of state-specific regulation over the production and sale of malt beverages. For the wine industry, the authenticity of boutique products relies heavily on a federally managed appellation system verifying the source of grapes. Many boutique wineries also depend on direct shipments of wines to consumers across state boundaries. (The legality of such transactions is under fire in some places.) Should these laws and practices be extended to other areas and types of firms? Or should they be reexamined in their current application? The answers are of more than academic interest.

Various interest groups and lobbies currently advocate changes favoring their constituents. For instance, we are sure that large breweries would jump at the chance to own brewpubs. As the market presence of these outlets grows, large breweries will likely demand (in courts and legislatures) equal treatment under the law. Although we have no desire to determine the outcomes of these kinds of struggles, we are also dismayed by the lack

---

designed to obtain nationally representative samples and use true probability sampling methods. Both sets use lengthy and confidential face-to-face interviewing methods. The detailed organizational and demographic data would allow close examination of these relationships in communities throughout the United States.

of social welfare analysis that might inform these decisions. Why does no one think about the impact of these changes on consumption patterns and abuse levels? In our view, the likely societal consequences of proposed legal and regulatory changes ought to be considered in addition to the interests and rights of the various producers, distributors, and their employees. We believe that developing corporate demography would assist in balancing these other policy debates.

20.2 Careers and Inequality

It takes little insight to realize that individuals experience wide variations in their career paths and rewards in modern society. What accounts for such career differences? Some of the diversity no doubt reflects hetero-geneity among individuals' abilities and tastes, some reflects differences in resources of families of origin, and so forth. Both sociological (e.g., status-attainment) and economic (e.g., human-capital) theorists emphasize the importance of initial conditions: differences in advantage of families of origin or differences in parental investment. Both lines of theory hold that small initial differences persist over the career cycle and might be amplified under certain conditions.

What if we used a different lens and looked at the heterogeneity among employers in a system rather than among the members of cohorts entering employment? To put the issue in sharp relief, consider two polar cases. One case is the extreme of low diversity with either one dominant employer (e.g., a classic company town or an extreme form of a Lenin-ist state) or a set of essentially indistinguishable employers (e.g., a coffee plantation economy—see Paige (1997)). The other case has a great variety of firms offering employment, as in central regions of modern capitalist economies such as Silicon Valley, the region surrounding Amsterdam (the Randstadt), and South-East England.

Suppose that the average outcomes of individuals do not differ in the prototype low-diversity and high-diversity systems. That is, assume that the average returns to education and other forms of investment in human cap-ital and stability of employment do not differ in the two cases. Would the difference in diversity of employers make any difference for individuals? Hannan (1988) argued that the diversity of organizations controlling jobs will affect the diversity of outcomes in the population of job-holders and job-seekers. A system with low diversity among its organizations presum-ably favors one (or a few) particular bundle of skills. For instance, a classic plantation economy or Fordist industrial system does not require a high diversity of skills and information. Individuals with the favored skills and positions in information networks do relatively well on average and those with different sets of skills and access to different kinds of information do not do well on average.

Moreover, individuals with the less favored set of skills and positions have few alternatives, because lateral mobility does not increase payoffs. Systems with high organizational diversity are less likely to favor any particular set of abilities and training. Although each employer might favor a narrow set of skills, various employers need not favor the same set.

Consider, for instance, the set of firms studied in The Stanford Project on Emerging Companies (Chapter 9). Founders and CEOs of some of these companies report that they want to hire only those with extensive industry experience on the grounds that they do not have the time to conduct training. Others, facing the same competitive environment, report that they favor applicants fresh from university, because they have not yet been exposed to poor organizational practice and thus have less to "unlearn" than experienced workers. On a different dimension, some founders and CEOs want to hire technical/scientific "stars" but others report that they want only "team players" and will not hire "prima donnas." In this context, different firms value different characteristics, and no one group is favored. Thus we would expect to find diminished inequality in career outcomes in such a community.

Diversity of career lines presumably affects the *inequality* of outcomes. When only a few kinds of careers can be fashioned, the significance of initial differences in abilities, training, and social ties gets magnified. The result is a high level of inequality. When many, diverse career paths are possible, heterogeneity in abilities and ties among workers matters less. In other words, organizational diversity among employers interacts with the distribution of initial advantage in determining levels of inequality. High diversity mutes the impact of differences in initial advantage; low diversity magnifies it. Thus the general argument is that the diversity of careers is proportional to the diversity of organizations in the system (Hannan 1988).

Dimensions of Demographic Diversity

Consider the implications of this argument in terms of two easily measured demographic dimensions of organizational diversity: size distributions and age distributions of firms. The best empirical research on the connections between attributes of firms and careers finds that size of firm has stronger effects on careers than any other organizational attribute (Baron and Bielby 1984; Carroll and Mayer 1986). Workers in large firms are less likely to move to other firms but have higher rates of mobility within firms, suggesting that large firms do indeed develop internal labor markets.

Size distributions of firms differ considerably among industries (compare the highly concentrated aircraft and pharmaceutical industries with the unconcentrated health care and garment industries) and among communities (compare company towns with commercial centers). Hannan (1988) hypothesized that the size distribution of firms or establishments affects levels of income or wage inequality in industries and communities net of distributions of individual characteristics (reflecting investments in human capital).

Greve (1994) confirmed this hypothesis in an analysis of career-history data on the cohort of 1000 men who entered employment in Norway in 1971 (taken from the Norwegian Life History Study). He found that the size diversity of firms in industry affected rates of mobility within and outside industries (net of the effects of the person's level of education, number of previous jobs, tenure in the firm and the job, and the size of the employing organization). The lower the diversity of sizes within an industry, the lower the rate of mobility within the industry and the higher the rate of leaving the industry. Fujiwara-Greve and Greve (1997) find a similar pattern of effects for the size diversity of firms within local areas.

It seems likely that age of employing organization and age distribution in the relevant system affect career paths. The most obvious effect concerns the fact that new organizations tend to have high mortality rates.[2] Employment in a younger firm tends to be associated with shorter spells of employment, whatever an individual's characteristics. Movement between firms caused by organizational mortality presumably increases the average time in states of unemployment. Long spells of unemployment damage chances of success strongly for young workers, because such interruptions delay the accumulation of experience and makes workers less attractive to alternative employers.

Presumably, the age of a firm also affects chances for advancement within it, because new organizations almost inevitably hire workers in a situation in which the firm's age distribution across ranks falls short of a "stable population." In the common circumstance of a new firm filling all of its ranks with relatively young individuals, few vacancies are caused by retirement or death at higher ranks. Thus, holding rate of firm growth constant, chances for promotion and salary increases are lower in younger organizations (assuming the initial staffing patterns discussed above).

The age distribution of a set of firms might also affect careers and inequality through its connection with diversity of organizational forms. As we noted in Chapter 9, cohorts of organizations exhibit patterned diversity of forms. Each cohort tends to incorporate prevailing social and political arrangements—not to mention fads and fashions in management—into organizational designs and to retain these distinctive features long after

---

[2]Chapter 14 shows that at least some of this association likely reflects the fact that young organizations tend to be small and small organizations have high hazards of mortality.

founding. According to this imprinting argument, the diversity of organizational forms in a system is affected by the age distribution of organizations. Industries whose firms were founded in a brief period (e.g., the railroad industry and the computer industry) should be less diverse than industries whose firms were founded relatively uniformly over a longer period of time (e.g., the investment banking and retail trades).

Inequality within Ethnic Communities

According to Hannan (1988), issues of organizational diversity might also explain some features of inequality within ethnic communities. By most informed accounts (beginning with Wilson (1978)), inequality within the African-American population has grown sharply relative to inequality within the white population.[3] Hout (1985, 321) concluded his analysis of patterns of occupational mobility of African-American men between 1962 and 1973 as follows: "Wilson is right: class became substantially more important for occupational chances of black men over the course of the 1960s." This research suggests that the African-American population was bifurcating into a relatively advantaged population (whose careers differ little from those in the white population) and an underclass. There are numerous possible explanations for this trend. One that has not received attention concerns the effects of organizational diversity. We suggest two ways that trends in diversity might be partly responsible for the trend toward increasing inequality with the African-American population.

First, discussion of "ethnic enclaves" suggests that the African-American population in the United States has been less successful than at least some other ethnic minority populations in creating and maintaining a diverse set of firms within its segregated communities. Some argue that the greater success of Cuban and Japanese migrant communities reflects the higher density of firms within the ethnic enclaves (Wilson and Martin 1982; Portes and Bach 1985). However, Sanders and Nee (1987) show that participation in an enclave economy per se does not explain the relatively greater success of Asians and Cubans in the United States.

These two observations might be reconciled by examining the possibility that the diversity of firms within an ethnic community affects the degree of inequality in success in the community. If the diversity of firms within predominantly black communities has remained low while the diversity of firms in other communities has risen, the level of inequality in black communities would rise relative to those in others.

---

[3] Farley (1984) shows that this claim is correct if income inequality is measured as the interquartile range but not if the Gini index is used.

The second aspect of organizational diversity affecting levels of inequality in the African-American community involves increased standardization of the employment relation. A number of laws and regulations, beginning mainly with the New Deal, have placed limits on the employment relation. These rules include minimum wage laws, health and safety regulations, child labor laws, and affirmative action rulings. While most of these regulations have been designed to improve the working conditions of less advantaged workers, they might have had the unintended consequence of increasing inequality. They have almost certainly reduced the diversity of employment conditions and employment relations, especially in those portions of the labor market(s) facing many African-Americans. In short, they have reduced organizational diversity with respect to the employment relation. According to the general argument, such changes increase the level of inequality in the population.

Effects of Careers on Organizational Diversity

As demonstrated throughout this book, organizational diversity in an industry or organizational population depends on: rates of innovation in organizational forms, the founding rate, the diversity of new entrants, the merger rate, and the disbanding rate. Diversity also depends on rates of environmental change and the adaptive capacities of individual organizations. Not only does organizational diversity influence careers, but also the distribution of career choices also greatly affects organizational diversity. This reverse causal process is also potentially very interesting.

The dynamics of career effects on organizational diversity can be specified in terms of any of the component rates of organizational change. Perhaps the most interesting class of processes are those that link career dynamics to the rate of innovation in organizational forms and the founding rate. An obvious, but easily overlooked, fact is that new firms and new organizational forms get created by individuals trying to fashion careers. When individual organizations have long life expectancies, when the flow of vacancies down a hierarchy of jobs matches the flow of entrants into the lower-level jobs, and when diversity of firms in a labor market is high, individuals with high ability and scarce training can develop rewarding careers within the existing set of organizations. Under such circumstances, the potential gains from starting or joining a new, novel organization rarely offset the high uncertainty of the new venture. Good career prospects within firms translate into low rates of innovation in forms and low founding rates.

When favorable prospects for developing careers within firms depress rates of innovation and firm founding, organizational diversity declines as mortality and adaptive change lead to the dominance of a small number of organizational forms. Declining diversity affects the gains from organizational innovation in two ways. First, if diversity declines due to mortality of some organizational forms, then workers in the failed organizations cannot move to other similar firms and a pool of available members is created. If the decrease in diversity occurs largely through adaptive change by existing organizations towards a common form, then the diversity of careers declines and mobility chances for some subpopulations of workers decline. In either case, the number of workers who can expect rewarding careers within the set of existing firms declines.

Decreases in the diversity of firms in a market tend to result in some potential demand being ignored. As the portion of unfilled and dissatisfied demand for services grows, the gains from creating organizations specially tailored to meet that demand grow. This circumstance combines with a set of interrupted and/or blocked careers and a set of "empty niches" in which to innovate. Such circumstances increase the frequency of attempted innovation in organizational forms and establishment of new firms using existing forms.

Stinchcombe (1965) argued that blocked mobility sparks social revolutions and sets off cascades of organization-building as labor and material resources become freed from constraints. Social revolutions provide just one instance of a class of social situations in which individual response to blocked opportunity within a set of organizational arrangements creates new organizational forms. These situations have in common that many individuals have acquired general skills of use in organization-building (e.g., literacy), have invested little in firm-specific human capital, and find that the existing set of organizations provides limited opportunities. The limitations on opportunity might reflect the actions of monopolies or it might reflect low levels of organizational diversity.

Empirical study of the effects of career dynamics on rates of innovation in organizational forms and rates of founding firms could focus on individuals and firms in bounded industries over the "life cycle" of the industry. Such study could evaluate the claim that the structure of careers decisively molds the industry in the crucial take-off period when technology and structure change rapidly. Brittain and Freeman (1986) analyzed the effects of work arrangements on the rate at which engineers in the semiconductor manufacturing industry leave firms to begin new ones. They find that firms trying to compete by staying at the leading edge of technical change (rather than producing standard products at low cost) have higher rates of entrepreneurial exits. They argue that this relationship arises because engineers in innovating firms have good information about impending technical changes and their employers cannot quickly exploit the opportunities arising from such changes. What has not yet been investigated is whether the rate of entrepreneurial exits also depends on the demography of opportunity within the firm and the diversity of organizational forms within the industry. Exploring such links would clarify the role of career paths in affecting organizational diversity.

Research on this issue could also profitably be framed at the level of the community or larger social system so as to incorporate the effects of changed career patterns among those not yet in an industry. For example, it would be interesting to explore the consequences of the rapid shift in career patterns of women in many societies on the diversity of firms. Clearly, this change increases diversity in the shortterm: women have created new organizations to deal with their special interests and problems as they have obtained increasing control over resources. What are the likely longterm impacts on diversity of a convergence of career patterns of men and women? One can easily imagine that the consequence is reduced diversity in the world of firms, as those that specialize in exploiting wage differences between equally qualified men and women adapt to changing conditions or disappear. On the other hand, it might turn out that the rapid change in the career paths of women has given rise to new organizational forms that persist as part of a new equilibrium.

Internal Organizational Demography

As reviewed in Chapter 2, research on internal organizational demography has proliferated in contemporary organizational research. It examines the effects of diversity (heterogeneity) in the tenure or length of service (LOS) distributions of individuals within an organization on organizational outcomes. Although most researchers apparently do not see a connection between internal demographic processes and the demography of corporations and industries, the underlying processes must be linked—if for no other reason than the simple fact that organizational vital events strongly affect the tenures of individuals (Chapter 19). Further development of these links might examine how population processes generating organizational diversity affect LOS heterogeneity or vice versa.

One recent study of these issues by Sørensen collected data on commercial television stations in the largest U.S. broadcast markets from 1961 to 1988 and analyzed the rates of growth/decline in viewership of individual firms (Sørensen 2000b; Sørensen 2000c). This project focused on the effect of the LOS distributions of top managers. Sørensen reviewed the extensive research that shows that the competitive environments in which managers have operated affects: (1) their capabilities, and (2) their stock of social ties (which affects the kinds of information that they can access). Differences in capabilities and social ties influence the kinds of competitive strategies that managers pursue. Thus, firms that recruit managers from similar sources will tend to develop similar strategies. Because the strength of competition between firms in a local system increases with the similarity of their strategies, similarity in patterns of executive recruitment will increase the intensity of competition among a set of firms. Sørensen (2000c) tested this conjecture by measuring the similarity of a given firm's pattern of executive recruitment with those of its local rivals and relating overlap in recruitment patterns to growth rates. The hypothesis receives strong support: growth rates dampen when a firm's pattern of executive recruitment overlaps substantially with those of its rivals.

Sørensen (2000b) also developed and tested another hypothesis about LOS distributions that was based on demographic and ecological reasoning. He relied on imprinting imagery (Chapter 9) to argue that the experiences that generate managers' capabilities and social ties are tied to the timing of their entry into management teams. Cohorts of managers who enter in different periods tend to have different experiences and to favor different strategies according to this argument. Sørensen (2000b) hypothesizes that sets of firms whose LOS distributions among top management teams are similar will follow more similar strategies than sets with less similar LOS distributions. This hypothesis too finds support in an analysis of growth rates of television stations: net of the effects of many relevant control variables, overlap in LOS distributions with competitors significantly lowers growth rates.

20.3 Toward a Community Ecology of Corporations

We have steadfastly maintained a population focus in this book. We have argued that designing research on populations of corporations is the most reliable strategy for uncovering empirical regularities and for cumulating knowledge about the demography of organizations. The foregoing sections illustrate that this strategy also has potential for shedding light on the more complex questions of how the evolution of populations of organizations affects the communities and societies in which they operate.

Once we open the question of broader impacts, we need to rethink some of the strategic issues. Many interesting and important societal outcomes are affected jointly by diverse sets of organizational populations, not just one. A thoroughgoing pursuit of the implications of organizational diversity might want to consider the implications of the diversity over sets of populations. If this strategy is adopted, then a scientifically sound multipopulation design likely needs to be developed. We think that an important next step in developing the demography of corporations and industries will design and conduct research on the communities of interacting populations of corporations and industries.

References

Aalen, Odd O. 1978. "Nonparametric Inference for a Family of Counting Processes." *Annals of Statistics* 6:701–26.

Aaronovitch, S., and M. C. Sawyer. 1975. "Mergers, Growth and Concentration." *Oxford Economic Papers* 27:136–55.

Abernathy, William J., Kim Clark, and A. Kantrow. 1983. *Industrial Renaissance*. New York: Basic Books.

Abernathy, William J., and James M. Utterback. 1978. "Patterns of Industrial Innovation." *Technology Review* 80:2–9.

Aitchison, J., and J. A. C. Brown. 1957. *The Lognormal Distribution*. Cambridge: Cambridge University Press.

Aldrich, Howard E., and Ellen R. Auster. 1993. "Even Dwarfs Started Small: Liabilities of Age and Their Strategic Implications." Pp. 165–98 in *Research in Organizational Behavior*, Volume 15, edited by L. Cummings and B. Staw. Greenwich, Conn.: JAI.

Aldrich, Howard E., and Peter V. Marsden. 1988. "Environments and Organizations." Pp. 361–92 in *Handbook of Sociology*, edited by N. Smelser. Beverley Hills, Calif.: Sage.

Aldrich, Howard E., Catherine R. Zimmer, Udo H. Staber, and John J. Beggs. 1994. "Minimalism, Mutualism, and Maturity: The Evolution of American Trade Association Populations in the 20th Century." Pp. 223–39 in *Evolutionary Dynamics of Organizations*, edited by J. Baum and J. Singh. New York: Oxford University Press.

Alexander, Peter J. 1996. "Entropy and Popular Culture: Product Diversity in the Music Recording Industry." *American Sociological Review* 61:171–74.

Alison, R. I., and K. P. Uhl. 1964. "Influence of Beer Brand Identification on Taste Perception." *Journal of Marketing Research* 1:36–39.

Altshuler, Alan, Martin Anderson, Daniel Jones, Daniel Roos, and James Womack. 1984. *The Future of the Automobile*. Cambridge: MIT Press.

Amburgey, Terry L., Tina Dacin, and Dawn Kelly. 1994. "Disruptive Selection and Population Segmentation: Interpopulation Competition as a Selection Process." Pp. 240–54 in *Evolutionary Dynamics of Organizations*, edited by J. Baum and J. Singh. New York: Oxford University Press.

Amburgey, Terry L., Dawn Kelly, and William P. Barnett. 1993. "Resetting the Clock: The Dynamics of Organizational Change and Failure." *Administrative Science Quarterly* 38:51–73.

Amburgey, Terry L., Marjo-Ritta Lehtisalo, and Dawn Kelly. 1988. "Suppression and Failure in the Political Press: Government Control, Party Affiliation, and Organizational Life Chances." Pp. 153–74 in *Ecological Models of Organizations*, edited by G. Carroll. Cambridge, Mass.: Ballinger.

Andersen, Per Kragh, Ørnuff Borgan, Richard Gill, and Niels Keiding. 1993. *Statistical Models Based on Counting Processes*. Berlin: Springer-Verlag.

Anderson, Philip, and Michael L. Tushman. 1990. "Technological Discontinuities and Dominant Design: A Cyclical Model of Technological Change." *Administrative Science Quarterly* 35:604–33.

Arrow, Kenneth J. 1974. *The Limits of Organization*. New York: Norton.

Arthur, W. Brian. 1989. "Competing Technologies, Increasing Returns, and Lock-In by Historical Events." *Economic Journal* 99:116–31.

Arthur, W. Brian, Y. M. Ermoliev, and Y. M. Kaniovski. 1987. "Path-Dependent Processes and the Emergence of Macro-Structure." *European Journal of Operational Research* 30:294–303.

Atwood, Roy. 1984. "Telephony and Its Cultural Meanings in Southeastern Iowa, 1900–1917." Ph.D. dissertation, University of Iowa.

Automotive News. 1993. "America at the Wheel: 100 Years of the Automobile in America (Special Issue)."

Banaszak-Holl, Jane. 1991. "Incorporating Organizational Growth into Models of Organizational Dynamics: Manhattan Banks, 1791–1980." Ph.D. dissertation, Cornell University.

Barley, Stephen, John Freeman, and Ralph C. Hybels. 1992. "Strategic Alliances in Biotechnology." Pp. 311–47 in *Networks and Organizations*, edited by N. Nohria and R. Eccles, Harvard Business School Press.

Barnett, William P. 1990. "The Organizational Ecology of a Technological System." *Administrative Science Quarterly* 35:31–60.

—— 1994. "The Liability of Collective Action: Growth and Change Among Early Telephone Companies." Pp. 337–54 in *Evolutionary Dynamics of Organizations*, edited by J. Baum and J. Singh. New York: Oxford University Press.

—— 1995. "Telephone Industries." Pp. 277–89 in *Organizations in Industry*, edited by G. Carroll and M. Hannan. New York: Oxford University Press.

—— 1997. "The Dynamics of Competitive Intensity." *Administrative Science Quarterly* 42:128–60.

Barnett, William P., and Glenn R. Carroll. 1987. "Competition and Mutualism Among Early Telephone Companies." *Administrative Science Quarterly* 30:400–421.

—— 1993. "How Institutional Constraints Affected the Organization of Early U.S. Telephony." *Journal of Law, Economics, and Organization* 9:98–126.

—— 1995. "Modeling Internal Organizational Change." *Annual Review of Sociology* 21:217–36.

Barnett, William P., and John Freeman. 1997. "Too Much of a Good Thing? Product Proliferation and Organizational Failure." Unpublished paper. Stanford Graduate School of Business.

Barnett, William P., and Morton T. Hansen. 1996. "The Red Queen in Organizational Evolution." *Strategic Management Journal* 17:139–58.

Barnett, William P., and David G. McKendrick. 1998. "The Evolution of Global Competition in the Hard Disk Drive Industry." Presented at Academy of Management Meetings.

Barnett, William P., Gary A. Mischke, and William Ocasio. 2000. "The Evolution of Collective Strategies Among Organizations." *Organization Studies,* forthcoming.

Barnett, William P., and Olav Sorenson. 1998. "The Red Queen in Organizational Creation and Development." Presented at the 14th Colloquium of the European Group on Organization Studies.

Baron, James N. 1984. "Organizational Perspectives on Stratification." *Annual Review of Sociology* 10:37–69.

Baron, James N., and William T. Bielby. 1984. "The Organization of Work in a Segmented Economy." *American Sociological Review* 49:454–73.

Baron, James N., M. Diane Burton, and Michael T. Hannan. 1996. "The Road Taken: Origins and Early Evolution of Employment Systems in Emerging Companies." *Industrial and Corporate Change* 5:239–76.

—— 1999. "Engineering Bureaucracy: The Genesis of Formal Policies, Positions, and Structures in High-Technology Firms." *Journal of Law, Economics, and Organization,* 15:1–41.

Baron, James N., Michael T. Hannan, and M. Diane Burton. 1999. "Building the Iron Cage: Determinants of Managerial Intensity in the Early Years of Organizations." *American Sociological Review,* in press.

Baron, James N., Brian S. Mittman, and Andrew E. Newman. 1991. "Targets of Opportunity: Organizational and Environmental Determinants of Gender Integration Within the California Civil Service, 1979–1985." *American Journal of Sociology* 96:1362–1401.

Baron, James N., and Andrew E. Newman. 1990. "For What It's Worth: Organizations, Occupations, and the Value of Work Done by Women and Nonwhites." *American Sociological Review* 55:155–75.

Barron, David N. 1992. "The Analysis of Count Data: Overdispersion and Autocorrelation." Pp. 179–220 in *Sociological Methodology 1992*, edited by P. Marsden. Oxford: Basil Blackwell.

—— 1995. "Credit Unions." Pp. 137–61 in *Organizations in Industry*, edited by G. Carroll and M. Hannan. New York: Oxford University Press.

—— 1998. "Pathways to Legitimacy Among Consumer Loan Providers in New York City, 1914–1934." *Organization Studies* 19:207–33.

—— 1999. "The Structuring of Organizational Populations." *American Sociological Review,* 64:421–45.

Barron, David N., and Michael T. Hannan. 1991. "Assessing Autocorrelation in Models of Organizational Founding Rates: Quasi-Likelihood Estimation." *Sociological Methods and Research* 20:218–41.

Barron, David N., Elizabeth West, and Michael T. Hannan. 1994. "A Time to Grow and a Time to Die: Growth and Mortality of Credit Unions in New York, 1914–1990." *American Journal of Sociology* 100:381–421.

—— 1995. *Competition, Deregulation, and the Fortunes of Credit Unions in New York.* Madison, Wisc.: Filene Research Institute.

——— 1998. "Deregulation and Competition in Populations of Credit Unions." *Industrial and Corporate Change* 7:1–32.

Baum, Joel A. C. 1996. "Organizational Ecology." Pp. 77–114 in *Handbook of Organizations*, edited by S. Clegg, C. Hardy, and W. Nord. Thousand Oaks, Calif.: Sage.

Baum, Joel A. C., and Stephen J. Mezias. 1992. "Localized Competition and Organizational Failure in the Manhattan Hotel Industry, 1898–1990." *Administrative Science Quarterly* 37:580–604.

Baum, Joel A. C., and Christine Oliver. 1991. "Institutional Linkages and Organizational Mortality." *Administrative Science Quarterly* 36:187–218.

Baum, Joel A. C., and Jitendra V. Singh. 1994. "Organizational Niches and the Dynamics of Organizational Mortality." *American Journal of Sociology* 100:346–80.

Baum, Joel A.C., Helain J. Korn, and Suresh Kotha. 1995. "Dominant Designs and Population Dynamics in Telecommunications Services: Founding and Failure of Fascimile Service Organizations, 1965–1992." *Social Science Research* 37:580–604.

Bigelow, Lyda. 1999. "Transaction Cost Alignment and Organizational Survival in the Early American Automobile Industry." Ph.D. dissertation, University of California at Berkeley.

Bigelow, Lyda S., Glenn R. Carroll, Marc-David Seidel, and Lucia Tsai. 1997. "Legitimation, Geographical Scale, and Organizational Density: Regional Patterns of Foundings of American Automobile Producers, 1885–1981." *Social Science Research* 26:377–98.

Birch, David. 1981. *Firm Behavior as a Determinant of Economic Change*. Cambridge: MIT Program on Neighborhood and Regional Change.

Blau, Judith R. 1995. "Art Museums." Pp. 87–120 in *Organizations in Industry*, edited by G. Carroll and M. Hannan. New York: Oxford University Press.

Blau, Judith R., and Cheryl Elman. 1998. "Where Parties Come From: Patronage Newspapers and the Institutionalization of Federal U.S. Political Parties." Unpublished manuscript. University of North Carolina, Chapel Hill.

Blossfeld, Hans-Peter, and Götz Rohwer. 1996. *Techniques of Event-History Modeling: New Approaches to Causal Analysis*. Mahwah, N.J.: Erlbaum.

Boone, Christophe, Vera Bröcheler, and Glenn R. Carroll. 2000. "Custom Service: Application and Tests of Resource Partitioning Among Dutch Auditing Firms From 1880 to 1982." *Organization Studies,* forthcoming.

Boone, Christophe, Glenn R. Carroll, and Arjen van Witteloostuijn. 1999. "Market Resource Distributions and Partitioning in the Dutch Newspaper Industry." Unpublished paper. University of Maastricht.

Boone, Christophe, and Woody Van Olffen. 1997. "The Confusing State of the Art in Top Management Composition Studies: A Theoretical and Empirical Review." Research Memorandum No. 97–11. Netherlands Institute of Business Organization and Strategy, Maastricht.

Borgatti, Stephen P., and Martin G. Everett. 1992. "Notions of Position in Social Network Analysis." Pp. 1–36 in *Sociological Methodology 1992*, edited by P. Marsden. Cambridge: Blackwell.

Boswell, Jonathan. 1973. *The Rise and Decline of Small Firms*. London: Allen & Unwin.

Brandon, Robert N. 1996. *Concepts and Methods in Evolutionary Biology*. Cambridge: Cambridge University Press.

Brittain, Jack. W., and John Freeman. 1986. "Entrepreneurship in the Semiconductor Industry." Presented at the Academy of Management Meetings.

Brock, Gerald W. 1981. *The Telecommunications Industry*. Cambridge: Harvard University Press.

Brooks, John. 1976. *Telephone: The First Hundred Years*. New York: Harper & Row.

Brüderl, Josef, and Peter Preisendörfer. 1998. "Fast Growing Businesses: Empirical Evidence from a German Study." Unpublished paper. University of Mannheim.

Brüderl, Josef, Peter Preisendörfer, and Rolf Ziegler. 1989. "Intraorganizational Career Mobility: The Effects of Individual Characteristics, Hierarchy, Opportunity Structure, Growth, and Cohort Size." Unpublished paper. University of Munich.

Brüderl, Josef, Peter Preisendörfer, and Rolf Ziegler. 1996. *Der Erfolg neugegründeter Betriebe*. Berlin: Duncker & Humbolt.

Brüderl, Josef, and Rudolph Schüssler. 1990. "Organizational Mortality: The Liabilities of Newness and Adolescence." *Administrative Science Quarterly* 35:530–37.

Buijink, W., S. Majoor, A. van Witteloostuijn, and M. Zinken. 1993. "The Evolution of the Structure of the Dutch Audit Industry: An Empirical Study." Unpublished paper. University of Limburg.

Bull, Donald, Manfred Friedrich, and Robert Gottschalk. 1984. *American Breweries*. Trumball, Conn.: Bullworks.

Bundt, T. P., T. F. Cosimano, and J. A. Halloran. 1992. "DIDMCA and Bank Market Risk: Theory and Evidence." *Journal of Banking and Finance* 16:1179–93.

Burt, Ronald S. 1987. "Social Contagion and Innovation: Cohesion versus Structural Equivalence." *American Journal of Sociology* 92:1287–1335.

—— 1993. *Structural Holes: The Social Structure of Competition*. Cambridge: Harvard University Press.

Cafferata, Gail L. 1982. "The Building of Democratic Organizations: An Embryological Metaphor." *Administrative Science Quarterly* 27:280–303.

Carroll, Glenn R. 1983. "A Stochastic Model of Organizational Mortality: Review and Reanalysis." *Social Science Research* 12:303–29.

—— 1984a. "Dynamics of Publisher Succession in the Newspaper Industry." *Administrative Science Quarterly* 29:93–113.

—— 1984b. "Organizational Ecology." *Annual Review of Sociology* 10:71–93.

—— 1985. "Concentration and Specialization: Dynamics of Niche Width in Populations of Organizations." *American Journal of Sociology* 90:1262–83.

—— 1987. *Publish and Perish: The Organizational Ecology of Newspaper Industries.* Greenwich, Conn.: JAI Press.

—— 1997. "Long-Term Evolutionary Change in Organizational Populations: Theory, Models, and Findings in Industrial Demography." *Industrial and Corporate Change* 6:119–43.

Carroll, Glenn R., Lyda Bigelow, Marc-David Seidel, and Lucia Tsai. 1996. "The Fates of De Novo and De Alio Producers in the American Automobile Industry, 1885–1982." *Strategic Management Journal* 17:117–37.

Carroll, Glenn R., and Jacques Delacroix. 1982. "Organizational Mortality in the Newspaper Industries of Argentina and Ireland: An Ecological Approach." *Administrative Science Quarterly* 27:169–98.

Carroll, Glenn R., Jacques Delacroix, and Jerry Goodstein. 1988. "The Political Environments of Organizations: An Ecological View." Pp. 359–92 in *Research in Organizational Behavior*, Volume 10, edited by B. Staw and L. Cummings. Greenwich, Conn.: JAI Press.

Carroll, Glenn R., and Michael T. Hannan. 1989a. "Density Delay in the Evolution of Organizational Populations: A Model and Five Empirical Tests." *Administrative Science Quarterly* 34:411–30.

—— 1989b. "Density Dependence in the Evolution of Newspaper Populations." *American Sociological Review* 54:524–41.

—— 1995a. "Automobile Manufacturers." Pp. 195–214 in *Organizations in Industry*, edited by G. Carroll and M. Hannan. New York: Oxford University Press.

Carroll, Glenn R., and Michael T. Hannan, editors 1995b. *Organizations in Industry: Strategy, Structure, and Selection.* New York: Oxford University Press.

Carroll, Glenn R., Michael T. Hannan, Lyda Bigelow, Marc-David Seidel, Albert Teo, and Lucia Tsai. 1994. "Before Production: Organizing Activities and Founding Events in the American Automobile Industry, 1886–1982." Technical Report 94-14, Center for Research on Management, University of California at Berkeley.

Carroll, Glenn R., and J. Richard Harrison. 1994. "On The Historical Efficiency of Competition Between Organizational Populations." *American Journal of Sociology* 100:720–49.

—— 1998. "Organizational Demography and Culture: Insights from a Formal Model and Simulation." *Administrative Science Quarterly* 43:637–67.

Carroll, Glenn R., Heather A. Haveman, and Anand Swaminathan. 1990. "Karrieren in Organizationen: Eine ökologische Perspektive." *Kölner Zeitschrift für Soziologie und Sozialpsychologie* (Sonderheft) 31:146–78.

—— 1992. "Careers in Organizations: An Ecological View." Pp. 111–44 in *Life-Span Development and Behavior*, Volume 11, edited by D. Featherman et al. Hillsdale, N.J.: Earlbaum.

Carroll, Glenn R., and Yangchung Paul Huo. 1988. "Organizational and Electoral Paradoxes of the Knights of Labor." Pp. 175–94 in *Ecological Models of Organizations*, edited by G. Carroll. Cambridge, Mass.: Ballinger.

Carroll, Glenn R., and Karl Ulrich Mayer. 1986. "Job Shift Patterns in the Federal Republic of Germany: The Effects of Social Class, Industrial Sector, and Organizational Size." *American Sociological Review* 51:323–41.

Carroll, Glenn R., and Elaine Mosakowski. 1987. "The Career Dynamics of Self-Employment." *Administrative Science Quarterly* 51:323–41.

Carroll, Glenn R., Peter Preisendorfer, Anand Swaminathan, and Gabriele Wiedenmayer. 1993. "Brewery and Brauerei: The Organizational Ecology of Brewing." *Organization Studies* 14:155–88.

Carroll, Glenn R., and Anand Swaminathan. 1991. "Density Dependent Organizational Evolution in the American Brewing Industry from 1633 to 1988." *Acta Sociologica* 34:155–75.

—— 1992. "The Organizational Ecology of Strategic Groups in the American Brewing Industry From 1975 to 1990." *Industrial and Corporate Change* 1:65–97.

—— 1998. "Why the Microbrewery Movement? Organizational Dynamics of Resource Partitioning in the American Brewing Industry After Prohibition." Presented at the 14th Colloquium of the European Group on Organizational Studies.

Carroll, Glenn R., and Albert C. Y. Teo. 1996. "Creative Self-Destruction among Organizations: An Empirical Study of Technical Innovation and Organizational Failure in the American Automobile Industry, 1885–1982." *Industrial and Corporate Change* 6:619–44.

—— 1998. "How Regulation and Globalization Affected Organizational Legitimation and Competition Among Commercial Banks in Singapore, 1840–1994." Presented at the Annual Meetings of the Academy of Management.

Carroll, Glenn R., and James B. Wade. 1991. "Density Dependence in the Organizational Evolution of the American Brewing Industry Across Levels of Analysis." *Social Science Research* 20:271–302.

Center for Economic Studies. 1995. *U.S. Bureau of the Census Center for Economic Studies Annual Report 1994-1995*. Washington: U.S. Government Printing Office.

Chandler, Alfred D. Jr. 1990. *Scale and Scope: The Dynamics of Industrial Capitalism*. Cambridge: Harvard University Press.

Chesnais, Jean-Claude. 1992. *The Demographic Transition*. New York: Oxford University Press.

Child, John, and Alfred Kieser. 1981. "Development of Organizations Over Time." Pp. 28–64 in *Handbook of Organizational Design*, Volume 1, edited by W. Starbuck and P. Nystrom. New York: Oxford University Press.

Cody, Martin L., and Jared M. Diamond. 1975. *Ecology and Evolution of Communities*. Cambridge: Harvard University Press.

Cohen, Joel E. 1976. "Irreproducible Results and the Breeding of Pigs, or Nondegenerate Limit Random Variables in Biology." *BioScience* 26:391–94.

Colburn, F. D. 1986. *Post Revolutionary Nicaragua*. Berkeley and Los Angeles: University of California Press.

Coleman, James S. 1964. *Introduction to Mathematical Sociology*. New York: Free Press.

—— 1990. *Foundations of Social Theory*. Cambridge: Harvard University Press.

Converse, Paul. 1932. "Business Mortality of Illinois Retail Stores from 1925 to 1930." Bulletin No. 1. University of Illinois: Bureau of Business Research.

Cover, J. 1933. *Business and Personal Failures and Readjustment in Chicago*. Chicago: University of Chicago Press.

Cox, D. R. 1975. "Partial Likelihood." *Biometrika* 62:269–76.

Cox, D. R., and D. Oakes. 1984. *Analysis of Survival Data*. London: Chapman & Hall.

Crum, William L. 1953. *The Age Structure of the Corporate System*. Berkeley and Los Angeles: University of California Press.

Danielian, Noobar R. 1939. *AT&T: The Story of Industrial Conquest*. New York: Vanguard.

David, Paul. 1985. "Clio and the Econometrics of QWERTY." *American Economic Review* 75:332–37.

Davis, Gerald F. 1991. "Agents Without Principles: The Spread of the Poison Pill Through the Intercorporate Network." *Administrative Science Quarterly* 36:583–613.

Davis, Gerald F., and Henrich R. Greve. 1997. "Corporate Elite Networks and Governance Changes in the 1980s." *American Journal of Sociology* 103:1–37.

Davis, Horace B. 1939. "Business Mortality: The Shoe Manufacturing Industry." *Harvard Business Review* 17:331–38.

Davis, Kingsley. 1945. "The World Demographic Transition." *Annals of the American Academy of Political and Social Science* 273:1–11.

Davis, Steven J., John Haltiwanger, and Scott Schuh. 1994. *Job Creation and Destruction in U.S. Manufacturing: Technical Appendix*. Washington. U.S. Census Bureau Monograph.

—— 1996. *Job Creation and Destruction*. Cambridge: MIT Press.

Delacroix, Jacques, and Glenn R. Carroll. 1983. "Organizational Foundings: An Ecological Study of the Newspaper Industries of Argentina and Ireland." *Administrative Science Quarterly* 28:274–91.

Delacroix, Jacques, and Anand Swaminathan. 1991. "Cosmetic, Speculative, and Adaptive Organizational Change in the Wine Industry." *Administrative Science Quarterly* 36:631–61.

Delacroix, Jacques, Anand Swaminathan, and Michael E. Solt. 1989. "Density Dependence versus Population Dynamics: An Ecological Study of Failings in the California Wine Industry." *American Sociological Review* 54:245–62.

DiMaggio, Paul J., and Walter W. Powell. 1983. "The Iron Cage Revisited: Institutional Isomorphism and Collective Rationality in Organizational Fields." *American Sociological Review* 48:147–60.

DiPrete, Thomas A. 1987. "The Professionalization of Administration and Equal Employment Opportunity in the U.S. Federal Government." *American Journal of Sociology* 93:119–40.

Dobbin, Frank, and Timothy Dowd. 1997. "How Policy Shapes Competition: Early Railroad Foundings in Massachusetts." *Administrative Science Quarterly* 42:501–29.

Dobbs, Michael E. 1999. "Playing for Keeps: Age Dependence, Density Dependence, and Growth Dependence in the Mortality Rates of Professional Sports Leagues, 1871–1997." Unpublished paper. University of Texas at Dallas.

Dobrev, Stanislav D. 1997. "The Dynamics of the Bulgarian Newspaper Industry in a Period of Transition." Ph.D. dissertation, Stanford University.

—— 1998. "Revisiting Organizational Legitimation: Cognitive Diffusion and Sociopolitical Factors in the Evolution of Bulgarian Newspaper Enterprises, 1846–1992." Presented at the 14th Colloquium of the European Group on Organizational Studies.

—— 1999. "The Dynamics of the Bulgarian Newspaper Industry in a Period of Transition: Organizational Adaptation, Structural Inertia, and Political Change." *Industrial and Corporate Change,* 8:573–605.

—— 2000. "Decreasing Concentration and Reversibility of the Resource Partitioning Model: Supply Shortages and Deregulation in the Bulgarian Newspaper Industry, 1987–1992." *Organization Studies,* forthcoming.

Doeringer, Peter B., and Michael J. Piore. 1971. *Internal Labor Markets and Manpower Analysis.* Lexington, Mass.: Heath.

Dosi, Giovanni. 1982. "Technological Paradigms and Technological Trajectories." *Research Policy* 11:147–62.

Dowell, Glen, and Anand Swaminathan. 2000. "Racing and Back-Pedaling into the Future: New Product Introduction and Organizational Mortality in the U.S. Bicycle Industry, 1880–1918." *Organizational Studies,* forthcoming.

Dun and Bradstreet. 1988. *Business Starts Records.* New York: Dun and Bradstreet Corp.

Dunne, Timothy, Mark J. Roberts, and Larry Samuelson. 1989. "The Growth and Failure of U.S. Manufacturing Plants." *Quarterly Journal of Economics* 104:671–98.

Durkheim, Emile. 1947. *The Division of Labor in Society.* Glencoe, Ill.: Free Press. [Originally published in 1893].

Eck, Allan. 1984. "New Occupational Separation Data Improve Estimates of Job Replacement Needs." *Monthly Labor Review* March:3–11.

Edelman, Lauren B. 1990. "Legal Ambiguity and Symbolic Structures: Organizational Mediation of Civil Rights Law." *American Journal of Sociology* 97:1531–76.

Edwards, Bob, and Sam Marullo. 1995. "Organizational Mortality in a Declining Social Movement: The Demise of Peace Movement Organizations in the End of the Cold War Era." *American Sociological Review* 60:908–27.

Eggenberger, F., and G. Polya. 1923. "Über die Statistik verketteter Vorgänge." *Zeitschrift für angewandte Mathematik und Mechanik* 3:279–89.

Engwall, L. 1968. "Size Distribution of Organizations, A Stochastic Model." *Swedish Journal of Economics* 70:138–57.

Epstein, Ralph C. 1927. "The Rise and Fall of Firms in the Automobile Industry." *Harvard Business Review* 2:157–74.

——— 1972. *The Automotive Industry*. New York: Arno Press.

Ernst & Young. 1996. *Biotech96: Pursuing Sustainability*. New York: Ernst & Young.

Evans, David S. 1987. "The Relationship Between Organization Growth, Size, and Age: Estimates for 100 Manufacturing Industries." *Journal of Industrial Economics* 35:567–81.

Evans, M.D.R. 1989. "Immigrant Entrepreneurship: Effects of Ethnic Market Size and Isolated Labor Pools." *American Sociological Review* 54:950–62.

Farley, Reynolds J. 1984. *Blacks and Whites: Narrowing the Gap?* Cambridge: Harvard University Press.

Federal Communications Commission. 1939. *Investigation of the Telephone Industry in the United States*. Washington: U.S. Government Printing Office.

Fichman, Mark, and Daniel A. Levinthal. 1991. "Honeymoons and the Liability of Adolescence: A New Perspective on Duration Dependence in Social and Organizational Relationships." *Academy of Management Review* 16:442–68.

Fier, Andreas, and Michael Woywode. 1997. "Entry Processes of Companies and the Evolution of Industries in East Germany after the Fall of the Berlin Wall." Presented at the EMOT Final Conference, Stresa, Italy.

Fink, Gary, editor 1977. *National Labor Unions*. Greenwood, Ala.: Greenwood Press.

Finkelstein, Sydney, and Donald C. Hambrick. 1990. *Strategic Leadership*. Minneapolis/St. Paul: West.

Fischer, Claude S. 1994. *America Calling: A Social History of the Telephone to 1940*. Berkeley and Los Angeles: University of California Press.

Flammang, James M. 1989. *Standard Catalog of American Cars 1976–1986*. Second edition. Iola, Wisc.: Krause.

Fligstein, Neil. 1990. *The Transformation of Corporate Control*. Cambridge: Harvard University Press.

Fligstein, Neil, and Peter Brantley. 1992. "Bank Control, Owner Control, or Organizational Dynamics: Who Controls the Large Modern Corporation?" *American Journal of Sociology* 98:280–307.

Flink, James J. 1988. *The Automobile Age*. Cambridge: MIT Press.

Frasure, William Wayne. 1952. *Longevity of Manufacturing Concerns in Allegheny County*. Pittsburgh: University of Pittsburgh Press.

Freeman, John. 1978. "The Unit of Analysis in Organizational Research." Pp. 335–51 in *Environments and Organizations*, edited by M. Meyer et al. San Francisco: Jossey–Bass.

—— 1986. "Data Quality and the Development of Organizational Science." *Administrative Science Quarterly* 31:298–303.

—— 1996. "The Economy of Time." Unpublished paper. Haas School of Business, University of California, Berkeley.

Freeman, John, Glenn R. Carroll, and Michael T. Hannan. 1983. "The Liability of Newness: Age Dependence in Organizational Death Rates." *American Sociological Review* 48:692–710.

Freeman, John, and Michael T. Hannan. 1975. "Growth and Decline Processes in Organizations." *American Sociological Review* 40:215–28.

Freeman, John, and Alessandro Lomi. 1994. "Resource Partitioning among Banking Cooperatives in Italy." Pp. 269–93 in *Evolutionary Dynamics of Organizations*, edited by J. Baum and J. Singh. New York: Oxford University Press.

Fujiwara-Greve, Takako, and Henrich R. Greve. 1997. "Industry Diversity, Inequality, and Reputational Effects on Wages: Evidence from Norwegian Data." Presented at the Annual Meetings of the Academy of Management.

Gabel, Richard. 1969. "The Early Competitive Era in Telephone Communications, 1893–1920." *Law and Contemporary Problems* 34:340–59.

Gibrat, Robert. 1931. *Les Inégalités Économiques*. Paris: Sirey.

Glick, William H., C. C. Miller, and George P. Huber. 1993. "The Import of Upper-Echelon Diversity on Organizational Performance." Pp. 176–214 in *Organizational Change and Redesign*, edited by G. Huber and W. Glick. New York: Oxford University Press.

Gort, M., and Steven Klepper. 1982. "Time Paths in the Diffusion of Product Innovations." *Economic Journal* 92:630–53.

Grabher, Gernot, and David Stark. 1997. "Organizing Diversity: Evolutionary Theory, Network Analysis, and Post-Socialism." Pp. 1–32 in *Restructuring Networks in Post-Socialism*, edited by G. Grabher and D. Stark. New York: Oxford University Press.

Gray, Virginia, and David Lowery. 1996. *The Population Ecology of Interest Representation*. Ann Arbor: University of Michigan Press.

Greiner, Larry E. 1972. "Evolution and Revolution as Organizations Grow." *Harvard Business Review* 50:37–46.

Greve, Henrich R. 1994. "Industry Diversity Effects on Job Mobility." *Acta Sociologica* Series A 37:119–39.

—— 1998. "The Spatial Dynamics of Organizational Founding: Tokyo Banking 1894–1936." Presented at the SCANCOR Conference, Stanford University.

Gunnell, John A., Dennis Schrimpf, and Kevin Buttolph. 1987. *Standard Catalog of American Cars 1946–1975*. Second edition. Iola, Wisc.: Krause.

—— 1992. *Standard Catalog of American Cars 1946–1975*. Third edition. Iola, Wisc.: Krause.

Guo, Guang. 1993. "Event-History Analysis for Left-Truncated Data." Pp. 217–44 in *Sociological Methodology 1993*, edited by P. Marsden. Oxford: Blackwell.

Gusfield, Joseph R. 1957. "The Problem of Generations in an Organizational Structure." *Social Forces* 35:323–30.

Haberman, Shelby J. 1977. "Log-Linear Models and Frequency Tables With Small Expected Cell Counts." *Annals of Statistics* 5:1148–65.

Hall, Bronwyn. 1987. "The Relationship Between Firm Size and Firm Growth in the U.S. Manufacturing Sector." *Journal of Industrial Economics* 35:583–606.

Hall, Robert E. 1982. "The Importance of Lifetime Jobs in the U.S. Economy." *American Economic Review* 72:716–24.

Halliday, Terence C., Michael J. Powell, and Mark W. Granfors. 1993. "After Minimalism: Transformations of State Bar Associations from Market Dependence to State Reliance, 1918–1950." *American Sociological Review* 58:515–35.

Han, Joon. 1998. "The Evolution of the Japanese Banking Industry: An Ecological Analysis, 1873–1945." Ph.D. dissertation, Stanford University.

Hannah, Leslie. 1999. "'Marhsall's 'Trees' and the Global 'Forest': Were 'Giant Redwoods' Different?" Pp. 253-93 in *Learning by Doing in Markets, Firms, and Countries*, edited by N. Lamoreaux, D. Raff, and P. Termin. Chicago: University of Chicago Press.

Hannan, Michael T. 1986a. "Competitive and Institutional Processes in Organizational Ecology." Technical Report 86–13, Department of Sociology, Cornell University.

—— 1986b. "Uncertainty, Diversity and Organizational Change." Pp. 73–94 in *Social and Behavioral Sciences: Discoveries over Fifty Years*, edited by N. Smelser and D. Gerstein. Washington: National Academy Press.

—— 1988. "Social Change, Organizational Diversity, and Individual Careers." Pp. 161–74 in *Social Structures and Human Lives*, edited by M. Riley. Newbury Park, Calif.: Sage.

—— 1989. "Age Dependence in the Mortality of National Labor Unions: Comparisons of Parametric Models." *Journal of Mathematical Sociology* 15:1–30.

—— 1995. "Labor Unions." Pp. 121–36 in *Organizations in Industry*, edited by G. Carroll and M. Hannan. New York: Oxford University Press.

—— 1996. "The Logic of Social Selection Mechanisms." Presented at the Conference on Social Mechanisms, Stockholm.

—— 1997. "Inertia, Density, and the Structure of Organizational Populations: Entries in European Automobile Industries, 1886–1981." *Organization Studies* 18:193–228.

—— 1998. "Rethinking Age Dependence in Organizational Mortality: Logical Formalizations." *American Journal of Sociology* 104:85–123.

Hannan, Michael T., David N. Barron, and Glenn R. Carroll. 1991. "On the Interpretation of Density Dependence in Rates of Organizational Mortality: A Reply to Petersen and Koput." *American Sociological Review* 56:410–15.

Hannan, Michael T., M. Diane Burton, and James N. Baron. 1996. "Inertia and Change in the Early Years: Employment Relations in Young, High-Technology Firms." *Industrial and Corporate Change* 5:503–36.

Hannan, Michael T., and Glenn R. Carroll. 1992. *Dynamics of Organizational Populations: Density, Legitimation, and Competition*. New York: Oxford University Press.

—— 1995. "Theory Building and Cheap Talk About Legitimation: Reply to Baum and Powell." *American Sociological Review* 60:539–44.

Hannan, Michael T., Glenn R. Carroll, Stanislav D. Dobrev, and Joon Han. 1998a. "Organizational Mortality in European and American Automobile Industries, Part I: Revisiting the Effects of Age and Size." *European Sociological Review* 14:279–302.

Hannan, Michael T., Glenn R. Carroll, Stanislav D. Dobrev, Joon Han, and John C. Torres. 1998b. "Organizational Mortality in European and American Automobile Industries, Part II: Coupled Clocks." *European Sociological Review* 14:302–13.

Hannan, Michael T., Glenn R. Carroll, Elizabeth A. Dundon, and John C. Torres. 1995. "Organizational Evolution in Multinational Context: Entries of Automobile Manufacturers in Belgium, Britain, France, Germany, and Italy." *American Sociological Review* 60:509–28.

Hannan, Michael T., and John Freeman. 1977. "The Population Ecology of Organizations." *American Journal of Sociology* 82:929–64.

—— 1984. "Structural Inertia and Organizational Change." *American Sociological Review* 49:149–64.

—— 1986. "Where Do Organizational Forms Come From?" *Sociological Forum* 1:50–57.

—— 1987. "The Ecology of Organizational Mortality: American Labor Unions, 1836–1985." *American Journal of Sociology* 92:910–43.

—— 1988. "The Ecology of Organizational Founding: American Labor Unions, 1836–1985." *American Journal of Sociology* 94:25–52.

—— 1989. *Organizational Ecology*. Cambridge: Harvard University Press.

Hannan, Michael T., and James Ranger-Moore. 1990. "The Ecology of Organizational Size Distributions: A Microsimulation Approach." *Journal of Mathematical Sociology* 15:67–90.

Hannan, Michael T., James Ranger-Moore, and Jane Banaszak-Holl. 1990. "Competition and the Evolution of Organizational Size Distributions." Pp. 246–68 in *Organizational Evolution: New Directions*, edited by J. Singh. Newbury Park, Calif.: Sage.

Hannan, Michael T., Elizabeth West, and David N. Barron. 1994. *Dynamics of Credit Unions in New York*. Madison, Wisc.: Filene Research Institute.

Harhoff, Dieter, Konrad Stahl, and Michael Woywode. 1995. "Survival and Growth of West German Firms: The Role of Limited Liability." Unpublished paper. University of Mannheim.

Hart, P. E. 1962. "The Size and Growth of Organizations." *Economica* 29:29–39.

Hart, P. E., and S. J. Prais. 1956. "The Analysis of Business Concentration." *Journal of the Royal Statistical Society* Part II, 1:150–91.

Haunschild, Pamela R. 1993. "Intraorganizational Imitation: The Impact of Corporate Interlocks on Acquisition Premia." *Administrative Science Quarterly* 38:564–92.

Hauser, Philip M., and Otis Dudley Duncan. 1959. *The Study of Population.* Chicago: University of Chicago Press.

Haveman, Heather A. 1992. "Between a Rock and a Hard Place: Organizational Change and Performance under Conditions of Fundamental Environmental Transformation." *Administrative Science Quarterly* 37:48–75.

—— 1993a. "Follow the Leader: Mimetic Isomorphism and Entry Into New Markets." *Administrative Science Quarterly* 38:593–627.

—— 1993b. "Organizational Size and Change: Diversification in the Savings and Loan Industry After Deregulation." *Administrative Science Quarterly* 38:20–50.

—— 1994. "The Ecological Dynamics of Organizational Change: Density and Mass Dependence in Rates of Entry into New Markets." Pp. 152–66 in *Evolutionary Dynamics of Organizations*, edited by J. Baum and J. Singh, New York: Oxford University Press.

Haveman, Heather A., and Lisa E. Cohen. 1994. "The Ecological Dynamics of Careers: The Impact of Organization Founding, Dissolution, and Merger on Job Mobility." *American Journal of Sociology* 100:104–52.

Haveman, Heather A., and Lynne Nonnenaker. 1998. "Competition in Multiple Geographic Markets: The Impact of Market Entry." Unpublished paper. Johnson School, Cornell University.

Hawley, Amos H. 1950. *Human Ecology: A Theory of Community Structure.* New York: Ronald Press.

Heckman, James J., and Burton Singer. 1984. "A Method for Minimizing the Impact of Distributional Assumptions in Econometric Models of Duration Data." *Econometrica* 52:271–320.

Hedström, Peter. 1994. "Contagious Collectives: On the Spatial Diffusion of Swedish Trade Unions, 1890–1940." *American Journal of Sociology* 99:1157–79.

Heilman, Ernest A. 1935. "Mortality of Business Firms in Minneapolis, St. Paul and Duluth, 1926–1930." Studies in Economics and Business, University of Minnesota.

Henderson, Rebecca, and Ian Cockburn. 1995. "Managing Product Development Across Organizational Boundaries: Exploring the Diffusion of 'Rational' Drug Discovery." Presented at the Academy of Management Meetings.

Hinz, Thomas, and Rolf Ziegler. 1998. "Organizational Performance of New Businesses in East and West Germany." Presented at the 14th Colloquium of the European Group on Organization Studies.

Hougaard, P. 1987. "Modeling Multivariate Survival." *Scandinavian Statistical Journal* 5:291–304.

Hounshell, David A. 1984. *From the American System to Mass Production, 1800–1932: Development of Manufacturing Technology in the United States.* Baltimore: Johns Hopkins University Press.

Hout, Michael. 1985. "Occupational Mobility of Black Men: 1962 to 1973." *American Sociological Review* 49:308–22.

Hutchinson, R. G., A. R. Hutchinson, and Mabel Newcomer. 1938. "A Study in Business Mortality." *American Economic Review* 28:497–514.

Hybels, Ralph C., Alan R. Ryan, and Stephen R. Barley. 1994. "Alliances, Legitimation, and Founding Rates in the U.S. Biotechnology Field, 1971–1989." Presented at the Academy of Management Meetings.

Hymer, Stephen, and Peter Paskigian. 1962. "Firm Size and Rate of Growth." *Journal of Political Economy* 70:556–69.

Iansiti, Marco, and T. Khanna. 1995. "Technological Evolution, System Architecture and the Obsolescence of Firm Capabilities." *Industrial and Corporate Change* 4:333–61.

Ijiri, Yuji, and Herbert A. Simon. 1977. *Size Distributions and the Sizes of Business Firms.* New York: North Holland.

Ingram, Paul. 1996. "Organizational Form as a Solution to the Problem of Credible Commitment: The Evolution of Naming Strategies Among U.S. Hotel Chains, 1890–1980." *Strategic Management Journal* 17:85–98.

Ingram, Paul, and Joel A. C. Baum. 1997. "Chain Affiliation and the Failure of Manhattan Hotels, 1898–1980." *Administrative Science Quarterly* 42:68–102.

Ingram, Paul, and Crist Inman. 1996. "Institutions, Intergroup Competition, and the Evolution of Hotel Populations Around Niagara Falls." *Administrative Science Quarterly* 41:629–58.

Jacobson, L. 1984. "A Tale of Employment Decline in Two Cities: How Bad Was the Worst of Times?" *Industrial and Labor Relations Review* 37:557–69.

Jacoby, J., J. C. Olson, and R. A. Haddock. 1971. "Price, Brand Name and Product Composition Characteristics as Determinants of Perceived Quality." *Journal of Applied Psychology* 55:570–79.

Jepperson, Ronald L. 1991. "Institutions, Institutional Effects, and Institutionalism." Pp. 143–63 in *The New Institutionalism in Organizational Analysis*, edited by W. Powell and P. DiMaggio. Chicago: University of Chicago Press.

Kalbfleisch, John D., and Ross L. Prentice. 1980. *Statistical Analysis of Failure Time Data.* New York: Wiley.

Kalecki, M. 1945. "On the Gibrat Distribution." *Econometrica* 13:161.

Kalleberg, Arne, David Knoke, Peter V. Marsden, and Joe L. Spaeth. 1996. *Organizations in America: Analyzing Their Structures and Human Resource Practices.* Thousand Oaks, Calif.: Sage.

Kalleberg, Arne, Peter Marsden, Howard Aldrich, and James W. Cassell. 1990. "Comparing Organizational Sampling Frames." *Administrative Science Quarterly* 35:658–88.

Kalleberg, Arne L., and Aage Sørensen. 1979. "The Sociology of Labor Markets." *Annual Review of Sociology* 5:351–79.

Kamien, Morton, and N. Schwartz. 1982. *Market Structure and Innovation*. Cambridge: Cambridge University Press.

Kaplan, E. L., and P. Meier. 1959. "Nonparametric Estimation From Incomplete Observations." *Journal of the American Statistical Association.* 53:457–81.

Kapteyn, J. C. 1903. *Skew Frequency Curves in Biology and Statistics*. Astronomical Laboratory, Groningen: Noordhoff.

Kay, E. 1987. "The Impact of Mergers, Acquisitions and Downsizing." Speech presented at the New England Society of Applied Psychologists, Chestnut Hill, Mass.

Kelly, Dawn, and Terry L. Amburgey. 1991. "Organizational Inertia and Momentum: A Dynamic Model of Strategic Change." *Academy of Management Journal* 34:591–612.

Keyfitz, Nathan. 1971. "Models." *Demography* 8:571–80.

—— 1973. "Individual Mobility in a Stationary Population." *Population Studies* 27:335–52.

—— 1977. *Applied Mathematical Demography*. New York: Wiley.

Kim, S., R. D. Roderick, and J. R. Shea. 1973. *Dual Careers: A Longitudinal Study of Labor Market Experience of Women*. Washington: U.S. Government Printing Office.

Kim, Tai-Young. 1998. "Mutualism, Competition and an Organization's Position: Film Production Companies in Britain, 1895–1960." Presented at the Sunbelt Social Network Conference.

Kimberly, John. 1976. "Organizational Size and the Structuralist Perspective: A Review, Critique and Proposal." *Administrative Science Quarterly* 21:571–97.

Kimes, Beverly Rae, and Henry Austin Clark. 1989. *Standard Catalog of American Cars 1805–1942*. Second edition. Iola, Wisc.: Krause.

—— 1996. *Standard Catalog of American Cars 1805–1942*. Third edition. Iola, Wisc.: Krause.

Kirchhoff, Bruce A., and Bruce D. Phillips. 1988. "The Effect of Firm Formation and Growth on Job Creation in the United States." *Journal of Business Venturing* 3:261–72.

Kirk, Dudley. 1944. "Population Change and the Postwar World." *American Sociological Review* 9:28–35.

Klepper, Steven, and Kenneth L. Simons. 1997. "Technological Extinctions of Industrial Firms: An Inquiry into Their Nature and Causes." *Industrial and Corporate Change* 6:379–460.

Kohen, A. I., and P. J. Andrisani. 1974. *Careers Thresholds: A Longitudinal Study of the Educational and Labor Market Experience of Male Youth*. Washington: U.S. Government Printing Office.

Kreps, David M. 1990. *Game Theory and Economic Modelling*. Oxford: Oxford University Press.

——— 1996. "Markets and Hierarchies and (Mathematical) Economic Theory." *Industrial and Corporate Change* 5:561–96.

Krugman, Paul R. 1991. "Increasing Returns and Economic Geography." *Journal of Political Economy* 99:483–99.

Kutner, Robert M. 1974. *The Complete Guide to Kit Cars, Auto Parts and Accessories*. Wilmington, Del.: Auto Logic.

Lancaster, Tony. 1990. *The Econometric Analysis of Transition Data*. Cambridge: Cambridge University Press.

Land, Kenneth C., Walter R. Davis, and Judith R. Blau. 1994. "Organizing the Boys of Summer: The Evolution of U.S. Minor League Baseball, 1883–1990." *American Journal of Sociology* 100:781–813.

Landry, A. 1909. "Les Trois Théories Principales de la Population." *Scientia* 6:3–29.

——— 1934. *La Révolution Demographique: Études et Essais Sur Les Problèmes de la Population*. Paris: Librairie Sirey.

Laux, James M. 1976. *In First Gear: The French Automobile Industry to 1914*. Montreal: McGill–Queen's University Press.

——— 1992. *The European Automobile Industry*. New York: Twanyne.

Lee, Ronald D. 1987. "Population Regulation in Humans and Other Animals." *Demography* 24:443–65.

Lehrman, William G. 1994. "Diversity in Decline: Institutional and Organizational Failure in the American Life Insurance Industry." *Social Forces* 73:605–36.

Leonard, Jonathan. 1987. "In the Wrong Place at the Wrong Time." Pp. 141–63 in *Unemployment and the Structure of Labor Markets*, edited by K. Lang and J. Leonard. New York: Blackwell.

Leslie, P. H. 1959. "The Properties of a Certain Lag Type of Population Growth and the Influence of an External Random Factor on the Number of Such Populations." *Physiological Zoölogy* 3:151–59.

Levinthal, Daniel. 1991. "Random Walks and Organizational Mortality." *Administrative Science Quarterly* 36:397–420.

Lewchuk, Wayne. 1987. *American Technology and the British Vehicle Industry*. New York: Cambridge University Press.

Lincoln, James R., and Michael L. Gerlach. 1996. "Keiretsu Networks and Corporate Performance in Japan." *American Sociological Review* 61:67–88.

Lippitt, G. L., and W. H. Schmidt. 1967. "Crises in a Developing Organization." *Harvard Business Review* 45:102–12.

Lomi, Alessandro. 1995a. "The Population and Community Ecology of Organizational Founding: Italian Cooperative Banks, 1936–1989." *European Sociological Review* 11:75–98.

—— 1995b. "The Population Ecology of Organizational Founding: Location Dependence and Unobserved Heterogeneity." *Administrative Science Quarterly* 40:111–45.

—— 2000. "Density Dependence and Spatial Duality in Organizational Founding Rates: Danish Commercial Banks, 1846–1989." *Organization Studies,* forthcoming.

Lopes, Paul. 1992. "Innovation and Diversity in the Popular Music Industry, 1969–1990." *American Sociological Review* 57:56–71.

MacArthur, Robert H. 1972. *Geographical Ecology.* New York: Harper & Row.

MacMeal, H. B. 1934. *The Story of Independent Telephony.* Chicago: Independent Pioneer Telephone Association.

Magnet, M. 1984. "Help! My Company Has Just Been Taken Over." *Fortune* 9 (July):44–49.

Manigart, Sophie. 1994. "The Founding Rates of Venture Capital Firms in Three European Countries (1970–1990)." *Journal of Business Venturing* 9:525–41.

Mansfield, Edwin. 1962. "Entry, Gibrat's Law, Innovation, and the Growth of Organizations." *American Economic Review* 52:1023–51.

March, James G. 1988. *Decisions in Organizations.* New York: Blackwell.

—— 1991. "Exploration and Exploitation in Organizational Learning." *Organization Science* 2:71–87.

March, James G., and Johan P. Olsen. 1989. *Rediscovering Institutions: The Organizational Basis of Politics.* New York: Free Press.

Mata, Jose, and Pedro Portugal. 1997. "The Survival of New Foreign and Domestic Firms." Banco de Portugal, Portugal.

Mayer, Kurt B., and Sidney Goldstein. 1961. *The First Two Years: Problems of Small Firm Growth and Survival.* Washington: U. S. Government Printing Office.

McCarthy, John D., Mark Wolfson, and David P. Baker. 1988. "The Founding of Social Movement Organizations: Local Citizens' Groups Opposing Drunk Driving." Pp. 71–84 in *Ecological Models of Organizations,* edited by G. Carroll. Cambridge, Mass.: Ballinger.

McCullagh, P. 1983. "Quasi-Likelihood Functions." *The Annals of Statistics* 11:59–67.

McCullagh, P., and J. Nelder. 1989. *Generalized Linear Models.* Second edition. London: Chapman & Hall.

McCune, William W. 1994. "Otter 3.0 Reference Manual and Guide (revised)." Technical Report NAL–94/6, Argonne National Laboratory.

McGarry, Edmund D. 1947. "The Mortality of Independent Grocery Stores in Buffalo and Pittsburgh, 1919–1941." *The Journal of Marketing* 12:14–24.

McPherson, J. Miller. 1982. "Hypernetwork Sampling: Duality and Differentiation in Voluntary Associations." *Social Networks* 3:225–49.

—— 1983. "An Ecology of Affiliation." *American Sociological Review* 48:519–35.

McPherson, J. Miller, Pamela Popielarz, and Sonja Drobnič. 1992. "Social Networks and Organizational Dynamics." *American Sociological Review* 57:153–70.

Merton, Robert K. 1987. "Three Fragments from a Sociologist's Notebooks: Establishing the Phenomenon, Specified Ignorance, and Strategic Research Materials." *Annual Review of Sociology* 13:1–28.

Meyer, John W., and Brian Rowan. 1977. "Institutionalized Organizations: Formal Structure as Myth and Ceremony." *American Journal of Sociology* 83:340–63.

Meyer, John W., and W. Richard Scott. 1992. *Organizational Environments: Ritual and Rationality.* Updated edition. Newbury Park, Calif.: Sage.

Meyer, John W., W. Richard Scott, and David Strang. 1987. "Centralization, Fragmentation, and School District Complexity." *Administrative Science Quarterly* 32:186–201.

Meyer, Marshall W., and V. Gupta. 1994. "The Performance Paradox." Pp. 309–69 in *Research in Organizational Behavior*, Volume 16, edited by L. Cummings and B. Staw. Greenwich, Conn: JAI.

Midanik, Lorraine T., and Walter B. Clark. 1995. "Drinking-Related Problems in the United States: Description and Trends, 1984–1990." *Journal of Studies on Alcohol* 56:395–402.

Midanik, Lorraine T., and Robin Room. 1992. "The Epidemiology of Alcohol Consumption." *Alcohol Health and Research World* 16:183–90.

Miller, Danny, and Minder J. Chen. 1994. "Sources and Consequences of Competitive Inertia: A Study of the U.S. Airline Industry." *Administrative Science Quarterly* 39:1–23.

Miner, Anne S., Terry L. Amburgey, and Timothy M. Stearns. 1990. "Interorganizational Linkages and Population Dynamics: Buffering and Transformation Shields." *Administrative Science Quarterly* 35:689–713.

Minkoff, Debra C. 1993. "The Organization of Survival: Women's and Racial Ethnic Voluntarist and Activist Organizations, 1955–1985." *Social Forces* 71:887–908.

—— 1997. "The Sequencing of Social Movements." *American Sociological Review* 62:779–99.

Mitchell, Will. 1994. "The Dynamics of Evolving Markets: The Effects of Business Sales and Age on Dissolutions and Divestitures." *Administrative Science Quarterly* 39:575–602.

—— 1995. "Medical Diagnostic Imaging Manufacturers." Pp. 244–72 in *Organizations in Industry*, edited by G. Carroll and M. Hannan. New York: Oxford University Press.

Mittleman, Edward B. 1927. "Trade Unionism (1833–1839)." In *History of Labor in the United States*, Volume 1, edited by J. Commons et al. New York: Macmillan.

Moe, Terry M. 1990. "Political Institutions: The Neglected Side of the Story." *Journal of Law, Economics and Organization* 6:S213–53.

Mott, Frank Luther. 1962. *American Journalism.* New York: Macmillan.

Nelson, Richard R. 1995. "Recent Evolutionary Theorizing About Economic Change." *Journal of Economic Literature* 33:48–90.

Nelson, Richard R., and Sidney Winter. 1982. *An Evolutionary Theory of Economic Change*. Cambridge: Harvard University Press.

Nelson, W. 1972. "Theory and Application of Hazard Plotting for Censored Data." *Technometrics* 14:945–65.

Notestein, F. W. 1945. "Population: The Long View." Pp. 36–57 in *Food for the World*, edited by E. Schultz. Chicago: University of Chicago Press.

Ohanian, Nancy Kane. 1994. "Vertical Integration in the U.S. Pulp and Paper Industry, 1900–1940." *Review of Economics and Statistics* 76:202–7.

Olzak, Susan. 1989. "Analysis of Events in Studies of Collective Action." *Annual Review of Sociology* 15:119–41.

—— 1992. *Dynamics of Ethnic Competition and Conflict*. Stanford: Stanford University Press.

Olzak, Susan, and Elizabeth West. 1991. "Ethnic Conflicts and the Rise and Fall of Ethnic Newspapers." *American Sociological Review* 56:458–74.

O'Reilly, Charles A., David Caldwell, and William P. Barnett. 1989. "Work Group Demography, Social Integration, and Turnover." *Administrative Science Quarterly* 34:32–37.

Padgett, John F., and Christopher K. Ansell. 1992. "Robust Action and the Rise of the Medici, 1400–1434." *American Journal of Sociology* 101:993–1028.

Paige, Jeffrey M. 1997. *Coffee and Power: Revolution and the Rise of Democracy in Central America*. Cambridge: Harvard University Press.

Park, Douglas Y., and Joel M. Podolny. 1998. "The Competitive Dynamics of Status and Niche Width: U.S. Investment Banking, 1920–1950." Unpublished paper. Stanford Graduate School of Business.

Parnes, H. S., K. Egge, and P. J. Andrisani. 1973. *The Pre-Retirement Years: A Longitudinal Study of the Labor Market Experience of Men*. Washington: U.S. Government Printing Office.

Parnes, H. S., B. M. Fleisher, R. C. Miljus, R. S. Spitz, and Associates. 1970. *The Pre-Retirement Years: A Longitudinal Study of the Labor Market Experience of Men*. Washington: U.S. Government Printing Office.

Parsons, Talcott. 1951. *The Social System*. Glencoe, Ill.: Free Press.

Pearce, D. K. 1984. "Recent Developments in the Credit Union Industry." *Economic Review, Federal Reserve Bank of Kansas City* 69:3–19.

Péli, Gábor. 1997. "The Niche Hikers Guide to Population Ecology: A Reconstruction of Niche Theory Using Logic." Pp. 1–46 in *Sociological Methodology 1997*, edited by A. Raftery. Cambridge: Blackwell.

Péli, Gábor, Jeroen Bruggeman, Michael Mausch, and Breanndán Ó Nualláin. 1994. "A Logical Approach to Organizational Ecology: Formalizing the Inertia Fragment in First-Order Logic." *American Sociological Review* 59:571–93.

Péli, Gábor, and Bart Nooteboom. 1999. "Market Partitioning and the Geometry of Resource Space." *American Journal of Sociology* 104:1132–53.

Péli, Gábor, László Pólos, and Michael T. Hannan. 1998. "Back to Inertia: Logical Formalizations." Technical Report 98B23, Faculty of Management, University of Groningen.

—— 1999. "Szervezeti tehetetlenség. Formalizálási stílusok, elméleti következmények." *Szociologiai Szemle,* 1/99:120–42.

Perrow, Charles. 1986. *Complex Organizations: A Critical Essay.* Third edition. Glencoe, Ill.: Scott Foresman.

Petersen, Trond. 1991. "Time-Aggregation Bias in Continuous-Time Hazard-Rate Models." Pp. 263–90 in *Sociological Methodology 1991,* edited by P. Marsden. Cambridge: Blackwell.

Petersen, Trond, and Kenneth W. Koput. 1991. "Legitimacy or Unobserved Heterogeneity: On the Source of Density Dependence in Organizational Death Rates." *American Sociological Review* 56:399–409.

Peterson, Richard A., and David G. Berger. 1996. "Measuring Industry Concentration, Diversity and Innovation in Popular Music." *American Sociological Review* 61:175–77.

Pfeffer, Jeffrey. 1983. "Organizational Demography." Pp. 299–357 in *Research in Organizational Behavior,* Volume 5, edited by L. Cummings and B. Staw. Greenwich, Conn.: JAI.

—— 1992. *Managing with Power.* Boston: Harvard Business School Press.

Phillips, Charles F. 1985. *The Regulation of Public Utilities: Theory and Practice.* Arlington, Virg.: Public Utilities Reports, Inc.

Podolny, Joel M. 1993. "A Status-Based Model of Market Competition." *American Journal of Sociology* 98:829–72.

—— 1998. "Networks: The Pipes and Prisms of the Market." Unpublished paper. Stanford Graduate School of Business.

Podolny, Joel M., and Karen L. Page. 1998. "Network Forms of Organization." *Annual Review of Sociology* 24:57–76.

Podolny, Joel M., and Toby E. Stuart. 1995. "A Role-Based Ecology of Technical Change." *American Journal of Sociology* 100:1224–60.

Podolny, Joel M., Toby E. Stuart, and Michael T. Hannan. 1996. "Networks, Knowledge, and Niches: Competition in the Worldwide Semiconductor Industry, 1984–1991." *American Journal of Sociology* 102:659–89.

Pólos, László, Michael T. Hannan, and Glenn R. Carroll. 1998. "Form and Identity: On the Structure of Organizational Forms." Presented at the 14th Colloquium of the European Group on Organization Studies.

—— 1999. "Identities, Forms, and Populations." Unpublished paper, University of Amsterdam.

Pólos, László, Michael T. Hannan, and Jaap Kamps. 1999. "Aging By Default: Building Theory from Fragmentary Materials." Pp. 207–19 in *Proceedings of the Fourth Dutch–German Workshop on Non-monotonic Reasoning Techniques and Their Applications,* edited by H. Rott, C. Albert, G. Brewka, and C. Witteveen. Amsterdam: ILCC Scientific Publications.

Porter, Michael E. 1980. *Competitive Strategy: Techniques for Analyzing Industries and Competitors*. New York: Free Press.

—— 1990. *The Competitive Advantage of Nations*. New York: Free Press.

Portes, Alejandro, and Robert Bach. 1985. *Latin Journey: Cuban and Mexican Immigrants in the United States*. Berkeley and Los Angeles: University of California Press.

Rae, John B. 1984. *The American Automobile Industry*. Boston: Twayne.

Ranger-Moore, James. 1997. "If Bigger Is Better, Is Older Wiser? Organizational Age and Size in the New York Life Insurance Industry." *American Sociological Review* 58:901–20.

Ranger-Moore, James, Jane Banaszak-Holl, and Michael T. Hannan. 1991. "Density Dependence in Regulated Industries: Founding Rates of Banks and Life Insurance Companies." *Administrative Science Quarterly* 36:36–65.

Ranger-Moore, James, Robert S. Breckenridge, and Daniel L. Jones. 1995. "Patterns of Growth and Size-Localized Competition in the New York State Life Insurance Industry, 1860–1985." *Social Forces* 73:1027–49.

Rao, Hayagreeva. 1994. "The Social Construction of Reputation: Certification Contests, Legitimation, and the Survival of Organizations in the American Automobile Industry, 1895–1912." *Strategic Management Journal* 15:29–44.

Reich, Michael, and Theresa Ghilarducci. 1997. "Pensions, Unions and Training." Unpublished paper. University of California, Berkeley.

Roderick, R. D., and A. I. Kohen. 1976. *Years for Decision: A Longitudinal Study of the Educational and Labor Market Experience of Young Women*. Washington: U.S. Government Printing Office. Volume 3 of U.S. Employment and Training Administration.

Rohwer, Götz, and Ulrich Pötter. 1998. "Transition Data Analysis 6.2: Users' Manual." Technical report, Ruhr Universität Bochum. (Available at http://www.ruhr-uni-bochum.de/sowi).

Romanelli, Elaine. 1991. "The Evolution of New Organizational Forms." *Annual Review of Sociology* 17:79–103.

Rose, Peter S. 1986. *Money and Capital Markets*. Plano, Tex.: Business Publications.

Rosenbaum, James E. 1984. *Career Mobility in a Corporate Hierarchy*. New York: Academic Press.

Rosenfeld, C. 1979. "Occupational Mobility During 1977." *Monthly Labor Review* 102 (October):44–48.

Roughgarden, Jonathan. 1979. *The Theory of Population Genetics and Evolutionary Ecology*. New York: Macmillan.

Russell, Raymond. 1995. *Utopia in Zion*. Albany: State University of New York Press.

Ryder, Norman B. 1965. "The Cohort as a Concept in the Study of Social Change." *American Sociological Review* 30:843–61.

Salem, Fredrick W. 1880. *Beer, Its History and Its Economic Value as a National Beverage*. Hartford, Conn.: F. W. Salem.

Sanders, Jimmy, and Victor Nee. 1987. "Limits of Ethnic Solidarity in the Enclave Economy." *American Sociological Review* 52:745–67.

Saxenian, Analise. 1994. *Regional Advantage: Culture and Competition in Silicon Valley and Route 128*. Cambridge: Harvard University Press.

Schmalansee, Richard. 1989. "Interindustry Studies of Structure and Performance." Pp. 952–1009 in *Handbook of Industrial Organization*, edited by R. Schmalansee and R. Willig. Amsterdam: Elsevier.

Schudson, Michael. 1978. *Discovering the News*. New York: Basic Books.

Seheer-Thoss, Hans C. Graf von. 1979. *Die deutsche Automobilindustrie: Eine Dokumentation von 1886 bis 1979*. Stuttgart: Deutsche Verlags–Anstalt.

Sehgal, E. 1984. "Occupational Mobility and Job Tenure in 1983." *Monthly Labor Review* (October):18–23.

Seidel, Marc-David. 1997. "Competitive Realignment in the Airline Industry: A Dynamic Analysis of Generalist and Specialist Organizations Under Different Network Structures." Ph.D. dissertation, University of California at Berkeley.

Shapiro, Carl. 1989. "The Theory of Business Strategy." *RAND Journal of Economics* 20:125–37.

Shryock, H. S., and J. S. Siegel. 1971. *The Methods and Materials of Demography*. Washington: U.S. Bureau of the Census.

Simon, Herbert A. 1955. "On a Class of Skew Distribution Functions." *Biometrika* 52:425–40.

Simon, Herbert A., and Charles P. Bonini. 1958. "The Size Distributions of Business Firms." *American Economic Review* 48:607–17.

Singh, Ajit, and Geoffrey Whittington. 1975. "The Size and Growth of Organizations." *Review of Economic Studies* 42:15–26.

Singh, Jitendra V., Robert J. House, and David J. Tucker. 1986. "Organizational Change and Organizational Mortality." *Administrative Science Quarterly* 31:587–611.

Singh, Jitendra V., and Charles J. Lumsden. 1990. "Theory and Research in Organizational Ecology." *Annual Review of Sociology* 16:161–95.

Singh, Jitendra V., David J. Tucker, and Agnes G. Meinard. 1991. "Institutional Change and Ecological Dynamics." Pp. 390–422 in *New Institutionalism in Organizational Analysis*, edited by W. Powell and P. DiMaggio. Chicago: University of Chicago Press.

Smith, Adam. 1976. *An Inquiry in the Nature and Causes of the Wealth of Nations*. Chicago: University of Chicago Press. [originally published in 1776].

Smith, Ken G., K. A. Smith, J. D. Ollian, H. P. Sims, D. P. O'Bannon, and J. A. Scully. 1994. "Top Management Team Demography and Process: The Role of Social Integration and Communication." *Administrative Science Quarterly* 39:412–38.

Sober, Elliot. 1984. *The Nature of Selection: Evolutionary Theory in Philosophical Focus*. Cambridge: MIT Press.

Sober, Elliot. 1993. *Philosophy of Biology.* Boulder, Colo.: Westview.

Sørensen, Jesper B. 2000a. "Changes in Group Composition and Turnover." *American Sociological Review,* forthcoming.

—— 2000b. "The Ecology of Organizational Demography: Managerial Tenure Distributions and Organizational Competition." *Industrial and Corporate Change,* in press.

—— 2000c. "Executive Migration and Interorganizational Competition." *Social Science Research,* forthcoming.

Sørensen, Jesper B., and Toby E. Stuart. 1998. "Aging, Obsolescence, and Organizational Innovation." Unpublished paper. University of Chicago: Graduate School of Business.

Spilerman, Seymour. 1977. "Careers, Labor Market Structure and Socioeconomic Achievement." *American Journal of Sociology* 83:551–93.

Staber, Udo. 1989. "Age Dependence and Historical Effects on the Failure Rates of Worker Cooperatives." *Economic and Industrial Democracy* 10:59–80.

Stark, David. 1996. "Recombinant Property in East European Capitalism." *American Journal of Sociology* 101:993–1027.

Starr, G. W., and G. A. Steiner. 1939. "Business Turnover of Indiana Retail Trades." Technical Report 19, Bureau of Business Research, School of Business, Indiana University.

Stehman, Warren J. 1925. *The Financial History of the American Telephone and Telegraph Company.* New York: Houghton Mifflin.

Steindl, Josef. 1965. *Random Processes and the Growth of Firms: A Study of the Pareto Law.* New York: Hafner.

Stewman, Shelby, and Suresh Konda. 1983. "Careers and Organizational Labor Markets: Demographic Models of Organizational Behavior." *American Journal of Sociology* 88:637–85.

Stigler, George. 1958. "The Economies of Scale." *Journal of Law and Economics* 1:54–71.

Stinchcombe, Arthur L. 1965. "Social Structure and Organizations." Pp. 142–93 in *Handbook of Organizations,* edited by J. March. Chicago: Rand McNally.

—— 1968. *Constructing Social Theories.* Chicago: University of Chicago Press.

—— 1979. "Social Mobility and the Industrial Labor Process." *Acta Sociologica* 22:217–45.

Storey, David J. 1994. *Understanding the Small Business Sector.* London: Routledge.

Storey, David J., and S. Johnson. 1987. *Job Generation and Labor Market Change.* Houndmills: Macmillan.

Strang, David. 1995. "Health Maintenance Organizations." Pp. 163–82 in *Organizations in Industry,* edited by G. Carroll and M. Hannan. New York: Oxford University Press.

Strong, Donald R., Daniel Simberloff, Jr., Lawrence G. Abele, and Anne B. Thistle. 1984. *Ecological Communities: Conceptual Issues and Evidence.* Princeton: Princeton University Press.

Stuart, Toby E. 1998. "Network Positions and Propensities to Collaborate: An Investigation of Strategic Alliance Formulation in a High-Technology Industry." *Administrative Science Quarterly* 43:668–98.

Sutton, John. 1997. "Gibrat's Legacy." *Journal of Economic Literature* 35:40–59.

—— 1999. *Technology and Market Structure*. Cambridge: MIT Press.

Sutton, John R., Frank Dobbin, John W. Meyer, and W. Richard Scott. 1994. "The Legalization of the Workplace." *American Journal of Sociology* 99:944–71.

Swaminathan, Anand. 1995. "The Proliferation of Specialist Organizations in the American Wine Industry, 1941–1990." *Administrative Science Quarterly* 40:653–80.

—— 1996. "Environmental Conditions at Founding and Organizational Mortality: A Trial-by-Fire Model." *Academy of Management Journal* 39:1350–77.

—— 1998. "Resource Partitioning and the Evolution of Specialist Organizations in the American Wine Industry." Presented at the Stanford Strategy Conference.

Swaminathan, Anand, and Glenn R. Carroll. 1995. "Beer Brewers." Pp. 223–43 in *Organizations in Industry*, edited by G. Carroll and M. Hannan. New York: Oxford University Press.

Swaminathan, Anand, and Gabriele Wiedenmayer. 1991. "Does the Pattern of Density Dependence in Organizational Mortality Rates Vary Across Levels of Analysis? Evidence from the German Brewing Industry." *Social Science Research* 20:45–73.

Teo, Albert C. Y., Chee-Leong Chong, Gjee-Soon Lim, and Edmund Kuan-Pheng Ng. 1998. "Foundings of Cooperative Societies in Singapore, 1925–1994: Density Dependence at Community and Population Levels." Unpublished paper. National University of Singapore.

Thomas, R. P. 1965. "An Analysis of the Pattern of Growth of the Automobile Industry, 1895–1929." Ph.D. dissertation, Northwestern University.

Tilly, Charles. 1984. "Social Movements and National Politics." In *Statemaking and Social Movements*, edited by C. Bright and S. Harding, Ann Arbor: University of Michigan Press.

Torres, John C. 1995. "The Dynamics of the U.K. Motor Industry, 1894–1990." Ph.D. dissertation, Stanford University.

Tremblay, Victor J. 1993. "The Organizational Ecology of Strategic Groups in the American Brewing Industry: A Comment." *Industrial and Corporate Change* 2:91–98.

Tsai, Lucia. 1999. "The Spatial Aggregation of Automobile Manufacturing Activities in the American Midwest." Ph.D. dissertation, University of California at Berkeley.

Tsiatis, A. 1978. "A Nonidentifiability Aspect of the Problem of Competing Risks." *Proceedings of the National Academy of Sciences* 72:20–22.

Tuljapurkar, Shripad. 1987. "Cycles in Nonlinear Age-Structured Models I: Renewal Equations." *Theoretical Population Biology* 32:26–41.

Tuma, Nancy Brandon, and Michael T. Hannan. 1984. *Social Dynamics: Models and Methods*. Orlando, Fl.: Academic Press.

Turner, Ralph. 1960. "Modes of Social Ascent through Education: Sponsored and Contest Mobility." *American Sociological Review* 25:855–67.

Tushman, Michael, and Philip C. Anderson. 1986. "Technological Discontinuities and Organizational Environments." *Administrative Science Quarterly* 31:439–65.

Tushman, Michael L., and Elaine Romanelli. 1985. "Organizational Evolution: A Metamorphosis Model of Convergence and Reorientation." Pp. 171–222 in *Research in Organizational Behavior*, Volume 7, edited by L. Cummings and B. Staw, Greenwich, Conn.: JAI.

Uchitelle, Louis, and N. R. Kleinfield. 1996. "The Price of Jobs Lost." Pp. 3–36 in *The Downsizing of America*, edited by The Reporters of New York Times. New York: Times Books.

Utterback, James. 1994. *Mastering the Dynamics of Innovation*. Boston: Harvard Business School Press.

Utterback, James, and Eduardo Suarez. 1993. "Innovation, Competition and Industry Structure." *Research Policy* 22:1–21.

Vaile, Roland. 1932. "Grocery Retailing, With Special Reference to the Effects of Competition." Technical report, University of Minnesota.

Van Valen, L. 1973. "A New Evolutionary Law." *Evolutionary Theory* 1:1–30.

Vaupel, James W., Kenneth G. Manton, and Eric Stallard. 1979. "The Impact of Heterogeneity in Individual Frailty on the Dynamics of Mortality." *Demography* 6:439–54.

Wachter, Kenneth W. 1988. "Elusive Cycles: Are There Dynamically Possible Lee–Easterlin Models for U.S. Births?" Technical Report 9, Institute of International Studies, University of California at Berkeley.

Wade, James B. 1996. "A Community-Level Analysis of Sources and Rates of Technological Variation in the Microprocessor Market." *Academy of Management Journal* 5:1218–44.

Wade, James B., Anand Swaminathan, and Michael Scott Saxon. 1998. "Normative and Resource Flow Consequences of Local Regulations in the American Brewing Industry, 1845–1918." *Administrative Science Quarterly,* 43:905–35.

Wagner, W. Gary, Jeffrey Pfeffer, and Charles A. O'Reilly. 1984. "Organizational Demography and Turnover in Top-Management Groups." *Administrative Science Quarterly* 29:74–92.

Weber, Max. 1968. *Economy and Society: An Outline of Interpretive Sociology*. New York: Bedmeister. 3 vols. [Originally published in 1924].

Wedervang, F. 1965. *Development of a Population of Industrial Firms*. Oslo: Universitetsforlaget.

West, Elizabeth. 1995. "Organization Building in the Wake of Ethnic Conflict: A Comparison of Three Populations." *Social Forces* 73:1333–64.

Westphal, James D., and Edward J. Zajac. 1994. "Substance and Symbolism in CEO's Long-Term Incentive Plans." *Administrative Science Quarterly* 39:587–90.

White, Harrison C. 1970. *Chains of Opportunity*. Cambridge: Harvard University Press.

—— 1981. "Where Do Markets Come From?" *American Journal of Sociology* 87:517–47.

Wholey, Douglas R., Jon B. Christianson, and Susan M. Sanchez. 1992. "Organizational Size and Failure among Health Maintenance Organizations." *American Sociological Review* 57:829–42.

Wilkinson, Paul. 1971. *Social Movements*. London: Pall Mall.

Williamson, Oliver E. 1975. *Markets and Hierarchies: Analysis and Antitrust Implications*. New York: Free Press.

—— 1985. *The Economic Institutions of Capitalism*. New York: Free Press.

Wilson, Edward O., and William H. Bossert. 1971. *A Primer of Population Biology*. Stamford, Conn.: Sineaur.

Wilson, Kenneth, and W. Allen Martin. 1982. "Ethnic Enclaves: A Comparison of the Cuban and Black Communities of Miami." *American Journal of Sociology* 88:135–60.

Wilson, William Julius. 1978. *The Declining Significance of Race*. Chicago: University of Chicago Press.

Winter, Sidney G. 1984. "Schumpeterian Competition in Alternative Technological Regimes." *Journal of Economic Behavior and Organization* 5:287–320.

—— 1990. "Survival, Selection, and Inheritance in Evolutionary Theories of Organizations." Pp. 269–97 in *Organizational Evolution: New Directions*, edited by J. Singh. Newbury Park, Calif.: Sage.

Zellner, Arnold. 1962. "An Efficient Method of Estimating Seemingly Unrelated Regressions and Tests for Aggregation Bias." *Journal of the American Statistical Association*. 57:348–68.

Zucker, Lynne G. 1987. "Normal Change or Risky Business: Institutional Effects on the 'Hazard' of Change in Hospital Organizations, 1959–1979." *Journal of Management Studies* 24:671–700.

Zuckerman, Ezra W. 1999. "The Categorical Imperative: Securities Analysts and the Legitimacy Discount." *American Journal of Sociology*, 104:1398–1438.

Index